Archaeology
OF THE Night

Archaeology
OF THE Night

LIFE AFTER DARK
IN THE ANCIENT WORLD

EDITED BY
Nancy Gonlin & April Nowell

UNIVERSITY PRESS OF COLORADO
Louisville

Published by University Press of Colorado
245 Century Circle, Suite 202
Louisville, Colorado 80027

 The University Press of Colorado is a proud member of
the Association of University Presses.

The University Press of Colorado is a cooperative publishing enterprise supported, in part, by Adams State University, Colorado State University, Fort Lewis College, Metropolitan State University of Denver, Regis University, University of Colorado, University of Northern Colorado, University of Wyoming, Utah State University, and Western Colorado University.

∞ This paper meets the requirements of the ANSI/NISO Z39.48-1992 (Permanence of Paper).

ISBN: 978-1-60732-677-9 (cloth)
ISBN: 978-1-64642-124-4 (paperback)
ISBN: 978-1-60732-678-6 (ebook)
DOI: 10.5876/9781607326786

Library of Congress Cataloging-in-Publication Data

Names: Gonlin, Nancy, editor. | Nowell, April, 1969– editor.
Title: Archaeology of the night : life after dark in ancient world / edited by Nancy Gonlin and April Nowell.
Description: Boulder : University Press of Colorado, [2017] | Includes bibliographical references and index.
Identifiers: LCCN 2017018223 | ISBN 9781607326779 (cloth) | ISBN 9781646421244 (pbk) | ISBN 9781607326786 (ebook)
Subjects: LCSH: Night—Social aspects. | Night—Religious aspects. | Antiquities, Prehistoric.
Classification: LCC GT3408 .A74 2017 | DDC 304.2/37—dc23
LC record available at https://lccn.loc.gov/2017018223

The University Press of Colorado gratefully acknowledges the generous support of the University of Victoria toward the publication of this book.

Cover photograph © Justin Kerr file no. 5877

NAN: For my incredible siblings—Alice, James, Jeffrey, Robert, Thomas, Richard, and Patti—with heartfelt appreciation and love for sharing fun-filled childhood nights, complete with monsters and moonlight

APRIL: For Jon, Ruka, and James; and for Mom and Stephen with much love

Contents

Section VI: Nighttime Practices

Section VII: Concluding the Night

Figures

Tables

Foreword

JERRY D. MOORE

. . . and the darkness He called Night.

—GENESIS 1:5

The most astonishing fact about a volume on the *Archaeology of the Night* is that it does not already exist. Perhaps we should not be surprised. As the eighteenth-century scientist Georg Christoph Lichtenberg observed, "our entire history is only the history of waking men" (quoted in Ekirch 2005, 262), and the cultures of night have been largely overlooked by archaeologists as well as by anthropologists and social historians (Dewdney 2004; Ekirch 2005; Galinier et al. 2010; Palmer 2000). The essays in this volume are initial sorties into what the anthropologist and essayist Loren Eiseley (1971) referred to as "The Night Country." It is not a singular destination, nor are the following explorations reducible to a simple, unifying theme. Rather, the reader will discover a range of distinct inquiries, intersecting and complementary probings into what an archaeology of the night might entail.

In this foreword, I want to highlight some common themes found throughout this volume. These reflect diverse and engaging intellectual forays, ranging from the technologies of illumination, the significance of lunar and stellar observations in creating cultural landscapes, the existence of complex nocturnal ontologies, to the specific valences, transgressions, and meanings associated with darkness. Before discussing the themes explored in this volume, I want to convey to the reader what an archaeology of the night could involve by summarizing a pair of previous studies of nocturnal culture among two very different societies, the Ju/'hoansi of the Kalahari (Wiessner 2014) and monks in Late Antiquity and Medieval Europe (Helms 2004). These case studies embody many of the specific themes explored by the contributors to this volume, themes that I discuss subsequently.

Polly Wiessner (2014) presents a fascinating study of daytime versus nighttime conversations among the Ju/'hoansi living in northeast Namibia and northwest Botswana. In 1974 Wiessner recorded information on 174 conversations, discussions that lasted more than twenty to thirty minutes and involved five or more adults; the 1974 data were supplemented in 2011–2013 by additional interviews and recordings (Wiessner 2014, 14028). In the 1970s, the Ju/'hoansi were still mobile foragers, although in the process of settling in permanent villages and engaging in a mixed economy including wage labor, craft sales, agriculture, and government pensions. Ju/'hoansi daytime talk was dominated by the three C's: "criticism, complaint, and conflict" (Wiessner 2014, 14029). "Verbal criticism, complaint, and conflict (CCC) were the spice of Ju/'hoan life that made group living viable; if not worked out by talk, people voted with their feet and departed" (Wiessner 2014, 14029). Interestingly, the vast majority of CCC exchanges were directly between the parties involved, rather than complaining in an offender's absence, except when directed against "big shots" whose verbal deflation was "everybody's sport" (Wiessner 2014, 14029). On two occasions, daytime complaints escalated to threats of death with poisoned arrows, although the protagonists were restrained.

Night talk was different in tone and topic: over 80% of Ju/'hoansi conversations were devoted to stories. "After dinner and dark," Wiessner observes, "the harsher mood of the day mellowed, and people who were in the mood gathered around single fires to talk, make music, or dance . . . The focus of conversation changed radically as economic matters and social gripes were put aside" (Wiessner 2014, 14029). Female and male storytellers recounted tales that "captured the workings of entire institutions in a small-scale society with little formal teaching": stories about marriages; the reciprocal exchanges of nonfood items (known as *hxaro* exchange) between Ju/'hoansi and neighboring groups, sometimes between partners living hundreds of kilometers apart; and the journeys to supernatural worlds made by trance healers. Adept storytellers transformed their "listeners stunned with suspense, nearly in tears, or rolling with laughter; they arrived at a similar emotional wavelength as their moods were altered" (Wiessner 2014, 14029).

In an equally fascinating essay regarding a very different cultural setting, Mary Helms (2004) explored nightly practices among Christian monks in Western Europe during Late Antiquity and the Early Middle Ages. Helms focused on cenobitic monasteries, "in which a master and disciples lived in a close village-like or communal setting" (Helms 2004, 177). Found across Europe, these walled communities housed thousands of men and women in religious orders that rejected the chaos and intentionally withdrew from the temptations of Satan and of the Flesh (Moore 2012, 132–134). "For monks," Helms (2004, 180) writes, "who, by definition, renounced the superficial things of the secular world of the day, the spiritual side of night held a particular attraction. Night provided deep silence and quietude when one's thoughts could be more readily drawn to supernatural mysteries." Darkness cloaked the shared communion of prayers, including the nightly liturgical prayers, or nocturns. For example, Benedictine monks slept fully dressed in a common room lit by a single candle, rising to sing psalms within throughout the night in a darkened church (183).

The significance of the nocturns is indicated by the number of psalms sung during each night's ceremony. Documents describing monastic offices in the fifth-century report that nocturns required as many as 18 psalms to be sung on a winter night; by the sixth century this had grown to a staggering 99 psalms on Saturday and Sunday night vigils during the winter, an exhausting program in which monks slept only 5–7 hours (depending on the seasonal length of night) before rising around 2 a.m. to sing through the night as they spiritually prepared for the dawn. Helms observes that "the office of nocturns (sometimes called vigils), [were] by far the longest and most important of the 'daily' liturgical services' and the office that was chanted in the depths of every night in a virtually unlit, pitch black church, manifested darkness. It can be essentially understood as connecting the monks with the primordial and pre-creational dark that both preceded and accompanied the original creation of the world as described in Genesis and with the power of the numinous that was felt to be present in its infinite depths" (Helms 2004, 177–178). This complex nocturnal ritual involved the rejection of sin, the search for Adamic innocence, and the defeat of death. "These intertwined monastic goals present early medieval monks both as creatures of the night who ritually explored the extraordinary supernatural realm manifested by darkness and as watchers for the coming day for whom the dark was the setting, the backdrop, for liturgy that anticipated its annihilation and conquest by the light" (187).

I have summarized these two very different cases to give the reader some sense of the complex range of behaviors that an archaeology of night might encounter.

On one hand, these two examples of nocturnal behaviors are separated by time, place, cultural traditions, and ontology, and yet there are fascinating intersections between them: the special behaviors associated with nightly practices, the change between day and night in the sounds and subjects of human voices, and the rich cultural associations with darkness and night. These two cases suggest what an archaeology of the night could illuminate, foreshadowing exciting lines of inquiry developed by the contributors to this volume.

Despite spending roughly half of our lives in the night, our archaeological inquiries have been relentlessly diurnal. One fruitful approach would be to examine the technologies of illumination, which has been done by historians and sociologists interested in the consequences of artificial illumination in nineteenth-century European and North American cities (Bowers 1998; Melbin 1987; Nye 1992; Schivelbusch 1988). In his study of artificial lighting in the nineteenth century, Schivelbusch (1988, 221) notes, "the power of artificial light to create its own reality only reveals itself in darkness. In the dark, light is life." Ironically, in the twenty-first century, technologies of illumination have rendered darkness into an environmental quality requiring preservation efforts by groups such as the International Dark-Sky Association (see http://darksky.org/ accessed electronically, September 11, 2016; see also Bogard 2013).

In the ancient world, the technologies of artificial light were basic, of limited luminance, and often multifunctional, such as hearths that provided both heat and light. Although there are some challenges in understanding these artifacts and features, the difficulties are not insurmountable. Rather, we archaeologists have been blinded to entire classes of nocturnal problems and objects, as in what Meghan Strong (chapter 12) calls the "entrenched apathy" when thinking about the role of artificial illumination in funeral ceremonies in New Kingdom Egypt that has led to "a false idea that there is little information to gain from an examination of light."

Yet, technologies of illumination have a deep prehistory. As April Nowell reports (chapter 2), stone lamps from Upper Paleolithic sites—caves, rockshelters, and open-air sites—were made from carved sandstone or limestone and burned animal fats from bovids and suids, resulting in a low glimmer. Torches and hearths were used deep inside caves and in open sites, in all cases extending light into darkness. The experimental study by Erin McGuire (chapter 13) reproducing Viking fish-oil-burning lamps challenges archaeological assumptions about materials and illumination toward the end of the so-called Dark Ages. McGuire's study shows how lamps created small pools of light in the smoky interiors of Viking dwellings and outbuildings—flickering consolations during long northern nights in a cosmos inhabited by dark figures such as werewolves, shape-changers, and berserkers (Byock 1986). Cynthia Van Gilder's (chapter 8) wide-ranging discussion of the night in ancient Polynesia examines traditional forms of artificial illumination, including the *kukui* nut (*Aleurites moluccana*), known in English as the "candlenut." Ethnographic accounts describe how kukui nuts were baked, cracked, threaded on reeds or palm leaves, and lighted, forming artificial illumination that left durable traces of charred fragments of endocarps. In her excavations on Maui, Van Gilder documented the relative densities of kukui in different archaeological structures—dwellings, men's houses, and temples—an examination of "night activities across a landscape."

Different forms of artificial illumination may have distinct associations. For example, we might set a special dinner table with glowing candlelight but not an unshaded and strident bare light bulb. Similarly, Minette Church (chapter 5) explores how campfires, candles, oil lamps, and even starlight gave way to incandescent and fluorescent bulbs in the nineteenth- and twentieth-century American Southwest. Older residents expressed in wistful recollections about the pre-electric lighting that was part of "el refresco de la noche," while younger residents report "la luz de aciete es triste." Church articulates a recurrent theme in this volume "about resituating commonplace archaeological finds in a nocturnal context."

While some objects—such as the technology of illumination—may be uniquely connected to the night, other objects and features deployed in nightly practices also may have diurnal uses. This situation results in what Shadreck Chirikure and Abigail Moffett (chapter 17) characterize as "the ambivalence of the archaeological record" in which "the material manifestation of daily performance is difficult to differentiate from that of nocturnal practices." They write, "a winnowing basket used for grain processing during the day, provided 'transport' for witches during ritual activities, while mortars were used as decoys in the same rituals. Pots and wooden plates used for rituals during ancestor supplication were similar to those used for daily activities." For such reasons, nightly practices present distinct—but not insurmountable—challenges.

Scholars in related fields who have explored nightly behaviors, such as ethnographers and historians, suggest some of the diverse lines archaeologists could pursue. For example, a review of ethnographic studies and cases focusing on the night identified such topics as sleep patterns, myths about the night, special nocturnal vocabularies, and eroticism among such different groups as the Maya, the Otomi, the Inuit, and Parisian cabaret performers (Galinier et al. 2010). Such an eclectic list reflects exploratory possibilities rather than a focused inquiry, as Ekirch (2010) has observed.

This volume follows similarly eclectic, exploratory, initial steps into an archaeology of the night. For example, several of the chapters in this volume explore matters of illumination, obscurity, and ceremony. April Nowell (chapter 2) considers "the nocturnal soundscapes in the European Upper Paleolithic," drawing attention to the artifactual evidence for music—flutes, whistles, pipes, and bull-roarers—but also to the acoustic properties of caves themselves as particular surfaces apparently chosen not only as lithic "canvases" for art, but also because of their sound resonance, combining visual and audial properties in the creation of sacred spaces.

Deployed in ritual, artificial illumination was not simply a passive radiance: it punctuated darkened and nocturnal ceremonies. As noted above, Strong explores the role of artificial illumination in New Kingdom Egypt, not just as technology, but also as luminous aspects of funeral rites in which light marked the liminal stage of "the transition from day/life to night/death and rebirth." Similarly, Tom Dillehay (chapter 9) discusses the nocturnal rituals of Mapuche female shamans (*machi*) who "complement [the multiday public ceremonies of] their male counterparts through religious and ritual practices primarily at night and through support provided by the spiritual and ancestral world." As Jeremy Coltman (chapter 10) discusses for the ancient Maya, "night was the chaotic antithesis to the bright diurnal day" a nocturnal field that extended to the darkness of caves, zones imbued with "wild and untamed darkness" that referenced "a return to primordial time and chaos that made the night so potent."

"There are good reasons to expect that what transpires socially will differ between day and night," Wiessner (2014, 14027) notes. As a preeminently visual primate, humans react in similar ways to the absence of light. Kathryn Kamp and John Whittaker (chapter 4) provide a brief overview of the physiology of vision, but then argue that archaeologists should employ the more inclusive phenomenological notion of "sensescapes" in which hearing, smell, taste, and touch are added to sight. In their discussion of the sensescapes at three Sinagua sites they have studied, Kamp and Whittaker borrow the concept of "affordances" from the psychologist James L. Gibson. "The affordances of the environment are what it offers the animal, what it provides or furnishes, either for good or ill," Gibson wrote (1979, 127). There is room to further develop the concept of affordance, as has been done by Montello and Moyes (2013) in their work on Mesoamerican cave sites. Specifically, it would be useful to expand on the subjective properties of Sinagua sensescapes in light of Gibson's caution that, a specific affordance cannot be reduced to either "an objective property [or] a subjective property . . . An affordance cuts across the dichotomy of subjective-objective and helps us to understand its inadequacy. It is equally a fact of the environment and a fact of behavior. It is both physical and psychical, yet neither. An affordance points both ways, to the environment and to the observer" (Gibson 1979, 129). Thus, even if common physiological responses are universal, it is also true that observers vary in their responses to dark worlds, as the other articles in this volume demonstrate, posing additional and unexamined challenges in implementing the concept of "sensescape."

An interesting theme visible in this volume references darkness and the night as domains of creation. The epigram from Genesis at the beginning of this foreword is a fragment of a great cosmogony in which the acts of creation result from gestures of distinction imposed upon a formless void, as Heaven was distinguished from Earth, Light from Darkness, Day from Night, and Land from Seas. The connection between darkness and creation is implicated in the Classic Maya phrase *ch'ab'-ak' ab*, which in addition to referencing kingship and ritual duties, as Coltman (chapter 10) notes, "may also relate to the invocation of primordial time rooted in the chaos of creation." An analogous connection between darkness and creation is found in the ancient Polynesian concept of *'pō'* which, as Van Gilder (chapter 8) writes, "referred to the source of creation, the depths of the sea, the spirit world, and the time of darkness that followed each day of tropical sun." Van Gilder points out that pō referred to the nighttime and to a 24-hour cycle that began at sunset: "Our evening, a transition to an end, would have been felt as a transition to a beginning." The Polynesian night was also a period of potential transformations, "a time when even an ordinary soul might slip from the *pō* of the world and into the *pō* of this one." As the Hawaiian scholar Mary Kawena Pukui recorded, *"Mai ka pō mai ka 'oiā'I'o"*: "truth comes from the night" (Van Gilder, chapter 8).

Other kinds of creative activities—including those that subvert the day-time order—may occur after sunset. In his essays on Western experiences of night between the Middle Ages and the modern era, Bryan Palmer (2000, 17–18) argues, "the dark cultures of the night are thus not unified in any categorical history of sameness. Rather they are . . . moments excluded from histories of the day, a counterpoint with the time, space and place governed and regulated by the logic and commerce of economic rationality and the structures of political rule . . . [N]ight has also been a locale where estrangement and marginality found themselves a home." Among the different studies in this volume, an outstanding example of estrangement and marginality is found in chapter 15 by Glenn Storey on nightlife in ancient Rome, in which the emperor Nero disguised himself as a common thug and rousted through the dark streets of Rome, stabbing men and throwing them into sewers, and—most shockingly—becoming a nocturnal model for other brigands who attacked passersby in the name of the emperor!

"The cover of darkness opened the door to different types of ritual performances," Shadreck Chirikure and Abigail Joy Moffett note (chapter 17), some that complemented and others that subverted diurnal practices, such as rituals that called on ancestors to intercede with deities, divinations, traditional healing practices, witchcraft, and sexual instruction. Jane Eva Baxter provides a fascinating example of night's subversive potential in discussing Junkanoo, a Bahamian festival with deep roots and meanings created by eighteenth- and nineteenth-century African slaves and still celebrated by their descendants. As Baxter writes, "enslaved peoples, who had been brought to the Bahamas carrying only intangible culture, had limited outlets in their day-to-day lives to express memory, culture, and identity" (chapter 18). A secretly organized ceremony involving choreographed dances performed to the call-and-response music of brass instruments, cowbells, and goatskin drums, the Junkanoo ceremony "is not just one of resistance and transgression, but also one of cultural creativity, ethnogenesis, and memory practice where identities and meanings were shaped and formed through intentional and deliberate actions." Moving beyond this specific ceremony, Baxter explores the Bahamian plantation landscapes. While plantation owners' houses were placed on commanding ridges to take advantage of cooling breezes and fewer insects, the panoptical advantage of owners' houses disappeared in the darkness of night. Rather, Baxter contends, the nocturnal landscapes and soundscapes of Bahamian plantations presented their own affordances that "offered the opportunity for enslaved peoples to interact without being overseen or overheard in the darkness," quiet nocturnal interactions that contrasted with the explosive brass and drummings of Junkanoo.

Another theme threading through this volume is the intertwining of darkness and placemaking. Alexei Vranich and Scott Smith (chapter 6) explore the role of nighttime astronomical observations as complex societies developed in the Titicaca Basin of the southern Andes. After approximately 1800 BCE, an architectural form—the sunken court—became common across the region, and it is one of the principal features at the urban center of Tiwanaku, the dominant settlement in the region between 500 and 1000 CE. The largest sunken court in the Titicaca Basin was constructed at Tiwanaku, a two-meter deep rectangular (28 m × 26 m) space flanked by fifty-seven large stone pillars set into the walls surrounding the court. Vranich and Smith contend that the sunken court was designed, at least in part, to view the night sky. Pillars aligned to the rising and setting of Alpha and Beta Centauri, which are interpreted in traditional Andean ethnoastronomy as the eyes of the Yacana, a dark cloud constellation in the form of a llama (Urton 1981). Colonial and ethnographic sources describe Yacana as one member in a procession of dark cloud constellations—zones of the night sky where no stars appear—that move across the Mayu, or "Celestial River," the astral feature Westerners refer to as "the Milky Way." Drawing on this, Vranich and Smith argue that Tiwanaku's sunken court was intentionally located in reference to the stars and constellations of darkness that journeyed through the Andean night. In a similar manner, places and astronomical observations in the night sky were essential for ancient Polynesians, as Van Gilder discusses, not only for navigating across the Pacific Ocean, but also for terrestrial concerns. The appearance of the Pleiades marked the Hawaiian New Year and the time for harvest festivals, and astrologists observed the heavens to predict propitious days for battles. Temples (*heiau*) and other constructions were oriented to cardinal directions and other celestial phenomena.

In an intriguing and wide-ranging essay considering celestial phenomena, Anthony Aveni (chapter 7) discusses human reactions to a different kind of night: the night of day created by a total solar eclipse. One might object that a discussion of eclipses—especially of total eclipses that are visible from a given location only once in four hundred years!—really does not fit into a volume on the archaeology of night, especially a volume that emphasizes the overlooked quotidian aspects of nocturnal life. Aveni argues for the need of "an anthropology of eclipse." For example, Aveni reports on the extraordinary ways that humans respond to darkness in the middle of the day. Noisemaking is prominent—drums are pounded, metal pots banged—although this behavior may be explained quite differently either as urging the sun to awaken or as applauding the sun as the eclipse fades and solar order is restored. Alternatively, a total solar eclipse may be explained as the moon biting the sun as among contemporary Maya or as the sun being swallowed by a demon in Hindu myth. Whatever their ontological frameworks, solar eclipses are seen as potential imbalances in the normal cosmos, and explaining those imbalances involves "lending familiarity to the unfamiliar" and in so doing "hope to find meaning" (chapter 7). In a recent insightful essay, Jocelyn Holland, a specialist on European scientific writings and literature during the Enlightenment and Romantic periods, has discussed the unique explanatory problems posed by total solar eclipses. Holland writes, "predictions of eclipses have operated at the intersection of scientific theory and cultural practices. As natural occurrences, eclipses are objects of scientific study that have been explained through increasingly sophisticated mathematical and astronomical models, allowing future eclipses to be predicted with precision and historical events to be dated even more exactly with reference to eclipses past. Yet, it is also true that throughout history eclipses have been perceived as the most supernatural of events, permitting superstition and fear to intrude, along with the strange darkness that disturbs the otherwise familiar oscillation of day and night" (Holland 2015, 216). It is exactly this "strange darkness" that makes total solar eclipse particularly unnerving for so many human societies, as Aveni documents in his essay.

Attempts to explain the differences between the realms of day and night lead to considerations of diurnal and nocturnal ontologies, an issue prominent in Dillehay's discussion of Mapuche female shamans (chapter 9). For the Classic Maya, Gonlin and Dixon (chapter 3) observe that the night was viewed as an ominous time and Coltman (chapter 10) discusses how the Maya associated night and the primordial darkness before creation, associations that imbued nighttime with distinctive dangers and potencies. The ontological associations between daylight, darkness, and gender are central to Susan Alt's discussion (chapter 11) of the Mississippian city of Cahokia. In the uplands east and southeast of Cahokia's core, a ridge was modified to align with the moon's standstill position, a zone of Cahokia known as the Emerald site. Significantly Emerald was directly connected to central Cahokia by a twenty-four-km-long formal avenue (Pauketat and Alt 2015). The Emerald site's ceremonial zone seems to have been created in the very earliest stages of Cahokia's existence, and it attracted pilgrims from throughout the American Midwest. In the core of the Emerald site, earthen mounds were constructed to align with the 53-degree azimuth, the point at which (as seen from Cahokia's latitude) the moon rises at its maximum northern standstill for several months every 18.6 years, before beginning its journey back to its southern extreme. Various structures were built at the Emerald site—sweat lodges, shelters for pilgrims, and shrine houses—but none were permanent dwellings. Alt documents how shrine houses were "decommissioned" with a "depositional liturgy" in which "every shrine was closed with water-washed silts, and most had burned materials on their [yellow clay plastered] floors, woven fabrics, and hides" (chapter 11). Alt writes, "Siouan oral histories tie the moon and the earth to women, the sun and the sky to men," but these and other polarities were essential, complementary, and ontologically diverse, involving humans, animals, nonhuman powers, and objects in a manner distinct form Cartesian distinctions. If specific zones of Cahokia's sacred landscape were associated with solar cycles and males—such as the "woodhenge" at Mound 72, whose posts marked solar solstices associated with burials of male and female elites—other powerful places were nocturnal and feminine. Alt writes, "the Mississippian night brought the moon and dreams. The night brought stories, histories, of intercourse between mother earth and father sky that created the people, spirits, and the world."

The Night Country is not only the domain of the esoteric, subversive, or otherworldly elements, but it is also the place of nocturnal quotidian activities, as many authors in this volume document. For example, Rita Wright and Zenobie Garrett (chapter 14) describe the "lavish system of water amenities" at Mohenjo-daro and other Indus valley cities, arguing that maintenance of the sanitation system occurred at night. Similarly, Chirikure and Moffett discuss how in southern Africa iron smelting occurred at night, a technological process imbued with sexuality as the clay smelting furnaces were female (including having molded breasts), the blow tubes were penises, and the resulting bloom of iron a baby. Storey discusses some of the "every night" activities in ancient Rome as heavy transport wagons lumbered through the streets, bread was baked, sex was purchased, and intellectuals—like the politician and general Pliny the Elder—thought, read, and wrote. Gonlin and Dixon list some of the nighttime tasks among the Maya, ranging from hunting and guarding gardens and fields to boiling beans, to soaking maize for *masa* or clay for pottery. In an intriguing study of irrigation practice in Oman, Smiti Nathan (chapter 16) discusses how irrigation water was allocated to different farmers' fields using traditional subsurface irrigation systems (*falaj*), and how the duration of allocations was measured by telling time from the stars in the night sky—the night being a cooler time for hard work in a hot desert.

In conclusion, the night is and was a prominent domain in human existence, and the chapters in this volume lead the reader to an exploration of its complex meanings, behaviors, and associations. What the reader will discover in the following chapters is a surprisingly complex array of nocturnal worlds. Simply put, there is no reason to assume that night was universally characterized by transgression or symbolic inversion, feared or embraced. Although Ekirch (2005, xxvii) has argued that "nocturnal culture was by no means monolithic, but people were more alike in their attitudes and conventions than they were different," he principally focuses on European traditions rather than on the cross-cultural variations in the Night Country. As the studies in this collection demonstrate, archaeologists and other scholars could do more to explore cross-cultural and diachronic variations in the notions and behaviors between dusk and dawn.

NOTE

1. Matins, prime, terce, sext, none, vespers, compline and nocturns.

REFERENCES

Bogard, Paul. 2013. *The End of Night: Searching for Natural Darkness in an Age of Artificial Light*. New York: Little, Brown.

Bowers, Brian. 1998. *Lengthening the Day: A History of Lighting Technology*. New York: Oxford University Press.

Byock, Jesse. 1986. "The Dark Figure as Survivor in an Icelandic Saga." In *The Dark Figure in Medieval German and Germanic Literature*, ed. E. R. Haymes and S. C. Van D'Elden, 151–163. Göppinger Arbeiten zur Germanistik 448. Göppingen: Kümmerle Verlag.

Dewdney, Christopher. 2004. *Acquainted with the Night: Excursions through the World After Dark*. London: Bloomsbury.

Eiseley, Loren. 1971. *The Night Country: Reflections of a Bone-Hunting Man*. New York: Charles Scribners.

Ekirch, A. Roger. 2005. *At Day's Close: Night in Times Past*. New York: W.W. Norton.

Ekirch, A. Roger. 2010. "Comment on Jacques Galinier et al., 'Anthropology of the Night: Cross-Disciplinary Investigations.'" *Current Anthropology* 51(6):838–839.

Galinier, Jacques, Aurore Monod Becquelin, Guy Bordin, Laurent Fontaine, Francine Fourmaux, Juliette Roullet Ponce, Piero Salzarulo, Philippe Simonnot, Michèle Therrien, and Iole Zilli. 2010. "Anthropology of the Night: Cross-Disciplinary Investigations." *Current Anthropology* 51(6):819–847. https://doi.org/10.1086/653691.

Gibson, James. 1979. *The Ecological Approach to Visual Perception*. Boston: Houghton Mifflin.

Helms, Mary. 2004. "Before the Dawn: Monks and the Night in Late Antiquity and Early Medieval Europe." *Anthropos* 99(1):177–191.

Holland, Jocelyn. 2015. "A Natural History of Disturbance: Time and the Solar Eclipse." *Configurations* 23(2):215–233. https://doi.org/10.1353/con.2015.0016.

Melbin, Murray. 1987. *Night as Frontier: Colonizing the World after Dark.* New York: Free Press.

Montello, Daniel, and Holley Moyes. 2013. "Why Dark Zones Are Sacred: Turning to Behavioral and Cognitive Sciences for Answers." In *Sacred Darkness: A Global Perspective on the Ritual Use of Caves*, ed. Holley Moyes, 385–396. Boulder: University Press of Colorado.

Moore, Jerry. 2012. *The Prehistory of Home.* Berkeley: University of California Press.

Nye, David E. 1992. *Electrifying America: Social Meanings of a New Technology, 1880–1940.* Cambridge, MA: The MIT Press.

Palmer, Bryan D. 2000. *Cultures of Darkness: Night Travels in the Histories of Transgression.* [*From Medieval to Modern.*] New York: Monthly Review Press.

Pauketat, Timothy R., and Susan M. Alt. 2015. "Religious Innovation at the Emerald Acropolis: Something New under the Moon." In *Something New under the Sun: Perspectives on the Interplay of Religion and Innovation*, ed. D. Yerxa. London: Bloomsbury Press. Accessed June 24, 2017. https://www.cahokia.illinois.edu/docu ments/Pauketat%20Alt%202016%20chapter%20draft.pdf.

Schivelbusch, Wolfgang. 1988. *Disenchanted Night: The Industrialization of Light in the Nineteenth Century.* Trans. Angela Davis. Berkeley: University of California Press.

Urton, Gary. 1981. "Animals and Astronomy in the Quechua Universe." *Proceedings of the American Philosophical Society* 125(pt. 2):110–127.

Wiessner, Polly. 2014. "Embers of Society: Firelight Talk among the Ju/'hoansi Bushmen." *Proceedings of the National Academies of Science* 11(39):14027–14035. https://doi.org/10.1073/pnas.1404212111.

Preface

It was a dark and stormy night.
—EDWARD BULWER-LYTTON (1830)

I (Nan Gonlin) was sitting by the fireplace one evening reading about daily practices. With wine glass in one hand and a book in the other, it occurred to me that I was using different artifacts and spaces than I do during the daytime. "What about nightly practices?" I thought. I Googled this term and found nothing. A search using synonyms did not produce archaeological publications either. I bounced this idea of ancient nocturnicity off my good friend Chris Dixon who encouraged me to delve into this matter wholeheartedly for she could think of no research on the matter either.

Enter April Nowell. On a return journey from an SAA meeting in 2011, I was fortunate to sit next to this expert on the Paleolithic. We were both heading back to the Pacific Northwest and had a flight of a few hours to spend talking about archaeology. With much in common, we stayed in touch and I approached April about the archaeology of the night. She was as excited as I

DOI: 10.5876/9781607326786.c000

about this new topic in our field and we agreed to put together two symposia. Easier said than done.

We contacted numerous archaeologists, many of whom responded with one of the following: "You want me to do what?" or "What can you say about 'the night'?" or "I have never heard of that!" or "Well, of course there's research out there on that topic" or "No, that would take too much work on my part since I have never thought about it." It was simply far too opacus a subject for most. The collected essays in this volume represent the brave few who affirmatively responded to our cry in the night, not knowing what they were getting themselves into (as we ourselves did not). Together we have journeyed into the darkness to explore the archaeology of the night.

The chapters in this volume originated from two symposia that April and I assembled, one at the 2015 American Anthropological Association in Denver ("From Dusk to Dawn: Nightly Practices in the Ancient World") and another at the 2016 SAA meetings in Orlando ("Archaeology of the Night"). Both were very well attended and well received, which encouraged us to continue forth. The discussant for the AAA symposium was Jerry Moore, and Polly Wiessner and Meg Conkey served as discussants for the SAA symposium. Jerry kindly agreed to write the Foreword for this volume while Meg summed up the volume in the Afterword. All offered critical insights from their vast anthropological experiences. We heartily thank Polly Wiessner for her contribution to anthropology in her seminal work on the Jo/hoansi and nighttime talk—truly inspirational. Polly opted out of participating in this publication, but we are very grateful for the contributions she made as a discussant.

April and I sincerely thank the contributors to this volume for adhering to our expedited publishing deadlines and to the University Press of Colorado for wholeheartedly embracing this novel idea. Jessica d'Arbonne, acquisitions editor, has been absolutely amazing with her swift support and rapid pace of quickly moving forward. She has been there for us at every step of the way. Other members of UPC, including Darrin Pratt, Dan Pratt, Laura Furney, and Beth Svinarich, have facilitated publication of this volume. Copy editor Karl Yambert provided exceptional input, and many thanks go to Linda Gregonis for composing the index. Our families have been incredibly supportive and have put up willingly with our lucubracious habits of late, despite the zeitgeber that darkness has descended. This volume is dedicated to our families.

Nancy Gonlin
Bellevue College
Bellevue, WA, USA

Archaeology
OF THE Night

Introduction

Introduction to the Archaeology of the Night

Nancy Gonlin and April Nowell

As twilight settled in the ancient world, a host of activities ensued, some of which were significantly different from what people did during the daytime. Some artifacts and features associated with these activities were particular to the dark, while other material culture was transformed in meaning as the sun set or just before it rose. While daily and nightly activities alike left their mark on the archaeological record through objects, features, iconography, writings, and even entire buildings, often archaeological reconstructions of the past privilege descriptions of daytime doings. But, as Minette Church (chapter 5) observes, our research subjects lived as many nights as days. Sleep, sex, socializing, stargazing, storytelling, ceremony, work and play—so much of our economic, social and ritual lives takes place at night that, in fact, some modern cities have begun appointing "night mayors" to oversee the ever expanding nocturnal economies of our urban centers (Henley 2016)—and yet relatively little archaeological research has been undertaken specifically on nightly quotidian practices. Does darkness obscure these activities for the archaeologist or is it that we need to learn to see them? There are, in fact, many questions we can frame around an

DOI: 10.5876/9781607326786.c001

inquiry into the night, such as what did people in the past do at night? How did our ancestors, before the advent of electricity, experience the night? What were their views and concerns about the night and darkness? What symbols, stories, myths, and rituals are specifically associated with the night? How did the night simultaneously liberate and confine? Perhaps most important for archaeologists, what are the archaeological signatures of these nighttime behaviors? We are just beginning to explore possible answers to these questions, answers that rest upon an enormous amount of comparative research and draw on evolutionary psychology, history, epigraphy, art history, biology, cultural astronomy, religious studies, literature, the four fields of anthropology, and many other related disciplines. Our purpose in writing this chapter and gathering together the case studies in this volume is to begin to make up for the lack of inquiry into the night from an archaeological perspective and to correct a bias that favors daytime doings in our reconstructions of the past.

NIGHT VISION

Archaeological studies of the night are best advanced from what is known as a parallax perspective, which essentially involves viewing one's subject from a different angle. The change in the position of the observer—in this case, our explicit orientation toward nightly practices rather than daily practices—has proven to be extremely productive. By viewing culture through what people did during the day *and* the night, we come to a more holistic understanding of the practices that have left their mark on the archaeological record. Studies of the night inform about human variation, what is unique about the night, how we humans have been able to adapt to the night, and much more. For these reasons, we asked authors of this volume to explicitly reimagine the sites where they have worked, the data they have amassed, the interpretations they have made, and the theories they have employed through the dark lens of the night to explore the past. We ask our readers to do the same, in essence, to evoke the parallax effect. Sarah Jackson (2017, 604) has effectively used a parallax perspective in her innovative analysis of Classic Maya materials from an emic viewpoint; the utilization of hieroglyphs reveals properties of material items previously understudied by Mesoamericanists. Her work, in turn, cites Faye Ginsburg's (1995) visual anthropology analysis. While Jackson and Ginsburg discuss the emic/etic differences in analyzing data, we utilize a night/day perspective as an analogy to the emic/etic one, and argue for a wider context within which to reconstruct past cultural behaviors that encompass the round-the-clock habits of our species.

ECOLOGICAL PARAMETERS OF THE NIGHT

Humans adapt to the night both biologically and culturally, so it is productive to begin by looking at the ecological parameters within which ancient humans lived their lives and the nightscapes they faced. There are several environmental changes to the Earth that occur as night settles in and light wanes. Temperatures cool for both animate and inanimate objects. In general, the night is a quieter time than the day for humans, but sounds at night emanate from different sources. In the cities, sounds of the "night shift" take over, while outside urban areas, numerous animals such as bats, owls, and crepuscular felines become active as darkness falls and the croaking of amphibians and the humming of insects begins. Even the aroma of night differs from daytime, with some flowers, whose growth is in response to moonlight, opening as the moon rises and closing as it descends. The length of the night varies from season to season and from latitude to latitude, from the long-lasting nights of the northern hemisphere during winter time and midnight suns during the summer to the nearly equal lengths of days and nights year round near the equator.

Chronobiology is the field that studies circadian rhythms. There are several physiological, biochemical, and behavioral changes that occur in the human body (as well as in the bodies of numerous other species) in response to variation in the amount of light (Burton 2009). Body temperature, urine production, and blood pressure generally drop at night, as does one's alertness while metabolism slows (Dewdney 2004). Hormonal changes include an increased production of melatonin and human growth hormone, while cortisol peaks just before rising to assist one in awakening (Burton 2009; see also Nowell, chapter 2, this volume). The cultural adaptations that humans have made to accommodate their circadian rhythms are numerous. Some of the obvious ones with which most humans are familiar are the invention of coverings, clothing, and safe places for sleeping. We also create myths about the night to explain the absence of the sun, the presence of the stars, and the possibility of harm from creatures both real and imagined. Many rituals center on the gloaming and the hopes of a new sunrise.

Night represents a study of time as humans experience it, rather than the longitudinal framework of scientists who can view chronology through millions and billions of years. Recent interpretations of the past call for such types of analyses (Ashmore 2015, 214; Golden 2002; 2010) because ancient peoples did not live for periods as long as a ceramic phase or for the duration of a dynasty. While we collectively study such phenomena as the "Upper Paleolithic" or the "Classic period," we can never experience such longevity ourselves. Furthermore, humans live in ecological time rather than geological time. The turning of night into day, winter into spring, or the annual solar cycle is how humans experience the world within their framework of reckoning time and social life (Lucas 2005). Such experiences mark the archaeological record and it is through their remains that we can further our knowledge of the past.

EXTENDING LIGHT INTO THE NIGHT

With the advent of the controlled use of fire millennia ago, our ancestors first began their quest to conquer the night and extend the availability of the light, warmth, and security naturally afforded by the sun. The earliest evidence for anthropogenic fires dates to 1.8 million years ago at Lake Turkana in Northern Kenya, but most paleoanthropologists agree that the controlled use of fire dates to approximately 500,000 years ago (Gowlett 2016). Richard Wrangham (2009, 2016) writes extensively about the controlled use of fire in cooking, which was essential for plant detoxification and softening foods for infants. Instrumental in this use of technology are the effects it had on brain size increase and gut size decrease (Gowlett and Wrangham 2013). Humans made good use of fire in many other capacities (see chapter 2, this volume). Fire as light lengthened productive hours, changed our circadian rhythms, and increased social interactions (Burton 2009; Gowlett 2012).

Most important for our purposes here, the controlled-use of fire extended the daylight hours—and for the first time in human history—altered our circadian rhythms by providing greater opportunities for socializing during what were previously nonproductive hours (Burton 2009; Gowlett 2012). "Day talk" and "night talk" differ substantially among hunter-gatherers, per Polly Wiessner's (2014) ethnographic research. While mundane and businesslike operations as well as gossip are the norm for conversation during the day, firelight intensifies interactions and other topics of conversation become customary. This qualitative difference in communication involves not only the spoken word but also dance, song, ceremony, and storytelling once the sun goes down (see also chapter 2, this volume). The benefits of such ritualized behaviors extend to the entire group in terms of reinforcing social mores and group cohesion and identity. The transformational impact of fire on the biological, social, and cultural development of our ancestors has prompted some anthropologists to argue that fire is in fact what made us "human" (Boyd 2009; Coe et al. 2006; Dunbar 2014; Gottschall 2012; Wiessner 2014).

THE DISAPPEARING NIGHT

In modern times, we face a disappearing night (Bogard 2008, 2013) as stars fade into the glow of cities and only the biggest and brightest of astronomical bodies are visible on even the clearest of nights (Bortle 2001). Only in recent human history have humans conquered the night with an intensity that sometimes outshines the day (Brox 2010; Edensor 2015). In fact, the abundance of artificial light pollution today is a significant concern for life on our planet. Recent research demonstrates that the circadian cycle controls between 10% and 15% of our genes, and its disruption has been linked to several medical disorders in humans, including depression, insomnia, and cardiovascular disease (Chepesiuk 2009; Naiman 2014). Further research suggests that early humans experienced selective pressure to fulfill sleep needs in the shortest time possible. Human sleep is shorter, deeper, and exhibits a higher proportion of REM than other primates to enable longer active periods in which to acquire and transmit new skills and knowledge (Samson and Nunn 2015). Even though humans have been described as the only "nocturnal ape" (Hill et al., 2009), we may be reaching our limits.

The adoption of electricity also had social consequences from the household to larger society. "When gas light and kerosene lamps disappeared, so did the last vestige of a central fire in the home. Electric light was everywhere, yet concentrated nowhere; everyone sat in the halo of his or her own lamp" (Brox 2010, 171). However, electricity provided a new hearth in the form of the radio (Brox 2010, 171) and later the television, although this is no longer the case in many households globally as each family member hunkers over his or her own cellular or computer screen. In light of these biological and social changes, Jane Brox (2010, 303) encourages us "to think back to the past, to ask ourselves whether we are hampered more by the brilliance than our ancestors ever were by the dark."

CHALLENGES TO STUDYING THE NIGHT

The excavation of sites is largely a daytime occupation. As archaeologists, we rarely experience our sites at night or in the darkness. Daytime digs are the norm since light is necessary for documenting what one is uncovering. However, when digging in dark places such as caves or tunnels deep inside pyramids, just as critical as the trowel is a source of light, and these digs usually occur during the day. Only under extraordinary circumstances, such as the excavation of royal Mochica tombs in Sipán, Peru (Alva and Donnan 1993), do we ever conduct nocturnal excavations or experience the sites we excavate at night. Dark doings, such as looting, the antithesis of professional excavation, are envisioned to take place at night. When in the field, nighttime is for lab work, research, report writing, and refreshment, all occurring under artificial light. For those of us in academia, similar activities ensue at night with a heavy dose of grading, lecture preparation, and committee work thrown in as well. It is no wonder then, that our bias toward the day is an occupational hazard.

Remains of the night, like other types of archaeological remains, will be biased toward the durable. Drawing on the usual suspects of stone and ceramic, we can learn a great deal from these items that previously went unnoticed or unremarked upon by asking new "night-focused" questions. Complex societies left more durable buildings, monuments, and in some cases, writing than less complex ones. These hierarchical societies' artifacts and features will be prominently seen, as will the possessions of royalty and elite, while the remains of their followers are sometimes cast into shadow. Nonetheless, the challenges that we face in understanding ancient nights are no greater than the challenges we as archaeologists normally face. Once our perspective has shifted, our night vision is enhanced (Van Gilder, chapter 8, this volume).

For most of us studying the past, the day is the default setting in our research orientation. We presume, for better or worse, that an object, space, or building was used during the day. While we have no reason to make such assumptions, they exist and once we are aware of them, only then can we reorient our research toward the night. Rarely have we stopped and questioned ourselves, "How do I know that artifact was used during the day?" Many objects have both day and night uses, as aptly pointed out by Shadreck Chirikure and Abigail Joy Moffett (chapter 17, this volume), which can be quite different: for the Shona, a broom for cleaning during the day is a witch's nocturnal vehicle. By resetting our perspective to envision how material remains would have been used at night, we will be able to switch from the "neutral" daytime and include activities of the night (Church, chapter 5, this volume). The task before us is to distinguish between daily artifacts that we find to be used at night and whether there are indeed artifacts/sites/places that pertain entirely to the night; only then can we begin to build an understanding of "nighttime culture" (K. Landau, pers. comm., November 2016).

APPROACHES TO STUDYING THE NIGHT

Despite the challenges, there are a number of productive ways in which theorizing about the night can be advanced. While with notable exceptions (Galinier et al. 2010; Handelman 2005; Monod Becquelin and Galinier 2016; Schnepel and Ben-Ari 2005), nighttime has been a neglected topic in anthropology and more specifically in archaeology, researchers in other disciplines have embraced this topic. Historians of European and Western history (e.g., Ekirch 2005; Koslofsky 2011; Palmer 2000) have more directly and extensively examined the night. Craig Koslofsky noted (2011:14), "we can see the night as part of a broader form of analysis, rather than as a self-contained topic . . . daily life as a category of historical analysis [can be used] to understand the reciprocal relationship between night and society."

The basis of any approach for archaeologists, however, is the assumption that behaviors at night, like many human behaviors, will have some material correlates that have survived in the archaeological record (e.g., Elson and Smith, 2001). We advocate approaching the night from wide theoretical perspectives and interdisciplinary viewpoints. This subject is best advanced through a holistic, cross-cultural, comparative framework as the investigation of the night involves various data sets and lends itself well to the four-field approach of American anthropology. The methodological and theoretical approaches of household archaeology, Pierre Bourdieu's practice theory, and phenomenology are three readily applicable vehicles for guiding and interpreting these inquiries, as well as approaching the night through a human adaptation perspective. All of these theoretical orientations have been readily and successfully applied to understand daily activities, yet explicit consideration of nightly activities has been notably absent in our analysis of the archaeological record.

Household Archaeology

Most humans, contemporary and ancient, spend the night at home. Fortunately, the remains of houses/habitation structures are the most numerous type of archaeological site on the landscape. Household archaeology has become a prominent and productive form of analysis for the remains of residences, whether they are humble abodes or dwellings of the rich and famous (e.g., Douglass and Gonlin 2012; Parker and Foster 2012). Nighttime household archaeology relies on the same types of data that household archaeologists depend upon to reveal information about production, distribution, transmission, reproduction, and coresidence (following Wilk and Netting 1984). Activities do not stop after the sun sets; to the contrary, this time period can be extremely productive. By tweaking the types of questions we ask, we open up a new way of thinking about the past. Our inquiries can include questions such as: how was culture transmitted at night? what tasks did household members routinely perform at night, especially through engendering the night? (Gero and Conkey 1991). Men's nighttime household activities often differed from those of women, especially for the unmarried. Children may have been safely tucked into bed or working, particularly in agricultural communities when harvest season was in full swing. Evidence for the transmission of culture at night through ritual can be found in households as Yosef Garfinkel (2003) has successfully demonstrated for early agricultural villages in the Near East. Many cultures have particular artifacts associated with the night, such as the sleeping benches and mats of the Classic Maya, which inform us about nightly coresidence (see Gonlin and Dixon, chapter 3, this volume). A traditional emphasis on activity areas can be enhanced by considering not only the time of day in which an activity was performed, but also an analysis of the lighting situation: those working at night likely worked where the light was strongest and perhaps relied upon other senses such as touch as well (Dawson et al. 2007; McGuire, chapter 13, this volume).

Practice Theory

Pierre Bourdieu's (1977) practice theory can be used to examine "nightly practices" in the same manner that daily practices enlighten our understanding of the past (Bourdieu 1979). While some nightly practices are every, or almost every, night (e.g., sleeping), other activities of the night might be less frequent (e.g., hunting or drying pottery). The use of the term *nightly practices* is used to complement the term *daily practices* in our advancing an archaeology of the

night. The reorientation of our perspective to the night informs us about artifacts and features we commonly recover as archaeologists. For example, not
only does the hearth represent the controlled use of fire and cooking (Pyburn
1989), but it reveals information about the practice of warming up the night,
of "fire talk," of socializing (Wiessner 2014). Firelight intrudes into the darkness
to assist in other practices such as toolmaking. Traditions that are maintained
and practiced over time are more likely to become part of the archaeological
record. Archaeologists working in different parts of the world have successfully
used Bourdieu's framework to inform us about everyday life (e.g., Pauketat 2001;
Robin 2013); we anticipate that a similar orientation will equally inform us about
nightly life.

Phenomenology

Don Handelman advocates the phenomenological approach to research, explaining that

> Thinking of night as a phenomenon might begin with elementary ideas of planes
> of human movement and synchronisation in the life-world. Phenomenologists
> commonly write of the everyday, not of the everynight life-world (Schutz and
> Luckmann 1973:21). Yet the task is to begin thinking of the (neologists) everynight,
> perhaps by contrasting this with the everyday. For this, at a minimum, we need
> ideas of horizon and trajectory, or others similar to these. (2005, 250)

At night, our horizons and trajectories alter significantly. The horizon
becomes physically limited as it is no longer possible to see its edges, its extent.
Our trajectories too, become limited as social contacts narrow. Darkness closes
in around us during the night and our daytime eyesight changes from polychro-
matic to monochromatic (Handelman 2005, 253). Our sensualities change and
the nightscape looks and feels different. Handelman advocates for "a more phenomenological perspective to nightness within anthropology, one that joins the
phenomenal to the social and both to space and time" (2005, 250).

Sensescapes and Timescapes

Building on phenomenological approaches to how humans experience the
night, we turn to consider the other senses. Anthropologists have emphasized
the visual in our analyses of culture, grossly reflected in how we "see" the world.
Many aspects of the English language reflect this bias, such as idioms ("I see
what you mean"), metaphors ("we shed light on this idea"), and similes ("eyes
like saucers"). We cannot easily see the night for it is dark, literally, so we must
train ourselves to do so by relying upon other senses. Sensory anthropology is
a relatively new field that emphasizes not only how visual, but auditory, hap-
tic, gustatory, and olfactory senses vary cross-culturally. Archaeologists have

contributed substantially to this field (Boivin et al. 2007; Claasen 1997; Day 2013; Hamilakis 2013; Houston et al. 2009; Houston and Newman 2015; Houston and Taube 2000; Scarre and Lawson 2006; *inter alia*) in recent years.

The sociologist Murray Melbin (1978) approaches the "night as frontier," a medium to be occupied and expanded into by humans, much like geographical space. He draws many parallels between the Western expansion of Euro-Americans into the United States in the 1800s and the gradual occupation of the night. Among these parallels that we may be able to examine archaeologically are numerous similarities between "land frontiers and time frontiers" (Melbin 1978, 6). Many of these sociological observations can be tested with archaeological, ethnohistoric, and ethnographic data, as similar patterns will emerge as those stated above for contemporary society. We have gradually come to occupy the night and much of that occupation can be attributed to changes in technology (Bowers 1998; Brox 2010; Jonnes 2004; O'Dea 1958), some of which were intentional while others were not. At any point in time during the night, one can expect fewer individuals up and about, except for special occasions—or as Handelman (2005, 248–249) puts it "night-time sociality may cohere especially within highly specialised settings," such as the Chorti midnight hunting ritual recorded by Wisdom (1940, 71) and in recent work by Linda Brown (2004, 2009) among the Maya, or feasting, where perhaps an entire community participates, leaving its mark on the archaeological record (e.g., Baron 2016; Hayden 2014; LeCount 2001).

WHAT THE NIGHT MEANS

The dichotomy between night and day that some cultures envision (figure 1.1) is stark, while in other cultures, the difference may be viewed as a continuous one. As darkness descends, the astronomical phenomenon of the setting sun is variously hailed and feared across the globe (Aveni, chapter 7, this volume). Nocturnal beings emerge, real or fantastical, to claim the night as their own, just as nightlife emerges as the sun sinks below the horizon. The night has often been used as a metaphor for hell, death, danger, evil, challenges, loneliness, hopelessness, and suffering (Alvarez 1995), particularly as it applies to the Holocaust (Wiesel 1955) in modern times. Nightmares occur in the deepest darkest hours. In this vein, night is opposed to light, or day, which represents truth, hope, and enlightenment. Night is used for plotting, scheming, escaping, and raiding. The night is associated with deviance, for better or worse. Night is primal and wild, something to be domesticated and colonized; day is civilized. But night also has positive attributes, as it is associated with dreaming (e.g., Shakespeare's a *Midsummer Night's Dream)*, relaxation, (witness the large number of late-night television shows), frivolity, worshipping and devotion, contemplation, and meditation. The question that we, as anthropologists, must address is how widespread spatially and temporally such metaphors are.

FIGURE 1.1. *Classic Maya plate, illustrating the boundary between (bottom) night and (top) day, with a form of the vision serpent in both hemispheres. (Photograph © Justin Kerr file no. K5877)*

All that Is Dark Is Not the Night

An emerging field of study that is complementary to the archaeology of the night is the inquiry into darkness. Leaders in this area, Marion Dowd and Robert Hensey, have published on a variety of conditions in which darkness is an overarching environmental characteristic (Dowd and Hensey 2016). Contributors to their edited volume explore caves, mines, the northern Arctic, megaliths, and the emotional and psychological impact that darkness has on the human spirit and psyche. Others (e.g., Brady and Prufer 2005; Moyes 2012) focus explicitly on caves to highlight the unique role that such geological features have played for our species over thousands of years (Nowell, chapter 2, this volume). The parameter of darkness is intricately related to the night, and many of this volume's authors delve into the symbolism of darkness to elucidate the night. However, rather

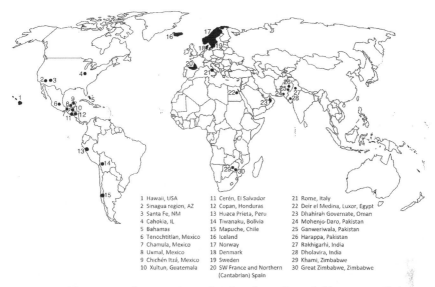

1 Hawaii, USA	11 Cerén, El Salvador	21 Rome, Italy
2 Sinagua region, AZ	12 Copan, Honduras	22 Deir el Medina, Luxor, Egypt
3 Santa Fe, NM	13 Huaca Prieta, Peru	23 Dhahirah Governate, Oman
4 Cahokia, IL	14 Tiwanaku, Bolivia	24 Mohenjo-Daro, Pakistan
5 Bahamas	15 Mapuche, Chile	25 Ganweriwala, Pakistan
6 Tenochtitlan, Mexico	16 Iceland	26 Harappa, Pakistan
7 Chamula, Mexico	17 Norway	27 Rakhigarhi, India
8 Uxmal, Mexico	18 Denmark	28 Dholavira, India
9 Chichén Itzá, Mexico	19 Sweden	29 Khami, Zimbabwe
10 Xultun, Guatemala	20 SW France and Northern (Cantabrian) Spain	30 Great Zimbabwe, Zimbabwe

FIGURE 1.2. *Major sites and areas mentioned in the volume. (Compiled by Jeremy Beller)*

than looking at darkness as the defining criterion of analysis, a particular time of day is given primacy.

CASE STUDIES OF THE NIGHT

The best way to show how productive an archaeological inquiry into the night can be is by showcasing a number of case studies from around the world (figure 1.2) that pertain to different time periods (figure 1.3), rather than concentrating on a single ancient culture, area, chronology, theoretical orientation, or specialty. This volume is divided into six main areas. Together, the foreword by Jerry Moore and this chapter introduce the reader to the topic of the archaeology of the night. Moore's cross-cultural work (e.g., Moore 2012) lends a much-needed perspective for investigating this topic.

Section II on "Nightscapes" provides examples of experiencing the night from four different time periods and locations. The Upper Paleolithic of Europe coincided with the last reaches of the Pleistocene epoch, creating a unique natural and cultural environment. Drawing on archaeological and neuropsychological data, April Nowell (chapter 2) proposes a model of a cultural Paleolithic soundscape set against the natural soundscape of the Pleistocene world as day turned to night. Various forms of lighting were created and used, and had different impacts on the people using them. Evidence for music is at the core of establishing the emotional resonance of early Europeans. Chapter 3 by Nancy Gonlin and Christine Dixon portray the Classic Maya sites of Copan, Honduras, and Cerén, El Salvador, from the dark perspective of the night. Enlisting cultural

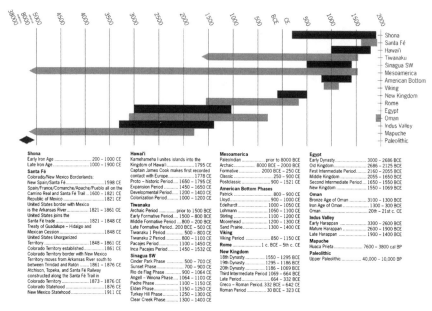

The timeline chart scale labels: 38000 BCE, 8000, 5000, 4500, 4000, 3500, 3000, 2500, 2000, 1500, 1000, 500, BCE, CE, 500, 1000, 1500, 2000

Timeline labels (right side): Shona, Santa Fé, Hawai'i, Tiwanaku, Sinagua SW, Mesoamerica, American Bottom, Viking, New Kingdom, Rome, Egypt, Oman, Indus Valley, Mapuche, Paleolithic

Shona
Early Iron Age .... 200 – 1000 CE
Late Iron Age .... 1000 – 1900 CE

Santa Fé
Colorado/New Mexico Borderlands:
New Spain/Santa Fé .... 1598 CE
Spain/France/Comanche/Apache/Pueblo all on the
Camino Real and Santa Fé Trail .. 1600 – 1821 CE
Republic of Mexico .... 1821 CE
United States border with Mexico
is the Arkansas River .... 1821 – 1861 CE
United States joins the
Santa Fé trade .... 1821 – 1848 CE
Treaty of Guadalupe – Hidalgo and
Mexican Cession .... 1848 CE
United States Unorganized
Territory .... 1848 – 1861 CE
Colorado Territory established .... 1861 CE
Colorado Territory border with New Mexico
Territory moves from Arkansas River south to
between Trinidad and Ratón .... 1861 – 1876 CE
Atchison, Topeka, and Santa Fé Railway
constructed along the Santa Fé Trail in
Colorado Territory .... 1873 – 1876 CE
Colorado Statehood .... 1876 CE
New Mexico Statehood .... 1911 CE

Hawai'i
Kamehameha I unites islands into the
Kingdom of Hawai'i .... 1795 CE
Captain James Cook makes first recorded
contact with Europe .... 1778 CE
Proto – historic Period .... 1650 – 1795 CE
Expansion Period .... 1450 – 1650 CE
Developmental Period .... 1200 – 1400 CE
Colonization Period .... 1000 – 1200 CE

Tiwanaku
Archaic Period .... prior to 1500 BCE
Early Formative Period .... 1500 – 800 BCE
Middle Formative Period .. 800 – 200 BCE
Late Formative Period .. 200 BCE – 500 CE
Tiwanaku 1 Period............ 500 – 800 CE
Tiwanaku 2 Period............ 800 – 1100 CE
Pacajes Period .... 1100 – 1450 CE
Inca Pacajes Period ...... 1450 – 1532 CE

Sinagua SW
Cinder Park Phase .... 500 – 700 CE
Sunset Phase................... 700 – 900 CE
Rio de Flag Phase .... 900 – 1064 CE
Angell – Winona Phase .. 1064 – 1100 CE
Padre Phase................... 1100 – 1150 CE
Elden Phase.................... 1150 – 1250 CE
Turkey Hill Phase............ 1250 – 1300 CE
Clear Creek Phase.......... 1300 – 1400 CE

Mesoamerica
Paleoindian .... prior to 8000 BCE
Archaic.................. 8000 BCE – 2000 BCE
Formative .... 2000 BCE – 250 CE
Classic .... 250 – 900 CE
Postclassic .... 900 – 1521 CE

American Bottom Phases
Patrick .... 800 – 900 CE
Lloyd............................... 900 – 1000 CE
Edelhardt .... 1000 – 1050 CE
Lohmann .... 1050 – 1100 CE
Stirling .... 1100 – 1200 CE
Moorehead .... 1200 – 1300 CE
Sand Prairie................. 1300 – 1400 CE

Viking
Viking Period .... 850 – 1150 CE

Rome .... 1 c. BCE – 5th c. CE

New Kingdom
18th Dynasty.............. 1550 – 1295 BCE
19th Dynasty.............. 1295 – 1186 BCE
20th Dynasty.............. 1186 – 1069 BCE
Third Intermediate Period 1069 – 664 BCE
Late Period.................... 664 – 332 BCE
Greco – Roman Period. 332 BCE – 642 CE
Roman Period .... 30 BCE – 323 CE

Egypt
Early Dynasty................. 3000 – 2686 BCE
Old Kingdom................. 2686 – 2125 BCE
First Intermediate Period..... 2160 – 2055 BCE
Middle Kingdom .... 2055 – 1650 BCE
Second Intermediate Period .. 1650 – 1550 BCE
New Kingdom................ 1550 – 1069 BCE

Oman
Bronze Age of Oman .... 3100 – 1300 BCE
Iron Age of Oman.......... 1300 – 300 BCE
Oman .... 20th – 21st c. CE

Indus Valley
Early Harappan .... 3300 – 2600 BCE
Mature Harappan .... 2600 – 1900 BCE
Late Harappan .... 1900 – 1400 BCE

Mapuche
Huaca Prieta .... 7600 – 3800 cal BP

Paleolithic
Upper Paleolithic............. 40,000 – 10,000 BP

FIGURE 1.3. *Major phases/periods/events highlighted in the volume. (Compiled by David M. Reed)*

ecology, practice theory, and household archaeology as interpretive frameworks, these authors greatly add to our understanding of the Classic Maya commoners and elites alike, who are usually viewed through a daytime lens. In chapter 4, Kathryn Kamp and John Whittaker help us experience the night as the Sinagua of the American Southwest would have. Contrasting the diurnal landscape with the nocturnal one, senses other than vision predominated. The authors advocate taking a multisensorial approach to further our understanding of the night. Historical archaeology lends an added dimension for us to understand the past and the night in particular, as reported on by Minette Church in chapter 5. The glow from an oil lamp or candle was appreciated by older residents in the American Southwest. Electrification is most often viewed as a positive symbol of modernization; however, in this case, its rejection was based on more than simply technological considerations. Church makes numerous astute observations that are applicable to any archaeological study of the night.

The "Night Sky," Section III, had an effect on emotions, politics, work, rituals, warfare, and more. For the highland Bolivian center of Tiwanaku, Alexei Vranich and Scott Smith (chapter 6) make a convincing case that the nighttime sky played a critical role in the founding of this center. Their work connects the celestial bodies and sacred mountains with community development and social complexity. Anthony Aveni (chapter 7) brings to our attention that very little research has been conducted on how people experience full solar eclipses, despite the voluminous astronomical publications on the topic. He supports the creation of an "anthropology of eclipses" to rectify the situation. A short cross-cultural survey of responses to eclipses is provided to contextualize Aveni's discourse on the ancient Maya, who were able to predict and provide warning of such events. Drawing upon ethnohistoric, ethnographic, linguistic, and archaeological data, Cynthia Van Gilder (chapter 8) reveals how Polynesians performed sacred and mundane nocturnal activities. The sea played a critical role in their conception of the night.

In Section IV, authors address "Nocturnal Ritual and Ideology" and how ancient peoples conceived of and dealt with the night. Tom Dillehay (chapter 9) concentrates his work on the remains of fires from Huaca Prieta on the north coast of Peru and illustrates their significance with ethnographic work among Mapuche shamans. Nighttime rituals affect both ritual specialists and participants, and fire played a critical role in the mesmerizing ceremonies for ancients and moderns alike. Jeremy Coltman (chapter 10) tackles the difficult subject of ancient Maya thought through the analysis of dark spaces and dark beings, which were connected to the night. Epigraphy and iconography across Mesoamerica are used amply to offer a reinterpretation of the ancient Maya underworld. Using Cahokia as a case study (chapter 11), Susan Alt is able to remark upon sex and reproduction and focus on women, all of which are intricately intertwined with the night. By combining oral histories and archaeology, Alt shows how the Emerald site and numerous well-known statues embody feminine principles.

Artificial illumination harks back thousands of years as humans throughout history creatively produced technological solutions to extend the daylight, as evidenced by the authors in Section V, "Illuminating the Night." Meghan Strong (chapter 12) weighs in on sources of artificial light in ancient Egypt and their transformation from the mundane to the sacred realm. The sun has received much attention in Egyptian studies but once the sun set, there were numerous choices to light up the night, including oil lamps, torches, and braziers. Erin McGuire's (chapter 13) use of experimental archaeology in her quest to deconstruct Viking lighting practices stands as an example of innovation and persistence.

Our authors approach studying ancient nights from a variety of perspectives. The five chapters in Section VI on "Nighttime Practices" illustrate how ethnographic and historic research can greatly contribute to our understanding of nightly practices. Nighttime work was often conducted outdoors under the stars, as Rita Wright and Zenobie Garrett discuss the dirty business of night soil and its pickup in the Indus civilization in chapter 14. Given the extensive network of drains, wells, and other features related to water and waste disposal in the ancient city of Mohenjo-daro, it is likely that certain tasks took place under the cover of darkness. Analogy with the sewer workers of New York City gives insight into the conditions of such employees and their relationship with the night. Twenty-first-century humans are not the first to make the most of the night, as Glenn Storey (chapter 15) tells us about the boisterous nightlife in the Roman Empire. Historical sources combined with archaeological data produce a robust chapter on nocturnal practices. The Early Bronze Age in Oman and its oases are the subject of Smiti Nathan's chapter 16, which focuses on select nightly activities of irrigation and plant propagation. With the judicious use of ethnographic investigations among contemporary farmers, Nathan is able to show that nighttime agricultural activities were ideal for desert climes where precious irrigation waters go farther during the night. Shadreck Chirikure and Abigail Joy Moffett (chapter 17) rightly chastise us archaeologists of being "afraid of the dark." They compare Iron Age houses in southern Africa with the modern Shona to reveal nocturnal practices of the household, including reproduction and ritual. Jane Eva Baxter (chapter 18) examines how the night served as a reprieve from the demanding duties of enslaved Africans on the Bahamian island of San Salvador. The privacy that darkness afforded enabled slaves to maintain their cultural traditions and resist the status quo. The festival of Junkanoo emanated from these practices and continues today. Meg Conkey wraps up the night in her thoughtful afterword that brings together the volume. Conkey compares the perspective of her seminal work on gender and archaeology to the view of looking at the archaeological record through night vision, and she urges us to pursue the archaeology of the night.

CONCLUSIONS

From poets to biologists, psychologists, and astrophysicists, the night has fascinated modern and ancient humans alike. However, while scholars of European history such as Roger Ekirch (2005) and Craig Koslofsky (2011) have directly and extensively examined this topic, anthropologists have only begun to explicitly study the night (Becquelin and Galinier 2016). The authors in this volume take a holistic and multidisciplinary approach to studying the night by incorporating data from the four fields of anthropology as well as evolutionary psychology, history, epigraphy, art history, biology, cultural astronomy, religious studies, and literature, among other disciplines and subdisciplines. Guiding their inquiries are methodological and theoretical approaches ranging from household archaeology to Bourdieu's practice theory to phenomenology, and the archaeologies of memory and space and place, among others. Such perspectives have been readily and successfully applied to daily activities, yet explicit consideration of nightly practices has been notably absent in our analyses before now. We thank you, the reader, for joining us as we embark together on this adventure into the night.

ACKNOWLEDGMENTS

We sincerely thank K. Viswanathan, Kristin Landau, Christine C. Dixon, David M. Reed, and two anonymous reviewers for their insights and edits, and for alerting us to pertinent literature. We were fortunate to receive feedback on our introductory symposium papers from Jerry Moore, Polly Wiessner, and Meg Conkey, all of whom helped to refine our ideas presented here. Jessica D'Arbonne, acquisitions editor for the University Press of Colorado, embraced this project from the beginning and we are truly grateful for her faith in us and all of our authors, and for expediting the publication process. Justin Kerr readily agreed to allow us to publish images from the Maya Vase Database. Jeremy Beller composed the world map that highlights the sites and areas featured in this volume. David M. Reed graciously provided a chronology chart of the various time periods discussed by the authors of this volume. Benayah Israel is Bellevue College's interlibrary loan expert who tirelessly filled Nan's numerous requests. Much of the initial research for this project was conducted during a sabbatical granted by Bellevue College to Nan during 2015–2016. Partial funding for this project was provided by a University of Victoria book subvention grant to April.

REFERENCES

Alva, Walter, and Christopher B. Donnan. 1993. *Royal Tombs of Sipán*. Los Angeles: Regents of the University of California and the Fowler Museum of Cultural History.

Alvarez, A. 1995. *Night: Night Life, Night Language, Sleep, and Dreams*. New York: W.W. Norton.

Ashmore, Wendy. 2015. "Contingent Acts of Remembrance: Royal Ancestors of Classic Maya Copan and Quirigua." *Ancient Mesoamerica* 26(2):213–231. https://doi.org/10.1017/S095653611500019X.

Baron, Joanne. 2016. "Patron Deities and Politics among the Classic Maya." In *Political Strategies in Pre-Columbian Mesoamerica*, ed. Sarah Kurnick and Joanne Baron, 121–152. Boulder: University Press of Colorado. https://doi.org/10.5876/9781607324164.c005.

Becquelin, Aurore Monod, and Jacques Galinier, eds. 2016. *Las Cosas de la Noche: Una Mirada Diferente*. Nouvelle édition. [online] México: Centro de Estudios Mexicanos y Centroamericanos. https://doi.org/10.4000/books.cemca.4201.

Bogard, Paul, ed. 2008. *Let There Be Night: Testimony on Behalf of the Dark*. Reno: University of Nevada Press.

Bogard, Paul. 2013. *The End of Night: Searching for Natural Darkness in an Age of Artificial Light*. New York: Little, Brown and Company.

Boivin, Nicole, Adam Brumm, Helen Lewis, Dave Robinson, and Ravi Korisettar. 2007. "Sensual, Material, and Technological Understanding: Exploring Prehistoric Soundscapes in South India." *Journal of the Royal Anthropological Institute* 13(2):267–294. https://doi.org/10.1111/j.1467-9655.2007.00428.x.

Bortle, John E. 2001. "Introducing the Bortle Dark-Sky Scale." *Sky and Telescope* (February):126–129.

Bourdieu, Pierre. 1977. *Outline of a Theory of Practice.* Cambridge: Cambridge University Press. https://doi.org/10.1017/CBO9780511812507.

Bourdieu, Pierre. 1979. *Algeria 1960: The Disenchantment of the World, The Sense of Honour, The Kabyle House or The World Reversed—Essays by Pierre Bourdieu.* Cambridge: Cambridge University Press.

Bowers, Brian. 1998. *Lengthening the Day: A History of Lighting Technology.* Oxford: Oxford University Press.

Boyd, Brian. 2009. *On the Origin of Stories: Evolution, Cognition, and Fiction.* Cambridge, MA: The Belknap Press of Harvard University Press.

Brady, James E., and Keith M. Prufer, eds. 2005. *In the Maw of the Earth Monster: Mesoamerican Ritual Cave Use.* Austin: University of Texas Press.

Brown, Linda A. 2004. "Dangerous Places and Wild Spaces: Creating Meaning with Materials and Space at Contemporary Maya Shrines on El Duende Mountain." *Journal of Archaeological Method and Theory* 11(1):31–58. https://doi.org/10.1023/B:J ARM.0000014347.47185.f9.

Brown, Linda A. 2009. "Communal and Personal Hunting Shrines Around Lake Atitlan, Guatemala." In *Maya Archaeology 1,* ed. Charles Golden, Stephen Houston, and Joel Skidmore, 36–59. San Francisco: Precolumbia Mesoweb Press.

Brox, Jane. 2010. *Brilliant: The Evolution of Artificial Light.* New York: Houghton Mifflin.

Burton, Frances D. 2009. *Fire: The Spark that Ignited Human Evolution.* Albuquerque: University of New Mexico Press.

Chepesiuk, Ron. 2009. "Missing the Dark: Health Effects of Light Pollution." *Environmental Health Perspectives* 117(1):A20–A27. https://doi.org/10.1289/ehp.117-a20.

Claasen, Constance. 1997. "Foundations for an Anthropology of the Senses." *International Social Science Journal* 153:401–412.

Coe, Kathryn, Nancy E. Aiken, and Craig T. Palmer. 2006. "Once Upon a Time: Ancestors and the Evolutionary Significance of Stories." *Anthropological Forum* 16(1):21–40. https://doi.org/10.1080/00664670600572421.

Dawson, Peter, Richard Levy, Don Gardner, and Matthew Walls. 2007. "Simulating the Behaviour of Light Inside Arctic Dwellings: Implications for Assessing the Role of Vision in Task Performance." *World Archaeology* 39(1):17–35. https://doi.org/10.1080/00438240601136397.

Day, Jo, ed. 2013. *Making Senses of the Past: Toward a Sensory Archaeology.* Center for Archaeological Investigations, Occasional Paper No. 40. Carbondale: Southern Illinois University Press.

Dewdney, Christopher. 2004. *Acquainted with the Night: Excursions through the World after Dark.* New York: Bloomsbury Publishing.

Douglass, John G., and Nancy Gonlin, eds. 2012. *Ancient Households of the Americas: Conceptualizing What Households Do.* Boulder: University Press of Colorado.

Dowd, Marion, and Robert Hensey, eds. 2016. *Darkness: Archaeological, Historical and Contemporary Perspectives.* Oxford: Oxbow Books.

Dunbar, Robin I.M. 2014. "How Conversations around Campfires Came To Be." *Proceedings of the National Academy of Sciences of the United States of America* 111(39):14013–14014. https://doi.org/10.1073/pnas.1416382111.

Edensor, Tim. 2015. "The Gloomy City: Rethinking the Relationship between Light and Dark." *Urban Studies (Edinburgh, Scotland)* 52(3):422–438. https://doi.org/10.1177/0042098013504009.

Ekirch, A. Roger. 2005. *At Day's Close: Night in Times Past.* New York: W.W. Norton.

Elson, Christina M., and Michael E. Smith. 2001. "Archaeological Deposits from the Aztec New Fire Ceremony." *Ancient Mesoamerica* 12(2):157–174. https://doi.org/10.1017/S0956536101122078.

Galinier, Jacques, Aurore Monod Becquelin, Guy Bordin, Laurent Fontaine, Francine Fourmaux, Juliette Roullet Ponce, Piero Salzarulo, Philippe Simonnot, Michèle Therrien, and Iole Zilli. 2010. "Anthropology of the Night: Cross-Disciplinary Investigations." *Current Anthropology* 51(6):819–847. https://doi.org/10.1086/653691.

Garfinkel, Yosef. 2003. *Dancing at the Dawn of Agriculture.* Austin: University of Texas Press.

Gero, Joan J., and Margaret W. Conkey, eds. 1991. *Engendering Archaeology: Women and Prehistory.* Oxford: Basil Blackwell Ltd.

Ginsburg, Faye. 1995. "The Parallax Effect: The Impact of Aboriginal Media on Ethnographic Film." *Visual Anthropology Review* 11(2):64–76. https://doi.org/10.1525/var.1995.11.2.64.

Golden, Charles. 2010. "Frayed at the Edges: Collective Memory and History on the Borders of Classic Maya Polities." *Ancient Mesoamerica* 21(2):373–384. https://doi.org/10.1017/S0956536110000246.

Golden, Charles W. 2002. "Bridging the Gap Between Archaeological and Indigenous Chronologies: An Investigation of the Early Classic/Late Classic Divide at Piedras Negras, Guatemala." PhD diss., University of Pennsylvania, Philadelphia.

Gottschall, Jonathan. 2012. *The Storytelling Animal: How Stories Make Us Human.* Boston: Houghton Mifflin Harcourt.

Gowlett, John A.J. 2012. "Firing Up the Social Brain." In *Social Brain, Distributed Mind*, ed. Robin Dunbar, Clive Gamble, and John Gowlett, 341–366. Oxford: Oxford University Press.

Gowlett, John A.J. 2016. "The Discovery of Fire by Humans: A Long and Convoluted Process." *Philosophical Transactions of the Royal Society of London. Series B, Biological Sciences,* 371(1696):20150164. https://doi.org/10.1098/rstb.2015.0164.

Gowlett, John A.J., and Richard W. Wrangham. 2013. "Earliest Fire in Africa: Towards the Convergence of Archaeological Evidence and the Cooking Hypothesis." *Azania* 48(1):5–30. https://doi.org/10.1080/0067270X.2012.756754.

Hamilakis, Yannis. 2013. *Archaeology of the Senses: Human Experience, Memory, and Affect.* New York: Cambridge University Press. https://doi.org/10.1017/CBO9781139024655.

Handelman, Don. 2005. "Epilogue: Dark Soundings—Towards a Phenomenology of Night." *Paidemua: Mitteilungen zur Kulturkunde,* Bd. 51:247–261.

Hayden, Brian. 2014. *The Power of Feasts: From Prehistory to the Present.* New York: Cambridge University Press. https://doi.org/10.1017/CBO9781107337688.

Henley, Jon. 2016. "The Stuff of Night Mayors: Amsterdam Pioneers New Way to Run Cities After Dark." *The Guardian,* March 21, 2016. https://www.theguardian.com/cities/2016/mar/21/night-mayor-amsterdam-holland-mirik-milan-night-time-commission.

Hill, Kim, Michael Barton, and A. Magdalena Hurtado. 2009. "The Emergence of Human Uniqueness: Characters Underlying Behavioral Modernity." *Evolutionary Anthropology* 18(5):187–200. https://doi.org/10.1002/evan.20224.

Houston, Stephen, Claudia Brittenham, Cassandra Mesick, Alexandre Tokovinine, and Christina Warinner. 2009. *Veiled Brightness: A History of Ancient Maya Color.* Austin: University of Texas Press.

Houston, Stephen, and Sarah Newman. 2015. "Flores fragantes y bestias fétidas: El olfato entre los mayas del Clásico." *Arqueología Mexicana* 23 (135): 36–43.

Houston, Stephen, and Karl Taube. 2000. "An Archaeology of the Senses: Perception and Cultural Expression in Ancient Mesoamerica." *Cambridge Archaeological Journal* 10(2):261–294. https://doi.org/10.1017/S095977430000010X.

Jackson, Sarah. 2017. "Envisioning Artifacts: A Classic Maya View of the Archaeological Record." *Journal of Archaeological Method and Theory* 4:579–610.

Jonnes, Jill. 2004. *Empires of Light: Edison, Tesla, Westinghouse, and the Race to Electrify the World.* New York: Random House.

Kerr, Justin. n.d. Maya Vase Database. Accessed November 14, 2015. http://research.mayavase.com/kerrmaya.html.

Koslofsky, Craig. 2011. *Evening's Empire: A History of the Night in Early Modern Europe.* Cambridge: Cambridge University Press. https://doi.org/10.1017/CBO9780511977695.

LeCount, Lisa J. 2001. "Like Water for Chocolate: Feasting and Political Ritual Among the Late Classic Maya at Xunantunich, Belize." *American Anthropologist* 103(4):935–953. https://doi.org/10.1525/aa.2001.103.4.935.

Lucas, Gavin. 2005. *The Archaeology of Time.* New York: Routledge.

Melbin, Murray. 1978. "Night as Frontier." *American Sociological Review* 43(1):3–22. https://doi.org/10.2307/2094758.

Monod Becquelin, Aurore, and Jacques Galinier, eds. 2016. *Las cosas de la noche: Una mirada diferente*. New Edition (on line). México: Centro de Estudios Mexicanos y Centroamericanos. https://doi.org/10.4000/books.cemca.4201.

Moore, Jerry D. 2012. *The Prehistory of Home*. Los Angeles: University of California Press.

Moyes, Holley, ed. 2012. *Sacred Darkness: A Global Perspective on the Ritual Use of Caves*. Boulder: University Press of Colorado.

Naiman, Rubin R. 2014. *Healing Night: The Science and Spirit of Sleeping, Dreaming, and Awakening*. 2nd ed. Tucson, AZ: NewMoon Media.

O'Dea, William T. 1958. *The Social History of Lighting*. London: Routledge & Kegal Paul.

Palmer, Bryan D. 2000. *Cultures of Darkness: Night Travels in the Histories of Transgression (from Medieval to Modern)*. New York: Monthly Review Press.

Parker, Bradley J., and Catherine P. Foster, eds. 2012. *New Perspectives on Household Archaeology*. Winona Lake, IN: Eisenbrauns.

Pauketat, Timothy R. 2001. "Practice and History in Archaeology: An Emerging Paradigm." *Anthropological Theory* 1(1):73–98. https://doi.org/10.1177/14634 990122228638.

Pyburn, K. Anne. 1989. "Maya Cuisine: Hearths and the Lowland Maya Economy." In *Prehistoric Maya Economies of Belize*, ed. Patricia A. McAnany and Barry L. Isaac, 325–344. Research in Economic Anthropology, Supplement 4. Greenwich: JAI Press.

Robin, Cynthia. 2013. *Everyday Life Matters: Maya Farmers at Chan*. Gainesville: University of Florida Press. https://doi.org/10.5744/florida/9780813044996.001.0001.

Samson, David R., and Charles L. Nunn. 2015. "Sleep Intensity and the Evolution of Human Cognition." *Evolutionary Anthropology* 24(6):225–237. https://doi.org/10.1002/evan.21464.

Scarre, Chris, and Graeme Lawson, eds. 2006. *Archaeoacoustics*. Cambridge: MacDonald Institute for Archaeological Research.

Schnepel, Burkhard, and Eyal Ben-Ari. 2005. "Introduction: 'When Darkness Comes . . .': Steps Toward an Anthropology of the Night." *Paidemua: Mitteilungen zur Kulturkunde* 51:153–163.

Schutz, Alfred, and Thomas Luckmann. 1973. *The Structures of the Life-World*. Evanston: Northwestern University Press.

Wiesel, Elie. 1955. *Night*. New York: Hill and Wang.

Wiessner, Polly W. 2014. "Embers of Society: Firelight Talk Among the Ju/'hoansi Bushmen." *Proceedings of the National Academy of Sciences of the United States of America* 111(39):14027–14035. https://doi.org/10.1073/pnas.1404212111.

Wilk, Richard R., and Robert McC. Netting. 1984. "Households Changing Forms and Functions." In *Households: Comparative and Historical Studies of the Domestic Group*, ed. Robert McC. Netting and Richard R. Wilk, 1–28. Berkeley: University of California Press.

Wisdom, Charles. 1940. *The Chorti Indians of Guatemala*. Chicago: The University of Chicago Press.

Wrangham, Richard. 2009. *Catching Fire: How Cooking Made Us Human*. New York: Basic Books.

Wrangham, Richard. 2016. "The Curiously Long Absence of Cooking in Evolutionary Thought." *Learning & Behavior* 44(2):116–117. https://doi.org/10.3758/s13420-016 -0223-4.

Nightscapes

Upper Paleolithic Soundscapes and the Emotional Resonance of Nighttime

APRIL NOWELL

As archaeologists, we tend to privilege the visual and the tactile at the expense of other senses. Out of necessity, we favor things we can see and touch in our analyses and in our reconstructions rather than emphasizing the auditory and the kinetic. But as Iain Morley (2013) observes, in our visually dominated society it is easy to overlook how much information about the world around us we derive from sound and this lapse is apparent in most archaeologists' models of the Paleolithic period. Nocturnal soundscapes in the European Upper Paleolithic (40,000–10,000 BP) would have varied through time and space. Nonetheless, we can reasonably infer from fossil, archaeological, and paleoenvironmental data that they would have included the calls of nocturnal animals, the crackle of campfires and, of course, the resonance of the spoken human voice. Sounds of the night also likely included music, as music is believed to be ubiquitous in human cultures (Fukui and Toyoshima 2014). Upper Paleolithic peoples were hunter-gatherers and music in contemporary and historically documented hunter-gatherer societies is often communal and accompanied by rhythmic dance and elaborate storytelling (Morley 2013). These behaviors

DOI: 10.5876/9781607326786.c002

are believed to galvanize human emotion, promoting social cohesion, and can act as a mnemonic permitting people to learn about the world around them through embodied gestural activity (Morley 2013). Music, dance, and storytelling are commonly part of the nocturnal soundscapes of hunter-gatherers (Wiessner 2014) and may have been selected for precisely because their emotional resonance is heightened at night.

In this chapter, the situating of Upper Paleolithic peoples as fully human will be briefly discussed, followed by a consideration of lighting options used by early Europeans during this time period. Drawing on archaeological and neuropsychological data, this chapter then reviews the evidence for music in the European Upper Paleolithic and the relationship between nighttime and the perception of emotion in music, offering new lines of inquiry into the social lives and embodied cognition of people living during the Upper Paleolithic.

LIFE IN THE EUROPEAN UPPER PALEOLITHIC

Upper Paleolithic (figures 1.2–1.3) peoples were nomadic to semisedentary hunter-gatherers who lived during the late Pleistocene. The Pleistocene epoch (2.5 million to 11,700 years ago) as a whole is characterized by climatic instability with frequent and often dramatic fluctuations between periods of intense cold, when glaciers advanced, and periods of relative warmth (interglacials), when glaciers retreated (Burroughs 2005). In northern and central Europe as climates shifted between interglacial and glacial periods, landscapes and ecosystems were transformed from mostly woodland vegetation to windswept and mostly treeless steppe-tundra (Woodward 2014). Steppe-tundra, also known as Mammoth Steppe, is characterized by low-growing vegetation adapted to short growing seasons. Throughout the Upper Paleolithic, mammoths, reindeer, and other large herbivores lived south of the ice sheets and were hunted by Upper Paleolithic peoples (Woodward 2014).

During the last glacial maximum (LGM) (ca. 23,000 to 18,000 years ago), ice sheets, as much as 1.5 to 3.0 km thick, covered 30% of the Earth's landmass and captured so much of the Earth's water that global sea levels fell 125 m, exposing land bridges and connecting Britain to the rest of Europe. During this time, much of northern and central Europe was cold and extremely arid with winds coming off the ice sheets. Thick layers of loess (wind-blown dust) suggest that dust storms were frequent (Guthrie 2001). It is this combination of cold and intense aridity that leads some researchers to argue that there are no modern analogues for this biome (Guthrie 2001). Unlike the nightscapes of glacial and tundra landscapes today with their skies of glittering stars and shimmering moons, Upper Paleolithic nightscapes would have been much hazier because of the amount of dust in the air. While northern and central Europe experienced glacial conditions, parts of southern Europe acted as refugia, supporting high biodiversity of plants and animals that eventually spread northward as the climate warmed (Woodward 2014).

After 14,000 years ago, the glacial ice sheets were in retreat (except during the Younger Dryas) leaving behind lakes and bogs (Woodward 2014). From the archaeological data, it is clear that modern humans rapidly dispersed into Europe between 50,000 and 35,000 years ago (Higham et al. 2014) tolerating a wide variety of climates (Woodward 2014), while our closest living relatives, the Neandertals, died out shortly after modern humans arrived on the continent (Higham et al. 2014).

Upper Paleolithic peoples were fully modern in their anatomy and their behavior. Contrary to our caveman stereotype, it is clear that these individuals lived rich lives. Studies of their material culture suggest that by at least 25,000 years ago, they participated in communities of practice centered on the production of textiles (including spun, dyed fabrics), ceramics, music, paintings, engravings, and tools and weaponry, among other types of artifacts (Conkey 2010; Nowell 2015a; Soffer and Conkey 1997). Through trade and migration, goods such as mammoth ivory and seashells moved across the continent far from their places of origin. Their knowledge of materials and their ability to employ metaphorical thinking (Nowell 2015b) are evident in the cave paintings they produced, which frequently took advantage of the cave's natural topography to lend three-dimensionality to images. They often adorned their bodies and their clothing with exquisitely made and highly standardized personal ornaments (White 2007) and during the Gravettian period (ca. 28,000–21,000 years ago), in particular, they at times engaged in elaborate funerary rites (Formicola 2007). They were, as Conkey (1993) has observed, both materialists and symbolists.

SOURCES OF ARTIFICIAL LIGHT IN THE UPPER PALEOLITHIC

The extremely cold and dark nights of the Pleistocene were faced in many different ways by our ancestors. Hunkering down for the night in either rockshelters, open-air sites with mammoth-bone huts (e.g., Dolní Věstonice), or in shallow caves, light and warmth would have been vital components of their nocturnal lives. In addition to the examples of technical knowledge described above, Upper Paleolithic peoples possessed sophisticated pyrotechnical capabilities. Three known sources of artificial light were available to Upper Paleolithic peoples in Europe: (1) stone lamps, (2) torches, and (3) hearths or campfires. Each of these inventions is considered in turn below.

Stone Lamps

Most of what we know about lamps (figure 2.1) during the Upper Paleolithic comes from studies conducted by Sophie de Beaune (1987; de Beaune and White 1993) and her work remains the most complete survey of Upper Paleolithic lamps

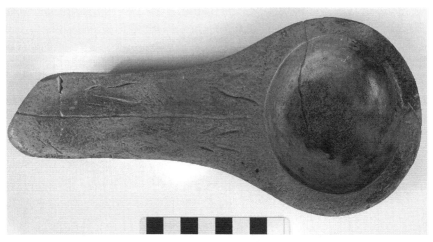

FIGURE 2.1. *Replica of ca. 17,500-year-old Upper Paleolithic stone lamp from Lascaux, France. (Photo by April Nowell)*

to date. According to de Beaune (1987), there are at least 302 probable lamps from at least 105 sites concentrated mainly in southwest France. Lamps outside this region and outside France, more broadly, are exceedingly rare. On average, the French sites contain two to three lamps, with the site of Lascaux being unusual in that 70 lamps have been recovered there. The lamps were carved from limestone or sandstone, and residue analysis conducted on a sample of lamps indicates that Upper Paleolithic peoples used animal fat, particularly from suids and bovids (de Beaune 1987), as fuel. Wicks tended to be made from mostly conifer, juniper, grass, and "non-woody" organics—based on ethnographic analogy and experimental archaeology. This latter category most likely included lichen or moss (de Beaune 1987; see Strong, chapter 12, and McGuire, chapter 13, this volume, for more on ancient lamps).

The majority of lamps are found at sites where it would have been possible to navigate without a reliance on artificial light (i.e., rockshelters, shallow caves, and open-air sites), suggesting that perhaps torches or hearths were the preferred method of generating artificial light in deep caves (de Beaune 1987). This preference may be for two reasons. First, while they have an advantage over hearths in that they are portable, lamps may not be as reliable or as long lasting as torches and hearths. Second, it may be difficult to navigate through some of the caves while carrying a lamp, given that the bowls or "active" parts of the lamps are often very shallow.

When the exact provenience of the lamps is known, it appears that they are often found at cave entrances where cave galleries intersect and along walls. De Beaune (1987) argues that these points may be strategic ones where lamps would be left to be used again at a later date. Often lamps are found in pairs, further suggesting that they have been stored in a particular locale for reuse, possibly by groups of two or more people. Many of the lamps are overturned either by accident or, as some have suggested, as a way to extinguish them (de Beaune 1987). Upper Paleolithic stone lamps cast very little light, approximately 2 lumens per m²—less than that generated by a standard candle, which casts about 13 lumens (The LED Light 2017)—but it is argued that this amount would have been sufficient to find one's way in a cave or even to engage in the production of imagery requiring fine detail, provided that the lamp was placed in close proximity to the image (de Beaune 1987; de Beaune and White 1993).

Torches

The second source of artificial light in the Upper Paleolithic is the torch. Functionally, torches are equivalent to lamps, since both are portable sources of light, but there may be as yet untested differences in longevity, reliability, and maneuverability between them. There is little archaeological evidence for torches other than rubbings. The practice of "rubbing" a torch along a cave wall functions to increase the amount of oxygen available, allowing the torch to burn more brightly. These marks are sometimes used in AMS dating of painted caves, most famously perhaps at France's Chauvet cave (Quiles et al. 2016). It is possible that torches may also have been used to facilitate hunting strategies, such as communal drives. There are examples of communal drives among modern humans (e.g., at the French site of Le Solutré) (Olsen 1989) and possibly among Neandertals (e.g., at the site of La Cotte de Saint-Brelade on the Channel Island of Jersey) (Scott 1980, 1986; but see Scott et al. 2014 for a reevaluation of this site).

Hearths and Campfires

Finally, the third type of artificial light in the Upper Paleolithic is the hearth or campfire. There is a general consensus in Paleolithic archaeology that while the opportunistic use of fire may date to 1 million years ago or more (Berna et al. 2012), the habitual use and control of fire dates back to half that amount of time (Roebroeks and Villa 2011). Hearths are associated with a variety of premodern hominin species, including the Neandertals, however, hearths in the Upper Paleolithic tend to be more structured than earlier ones. For example, people at this time often dug channels into the side of hearths to increase the amount of oxygen reaching the fire, and rocks were used for warmth banking and parching activities (Bar-Yosef 2002). The regular use of fire is thought to be associated with cooking/detoxifying plants and other foods (some of which may have been used as weaning foods), warmth, protection from predators, modification of the landscape, and tool production (e.g., fire-hardened spears and heat-treated lithics) (Burton 2009; Samson and Nunn 2015; Wrangham 2009; Wrangham and

Carmody 2010). Most important for our purposes here, the controlled use of fire extended the daylight hours, altering our circadian rhythms (Burton 2009; Gowlett 2012) and providing greater opportunities for socializing during what were previously nonproductive hours (Wiessner 2014; see also Gowlett 2012).

HUMAN INTERACTION AT NIGHT AND DURING THE DAY

All three sources of artificial light—lamps, torches, and hearths—appear to have been used both inside and outside caves and rockshelters, likely both during the day and at night. However, hearths, as a fixed point on a landscape and a feature large enough to accommodate groups of people sitting or dancing around them, are the only source of lighting that has an obvious social dimension. In a recent publication, Polly Wiessner (2014) documented the differences between "day talk" and "night talk" among a variety of hunter-gather societies. She observed that while day talk most often involved gossip and economic matters, the transition to nighttime saw people engaging in qualitatively different forms of social communication. Specifically, Wiessner noted that people participated in singing, dancing, ceremony, and storytelling around camp fires. These kinds of activities are well documented to promote social cohesion and adherence to social values and norms and/or to galvanize people to action. It is reasonable to assume that hunter-gatherer peoples living during the Upper Paleolithic may have also engaged in similar nighttime activities.

ARCHAEOLOGICAL EVIDENCE OF DANCE, STORYTELLING, AND MUSIC IN THE UPPER PALEOLITHIC

Dance

Most of the activities that Wiessner describes leave few traces in the prehistoric archaeological record. Possible exceptions include the panel of dots which may represent a bison or rhinoceros (Mohen 2002) or a mammoth (Clottes 2010) at the French Aurignacian site of Chauvet (figure 2.2). Forensic studies of the palm prints that comprise it suggest to researchers that there is a performative dimension to its production, as a number of different people's hands were involved in its rendering (Clottes 2003), and Leslie Van Gelder (pers. comm., May 2016) has suggested that perhaps some finger flutings, lines drawn in soft sediment on cave walls and ceilings (quite literally the residue of touch), may have been created during dance. At one time it was thought that 183 heel prints in the French cave Tuc D'Audoubert were the product of young individuals dancing, perhaps as part of an initiation ritual (Bégouën et al. 2009). A recent study that relied on the expertise of three professional trackers from the Ju/'hoan San failed to corroborate this initial interpretation (Pastoors et al. 2015). Instead, the heel marks have been reinterpreted as the normal stride of a man and adolescent boy collecting

FIGURE 2.2. *Panel of dots at Chauvet cave, France, dating to approximately 34,000 years ago, described variously as a bison, a rhinoceros (Mohen 2002), or a mammoth (Clottes 2010). The image was created by several people dipping their palms into pigment and then pressing their hands onto the cave wall to form a coherent image. (Photo by and permission of Prof. Jean Clottes)*

clay from a pit located 15 m away from a pair of beautiful clay bison. The trackers noted that the main reason to walk on your heels is to remain anonymous, as a knowledgeable tracker can recognize an individual from a complete footprint (Pastoors et al. 2015).

Storytelling

With regards to storytelling, Jean Clottes (1997) has argued that the changing subject matter of prehistoric art may reflect changes in peoples' stories and myths. For example, dangerous animals such as mammoths and cave lions over time begin to drop out of artists' repertoires. Similarly, it has been observed that over time there is a divergence between the animals Upper Paleolithic peoples consumed and the ones they depicted (Bahn 2016), suggesting that these images were not simply iconic representations of the world around them but may have held symbolic meaning(s) as well.

Azéma and Rivère (2012) have further developed this notion of storytelling by arguing that Upper Paleolithic images of single animals depicted with multiple horns, legs, or tails should be interpreted not as a herd of animals but rather as one animal in motion—a type of primitive animation. The cinematic effect is enhanced by changes in shadow and color saturation. Observing images by lamplight in the cave of Le Mouthe, Edward Wachtel (1993, 137) describes the experience thusly: "In the space of a few moments, I saw cuts and dissolves, change and movement. Forms appeared and disappeared. Colors shifted and changed. In short, I was watching a movie." Other attempts to depict motion from still images include breaking up a narrative over several panels or "scenes," such as the Panel of Lions at Chauvet cave, where artists depicted cave lions stalking and then lunging after fleeing bison (Azéma and Rivère 2012). (For a detailed discussion of the ability of Upper Paleolithic peoples to move between two, three, and four [i.e., time] dimensions in their art, see Nowell 2015a).

Music

In contrast to the often more ephemeral traces of dance and storytelling, in the Upper Paleolithic there is a substantial amount of material evidence for music in the form of instrumentation including more than 144 fragments of technologically sophisticated flutes, whistles, and pipes (Conard et al. 2009; Lawson and d'Errico 2002; Morley 2013). The flutes, many dating to the Aurignacian (ca. 40,000–30,000 BP), are particularly striking. Most derive from the sites of Geißenklösterle, Vogelherd, and Hohle Fels in Germany (Conard 2011; Conard et al. 2009), and from Isturitz in France (d'Errico et al. 2003; Lawson and d'Errico 2002). The instruments are made from bone (swan and vulture radii) and mammoth ivory. The ivory flutes are especially remarkable for their complexity. To fashion a flute from ivory one must cut a tube from the ivory, split it in half, hollow out each half and then seamlessly fit the two pieces back together. The flute makers incised small notches in each piece to guide themselves and they manufactured a sealant to make the flute air tight (Conard et al. 2009). Experimental work demonstrates that these ancient instruments were capable of producing a wide range of tones (Conard 2011).

Adding to the cacophony of sound were bullroarers and rasps. A bullroarer (figure 2.3A), known from France and Spain, is a "flat, perforated piece of wood, stone, bone, antler, or ivory tied onto the end of a cord, which creates a whirring sound when swung in a circular motion" (Morley 2013, 105). The sound varies based on the size of the bullroarer, the length of string, and the rate of rotation (Morley 2013). A rasp or scraped idiophone is a piece of "wood, bone or stone with grooves cut into it perpendicular to its length, which are then rubbed with another object to create a staccato vibration" (Morley 2013, 109–110). Some researchers have argued that the so-called Venus of Laussel, from France, is holding a rasp (Huyge 1991) (figure 2.3B). There are also percussive instruments at the Upper Paleolithic sites of Mezin and Mezirich in the Ukraine. At Mezin, for example, in what has been described as a central, nonresidential hut, researchers

FIGURE 2.3. *(A) Venus of Laussel, holding what may be a rasp. (Photo: Wikimedia Commons, https://commons.wikimedia.org/wiki/File%3AVenus-de-Laussel-vue-generale-noir.jpg) (B) Replica of a bullroarer from the Upper Paleolithic of Spain. (Photo by April Nowell)*

uncovered mammoth bones that had been struck multiple times and were found in association with reindeer-antler mallets and possible "rattles" (Morley 2013).

Finally, the painted caves may have played a significant role in the production of music during the Upper Paleolithic. A study conducted at 10 French caves by Iegor Reznikoff (2002; Reznikoff and Dauvois 1988) found a consistent correlation between places with the best resonance and places where art was located—often within 1 m of best resonance. According to Reznikoff (2002), the quality of resonance may explain why some panels that look ideal for painting were left untouched. In addition to the acoustic properties of caves, sometimes stalactites and other natural calcareous depositions in caves have chips and other percussive damage, suggesting they functioned as lithophones. The best-known example is the Spanish site of Nerja with its "organ," which consists of more than 200 folds of calcareous deposits, almost all decorated with nonfigurative signs such as lines and dots in black and red (Dams 1984, 1985; Morley 2013).

THE DIFFERENCE THE NIGHTTIME MAKES

From the above discussion, it is clear that there is a significant amount of evidence to support the existence of well-developed musical traditions throughout the European Upper Paleolithic. If Wiessner's (2014) observations about the nature of nocturnal social interactions can reasonably be projected onto our Upper Paleolithic hunter-gatherer past, the question is why these activities are temporally distributed in this particular manner. Arguably, music, dance, storytelling, and similar behaviors function to promote social cohesion, whether they are performed during the day or night. At the same time, there may be some very practical reasons for why such activities more often take place at night. The economic necessities of the foraging lifestyle may have prevailed during the day: hunting is likely more dangerous at night, and gathering would be more difficult in the near absence of light, given that it may not be convenient to carry torches or stone lamps. Therefore, one could legitimately argue that there is more "free" time in the evenings. These caveats notwithstanding, is it possible that there was something "special" or particularly effective about participating in these behaviors at night that might have been selected for evolutionarily? This broad question can be broken into three sub-questions: (1) Are people more sensitive to emotions at night? (2) How effectively do humans perceive emotion in music? and (3) Does emotion perceived in music have any residual effects that can be transferred to other contexts?

Sleep and the Emotional Brain

The first question to address is whether people are more emotionally sensitive at night. Emotion is normally defined as "relatively intense affective responses that usually involve a number of subcomponents—subjective feeling, physiological arousal, expression, action, tendency and regulation . . . which lasts minutes to a few hours" (Marin and Bhattacharya 2009, 3). Emotions are distinguished from "moods," which are "affective states that feature a lower intensity than emotions, that do not have a clear object and that last much longer than emotions—several hours to several days" (Marin and Bhattacharya 2009, 3; see also Goldstein and Walker 2014). While there has been little research on the role of sleep in regulating human emotions, clinical evidence does suggest that sleep deprivation can lead to affective imbalance (Yoo et al. 2007). The amygdala, gray matter located in both cerebral hemispheres, is involved in the experiencing of emotion (Yoo et al. 2007) and in clinical settings, patients who were well rested showed greater connectivity between the amygdala and the medial prefrontal cortex (MPFC). This connection is significant because the MPFC controls and inhibits amygdala function in what is described as a "top-down" manner, resulting in appropriate emotional responses in a given context (Yoo et al. 2007). Conversely, in people suffering from sleep deprivation, there is a weakened connection between the amygdala and the MPFC, and as a result, they exhibit an "amplified hyper-limbic response of the amygdala" because of the failure of the MPFC to exert this "top-down" inhibiting effect (Yoo et al. 2007, R878). In other words, researchers found that sleep-deprived people exhibited enhanced or exaggerated emotional responses to both negative and positive stimuli (Goldstein and Walker 2014; Gujar et al. 2011; Yoo et al. 2007).

However, sleep deprivation is not the same phenomenon as being tired at the end of a day. In physically and mentally healthy adults, sleep deprivation is rare and may occur occasionally due to life events such as changes in routine (e.g., adjusting to a new work schedule, caring for an infant, or traveling), illness, hormonal changes, or temporary stress. By contrast, our daily lives are regulated by a circadian cycle, or "biological clock." Our circadian ("24-hour") cycle relies primarily on the hormone melatonin to convert external light cues into biological rhythms (Burton 2009). All life forms, from single-celled organisms to humans, respond to sequences of light and darkness (Burton 2009). This response, referred to as photoperiodicity, is a function of the amount of the light hitting the earth at a particular time and place and it underlies species' specific patterns of activity, growth, and reproduction (Burton 2009). Unlike culturally conditioned patterns of sleep and wakefulness (e.g., see Storey, chapter 15, this volume, for a discussion of "first" and "second" sleep in Ancient Rome), circadian rhythms are genetically based and "hard-wired" within a species (Burton 2009; Gowlett 2012). According to Burton (2009, 47), this characteristic is because "the retina contains special nonvisual photoreceptors that convert light stimuli to chemical substances, which themselves affect a variety of target organisms." This system is what regulates our circadian rhythms and the 24-hour cycle that is characteristic of humans, and is in fact a mammalian-wide pattern (Burton 2009). In diurnal mammals like humans, circadian cycles function to counteract the need for sleep during the day while facilitating it at night (Waterhouse, Yumi, and Takeshi 2012). The circadian cycle influences the ideal time for sleep. All things being equal, an adult in synchronicity with the sun will naturally fall asleep a few hours after sunset.

Throughout our cycles, humans have "peak" and "off-peak" periods in energy levels and alertness, and evidence shows we have more difficulty regulating our emotions at off-peak times (Tucker et al. 2012; see also van Eekelen et al. 2003, 2004). It is possible that sitting around a campfire might have actually served to increase hominin alertness because the emission of light from a campfire would inhibit melatonin production (Burton 2009). However, as Frances Burton (2009) acknowledges, there is a crucial difference between light emission and light reception (i.e., how much light is actually hitting the retina). Glickman and colleagues (2003) demonstrated that the photoreceptors of the inferior retina are the most sensitive to light and they play the most significant role in melatonin suppression. In order for light from a campfire to heighten alertness in our Upper Paleolithic ancestors, they would have had to be in close proximity to it (approximately 1 m) and, more importantly, be gazing up at the fire (i.e., be lying down) (Burton 2009). If people were sitting, standing, walking, or dancing around a campfire and in the process gazing down at, directly at, across, around, or away from the firelight, the fire's luminosity would have provided enough light to see, but would have had negligible effects on hominin alertness.

While Tucker and colleagues (2012) studied emotional responses in humans to stimuli at 9 a.m. and 4 p.m., it is clear that an off-peak time for humans regulated by the distribution of sunlight, as our Upper Paleolithic ancestors would have been, is within those initial hours after sunset. Drawing a reasonable ethnographic analogy based on Wiessner's (2014) work, this time of day is also when groups would have been most likely assembled around a campfire. Thus, the answer to our first question—are humans more sensitive to emotion at night?— appears to be yes, with all things being equal, sensitivity to emotion and our ability to regulate emotional responses correlate with the peaks and troughs in energy and alertness that characterize an individual's circadian clock and one of these troughs occurs within the hours just after sunset.

Perception of Emotion in Music

The second question addresses how effectively humans perceive emotion in music. Music is argued to be a powerful and universal means of evoking emotion in humans (Andrade and Bhattacharya 2003; Marin and Bhattacharya 2009) and when we listen to our favorite music, brain areas associated with pleasure or rewards are activated (Andrade and Bhattacharya 2003; Blood and Zatorre 2001; Marin and Bhattacharya 2009). Researchers argue that, in contrast to most other kinds of stimuli in the everyday lives of people, "what is unique about musical emotions is not the underlying mechanisms or the emotions they evoke, but the rather the fact that music . . . is often intentionally designed to induce emotion, using whatever means available" (Juslin and Västfjäll [2008:572] as cited in Marin and Bhattacharya [2009]). In fact, studies demonstrate that professional musicians are able to communicate emotion through music almost as effectively as humans more generally express emotions through facial and vocal cues (Logeswaran and Bhattacharya 2009). Thus the answer to our second question—how effectively do humans perceive emotion in music?—is that data support the assertion that music is a highly effective means of communicating emotion and that humans are particularly sensitive and susceptible to both positive and negative emotion in music.

Residual Effects of Emotions Perceived through Music

A third line of inquiry raises the question as to whether emotion perceived in music has any lasting effects. In a recent study of the cross-modality of emotion perception, Nidhya Logeswaran and Joydeep Bhattacharya discovered that listening to even short excerpts of music that listeners perceived as "happy" or "sad" influenced subsequent interpretation of images of human faces, especially neutral faces that by definition contain less information about emotion (Logeswaran and Bhattacharya 2009). The researchers write, "behavioural data clearly showed that listening to musical excerpts . . . could significantly influence subsequent explicit evaluation of visual emotional stimuli" (Logeswaran and Bhattacharya 2009, 133). Similarly, other studies have found that listening to "positive" music impacts sense of taste (Marin and Bhattacharya 2009) and even sensitivity to false memory production (Marin and Bhattacharya 2009; Storbeck and Clore 2005). Hajime Fukui and Kumiko Toyoshima found that after listening to preferred music, participants were more altruistic (Fukui and Toyoshima 2014). Listening to music they disliked made participants less altruistic, whereas silence had no impact on subsequent behaviors. Although listening to preferred music is not the same as perceiving emotion in music, emotion is still being generated in the listener that influences later behaviors. As Mark Changizi (2009) notes, "the lion's share of emotionally evocative stimuli in the lives of our ancestors would have been the faces and bodies of other people." One possible implication of these cross-model studies of music and emotion is that positive or negative emotion perceived in and generated through music in Upper Paleolithic societies could have been redirected or manipulated to influence how individuals perceive others within or outside their groups and to modify subsequent action. Thus, the answer to our third question—does emotion perceived in music have any lasting effects?—is tentatively yes. Cross-modal studies of this nature are still in their infancy and more research into the duration and nature of these residual effects is needed but the preliminary data are compelling.

CONCLUSIONS

In thinking about music and emotion, the performative nature of music is key. Most contemporary and historically documented hunter-gather music is produced without instrumentation, relying instead on the voice for melody and the body for percussion (Morley 2013). As Morley (2013) notes, what instruments are incorporated into the performance are most often percussive. Thus, in this sense, instrumentation becomes an extension of the body. Before the advent of recording devices, people had to experience music as it was happening, and Marin and Bhattacharya (2009) argue that this relationship between listeners and the musicians / music-makers enhanced the emotional resonance of the experience. These researchers are referring to a mostly passive listener, so one can infer that music's affective impact is heightened when we consider that with hunter-gatherers, we should be thinking in terms of embodied, performative acts.

In conclusion, we know from fossil, archaeological, and paleoenvironmental data that Upper Paleolithic nocturnal soundscapes would have included the calls of nocturnal animals, the crackle of campfires, and the resonance of human communication. The ethnographic work of Polly Wiessner and Iain Morley suggests that Upper Paleolithic nights would also have been filled with song, dance, and storytelling. While these behaviors can and do take place during the day, evidence from neurobiology and psychology suggests that their ability to promote social cohesion and to galvanize people into action may be particularly effective at night. As we have seen, music is a highly potent means of communicating emotion and this emotion can be transferred to other senses and other contexts. As fully modern humans, Upper Paleolithic peoples would have been sensitive to both positive and negative emotion in music, particularly as the sun set and their circadian clocks prepared them for the restorative sleep to come.

REFERENCES

Andrade, Paulo Estévão, and Joydeep Bhattacharya. 2003. "Brain Tuned to Music." *Journal of the Royal Society of Medicine* 96(6):284–287. https://doi.org/10.1258/jrsm.96.6.284.

Azéma, Marc, and Florent Rivère. 2012. "Animation in Palaeolithic Art: A Pre-Echo of Cinema." *Antiquity* 86(332):316–324. https://doi.org/10.1017/S0003598X00062785.

Bahn, Paul. 2016. *Images of the Ice Age*. Oxford: Oxford University Press.

Bar-Yosef, Ofer. 2002. "Upper Paleolithic Revolution." *Annual Review of Anthropology* 31(1):363–393. https://doi.org/10.1146/annurev.anthro.31.040402.085416.

Bégouën, Robert, Carole Fritz, Gilles Tosello, Jean Clottes, A. Pastoors, and F. Faist. 2009. *Le sanctuaire secret des bisons: Il y a 14 000 ans dans la caverne du Tuc d'Audoubert*. Paris: Somogy.

Berna, Francesco, Paul Goldberg, Liora Kolska Horwitz, James Brink, Sharon Holt, Marion Bamford, and Michael Chazan. 2012. "Microstratigraphic Evidence of In Situ Fire in the Acheulean Strata of Wonderwerk Cave, Northern Cape Province, South Africa." *Proceedings of the National Academy of Sciences of the United States of America* 109(20):E1215–E1220. https://doi.org/10.1073/pnas.1117620109.

Blood, Anne J., and, Robert J. Zatorre. 2001. "Intensely Pleasurable Responses to Music Correlate with Activity in Brain Regions Implicated in Reward and Emotion." *Proceedings of the National Academy of Sciences* 98:11818–11823. https://doi.org/10.1073/pnas.191355898.

Burroughs, William J. 2005. *Climate Change in Prehistory: The End of the Reign of Chaos*. Cambridge: Cambridge University Press. https://doi.org/10.1017/CBO9780511535826.

Burton, Frances. 2009. *Fire: The Spark that Ignited Human Evolution*. Albuquerque: University of New Mexico Press.

Changizi, Mark. 2009. "Why Does Music Make Us Feel?" *Scientific American*. https://www.scientificamerican.com/article/why-does-music-make-us-fe/.

Clottes, Jean. 1997. "Art of the Light and Art of the Depths." In *Beyond Art: Pleistocene Image and Symbol*, ed. Margaret W. Conkey, Olga Soffer, Deborah Stratmann, and Nina Jablonski, 203–216. Memoirs of the California Academy of Sciences 23. San Francisco: California Academy of Sciences.

Clottes, Jean. 2003. *Chauvet Cave: The Art of Earliest Times*. Salt Lake City: University of Utah Press.

Clottes, Jean. 2010. *Cave Art*. New York: Phaidon.

Conard, Nicholas J. 2011. "The Demise of the Neanderthal Cultural Niche and the Beginning of the Upper Paleolithic in Southwestern Germany." In *Neanderthal Lifeways, Subsistence and Technology: One Hundred Fifty Years of Neanderthal Study*. Vertebrate Paleobiology and Paleoanthropology 19, ed. Nicholas Conard and Jürgen Richter, 223–240. New York: Springer. https://doi.org/10.1007/978-94-007-0415-2_19.

Conard, Nicholas, Marina Malina, and Susanne Münzel. 2009. "New Flutes Document the Earliest Musical Tradition in Southwestern Germany." *Nature* 460:737–740.

Conkey, Margaret. 1993. "Humans as Materialists and Symbolists: Image Making in the Upper Paleolithic." In *The Origin and Evolution of Humans and Humanness*, ed. David Tab Rasmussen, 95–118. Boston: Jones and Bartlett.

Conkey, Margaret. 2010. "Images without Words: The Construction of Prehistoric Imaginaries for Definitions of 'Us.'" *Journal of Visual Culture* 9(3):272–283. https://doi.org/10.1177/1470412910380341.

d'Errico, Francesco, Christopher Henshilwood, Graeme Lawson, Marian Vanhaeren, Anne-Marie Tillier, Marie Soressi, Françoise Bresson, Bruno Maureille, April Nowell, Joseba Lakarra, et al. 2003. "Archaeological Evidence for the Emergence of Language, Symbolism, and Music: An Alternative Multidisciplinary Perspective." *Journal of World Prehistory* 17(1):1–70. https://doi.org/10.1023/A:1023980201043.

Dams, Lya. 1984. "Preliminary Findings at the 'Organ Sanctuary' in the Cave of Nerja, Malaga, Spain." *Oxford Journal of Archaeology* 3(1):1–14. https://doi.org/10.1111/j.1468-0092.1984.tb00112.x.

Dams, Lya. 1985. "Paleolithic Lithophones: Descriptions and Comparisons." *Oxford Journal of Archaeology* 4(1):31–46. https://doi.org/10.1111/j.1468-0092.1985.tb00229.x.

de Beaune, Sophie A. 1987. "Paleolithic Lamps and Their Specialization: A Hypothesis." *Current Anthropology* 28(4):569–577. https://doi.org/10.1086/203565.

de Beaune, Sophie A., and Randall White. 1993. "Paleolithic Lamps." *Scientific American* 266(3):108–113. https://doi.org/10.1038/scientificamerican0393-108.

Formicola, Vincenzo. 2007. "From the Sunghir Children to the Romito Dwarf: Aspects of the Upper Paleolithic Funerary Landscape." *Current Anthropology* 48(3):446–453. https://doi.org/10.1086/517592.

Fukui, Hajime, and Kumiko Toyoshima. 2014. "Chill-Inducing Music Enhances Altruism in Humans." *Frontiers in Psychology* 5:1215. https://doi.org/10.3389/fpsyg.2014.01215.

Glickman, Gena, John P. Hanifin, Mark D. Rollag, Jenny Wang, Howard Cooper, and George C. Brainard. 2003. "Inferior Retinal Light Exposure Is More Effective than

Superior Retinal Exposure in Suppressing Melatonin in Humans." *Journal of Biological Rhythms* 18(1):71–79. https://doi.org/10.1177/0748730402239678.

Goldstein, Andrea, and Matthew P. Walker. 2014. "The Role of Sleep in Emotional Brain Function." *Annual Review of Clinical Psychology* 10(1):679–708. https://doi.org/10.1146/annurev-clinpsy-032813-153716.

Gowlett, John. 2012. "Firing Up the Social Brain." In *Social Brain, Distributed Mind*, ed. Robin Dunbar, Clive Gamble, and John Gowlett, 341–366. Oxford: Oxford University Press.

Gujar, Ninad, Seung-Schik Yoo, Peter Hu, and Matthew P. Walker. 2011. "Sleep Deprivation Amplifies Reactivity of Brain Reward Networks, Biasing the Appraisal of Positive Emotional Experiences." *Journal of Neuroscience* 31(12):4466–4474. https://doi.org/10.1523/JNEUROSCI.3220-10.2011.

Guthrie, R. Dale. 2001. "Origin and Causes of the Mammoth Steppe: A Story of Cloud Cover, Woolly Mammal Tooth Pits, Buckles, and Inside-Out Beringia." *Quaternary Science Reviews* 20(1-3):549–574. https://doi.org/10.1016/S0277-3791(00)00099-8.

Higham, Tom, Katerina Douka, Rachel Wood, Christopher Bronk Ramsey, Fiona Brock, Laura Basell, Marta Camps, Alvaro Arrizabalaga, Javier Baena, Cecillio Barroso-Ruíz, et al. 2014. "The Timing and Spatiotemporal Patterning of Neanderthal disappearance." *Nature* 512(7514):306–309. https://doi.org/10.1038/nature13621.

Huyge, Dirk. 1991. "The 'Venus' of Laussel in the Light of Ethnomusicology." *Archaeologie in Vlaanderen* 1:11–18.

Lawson, Graeme, and Francesco d'Errico. 2002. "Microscopic, Experimental and Theoretical Reassessment of Upper Paleolithic Bird-Bone Pipes from Istiritz, France: Ergonomics of Design, Systems of Notation and the Origins of Musical Traditions." In *Studien zur Musikarchäologie III*, ed. Ellen Hickman, Anne Kilmer, and Ricardo Eichman, 119–142. Rahden: Verlag Marie Leidorf.

The LED Light. 2017. "What Today's Consumers Need to Know about Lumens." Accessed June 24, 2017. www.theledlight.com/lumens.html.

Logeswaran, Nidhya, and Joydeep Bhattacharya. 2009. "Crossmodal Transfer of Emotion by Music." *Neuroscience Letters* 455(2):129–133. https://doi.org/10.1016/j.neulet.2009.03.044.

Marin, Manuela M., and Joydeep Bhattacharya. 2009. "Music Induced Emotions: Some Current Issues and Cross-Modal Comparisons." In *Music Education*, ed. Joao Hermida and Mariana Ferrero, 1–38. Hauppauge, NY: Nova Science.

Mohen, Jean-Pierre. 2002. *Prehistoric Art*. Paris: Éditions Pierre Terrail.

Morley, Iain. 2013. *The Prehistory of Music: Human Evolution, Archaeology and the Origins of Musicality*. Oxford: Oxford University Press. https://doi.org/10.1093/acprof:osobl/9780199234080.001.0001.

Nowell, April. 2015a. "Learning to See and Seeing to Learn: Children, Communities of Practice and Pleistocene Visual Cultures." *Cambridge Archaeological Journal* 25(4):889–899. https://doi.org/10.1017/S0959774315000360.

Nowell, April. 2015b. "Children, Metaphorical Thinking and Upper Paleolithic Visual Cultures." *Childhood in the Past* 8(2):122–132. https://doi.org/10.1179/1758571615Z .00000000034.

Olsen, Sandra. 1989. "Solutré: A Theoretical Approach to the Reconstruction of Upper Palaeolithic Hunting Strategies." *Journal of Human Evolution* 18(4):295–327. https://doi.org/10.1016/0047-2484(89)90034-1.

Pastoors, Andreas, Tilman Lenssen-Erz, Tsamkxao Ciqae, Ui Kxunta, Thui Thao, Robert Bégouën, Megan Biesele, and Jean Clottes. 2015. "Tracking in Caves: Experience Based Reading of Pleistocene Human Footprints in French Caves." *Cambridge Archaeological Journal* 25(3):551–564. https://doi.org/10.1017/S0959774315000050.

Quiles, Anita, Hélène Valladas, Hervé Bocherens, Emmanuelle Delqué-Količ, Evelyne Kaltnecker, Johannes van der Plicht, Jean-Jacques Delannoy, Valérie Feruglio, Carole Fritz, Julien Monney, et al. 2016. "A High-Precision Chronological Model for the Decorated Upper Paleolithic Cave of Chauvet-Pont d'Arc, Ardèche, France." *Proceedings of the National Academy of Sciences of the United States of America* 113(17):4670–4675. https://doi.org/10.1073/pnas.1523158113.

Reznikoff, Iegor. 2002. "Prehistoric Paintings, Sound and Rocks." In *The Archaeology of Sound: Origin and Organization,* Papers from the 2nd Symposium of the International Study Group on Music Archaeology, ed. Ellen Hickmann, Anne D. Kilmer, and Ricardo Eichmann, 39–56. Berlin: Orient-Archäologie.

Reznikoff, Iegor, and Michel Dauvois. 1988. "La Dimension Sonore Des Grottes Ornées." *Bulletin de la Société Préhistorique Française* 85(8):238–246. https://doi.org/10.3406/bspf.1988.9349.

Roebroeks, Wil, and Paola Villa. 2011. "On the Earliest Evidence for Habitual Use of Fire in Europe." *Proceedings of the National Academy of Sciences of the United States of America* 108(13):5209–5214. https://doi.org/10.1073/pnas.1018116108.

Samson, David R., and Charles L. Nunn. 2015. "Sleep Intensity and the Evolution of Human Cognition." *Evolutionary Anthropology* 24(6):225–237. https://doi.org/10.1002/evan.21464.

Scott, Beccy, Martin Bates, Richard Bates, Chantal Conneller, Matt Pope, Andrew Shaw, and Geoff Smith. 2014. "A New View From La Cotte de St Brelade, Jersey." *Antiquity* 88(339):13–29. https://doi.org/10.1017/S0003598X00050195.

Scott, Katharine. 1980. "Two Hunting Episodes of Middle Palaeolithic Age at La Cotte de Saint Brelade, Jersey." *World Archaeology* 12(2):137–152. https://doi.org/10.1080/00438243.1980.9979788.

Scott, Katharine. 1986. "The Bone Assemblages from Layers 3 and 6." In *La Cotte de St Brelade 1961–1978,* ed. Paul Callow and Jean M. Cornford, 59–85. Norwich: Geo.

Soffer, Olga, and Margaret W. Conkey. 1997. "Studying Ancient Visual Cultures." In *Beyond Art: Pleistocene Image and Symbol,* ed. Margaret W. Conkey, Olga Soffer,

Deborah Stratmann, and Nina G. Jablonski, 1–16. Memoirs of the California Academy of Sciences 23. San Francisco: California Academy of Sciences.

Storbeck, Justin, and Gerald L. Clore. 2005. "With Sadness Comes Accuracy; with Happiness, Falsememory: Mood and the False Memory Effect." *Psychological Science* 16(10):785–91.

Tucker, Adrienne M., Rebecca Feuerstein, Peter Mende-Siedlecki, Kevin N. Ochsner, and Yaakov Stern. 2012. "Double Dissociation: Circadian Off-Peak Times Increase Emotional Reactivity; Aging Impairs Emotion Regulation Via Reappraisal." *Emotion (Washington, DC)* 12(5):869–874. https://doi.org/10.1037/a0028207.

van Eekelen, Alexander P.J., Jan H. Houtveen, and Gerard A. Kerkhof. 2004. "Circadian Variation in Cardiac Autonomic Activity: Reactivity Measurements to Different Types of Stressors." *Chronobiology International* 21(1):107–129. https://doi.org/10.1081/CBI-120027983.

van Eekelen, Alexander P. J., Gerard A. Kerkhof, and Jan G. C. Amsterdam. 2003. "Circadian Variation in Cortisol Reactivity to an Acute Stressor." *Chronobiology International* 20(5):863–878. https://doi.org/10.1081/CBI-120024212.

Wachtel, Edward. 1993. "The First Picture Show: Cinematic Aspects of Cave Art." *Leonardo* 26(2):135–140. https://doi.org/10.2307/1575898.

Waterhouse, Jim, Fukuda Yumi, and Morita Takeshi. 2012. "Daily Rhythms of the Sleep-Wake Cycle." *Journal of Physiological Anthropology* 31(5):1–14. https://doi.org/10.1186/1880-6805-31-5.

White, Randall. 2007. "Systems of Personal Ornamentation in the Early Upper Paleolithic: Methodological Challenges and New Observations." In *Rethinking the Human Revolution*, ed. Paul Mellars, Katie Boyle, Ofer Bar-Yosef, and Christopher Stringer, 287–302. Cambridge: MacDonald Institute.

Wiessner, Polly W. 2014. "Embers of Society: Firelight Talk Among the Ju/'hoansi Bushmen." *Proceedings of the National Academy of Sciences of the United States of America* 111(39):14027–14035. https://doi.org/10.1073/pnas.1404212111.

Woodward, Jamie. 2014. *The Ice Age: A Very Short Introduction.* Oxford: Oxford University Press. https://doi.org/10.1093/actrade/9780199580699.001.0001.

Wrangham, Richard. 2009. *Catching Fire: How Cooking Made Us Human.* New York: Basic Books.

Wrangham, Richard, and Rachel Carmody. 2010. "Human Adaptation to the Control of Fire." *Evolutionary Anthropology* 19(5):187–199. https://doi.org/10.1002/evan.20275.

Yoo, Seung-Schik, Ninad Gujar, Peter Hu, Ferenc A. Jolesz, and Matthew P. Walker. 2007. "The Human Emotional Brain Without Sleep—A Prefrontal Amygdala Disconnect." *Current Biology* 17(20):R877–R878. https://doi.org/10.1016/j.cub.2007.08.007.

CHAPTER 3

Classic Maya Nights at Copan, Honduras and El Cerén, El Salvador

NANCY GONLIN AND CHRISTINE C. DIXON

Anthropologists have extensively studied Mesoamerica, which provides fertile ground for exploring the vast amount of evidence of ancient people's nightly practices.[1] A fundamental question we address in this chapter is how the perspective of viewing ancient Mesoamerican practices through the lens of the night enriches our understanding of the past (Ekirch 2005; Koslofsky 2011; Galinier et al. 2010; Monod Becquelin and Galinier 2016). As a culture area, Mesoamerica, which encompasses the modern countries of Guatemala, Honduras, Belize, El Salvador, and most of Mexico (figure 1.2), has many features in common across the myriad regions and diversity of lifeways (see Aveni, chapter 7, and Coltman, chapter 10, this volume, for more on Mesoamerica). Complexly organized societies dominated the region as early as a few thousand years ago (Evans 2013; Joyce 2004). Here, we concentrate on the Lowland Classic Maya, well known for their hieroglyphic writing and sophisticated iconography, who built the vast majority of their cities from approximately 250 to 900 CE (figure 1.3) which corresponds to the dates of the Classic period in Mesoamerica. Two major types of data figure in this study: material items (artifacts, features, architecture) from the remains of

DOI: 10.5876/9781607326786.c003

a range of household sizes and statuses, and symbolic representations recorded in iconography and epigraphy. Data are complemented by ethnography, ethnohistory, and cultural astronomy, for enhanced "night vision." Particular attention is given to the sites of Copan in Honduras and El Cerén in El Salvador. Copan represents the types of remains typical to a tropical environment with poor preservation of organic remains and highly eroded materials as the norm, whereas Cerén offers us a snapshot preserved in time: just as the sun set on this community, it was buried under meters of volcanic ash, resulting in extraordinary preservation of an agricultural community at night. This rapidly abandoned site (Inomata and Sheets 2000) offers an unprecedented opportunity to study the night. The contrast between these two sites is quite informative and complements each other in what we can learn about the past (e.g., Gonlin 2004; Webster, Gonlin, and Sheets 1997). Furthermore, these two sites have been heavily investigated by the authors.

Like many peoples past and present, the Classic Maya often viewed the night as an ominous time. It was a time of uncertainty when the gods of the Underworld, or Xibalba, became active—when one hoped that the sun would rise once again on the following day. The Mesoamerican night also had cosmological significance for time keeping, astrological observations (Aveni, chapter 7, this volume), spiritual beliefs, and nocturnal practices (Coltman, chapter 10, this volume). Nighttime rituals and celebrations took place on auspicious dates. When one did sleep, one's companion spirit (co-essence) could roam about (Houston and Stuart 1989, 2; Freidel et al. 1993, 192). The Classic Maya named this spirit *way*, which "derives from the words 'to sleep' and 'to dream'" (Freidel et al. 1993, 192). Ethnographers of contemporary descendants (Mothré and Monod Becquelin 2016; Reyna 1962 as cited in Hofling 1993; Wisdom 1941) have commented upon the respect afforded the night. Complementary dualities are well-known in Maya cosmovision (Freidel et al. 1993) and the contrast between night and day is one of the most ubiquitous cross-cultural dualities. The night can be perceived as a boundary, a border that one negotiates within a cultural context (figure 1.1). The Classic Maya nightscape was composed of both natural and cultural elements that together created a world of its own that had to be properly negotiated in order to prosper.

In this chapter, we focus on the night as it is connected to the concept of darkness and the existence of darkness in the natural and built environment, including emic classifications of artifacts (Jackson 2016). Darkness is one of the many conditions of the night, but there are other places where darkness occurs (Dowd and Hensey 2016) and where analogies with night are abundant, such as in the experience of volcanic eruptions (Egan 2017) and total eclipses (see Aveni, chapter 7, this volume) or in special locations like caves (see Nowell, chapter 2, this volume, for caves and darkness). James Brady and Keith Prufer (Brady and Prufer 2005), as well as many others (e.g., Moyes 2012), have contributed

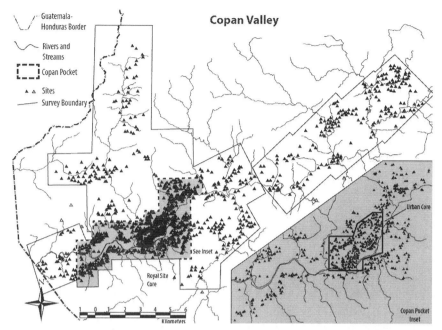

FIGURE 3.1. *Copan valley, Honduras, illustrating sites located on the survey (triangles). The inset shows the Copan Pocket, the largest expanse of alluvial land in the valley. Here is located the Main Group along with urban neighborhoods of Las Sepulturas and El Bosque, all of which comprise the urban core. (Map courtesy of and with permission from David M. Reed and W. Scott Zeleznik)*

greatly to our understanding of caves in Mesoamerica, and while not explicitly dealt with in this chapter, cave research holds great potential to contribute to our study of ancient nights and experiences of darkness in the past.

COPAN AND CERÉN

The case studies of Copan and Cerén afford unique access points for examining the Classic Maya and a useful contrast of archaeological preservation, settlement size, and location within the Maya area. Copan is the southernmost expression of Classic Maya high culture located in western Honduras. The Copan Maya flourished for centuries along the Río Copan in an interior valley of the tropical highlands (figure 3.1). Resources are abundant and the valley is ideal for agriculture because both alluvial and upland soils can be productively farmed (Wingard 2016). This site has been heavily researched over decades of archaeological investigations that encompass a range of settlement from commoner residences to palatial ones, resulting in a substantial amount of information about the houses in which people of varying social statuses lived their lives and spent their nights

(Andrews and W. Fash 2005; W. Fash 2001; Sanders 1986–1990; Webster et al. 2000; Willey et al. 1994). Settlement surveys and testing, as well as chronological analysis, were carried out in all major tributaries of the Río Copan, so the distribution of the population through time is well known (W. Fash 1983; Freter 1988; Willey and Leventhal 1979). A dynasty of sixteen kings ruled Copan for about a four-hundred-year period from 426 to 822 CE, with a peak population size around twenty thousand during the seventh and eighth centuries (Webster 2014, 352). Intensive excavations of the royal compounds provide historical details about the kings and queens, and their lives and deaths (Agurcia Fasquelle 2004; Andrews and Bill 2005; Bell et al. 2004; Sharer et al. 1999; *inter alia*). Royal precincts were centered in an area referred to variously as the Main Group or Principal Group. Two urban neighborhoods (Las Sepulturas and El Bosque) surrounded the royal establishment and, with the Main Group, collectively formed what is called the urban core. Settlement thinned out as one moved from the urban core to the hinterlands, which have also been heavily investigated.

Because of its remarkable preservation, Cerén, a farming community buried beneath several meters of volcanic ash, offers a particularly informative case study to search the archaeological record for nocturnal activities (Dixon 2013; Sheets 2002, 2006; Sheets et al. 2015). Located in the Zapotitán Valley of El Salvador, inhabitants may have been under the domain of local elites who resided at San Andrés or other nearby centers within a few kilometers, though evidence suggests the Cerén community maintained significant autonomy (Dixon 2013; Sheets et al. 2015). "The Loma Caldera eruption was disastrous for Ceren and nearby settlements, but only within a diameter of 2–3 km from the epicenter" (Sheets 2012, 50). The serendipitous discovery of Cerén is unparalleled in the valley, meaning that nearby neighbors are currently unknown. Payson Sheets has hypothesized that the Loma Caldera eruption that buried Cerén in 630 CE occurred just after sunset, before tools for daily activities had been put away, before dishes were cleaned, before sleeping mats were retrieved from the rafters, and before the occupants had returned home—the front doors of domiciles were tied shut (Sheets 2006, 37). Sheets (2002) has suggested that this community of approximately a hundred residents was in the midst of a ritual harvest feast when the eruption occurred. Thus, because of the time of the eruption and the extraordinary preservation, the site provides an unprecedented opportunity to examine nightly practices in Mesoamerica. To date, twelve earthen structures have been completely excavated and restored at the site; these are divided among four separate households (McKee 2002), each with a public community structure in close proximity (figure 3.2). Agricultural fields and an earthen road (*sacbe*) have also been recovered, greatly adding to our knowledge of ancient farming and community organization. The amount of detail on ancient life that is preserved is astounding, to say the least. The differences in the nature of

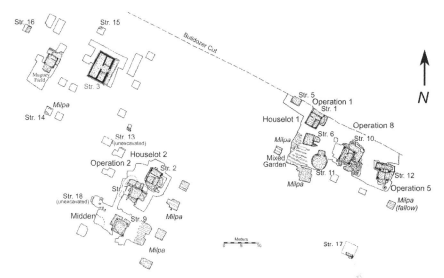

FIGURE 3.2. *Cerén, El Salvador, excavated structures. Each of the four households contains a public/community structure. (Courtesy of and with permission from Payson Sheets)*

preservation, the scale of research, settlement size, and excavation methodology between Cerén and Copan provide complementary data sets for reconstructing nightly practices of the Classic Maya.

THEORETICAL ORIENTATIONS TO INVESTIGATE THE NIGHT

In general, the archaeological record has not been explicitly or consistently examined for nightly practices, let alone those common among the Classic Maya. We draw upon two major theoretical perspectives that enhance each other: household archaeology and practice theory (Bourdieu 1977) (see Gonlin and Nowell, chapter 1, this volume, for more on theoretical orientations). These two different approaches have in common an interest in how people dealt with life on a daily basis. They explore the ways that human behaviors construct, maintain, resist, and deconstruct the specific cultural, social, historical, and environmental contexts that in turn construct, maintain, and deconstruct human practices.

A vast amount of research has been conducted on the remains of ancient households in Mesoamerica, making this approach ideal to investigate commoners, elites, and royalty alike (Acosta Ochoa 2012; Carballo 2011; Douglass and Gonlin 2012; Flannery 1976; Haviland 1985; Hendon 2010; Inomata and Houston 2001; Joyce and Gillespie 2000; Lohse and Valdez 2004; Manzanilla 1986; McEachern et. al 1989; Robin 2013; Santley and Hirth 1992; Sheets 2006; Smith 2016; Webster 1989; Wilk and Ashmore 1988; *inter alia*). The same information that archaeologists have gathered to answer a myriad of questions about household function, social organization, political connections, ideology, and more, can be reoriented to successfully determine nightly activities—essentially establishing a record of nighttime household archaeology. Most ancient people spent the night at home, a place that offered comfort in material and nonmaterial ways. Once safely inside, they involved themselves in several activities, including the obvious ones, such as sleeping and, perhaps, sex.

Many archaeologists have successfully applied elements of practice theory (Bourdieu 1977) to interpret the past (e.g., Hodder 1995; Overholtzer 2012; Pauketat 2001; Robin 2013), thereby exploring the inextricable connection between human practices and the social, political, cultural, environmental, and historical contexts that shape and are shaped by such practices. Individuals, actions, and their agency are given primacy and are used as explanatory mechanisms (Giddens 1984). Much of archaeological research in this theoretical domain has focused on the daily practices of people in the past and emphasized how social change is the result of the choices and actions of all individuals in a social group. While the term *daily practices* is not meant to include only those activities between sunrise and sunset, limitations of our resolution of the past have often favored activities of the daytime. Here we begin to explore the practices of the night.

SETTING OF THE NEOTROPICAL NIGHTSCAPE

Nightly conditions of dark and cold differ from those of day world over, meaning that humans must adjust each day to a transformed environment. Human eyesight is compromised, body temperature drops, and hormonal changes occur as the sun sets. Nocturnal beasts and birds (jaguars, coyotes, bats, toads, owls, night herons, kinkajous, etc.) emerge as darkness rises (Benson 1997) and some tropical plants flourish in the moonlight (Slotten 2017). In the northern latitude tropics (defined as from the equator to 23.5°N), the season will have an impact on the amount of darkness and sunlight received diurnally (NASA 2016). In addition to the season, variations in the amount and intensity of sunlight received per day depend on cloud coverage (Solar Illumination: Seasonal and Diurnal Patterns 2016); however, night and day are similar in length in tropical regions, resulting in a more consistent experience in the amount of daytime and nighttime throughout the year. In terms of climate, both Copan (600 masl) and Cerén (450 masl) fall into what is classically known as the *tierra caliente*, or literally "hot lands" (Vivó Escoto 1971, 188), that are below 1,000 m in elevation. "High, but not excessive, daytime temperatures (29°–32°C) [84°–90°F] contrast with cool nights (20°–24°C) [68°–75°F]. The common adage 'night is the winter of the tropics' is quite true of the lowlands, where daily range of temperature exceeds the annual range by many degrees" (Vivó Escoto 1971, 199). Both Cerén (Sheets 2002, 1) and Copan (Webster et al. 2000, 16) are classified as *Aw* in the Köppen system, known as tropical wet-dry, which means that this humid tropical climate has a dry season that occurs during the winter (Vivó Escoto 1971, 205). Most of the precipitation in the form of rain falls from June through November (Vivó Escoto 1971, 212). Rainy-season nights may have involved different practices than dry-season nights (Kristin Landau, personal communication). Downpours often occur in late afternoon, resulting in cooler evening air. Sound attenuation is higher for drier air; that is, sound travels farther when the relative humidity is higher (Shields and Bass 1977). Therefore, as the sharpness of human eyesight diminishes at night, hearing acuity increases and is assisted by the night air. These data provide information on the natural conditions to which Classic Maya people had to adapt and they set the scene for examining the nighttime practices.

NIGHTTIME PRACTICES AMONG THE CLASSIC MAYA

How did the Classic Maya adapt to the night? What did they do during the night, or what were their practices? Some practices were quotidian in nature, such as keeping warm on a cool night during the rainy season or keeping cool on a warm night during the dry season. Whether ruler or farmer, these aspects of the nightscape had to be dealt with; however, wide differences in housing moderated one's experience. Other practices involved the supernatural and occurred on only certain occasions rather than on a nightly basis. Here we first look at the place where most people spent the night, at home.

At Home at Night

Throughout the Classic Maya world, people built and used a range of housing types (Halperin 2017). The highest class and fewest residences are those made entirely of stone. Some stone structures sported beam-and-mortar roofs with plaster capping, while there were also buildings with substantial walls that had thatch roofs. Adobe housing was also known for the Maya area. The most numerous type of domiciles, however, were those constructed of wattle and daub with a thatch roof. Structures built of poles lashed together and topped with thatching were also constructed and usually functioned as kitchens, as was the case at Cerén (Calvin 2002, 72–73). This variety in structure types directly affected one's nightly experiences, whether commoner or king.

Heating imbalances occurred on an annual cycle in the tropics, with less heat from the sun reaching the northern tropics during a time period that coincides with the rainy season (NASA 2016), coalescing to make conditions cool and damp. In his book on Maya building practices, Elliot Abrams (1994) contrasts two primary house forms at Copan that are points along a continuum of residential buildings: (1) wattle-and-daub structure with a thatched roof and (2) the improved house form with both substructure and superstructure built of stone. Abrams (1994, 33) contrasts heating costs in each:

The size of individual rooms varies considerably between the basic form and the improved form. Rooms in the improved form tend to be smaller, self-contained, and more enclosed units, whereas those in the basic form are in effect one large room partitioned into spaces that are physically connected. This difference in room size has an influence on the ability to heat individual rooms, particularly during the cooler nights. During the winter evenings at Copan, the temperature can drop as low as 30 degrees F. The smaller, self-contained rooms of the improved form would have been better heat retainers; in addition, they would have been easier and more efficient to heat in terms of fuelwood needs. The more open spaces within the basic form would have led to greater heat loss and a less efficient use of fuelwood. Notably, then, the elite, who had better access to fuelwood, required less of this important raw material to heat their homes.

Differences in heating reflected differences in status and were expressions of inequality as much as building materials and house size. Rooms in structures with stone roofs are narrow, since the corbel-vault arch employed in Maya buildings allowed for only a small span when compared to a true arch. If windows existed, they were very small, so there would be little to no natural light in such rooms, although the resulting darkness would enhance privacy. However, many of these rooms faced outward, allowing for sunlight, moonlight, and any forms of artificial light to penetrate inward through doorways. Curtains were often placed at such openings, as shown by cordholders on either side of an entrance (figure 3.3). At night, stone-walled buildings would have been much darker than those with wattle-and-daub or pole-and-thatch walls. The majority of buildings in the Copan valley were constructed of perishable materials, just as they were at Cerén, allowing for the interior to breathe, and light, heat, and cold to slip in. Impenetrable stone roofs and those plastered over may have amplified night sounds, such as rain. Thatched roofs, found on the majority of homes, provided a softer landing for raindrops; but such coverings also harbored a menagerie of vermin such as insects and rats. Late night scuttling about in the rafters can be a noisy affair. A hole in the roof, whether made of thatch or stone, would make for a long night when tropical storms moved in.

Sleep

For those times when warmth was needed, another way of sustaining heat in the night included sleeping together. Sleep is a biological necessity for our species, but how one sleeps and where, on what and with whom are culturally shaped (Glaskin and Chenhall 2013). Sleeping is anything but a passive activity, and oneiric studies (de la Garza 1990; Tedlock 1992) reveal the importance of dreams in structuring interactions in contemporary societies. Sleep and the night often coincide but they are very different entities (Ekirch 2010, 838). In

FIGURE 3.3. *Elite structures from the Las Sepulturas urban neighborhood, Copan, Honduras. (A) Stone bench with remaining plaster (Group 8N-11, Structure 66C, Room 2, North wall). Note cordholders (which are notches in stone blocks) that would have been used to attach material for privacy. (B) Burn marks on plaster floor, which likely resulted from indoor use of fire (Group 9N-8, Plaza A, Structure 83, central room). Also note bench and plaster remains atop it. (Photos courtesy of and with permission from David Webster)*

many cases, ancients and moderns alike used special artifacts and features associated with sleep, but not necessarily exclusive to it. (Think of the several uses of the "night stand" or "night gown" in Western cultures.) While people the world over, both past and present, sleep on the floor, features associated with repose also exist. The Maya used benches to elevate sleeping bodies from the level of the floor, protecting them from the cold, dampness, and pests. Stone benches most commonly survive in typical tropical conditions, greatly biasing the archaeological record toward "improved" elite and urban households, whose residents most often chose such construction. Stone benches are commonly located in the back or corner of rooms, possibly indicating more private space and they were typically plastered over, making the white surface more visible in the dark interiors (figure 3.3A). It is likely, however, that such bright surfaces were covered with plush materials, such as mats and cloth (as sometimes portrayed on Late Classic Maya ceramics), to make the hard surface more comfortable. In the royal precinct of Copan, in Group 10L-2, "Structure 33 south was clearly a sleeping room, for most of it was filled with a large, C-shaped bench" (B. Fash 2011, 156). This royal domestic structure was in a private location of Courtyard A (Andrews and Bill 2005, 264). Stone benches are ubiquitous throughout the urban residential neighborhood of Sepulturas, just southeast of Copan's royal precinct, and such surfaces were built at every major Classic Maya site. Copan's rural commoners were more likely to have slept on the floor or perhaps on perishable earthen or wooden benches, based on the paucity of stone benches recovered in households of this population (Gonlin 1993;

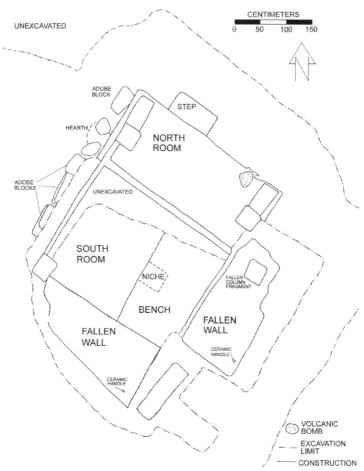

FIGURE 3.4. *Cerén, El Salvador. Structure 2, domicile of Household 2. Note bench in interior of structure. (Figure courtesy of and with permission from Brian McKee)*

2004)—at only two of eight completely excavated rural commoner farmsteads are the remains of stone benches found.

Here Cerén is informative because earthen benches were built in both domiciles and public structures. In general, benches are multipurpose, serving as work areas and political platforms during the day, and sleeping platforms at night. Based on the size of Cerén's sleeping benches (figure 3.4), it is estimated that two adults could have slept on each bench with two to three children on the floor (Sheets 2002). This pattern of floor sleeping for children has been recorded ethnographically (e.g., Wisdom 1941, 134), so we cannot assume that only benches were appropriate places for resting. At the time the volcano erupted at Cerén, sleeping mats, that would have been placed on either benches or floors, were not in use, since these items were found rolled and stored in the thatch roof (Sheets 2002; 2006, 37).

Evidence for the daytime use of benches, whether of stone, earth, or wood, exists at Copan. For example, at the elite residence of 9N-8, Patio H, in Copan's Las Sepulturas neighborhood, *in situ* lapidary remains were found on benches in Structures 110A and 110B (Widmer 2009, 177–180). When privacy was desired, curtains were employed to keep out sound and light (Mongelluzo 2013), as evidenced by the cordholders that were chiseled into stone blocks (figure 3.3A). While stone cordholders are common in elite architecture, residents at Cerén recycled ceramic loop handles for such purposes in both domiciles and public structures (figure 3.4), suggesting that the latter facilities were perhaps multipurpose (Sheets 2006). Loop handles are common items recovered in Mesoamerican excavations; this repurposing of them gives new meaning to those vast collections of this artifact.

Sex

Sex is one activity often associated with the night that is practiced both in light and dark (see Chirikure and Moffett, chapter 17, this volume, for materials relating to sex). As is the case today, however, humans have sex at any time and any place, so assigning ancient sexual activities to a particular time of day or location proves to be difficult (see Storey, chapter 15, this volume, for the historical record of Roman sex) since we do not know the cultural conventions about these practices. Furthermore, material evidence of such practices may be nonexistent. One must rely upon representations that have survived the ravages of time and the accurate interpretation of them (e.g., Clarke and Larvey 2003 for the Roman Empire). Many cultures are known to have prohibitions on having sex at certain auspicious times or there are restrictions for certain individuals (e.g., Wisdom 1941, 209, 285); so we may surmise, though we cannot firmly state, that they existed for the Classic Maya as well. It is also unknown whether sex was an indoor and/or outdoor activity and whether benches played any role in this performance. But the generally small rooms (from a Western perspective) and lack of privacy (again from a Western perspective) may have encouraged couples to sneak away when and where they could. Sex, however, is not a subject about which the Classic Maya typically wrote and "actual scenes of coitus or other forms of sexual stimulation are extremely rare in Classic Maya imagery" (Houston et al. 2006, 43).

Night Soil

Another aspect associated by name with the night is night soil. This organic debris is recovered in only exceptional conditions of preservation, such as dry caves. Night soil surely must have existed at nearly every prehistoric domestic site, except perhaps those of the Indus Valley (see Wright and Garrett, chapter 14, this volume) where it was routinely removed by a well-constructed sewage system. Given that the site of Cerén does indeed exhibit such exceptional preservation, one must ponder why such remains have not been found there (Payson Sheets, personal communication). In general, residents kept their houselots clean, as domiciles, kitchens, community buildings, and gardens were all in close proximity (Sheets 2006); perhaps the recovery of night soil at Cerén would require the excavation of areas much further afield from the built environment, or the chemical analysis of the soil in close proximity, to examine whether it was enriched. Night soil was well known among the Classic Maya according to Sarah Newman's research on Maya trash and Stephen Houston's hieroglyphic interpretations: "In its Classic period glyphic rendering, the raw material for clay, earth, is marked by signs for its pungent smell—'a fertile night soil'" (Newman 2015, 96, quoting Houston 2014, 20).

Night Work

In an agricultural society, there is always work to be done. If one is not sleeping, then perhaps one would be working. The judicious use of ethnohistoric and ethnographic sources can provide general ideas into the types of nocturnal activities toward which we should turn our night vision. Ethnohistoric documents, such as Fray Diego de Landa's (1941) sixteenth-century *Relación* on the early colonial Maya in the Yucatan, provide information on social, political, economic, and religious activities (cf. Hendon 2004; cf. Restall and Chuchiak 2002). Conducting business and performing rituals (see below) were mentioned often as nocturnal activities, with leaders and priests busy at this time. The night would have been ideal for some economic activities, particularly in lowland tropical areas where cooler temperatures are conducive for a wide variety of undertakings. Reexamination of ethnographies reveals several activities performed by women and men throughout the night—the night, like other aspects of culture, is gendered (Gero and Conkey 1991). For instance, Wisdom (1941), in his lengthy work on the Chorti, reported on the nighttime activities of hunting and guarding the milpas, both of which were reported to have been performed by men, and soaking maize (de Landa 1941, 43), boiling beans, and soaking clay for pottery production, which were typically nocturnal activities reported for women.

Classic Maya pottery illustrates gendered activities providing evidence for nightly practices. For example, one ceramic vase portrays the association of hunting with the night—the Moon Goddess, and the Hero Twins (K3055)—and a plate shows the Moon Goddess astride a deer (K3069) (deer hunting is almost always done at night) (figure 3.5). Production and ritual are often intertwined. Contemporary hunting rituals that have been well documented by Linda Brown

FIGURE 3.5. *Classic Maya plate illustrating the Moon Goddess astride a deer. (Photograph ©
Justin Kerr file no. K3069)*

(2004, 2009, 2017) and Brown and Kitty Emery in the highlands of Guatemala
occur during both the night and day (Brown and Emery 2008).

NIGHTTIME USE OF ARTIFACTS AND FEATURES

Hearths and braziers used for warmth and light settled in the ancients for the night.
The recovery of hearths is perhaps one of the most direct material links to nightly
practices. While used throughout the day, at night hearths afford opportunities for
cooking, warmth, light, and ambiance after the sun set. However, hearths can be
difficult to recover in the archaeological record (Pyburn 1989), because some are
located outside of buildings in areas where archaeologists may not typically excavate. Threat of fire may have dictated the location of hearths outside, especially
for houses constructed of flammable materials. Furthermore, for the majority
of Maya who lived in wattle-and-daub houses, having a fire burning inside one's

home would light it up for those outside to see activities going on inside (K. Landau, personal communication). Commoner residents of rural Copan did not appear to build their hearths within domiciles, except for the kitchen building at one site (7D-6–2) (Gonlin 1993). Presumably the kitchen hearths would die down, though not entirely extinguish, at the end of the day's work. At Cerén, hearths are present in kitchen areas, but not in domiciles. The isolation of hearths in kitchen contexts suggests their use in cooking activities, but also might highlight fire prevention by keeping the fire away from storage rooms and domiciles. Cerén occupants also built a hearth in a non-kitchen context at the entrance to the feasting building, Structure 10. Given its location, one would expect its use to be different from that of the other hearths in the village, providing a necessary reminder that hearths have a variety of uses and meanings in the past and present.

Whether inside or outside a structure, hearths hold far more significance than their functional attributes indicate. Based on research by Karl Taube (1998, 432), the three-stone hearth represents an *axis mundi*: "As the first central place, the simple three-stone hearth may well constitute the original construction of creation, antedating even the erection of the four corner post." From ethnographic research on "fireside talk" by Polly Wiessner (2014), we know that the hearth served as a focal point for socialization, especially after the day's work had been completed (see Nowell, chapter 2, this volume, for the significance of Paleolithic hearths). Though Wiessner's study focused on the Ju/'hoansi foragers of southern Africa, one could envision similar differences in day talk and night talk among agriculturalists or even postindustrialists. Wiessner asks, "Does fire time simply extend the day or does it provide contexts for interactions of a different nature?" These provocative questions are timeless ones. Anyone who has ever sat around a camp fire and experienced its magic can testify to the significantly different types of interactions in this setting.

Braziers and censers are not universal in Mesoamerica (e.g., Kurnick 2009; Rice 1999) and their distribution at Copan shows that these vessels were more likely to be recovered from urban contexts than rural ones (Gonlin 1993; Willey et al. 1994). Elaborately decorated censers are most closely associated with rituals, however plain types are sometimes found inside buildings with charcoal in them, indicating their use in heating and producing smoke, perhaps as much to ward off pesky insects as to create an ephemeral screen for rituals. For example, Randolph Widmer (2009, 178) recovered a censer at Copan at the elite compound of 9N–8 "with copious amounts of charcoal . . . This censer is thought to have provided light for the apparently windowless room by functioning as a receptacle for a torch." Furthermore, photographic evidence of inhabitants' repeated use of indoor fires is seen in the picture of the floor of the central room of Structure 83, Group 9N-8 (House of the Bacabs) in Sepulturas (figure 3.3B). Torches are often pictured on ceramic vases of this time period, but they are held by individuals rather than set into either a device or the wall, and stone walls of houses throughout Copan show no evidence for built-in torch holders. Such evidence suggests that lighting the domicile needs to be further evaluated in terms of archaeological and iconographic evidence (Gonlin and Dixon 2017; see Bille and Sørensen 2007 for an anthropology of luminosity); standards of illumination from modern to ancient times surely varied.

EXPERIENCING THE NIGHT: CITY LIFE VERSUS COUNTRY LIVING

When we visualize the nocturnal experiences of ancient Maya people, one variable that we must consider (apart from building materials and artifacts described above) is location: urban (Hutson 2016) versus rural. In Copan's urban enclaves of El Bosque and Las Sepulturas, along with the Main Group, night life would have been radically different for city dwellers than for the kingdom's inhabitants who lived farther afield. "Before parts of Las Sepulturas were washed away by the river or buried under eroded soil from the hills, there were probably 1,400–1,800 buildings in an area of about 1 sq km—a density of residential structures higher than that found at any other Classic Maya center" (Webster et al. 2000, 7). Furthermore, Las Sepulturas was connected to the Main Group by a sacbe, or raised causeway (ibid.), which would have enabled foot traffic in both light and dark conditions. *Sacbeob* (Mayan plural for sacbe) are most typically white since they are either plastered over with lime or built from glistening white stone, as in the Yucatan Peninsula (Schwake 1999; Shaw 2001). Human vision is not as well adapted to the night, but light-colored objects are far easier for us to see in the dark than dark-colored ones. The sights and sounds that occurred in this dense urban setting would have carried throughout the neighborhoods (see Storey, chapter 15, this volume, to hear about noisy Roman nights). Families of different statuses commingled and would have known each other's business as they were firsthand witnesses to crowded living. Under the cover of dark, one could at least have some sense of privacy, though we recognize the vast range in cross-cultural conceptions of privacy in the past and present. Moving out to the countryside, isolated homesteads characterized both the Copan hinterlands and the farming community of Cerén. Small social groups of related families with similar status likely occupied such venues where they shared household duties. The degree of darkness and quiet that one would have experienced in such settings was very different from what modern people experience today (Bogard 2008, 2013). Without the hindrance of some type of lighting, the Milky Way, the planets, the moon, and thousands of stars would have sparkled in the night sky. Furthermore, it is more likely that dangerous animals would have been lurking about in rural areas than in the city centers. The sounds of insects busily buzzing about in the night would have been amplified, as would the calls of carnivores. The Classic Maya often marked these nocturnal creatures with the *ak'ab* symbol in their writing system, indicating darkness/night (see below). The threat of animals stalking prey and attacking under the cover of night could have led to associations between safety and inside spaces.

CELEBRATING THE NIGHT

Material evidence of feasting recorded by many archaeologists (e.g., LeCount 2001) might be evidence of nighttime celebrations. While there is a wide range of types of feasts, and not all feasts occurred at night, "the widespread distribution of feasting wares both spatially and economically in households" attests to the popularity and significance of this activity (Hayden 2014, 330–331). References to nocturnal activities are sprinkled throughout the archaeological literature and tease us into wanting to know more about the night. For example, Alexandre Tokovinine (2016) recently analyzed texts and images to reveal aspects of political networking among the Classic Maya. Of interest here is the interpretation of Panel 3 (carved in 782 CE) at Piedras Negras, Guatemala, where a ruler celebrates a twenty-year anniversary (749 CE) of his reign (Tokovinine 2016, 15): "According to the panels' main text, two days after the anniversary, the ruler of Piedras Negras danced at midnight and drank 'hot' or 'inebriating' cacao. Both text and image support the consumption of a possibly alcoholic beverage late at night as well as dancing." This provocative hieroglyphic passage provides us with a glimpse of an event that probably took place under the stars.

Such activities were apparently indulged in at both Copan and Cerén. In Copan's royal precinct, a dancing platform (Structure 25) measuring 8 m × 30 m (26 feet × 98 feet), was repeatedly used, requiring its surface to be plastered several times over (B. Fash 2011, 146). A large number of stone censers were recovered from this platform. Unlike their ceramic counterparts that burned incense or charcoal, it is thought that these large deep vessels functioned as receptacles for offerings (B. Fash 2011, 90–91). This smooth platform, which probably lacked a superstructure, is adorned by two upright jaguars, each with an "arm" on its hip and the other extended, perhaps already positioned in dance mode (B. Fash 2011, 90–91) (see Dillehay, chapter 9 for the use of small spaces for nocturnal rituals).

Classic Maya deities had a strong nocturnal presence. The Mesoamerican Lords of the Night presided over darkness as the Earth succumbed to its daily cycle. Elisabeth Wagner's (2000, 2006) interpretation of Structure 10L-22A (figure 3.6) at Copan is that this building features the nine Lords of the Night and is an ancestor shrine, contrary to the interpretation of this structure as a *popol na*, or council house, where Copan rulers may have met with their constituents in a form of shared governance (B. Fash 2011; Stomper 2001). Similarly, the toponyms on Structure 10L-22A all invoke the color or concept of "black." However, as Barbara Fash (2011, 147) explains, "the 'nine lords' concept is still little understood, but it is possible that people affiliated themselves and their social units

FIGURE 3.6. *Structure 10L-22A, Copan, Honduras. The iconography, according to Elisabeth Wagner (2000), illustrates the Nine Lords of the Night. She interprets this building as an ancestor shrine rather than a council house. The dancing platform (Structure 25) is located to the left of the building. (Photo courtesy of and with permission from W. Scott Zeleznik)*

with them as mythological or spiritual entities, and locations." Regardless of our current understanding of this structure, the associated dancing platform, Structure 25 (discussed above), appears to have been the stage for dancing and perhaps other ritual performances as well.

In fact, dancing may have been part of elite duties and identity (Jackson 2013, 67, 74), as there were numerous occasions that called for such performance (Grube 1992). However, it would be a mistake to envision only elites engaging in such practices. As mentioned above, Sheets (2006) has long hypothesized that the Cerén inhabitants were in the middle of a feast/harvest ceremony when the Loma Caldera erupted. Residents had tied shut their doors, dirty dishes were left for cleaning, and huge quantities of manioc had been previously harvested (Dixon 2013), perhaps to make beer for the occasion. One can easily imagine that dancing took place here as well.

A number of rituals were particular to the night in many different Mesoamerican contexts (e.g., Gonlin and Lohse 2007). Two are illustrated here: the New Fire Ceremony and bloodletting. The New Fire Ceremony occurred every fifty-two years when the cycles of two widely shared Mesoamerican calendars came together. The *tzolkin* (260-day year), or divinatory almanac, and the *haab* (365-day year), or solar calendar, "are meshed together, the result was a set of roughly 18,980 uniquely named days" (Evans 2013, 227) known as the Calendar Round. The ominous night before a new cycle began was celebrated with the

New Fire Ceremony. For example, it has been recorded through ethnohistoric documents that the Aztecs of Central Mexico extinguished hearth fires throughout the entire empire. Only with the New Fire Ceremony (figure 3.7), which took place at night, were such fires rekindled, as recorded in the *Codex Borbonicus* (1974). The Spanish chronicler Bernardino de Sahagún (1950–1982, VII:27) observed that "it was claimed that if fire could not be drawn, then [the sun] would be destroyed forever; all would be ended; there would evermore be night. Nevermore would the sun come forth. Night would prevail forever, and the demons of darkness [*tzitzimime*] would descend, to eat men." This process ensured the continuation of the empire through human sacrifice. The new calendar round began again and dawn brought the start of another 52-year cycle.

We can hypothesize that similar ceremonies were likely conducted in earlier civilizations of Mesoamerica, such as the Classic Maya, and anticipate that material remains of such will be uncovered as they have been for the Postclassic Aztec (Elson and Smith 2001). Interestingly, in Copan's royal compound, Structure 33 south in Group 10L–2, the sleeping house (see above), Barbara Fash (2011, 156) reports that "the crossed bundles, mirrors, and Tlaloc motifs are related to central Mexican motifs pertaining to the New Fire ceremony, as found on the final versions of Structure 26 (Ruler 15) and Structure 16 and on Altar Q (Ruler 16) on the Acropolis. The earlier Structure 33 seems to have been a forerunner in the dynastic lineage's sculptural proclamations reaffirming its affiliation with central Mexico and with this ceremony, previously celebrated at Teotihuacan."

Numerous images on Classic-period Maya painted vases and stone carvings show that royal persons were busy during the night, conducting ceremonies and propitiating ancestors and deities, and presumably procreating the next generation of rulers. Stone carvings provide information about ceremonies conducted at night with torches figuring prominently in these scenes. Royal nighttime rituals, or those performed in the dark, have been famously portrayed, such as the scene illustrated on Lintel 24 (Schele and Miller 1986, 186–187) of Structure 23 at Yaxchilan, Mexico, where Lady Xoc (*ix k'ab'al xook* [Miller and Martin 2004, 99]) engages in bloodletting, illuminated by the large torch wielded by King Shield Jaguar the Great (*itzamnaaj b'ahlam* [ibid.]) (figure 3.8). Bloodletting is common to Mesoamerican civilizations and is often portrayed in various media. Perhaps the large torch was necessary to supply illumination to the queen and her audience witnessing this act of devotion. The blue background of the lintel indicates that this scene may have taken place either at day or night, or perhaps the color blue is used to symbolize the sacredness of the event (Houston et al. 2009, 31). If at night, there was a waxing gibbous moon on Sunday, October 24, 709 CE, the hieroglyphic date associated with the lintel (Corpus of Maya Hieroglyphs 2016). Such a moon was 89.94% illuminated (Wolfram Alpha 2016) and likely provided light in addition to the torch.

FIGURE 3.7. Codex Borbonicus *(page 34), illustrating the Aztec New Fire Ceremony. Every 52 years, when two sacred calendars coincided, all fires were extinguished in the empire and then relit from the fires distributed by priests at a shrine on the hill called Citlaltepec. A new cycle was signaled by this event. (Image in public domain)*

THE NIGHT SKY

The night sky played an essential role in ancient Maya life (Aveni 2003, 2015; chapter 7, this volume). James Brady and Wendy Ashmore observe that "the night sky is a dynamic map of events in the mythical realm of creation, and trees, birds, and other wildlife are key players in the retelling of these events" (Brady and Ashmore 1999, 124). The perspective of the night sky as a map of ideological events indicates the significance of creation to Maya lives. Furthermore, the night sky created orientation in the built landscape. In a discussion of archaeological landscapes, Bernard Knapp and Ashmore (1999, 3) state, "perhaps more often than we have yet recognized, the sky provides the cues to spatial order on the terrestrial plan." When discussing social memory of place, perhaps it is

FIGURE 3.8. *Lady Xoc performs a bloodletting ceremony by perforating her tongue with a rope laced with sharp objects, while her husband King Shield Jaguar illuminates the scene by wielding a large torch. Late Classic Maya, Lintel 24, Structure 23, Yaxchilan, Mexico. Date: October 24, 709 CE. (Photo © The Trustees of the British Museum)*

FIGURE 3.9. *The earthen sacbe at El Cerén, El Salvador. Sacbe, or the "white way," has symbolic connections to the Milky Way. (Photo by Christine C. Dixon)*

appropriate to turn our gaze to the stars and examine how the night sky would provide a regular place of inscribed meaning, memory, and orientation. Celestial events and patterns in the sky were thought to impact affairs on earth (Aveni 2001; Stuart 2011). One had to pay close attention to the phases of the moon, whether it was for warfare, planting, or other symbolically laden activities.

Returning to Cerén, a strong symbolic connection to the night was recently uncovered: the sacbe, or earthen road (figure 3.9). Rather than constructing their sacbe of stone coated with limestone plaster, residents of Cerén used compacted Tierra Blanca Joven (TBJ) soil, named for the young, white tephra (Dixon and Sheets 2013). The whitest of the white soil was carefully chosen for the top layer of road construction, which would have afforded greater reflectivity at night. The sacbe averages 2 m wide by 20 cm high, with clearly defined drainage canals on each side (Dixon and Sheets 2013). The term *sacbe* likely takes its name from its white color (Folan 1991, 222) and translates to "white way" (Freidel et al. 1993, 77). This same term has also been connected to references of the Milky Way (ibid., 9), which is a primary symbol of creation, thus providing an aspect of the night sky directly associated with the built environment. Sacbeob are common features at many Maya sites, one of which was noted above for Copan's urban neighborhood of Las Sepulturas, and likely had both daytime and nighttime associations and functions, including providing a path easier and safer to travers in the dark.

EPIGRAPHY OF THE NIGHT AND DARKNESS

The Classic Maya wrote a lot, but they did not write about everything, nor did they record explicit information about all aspects of their culture. From the examples provided above, we can glimpse into the activities of the night as it was a component of some events. However, there are some Mayan glyphs that form key correlates for symbolic connections to the night (e.g., Matthews and Biro 2006) (see Coltman, chapter 10, this volume, for further insights). Mayan glyphs related to the night are numerous: "black," "darkness/night," "torch," "moon," "star/planet/constellation"; and for animals associated with the night, such as "bat," "firefly," "jaguar," and "owl" (Stone and Zender 2011).

Epigraphy relating to darkness prevails in many different contexts. For example, in their analysis of Late Classic Maya ceramic flasks, Loughmiller-Cardinal and Zagorevski (2016, 3) found that most of the figures that are wearing flasks, as depicted on codex-style vessels, are marked with either *ak'ab* ("darkness") or *cimi* ("death"). Another example comes from Sarah Jackson, who uses Classic Maya emic categories in labeling various types of material items with property markers: "In some cases, property qualifiers assign entities to particular realms that do not appear to relate to observable component materials or physical qualities of the items themselves. This can be seen, for instance, in the marking of nocturnal animals with a 'darkness' sign, as discussed by Stone and Zender (2011, 14, 189): animals like gophers, jaguars (see Sugiyama 2016 for jaguar iconography at Teotihuacan), fireflies, and bats are affiliated with a 'dark' category" (Jackson 2016, 23). At Copan, in Group 8N-11, a "Skyband" bench was built by the inhabitants of this elite group and featured the sun in both its day and night guises, as well as portraying the moon goddess with her well-known companion, the rabbit, on Panel C (Webster et al. 1998; Webster n.d.). Celestial imagery with warfare dominates the iconography of this carved bench. On Panel D of the bench, the Sun God in his night guise, sports an *ak'bal* symbol on his appendages and the direction west is indicated (Webster et al. 1998; Webster n.d.). The term for the color black is conflated with the direction west, toward the setting sun (Houston et al. 2009), on many different objects in Classic Mayan hieroglyphs. As we pay greater attention to the night, it will become more prominent in the interpretation of Maya writing.

CONCLUSIONS

Without a doubt the night comprised a vital aspect of ancient Maya life. The symbolic connections of the night, such as the stars, the moon, and deities, afforded a canvas upon which to record mythological stories and social memories of creation and cosmological significance. By incorporating investigation of the night, both in terms of material evidence and symbolism, we create a more complex and dynamic view of the ancient Maya. Archaeological reconstructions that consider nightly practices will advance our understanding of the adaptations that ancient peoples made to the natural darkness. The night was gendered as people of different identities performed differently at this time of day, just as they did after the sun rose. Variation in how the night was experienced cut across rural and urban communities, as well as elite and commoner segments of society. Housing figured significantly in experiencing the night, as the majority of the populace living in perishable structures had advantages and challenges that differed from the few who prospered in stone structures. Household archaeology holds great promise in advancing our understanding of Classic Maya nights, as the majority of people would have spent nighttime ensconced in the safety of their homes. The nightscape was an integral part of the Classic Maya experience and was shaped by natural and cultural features.

The few examples we have presented here show the cultural richness, variety, and significance of nighttime adaptations and practices of the Classic Maya. This new topic of the archaeology of the night is an engaging one that we should embrace and pursue. We need epigraphers, iconographers, art historians, ethnohistorians, and others with particular expertise to weigh in on this subject to further our knowledge of Classic Maya nights. We look forward to researching in more depth the topics on which we have presented here, as well as many others, to expand our understanding of life in the past, both in the days and the nights.

ACKNOWLEDGMENTS

Gratitude is due to K. Viswanathan, David Webster, Kristin Landau, April Nowell, David M. Reed, Payson Sheets, Anthony Aveni, Jeremy Coltman, and two anonymous reviewers for providing feedback. Special thanks to David Reed for supplying numerous resources on the archaeology of the night. Rosemary Joyce was most helpful by sharing her knowledge of Mesoamerican figurines and pottery with us. Glenn Storey provided information about Roman sex. Photos were generously contributed by David Webster and W. Scott Zeleznik, and Justin Kerr (n.d.) readily allowed us to publish images from the Maya Vase Database. Brian McKee cheerfully generated a drawing of Cerén's Structure 2 for us. Benayah Israel at Bellevue College continues to be a tireless provider of interlibrary loan materials, tracking down even the most obscure reference and producing it in a timely fashion. Polly Wiessner was an inspiration even before she knew it.

NOTE

1. Some material has been adopted from previous presentations by the authors at the 2015 AAA meetings and 2016 SAA meetings, and a blog by Nancy Gonlin on "The Archaeology of the Night":

Gonlin, Nancy, and Christine C. Dixon. 2015. "An Introduction to Nightly Practices in the Ancient World with Illustration from Mesoamerica." Paper presented at the 114th Annual Meeting of the American Anthropological Association, Denver, Colorado, November 18–21.

Gonlin, Nancy, and Christine C. Dixon. 2016. "Midnight Madness in Mesoamerica." Paper presented at the 81st Annual Meeting of the Society for American Archaeology, Orlando, Florida, April 6–10.

Gonlin, Nancy. 2016. Archaeology of the Night. http://www.upcolorado.com /about-us/blog/item/2951-archaeology-of-the-night.

REFERENCES

Abrams, Elliot. 1994. *How the Maya Built Their World: Energetics and Ancient Architecture.* Austin: University of Texas Press.

Acosta Ochoa, Guillermo, ed. 2012. *Arqueologías de la vida cotidiana: espacios domésticos y áreas de actividad en el México antiguo y otras zonas culturales.* Mexico: Instituto de Investigaciones Antropológicas, Universidad Nacional Autónoma de México.

Agurcia Fasquelle, Ricardo. 2004. "Rosalila, Temple of the Sun-King." In *Understanding Early Classic Copan,* ed. Ellen E. Bell, Marcello A. Canuto, and Robert J. Sharer, 101–112. Philadelphia: University of Pennsylvania Museum of Archaeology and Anthropology.

Andrews, E. Wyllys, and Cassandra R. Bill. 2005. "A Late Classic Royal Residence at Copán." In *Copán: The History of an Ancient Maya Kingdom,* ed. E. Wyllys Andrews and William L. Fash, 239–314. Santa Fe, NM: School of American Research Press.

Andrews, E. Wyllys, and William L. Fash, eds. 2005. *Copán: The History of an Ancient Maya Kingdom.* Santa Fe, NM: School of American Research Press.

Aveni, Anthony F. 2001. *Skywatchers: A Revised and Updated Version of Skywatchers of Ancient Mexico.* Austin: University of Texas Press.

Aveni, Anthony F. 2003. "Moctezuma's Sky: Aztec Astronomy and Ritual." In *Moctezuma's Mexico: Visions of the Aztec World,* revised ed., ed. Davíd Carrasco and Eduardo Matos Moctezuma, 149–158. Boulder: University Press of Colorado.

Aveni, Anthony F., ed. 2015. *The Measure and Meaning of Time in Mesoamerica and the Andes.* Washington, DC: Dumbarton Oaks Research Library and Collection.

Bell, Ellen E., Marcello A. Canuto, and Robert J. Sharer, eds. 2004. *Understanding Early Classic Copán.* Philadelphia: University of Pennsylvania Museum of Archaeology and Anthropology.

Benson, Elizabeth P. 1997. *Birds and Beasts of Ancient Latin America.* Gainesville: University Press of Florida.

Bille, Mikkel, and Tim Flohr Sørensen. 2007. "An Anthropology of Luminosity: The Agency of Light." *Journal of Material Culture* 12(3):263–284. https://doi.org/10.1177 /1359183507081894.

Bogard, Paul, ed. 2008. *Let There Be Night: Testimony on Behalf of the Dark*. Reno: University of Nevada Press.

Bogard, Paul. 2013. *The End of Night: Searching for Natural Darkness in an Age of Artificial Light*. New York: Little, Brown, and Company.

Bourdieu, Pierre. 1977. *Outline of a Theory of Practice*. Cambridge: Cambridge University Press. https://doi.org/10.1017/CBO9780511812507.

Brady, James E., and Wendy Ashmore. 1999. "Mountains, Caves, Water: Ideational Landscapes of the Ancient Maya." In *Archaeologies of Landscape: Contemporary Perspectives*, ed. Wendy Ashmore and A. Bernard Knapp, 124–145. Oxford: Blackwell Publishers.

Brady, James E., and Keith Prufer, eds. 2005. *In the Maw of the Earth Monster: Mesoamerican Ritual Cave Use*. Austin: University of Texas Press.

Brown, Linda A. 2004. "Dangerous Places and Wild Spaces: Creating Meaning with Materials and Space at Contemporary Maya Shrines on El Duende Mountain." *Journal of Archaeological Method and Theory* 11(1):31–58. https://doi.org/10.1023/B:JARM.0000014347.47185.f9.

Brown, Linda A. 2009. "Communal and Personal Hunting Shrines around Lake Atitlan, Guatemala." In *Maya Archaeology 1*, ed. Charles Golden, Stephen Houston, and Joel Skidmore, 36–59. San Francisco: Precolumbia Mesoweb Press.

Brown, Linda A. 2017. "Tz'utujil Maya Ritual Practitioners, Embodied Objects and the Night." Paper presented at the 82nd Annual Meeting of the Society for American Archaeology, Vancouver, British Columbia, Canada, March 29–April 2.

Brown, Linda A., and Kitty F. Emery. 2008. "Negotiations with the Animate Forest: Hunting Shrines in the Guatemalan Highlands." *Journal of Archaeological Method and Theory* 15(4):300–337. https://doi.org/10.1007/s10816-008-9055-7.

Calvin, Inga. 2002. "Structure 16: The Kitchen of Household 3." In *Before the Volcano Erupted: The Ancient Cerén Village in Central America*, ed. Payson Sheets, 72–73. Austin: University of Texas Press.

Carballo, David. 2011. "Advances in Household Archaeology of Highland Mesoamerica." *Journal of Archaeological Research* 19(2):133–189. https://doi.org/10.1007/s10814-010-9045-7.

Clarke, John R., and Michael Larvey. 2003. *Roman Sex: 100 B.C. to A.D. 250*. New York City: Harry N. Abrams.

Codex Borbonicus. 1974. Bibliothèque de l'Assemblée Nationale Paris.

Corpus of Maya Hieroglyphs. Yaxchilan, Lintel 24. Peabody Museum of Archaeology and Ethnology. Accessed March 15, 2016. https://www.peabody.harvard.edu/cmhi/detail.php?num=24&site=Yaxchilan&type=Lintel.

de la Garza, Mercedes. 1990. *Sueño y alucinación en el mundo náhuatl y maya*. Mexico City: Universidad Nacional Autónoma de México.

de Landa, Diego. 1941. *Relación de las Cosas de Yucatan*. Papers of the Peabody Museum of Archeology and Ethnology 18. Ed. Alfred Tozzer. Cambridge, MA: Harvard University.

Dixon, Christine, and Payson Sheets. 2013. Cerén Sacbe. *Report of the 2013 Research: The Sacbe and Agricultural Fields of Joya de Cerén*, ed. Payson Sheets and Christine Dixon, 32–72. Preliminary Report 2013 Enlance Academico Centroamericano, Fundacion Clic, San Salvador, El Salvador. http://www.colorado.edu/anthropology/sites/default/files/attached-files/2013cerenresearchreport.pdf.

Dixon, Christine C. 2013. "Farming and Power: Classic Period Maya Manioc and Maize Cultivation at Cerén, El Salvador." PhD diss., University of Colorado, Boulder.

Douglass, John G., and Nancy Gonlin, eds. 2012. *Ancient Households of the Americas: Conceptualizing What Households Do*. Boulder: University Press of Colorado.

Dowd, Marion, and Robert Hensey, eds. 2016. *Darkness: Archaeological, Historical and Contemporary Perspectives*. Oxford: Oxbow Books.

Egan, Rachel. 2017. "Extending the Notion of Night: Volcanic Eruptions in Mesoamerica." Paper presented at the 82nd Annual Meeting of the Society for American Archaeology, Vancouver, British Columbia, Canada, March 29–April 2.

Ekirch, A. Roger. 2005. *At Day's Close: Night in Times Past*. New York: W.W. Norton.

Ekirch, A. Roger. 2010. "Comment on Jacques Galinier et al., 'Anthropology of the Night: Cross-Disciplinary Investigations.'" *Current Anthropology* 51(6):838–839.

Elson, Christina M., and Michael E. Smith. 2001. "Archaeological Deposits from the Aztec New Fire Ceremony." *Ancient Mesoamerica* 12(2):157–174. https://doi.org/10.1017/S0956536101122078.

Evans, Susan Toby. 2013. *Ancient Mexico and Central America: Archaeology and Culture History*. 3rd ed. London: Thames & Hudson.

Fash, Barbara W. 2011. *The Copan Sculpture Museum: Ancient Maya Artistry in Stucco and Stone*. Cambridge, MA: Peabody Museum Press and David Rockefeller Center for Latin American Studies, Harvard University.

Fash, William L. 1983. "Reconocimiento y Excavaciones en el Valle." In *Introducción a la Arqueología de Copán, Honduras*, ed. Claude F. Baudez, 229–470. Tegucigalpa, DC: Secretaría de Estado en el Despacho de Cultura y Turismo.

Fash, William L. 2001. *Scribes, Warriors, and Kings: The City of Copán and the Ancient Maya*. New York: Thames & Hudson.

Flannery, Kent V., ed. 1976. *The Early Mesoamerican Village*. New York: Academic Press.

Folan, William J. 1991. "Sacbes of the Northern Maya." In *Ancient Road Networks and Settlement in the New World*, ed. Charles D. Trombold, 222–229. Cambridge: Cambridge University Press.

Freidel, David, and Linda Schele, with Joy Parker. 1993. *Maya Cosmos: Three Thousand Years on the Shaman's Path*. New York: William Morrow and Company, Inc.

Freter, AnnCorinne. 1988. "The Classic Maya Collapse at Copan, Honduras: A Regional Settlement Perspective." PhD diss., The Pennsylvania State University, University Park.

Galinier, Jacques, Aurore Monod Becquelin, Guy Bordin, Laurent Fontaine, Francine Fourmaux, Juliette Roullet Ponce, Piero Salzarulo, Philippe Simonnot, Michèle

Therrien, and Iole Zilli. 2010. "Anthropology of the Night: Cross-Disciplinary Investigations." *Current Anthropology* 51(6):819–847. https://doi.org/10.1086/653691.

Gero, Joan M., and Margaret W. Conkey. 1991. *Engendering Archaeology: Women and Prehistory*. Oxford: Blackwell.

Giddens, Anthony. 1984. *The Constitution of Society: Outline of the Theory of Structuration*. Berkeley: University of California Press.

Glaskin, Katie, and Richard Chenhall. 2013. *Sleep Around the World: Anthropological Perspectives*. New York: Palgrave MacMillan. https://doi.org/10.1057/9781137315731.

Gonlin, Nancy. 1993. "Rural Household Archaeology at Copan, Honduras." PhD diss., The Pennsylvania State University, University Park.

Gonlin, Nancy. 2004. "Methods for Understanding Classic Maya Commoners: Structure Function, Energetics, and More." In *Ancient Maya Commoners*, ed. Jon C. Lohse and Fred Valdez Jr., 225–254. Austin: University of Texas Press.

Gonlin, Nancy, and Christine C. Dixon. 2017. "Luminosity in Ancient Mesoamerica." Paper presented at the 82nd Annual Meeting of the Society for American Archaeology, Vancouver, British Columbia, Canada, March 29–April 2.

Gonlin, Nancy, and Jon C. Lohse, eds. 2007. *Commoner Ritual and Ideology in Ancient Mesoamerica*. Boulder: University Press of Colorado.

Grube, Nikolai. 1992. "Classic Maya Dance: Evidence from Hieroglyphs and Iconography." *Ancient Mesoamerica* 3(2):201–218. https://doi.org/10.1017/S095653610000064X.

Halperin, Christina T. 2017. "Vernacular and Monumental Maya Architecture: Translations and Lost in Translations during the Terminal Classic Period (ca. 800–950 CE)." In *Vernacular Architecture in the Pre-Columbian Americas*, ed. Christina T. Halperin and Lauren E. Schwartz, 113–137. London: Routledge.

Haviland, William A. 1985. *Excavations in Small Residential Groups at Tikal, Groups 4F–1 and 4F–2*. Tikal Report No. 19. Philadelphia: University Museum, University of Pennsylvania.

Hayden, Brian. 2014. *The Power of Feasts: From Prehistory to the Present*. New York: Cambridge University Press. https://doi.org/10.1017/CBO9781107337688.

Hendon, Julia A. 2004. "Postclassic and Colonial Period Sources on Maya Society and History." In *Mesoamerican Archaeology*, ed. Julia A. Hendon and Rosemary A. Joyce, 296–322. Malden, MA: Blackwell Publishing.

Hendon, Julia A. 2010. *Houses in a Landscape: Memory and Everyday Life in Mesoamerica*. Durham, NC: Duke University Press.

Hodder, Ian. 1995. *Theory and Practice in Archaeology*. New York: Routledge.

Hofling, Charles Andrew. 1993. "Marking Space and Time in Itzaj Maya Narrative." *Journal of Linguistic Anthropology* 3(2):164–184. https://doi.org/10.1525/jlin.1993.3.2.164.

Houston, Stephen. 2014. *The Life Within: Classic Maya and the Matter of Permanence*. New Haven, CT: Yale University Press.

Houston, Stephen, Claudia Brittenham, Cassandra Mesick, Alexandre Tokovinine, and Christina Warinner. 2009. *Veiled Brightness: A History of Ancient Maya Color*. Austin: University of Texas Press.

Houston, Stephen, and David Stuart. 1989. *The Way Glyph: Evidence for 'Co-Essences' among the Classic Maya*. Research Reports on Ancient Maya Writing 30. Washington, DC: Center for Maya Research.

Houston, Stephen, David Stuart, and Karl Taube. 2006. *The Memory of Bones: Body, Being, and Experience among the Classic Maya*. Austin: University of Texas Press.

Hutson, Scott R. 2016. *The Ancient Urban Maya: Neighborhoods, Inequality, and the Built Form*. Gainesville: University of Florida Press.

Inomata, Takeshi, and Stephen D. Houston, eds. 2001. *Royal Courts of the Ancient Maya*. Boulder: Westview Press.

Inomata, Takeshi, and Payson Sheets. 2000. "Mesoamerican Households Viewed from Rapidly Abandoned Sites: An Introduction." *Mayab* 13:5–10.

Jackson, Sarah E. 2013. *Politics of the Maya Court: Hierarchy and Change in the Late Classic Period*. Norman: University of Oklahoma Press.

Jackson, Sarah E. 2017. "Envisioning Artifacts: A Classic Maya View of the Archaeological Record." *Journal of Archaeological Method and Theory* 4:579–610.

Joyce, Rosemary A., and Susan D. Gillespie, eds. 2000. *Beyond Kinship: Social and Material Reproduction in House Societies*. Philadelphia: University of Pennsylvania Press.

Joyce, Rosemary A. 2004. "Mesoamerica: A Working Model for Archaeology." In *Mesoamerican Archaeology*, ed. Julia A. Hendon and Rosemary A. Joyce, 1–42. Malden, MA: Blackwell Publishing, Ltd.

Kerr, Justin. n.d. Maya Vase Database. Accessed November 14, 2015. http://research.mayavase.com/kerrmaya.html.

Knapp, A. Bernard, and Wendy Ashmore. 1999. "Archaeological Landscapes: Constructed, Conceptualized, Ideational." In *Archaeologies of Landscape: Contemporary Perspectives*, ed. Wendy Ashmore and A. Bernard Knapp, 1–31. Malden, MA: Wiley-Blackwell.

Koslofsky, Craig. 2011. *Evening's Empire: A History of the Night in Early Modern Europe*. Cambridge: Cambridge University Press. https://doi.org/10.1017/CBO9780511977695.

Kurnick, Sara. 2009. "Crossing Boundaries: Maya Censers from the Guatemala Highlands." *Expedition* March 51(1):25–32.

LeCount, Lisa J. 2001. "Like Water for Chocolate: Feasting and Political Ritual among the Late Classic Maya at Xunantunich, Belize." *American Anthropologist* 103(4):935–953. https://doi.org/10.1525/aa.2001.103.4.935.

Lohse, Jon C., and Fred Valdez, eds. 2004. *Ancient Maya Commoners*. Austin: University of Texas Press.

Loughmiller-Cardinal, Jennifer A., and Dmitri Zagorevski. 2016. "Maya Flasks: The 'Home' of Tobacco and Godly Substances." *Ancient Mesoamerica* 27(1):1–11. https://doi.org/10.1017/S0956536116000079.

Manzanilla, Linda R., ed. 1986. *Cobá, Quintana Roo: Analisis de dos Unidades de habitaciones mayas*. Instituto de Investigaciones Antropológicas, Serie Antropológica 82. Mexico City: Universidad Nacional Autónoma de México.

Matthews, Peter, and Peter Biro. 2006. Maya Hieroglyph Dictionary. Accessed July 4, 2016. http://research.famsi.org/mdp/mdp_index.php.

McEachern, Scott, David J.W. Archer, and Richard D. Garvin, eds. 1989. *Households and Communities*, Proceedings of the 21st Chacmool Conference. Calgary: The Archaeological Association of the University of Calgary.

McKee, Brian R. 2002. "Household 2 at Cerén: The Remains of an Agrarian and Craft-Oriented Corporate Group." In *Before the Volcano Erupted: The Ancient Cerén Village in Central America*, ed. Payson Sheets, 58–71. Austin: University of Texas Press.

Miller, Mary, and Simon Martin. 2004. *Courtly Art of the Ancient Maya*. New York: Thames & Hudson. San Francisco: Fine Arts Museums of San Francisco.

Mongelluzo, R. 2013. "Maya Palaces as Experiences: Ancient Maya Royal Architecture and Its Influence on Sensory Perception." In *Making Senses of the Past: Toward a Sensory Archaeology*, ed. Jo Day, 90–112. Center for Archaeological Investigations. Southern Illinois University, Carbondale. Occasional Paper No. 40. Carbondale: Southern Illinois University Press.

Monod Becquelin, Aurore, and Jacques Galinier, eds. 2016. *Las cosas de la noche: Una mirada diferente. New Edition (on line)*. México: Centro de Estudios Mexicanos y Centroamericano. https://doi.org/10.4000/books.cemca.4201.

Mothré, Ève, and Aurore Monod Becquelin. 2016. "La Profundidad de la Noche Maya." In *Las Cosas de La Noche: Una Mirada Diferente*, new ed. (online), ed. Aurore Monod Becquelin and Jacques Galinier, 99–112. México: Centro de Estudios Mexicanos y Centroamericano. https://doi.org/10.4000/books.cemca.4229.

Moyes, Holley, ed. 2012. *Sacred Darkness: A Global Perspective on the Ritual Use of Caves*. Boulder: University Press of Colorado.

NASA. 2016. Earth Observatory. Climate and Earth's Energy Budget: Heating Imbalances. Accessed July 21, 2016. http://earthobservatory.nasa.gov/Features/EnergyBalance/page3.php.

Newman, Sarah. 2015. "Rethinking Refuse: A History of Maya Trash." PhD diss., Brown University, Providence, RI.

Overholtzer, Lisa. 2012. "Empires and Everyday Material Practices: A Household Archaeology of Aztec and Spanish Imperialism at Xaltocan, Mexico." PhD Diss., Department of Anthropology, Northwestern University, Evanston, IL.

Pauketat, Timothy R. 2001. "Practice and History in Archaeology." *Anthropological Theory* 1(1):73–98. https://doi.org/10.1177/14634990122228638.

Pyburn, K. Anne. 1989. "Maya Cuisine: Hearths and the Lowland Maya Economy." In *Prehistoric Maya Economies of Belize*, ed. Patricia A. McAnany and Barry L. Isaac, 325–344. Research in Economic Anthropology, Supplement 4. Greenwich: JAI Press.

Restall, Matthew, and John F. Chuchiak, IV. 2002. "A Reevaluation of the Authenticity of Fray Diego de Landa's *Relación de las cosas de Yucatán.*" *Ethnohistory (Columbus, Ohio)* 49(3):651–669. https://doi.org/10.1215/00141801-49-3-651.

Reyna, Ruben E. 1962. "The Ritual of the Skull in Peten, Guatemala." *Expedition* 4(1):25–35.

Rice, Prudence M. 1999. "Rethinking Classic Lowland Maya Pottery Censers." *Ancient Mesoamerica* 10(1):25–50. https://doi.org/10.1017/S0956536199101020.

Robin, Cynthia. 2013. *Everyday Life Matters: Maya Farmers at Chan.* Gainesville: University Press of Florida. https://doi.org/10.5744/florida/9780813044996.001.0001.

Sahagún. Fray Bernardino de. 1950–1982 [1569]. *General History of the Things of New Spain (Florentine Codex).* 13 vols. Trans. with notes by A.J.O. Anderson and C. E. Dibble. Santa Fe, NM: The School of American Research; Salt Lake City: University of Utah Press.

Sanders, William T., ed. 1986–1990. *Excavaciones en el Area Urbana de Copán.* vol. 1–3. Tegucigalpa, Honduras: Secretaría de Cultura y Turismo and Instituto Hondureño de Antropología e Historia.

Santley, Robert S., and Kenneth G. Hirth. 1992. *Prehispanic Domestic Units in Western Mesoamerica: Studies of the Household, Compound, and Residence.* Boca Raton, FL: CRC Press.

Schele, Linda, and Mary Ellen Miller. 1986. *The Blood of Kings: Dynasty and Ritual in Maya Art.* New York, Fort Worth, TX: G. Braziller and Kimbell Art Museum.

Schwake, S. 1999. "On the Road: Excavation Along the Maya Sacbe at X-Ual-Canil, Cayo District, Belize." MA Thesis, Trent University, Peterborough, ON.

Sharer, Robert J., Loa P. Traxler, David W. Sedat, Ellen Bell, Marcello Canuto, and Christopher Powell. 1999. "Early Classic Architecture Beneath the Copan Acropolis: A Research Update." *Ancient Mesoamerica* 10(1):3–23. https://doi.org/10.1017/S0956 536199101056.

Shaw, Justine M. 2001. "Maya Sacbeob." *Ancient Mesoamerica* 12(2):261–272. https://doi.org/10.1017/S0956536101121048.

Sheets, Payson, ed. 2002. *Before the Volcano Erupted: The Ancient Cerén Village in Central America.* Austin: University of Texas Press.

Sheets, Payson. 2006. *The Cerén Site: An Ancient Village Buried by Volcanic Ash in Central America.* 2nd ed. Belmont, CA: Thomson Wadsworth.

Sheets, Payson. 2012. "Responses to Explosive Volcanic Eruptions by Small to Complex Societies in Ancient Mexico and Central America." In *Surviving Sudden Environmental Change: Answers from Archaeology,* ed. Jago Cooper and Payson Sheets, 43–65. Boulder: University Press of Colorado.

Sheets, Payson, Christine C. Dixon, David Lentz, Rachel Egan, Alexandria Halmbacher, Venicia Slotten, Rocío Herrera, and Celine Lamb. 2015. "The Sociopolitical Economy of an Ancient Maya Village: Cerén and its Sacbe." *Latin American Antiquity* 26(3):341–361. https://doi.org/10.7183/1045-6635.26.3.341.

Shields, F. Douglas, and Henry E. Bass. 1977. "Atmospheric Absorption of High Frequency Noise and Application to Fractional-Octave Band." NASA Contractor Report 2760.

Slotten, Venicia. 2017. "Mesoamerican Plants of the Night: A Paleoethnobotanical Perspective." Paper presented at the 82nd Annual Meeting of the Society for American Archaeology meetings, Vancouver, British Columbia, Canada, March 29–April 2.

Smith, Michael E. 2016. *At Home with the Aztecs: An Archaeologist Uncovers their Daily Life.* New York: Routledge.

Solar Illumination: Seasonal and Diurnal Patterns. 2016. Accessed July 21, 2016. http://science.jrank.org/pages/6261/Solar-Illumination-Seasonal-Diurnal-Patterns.html.

Stomper, Jeffrey Alan. 2001. "A Model for Late Classic Community Structure at Copán, Honduras." In *Landscape and Power in Ancient Mesoamerica*, ed. Rex Koontz, Kathryn Reese-Taylor, and Annabeth Headrick, 197–230. Boulder: Westview Press.

Stone, Andrea, and Marc Zender. 2011. *Reading Maya Art: A Hieroglyphic Guide to Ancient Maya Painting and Sculpture.* London: Thames & Hudson.

Stuart, David. 2011. *The Order of Days: The Maya World and the Truth about 2012.* New York: Harmony Books.

Sugiyama, Nawa. 2016. "La noche y el día en Teotihuacan." *Artes de Mexico* 121:30–35.

Taube, Karl A. 1998. "The Jade Hearth: Centrality, Rulership, and the Classic Maya Temple." In *Function and Meaning in Classic Maya Architecture*, ed. Stephen D. Houston, 427–478. Washington, DC: Dumbarton Oaks Research Library and Collection.

Tedlock, Barbara, ed. 1992. *Dreaming: Anthropological and Psychological Interpretations.* Santa Fe, NM: School of American Research Advanced Seminar Series.

Tokovinine, Alexandre. 2016. "'It Is His Image with Pulque': Drinks, Gifts, and Political Networking in Classic Maya Texts and Images." *Ancient Mesoamerica* 27(1):13–29. https://doi.org/10.1017/S0956536116000043.

Vivó Escoto, Jorge A. 1971. "Weather and Climate of Mexico and Central America." In *Handbook of Middle American Indians*, Volume 1, *Natural Environment and Early Cultures*, ed. Robert C. West, general ed., Robert Wauchope, 187–215. Austin: University of Texas Press.

Wagner, Elisabeth. 2000. "An Alternative View of the Meaning and Function of Structure 10L-22a, Copán, Honduras." In *The Sacred and the Profane: Architecture and Identity in the Maya Lowlands*, ed. Pierre Robert Colas, Kai Delvendahl, Marcus Kuhnert, and Annette Schubart, 25–49. European Maya Conference, University of Hamburg, November 1998. *Acta Mesoamericana*, Vol. 10. Markt Schwaben, Germany: Verlag Anton Sauerwein.

Wagner, Elisabeth. 2006. "Ranked Spaces, Ranked Identities: Local Hierarchies, Community Boundaries and an Emic Notion of the Maya Cultural Sphere at Late Classic Copán." In *Maya Ethnicity: The Construction of Ethnic Identity from Preclassic to*

Modern Times, ed. Frauke Sachse, 143–164. Proceedings of the Ninth European Maya Conference, Bonn, December 10–12. *Acta Mesoamericana*, Vol. 19. Markt Schwaben, Germany: Verlag Anton Sauerwein.

Webster, David, ed. 1989. *The House of the Bacabs, Copan, Honduras*. Studies in Precolumbian Art and Archaeology, No. 29. Washington, DC: Dumbarton Oaks.

Webster, David. 2014. "Maya Drought and Niche Inheritance." In *The Great Maya Droughts in Cultural Context: Case Studies in Resilience and Vulnerability*, ed. Gyles Iannone, 333–358. Boulder: University Press of Colorado.

Webster, David. n.d. "The Skyband Bench." Manuscript in possession of author.

Webster, David, Barbara Fash, Randolph Widmer, and Scott Zeleznik. 1998. "The Skyband Group: Investigation of a Classic Maya Elite Residential Complex at Copán, Honduras." *Journal of Field Archaeology* 25(3):319–343.

Webster, David. AnnCorinne Freter, and Nancy Gonlin. 2000. *Copán: The Rise and Fall of an Ancient Maya Kingdom*. Fort Worth, TX: Harcourt College Publishers.

Webster, David, Nancy Gonlin, and Payson Sheets. 1997. "Copan and Ceren: Two Perspectives on Ancient Mesoamerican Households." *Ancient Mesoamerica* 8(1):43–61. https://doi.org/10.1017/S0956536100001565.

Widmer, Randolph J. 2009. "Elite Household Multicrafting Specialization at 9N-8, Patio H, Copán." In *Housework: Craft Production and Domestic Economy in Ancient Mesoamerica*, ed. Kenneth G. Hirth, 174–204. Archaeological Papers of the American Anthropological Association, No. 19. Hoboken: Wiley.

Wiessner, Polly W. 2014. "Embers of Society: Firelight Talk among the Ju/'hoansi Bushmen." *Proceedings of the National Academy of Sciences of the United States of America* 111(39): 14027–14035. https://doi.org/10.1073/pnas.1404212111.

Wilk, Richard R., and Wendy Ashmore, eds. 1988. *Household and Community in the Mesoamerican Past*. Albuquerque: University of New Mexico Press.

Willey, Gordon R., and Richard M. Leventhal. 1979. "Prehistoric Settlement at Copan." In *Maya Archaeology and Ethnohistory*, ed. Norman Hammond and Gordon R. Willey, 75–102. Austin: University of Texas Press.

Willey, Gordon R., Richard M. Leventhal, Arthur A. Demarest, and William L. Fash, Jr. 1994. *Ceramics and Artifacts from Excavations in the Copan Residential Zone*. Papers of the Peabody Museum of Archaeology and Ethnology, vol. 80. Cambridge, MA: Harvard University.

Wingard, John D. 2016. "Complementary and Synergy: Stones, Bones, Soil, and Toil in the Copan Valley, Honduras." In *Human Adaptation in Ancient Mesoamerica: Empirical Approaches to Mesoamerican Archaeology*, ed. Nancy Gonlin and Kirk D. French, 73–93. Boulder: University Press of Colorado.

Wisdom, Charles. 1941. *The Chorti Indians of Guatemala*. Chicago: University of Chicago Press.

Wolfram Alpha computational knowledge engine. Accessed April 2, 2016. http://www.wolframalpha.com/input/?i=moon+phase+October+24,+AD+709.

The Night Is Different

Sensescapes and Affordances in Ancient Arizona

KATHRYN KAMP AND JOHN WHITTAKER

As night falls, illumination decreases. Simultaneously, temperatures drop and wind patterns change, bringing altered scent and humidity regimes. Some flowers open, others close; different mammals, birds, and insects emerge. With the transformed sights, sounds, smells, and tactile sensations come new resources, but also a new set of real or imagined obstacles. Thus the potentials for human action change. Humans perceive the night through both biological and cultural lenses. The sensescapes of night influence behaviors and are given cultural meanings, but humans also manipulate and alter the experience of night by modifications to the built environment. The tendency for archaeologists and even cultural anthropologists to concentrate their discussions on day and ignore the night, or to conflate day and night, produces at best an incomplete picture of human life.

We excavate and survey in the bright sun of northern Arizona, sharing the usual diurnal bias of archaeology as we study the Sinagua, who farmed, hunted, and gathered in what is now the Flagstaff area. The Sinagua were one of many regional archaeological "cultures" ancestral to the existing Pueblo tribes. The

DOI: 10.5876/9781607326786.c004

northern Sinagua occupied the zone of volcanic soils and cinder cones around the San Francisco Peaks and Sunset Crater, south and east of modern Flagstaff, Arizona. The population was small, depending on scattered pockets of good soil. Subsistence was based on dry farming maize, beans, squash, and cotton, and also depended heavily on wild plants and hunted game, mostly rabbit and deer. For most of Sinagua prehistory, from somewhat before the eruption of Sunset Crater in the late 1000s to their movement from the region around 1300, most people lived in small scattered homesteads and hamlets, with a few larger villages. The characteristic architecture of the region was pithouses, especially early, and masonry room blocks, which became increasingly typical through time. Awakening to the importance of night in the land of the Sinagua means reconsidering the structure of activities, the meaning and construction of group and individual identities, and the very configuration of the built environment.

Night simultaneously divides and unites. If the night is seen as more treacherous than day, because of spiritual, animal, or human threats, or because the terrain itself is hazardous as it is in the Sinagua area, mobility may be restricted for some or all individuals. The boundaries imposed by night act to reinforce spatial separation and may transform it into social distance, but these impositions may be diminished or exacerbated by human modifications to the social or physical environment. Those who are together at night, but separated from others, experience a sense of shared isolation which enhances social identification; thus stronger group identities based on residential locale may result from the restrictions of the night. Similarly, the development of gender, age, and other personal identities respond to the associations and separations of night and day.

AFFORDANCES AND SENSESCAPES OF THE NIGHT

The world is such a complex place that no one, even for an instant, perceives it in its totality. Since humans have evolved as diurnal animals with sensitive binocular vision and a heavy investment in brain and nerves to process information from the eyes, much of the human experience of the world is filtered through vision. Nevertheless, as geographer Yi-Fu Tuan (1974, 1977) has pointed out, we experience place with all of our senses simultaneously. Thus, the different worlds of day and night need to be thought of in terms of sensescapes, not just viewscapes. Consciousness of the world is an embodied experience that relies on all of our senses. The texture of crunching sand under foot, grass brushing calves, the rustling of a lizard, the smell of pinyon, and the taste of a smoky fire can all be as important in the experience of place as the visual landscape.

Our perceptions of the world, day or night, in terms of what we notice as well as how we interpret it, are influenced by the interactions between biology and culture. We acclimate to constants in the environment and filter out information that is perceived as extraneous. James J. Gibson (1986), a pioneer in the field of ecological psychology, argues that as we encounter the world we are constantly assessing the potential of the environment. Thus humans perceive the world not just in terms of attributes like "red" or "round," but also in terms of potentialities such as "edible," "knappable," or "climbable," which Gibson termed *affordances*. Affordances depend on both cultural and personal factors, such as age, gender, and physical abilities. While Gibson (1986) was primarily studying visual perception, subsequent studies have shown that the same principles apply to other senses as well (Gaver 1993). Biological realities such as the patterns of circadian rhythms and the physiological mechanisms of sight are important for understanding differences between the ways humans experience day and night.

Cones, the retina's color receptors, dominate vision when illumination is high, but when the light is low, vision is primarily the provenance of rods, and color vision is lost (See Buser and Imbert [1992] and McIlwain [1996] for overviews of the biology of vision). On a bright moonlit night or in other nighttime contexts with medium light levels, vision is actually mesopic, using a mix of rods and cones and with properties falling in-between photopic and scotopic vision. In normal daylight, the level of visual acuity is greater than in low illumination for a number of reasons that relate to neural processing of information rather than the simple responses of the rods and cones, which have similar sensitivity to light. Rods rely on convergence, a summing of receptor outputs to compensate for the decreased levels of illumination, while cones tend to have a more one-to-one relationship to retinal ganglia cells, which results in better perception of detail. In high illumination the photoreceptors exhibit a property called lateral inhibition, in which visual neurons respond less if a neighboring neuron is simultaneously stimulated, an effect that enhances the sharpness of edges. In low illumination, lateral inhibition is diminished. Thus, night vision not only lacks color, but is also less acute. Since cones are concentrated in the center of the retina, while rods are more peripheral, the optimal area of focus changes in the dark, so at night we may be more aware of objects on the periphery of our vision.

Soundscapes have been less studied by anthropologists (Day 2013; Samuels et al. 2010), but like viewscapes, they are affected by geophysical factors such as landform, substrate, and weather; biogenic properties like animal populations and vegetation; and anthropogenic ones like population dispersion and activities. Sound recordings in a variety of landscapes have demonstrated the localized variation in sound as well as revealing seasonal and daily patterns (Pijanowski et al. 2011). The phenomenon that occurs after or during a snowfall when the snow absorbs sound and the world seems preternaturally quiet is well known to those in colder climates. Since sounds themselves vary with temperature, humidity, and wind direction and velocity, sounds at night may differ systematically with these variables as well as with the changes in human activity (Pijanowski et al. 2011).

Most studies of the archaeological soundscape have dealt with ritual soundscapes (Boivin et al. 2007; Sanchez 2007), although recently archaeologists have begun to consider the effects of daily activities on the soundscape (Boivin et al. 2007; King and Santiago 2011). As with viewscapes, perception of a soundscape filters some components and emphasizes others. This selective attentiveness follows physical principles of habituation, but also takes into account affordances. In other words, humans hear sounds and understand them through a filter that is based on their cultural understandings and abilities. Attention focuses on affordances, those things that are meaningful and useful.

The perceptual characteristics of soundscapes differ from those of viewscapes in a number of ways. The differences are of course due to the physical differences between sight and hearing, but not all the implications are immediately obvious (Gaver 1993). Under most conditions, humans can see farther than they can hear. Paradoxically, however, some things that are close may be visually obscured by barriers, but can be heard. In general the characteristics of human sight put it at an advantage over hearing, but this is not true with respect to the sensory field. While the visual field is only about a 170° forward-facing arc, the auditory field is a complete 360°, accessible without having to move the head or body. To some extent, this advantage may be mitigated by the fact that humans find it harder to localize sounds than sights. It is more difficult to distinguish sounds coming from behind from those coming in front than it is to tell whether a sound is coming from the left or the right. The advantage of our auditory sense, especially at night, is that it is not impaired by the darkness and may even be enhanced, if the night is quieter with less ambient noise than the day. Some of the ambiguities of sound, such as the difficulties in identifying and localizing sounds, may tend to increase attention to sounds, particularly when vision is impaired. In practice, eyes and ears usually work together. Culturally significant or familiar sounds may be easily recognized, but less familiar sounds can be very difficult to interpret without accompanying visual cues.

Touch, smell, and taste are also parts of the sensescape. At night we may sense the temperature decreasing, the wind rising or blowing from a different direction, and new aromas arising, associated with the opening of flowers, the cooking of stews, or the lighting of new fires. Touch probably varies less with the change to night, but we may rely on it more, and pay attention to clues that are inconsequential during the day. In the lower illumination of night, vision becomes less acute and reliable, so the importance of other senses increases. It is a common belief that these senses are actually better at night as vision is reduced, but this belief is not true; it is merely that they are attended to more carefully and thus become more important for the overall perception of the environment. Thus awareness of things behind us and in the periphery as well as of sounds and tactile sensations that might be ignored during the day is enhanced at night.

FEAR AND THE NIGHT: GREATER RELIANCE
ON THE NONDOMINANT SENSES

The perceptual changes discussed above demonstrate that for predominantly visual animals like humans the overall sensescape becomes more ambiguous in the dark of the night and that one of the possible ramifications is a heightened sense of danger. At night the visual world takes on new shapes and the realities of the day are transformed. A Kodachrome image becomes black and white; details once sharp are obscured; objects are seen in silhouette; eyes see poorly resolved and potentially threatening peripheral images. As consciousness becomes more alert to the nonvisual world, sensations ignored during the day may be perceived. Sounds come from all directions and are difficult to pinpoint. Familiar sounds are no problem, but the unfamiliar can be interpreted as threatening. Reliance on perceptions from senses other than vision may be, and also may be seen as, less trustworthy to visually oriented humans. Thus, simply because of perceptual differences, the night may be seen as more dangerous than day. The clear becomes ambiguous; the familiar, strange; and the unfamiliar, dangerous. Cultures worldwide consider night to be threatening, the realm of the unknown, the hidden, and perhaps the unknowable (Schnepel and Ben-Ari 2005; Tuan 1979).

The affordances people see in the animal world change at night (and seasonally), but so too do hazards. Humans in the prehistoric Southwest probably did not have to worry too much about predators, with the exception of bears and mountain lions (Beaglehole 1936:3). Snake bites can be dangerous, but alert humans and snakes do their best to avoid each other, which is possibly why the reptiles have evolved an auditory warning system. Rattlesnakes are rare today in the northern Sinagua area, but warm nights are when they are likely to be out, and mutual avoidance is not as easy as during the day. The spiritual aspects of night animals were probably of more concern to the Sinagua than the slight hazard of snakebites and the minor nuisance of insect stings. Ethnographically, most Native American cultures consider owls to be messengers of misfortune, and snakes are creatures that travel between this world and the underworld and should be treated with circumspection.

It is probably no accident that many dangerous encounters in stories from the ethnographic Pueblos, with tricksters like Coyote, or menacing deities like Maasaw, involve shapeshifting and ambiguous perceptions (Malotki and Lomatuway'ma 1984, 1990). Creatures wear disguises, witches travel in the form of animals, a fire at night reveals something you did not want to see, and a beautiful maiden becomes a hag. In several Puebloan stories the visions of the night are proven to be false in the daylight (Tyler 1964). For example, the maiden Huru'ing Wuhti (Hard Substances Woman, a goddess of the earth associated with items such as turquoise and shell) transforms from young and beautiful at night to old and ugly during the day. Frank Cushing's *Zuni Folk Tales* (1901:428) records the story of a youth who falls in love with a female eagle and finds a city of the dead, active only at night. While we do not know the specifics of Sinagua beliefs about the night, it is highly likely that they included nuances of distrust, if not outright fear.

NIGHT AFFORDANCES AND THE SINAGUA

The sensescape affordances of night are intertwined in complex ways. Just as places deemed safe during the day may be or be seen as less safe in the dark; the accessible may become less accessible. It may be easier to hide and harder to find the hidden. Crepuscular animals replace diurnal ones and are in turn replaced by nocturnal resources. Of course, these changes in affordances pertain in various degrees to each individual depending on their personal characteristics. Changes in affordances imply changed patterns of human activity and new, possibly aged and gendered, definitions of place and space. We should see the effects of the night directly in archaeological sites, in the form of modifications to the built environment and new facilities constructed specifically to respond to the needs of night.

Regardless of difficult travel or fear of the dark, both social and economic circumstances probably encouraged the Sinagua to be abroad at night. The social world of the Sinagua tended to be somewhat dispersed with small interrelated sites functioning as communities. Even some larger sites are organized on this principle, requiring movement between dispersed residential units. Three Sinagua sites that we have excavated—Lizard Man Village (Kamp 1998; Kamp and Whittaker 1999), Fortress Hills Pueblo, and New Caves Pueblo (Kamp and Whittaker 2009; Whittaker and Kamp 2012) (figure 1.2; figure 4.1), all occupied from about 1150 to 1300 CE during the Elden and subsequent Turkey Hill phases (figure 1.3)—will provide much of the focus of our discussion.

Lizard Man Village and Fortress Hills Pueblo are two of many small- to medium-sized villages from the earlier part of this time frame. A few resident families lived in room blocks composed of contiguous flat-roofed masonry rooms. Most of the rooms were aboveground, but subterranean or semisubterranean rooms were not uncommon, especially located on the eastern aspect of the room blocks. The core of Fortress Hills Pueblo was a single small five- to six-room room block, perhaps occupied by an extended family, while the contemporaneous Lizard Man Village had two similar room blocks. Lizard Man Village had two subterranean rooms with benches, which are interpreted in the Sinagua area as the equivalent of Hopi *kivas* (Kamp and Whittaker 1999). Ethnographically, kivas function as ceremonial rooms, but are also used by single and visiting men for sleeping and provide areas for men's craft production and other male activities (Dozier 1970; Hill 1970). As such, they are the male counterpoint to the more female-dominated domestic spaces.

FIGURE 4.1. *Arizona: locations of the Sinagua sites mentioned in the chapter. Inset shows modern cities in relation to the study area.*

The elements of New Caves Pueblo, scattered atop the O'Neill Crater cinder cone, include small room blocks, clusters of semisubterranean masonry rooms, and a row of cavates (modified overhangs and caves) on the eastern cliff of the cinder cone. Many of the room groups include kivas, meaning that this room type is dispersed throughout the site. These groups of rooms may be the social equivalents of smaller sites like Lizard Man Village and Fortress Hills Pueblo, possibly forming as part of a general migration to a few larger sites like Turkey Hills, Elden Pueblo, Old Caves, and the New Caves complex that includes Bench Pueblo. While initially contemporary to the other two sites, New Caves Pueblo persisted until the Sinagua moved from the Flagstaff region as a whole to other areas, such as Anderson Mesa.

A consideration of the possibilities of movement within Sinagua communities is illuminating. As described above, Fortress Hills Pueblo and Lizard Man Village are both quite small. New Caves Pueblo is much larger, but the distance between any room block and its nearest neighbor is generally a matter of tens of meters (figure 4.2). Nevertheless, it is not always as easy to move from one to

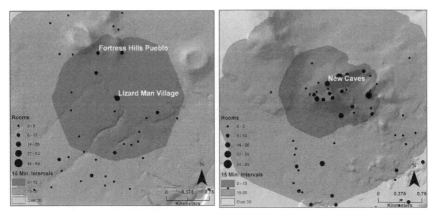

FIGURE 4.2. *Room block clusters and sites in the vicinity of (left) Lizard Man Village and (right) New Caves Pueblo. Concentric rings represent modeled 15-minute distances from the center of Lizard Man Village or the New Caves Pueblo Community Room, respectively.*

another as one might think. Today, the terrain on top of O'Neill Crater is tough even in the daylight. The surface is mostly composed of small loose volcanic rocks, and where the larger stable pieces that compose the "bedrock" of the cinder cone protrude, they are sharp and abrasive. Frequent gusty winds make balance even more difficult. On a wider scale, houses you can see or hear, for instance those plainly visible across the crater, are not always rapidly reached.

We can expect that humans modified the terrain to make travel on habitual routes easier. We know that ladders and ropes were in constant use in the Southwest, and some of these mundane and perishable artifacts have survived in sites elsewhere (e.g., Lister and Lister 1987, 50). There are many sets of pecked hand- and footholds going up and down cliffs as well. Built trails are a feature that we can expect to have survived, at least partially and in some form (Snead 2008). The obvious and well-traveled routes on the surface of O'Neill Crater today would probably have been used prehistorically as well, and ephemeral improvements like brush clearance would have made them even more obvious. The trail up from the plains below passes through a walled plaza and is probably close to the prehistoric access route. This path may have been what Snead (2008) calls a gateway trail, the symbolically bounded and defined "main" entrance to the community. We have recorded masonry steps in some of the canyon settlements in the southern Sinagua sphere, although we have seen none among the masonry rooms, wing walls, and terracing at New Caves. On the shifting mountain face of O'Neill Crater, where the front walls of cavate rooms and the cliff face itself has been collapsing for 700 years, the ledges and trails that served this part of the settlement have been largely swept away, and the current trails clamber over rubble. It is possible, but difficult, to climb up the loose volcanic talus slope to the cliff rooms and the rest of the community from the crater's interior. The gentler slope of the opposite side of the mountain was fortified with a massive wall. The second logical route of entry would have been along the sloping spine to the east, where groups of rooms are strung along the ridgetop. There would have been no need to scramble over fallen wall rocks when these rooms were occupied, and the trail would have been clear and familiar.

Both visibility and familiarity of trails become even more important at night when different senses inform movement. A trodden surface cleared of small debris sounds different under foot, feels different especially with bare feet or through the cordage sandals probably worn by the Sinagua (Teague and Washburn 2013), and keeps the traveler on track. Clearing brush along trails prevents unpleasant encounters with invisible sharp branches at night. While it seems likely that movement was facilitated by paths, the large and dispersed nature of New Caves in conjunction with the rough terrain and the existence of multiple, spatially segregated room clusters, many of which included kivas, may suggest that at night most people remained within their residential clusters.

Movement between neighboring communities was probably common during the day. Even before the Sinagua coalesced into fewer and larger villages, one hamlet was often fairly close to the next. During the day, visits to other sites were doubtless easy. From Lizard Man Village, for instance, it is a short day's walk for an active individual to reach larger communities in Walnut Canyon, less than 5 miles (7.5 km) away as the raven flies, although longer on foot. It is a matter of only a couple of hours to get from the area of Lizard Man Village to the top of New Caves, although this trek requires some good healthy exercise. From New Caves on top of its mountain, you can see most of what we now consider the northern Sinagua culture area. Surveying by our projects, the Coconino National Forest, and others shows that most sites in this landscape are within a very short walk of several other sites (figure 4.2). There are an estimated 14 contemporary (within the limits of archaeological dating) sites within a brief 15-minute walk from Lizard Man Village. The average distance to the nearest site is 273 m and all of the sites are less than a half kilometer from the nearest neighbor. A visit to the Walnut Canyon communities could have been routed to pass by several other villages that may have been occupied at the time of Lizard Man. At New Caves the calculations are more complex, since there are multiple room clusters on the cinder cone (and a complex history of the ways that site numbers were allocated). There are 24 room clusters that we identified within 15 minutes of the New Caves Community Room, although this number should not necessarily be interpreted as 25 distinct communities. The average distance here is only 123 m.

As farmers, the Sinagua would have been intimately familiar with their fields and field locations. Many important game animals, such as deer and rabbits, are crepuscular, feeding and moving most at dusk and dawn. The changing affordances prescribed by animal behavior imply that Sinagua hunters, probably male, made frequent forays before dawn and often returned home in the early night. Dawn and dusk are also the times when crops would need most protection. Based in part on ethnographic analogies, we have argued elsewhere (Kamp 2002, 2012) that a major task for children would have been chasing pests from fields, so they, too, may have been out and about as darkness began to fall and as the sun rose. One likely solution to the problem of travel in the dark could be field houses, which, interpreted by analogy to modern Pueblo practice, are small single-room or shelter sites with evidence of limited occupation. They are usually near potential field areas, sometimes at a distance from the main habitation sites, and likely represent occasional or seasonal stays by a few people tending agricultural fields.

As our description of the site of New Caves implies, the natural environment in which the Sinagua lived is rugged, one of mountains, canyons, volcanic lava flows, and cinder cones, interspersed with more gentle parklands. At night the terrain would have been even more difficult to navigate, and a good trail system of habitual routes, like those documented around Tapamveni by Snead (2008), would likely have been in place, but now are not recognizable. Lewis (1976), working with native peoples in Australia, found that their powers of memory for travel in landscapes with subtle features was enormous. His informants relied on a constantly updated "dynamic mental map" as they traveled. For them, there was "no such thing as a featureless landscape," not only because they were aware of the markers, but because the human landscape is filled with meaning. Every route and feature was associated with the paths of sacred ancestral beings of the Dreaming, and singing the tales served as a mnemonic, even for areas where humans had never traveled. The Sinagua landscape was surely also marked for them with meanings now lost, as it is for all groups in the ethnographic Southwest (Basso 1996; Ferguson and Hart 1985; Ortiz 1972).

SEEING OTHER COMMUNITIES AT NIGHT

Visual connections would also have been a component of Sinagua identity. A viewshed analysis that assumes 2-m-high structures (figure 4.3) suggests that all of the sites within a 15-minute walk from Lizard Man Village could have been visible from it. Today this visibility would not exist because of fairly dense tree cover. We do not know what vegetation patterns would have been like in the past, but, since crops were being grown in the vicinity and wood was used for both building and making fires, the wooded acreage would presumably have been less. At the very least, smoke from fires at some of the nearby villages would have been visible during the day.

The steep terrain at New Caves causes visibility of neighbors to vary considerably from place to place on the site, but the height of the site generally provides

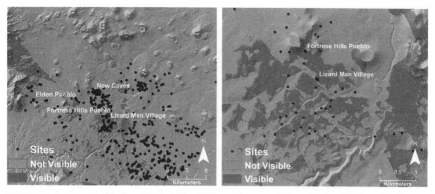

FIGURE 4.3. *Sites visible from Lizard Man Village: the overall distribution* (left) *and a close-up of the more immediate area of Lizard Man Village* (right).

excellent views (figure 4.4). While all dwellings on the crater would have been in sight of some other structures, there is no single place with a view of the complete site. For both Lizard Man and New Caves it may have been hard to see other villages at night unless exterior fires were burning. We do know from archaeological evidence that such fires existed. Usually they were quite small, but occasionally they appear to have been much larger. For example, at Lizard Man Village, we excavated one shallow plaster-lined pithouse that had a huge post-abandonment fire feature in the center. Surely this blaze would have been highly visible from quite a distance, especially at night. The meaning of fires in the night is less obvious than their existence. While seeing the fires of another community might have engendered a sense of mutual belonging and occupation, it may also have visually reinforced the idea of the other.

LIGHTING AND FIRE FEATURES

Fires are the only known sources of manufactured night light for the Sinagua. During the day and on bright, moonlit nights, smoke holes, entry hatches, and doorways would have provided interior light. During daily patterns of activity, fires drew villagers to particular locales and facilitated interactions in their vicinity. The nature of fires and fireside activities would have had a profound effect on the nature of social groupings and identities.

Within New Caves, Fortress Hills Pueblo, Lizard Man Village, and other Sinagua sites, fire features occur both inside structures and in exterior areas. Fire is necessary for heating and cooking as well as light, and most interpretations of Pueblo room functions see fire features as a minimum qualification for both living rooms and kivas, although other room types may or may not have included fire features (Hill 1970; Kamp and Whittaker 1999, 28; Lowell 1999; Stone 2009). The relatively modest size of interior fire features in our Sinagua

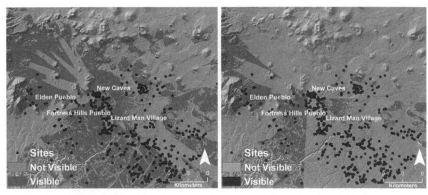

FIGURE 4.4. *The viewshed from the summit of New Caves* (left) *contrasts with the much more restricted view from the lower community room* (right).

sites (table 4.1) makes sense not only in terms of fire safety inside wooden structures, but also in the context of occupied environments where wood probably became increasingly scarce. Some evidence (Sobolik et al. 1997) suggests that harder woods, which burn longer and produce less smoke, tend to be used for interior fires. The ramification is that the interior fires would have provided only modest light.

While New Caves does have a community room structure that is rather centrally located within the site, our excavation found no central fire feature, nor was much ash found in the fill. Sinagua community rooms are large, walled structures, usually rectangular, and with or without roofs. They are interpreted as the setting for social and ritual gatherings, perhaps equivalent to great kivas in other parts of the Southwest. At New Caves, the adjoining plaza was not excavated, so we do not know whether fires were burned there. Nevertheless, the lack of a fire in the community room does raise an issue about the extent to which the New Caves community aggregated indoors in large groups at night.

Exterior fire features are undoubtedly underrepresented in our excavations, which emphasized the exploration of room areas, as is common in Southwestern archaeology. In addition, it is not possible to discern which exterior fire features burned at night and which during the day. The twelve we have excavated are on average larger than interior fire features, which are quite small, but not dramatically so (table 4.1). Whether indoors or out, in the low illumination of the night, some activities such as craft production would have been less feasible, although to some extent visual acuity may have been compensated for through greater reliance on other senses such as touch (Dawson et al. 2007). Thus the degree of lighting and the resulting distribution of human activity would have affected the sounds, smells, and entire sensescapes of communities.

TABLE 4.1. Size of interior fire features at three Sinagua sites.

Type of Firepit	N	Average Diameter or Maximum Dimension (cm)	Average Depth (cm)
Stone rings (exterior)	6	59	7.8
Slab-lined	5	31	25.6
Clay-lined	30	28.9	15.1
Clay unlined	11	33.4	11.9

Fires would have created on- and off-stage areas with those near the fire illuminated and those in the periphery less visible. Even people removed from the visual stage, however, would have been able to hear and be heard, creating varying levels and types of participation. When illumination is sparse but concentrated, patterns of light and darkness will develop. In a dwelling lit by a fire, those closest to the fire will be better lit than those farther away. In social interactions, lighting may be key in specifying who has the stage and who does not. Thus, Cushing was told that on entering a Zuñi ceremonial room and interacting with clowns, he should move into the light of the fire before repeating a specific phrase in Zuñi (Green 1979, 82, originally 1882, 1883). The small size of fires would also have mandated the physical proximity of those who gathered around, producing a sensescape of shared human community through touch, smell, and even the intimate sound of breathing.

While we cannot reconstruct all of the activities that would have occurred at night around the fire, we can be pretty certain that some cooking and eating did occur. The sensory ramifications of these activities are great, since both taste and smell are emotionally evocative. Like the close proximity of gathering near a fire, sharing food around a fire at night would create a sense of unity and identity. It is thus necessary to consider who might have been participating in these communal experiences. Were the groups familial or did they include neighbors? What about strangers? Were they multi-age and/or multigenerational? Were the genders mixed?

These types of questions are particularly central with respect to the story-telling and ritual that undoubtedly occurred around the fire. Polly Wiessner (2014) has provided one of the few ethnographic studies of nighttime behavior, finding that among the Kalahari folk she studied, talk around the fire focused on stories and social relationships, shifting away from the economic concerns of daylight conversations. One suspects that this pattern holds across cultures. Some important social business can be transacted only at night. In the ethnographic Southwest, some offerings are appropriately made at that time, communication with night-dwelling spirits occurs, and some pueblo dances and other ceremonies must be performed at night. The theatrical possibilities of darkness are obvious. If night is the time when some of the normal activities of the day are suspended and people gather around the fire to gossip, to listen to the wisdom of the elders, and especially to tell stories, the composition of the fireside group strongly influences the pathways for the transmission of knowledge. To the extent that kivas are not only ritually significant but also as places where exclusively men would gather, the implication is that some of the bonding experiences of night are gender segregated, and that some of this night knowledge also was transmitted along gendered lines. If, as some cross-cultural evidence suggests, young children of both genders are more likely to spend time with women, the implication is that women are the predominant enculturating force.

SLEEP

If we ask where the Sinagua slept, we have an even thornier problem, with little real evidence and many possible bits of information that may or may not apply. Humans are universally somewhat vulnerable as they sleep, eyes closed in the dark, a sort of "double blindness" (Musharbash 2013). Yasmine Musharbash's work in Australia can be used to suggest that there are two common approaches to this problem that are not mutually exclusive. While Australians of European culture tend to "fortify" themselves inside houses and expect individual privacy, her Warlpiri informants prefer to sleep outside, even if they have been settled in government housing. They sleep close together in named (*yunta*) rows, with unmarried women to the west, men to the east, and couples in the center row. The Warlpiri fear night and its sensory limitations. It is hard to see snakes, scorpions, *kurdaitcha* evil spirits, and the approach of hostile humans, drunks, and fighting dogs. Accordingly, some senior member of the appropriate group, not necessarily the eldest, is positioned on the ends of the rows to protect those in the middle by wakefulness and awareness. Musharbash reports a sense of security and comfort in sleeping thus and notes that individuals and families sometimes move or camp together specifically so they can sleep with others who provide this sense.

The Sinagua may have slept indoors or sleeping patterns may have varied seasonally. While the snows and cold of winter would have encouraged sleeping indoors, in hot weather it would have been more comfortable to sleep outside. Unknowable issues of appropriate behavior toward privacy, relatives, sexuality, and so on complicate the issue. The proximity of neighboring houses may suffice to provide a sense of protection.

A knowledge of who generally slept together may be as critical as knowing where people slept. Did men often sleep together, perhaps in the rooms we are interpreting as kivas, rather than at home? Did unmarried young males generally gather there, talk, and then sleep? What about children? Did they sleep where they fell or was it seen as necessary to return home at night? What about women? What type of flexibility did they have in where they slept?

UNITING/DIVIDING: VISION AND ACOUSTICS

One of the important considerations for an understanding of the night is the extent to which it divides people. We have argued that the experience of gathering around a fire tends to unite. Sound unites neighbors during the night. Those outside the ring of light shed by a fire could hear and be heard. It is not clear how far the auditory range would have extended in a Sinagua village. We need more and better studies of the acoustics of the dwellings used by Sinagua and other Puebloan groups in order to be able to understand what could and could not be overheard from the outside or from neighboring dwellings, whether pithouses of a variety of types, or pueblo rooms.

CONCLUSIONS: THE VILLAGE SENSESCAPE

Night in a Sinagua village would have brought obvious visual changes in what could be seen, but the rest of the sensescape is altered too. At night some of the sounds heard during the day would disappear, because the activities they represent are not efficiently done in lower illumination. The distinctive crack of flintknapping and the rhythmic pounding of metate manufacture were probably absent. Hopi women grind corn during the day; in fact, there are taboos against doing this task and others at night (Malotki and Lomatuway'ma 1990:89–98). The cheerful sound of whistling, for instance, is also dangerous at night.

Given the seasonal variability that the Sinagua would have experienced, the sensescape of the night was not constant. Snow in the winter contrasted with pleasant warm weather in the summer; dry conditions were interspersed with seasonal rainy spells; and, especially at the higher elevations of New Caves, the possibility of strong winds. In particular, during the cold winter months much nighttime human activity probably occurred indoors, while during the summer, sleeping, eating or just gathering outdoors was probably more pleasant.

The worlds of day and night are cultural as well as physical since all experience is filtered through a cultural lens that specifies appropriate activities, and influences beliefs and attitudes. Human activities change in response to nightfall, often in ways that are shaped by social variables such as age, gender, and group membership, and in turn act to shape social identities. The 'built environment' that people create around themselves must always include facilities for night activities as well as for daylight ones. The phenomenological approaches suggested by some current theorists (Hegmon 2013) wisely encourage us to consider what it would have been like to experience our sites as inhabitants, and this perspective should lead us to think about obvious but neglected issues such as life at night. Nightlife, like daylife, is lived through culturally defined and patterned activities, and thus must leave interpretable patterns for our archaeological understanding.

REFERENCES

Basso, Keith. 1996. *Wisdom Sits in Places: Landscape and Language among the Western Apache.* Albuquerque: University of New Mexico Press.

Beaglehole, Ernest. 1936. *Hopi Hunting and Hunting Ritual.* Yale University Publications in Anthropology No. 4. New Haven, CT: Yale University Press.

Boivin, Nicole, Adam Brumm, Helen Lewis, Dave Robinson, and Ravi Korisettar. 2007. "Sensual, Material, and Technological Understanding: Exploring Prehistoric Soundscapes in South India." *Journal of the Royal Anthropological Institute* 13(2):267–294. https://doi.org/10.1111/j.1467-9655.2007.00428.x.

Buser, Pierre, and Michel Imbert. 1992. *Vision.* Cambridge, MA: The MIT Press.

Cushing, Frank Hamilton. 1901. *Zuñi Folk Tales.* New York: G. P. Putnam's Sons.

Dawson, Peter, Richard Levy, Don Gardner, and Matthew Walls. 2007. "Simulating the Behaviour of Light inside Arctic Dwellings: Implications for Assessing the Role of Vision in Task Performance." *World Archaeology* 39(1):17–35. https://doi.org/10.1080/00438240601136397.

Day, Jo, ed. 2013. *Making Senses of the Past: Toward a Sensory Archaeology.* Center for Archaeological Investigations Occasional Paper No. 40. Carbondale: Southern Illinois University Press.

Dozier, Edward P. 1970. "Making Inferences from the Present to the Past." In *Reconstructing Prehistoric Pueblo Societies,* ed. William A. Longacre, 202–213. Albuquerque: University of New Mexico Press.

Ferguson, T. J., and E. R. Hart. 1985. *A Zuni Atlas.* Norman: University of Oklahoma Press.

Gaver, William W. 1993. "What in the World Do We Hear?: An Ecological Approach to Auditory Event Perception." *Ecological Psychology* 5(1):1–29. https://doi.org/10.1207/s15326969eco0501_1.

Gibson, James J. 1986. *The Ecological Approach to Visual Perception.* Boston: Houghton Mifflin.

Green, Jesse. 1979. *Zuñi: Selected Writings of Frank Hamilton Cushing.* Lincoln: University of Nebraska Press.

Hegmon, Michelle. 2013. "The Archaeology of the Human Experience." *SAA Archaeological Record* 13(5):16–19.

Hill, James N. 1970. *Broken K Pueblo: Prehistoric Social Organization in the American Southwest.* Anthropological Papers No. 18. Tucson: University of Arizona Press.

Kamp, Kathryn. 1998. *Life in the Pueblo: Understanding the Past Through Archaeology.* Prospect Heights, IL: Waveland Press.

Kamp, Kathryn. 2002. "Working for a Living: Childhood in the Prehistoric Puebloan Southwest." In *Children in the Prehistoric Puebloan Southwest,* ed. Kathryn A. Kamp, 71–89. Salt Lake City: University of Utah Press.

Kamp, Kathryn. 2012. "Children of the Sierra Sin Agua." In *Hisatsinom: People of the Land without Water*, ed. Chris Downum, 89–95. Santa Fe, NM: School of American Research.

Kamp, Kathryn, and John Whittaker. 1999. *Surviving Adversity: The Sinagua of Lizard Man Village*. University of Utah Anthropological Papers No. 120. Salt Lake City: School of American Research Press.

Kamp, Kathryn, and John Whittaker. 2009. "A Sinagua Acropolis: Architectural Adaptation at New Caves, Arizona." *Kiva* 74(3):281–304. https://doi.org/10.1179/kiv.2009.74.3.002.

King, Stacie M., and Gonzalo Sánchez Santiago. 2011. "Soundscapes of the Everyday in Ancient Oaxaca, Mexico." *Archaeologies* 7(2):387–422. https://doi.org/10.1007/s11759-011-9171-y.

Lewis, David. 1976. "Observations on Route Finding and Spatial Orientation among the Aboriginal peoples of the Western Desert Region of Central Australia." *Oceania* 46(4):249–282. https://doi.org/10.1002/j.1834-4461.1976.tb01254.x.

Lister, Robert H., and Florence C. Lister. 1987. *Aztec Ruins on the Animas: Excavated, Preserved, and Interpreted*. Albuquerque: University of New Mexico Press.

Lowell, Julia C. 1999. "The Fires of Grasshopper: Enlightening Transformations in Subsistence Practices through Fire-Feature Analysis." *Journal of Anthropological Archaeology* 18(4):441–470. https://doi.org/10.1006/jaar.1999.0338.

Malotki, Ekkehart, and Michael Lomatuway'ma. 1984. *Hopi Coyote Tales: Istutuwutsi*. Lincoln: University of Nebraska Press.

Malotki, Ekkehart, and Michael Lomatuway'ma. 1990. *Maasaw: Profile of a Hopi God*. Lincoln: University of Nebraska Press.

McIlwain, James T. 1996. *An Introduction to the Biology of Vision*. Cambridge, UK: Cambridge University Press. https://doi.org/10.1017/CBO9781139174473.

Musharbash, Yasmine. 2013. "Night, Sleep, and Feeling Safe: An Exploration of Aspects of Warlpiri and Western Sleep." *Australian Journal of Anthropology* 24(1):48–63. https://doi.org/10.1111/taja.12021.

Ortiz, Alfonso. 1972. *The Tewa World: Space, Time, Being, and Becoming in a Pueblo Society*. Chicago: University of Chicago Press.

Pijanowski, Bryan C., Luis J. Villanueva-Rivera, Sarah L. Dumyahn, Almo Farina, Bernie L. Krause, Brian M. Napoletano, Stuart H. Gage, and Nadia Pieretti. 2011. "Soundscape Ecology: The Science of Sound in the Landscape." *Bioscience* 61(3):203–216. https://doi.org/10.1525/bio.2011.61.3.6.

Samuels, David W., Louise Meintjes, Ana Maria Ochoa, and Thomas Porcello. 2010. "Soundscapes: Toward a Sounded Anthropology." *Annual Review of Anthropology* 39(1):329–345. https://doi.org/10.1146/annurev-anthro-022510-132230.

Sanchez, Julia L. J. 2007. "Procession and Performance: Recreating Soundscapes among the Ancient Maya." *World of Music* 49(2):35–44.

Schnepel, Burkhard, and Eyal Ben-Ari. 2005. "Introduction: 'When Darkness Comes . . . ': Steps toward an Anthropology of the Night." *Paideuma: Mitteilungen zur Kulturkunde* 51:153–163.

Snead, James E. 2008. *Ancestral Landscapes of the Pueblo World.* Tucson: University of Arizona Press.

Sobolik, Kristen D., Laurie S. Zimmerman, and Brooke Manross Guilfoyl. 1997. "Indoor versus Outdoor Firepit Usage: A Case Study from the Mimbres." *Kiva* 62(3):283–300. https://doi.org/10.1080/00231940.1997.11758336.

Stone, Tammy. 2009. "Room Function and Room Suites in Late Mogollon Pueblo Sites." *Kiva* 75(1):63–86. https://doi.org/10.1179/kiv.2009.75.1.004.

Teague, Lynn Shuler, and Dorothy K. Washburn. 2013. *Sandals of the Basketmaker and Pueblo Peoples: Fabric Structure and Color Symmetry.* Albuquerque: University of New Mexico Press.

Tuan, Yi-Fu. 1974. *Topophilia: A Study of Environmental Perception, Attitudes, and Values.* Englewood Cliffs, NJ: Prentice Hall.

Tuan, Yi-Fu. 1977. *Space and Place: The Perspective of Experience.* Minneapolis: University of Minnesota Press.

Tuan, Yi-Fu. 1979. *Landscapes of Fear.* Minneapolis: University of Minnesota Press.

Tyler, Hamilton. 1964. *Pueblo Gods and Myths.* Norman: University of Oklahoma Press.

Whittaker, John C., and Kathryn Kamp. 2012. "The Troubled End of Pueblo Life in the Sierra Sin Agua: Evidence from the Site of New Caves." In *Hisat'sinom: Ancient Peoples in a Land without Water*, ed. Christian E. Downum, 148–154. Santa Fe, NM: School for Advanced Research Press.

Wiessner, Polly W. 2014. "Embers of Society: Firelight Talk among the Ju/'hoansi Bushmen." *Proceedings of the National Academy of Sciences of the United States of America* 111(39):14027–14035. https://doi.org/10.1073/pnas.1404212111.

"La Luz de Aceite es Triste"

*Nighttime, Community, and Memory in the
Colorado–New Mexico Borderlands*

MINETTE C. CHURCH

*Weather forecast for tonight: dark. Continued dark
overnight, with widely scattered light by morning.*
—GEORGE CARLIN

Consideration of specifically nocturnal contexts for human behavior is not new but it is still strangely uncommon for archaeologists, given the unremitting inevitability of sunless hours the world over. It is perhaps less so for ethnographers and historians (Ekirch 2006; Glassie 1982). Folklorist Henry Glassie writes evocatively of community-building and placemaking *ceilies*, or late evening social "entertainments" in the dispersed, rural Ulster community of Ballymenone, "when tea appears and talk cracks, when the neighbors bring a little happiness into the night while reaffirming the relations that make them more than people who chance to live near one another" (Glassie 1982, 77). In contrast, archaeologists tend to focus on technologies of lighting after dark: more on the lantern bits, less on the broken teacups. At the other extreme, archaeoastronomers outline highly symbolic and ritualized intersections of nighttime and the landscape. Recent popular history

DOI: 10.5876/9781607326786.c005

(Ekirch 2006) has examined night as an exceptional time of misrule, misbehavior, and exotic social settings rather than hosting repetitive and sometimes prosaic activities. Here, I focus on archaeology of nighttime as both more socially situated in memory and routine, and less exceptional and monumental. Rather than a time of extraordinary behavior and "nocturnal license" (Ekirch 2006) I consider nighttime and different technologies of lighting as context for the mundane bits and pieces used in "everynight" rather than everyday activities.

In the nineteenth-century Colorado borderlands (figures 1.2 and 1.3), the night was a time for work and travel as well as a time for framing social memory through storytelling and social reproduction, and these were not always separable classes of activity. In contrast, by the mid-twentieth century this social context was changing with the replacement of oil light by electric bulbs, and of fiddle and harmonica by transistor radios. A generation earlier, community-building and placemaking, primarily lit by evening fire and oil light, was critical in a region where settlement was dispersed and rural, and boundaries were fluid and contested; community membership needed to be repeatedly, if implicitly, defined and sustained among neighbors. Thus nighttime activities, both solitary and social, frame the architecture, landscape, and artifacts we find on the seemingly isolated farmstead sites we explore and the often-ignored communicating terrain between them. Along the Purgatoire River of the southern Colorado–New Mexico borderlands, as along the disputed borders of Glassie's Ulster, religious ritual and meaning, class, nationality, and gendered ideologies were entangled with and structured nighttime activities, perhaps even more so as these areas were politically, ethnically, and at times violently contested rural spaces. It is time we start looking at artifacts, architecture, and features of terrain divested of assumptions about daylight hours.

For decades, archaeologists engaged in purportedly "gender neutral" archaeology while in effect excluding women (Claassen and Conkey 1991; Gero and Conkey 1991). The same can be said about archaeologies of non-binary genders (Schmidt and Voss 2005), the elderly, and children. In another example, even when archaeologists finally acknowledged that we should be examining the lives and built environment of enslaved labor in the United States, we often started with "the quarters" and it took more decades to acknowledge that the "big house"—Monticello or the White House—along with entire historical economies were also built by people enslaved and indentured. These monuments represent the material footprint of their lives and their achievements (Allen 2005; Battle-Baptiste 2011). When looking for the material signature of nighttime activities, it becomes clear that we should not begin by looking for "nighttime artifacts" or spaces. Looking for some sort of signature "women's artifacts" or "African American artifacts" long blinded us to the fact that the vast majority of artifacts on any given site were used by everyone at one time or another, or if not, were gendered or assigned by race according to a cultural logic that usually differed from that of most researchers.

Of course recognizing nighttime activities generally does not have anything like the sort of social justice ramifications as do these other examples of researcher bias. Nevertheless, the interpretive pitfall is similar; where the default or "neutral" stance has been that people act during the day and rest at night, this perspective should not be a default interpretive position simply because that is considered the norm (or at least the ideal) now. When encountering architectural spaces, landscape features, and artifacts, we should make no a priori assumptions about when the activities represented took place.

Concentrating on "daily" lives, archaeologists and historians have ignored the fact that our research subjects lived as many nights as they did days. The bread and butter of archaeology in southern Colorado, which was a United States–Republic of Mexico borderland until 1848, are plaza and household architectural spaces, churches, and landscapes dissected by trails, roads, fence lines, and irrigation ditches. All provided settings for the changing material culture that emerged with the advent of railroads and access to merchandisers such as Sears, Roebuck and Co. Rarely have we explored any of these "everyday" material traces in the context of nighttime.

DISCUSSION

When writing on landscape archaeology out on the Colorado plains, sometimes described as "Big Sky country," one must first acknowledge that the sky is easily 60 percent or more of the perceptible landscape in terms of "viewshed." As someone working in archaeoastronomy, Lionel Sims (2009, 389) recommends archaeologists broaden definitions of landscape to include skyscape. Though it should be obvious that roughly half of the time that sky is dark (depending on latitude), lit by stars and periodic moon, those of us not dealing specifically in archaeoastronomy have not always engaged with nocturnal cultural skyscapes as we should. In contrast, it is not at all surprising when researching settlement on the plains to find that nineteenth-century memoirists dedicate large chunks of prose to the sky and what falls from it, blows across it, or fails to fall from it, including delightful sayings such as "ditches and manure piles smell stronger before a rain" (Book Committee 1993). Tim Ingold (2007, 20) titled a paper "Earth, Sky, Wind, and Weather," arguing that people who live wholly or part-time "in the open" do not live on the ground and under the sky but instead mingle with "wind, light, and moisture of the sky" as they are bound with "substances of the earth in the continual forging of a way through the tangle of life-lines that comprise the land."

In academic buildings it makes little difference what the weather is like, or whether it is still light when university faculty emerge, blinking like trolls, into the parking lot to go home. City lights obscure the stars, and we need not navigate home by them in some variant of a prairie schooner (Conestoga wagon) or ox-drawn Santa Fé *carreta* (wooden cart). According to Ingold (2007, S32), this interior and artificially lit context of research can affect the investigation we do:

> I have suggested that because we generally think and write indoors, the world we describe in our writing is one that has been imaginatively remodeled as if it were already set up within an enclosed, interior space. In this as if world, populated only by people and objects, those fluxes of the medium that we experience as wind and rain, sunshine and mist, frost and snow, and so on, are simply inconceivable. This, I believe, accounts for their absence from practically all discussions concerning the relations between human beings and the material world.

Archaeological fieldwork is another matter. While working on one of the sites discussed here, students slept in tents in a maze of canyons, more than an hour from the nearest town by two-track and gravel roads. The sense of isolation is strong in the vast expanses of twenty-first-century Forest Service and adjacent military lands, set in turn among enormous ranches. However, we know from memoirs and newspapers that a century ago, a sense of rural community was correspondingly strong *because* it was both dispersed and sometimes contested.

We spent our days here in the relentless June sunshine of the high-altitude plains, where it can easily reach over 100 degrees Fahrenheit by noon. This kind of climate strengthens the appeal of a midday rest in the shade, and students often dozed during half-hour lunch spans. Archaeologists often assume work happens by day, and sleep by night. However, far from resting only at night, we know that Loretta Lopez, matriarch of the family who built the site we were exploring, took a traditional daily *siesta* and as her daughter Julia (Juanita) emphasized in her memoir: woe and a "willow switch" to the child who wandered too far while her mother was sleeping. Students quickly learned the value of going out as early as the light allowed and heading back to camp in the early afternoon to take refuge in the relative cool provided by the thick adobe walls surrounding the field lab, a nineteenth-century ranch house. In contrast, the arid high-altitude nights cool quickly, and students spent them outside by a wood fire or Coleman lantern, listening to coyotes and nighthawks under a bright Milky Way. Sometimes we discussed journal articles or entered map data onto laptops. More often, we planned work strategies for the next day, told stories, and broke out instruments to play music.

As it turns out, these day and nighttime rhythms of field archaeology were in some respects like those of the homesteaders whose sites we explored in these canyons along the river. In memoirs and interviews, there is talk of dances that went on most of the night. Some people met future spouses at these community events. At field school, even though we got up at dawn to get into the field while it was cool, and we stayed up past dark visiting, playing music, and mending equipment, we honestly had not thought much about the archaeological signatures or the meanings of after-dark activities.

LIGHTING TECHNOLOGY AND CHANGE

One class of artifacts and features that we can assign to nighttime relatively securely is that associated with lighting technologies such as lamp and lantern parts, or fire pits (see Nowell, chapter 2; Strong, chapter 12; and McGuire, chapter 13, this volume). As archaeologists, we like technology. It leaves behind visible and relatively easily interpreted bits and pieces; we can count them, measure them, map them in space, date them precisely, quantify their prevalence relative to other objects, and assign basic functionality. The technology around seeing after dark is evident on virtually every nineteenth-century site in the western United States. Parks Canada has a very useful book (Woodhead et al. 1984) devoted to dating and typing archaeological evidence of lighting devices of various historical periods, and with that kind of help, archaeologists are good at identifying and dating candlesnuffers and kerosene lamp diffusers.

However, there are also productive research questions to ask about what people were doing by the light of all those candles and kerosene lamps, and what changing technologies around lighting through time allowed them to do or, alternatively, discouraged. In his discussions of Ulster Irish contexts, Glassie (1982) notes that by the second half of the twentieth century, radio and then television sometimes disrupted the culture of nighttime ceili "entertainments" and storytelling in rural country homes. More particularly, this Colorado discussion will be about what was gained and what was lost after each new lighting innovation spread in popularity and affordability, decades before the advent of radio and TV. New lighting technologies changed lives in the last years of the nineteenth century and continue to do so now, so archaeological interpretation of nighttime activities must change to encompass how the context around lantern and lightbulb bits changed through time.

A phenomenological approach to an embodied sense of place and landscape requires that we consider these contexts and technological changes as intertwined (Johnson 1999; Sims 2009). Consider tungsten lighting, as compact fluorescent and LED lighting have almost replaced it. These are not just newer and more efficient technologies, they effectively change the quality of light in which we immerse ourselves for large chunks of our lives after sunset or before dawn, and the sheer quantity of light is increasing as well. Artificial light is becoming inescapable. The International Dark Sky Association declares prominently on its website: "Eight out of ten people live under a light-polluted night sky" (http://darksky.org/, accessed July 2020). With each new technology, people gain productive time after the sun goes down. People also lose intimacy with the night sky and knowledge of how to tell time by it or navigate by it. "Instead of being in its own right qualitatively mysterious and uncanny, now [night] is simply regarded as the temporary absence or suspension of light that should be gotten through as quickly and insensibly as possible" (Helms 2004, 179). Working productively into the night comes at a cost (Ekirch 2006); we lose the intimacy and community of neighborly visits. People forget stories told by the dim light of stars, trading it for the flickering blue light of "prime time" (i.e., nighttime) on TVs. By combining available documentary evidence of nighttime activities with the artifacts we find archaeologically, we can triangulate data on the sorts of activities occurring after dark before rural electrification, ranging from the prosaic to the sacred, as well as the changes that emerging modernity brought.

MOONLIGHT, STARLIGHT, FIRELIGHT, LANTERN LIGHT

At its most basic and pragmatic, firelight has been available for certain activities since the Paleolithic (see Nowell, chapter 2, this volume). We know that for our hominid ancestors, fires cooked meat, hardened spears, warmed bodies, and deterred nocturnal predators. They may have done more; Thomas Wynn (2012) recently wrote in *Smithsonian Magazine* about how staring into campfires, mesmerized by the flicker, might well have played a role in early human cognitive development. For the nineteenth century, our interpretations are perhaps less grand and evolutionary, or at least more proximate and gendered. We find that a wood fireplace or stove in the home is part-and-parcel of a woman's work never being done. At the Lopez homestead in southeastern Colorado, a cluster of straight pins lay scattered on the oxidized earthen floor before the hearth in what was the main house (figure 5.1).

> On these small ranches the people at the harvest season gathered in the home
> of one of their neighbors and there husked corn. The women ground it and put
> the leaves aside to be used for rolling cigarettes, for both men and women smoke.
> This work was done . . . but by the light of an *ocote* [pine] log. This pitch-wood
> served a double purpose, of fuel and light. (Otero Warren 1936)

In Ulster, "If neighbors enter the kitchen, the first and central space of the home, a ceili might develop, but if no one comes the scene is one of 'fireside.' Its participants are not ceiliers but members of the family" (Glassie 1982, 77). Some social activities in the Lopez household took place by candle or kerosene lamp, but firelight gave both heat and light, and candles and oil for lamps were costly.

Part of the focus of research at the Lopez Plaza Site is on an archaeology of parenting in the Colorado–New Mexico border area. The research deals with the changes evident in contrasting memoirs penned by two of the Lopez children who grew up along the Purgatoire River, born 16 years apart. These documentary data are enriched and checked with archaeological data from the site where they both lived. Elfido, the eldest of 12 surviving children, was born

FIGURE 5.1. *Maclovia Lopez (no relation to the Lopez homestead, so far as the author knows), wife of the mayordomo, spinning wool by the light of the fire, Trampas, New Mexico. (John Collier, 1943; Library of Congress, Prints & Photographs Division, FSA/OWI Collection LC-DIG-fsa-8d38302)*

in 1869. Julia (Juanita), the second-to-youngest, was born in 1885. Elfido spent a few childhood years in the village of Las Animas, Colorado, but for the most part, they grew up on the same site with the same parents. Nevertheless, their childhoods were different in innumerable ways. Elfido grew up in the 1870s after his father Domacio, a Santa Fé trader, lost his ox cart in the Purgatoire River. Domacio had to re-earn capital by working on construction of the Atchison, Topeka, and Santa Fe Railroad through the new town of West Las Animas where little Elfido, from age seven, herded cattle. In contrast, by the time Julia was growing up in the 1890s, *Don* Domacio ran the post office and general store on their homestead. She writes: "By the time I was born in 1885 Papa had prospered" (Hudson 1987a). These different circumstances had, of course, a profound impact on the archaeological record produced, and the material context in which each of them lived.

Both siblings describe camping out on trips with parents to Trinidad, Colorado, but their descriptions are telling. On his way with his father to grind wheat in town, Elfido writes:

> After night came there were lots of buggies going from Trinidad to El Moro and back. They had lights on the corners of the buggies and the horses were trotting. I thought it was the prettiest sight I had ever seen. I don't think I slept hardly any. It sure looked good to me." (Lopez 1998, 28)

Wagon parts and associated livestock tack are ubiquitous on sites of this era, as are footpaths, two-tracks, and roads. Yet in all the scholarship about Santa Fé Trail's freighting, international trade, and travel, there is little discussion of transportation after darkness fell and cooler temperatures prevailed. In the summer months, daytime temperatures in the southern plains and Southwest can be brutally hot. Accounts like Elfido's provide archaeologists and historians a glimpse of this nighttime travel.

The fact that so few have described such nighttime journeys may be related to the fact that US scholars have relied most heavily on English-language reports by Anglo American travelers rather than those written in Spanish. The experience of travel through familiar spaces, homelands, is of course different from that of travel through novel and foreign landscapes with unfamiliar and occasionally hostile inhabitants (Sunseri 2015). One does not come across accounts of night travel too often in the travel journals of English-speaking easterners; it is more common to find wagons circled at nightfall against potential Indian attack, real or perceived. Yet non-Indian people born and raised in the borderlands had different relationships with Native Americans, who were sometimes enemies but just as often *vecinos* (neighbors), friends, and often family (Frank 2007, Sunseri 2018).

Susan Magoffin (1962), an easterner married to an Irish American trader, is perhaps the most famous Anglo American woman to travel along the Santa Fé Trail in the nineteenth century because we still have her detailed diary. Riding south from Santa Fé into Chihuahua, Mexico, in 1846, she is unnerved by the fact that the borderlands-based traders chaperoning that leg of their journey preferred to travel at night and avoid the heat of the day.

> La Luna [the moon] made her appearance about 10—and afforded us a beautiful light to travel by: the road is hard and level and we made fine progress, arriving at this place about 25 miles by 2 [o'clock] this morning . . . I am not an advocate

though, for night travelling when I have to be shut up in the carriage in a road I know nothing of, and the driver nodding all the time, and letting the reins drop from his hands to the entire will of the mules. I was kept in a *fever* the whole night, though everyone complained bitterly of cold. (Magoffin 1962, 199)

In this way she describes their passage through the *Jornada del Muerto* (day's journey of the dead man), a portion of *El Camino Real* (royal road) between Santa Fé and Chihuahua that notoriously afforded travelers little to no water. Like most deserts, it can be beastly hot during the day and correspondingly chilly at night. In such circumstances travel at night, lit by lanterns such as those witnessed by Elfido as a boy, was much easier on the oxen and other livestock.

Clearly, travelers like Magoffin had a far different experience of traversing this moonlit landscape than did locals like her sleepy driver. The light of stars in the broad expanse of the Great Plains is significant, but the light of the moon provides particularly clear light three-quarters of the nighttime in a climate with few clouds. Roads were lined with rocks, cleared of brush, marked by cairns, or grooved into two-tracks such that people or oxen could walk virtually unguided along the paths at night. Here, it is important to reach beyond archaeologists' comfort zone at the site and artifact level, to the moonlit landscapes of roads, fences, cairns, and footpaths in the borderlands: "The embodied accumulation of sensory and purposive experiences in space over time builds an accretion of memories into a sense of place" (Sims 2009, 386).

More than a decade after Elfido traveled and camped with his father, Julia describes overnight camping trips similar to those of her elder brother but this time with both parents and a sibling or two along:

Papa and Mama used to make an occasional trip to Trinidad [Colorado] for supplies and it was a great treat when two or three of us—the youngest—were permitted to go on the trip. We always went in the big wagon drawn by a team of big horses. We always camped out the first night. Around the campfire Papa would tell us exciting stories about the old settlers and early pioneer days. The campfire burned far into the night. We eventually fell asleep to the howling of the wolves and coyotes. We felt no fear; it was part of our upbringing. We knew that God watched over us. (Hudson 1987a: 5)

In a letter to her grandson, she added details:

It is lovely to sleep under the stars. Reminds me of the times when Papa and Mama . . . drove the big wagon to Trinidad for supplies and we slept in the shadows of the ruins of Old Bent's Fort. We considered it a big treat. It was an 85-mile ride and took two days to make it. We loved camping out and staying awake to hear Papa tell of their early years as homesteaders. Also about the marauding Indians. (Hudson 1987b: 58)

Here is an example of social reproduction and memory specifically saved for firelit nights such as these. It is not coincidental that these stories of family and regional history were told while camped at night among ruins of William Bent's old trading fort, nor is the fact that Julia recalls it twice in her written memories. "It is at times such as these, when individuals step back from the flow of everyday experience and attend self-consciously to places—when, we may say, they pause to actively sense them—that their relationships to geographical space are most richly lived and surely felt" (Basso 1996, 54). "The past lives as the land. Geography was the natural way to bring different speakers and different stories into aesthetic and social union" (Glassie 1982, 111). The past in this context for Julia is not abstract but plays into her girlhood roots of personal and social sense of self. "Persons thus involved may also dwell on aspects of themselves, on sides and corners of their own evolving identities" (Basso 1996, 55). As she internalized these campfire stories under the stars, Julia's sense of family history and identity, particularly her sense of the dangers of "marauding Indians," was clearly different than her older brother's recollections of Native American paternal kin and of playing together with a Ute child, from his memoir (Lopez 1937).

Beyond the changes in technologies of lighting, there clearly are associated changing memories and social contexts described in Elfido's and Julia's accounts. Between his experience of the 1870s and hers of the 1890s, there had been a shift in the perception of the night sky that was a result of changing Indian relations and gender roles as well as the lighting technologies familiar to each child. In Elfido's account he does not mention the stars at all. Having herded cattle alone from the age of seven, the night sky was no doubt familiar. Many early travelers described the Great Plains as like an ocean. "In the Arab world, the stars are used for navigation at sea and in the desert" (Agius 2005, 156–157; Varisco 1997; both cited in Nash 2007, 162). Elfido's father Domacio Lopez described grass so high in 1870 that when his oxen lay down in the bluestem, he could not find them (Lopez 1998, 28). When following the cows beyond the river bottoms out into grasses on "the flats" of the open prairie lands, the stars were a critical tool of navigation after dark for the small boys and men in charge of livestock (figure 5.2). When he was older, Elfido went to work on cattle drives for local ranchers and spent months of nights outside. "We sure did work hard. We would go to bed after dark and get up and have breakfast by firelight and be on our horses by daylight. I think we put in 15 to 16 hours a day as we had to get up and stand [guard] two hours at night" (Lopez 1998, 34).

In addition to running the cattle, there was crop work to be done at the Lopez place. There were irrigation ditches serving the property along the Purgatoire valley, watering alfalfa fields, an orchard, and a kitchen garden. In New Mexican villages as well as on ranches, boys and men were primarily responsible for managing the irrigation ditches for agricultural fields, sometimes at night (see

FIGURE 5.2. *Sunset and clouds over the southern Great Plains. (Photo by Minette Church)*

Nathan, chapter 16, this volume). *Acequias* (large primary irrigation canals) and branching irrigation subditches traverse the landscape at intervals along the rivers of the US borderlands, and archaeologists record old head gates and ditch remnants, some still active. We rarely think of these carefully managed waterways as specifically indicative of day *and* night activities. However, during times of drought, irrigation allotments were distributed over a 24-hour period, and so sometimes someone had to stay awake to monitor the ditch and open or close the gates as appropriate during the night. The New Mexican word *acequia* has roots in Arabic by way of Spain and Mexico. In a case study in Oman by Harriet Nash (2007), men and boys used the stars to time irrigation even when wristwatches were available.

> It appears that the use of stars survives mainly in smaller settlements still dependent on agriculture for livelihoods, where light pollution is less severe than in the towns, and where the community adheres to traditional practices. Many of the stars have different names to those given in the literature on Arabic stars, and the stars used for timing water vary somewhat from one village to another. The method of stargazing also varies among villages: in some the stars are watched rising above the horizon and in others the time is known by the rising or setting of the star above or below a man-made marker, or on its reaching the zenith. (Nash 2007, 157)

In the arid Colorado borderlands, village men and boys would have used the stars similarly to tell when their nighttime water allotment time began and ended, just as cowhands might have used the stars to tell when their two-hour night watch was over. They may not have had a sense of absolute time; stars' relative position in the sky shifted against the landscape as nights lengthened or shortened according to season. In these cases, as in Oman, allocation of water was divided into shares measured by the amount of time that it was allowed to flow into the field, not measured by any absolute amount of water, which meant that in times of drought everyone shared the pain.

> When called upon by circumstances, the water judges were responsible for ini-
> tiating and implementing strict rotations for water usage . . . Because physical
> conditions often made it necessary to set up the rotations on a twenty-four hour
> basis, and because few farmers preferred to irrigate their fields at night, irrigation
> times were drawn by lot. (Meyer 1996, 65)

On one hand, in an arid environment farmers got more moisture per unit of time at night when the rate of evaporation was low, but on the other hand nighttime irrigation meant there was no evaporative cooling to ameliorate the withering effects of high temperatures during the day. "When water is scarce one may see a man and his entire family up all night irrigating the small patches of ground, since the water may have been turned in his ditch for only twenty-four hours and he must get the entire benefit of it" (Otero Warren 1936, 62). In the early days of Spanish and Mexican settlement frontiers, there was no protection from enemies at night, Indian or otherwise, when out maintaining ditches (Jun Senseri, personal communication, August 2016). Nor was there protection from neighborly conflict.

Communities cohered and also fractured around the management of such a scarce resource. All this formality, hierarchy, and sometimes political position-ing around irrigation and water (Crawford 1988; Meyer 1996; Rodríguez 2006) stemmed from the fact that in the arid Southwest, skirmishes arose around access to water, just as conflict arose between cattle and sheep ranchers (the latter often Hispanos and the former often Anglo American), and between both of these groups and homesteaders. Associated acts of sabotage such as fence cutting and tampering with head gates (Rodríguez 2006) occurred at night. "In time of great drought conflicts are frequently brought into court and even kill-ings take place over the allotment of water" (Otero Warren 1936, 62). Structured delegation of ditch judges, *mayordomos* (local, elected officials), and other offi-cers was necessary. Along with abandoned remnants of irrigation ditches and head gates, archaeologists record the fence lines by which homesteaders con-troversially segmented the "open prairie," marked by posts of decaying wood or tilting limestone crisscrossing the Plains. All of these landscape features mark terrain that is potentially interpretable as a landscape of conflict (cf. Shackel 2003). Much of that conflict may have manifested at night.

Subversive nighttime activities reflected ruptures in nineteenth-century rural community identities. Such fractures arose in the face of social differences and emerging inequalities brought on, for example, by being the family at the end of the ditch that was chronically shorted water allotments by the rest of the upstream community. Tensions arose between Hispano sheepherders and Anglo American cattle ranchers, or resulted from frustrations on the part of those who, by the 1880s, felt increasingly impinged upon by new corporate, absentee-owned cattle operatives claiming and enclosing what was previously open prairie (Reed and Horn 1995).

The fact is that farm and ranch labor meant that substantial parts of men's and boys' lives were lived outside during the day and often during the night. So instead of remarking on the familiar stars that he saw while camping with his father as a boy, Elfido instead was entranced by the candle-lanterns mounted on the wagons that went by. His father and other families at the time were shoveling irrigation ditches with wooden shovels and plowing with wooden plows. Of 12 men who began the main irrigation ditch along the Purgatoire River, only six could afford metal shovels (Lopez 1998). Any manufactured goods we might find evidence of archaeologically, like lamps and bottles of lamp oil, would have come before rail transportation, by stage or wagon through intermediaries who drove up costs. By the time of Julia's childhood, transport of goods along the Atchison, Topeka, and Santa Fe Railroad expedited the arrival of such goods to her father's Post Office and general store.

Julia's special mention of the stars when she camped away from the homestead not only speaks to the fact that her parents had better access to oil lamps in the house at night by the time she was a child, it also speaks to social facts of the gendered geography of the homestead. The boys, whom she calls *"caballeros"* (gentlemen horsemen and cattlemen) in-training, bunked out in rooms around the livestock plaza, near the rooms of two hired hands from Taos Pueblo who did what she considered lower-status field and orchard work. The girls always slept inside the house. Sleeping (or not sleeping) under the night sky was novel to her in a way that it was not to her much older brother for complex reasons involving newly affordable lighting technologies but also the family's social mobility and gendered household practices and occupations.

Another account illustrates how Colorado–New Mexico borderland locals were variously familiar with night travel and how archaeologists should look at the communicating terrains of roads and footpaths accordingly. Adelina (Nina) Otero Warren tells a charming story of a nighttime journey. Doña Adelina was a native of the Southwest, suffragist, and Santa Fé School Superintendent, born in 1881, just four years before the birth of Julia Lopez. She rode a circuit to inspect rural schools that extended from New Mexico into southern Colorado.

Darkness comes upon us suddenly in the high mountains, like a curtain lowered to cover our eyes from too much grandeur: But we were fortunate. A moon rose over the ranges, shedding its white light upon the countryside. A breeze stirred the pine trees that they might give forth a fragrance and refresh their guests in the canyon—*el refresco de la noche* [the refreshment of the night]. Suddenly I heard a man singing. I looked back and noticed that he was following us on horseback. It was Teófilo, one of the school directors.

I asked him, "Teófilo, where are you going at this hour?"

"Para Santa Fe, Señora."

"To Santa Fe! It is thirty miles. You will not arrive there till late. Can I attend to your business for you?"

"No senora. *No tenga pensa[miento].*" [Do not be worried.]

We drove on. Our Indian boy never saying a word; Teófilo just keeping us in sight. The moon, as it rose, gave us more and more light. At first the tall pines seemed like sentinels one is afraid to approach, but gradually they became more friendly, and Teófilo began to sing: "*Alli en un bosque donde yo me——, solo se [oye] mi triste penar*" [Here in the forest where I hear my sad thoughts.]

The melody of it, the pathos, "*Solo se [oye] mi triste penar!*"

The little Spanish community; the mountains; the moon; Teófilo's voice breaking the great silence. *La hermosura de la noche!* [The beauty of the night!] We finally reached Nambé, and as I thanked and paid the Indian boy and got into my car, I noticed Teófilo was still following. He drew up to the car and addressed me:

"Are you alright Doña Adelina?"

"Si, gracias."

"You will not have trouble with your car?"

"I think not."

"Well then, *buenas noches, y Dios la cuide* [good night, and God go with you]. I shall return to Cundiyo. But first would you be so kind as to mail this letter for me in Santa Fé?"

"But you are not going there yourself then!?"

Teófilo smiled, bowed, donned on his coat, and rode off into the night. He had followed us for ten miles and wanted to be certain that we were not lost in the mountains. These are my people. (Otero 1931, 149–151)

"These are my people" certainly speaks to identity and social memory in this story built on landscape, community, and nighttime (cf. Basso 1996). As Glassie notes in Ulster, "it is courteous to be sure the cailier (visiting neighbor) finds the best route out of the territory the householder knows best."

The land is pocked with sloughs, netted with complicated routes through gaps in a maze of thorny hedges . . . Safe home, Henry. God bless, Peter. All the best. Safe home. God bless. Words continue at conversational pitch until I have walked them out of hearing, along the pass towards the road. The narrow lane, the trees walling it, the bog and fields beyond, the sky—all is one blackness. There is no light, utterly, no sound. (Glassie 107, 108)

Each of these stories is about people, Teófilo and Peter Flanagan, who, along roads and pathways, are actively incorporating visitors—school superintendent, folklorist—into a sense of local community. Hosting community as an evening domestic activity can be defined in excavated data by the odd bit of kerosene lamp, broken teacup, or candle lantern but should also cause us to see surrounding landscape in a new way. Roads and trails, horse tack, and yard spaces can be reinterpreted in light of such accounts.

Julia and her contemporaries note that it is in the cool of summer nights or warmth of winter evenings that they listened to their elders and learned about history, identity, and mythology. This enculturation includes learning songs and playing music. Doña Adelina goes on to describe typical households along her school circuit:

On the long winter evenings I may see this same family sitting in front of an open fireplace, the father playing the guitar, the children the flute or the mouth harp, and the rest joining in with the sheer joy of singing. (Otero 1931, 149–151)

The longer winter evenings would have provided most time for such gatherings. It is entirely possible that the Lopez boys played music on mouth harps during the long daylight hours of tending cattle, but it is also probable that the bits of accordion, concertina, or mouth harp (figure 5.3) we found in domestic areas at the Lopez site were used primarily during evening gatherings, whether at community dances or just with family. Julia wrote further about social evenings at their home:

John Littleton, a near neighbor, used to come evenings. Mela and I looked up to him because he was a college graduate. He usually brought books. One teacher, a Miss Beasley, is the one I remember so well as she stayed the longest. On Friday and Saturday nights the adults would often play cards. One game they enjoyed playing was called 'Hearts.' Mela and I were too young to play so we just watched, or read until bedtime. (Hudson 1987b, 47)

Reading until bedtime while adult neighbors became close friends was a pastime made possible by lamps, and one that her older brother was not afforded 16 years earlier; he did not learn to read until his future wife made learning to do so a condition of courting her (Lopez 1937). Nor was it something their mother ever did; like most New Mexican women of her generation, even with her well-heeled origins, Loretta d'Arcia Lopez did not know how to read. She appears in the 1870 Territorial Census (US Bureau of the Census 1870) as unable to read or write, and her son describes her in this way (Lopez 1998). Reading, writing, and

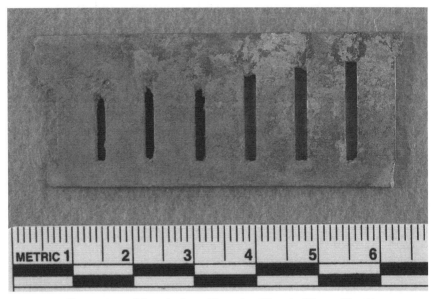

FIGURE 5.3. *Harmonica reed from the Lopez Plaza site. (Photo by Minette Church)*

bookkeeping in general was usually a men's evening activity for that generation, often lit by candle or lamp.

RELIGION AND COMMUNITY

The meanings of nighttime activities, and therefore archaeological interpretation of these spaces and artifacts, bridge the social and the ritual. Secular community-building undertaken in people's homes of an evening sometimes blended with those gatherings established within the Catholic Church calendar. Nighttime has long been a time of ritual in the Catholic Church; the liturgy of the hours can include Vespers (6 p.m.), Compline (9 p.m.), Matins (often midnight), and Lauds (dawn). Mary Helms (2004, 178) argues, "detailed scholarly discussions of early monastic life typically emphasize the activities of the day as much or more than those of the night and deeper ideological implications of an emphasis on the spirituality of the night remain largely unexplored." In contrast, she argues that early European monks "were quintessential men of the dark, for nocturns [or vigils], by far their longest liturgical office, was conducted each night, in the blackness of virtually unlit churches" (2004, 177). In a letter to her son, Julia Lopez Hudson wrote, "I like the quiet hours at night after prayers when I ask God's blessing for my children" (Hudson 1987b, 47).

Doña Adelina writes of a southern Colorado home she encountered on her circuit, providing some interpretive help for archaeologists interested in defining household spaces and Catholic ritual:

FIGURE 5.4. *Ruins of Mission Dolores, built by Don and Doña Lopez. (Photo by Minette Church)*

One room was set aside as a *sanctuario*, or little Chapel, where candles were burning that day in front of images of the saints and of our Lord. The family meets together every evening, light the candles, and say evening prayer. A devout, religious people whose religion permeates each thought and action. As these people watch the snow on the Sangre de Cristo range they feel that it is a sign from Dios that there will be water in the streams for their crops. "Why are we Catholics? Because we are Spanish." some of our people say. (Otero 1931, 149–151)

The houses of this period are not large, but they housed large and extended families. To dedicate an entire room, even temporarily, as a sanctuary chapel is a significant commitment of space for activities that occurred primarily, if not exclusively, at night.

Many of the borderlands households were served only by itinerate priests, and so routine Catholic ritual rested with individual households where religious observances often merged with practical concerns about water.

Yeah, well, nine days before the fiesta, we pray the novena each night. We get together in different houses, each one. They offer the homes for that. And we go to different houses. (Rodríguez 2006, 85)

Communities visited irrigation features on the landscape periodically in processions in honor of saints, blessing the acequia (primary ditch) and expressing gratitude for that scarcest resource, water (Rodríguez 2006, 85): "My husband and I pray[ed] the novena for them for 12 years before he died. And we go to the mayordomos [ditch bosses]." During such activities, Catholic ritual, day and night, is harnessed to honor or bless incoming and outgoing ditch managers.

Don and Doña Lopez built a small *visita* (small church lacking a resident priest) on their land (figure 5.4), called Mission Dolores, and built community by

FIGURE 5.5. *The mayordomo of Trampas, New Mexico, replacing the santos in their niches, after they have been borrowed by a chapel three miles away for a night of worship. (John Collier, 1943; Library of Congress, Prints & Photographs Division, FSA/OWI Collection LC-USW3-To1-015215-C)*

asking all canyon denizens of any creed to feel welcome there (Hudson 1987b). At such churches all over the borderlands, communities gathered at night to venerate patron saints and various iterations of "Our Lady" who stands on a crescent moon in a cloak decorated with stars (figure 5.5).

> We get together at the church, and then we go out in the procession with the santos on San Isidro's eve . . . Maybe about half an hour to pray it, and the singing

FIGURE 5.6. *Stoneware fragments from the Lopez Plaza site. (Photo by Minette Church)*

and all that, and then we ask, you know, the intercessions. We ask for God to bless the people that offer their home, and we ask for all the people who have died, and things like that. And then they sing the San Isidro song, and that's it. And then we just get together and have a party, have the eats. Some houses, they go all aboard. They go more than others. (Rodríguez 2006, 86)

Such a party would perhaps entail some of the elderberry wine that Julia remembers her mother making and storing in stoneware jugs (figure 5.6), the sherds of which litter the Lopez archaeological site (Hudson, 1987a). It is unlikely that the wine was consumed during the workday.

Otero Warren describes being the only woman at a ritual held in a *morada* (chapel) built by the *Los Hermanos de la Fraternidad Piadosa de Nuestro Padre Jesús Nazareno*, commonly known as the Penitente Brotherhood. The remains of moradas dot the Colorado–New Mexico borderlands landscape and are always associated with a well-worn processional trail marked by Stations of the Cross. Archaeologist Sims (2009, 391) suggests that "if we are to re-experience the monuments in the way their builders intended, then the minimum requirement is to walk through them as prescribed." Characteristically, Doña Adelina describes the ritual in very physical, experiential terms:

we all arose and filed out of the church. Two men with lanterns led the procession . . . It was now quite dark, though the stars appeared and partly illuminated the heavens . . . the path had been cleaned of *chamiza* [brushwood] but the way was rough and sandy . . . Suddenly, the light of the lantern reflected an object—the

Calvario [Calvary]. The scenes around me became distinct . . . Slowly we retraced our steps for a final prayer . . . A gust of wind extinguished the candles and I walked out into the night, in the full light of the moon. (Otero Warren 1936, 82)

Local households banded together for such rituals unsupervised by clergy, between visits from itinerate priests, and they built chapels to house Penitente activities separately and away from the formally consecrated visita mission churches. They were connected to settlements by footpaths and associated with formal processional pathways. Such pathways had to be navigable at nighttime. Nighttime visits between houses during the holy days around Christmas is still lit by *farolitos* (small candle lamps). Some of these lights were made of tinwork from recycled and punctured cans, the remains of which turn up archaeologically. A pathway at the Lopez site was cobbled with white limestone that would presumably reflect any low light. Memoirs note periodically clearing brush and overgrowth away from processional and communicating paths.

Again, fracturing of community is as active as creation thereof, and can be set in religious terms with ominous activity during nighttime hours. Witchcraft and prognostication are common subjects of *cuentas* (traditional stories) and appear in ethnographic accounts.

One man in the village reported that he had heard an owl hooting on a tree in his backyard one evening. He had gone out and shot it. The wounded bird flew away. The next morning, a little *viejita* [old woman], who lived alone nearby, was visited by a relative. The old woman was supposedly wounded. The man assumed that surely she was the owl that he had shot and told people so. (Valdez and Valdez de Pong 2005, 175)

The creature of omen in southwestern lore is the nocturnal owl. Stories of transformation and witchcraft, like those of fence cutting and fire setting, are almost always set at night. Stories such as this one illustrate the other side of Glassie's and Basso's picture of how stories can be a community's way of embracing others; instead stories can define certain individuals as out of bounds, even pariahs. Catholic iconography and related artifacts and architecture are much more visible in the archaeological record than are those we can associate firmly with accusations of witchcraft, although archaeologists have hypothesized about artifacts and osteological evidence from borderlands Pueblo communities (Darling 1998; Walker 1998).

CONCLUSIONS

This discussion has not been so much about finding the archaeological signature of nighttime activities as about resituating commonplace archaeological finds and landscape features in a nocturnal context. Beginning with the changing technologies of lighting, through the period of occupation for the Lopez Plaza (1870 to 1903), interpretation broadens to include social reproduction through repeated community gatherings for work or worship at night, and within those contexts, repeated narratives of origin and identity. Such acts of social memory and identity creation, whether at the family or community scale, change with each retelling as details are added, dropped, or altered (Halbwachs 1992; Hobsbawm and Ranger 1983; Glassie 1982; Shackel 2003), and the venues and opportunities for such events change with new technologies that influence how people interacted during evening hours, domestically and through landscape. Our changing experience of lighting, from fire to candle to oil to gas light to tungsten to florescent to LED, impacts family routine, storytelling, travel, rituals both individual and collective, and has come to impact our very ability to experience the night sky. In 2016 we can no longer do what Sims (2009, 391) suggests, and "re-experience the monuments in the way their builders intended" by walking out into an unadulterated night as Nina Otero Warren did in the early years of the twentieth century.

In the 1970s, when ethnographers Paul Kutsche and John R. Van Ness canvassed neighbors in the northern New Mexico town of Cañones, there were some elderly people who had resisted rural electrification when it became available in the early 1950s (Kutsche and Van Ness 1988). These old people, the *viejos*, argued that the softer light of oil and kerosene was more comfortable to them. A younger man, Antonio Serrano, summed up a generational difference in attitude, saying, *"la luz de aceite es triste"* (oil light is melancholy). The older residents cherished lifetimes of stories and memories primarily lit by fire, oil lamp, and candle light, or even starlight. Their sense of history and identity as well as neighborliness was swathed in candle and oil light, qualitatively different from the tungsten lighting and accompanying transistor radio options they were being offered. Surely nighttime was far less strange and fraught, and candle and oil light more familiar to nineteenth- and early twentieth-century villagers in the southwestern United States borderlands than it was to young Antonio in the 1970s.

Refocusing on the night as a context for human activity requires that we rethink the construction of social memory and communities in the context of indoor and outdoor nighttime activities. On a farm or ranch, during the day, people are farming or ranching. Often such tasks are solitary, and they separate parents and children, brothers and sisters into age-graded and gendered activities. It was during evening gatherings or while traveling that traditions were enacted, retold, and repeated, subject to all the omissions and changes that come with each new context of each retelling. As Glassie (1982, 77) notes on Ulster farms, "tomorrow they will be neighbors, people who work together and count on one another when troubles come." For the elderly people in 1950s Cañones confronted with the possibility of electric lighting, the night held meanings beyond the pragmatic technical challenges of simple illumination; far from finding softer oil and starlight saddening, they, like Nina Otero (1931), found sustenance in *"el refresco de la noche."*

ACKNOWLEDGMENTS

I would like to thank Nan Gonlin and April Nowell for including me in what turned out to be an exceptionally productive and just plain fun exploration of materiality and night, and for reading this over and providing useful comments and suggestions. I would also like to thank Tom Wynn, Audrey Horning, and Mark Gardiner—spanning Paleolithic, post-medieval, and medieval archaeology respectively—for reading and commenting thoughtfully and extensively on drafts of this chapter. It is improved and deepened as a result, but of course, the flaws are entirely mine.

REFERENCES

Agius, Dionisius A. 2005. *Seafaring in the Arabian Gulf and Oman: The People of the Dhow.* London/Bahrain: Kegan Paul Arabian Library.

Allen, William C. 2005. *History of Slave Laborers in the Construction of the United States Capital.* Washington, DC: Office of the Architect of the Capitol.

Basso, Keith H. 1996. *Wisdom Sits in Places: Landscape and Language among the Western Apache.* Albuquerque: University of New Mexico Press.

Battle-Baptiste, Whitney. 2011. *Black Feminist Archaeology.* Walnut Creek, CA: Left Coast Press.

Book Committee. 1993. *Bent County (Colorado) History.* Las Animas, CO: Book Committee.

Claassen, Cheryl, and Margaret W. Conkey, eds. 1991. *Exploring Gender through Archaeology: Selected Papers from the 1991 Boone Conference.* Monographs in World Archaeology No. 11. Madison, WI: Prehistory Press.

Crawford, Stanley G. 1988. *Mayordomo: Chronicle of an Acequia in Northern New Mexico.* Albuquerque: University of New Mexico Press.

Darling, J. Andrew. 1998. "Mass Inhumation and the Execution of Witches in the American Southwest." *American Anthropologist* 100(3):732–752. https://doi.org/10.1525/aa.1998.100.3.732.

Ekirch, A. Roger. 2006. *At Day's Close: Night in Times Past.* New York: W. W. Norton.

Frank, Ross. 2007. *From Settler to Citizen: New Mexican Economic Development and the Creation of Vecino Society, 1750–1820.* Berkeley: University of California Press.

Gero, Joan M., and Margaret W. Conkey, eds. 1991. *Engendering Archaeology: Women and Prehistory.* Malden, MA: Blackwell Publishers.

Glassie, Henry H. 1982. *Passing the Time in Ballymenone: Culture and History of an Ulster Community.* Publications of the American Folklore Society, New Series. Philadelphia: University of Pennsylvania Press.

Halbwachs, Maurice, ed. 1992. *On Collective Memory.* Trans. Lewis A. Coser. Chicago: University of Chicago Press.

Helms, Mary W. 2004. "Before the Dawn. Monks and the Night in Late Antiquity and Early Medieval Europe." *Anthropos,* Bd. 99, H. 1:177–191.

Hobsbawm, Eric J., and Terence O. Ranger. 1983. *The Invention of Tradition.* Cambridge, UK: Cambridge University Press.

Hudson, Julia. 1987a. Excerpts from the *Ranch Journal of Julia L. Hudson* and *Reminiscences of Her Early Life on a Cattle Ranch in Southeastern Colorado (on the Purgatoire River) 1885–1903,* edited by J. Paul Hudson. Manuscript in possession of USFS Office, 1420 E 3rd St, La Junta, CO 81050.

Hudson, Julia. 1987b. *Appendix I: Julia Hudson's Ranch Journal.* Manuscript in possession of USFS Office, 1420 E 3rd St., La Junta CO 81050.

Ingold, Tim. 2007. "Earth, Sky, Wind, and Weather." *Journal of the Royal Anthropological Institute* 13(s1):S19–S38. https://doi.org/10.1111/j.1467-9655.2007.00401.x.

Johnson, Matthew. 1999. *Archaeological Theory: An Introduction.* Oxford: Blackwell.

Kutsche, Paul, and John R. Van Ness. 1988. *Cañones: Values, Crisis, and Survival in a Northern New Mexico Village.* Salem, WI: Sheffield Publishing Company.

Lopez, Elfido. 1937. *Some Memories from My Life.* Elfido Lopez, Sr. Collection (MSS #813). Denver, CO: History Colorado.

Lopez, Elfido. 1998. "Some Memories from My Life, as Written by Elfido Lopez, Sr." Ed. and annotated by Richard Louden. In *La Gente: Hispano History and Life in Colorado,* ed. Vincent C. De Baca, 21–44. Denver: Colorado Historical Society.

Magoffin, Susan S. 1962. *Down the Santa Fe Trail and into Mexico: The Diary of Susan Shelby Magoffin, 1846–1847.* New Haven, CT: Yale University Press.

Meyer, Michael C. 1996. *Water in the Hispanic Southwest: A Social and Legal History, 1550–1850.* Tucson: University of Arizona Press.

Nash, Harriet. 2007. "Stargazing in Traditional Water Management: A Case Study in Northern Oman." *Proceedings of the Seminar for Arabian Studies,* Papers from the fortieth meeting of the Seminar for Arabian Studies held in London, July 27–29, 2006, 37:157–170. Oxford: Archaeopress Publishing Ltd.

Otero, Adelina. 1931. "My People." *Survey Graphic* (May): 139–151.

Otero Warren, Adelina. 1936. *Old Spain in Our Southwest.* Chicago: Rio Grande Press.

Reed, A. D., and C. Jonathan Horn. 1995. *Cultural Resource Inventory of a Portion of the Picketwire Canyonlands, Comanche National Grassland, Las Animas and Otero Counties, Colorado.* Report for the Pike and San Isabel National Forests Cimarron and Comanche National Grasslands by Alpine Archaeological Consultants, Inc. Denver: Office of Archaeology and Historic Preservation.

Rodríguez, Sylvia. 2006. *Acequia: Water Sharing, Sanctity, and Place*. Santa Fe, NM: School for Advanced Research Press.

Schmidt, Robert A., and Barbara L. Voss. 2005. *Archaeologies of Sexuality*. London: Routledge.

Shackel, Paul A. 2003. "Archaeology, Memory, and Landscapes of Conflict." *Historical Archaeology* 37(3):3–13. https://doi.org/10.1007/BF03376607.

Sims, Lionel. 2009. "Entering, and Returning from, the Underworld: Reconstituting Silbury Hill by Combining a Quantified Landscape Phenomenology with Archaeoastronomy." *Journal of the Royal Anthropological Institute* 15(2):386–408. https://doi.org/10.1111/j.1467-9655.2009.01559.x.

Sunseri, Jun Ueno. 2015. "A Horse-Travel Approach to Landscape Archaeology." *Historical Archaeology* 49(2):72–92.

Sunseri, Jun Ueno. 2018. *Situational Identities Along the Raiding Frontier of Colonial New Mexico*. Lincoln: University of Nebraska Press.

US Bureau of the Census. 1870. *Colorado Territory, Schedule 1: Las Animas County, Purgatory River East of Trinidad*. Washington, DC: National Archives and Records Service, General Services Administration.

Valdez, Olivama Salazar de, and D. Valdez de Pong. 2005. *Life in Los Sauces*. Monte Vista, CO: Adobe Village Press.

Varisco, Daniel M. 1997. *Medieval Folk Astronomy and Agriculture in Arabia and the Yemen*. Variorum Collected Studies Series, C8585. Aldershot/Brookfield: Ashgate Publishing.

Walker, William H. 1998. "Where Are the Witches of Prehistory?" *Journal of Archaeological Method and Theory* 5(3):245–308. https://doi.org/10.1007/BF02428071.

Woodhead, Eileen I., Catherine Sullivan, and Gérard Gusset. 1984. *Lighting Devices in the National Reference Collection, Parks Canada*. Studies in Archaeology, Architecture, and History. National Historic Parks and Sites Branch, Parks Canada. Ottawa, ON: National Historic Parks and Sites Branch, Parks Canada, Environment Canada.

Wynn, Thomas. 2012. "Spark of Genius: Did Fire Influence the Evolution of the Human Mind?" *Smithsonian* (December):16.

The Night Sky

CHAPTER 6

Nighttime Sky and Early Urbanism in the High Andes

Architecture and Ritual in the Southern Lake Titicaca
Basin during the Formative and Tiwanaku Periods

ALEXEI VRANICH AND SCOTT C. SMITH

ASTRONOMY AND SOCIAL COMPLEXITY IN THE AMERICAS

The role of ritual political theater in the development of complex society is well documented (e.g., Inomata and Coben 2006; Swenson 2011), and within the range of potential dramatic public events, the celebration of the solstice looms large in both public imagination and scholarship. The adoption of agriculture is conventionally seen as the major turning point in the development of civilization, and in order to effectively manage and expand this sustainable subsistence strategy, an elite class became knowledgeable in measuring the regular movements of the sun and presenting key events in an awe-inspiring and theatrical manner (Aveni 2001). In time, these dramatic ceremonies during key movements in the solar cycle served to associate social hierarchies to immutable truths of the cosmos, and to motivate populations to work collectively, thereby accomplishing undertakings as diverse as building pyramids and conquering territories. As opposed to the solar ceremonies that drove thousands into a collective frenzy, popular representations of stellar observations conveyed the impression of a solitary and more esoteric pursuit, an indigenous American version of Old World

DOI: 10.5876/9781607326786.c006

mathematics and philosophy that developed once the state was mature. This specialized knowledge, visible and comprehensible by a restricted number of individuals, allowed the priestly elites to predict and present to the impressionable masses awe-inspiring events such as solar eclipses. This volume presents a number of archaeological studies that have questioned this enduring framework that privileges solar observation over stellar with a view to explaining the development of social complexity (Gonlin and Nowell, chapter 1, this volume).

In this chapter, we present a counterexample to these conventional ideas that privilege the primacy of the solar cycle with a case study of the precolumbian societies of the Titicaca basin in the highland Andes of South America (figures 1.2 and 6.1). Lake Titicaca straddles the border between Peru and Bolivia at an elevation of 3,810 masl. This region lies at the northern end of the broad high plain known as the *altiplano,* a region bounded on the east by the peaks of the Cordillera Blanca and on the west by the Cordillera Negra. Our discussion centers on the southern end of the Lake Titicaca basin; in particular, we discuss archaeological sites in two adjacent valleys that are separated by the low hills of the Quimsachata-Chilla range. The northern Tiwanaku valley is cut by the Wila Jawira River, which drains into Lake Titicaca; the Upper Desaguadero valley to the south contains the Desaguadero River, which is the only drainage for Lake Titicaca. The Desaguadero River flows roughly 390 km south, eventually emptying into Lake Poopó near the modern city of Oruro, Bolivia.

The Lake Titicaca basin was the setting for a series of dramatic social changes between 1500 BCE and 1000 CE (figure 1.3). During the Formative period (1500 BCE to 500 CE), the region saw the development of a network of ceremonial centers characterized by monumental earthen platforms that incorporated sunken courts. Around 500 CE, one of these ceremonial centers, Tiwanaku, began to grow in monumentality and influence. As construction accelerated, the site emerged as a preeminent center that exerted influence throughout much of the south-central Andes. Known now for its "Temple of the Sun," "Gateway of the Sun," and popular tourist solstice festival, Tiwanaku has long been associated with solar observations (Posnansky 1945). Combined with the presence of an innovative form of cultivation that allowed intensive agriculture at high elevations (Erickson 1996), archaeologists have frequently rooted the development of social complexity at Tiwanaku in the capacity of incipient elites to orchestrate and manage an intensified, agriculturally based, productive economy (Posnansky 1945, Kolata 1993). Recent archaeoastronomical research (Benítez 2013), however, documents a wide range of celebrated astronomical observations, including an emphasis on the moon and the evening sky during the initial development of social complexity in the region. Furthermore, the initial period of sedentism of the Titicaca basin has of late come under greater scrutiny (Hastorf 1999; Janusek 2015), revealing a high degree of social complexity well before the construction

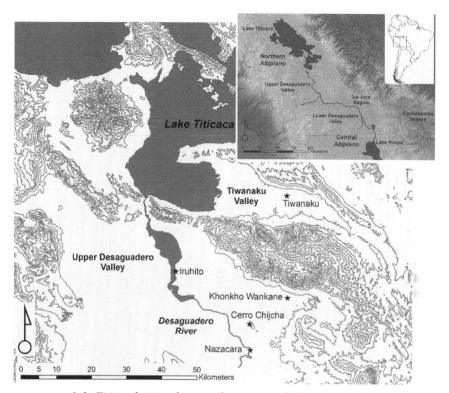

FIGURE 6.1. *Lake Titicaca basin and its initial environs, with the sites mentioned in the text.* (*Map by Alexei Vranich*)

of the more spectacular monuments at Tiwanaku as well as foregrounding the prominence of this early period to the development of complexity and the relationship of mobile populations, interregional trade, transhumance, and camelid pastoralism to social trajectories in the southern Lake Titicaca basin. Initial settlements developed at the confluence of such variables as nearby sources of water, fodder for animals, and loci of alignments between the nighttime sky and sacred mountains. Early public architecture was the setting for structured encounters between relatively dispersed sedentary people and transhumant groups, places that later matured into a form popularly called a "city."

THE LANDSCAPE OF THE TITICACA BASIN

The central feature of the basin is Lake Titicaca. This sacred body of water, considered by the Incas (1200–1534 CE) as the source of all water in the Andes (Sherbondy 1982), is surrounded in dramatic fashion by all the elements of the sacred Andean landscape: life-giving snowcapped mountains where the ancestors and gods live, natural springs that mark the places of divine creation, and exposed rock outcrops that are as vivid as the domestic and wild animals that inhabit the high plateau. This landscape, animated by sacred narratives recounted along local and regional pilgrimage routes, was conceptualized as living and intimately tied to the mythical origins of humans and llamas (Smith 2012). During the early colonial period, many Spanish observers (Albornoz 1989; Molina 1989; Sarmiento de Gamboa 1942) recorded origin myths that traced the original emergence of both humans and animals—in particular llamas—to mountain caves, springs, and rivers. In fact, they were amazed, even aghast, at the degree to which nearly everything in the natural world formed part of a sacred narrative antithetical to their Catholic beliefs.

In addition to their sacred connotations, the mountains, rivers, streams, and springs that anchored early settlement in the region were key places in the seasonal movements of local agropastoralists. The present-day Western visitor might find it difficult to envisage the Titicaca basin as one of the wealthiest and most productive areas in the Andes during precolumbian times due to the endless expanse of spiny grass. Up until modern times, lengthy meandrous caravans of llamas were the vehicles for a constant exchange of highland products, such as potatoes and dried meat, as well as products or foodstuffs from more temperate zones, such as the maize used in the preparation of *chicha*, a fermented beverage that played a central role in the economy and ritual life of both small- and large-scale societies (Morris 1979). As a result of this robust trading system, the various peoples of the Titicaca basin influenced a significant swath of the southern Andes. Today, Aymara agropastoralists in the altiplano balance the movements of herds with the agricultural cycle. Fields are plowed in July, August, or September, and planting occurs toward the end of the dry season, between September and November (Bruno 2011, 227–228). During these months, herds are pastured near the fields, on the lower-elevation *pampas* (grassy plains) and foothills below mountain ranges. After planting, as the rains increase between September and November, the herds are moved to higher-elevation pastures. Herders maintain secondary residences in these areas, often located near mountain streams and rivers (Gladwell 2007, 26; Tomka 2001). Camelid mating often occurs at these higher elevations; the birthing period extends through much of the rainy season (Flores Ochoa 1979; Tomka 2001, 149–152). These practices reinforce the conceptual link between mountain streams and rivers and camelid fertility (Smith 2016).

Nighttime Sky

The other dramatic aspect of this unique part of the world is the nighttime sky. At 13,000 feet above sea level the rarified air creates perfect celestial viewing conditions, and modern shamans know the best locations on the landscape to watch the stars "play" with each other and the sacred mountains along the horizon.

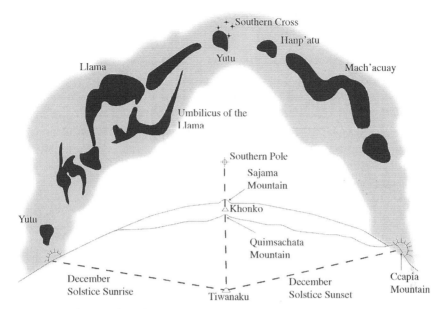

FIGURE 6.2. *The cosmological animals of the nighttime Andean sky.*

Stars are so numerous and brilliant that it is no wonder that Andean peoples found meaning in the dark areas that in their eyes took the form of sacred animals: the snake, the llama, the partridge, the fox, and the frog (Urton 1981, 1985). As the Milky Way rotates around the Southern Celestial Pole, a location not marked by a star as in the Northern hemisphere but by a murky space, these anthropomorphic "dark cloud" constellations—called *yana phuyu* in Quechua—interact with the horizon of the sacred landscape (figure 6.2). The Huarochiri manuscript, a colonial document written circa 1598 CE (Salomon and Urioste 1991), relates the story of one of these dark-cloud constellations called *Yacana*, a llama whose eyes are marked by the stars Alpha and Beta Centauri. Yacana is located in the Milky Way, which was called *Mayu* and conceptualized as a vast celestial river. The myth recounts that Yacana descends to the Pacific Ocean during the dry season to drink before returning to the highlands at the beginning of the rainy season to deposit water in the mountains, thus feeding the highland streams and rivers.

Dark-cloud constellations are particularly prevalent during the rainy season, and, according to the Huarochiri manuscript, Yacana was specifically associated with the beginning of the rainy season (Salomon and Urioste 1991, 132–133; Urton 1981, 111). The myth suggests that llamas and alpacas were metaphorically associated with mountain streams and rivers. In addition, Yacana is accompanied by a suckling calf, reinforcing the connection between the camelid birthing period that begins near the onset of the rainy season when Yacana first appears in the night sky (Smith 2016).

INITIAL DEVELOPMENT OF COMPLEXITY

The ability to move large quantities of goods across the ecologically diverse vertical Andean landscape has led to alternative perspectives on the development of complexity in the south-central Andes. Browman (1978, 1981) has argued that centers like Tiwanaku functioned as craft specialization and exchange hubs. Caravans transported resources from other regions, including lower-elevation zones, and exchanged these items for goods produced at the altiplano centers. Nuñez Atencio and Dillehay (Dillehay and Núñez Atencio 1988; Núñez Atencio 1996; Núñez Atencio and Dillehay 1995 [1979]) proposed a model, often referred to as the "circuit mobility model," that emphasizes the social impact of the caravan circuits themselves on the developmental trajectories in the region and envisions a landscape crossed by wide-ranging caravan circuits. Early centers, then, developed as axis settlements that anchored the movements of particularly influential caravans.

Other scholars have refined these ideas, shifting the focus from centers or axis settlements to the areas of occupation along caravan routes, sometimes referred to as "internodes" (Berenguer Rodríguez 2004; Nielsen 2006, 2013). They argue that internodal zones spurred sociopolitical change by "connecting elites in a complex interaction network focused on the exchange of religiously charged goods" (Smith and Janusek 2014, 686; see also Llagostera 1996). In fact, the relationship between the caravans and more sedentary people became mutually supportive and was reinforced through the establishment of kin relationships (Smith and Janusek 2014, 695).

These theories were tested recently in the upper Desaguadero valley, a region located south across the Quimsachata-Chilla mountain range from Tiwanaku (Janusek 2013, 2015; Smith 2016; Smith and Janusek 2014) (see figure 6.1). Settlement survey and selective excavations at several sites in this region suggest that shifting caravan circuits were central to the development of early politico-religious centers in this region. These circuits connected the altiplano with temperate valleys to the southeast, and facilitated the movement of resources, including maize, between these regions (Berryman 2010). Consequently, the fortunes of early centers were connected, in part, to the influence of these shifting caravan routes. As particular "leading" circuits became more powerful, the early centers that anchored these routes grew in influence. The trajectories of people, animals, objects, and ideas combined at these centers to create powerful politico-religious sites.

One influential caravan route seems to have followed the Desaguadero River, which connects Lake Titicaca with the central altiplano 150 km to the south. Early settlements in this region were concentrated along the river, near abundant water and fodder. During the Middle Formative period (800–200 BCE) the most significant settlements in the upper Desaguadero valley, Iruhito and Cerro Chijcha, were located along the river. In contrast, the settlement survey of a 44 km² inland region surrounding the later monumental inland site of Khonkho Wankane, conducted by Carlos Lémuz Aguirre (2011), recorded very few remains of this early period. Occupation along the river at Iruhito and Cerro Chijcha continued into the Late Formative period (200 BCE–500 CE), and said survey along the river documented an increase in both the number and total area of sites. At the same time, new sites were founded at inland locations where very little previous occupation existed. Khonkho Wankane, for example, was founded around 50 CE, and grew rapidly into an influential ritual center incorporating several sunken courts. Further south, another inland center was founded at Pajcha Pata (Pärssinen 1999), and around the same time, in the Tiwanaku valley to the north, new centers rose far from the lakeshore, at Kallamarka and Tiwanaku itself. Variability in rainfall during the Late Formative period is likely to have caused fluctuations in the level of the river, which opened up the opportunity for new, inland caravan circuits to flourish and new politico-religious centers to develop (Smith 2016). New circuits followed routes along the foothills of inland mountains, possibly to take advantage of mountain springs and streams. The earliest known sunken courts in the upper Desaguadero valley developed along one of these inland circuits at Khonkho Wankane.

TIWANAKU

The hallmark of public architecture is the sunken court, a general form that begins around 1800 BCE and continues until the end of the Middle Horizon (600–1000 CE). Sunken courts dot the landscape of the region, numbering as high as an estimated eight hundred across the entire basin. The lack of substantial infrastructure such as roads and fortresses, along with similarities in architectural form and a shared iconography, have fostered a consensus that these Formative communities participated in a shared religious tradition rather than forming part of a larger organization such as a state (K. L. M. Chávez 1988; S. J. Chávez and Chávez 1975). The largest and most elaborate sunken court was built in a fairly nondescript area of the southern basin, 15 km from the shore, at Tiwanaku (figure 6.3, *top*). Over the next millennium, other monumental sites in the southern basin would wither while some of the largest structures ever erected in the Andes would crowd around Tiwanaku's sunken court. In such a dynamic and disturbed setting, it is difficult to reconstruct the earliest form of Tiwanaku, but it seems that the sunken court was intentionally preserved and remained in use for nearly a millennium while the rest of the site was built and rebuilt many times over. Centuries of post-Tiwanaku erosion buried the

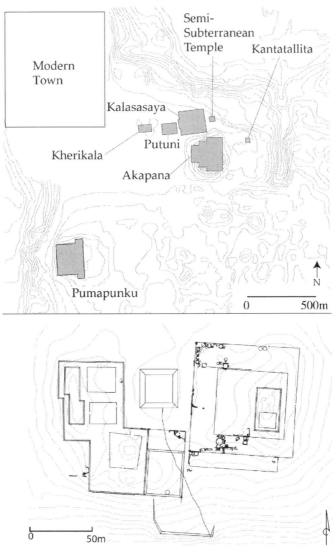

FIGURE 6.3. *The primary ritual buildings of Tiwanaku (top) and Khonko Wankane (bottom). (Map at top by Alexei Vranich; map at bottom by Scott C. Smith)*

structure, which perhaps accounted for its obscurity during the colonial period (beginning 1532 CE) until its excavation in 1903.

The form of this sunken court follows the general pattern of sunken courts, although its dimensions (28 m × 26 m and 2 m deep) make it the largest example of this type of architecture in the Titicaca basin (figure 6.4). The walls consist

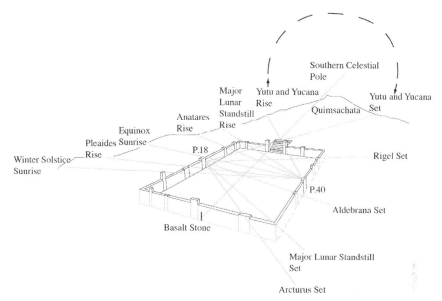

FIGURE 6.4. *Archaeoastronomical alignments of the Semi-Subterranean Temple at Tiwanaku. P.40 and P.18 are the only pillars with carved iconography. (Redrawn from Benítez [2013] by Alexei Vranich)*

of fifty-seven large vertical pillars interspersed among smaller cut-stone and carved tenoned heads. The heights of the pillars are variable; several peek over the elevation of the reconstructed wall. The pillars in the approximate center of the east and west walls show evidence of the subtle remains of heavily eroded carved iconography. A black basalt stone slab, the only such stone built into the structure and possibly in all of Tiwanaku, is set in the approximate center of the north wall. Opposite this slab of basalt, on the south side of the sunken court, sit broad overlapping sandstone slabs that form stairs framed on either side by the largest pillars in the structure. This monumental entrance appears to be in the middle of the south wall, but in fact it is set a near-meter off center. The Tiwanaku had a preference and ability to build along strict and precise mathematical lines, reaching accuracy to the millimeter (Protzen and Nair 2013). In the context of such an architectural tradition, the off-centered location of the entrance should be seen as an intentional decision rather than the result of the imprecisions of vernacular construction.

Though conventionally seen as a small restricted space reserved for an elite class that would consult in an oracle-like fashion with the ritual sculptures (Kolata 1993), we took the perspective that the sunken court is a place to view *from* rather than to look in to. The most common known method to present a view to an audience would be raising or placing the structure on high ground in a manner to appreciate a view, such as in the modern examples of a high balcony with a view of the city skyline, or a highway rest stop overlooking a particularly dramatic view of the natural landscape. The sunken court presents a selective view of the landscape by insetting the floor deep enough to the point that the majority of the natural horizon is hidden behind the edge of the sunken court. The east and the west horizons would be obscured from view and replaced with the edge of the sunken court, which functions as an architectural horizon punctuated with standing pillars (figure 6.4); to the north is the gentle grass covering the Taraco hills. Prior to 600 CE, when additional monuments were built in the center, any location within the sunken court would draw attention to the distant Quimsachata Mountain framed by the pillars of the singular entrance. For someone standing at the basalt stone along the north wall, the skewed angle to the off-center entrance places the Southern Celestial Pole—the point in the sky around which the Milky Way rotates—directly above the tallest peak of the Quimsachata Mountain.

The pillars with the iconography (P.40 and P.18 on figure 6.4) mark the location from which one can watch the rising and setting of the bright stars Alpha and Beta Centauri—the eyes of the llama—within the pillars of the entrance (figure 6.5). These celestial events correspond to the crucial period of moving herds between the highland and lowland pastures. Another notable alignment is along the west wall where the corners of the sunken court mark the positions of either end of the eighteen-year cycle of lunar standstills (see Alt, chapter 11, this volume, for more on lunar standstills). Overall, the majority of the alignments relate to stellar and lunar observations. The pillars also mark the locations to view the equinox sunrise and sunset; notwithstanding, the majority of the alignments are related to the evening sky.

The alignment created by the sunken court and the Southern Celestial Pole creates a route over the Quimsachata Mountain, which leads directly to the entrance of the sunken court at the site of Khonko Wankane (figure 6.3, *bottom*). This alignment, with an estimated margin of error of 50 m over a 70-km distance, shows an intentional association between the placements of these initial examples of public ritual architecture. In addition, several of the abovementioned astronomical and landscape alignments are also evident in the construction of the contemporaneous sunken court at Khonkho Wankane. This sunken court, the first of at least three built over the course of the site's occupation, was trapezoidal in form and roughly 1 m deep. The north wall measured 26 m in length, the south wall 21 m, the west wall 27.1 m, and the east wall 26 m (Smith 2016, 69). This court, like the one at Tiwanaku, was also constructed with vertically placed sandstone pillars interspersed with sandstone and limestone blocks. However, the Khonkho Wankane sunken court had an entrance in each wall. The southern threshold was the most elaborate entrance to the court, consisting of two vertical pillars framing a multicolored staircase consisting of one reddish sandstone

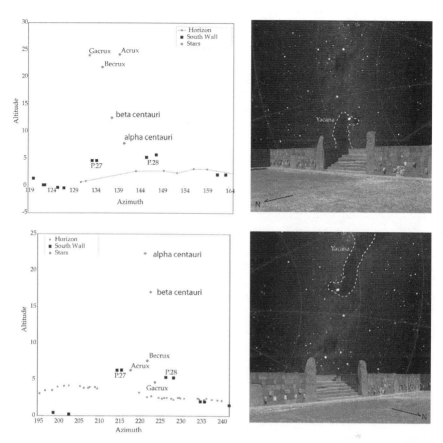

FIGURE 6.5. *Virtual reconstruction of the view of the Yacana constellation from the P.40 and P.18 pillars in the Semi-Subterranean Temple during the Formative period and prior to the construction of the Akapana platform. (From Benítez 2013, 99, figure 8.8)*

step, one white limestone step, and one gray-green andesite step. While this entrance was centrally located along the wall, the other three entrances to the court were off center, similar to the entrance to the Tiwanaku court described above. Investigation of the landscape and celestial alignments evident in the construction has suggested similar patterns to the Tiwanaku court (Benítez 2013). The central southern entrance frames the prominent snow-capped southern peak Sajama, while an observer standing in the northern entrance would see the mountain Cerro Chijcha, itself a significant archaeological site, framed in the western entrance. As was the case at Tiwanaku, the celestial llama Yacana is framed by the southern entrance: an observer standing in the western threshold would observe Alpha and Beta Centauri rise over the multicolored steps, framed by the sandstone pillars (Benítez 2013, 94–95).

DISCUSSION

The choice of settlement locations near sources of water and fodder and appropriate loci for observing the nighttime sky for stellar and lunar movements reveal the conditions required by herders. The initial modest public architecture formed the setting for structured encounters between transhumance groups and dispersed sedentary peoples. Most of these locations remained foci of cyclical communal gatherings defined by small-scale architecture. On rare occasions, a few of these locations became the nucleus for settlements that reached monumental proportions. After 500 CE, Khonkho Wankane was largely abandoned, but Tiwanaku began to expand its influence in the Lake Titicaca basin. The big question is why did Tiwanaku, over the other estimated eight hundred sunken courts across the basin, become the site of a primary city and state?

There must be several variables, but from an astronomical point of view, Tiwanaku was perfectly located to take advantage of the primary features of both the daytime and nighttime sky. To the west is the massive and sacred extinct volcano of Ccapia, where the highest peak coincides with the setting position of the winter solstice sun. While there does not appear to be any pillar marking this alignment, this mountain/astronomical alignment would be appreciated only 122 m north and south of the *sunken court*. In the Tiwanaku valley, which spans 15 km from north to south, there is approximately a 2% chance that a randomly chosen location will result in this alignment. The Quimsachata/Southern Celestial Pole alignment would be appreciated by all within the sunken court, and to a distance of 210 m on either side of the court. Based on the east-west expanse (32 km) of the Tiwanaku valley, there is roughly a 1% chance that a randomly chosen location would result in the alignment. Combining the probability of the Quimsachata /Southern Celestial Pole and the Ccapia/Winter Solstice alignment, the location of the sunken court was based on properly viewing these two topographical/astronomical alignments.

Another monument at Tiwanaku, the large Kalasasaya platform, was constructed with clear solar alignments, and over the centuries, the areas and the means to appreciate the solar alignments were expanded with surfaced plazas and elaborate andesite constructions (figure 6.4). The Kantatallita Complex—the "place where the sun rises" in Aymara—is built on the eastern edge of the site. Though the importance of the sun is evident, it would be simplistic to say that, with the advent of a more mature state, the solar cult replaced a stellar or lunar cult. In one case there is evidence that a particular nighttime view was not only still appreciated, but was changed at tremendous expense. The Akapana platform, now much reduced after centuries of looting, was built nearly a millennium after the sunken court. For all its size, it is, on closer inspection, a rather hastily built affair consisting entirely of reused ashlars (Vranich 2001). The purpose of the largest monument at Tiwanaku remains a mystery, and

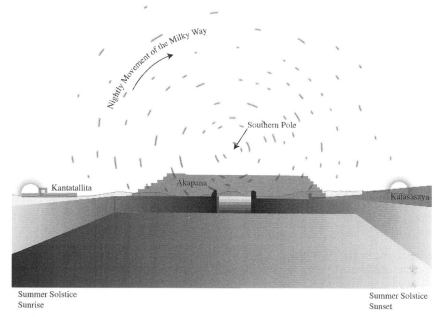

Summer Solstice
Sunrise

Summer Solstice
Sunset

FIGURE 6.6. *View of the Semi-Subterranean Temple during the Formative period, overlaid with later constructions during the later period (700–1000 CE) of the Tiwanaku polity. (Illustration by Alexei Vranich)*

unfortunately it is so heavily destroyed that it is difficult to determine its astronomical purpose. However, the view from the sunken court speaks volumes about how the people of Tiwanaku saw their world and what they thought of themselves (figure 6.6). As mentioned above, the view from the sunken court to the south framed the Southern Celestial Pole directly above the local sacred mountain. After nearly a millennium of this view, the platform was built just high enough to replace the mountain with its own form, and crowned itself with the Southern Celestial Pole. This remarkable exercise in forced perception literally brings the sacred mountain, and the point around which the cosmos rotates, to the site (Benítez 2013; Vranich 2016). It also shows that a nighttime observation, one of the primary variables in the placement and development of early complexity, remained a core aspect of the design for the later mature form of this primary city and state.

CONCLUSIONS

The Lake Titicaca basin was a landscape inscribed with the movement of herders and caravans. Objects, ideas, people, and animals moved along dynamic circuits connecting far-flung geographies. Resources from distant regions and nearby locales were transported along these routes, including andesite from the Ccapia source on the southern shores of Lake Titicaca, basalt from the Querimita source near Lake Poopó 300 km to the southeast, obsidian from at least five different sources, and corn from the Cochabamba region southeast of Lake Titicaca and the Moquegua valley to the west (Berryman 2010; Giesso 2003, 2006; Janusek 2004, 2008; Smith 2016; Wright, Hastorf, and Lennstrom 2003). This was also a landscape imbued with meaning, conceptualized as animate and intimately tied to the mythical origins of humans and llamas (Smith 2012). Agropastoralists moved herds from lower-elevation pampas and foothills during the dry season to higher-elevation secondary residences during the rainy season. It is often at these secondary residences, located near mountain streams and rivers, where camelids give birth. The conceptual connection between mountain streams and rivers and the fertility of the herds was noted by colonial-period Spanish observers, and continues to the present day in rural areas. Archaeological and iconographic evidence suggest that earlier populations held similar beliefs (Smith 2012). Ideas about the generative power of the mountainous landscape were inscribed in the constructed environments of Tiwanaku and Formative-period ritual centers. Constructed platforms and sunken courts were material icons of powerful animate mountains and streams. Some of these platform mounds and sunken court complexes, including those at Khonkho Wankane and Tiwanaku, integrated systems of over-engineered monumental canals that drained the copious amount of water during the rainy season. Significantly, at both Khonkho Wankane and Tiwanaku, the sunken courts were designed to frame the rise of Yacana and her nursing calf at the beginning of the wet season, heralding the rains to come and the migration of agropastoralists and herds to secondary higher elevation residences for the birthing season. The effort expended to create dramatic monumental settings to observe the sun reflected the agricultural priorities of the later Tiwanaku polity. However, Tiwanaku's initial location and its continued success in creating a location for the interaction between pastoralists and agriculturalists can be attributed to a life cycle based on the observation of the nighttime sky.

REFERENCES

Albornoz, Cristóbal de. 1989 [1581/1585]. "Instrucción para descubrir todas las huacas del Pirú y sus camayos y haziendas." In *C. de Molina and C. de Albornoz, Fábulas y mitos de los incas*, ed. Henrique Urbano and Pierre Duviols, 135–198. Crónicas de America, vol. 48. Madrid: Historia 16.

Aveni, Anthony. 2001. *Skywatchers*. Austin: University of Texas Press.

Benítez, Leonardo. 2013. "What Would Celebrants See? Sky, Landscape, and Settlement Planning in the Late Formative Southern Titicaca Basin." In *Advances in Titicaca Basin*

Archaeology II, ed. Alexei Vranich and Abigail R. Levine, 89–104. Los Angeles: Cotsen Institute of Archaeology at UCLA.

Berenguer Rodríguez, José. 2004. *Caravanas, Interacción y Cambio en el Desierto de Atacama*. Santiago: Ediciones Sirawi.

Berryman, Carrie Anne. 2010. "Food, Feasts, and the Construction of Identity and Power in Ancient Tiwanaku: A Bioarchaeological Perspective." PhD diss., Vanderbilt University.

Browman, David L. 1978. "Toward the Development of the Tiahuanaco (Tiwanaku) State." In *Advances in Andean Archaeology*, ed. David L. Browman, 327–349. The Hague: Mouton Publishers. https://doi.org/10.1515/9783110810011.327.

Browman, David L. 1981. "New Light on Andean Tiwanaku." *American Scientist* 69(4):408–419.

Bruno, Maria. 2011. "Farmers' Experience and Knowledge: Utilizing Soil Diversity to Mitigate Rainfall Variability on the Taraco Peninsula, Bolivia." In *Sustainable Lifeways: Cultural Persistence in an Ever-changing Environment*, ed. Naomi F. Miller, Katherine M. Moore, and Kathleen Ryan, 212–243. Philadelphia: University of Pennsylvania Museum of Archaeology and Anthropology. https://doi.org/10.9783/9781934536322.212.

Chávez, Karen L. Mohr. 1988. "The Significance of Chiripa in Lake Titicaca Basin Developments." *Expedition* 30(3):17–26.

Chávez, Sergio J., and Karen L. M. Chávez. 1975. "A Carved Stela from Taraco, Puno, Peru and the Definition of an Early Style of Stone Sculpture from the Altiplano of Peru and Bolivia." *Ñawpa Pacha* 13(1):45–83. https://doi.org/10.1179/naw.1975.13.1.005.

Dillehay, Tom D., and Lautaro Núñez Atencio. 1988. "Camelids, Caravans, and Complex Societies in the South-Central Andes." In *Recent Studies in Pre-Columbian Archaeology*, British Archaeological Reports International Series 421 (Part ii), ed. Nicholas J. Saunders and Olivier de Montmollin, 603–634. Oxford: British Archaeological Reports.

Erickson, Clark. 1996. *Investigación Arqueológica del Sistema Agrícola de los Camelloens en la Cuenca del Lago Titicaca del Perú*. La Paz, Bolivia: Programa Interinstitucional de Waru Waru and Centro para Información para el Desarrollo.

Flores Ochoa, Jorge A. 1979. *Pastoralists of the Andes: The Alpaca Herders of Paratía*. Trans. Ralph Bolton. Philadelphia: Institute for the Study of Human Issues.

Giesso, Martin. 2003. "Stone Tool Production in the Tiwanaku Heartland." In *Tiwanaku and Its Hinterland: Archaeology and Paleoecology of an Andean Civilization*. Volume 2, *Urban and Rural Archaeology*, ed. Alan L. Kolata, 363–383. Washington, DC: Smithsonian Institution Press.

Giesso, Martin. 2006. "Algunos Resultados del Análisis de Material Lítico de Khonkho Wankane." In *Khonkho Wankane: Segundo Informe Preliminar del Proyecto Arqueológico Jach'a Machaca*, ed. John W. Janusek and Victor Plaza Martinez, 204–206. Report submitted to the Unidad Nacional de Arqueología de Bolivia.

Gladwell, Randi. 2007. "El Rango de Machaca (Quimsachata) como Zona de Producción Pastoral: Implicaciones históricas para comprender Paisajes del Pasado." In *Khonkho e Iruhito: Tercer Informe Preliminar del Proyecto Jach'a Machaca (Investigaciones en 2006)*, ed. John W. Janusek and Victor Plaza Martínez, 22–65. Report submitted to the Unidad Nacional de Arqueología de Bolivia.

Hastorf, Christine. 1999. *Early Settlement at Chiripa, Bolivia: Research of the Taraco Archaeological Project*. Berkeley: Archaeological Research Facility, University of California at Berkeley.

Inomata, Takeshi, and Lawrence Coben, eds. 2006. *Archaeology of Performance: Theaters of Power, Community, and Politics*. New York: Altamira.

Janusek, John W. 2004. *Identity and Power in the Ancient Andes: Tiwanaku Cities through Time*. New York: Routledge. https://doi.org/10.4324/9780203324615.

Janusek, John W. 2008. *Ancient Tiwanaku*. Cambridge: Cambridge University Press.

Janusek, John W. 2013. "Jesús de Machaca before and after Tiwanaku: A Background to Recent Archaeology at Khonkho Wankane and Pukara de Khonkho." In *Advances in Titicaca Basin Archaeology II*, Alexei Vranich and Abigail R. Levine, 7–22. Los Angeles: Cotsen Institute of Archaeology.

Janusek, John W. 2015. "Incipient Urbanism at the Early Andean center of Khonkho Wankane, Bolivia." *Journal of Field Archaeology* 40(2):127–143. https://doi.org/10.1179/0093469014Z.000000000105.

Kolata, Alan. 1993. *The Tiwanaku*. Oxford: Basil Blackwell.

Lémuz Aguirre, Carlos. 2011. "Patrones de asentamiento arqueológico en el área de influencia del sitio de Khonkho Wankane." *Nuevos Aportes* 5:31–70.

Llagostera, M. Augustín. 1996. "San Pedro de Atacama: Nodo de complementariedad reticular." In *La integración sur andina cinco siglos después*, ed. Xavier Albó, María Inés Arratia, Jorge Hidalgo, Lautaro Núñez, Augustín Llagostera, María Isabel Remy and Bruno Revesz, 17–42. Cuzco: Centro de Estudios Regionales Andinos "Bartolomé de Las Casas."

Molina, Cristóbal de. 1989 [1576]. "Relación de las Fábulas y Ritos de los Incas." In *C. de Molina and C. de Albornoz, Fabulas y mitos de los incas*, ed. Henrique Urbano and Pierre Duviols, 135–198. Madrid: Crónicas de América.

Morris, Craig. 1979. "Maize Beer in the Economics, Politics, and Religion of the Inca Empire." In *Fermented Food Beverages in Nutrition*, ed. Clifford F. Gastineau, William J. Darby, and Thomas B. Turner, 21–34. New York: Academic Press. https://doi.org/10.1016/B978-0-12-277050-0.50008-2.

Nielsen, Axel E. 2006. "Estudios internodales e interacción interregional en los Andes circumpuneños: Teoría, método y ejemplos de aplicación." In *Esferas de interacción prehistóricas y fronteras nacionales modernas: Los Andes sur centrales*, ed. Heather Lechtman, 29–62. Lima: Instituto de Estudios Peruanos—Institute of Andean Research.

Nielsen, Axel E. 2013. "Circulating Objects and the Constitution of South Andean Society (500 BC–AD 1550)." In *Merchants, Markets, and Exchange in the Pre-Columbian World*, ed. Kenneth G. Hirth and Joanne Pillsbury, 389–418. Washington, DC: Dumbarton Oaks Research Library and Collection.

Núñez Atencio, Lautaro. 1996. "Movilidad Caravánica en el Área Centro Sur Andina: Reflexiones y Expectativas." In *La Integración Sur Andina Cinco Siglos Después*, ed. Xavier Albó, María Inés Arratia, Jorge Hidalgo, Lautaro Núñez, Augustín Llagostera, María Isabel Remy, and Bruno Revesz, 43–61. Cuzco: Centro de Estudios Regionales Andinos "Bartolomé de Las Casas."

Núñez Atencio, Lautaro, and Tom D. Dillehay. 1995 [1979]. *Movilidad giratoria, armonía social y desarrollo en los Andes meridionales: patrones de tráfico e interacción económica.* Antofagasto, Chile: Universidad Católica del Norte.

Pärssinen, Martti. 1999. "Pajcha Pata de Caquiaviri. Evidencias sobre el nuevo complejo arqueológico de Alto Formativo en la Provincia de Pacajes, Bolivia (0–375 d.C.)." *Revista Espanola de Antropologia Americana* 29:159–205.

Posnansky, Arthur. 1945. *Tihuacancu: The Cradle of the American Man.* New York: J. J. Augustín.

Protzen, Jean-Pierre, and Stella Nair. 2013. *The Stones of Tiahuanaco.* Los Angeles: Cotsen Institute of Archaeology Press.

Salomon, Frank, and George L. Urioste. 1991 [1598?]. *The Huarochiri Manuscript: A Testament of Ancient and Colonial Andean Religion.* Trans. Frank Salomon and George L. Urioste. Austin: University of Texas Press.

Sarmiento de Gamboa, Pedro. 1942 [1572]. *Historia de los Incas.* Buenos Aires, Argentina: Emecé Editores.

Sherbondy, Jeanette. 1982. "The Canal Systems of Hanan Cuzco." PhD diss., University of Illinois, Urbana-Champagne.

Smith, Scott C. 2012. *Generative Landscapes: The Step Mountain Motif in Tiwanaku Iconography.* Ancient America 46. Barnardsville: Boundry End Archaeology Research Center.

Smith, Scott C. 2016. *Landscape and Politics in the Ancient Andes: Biographies of Place at Khonkho Wankane.* Albuquerque: University of New Mexico Press.

Smith, Scott C., and John W. Janusek. 2014. "Political Mosaics and Networks: The Tiwanaku Expansion into the Upper Desaguadero Valley, Bolivia." *World Archaeology* 46(5):681–704. https://doi.org/10.1080/00438243.2014.953705.

Swenson, Edward. 2011. "Stagecraft and the Politics of Spectacle in Ancient Peru." *Cambridge Archaeological Journal* 21(2):283–313. https://doi.org/10.1017/S095977431100028X.

Tomka, Steve A. 2001. "'Up and Down We Move . . . ': Factors Conditioning Agro-pastoral Settlement Organization in Mountainous Settings." In *Ethnoarchaeology of Andean South America: Contributions to Archaeological Method and Theory*, ed.

Lawrence A. Kuznar, 138–162. Ann Arbor, MI: International Monographs in Prehistory.

Urton, Gary. 1981. "Animals and Astronomy in the Quechua Universe." *Proceedings of the American Philosophical Society* 125(2):110–127.

Urton, Gary. 1985. "Animal Metaphors and the Life Cycle in an Andean Community." In *Animal Myths and Metaphors in South America*, ed. Gary Urton, 251–284. Salt Lake City: University of Utah Press.

Vranich, Alexei. 2001. "La Pirámide de Akapana: Reconsiderando el Centro Monumental de Tiwanaku." In *Huari y Tiwanaku: Modelos vs. Evidencias*, ed. P. Kaulicke and W. H. Isbell, 295–308. Boletín de Arqueología 5. Lima: Fondo Editorial de la Pontífica Universidad Católica del Perú.

Vranich, Alexei. 2016. "Monumental Perception of the Tiwanaku Landscape." In *Political Landscapes of Capital Cities*, ed. Jessica Joyce Christie, Jelena Bogdanovic, and Eulogio Guzmán, 181–211. Boulder: University Press of Colorado. https://doi.org/10.5876/9781607324690.c005.

Wright, Melanie F., Christine A. Hastorf, and Heidi A. Lennstrom. 2003. "Pre-Hispanic Agriculture and Plant Use at Tiwanaku: Social and Political Implications." In *Tiwanaku and Its Hinterland: Archaeology and Paleoecology of an Andean Civilization*, Vol. 2, *Urban and Rural Archaeology*, ed. Alan L. Kolata, 384–403. Washington, DC: Smithsonian Institution Press.

Night in Day

Contrasting Ancient and Contemporary Maya and
Hindu Responses to Total Solar Eclipses

ANTHONY F. AVENI

Modern urban culture's disconnect with the night sky formally began at 5:25 p.m. on 21 December, 1880, when Thomas Edison threw a switch connecting a long string of incandescent lamps on lower Broadway between 14th and 26th Streets, Manhattan, to his nearby DC generator (Freidel and Israel 2010, 179). Thus he set the "Great White Way" aglow. In an instant the electric bulb turned night into day. Since then people in the developed world have scarcely ever found themselves in the dark. Unlike our ancestors, we no longer have the need to skywatch in our daily lives. Who knows the time the sun rose today or the current phase of the moon? The clocks that we use to pace our daily activities give us a distorted view of the dependence that day-night time periods have on circumstances that take place in the sky.

Though we may try, we cannot really appreciate the degree to which the minds of people of most other cultures, past and present, were/are preoccupied with astronomical pursuits. The heavens once touched nearly every aspect of culture; consequently, we find ancient astronomy woven into myth, religion, and astrology. So great was the reliance on the sun and the moon that

DOI: 10.5876/9781607326786.c007

they became deified. Representations of these luminaries adorned temples as objects of worship, and they were symbolized in sculpture and other works of art. People followed the sun god wherever he went, marking his appearance and disappearance with great care. His return to a certain place on the horizon told them when to plant the crops, when the river would overflow its banks, or when the monsoon season would arrive. The important days of celebration and festivity could be marked effectively using the celestial calendar. Equipped with a knowledge of mathematics and a method for keeping records, more hierarchically organized civilizations, such as ancient China and Mesoamerica, refined and expanded their knowledge of positional astronomy.

The acquisition of knowledge of the night sky is abundant in the literature on cultural astronomy (for an overview and bibliography see Aveni 2001, 2008, 2017). The purpose of this chapter is to highlight cross-cultural reactions to an extraordinary interruption of day-night periodicity: a total eclipse of the sun. I begin with as objective a description as can be managed of what takes place physically during a total eclipse of the sun, followed by a brief collection of infrequently published eclipse stories, the goal of which is to elicit further studies of this phenomenon in the anthropological community. To provide contrast in places where sufficient data are available, I will focus principally on past and present Maya and Hindu impressions and expressions of darkness occurring in the midst of daylight.

THE TOTAL SOLAR ECLIPSE: A DIFFERENT KIND OF NIGHT

Total solar eclipses are rare. They occur approximately once in four hundred years in a given location. Technically, totality requires 100% coverage of the sun, though annular eclipses, in which a ring of light remains around the lunar disk, are generally also classified as total. Solar coverage of 96% or greater, wherein the illumination is approximately equivalent to a full moonlit sky, produces most of the effects discussed in this chapter. When an eclipse of this extent does take place, unless forewarned, you do not realize night is about to descend until the landscape suddenly dims, not in one direction as at dawn or dusk, but all around the horizon. Shadows rapidly begin to sharpen. The sun looks different in the sky, a crescent imitating the waning moon at rapid speed. Spaces between the leaves on trees cast thousands of shimmering mini-crescents on the ground; the breeze picks up and the skin chills. Then, like a dark brooding storm in the distance, the moon's shadow approaches from the west. Liminality is upon you. As the daytime luminary thins out into a tiny ribbon of light, rippling shades run swiftly along walls and on the ground: the shadow bands. They resemble reflection patterns on the bottom of a swimming pool. Suddenly, a flash, like a diamond set into a luminous ring, pops out on the edge of the now black solar disk and tiny rose-colored flames decorate what remains on the lighted rim. Then a sudden plunge into night.

But the nature of this nighttime darkness refuses categorization in the ordinary epistemological and temporal framework in which those of us in the modern West situate our day-night sensory experiences. The quality of the faded light that accompanies a full eclipse (totality) challenges expression as well. Illuminated by the light of the sun's faint corona, it is a twilight of a different color, variously described as smoky topaz, peach, metallic gray, greenish, ruddy brown, yellow-brown, and sulfur. Stars pop out and the planets appear strung out on a line on either side of the pitch black disk, running parallel to the faint streamers that extend outward from the sun's corona. Expressing extraordinary sensory impressions to a nonparticipant in our own culture is difficult enough. I agree with Joscelyn Holland (2015), who explores the tension between scientific objectivity and religious awe in Western historical accounts of eclipses, that it is basically a problem of language.

Fear and superstition intrude on us to varying degrees once the lights go out. We are surrounded by that strange darkness, which itself has long been associated with uncertainty in our minds. It is the discontinuity, the disruption that is so bothersome, even if predictable. The eclipse is a mockery of the normal oscillation between light and dark that happens every day. Then there is the aesthetic component—the feeling of something sublime. Because the darkness of the eclipse corresponds to nothing else we experience in lived time, some witnesses to a solar eclipse, for want of a better term, choose death as a metaphor. One can imagine the irrational fears, as Holland suggests in her translation (from the German) of a nineteenth-century account of the quality of darkness experienced during totality:

> It was not a decrease of light as in evening twilight, through which something
> remains cheerful and vital through the yellow and red tints of the western sky;
> it was rather an extinguishing of light through which the colorless gray became
> darker, moment by moment, and which for the observer did not conjure the
> image of a peaceful drifting into sleep, but rather the image of the death of
> nature. (Holland 2015, 228, note 32)

Then, after just a few minutes, it is over. Time reverses itself: the diamond ring flashes out, the shadowy wave of darkness recedes off to the east, the stars are extinguished, and the scintillating crescents reappear as the ruddy brown twilight gradually brightens into broad daylight.

Every living form responds to this brief interlude of night in day. Zooplankton—microscopic organisms, or larger ones, drifting in the sea—seem to deal with the diurnal interruption as a purely reflexive phenomenon. Biologists note that layers of it rise slowly toward the surface as darkness ensues, as if looking to be nurtured by their vanished resource, only to recede back to their previous levels when daytime returns (Kampa 1975; Ferrari 1976). Such is not the case for insects and mammals. Honeybees en route to the hive become disoriented and angered, stinging their keepers. Squirrels scurry around madly, cows head for the barn and chickens toward the coop, with the degree of agitation caused by the sudden darkness depending on the chicken. The same occurs for dogs (Wheeler et al. 1935). Like zooplankton, zoo chimps migrate toward the light source (the tops of trees) as the light of day suddenly diminishes. At the onset of darkness, a chimp was reported to have looked directly at the black disk in the sky and gesture toward it (Branch and Gust 1986). I have done the same.

While there has been considerable research on reactions to eclipses in the biological world, what do we know about the anthropology of eclipses? Unfortunately not very much. Eclipse expeditions belong to the domain of astronomers, who migrate to the far reaches of the world to position themselves in the moon's shadow. There they spend their time documenting these treasured events in hopes of answering questions important to them—questions about the sun: What atomic components comprise the various layers of its atmosphere? What is the source of coronal light? How is the temperature in that region raised to well above that of the photosphere below? Any observations about people who share the eclipse stage with them are casual and uninformed.

Missing in the inquiry are the anthropologist's questions: What do people's portrayals of eclipses tell us about their religion, their beliefs in the afterlife, their social cohesion? How do they express what they see and feel in their material culture? Did they have the capacity to foretell eclipses? If so, what motivated them? How did this affect their politics, their concept of history? What stories did they tell? To answer these questions requires a study of the material record, ethnography, and ethnohistory of those whose reactions we seek, both on site and in the aftermath of the phenomenon. My survey of the literature reveals that the anthropology of eclipse watching is an almost totally unexplored inquiry.

ECLIPSES ACROSS CULTURE: MAKING NOISE

When it comes to human reactions to a total eclipse of the sun, the anthropologist is in no better position than the zoologist to collect data. They can confront, interview, and survey living descendants of people who witnessed eclipses, mindful that many reported beliefs have been influenced by European Christian doctrine. They can further explore continuities and disjunctions between cultural data from past and present; for example, they might look for eclipse lore embedded in myths passed down through oral traditions that offer a social context for behavior that has been passed off as a product of superstition. Unfortunately, the effects of totality on people are rarely mentioned in standard treatises on eclipses.

Of all the known reactions to eclipses, making noise, biting, eating, or swallowing stand out. We all make noise for different reasons: to attract attention, to warn a companion of imminent danger, or to scare away an animal we encounter in the woods. There is noisemaking, too, among contemporary cultures; for example, people banged together pans during the 1973 eclipse in South Sudan, and Zulu clapping and wailing lamentations could be heard from afar when the sun was eclipsed (Alcock 2014, 217). Witnesses say the people must awaken the solar deity from his lethargy, for his inattentiveness foretells a great calamity. Like the god, the people become sluggish: no man slept with his wife, women stopped brewing beer, men quit hunting and slaughtering, and cows went unmilked (Alcock 2014, 214). Noisemaking is also pervasive in eclipse watching in the contemporary Maya world. Ants, or alternatively jaguars, are devouring the sun, so we need to make as much noise as possible—even pinch our dogs to make them howl. Some Maya say eclipses are renewals of an old cosmic sibling rivalry. The two luminaries are fighting over the lies that the moon once told the sun about how people on earth have been behaving. Noise made during an eclipse is intended to get the sun's attention. We need to convince the sun that these stories are not true (Thompson 1939).

Some tribal cultures offer a sexual interpretation for the noisemaking during sun-moon interactions. The abnormal encounter of the two luminaries invokes the theme of incest. The Great Plains Arapaho interpret the sun and moon changing places in the sky during an eclipse as a gender role-reversal; in other words, the normal gender relationship—the sun as male and the moon as female—is violated when the two join together in eclipse. One mythological interpretation of Arapaho marriage is seen "as a monthly honeymoon interrupted at each dark moon by menstruation" (Knight 1997, 133). In effect a woman's monthly time division between sex with and seclusion from her husband is coded celestially as an alternation between the sun and the moon.

Knight notes the cross-cultural connection between incest and making noise in a number of rites associated with natural phenomena—especially eclipses, darkness, and storms—and the flow of blood and unruly behavior in general. The link between noisy rebellion, cooking, and incest appears in Levi-Strauss's (1970, 312; 1981, 219) account of a Brazilian myth, a version that has much in common compared with myths across Native America. A man had engaged in sex with his sister every night, but never revealed his identity. She stained his face with *genipa* (a relative of the gardenia) juice to identify him publicly. He went to live in the sky and there he became the moon. (Notice those spots on his face?) The sister followed him into the sky; they quarreled and she fell to earth, making a loud noise. Another brother learned of this and shot arrows at the moon. People below were spattered with his blood. When they attempted to smear it away, they acquired the colors of their dress plumage. They ceased cooking out of fear that the descending blood would pollute their food. Thus thoughts of lunar blood are triggered by eclipses (Knight 1997, 137).

Dynastic power and the meaning of history are also linked to the cosmos among the contemporary Lozi, an ethnic group comprising half a million people who live along the Zambezi River in Zambia. According to art historian Karen Milbourne (2012), continuity in rulership and balance in relation to its citizens are expressed in rites based on observing the way the sun and the moon interact. Elders say that at the beginning of time, their sun god, Nyambé, married Nesilele. Together they came down from heaven and gave birth to the first in the line of kings destined to govern the people of the region and to safeguard the secret knowledge of the mystery of the heavens. Every year, during the seasonal flooding of the river timed by the first full moon that follows inundation, they celebrate the Kuomboka pageant, recognizing the continuation of dynastic power. *Kuomboka* means "get out of the water"; its significance is to warn both royalty and subjects to vacate their houses and get to high ground. Royal drums give the signal as the illuminated lunar disk rises high in the sky. In the ceremony the Lozi kings lead their people away from danger by boarding a black-and-white-striped river barge, black for dark storm clouds and white for the cool drops of rain that emanate from them. Milbourne thinks that the black and white also stand, respectively, for death balanced by renewal and ancestorhood; both are lunar symbols. Kuomboka climaxes just before the arrival of the next new moon (first crescent visible in the west), when the barge reaches dry land. Amidst loud drumming and a cheering crowd, the king gestures to the setting sun while the onlookers clap their hands, reinforcing the connection between the two sky deities. Meanwhile his attendants move around the drums in a circle, the way the sun and moon cycle around the sky.

The Kuomboka ritual appears to be designed to show that the king of the Lozi acquires his legitimacy to rule from his ancestors and he must continually renew it in ceremonies carefully timed by the moon; however, as Milbourne points out, it is the sun who influences the way the king interacts with the people. Hand clapping is not generated out of fear; it is more like applause, part of the Lozi code of conduct for recognizing the sun as the force in the sky that seals the bond between the ruler and his people. A nineteenth-century account of this noisemaking tells of one company of men clapping in unison before their king: "and before taking their places [they] raised their hands above their heads and shouted the royal salutation, '*Yo sho, yo sho, yo sho!*'" (Milbourne 2012, note 27). Then, as they continued clapping, celebrants bowed toward the earth three times. The ceremonial clapping unites heaven and earth, restores order, achieves balance, and shows respect for their leader. The ritual persists today.

ECLIPSES ACROSS CULTURE: BITING, EATING, AND SWALLOWING

The moon biting the sun is another frequently reported eclipse metaphor. "Do people bite or eat one another in your country?" a Chamula Maya descendant asked anthropologist Gary Gossen (1974, 29) during an interview. "Of course not," came the obvious answer. "Do people bite and eat one another here?" Not now was the response, "but the first people did." As Gossen continued his line of questioning, he began to realize that, as far as the Maya were concerned, strangers lived on the outer fringes of the world and what lay far away in spatial distance also resided in ancient time. Even though the Chamula claim to have become civilized by creating social rules eliminating cannibalism and infanticide from contemporary space-time, they believed that such deviant behavior might still occur at the outer limits of the universe, thus the informant's question.

If the competing sources of good and evil yet reside in the cosmos, where the sun and moon also dwell, the eclipse becomes a reminder that the social order is always in danger of getting out of balance. The ideal society the Chamula envisage, free of the chaotic social behavior of ancient barbarism, has yet to be realized. Is this so different from the Christian celestial metaphor of the permanent darkness that will prevail upon sinners at the time of the final judgment? Far from something to be feared, the sudden nighttime serves as a platform for contemplation and discourse about the forces of nature for the contemporary Maya—just as it does in the modern West.

PREDICTING ECLIPSES: THE MAYA THEN AND NOW

There is little doubt that the ancestors of contemporary Maya people sought to forewarn of possible eclipses because of the potential imbalance of forces that might have threatened them. Omen texts that accompany an eclipse table in the *Dresden Codex*, surviving precolumbian documents dated to the fifteenth century, tell of dire prognostications that resonate in our minds with astrology. The hieroglyphic text is punctuated by suggestive pictures, for example, a feathered serpent eating the symbol for the sun, along with moon and sun hieroglyphs painted on half dark backgrounds (figure 7.1). The numbers that line up across the bottom of each half-page translate to a repeated chain of 177 days followed by an interval of 148 days. These six- and five-month periods are the key to eclipse prediction (Aveni 2001, 173–184). Another series of black dot-bar numerals is positioned a few lines above each of these numbers. If the lower number of a given column is added to the upper number of the previous column, one arrives at the upper number in the next column. Clearly, the latter are running totals.

Recent excavations at a ninth-century Maya city offer evidence that the Classic Maya (figure 1.3) were predicting eclipses several centuries prior to Hispanic contact. Now badly eroded, a microtext (2 inches high and 17 inches long) inscribed on a wall in Room 10K-2 at Xultun (figure 1.2) was excavated by archaeologist William Saturno in 2011. He and Maya epigrapher David Stuart were able to get a close-up view of the writing. They recognized a pattern in the rightmost three columns, the only decipherable ones in the set. The large numbers 4,784, 4,606 and 4,429, so painstakingly rendered by the scribe, are separated by intervals of 177 (or 178) days—sets of six months of lunar phases, or semesters (Saturno et al. 2012) (figure 7.2). Backtracking to preceding columns by repeatedly deducting 177

FIGURE 7.1. *An eclipse reference in the Maya Dresden Codex: a feathered serpent (bottom center) bites a half-darkened sun. (Graz: Akad. Druck-u Verlag)*

(or 178) from each successive entry, Stuart found perfect consistency with remnants in the surviving number fragments. The text tabulated 162 lunar months arranged in 27 columns of dot and bar numbers.

How are inscriptions penned on a refurbished wall in the ruins of a ninth-century Maya city and inscribed in one of their books of prognostications dated several centuries later, related? First, the black numerals in both texts are almost exactly the same size. Second, the length of time recorded in the black totals in the Dresden document is exactly two-and-a-half times the semester sequence inscribed on the wall of Room 10K-2. Maya mathematicians had a love affair with numbers—the bigger the better—that resonated with one another in the ratio of small whole multiples, like the 405 / 162, or 5 / 2 rhythm, that harmonizes the two texts.

The lunar semester table is directly relevant to the lunar series that appears in monumental inscriptions dated to the Classic period. Initially, we concluded there was no evidence in the text as it stands that bears any relation to eclipse

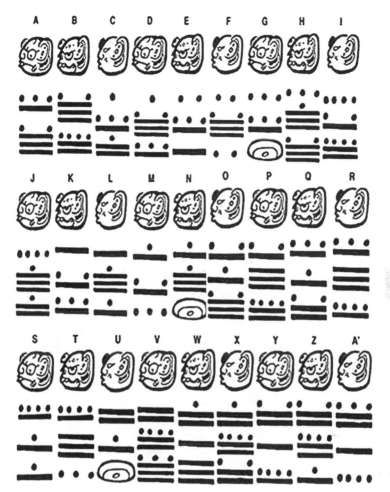

FIGURE 7.2. *Microtext on the wall of Str. 10K-2 at Xultun, Guatemala: restored version of the lunar semester table that was likely employed in setting eclipse warnings. (Original drawing by David Stuart appeared as a single line of text.)*

prediction (Aveni et al. 2013). For example, the 148-day intervals necessary for eclipse forecasting that are present in the Dresden table do not appear in the Xultun inscription. But later analysis of an adjacent inscription on the wall of Str. 10K-2 provided evidence of the back-calculation of eclipse phenomena to the previous Maya creation epoch. In that process, use was likely made of the semester table (Bricker et al. 2014).

Though scholars are not in agreement over which particular set of eclipses (and whether they were lunar or solar) was being recorded, most are convinced that the information written in the codex proves that the Dresden eclipse table has to do with warning of possible eclipses (Aveni 2001, 173–184) (for more on eclipses of possible historical eclipses visible in Yucatan, see Milbrath 2016). The most convincing evidence connecting the document with the Xultun text comes from the introductory page of the Dresden table, which records four Maya dates from around the time the Xultun inscriptions were written down: November 8, 755; November 23, 755; December 13, 755; and October 8, 818 CE. On the first of these dates a lunar eclipse took place, and fifteen days later (which is the second date), an eclipse of the sun occurred on the new moon that followed. The Dresden table is most likely a revised version of an earlier text, or perhaps a series comparable to succeeding editions of a contemporary farmer's almanac, updated and intended for consecutive years. Additional inscriptions adjacent to the Xultun lunar semester text suggest Maya astronomers were attempting to project eclipse calculations millennia backward in mythic time to the previous Maya creation era—the one that ended in 3114 BCE (Aveni et al. 2013; Bricker et al. 2014).

Recent excavations of the floor of Room 10K-2 revealed the remains of two high-status individuals wearing the same ornaments depicted in mural paintings beneath the inscriptions on the walls of the chamber (Rossi et al. 2015). The wall scene portrays three members of a school of scribes. A fourth, more elaborately garbed individual appears to be conferring with a royal personage on matters pertaining to the celebration of a New Year ritual. Hieroglyphs accompanying the images identify the two high-status individuals as senior and junior *taaj*, titles bearing the designation of ritual specialists who would possess the knowledge and skills necessary to calculate and write out calendrical tables. Next to one of the individuals Rossi found a bark beater and a plaster smoother—tools of the trade that could have found use in Maya bookmaking.

Since contemporary Maya use expressions related to being bitten, eaten, or blinded by forces from the underworld to describe what happens during an eclipse (sometimes the sun god is pictured blindfolded in eclipse texts), it may be that the agents are the bright planets nearby during totality, especially Venus (Milbrath 2000). Normally thought to be in the underworld when not visible as the morning or evening star, during an eclipse Venus suddenly flashes out, seeming to boldly attack the sun in broad daylight. Accompanying words referencing the end of days or years suggest the end of time that accompanies darkness in a broader sense—that is, the end of a Long Count cycle, such as a Maya creation era. Each such era ended with the death of the sun: thus the presence of instability that usually accompanies any period of transition. The Maya, then and now, believe that the rituals of renewal they conduct aid in the triumph over the forces of darkness (Vail 2015).

Why were ancient Maya astronomers so concerned about being precise? Knowledge is power—and the ability to decode rhythms in the cosmos would enable them to peer around time's corner and anticipate future events. Such information would prove invaluable to any ruler. The farther back in time you can plant your roots, the greater your legitimacy to rule. With the power of heaven vested in him, the ruler's presence would guarantee a perpetual universe, alive with the sacred power of fertility in the earth and in the human body, provided the rituals of sacrifice in debt payment to the Maya gods be made on time.

Foreknowledge of eclipses also had its practical side. The unknown Maya king who reigned at Xultun would have placed great value in seeking out the most expert skywatcher-mathematicians as court advisors. Charged with their royal task, the scribes who penned them were using the Xultun wall the way students might use a classroom blackboard or tablet to calculate what would become the finished product—an eclipse-warning table designed to fit at the appropriate place in a codex. There it could be consulted to time celestial phenomena that would deliver omens of impending drought, warfare, a marriage alliance—any sign in the sky that might threaten the dynasty. In effect their wall scribblings were seminal in charting the future course of the state.

SOLAR ECLIPSES IN INDIA

In parts of rural India solar eclipses serve as mediating forces between tradition and progress (Chakrabarti 1999). According to Hindu mythology, an eclipse of the sun occurs when the demon Rahu swallows the sun. Like the Maya, they say that ancient times were filled with chaos. The demons and the gods fought over who would rule the world. Out of the churning ocean, Lord Vishnu, protector of the universe, created a pot of Amrit, the elixir of immortality, for the contestants to consume. He disguised himself by changing into a woman before distributing the magical brew to both sides, who were seated in orderly rows. But Vishnu tricked the demons by offering them an imitation liquid. Seated next to the sun and moon deities, one clever demon realized he was being duped. He seized a goblet of Amrit and began to drink it. Vishnu suddenly assumed his real form and beheaded the demon on the spot so that the elixir could not take effect. The demon's head, called Rahu, swallowed the sun out of revenge. Whenever he gets the chance, Rahu repeats his act of consuming the sun.

A British visitor who came to India to witness the August 18, 1868, eclipse and heard of the Rahu eclipse myth commented: "European science has as yet produced but little effect upon the minds of the superstitious masses of India. Of the many millions who witnessed the eclipse of the 18th of August last there were comparatively few who did not verily believe that it was caused by the dragon Rahu in his endeavor to swallow up the Lord of the Day." Then he added: "The pious Hindu, before the eclipse comes on, takes a torch, and begins to search his house and carefully removes all cooked food, and all water for drinking purposes. Such food and water, by the eclipse, incur *Grahama seshah*, that is, uncleanliness, and are rendered unfit for use. Some, with less scruples of conscience, declare that the food may be preserved by placing on it *dharba* or *Kusa grass*" (Chambers 1904, 191–192).

Over a century later, a group of Indian anthropologists conducted a rare study of the response of diverse Hindu people to a solar eclipse, one that took place on October 24, 1995, and was total in the Ganges area of West Bengal (Chakrabarti 1999). They were interested specifically in the impact of the electronic media on traditional beliefs, such as the Rahu story. In the urban societies of the people with whom they worked, the anthropologists found that women in particular mentioned taboos on cooking, eating, and drinking—especially swallowing. One stay-at-home woman told an interviewer that she intended to avoid cooking; another said she planned to throw away the supply of drinking water in the house and discourage members of her family to swallow anything during the eclipse. Her educated, better-traveled young son said that he would obey his mother's wishes, not because he believed harm would come to him by swallowing any-thing, but rather not to hurt his mother's feelings or cloud family sentiment.

Another mother told of her intention to take a post-eclipse bath in the Ganges to remove any residual negative effects of Rahu. When questioned about these beliefs, her more educated daughter insisted that this is not so much a superstition as part of tradition: "Why should [I] indulge in violating the custom and risk the well-being of family members" (Chakrabarti 1999, 26). Just as some of us might withhold breaking with our family's cultural or religious traditions despite a more independent or secular personal view, younger family members pointed out that while they were perfectly well aware of the scientific explanation of eclipses, they chose to opt for the cohesive power of following family customs. Are not many of us conflicted as we try to cope with the implications of scientific discovery in a vast material universe with which we have lost intimacy?

Among more rural Hindu populations the anthropologists discovered that eclipse reactions were even more deeply embedded in tradition. Members of one tribe told a diluted version of the story of Rahu swallowing the sun: basically the moon god got angry with the sun god, so he swallowed him. One variation has it that the moon borrowed some rice, standard currency in ancient times, from the sun. Unable to pay it back he hid behind the sun out of remorse: that is what eclipses are about (Chakrabarti 1999, 42–43).

A variation on the rice-borrowing story finds the sun hiding behind the moon because he thinks the latter has returned for handout seconds. In one ritual that emanated from the rice debt account, people put some rice grains along with a coin (modern currency) in a packet on the thatched roof of the house. After the eclipse was over, the rice was kept for use in other sacred rituals. Some Hindus expose their agricultural and hunting implements, along with a piece of iron bar, to the eclipse by placing them on the roof. The bar becomes part of the material used to fabricate other household articles. If there is a newborn in the house, they place some of the exposed rice grains next to the child and later disperse it outside the house during the night to ward off any remaining evil shadows. Some nontribal people interpret the rice borrower to be a member of a lower caste. In effect they transfer the relationship between the eclipse and food spoilage to the idea of purity and pollution (Chakrabarti 1999, 40).

A NORTHERN ECLIPSE AMONG THE CANADIAN INUIT

Deep-seated social and religious beliefs about subsistence lie at the base of trans cultural eclipse watching. In the northeast Canadian Inuit province, Mark Ijjangiaq's eclipse story typifies the educated younger generation's loss of childhood fear. Though he tells it with some amusement, he still participates fully in the ritual:

> One afternoon when I was inland with my family for the summer there was an
> eclipse of the Sun. I was nine years old at the time and indeed I was horrified by
> the experience. It had the same effect as when one is wearing sunglasses. The
> Sun had the same characteristics as the Moon when it is just coming into its first
> or last quarter. My mother was still alive at the time. We had a place we drew
> water from—a small stream, very close to our tent. After the eclipse was over my
> mother asked me to go and fetch water with a small pail. But I did not want to
> go for I was afraid that once I went a little distance [from the tent] there might be
> another eclipse while I was all alone. (MacDonald 1998, 136)

The Inuit say that during an eclipse all animals and fish disappear. To get them back, hunters and fishermen gather samples of every kind of creature they consume and place them in a large sack. Carrying their burden they circuit the periphery of the village, acting out the direction of the movement of the sun. Once back in the center of town they empty the sack and distribute bits of each kind of flesh to residents to eat. Mutual respect between hunter and prey is an important part of Inuit culture. They tell inquiring anthropologists that the creatures remind them that they need their attention and the only way successful hunting can be resumed after the eclipse is for the men to perform this rite so that they can return safely. The eclipse becomes the medium through which humans engage beasts.

ECLIPSE EXPERIENCES IN PAPUA NEW GUINEA

Finally, the Suki of Papua New Guinea told Dutch anthropologists in the 1960s that eclipses happen because people's souls leave their bodies and throw themselves at the sun or the moon. If a soul fails to return to its body, the possessor will die. Those responsible for solar eclipses are members of the cassowary (large bird) moiety, one of paired kinship groups into which they divide themselves. This moiety is associated with water, the rainy season, darkness, and the moon, while the pig moiety relates to land, the dry season, and bright days; the latter tend to lunar eclipses (van Nieuwenhuijsen and van Nieuwenhuijsen-Riedeman 1975, 115).

Eclipses happen when members of one moiety cross over to the other, thus violating the natural order. After considerable difficulty getting anyone to talk about eclipses, the anthropologists finally spoke to two informants who had witnessed such events over the years and had been surprised by them. In each instance an appointed clansman from the tribe responsible climbed a tree and asked the sky gods for an interpretation of the daytime darkness. In one case four souls from sick people in the opposing clan were covering the sun. In another a woman whose husband had abused her was named. She died shortly after the eclipse. In a third incident the clansman went to the top of the tree and shouted "Nagaia Namagwaria, Gwauia, what is the matter?" Came the omen: "The man here is Tutie, we tried to send him back, but he did not obey us. We have cut his hair so that he will soon die" (van Nieuwenhuijsen and van Nieuwenhuijsen-Riedeman 1975, 116). When Tutie learned he'd been fingered he began to cry. He too, they said, died shortly after the eclipse. That the Suki seem to go to great lengths to conceal their eclipse traditions from outsiders suggests a deep commitment to their beliefs.

CONCLUSIONS

What puzzles us about eclipse stories that involve making noise, eating, biting, and swallowing is the apparent conflict between myth and cognition. Why should an animate sun and moon serve as the action figures in the reenactment of a narrative of life? How is it that these mental speculations continue to coexist alongside rational thought, so clearly evident in the Hindu eclipse reactions? In my view the common thread that knits together all people is deeply woven in the human desire to embrace intangible natural phenomena, whether they be black holes in an infinite universe or a total eclipse of the sun, by trying to make sense of what we see with what we experience in the tangible world. Only by lending familiarity to the unfamiliar can one hope to find meaning. The eclipse stories narrated in this chapter are examples of the way people project their social interactions into the world of nature, especially when the status quo is violated, for example, by threats to sustenance, breaching family ties, and political instability. People create stories about the world around them as a way of transporting that unpredictable realm closer to themselves. By discovering society mirrored in the cosmos, they become humanized.

In sum, it is not the eclipse that matters; it is the action triggered by what happens to the one who witnesses it. For the Maya, daytime darkness is a reminder of challenges to the social order and the need to engage a discourse to preserve it. The Hindu sun watcher recalls the obligation to debt payment and the cohesive power of family custom in the face of techno-modernity, while the Inuit, in a subsistence-challenged environment, perform a rite to sustain harmony between hunter and hunted. In societies outside the modern West, the sun and the moon are *not* members of a world apart—a world of matter devoid of spirit, as science teaches us. The celestial players involved in the cosmic drama of a solar eclipse offer a kind of dualistic imagery that reflect complementary social concepts in everyday life: male and female, pure and impure, good and evil, day and night. Far from amusing relics, eclipse stories from around the world are examples for the active mind to engage and contemplate, powerful agents in setting up a dialog between people and the sky about the meaning of human existence. They restore a lost moral component to the art of skywatching and they inspire us to pay closer attention to human diversity.

REFERENCES

Alcock, Peter. 2014. *Venus Rising: South African Astronomical Beliefs, Customs and Observations*. Durban: Astronomical Society of Southern Africa.

Aveni, Anthony. 2001. *Skywatchers: A Revised, Updated Version of* Skywatchers of Ancient Mexico. Austin: University of Texas Press.

Aveni, Anthony. 2008. *People and the Sky: Our Ancestors and the Cosmos*. London: Thames and Hudson.

Aveni, Anthony. 2017. *In the Shadow of the Moon: The Culture and Science Behind the Magic, Mystery, and Fear of Eclipses*. New Haven, CT: Yale University Press.

Aveni, Anthony, William Saturno, and David Stuart. 2013. "Astronomical Implications of Maya Hieroglyphic Notations at Xultun." *Journal for the History of Astronomy* 44(1):1–16. https://doi.org/10.1177/002182861304400101.

Branch, Jane, and Deborah Gust. 1986. "Effect of Solar Eclipse on the Behavior of a Captive Group of Chimpanzees (*Pan troglodytes*)." *American Journal of Primatology* 11(4):367–373. https://doi.org/10.1002/ajp.1350110407.

Bricker, Victoria, Anthony Aveni, and Harvey Bricker. 2014. "Deciphering the Handwriting on the Wall: Some Astronomical Interpretations of the Recent Discoveries at Xultun." *Latin American Antiquity* 25(2):152–169. https://doi.org/10.7183/1045-6635.25.2.152.

Chakrabarti, S. B. 1999. *Man, Myth, and Media: An Anthropological Enquiry into the Recent Total Solar Eclipse in Eastern India*. Calcutta: Anthropological Survey of India, Ministry of Human Resource Development, Department of Culture, Government of India.

Chambers, George. 1904. *The Story of Eclipses*. New York: Appleton.

Ferrari, Frank. 1976. "The Significance of the Response of Pelagic Marine Animals to Solar Eclipses." *Deep Sea Research and Oceanographic Abstracts* 23(7):653–654. https://doi.org/10.1016/0011-7471(76)90008-5.

Freidel, Robert, and Paul Israel. 2010. *Edison's Electric Light: The Art of Invention*. Baltimore: John Hopkins University Press.

Gossen, Gary. 1974. *Chamulas in the World of the Sun: Time and Space in a Maya Oral Tradition*. Cambridge, MA: Harvard University Press.

Holland, Joscelyn. 2015. "A Natural History of Disturbance: Time and the Solar Eclipse." *Configuration* 23(2):215–233. https://doi.org/10.1353/con.2015.0016.

Kampa, Elizabeth. 1975. "Observations of a Sonic-Scattering Layer During the Total Solar Eclipse 30 June, 1973." *Deep Sea Research and Oceanographic Abstracts* 22(6):417–420. https://doi.org/10.1016/0011-7471(75)90063-7.

Knight, Chris. 1997. "The Wives of the Sun and Moon." *Journal of the Royal Anthropological Institute* 3(1):133–153. https://doi.org/10.2307/3034369.

Levi-Strauss, Claude. 1970. *The Raw and the Cooked*. London: Cape.

Levi-Strauss, Claude. 1981. *The Naked Man*. London: Cape.

MacDonald, John. 1998. *The Arctic Sky: Inuit Astronomy, Sky Lore, and Legend*. Toronto: Royal Ontario Museum.

Milbourne, Karen. 2012. "Moonlight and the Clapping of Hands." In *African Cosmos: Lozi Cosmic Arts of Barotseland (Western Zambia)*, ed. Christine Kreamer, 283–300. New York: Monacelli.

Milbrath, Susan. 2000. *Star Gods of the Maya: Astronomy in Art, Folklore, and Calendars*. Austin: University of Texas Press.

Milbrath, Susan. 2016. "La Evidencia de la Agro-astronomia entre los Antiguos Mayas." *Estudios de Cultura Maya* 47:11–29. https://doi.org/10.19130/iifl.ecm.2016.47.738.

Rossi, Franco, William Saturno, and Heather Hurst. 2015. "Maya Codex Book Production and the Politics of Expertise: Archaeology of a Classic Period Household at Xultun, Guatemala." *American Anthropologist* 117(1):116–132. https://doi.org/10.1111/aman.12167.

Saturno, William, David Stuart, Anthony Aveni, and Franco Rossi. 2012. "Ancient Maya Astronomical Tables from Xultun, Guatemala." *Science* 336(6082):714–717. https://doi.org/10.1126/science.1221444.

Thompson, John Eric S. 1939. *The Moon Goddess in Middle America with Notes on Related Deities*. Carnegie Institution of Washington Publication No. 509, Contributions to American Anthropology and History No. 29. Washington, DC: Carnegie Institute of Washington.

Vail, Gabrielle. 2015. "Iconography and Metaphorical Expressions Pertaining to Eclipses: A Perspective from Postclassic and Colonial Maya Manuscripts." In *Cosmology, Calendars, and Horizon-Based Astronomy in Ancient Mesoamerica*, ed. Anne Dowd and Susan Milbrath, 163–196. Boulder: University Press of Colorado. https://doi.org/10.5876/9781607323792.c007.

van Nieuwenhuijsen, J. W., and C. H. van Nieuwenhuijsen-Riedeman. 1975. "Eclipses as Omens of Death." In *Explorations in the Anthropology of Religion: Essays in Honour of Jan van Baal*, ed. W.E.A. van Beek and J. A. Scherer, 112–121. The Hague: Martinus Nijhoff. https://doi.org/10.1007/978-94-017-4902-2_8.

Wheeler, William, Clint MacCoy, Ludlow Griscom, Glover Allen, and Harold Coolidge, Jr. 1935. "Observations on the Behavior of Animals During the Total Solar Eclipse of August 31, 1932." *Proceedings of the American Academy of Arts and Sciences* 70(2):33–70. https://doi.org/10.2307/20023118.

In the Sea of Night

Ancient Polynesia and the Dark

CYNTHIA L. VAN GILDER

The source of the darkness that made darkness
O ke kumu o ka po i po ai
The source of the night that made night
O ka lipolipo, o ka lipolipo
The intense darkness, the deep darkness
O ka lipo o ka la, o ka po
Darkness of the sun, darkness of the night
Po wale ho'i
Nothing but night.
Hanau ka po . . .
The night gave birth . . .
—*Kumulipo*[1]

(BECKWITH 1972)

To understand night (pō) in ancient Hawai'i, one must start at the very begin-ning, with creation. *Pō* is an ancient Polynesian word with cognates in most Eastern Polynesian and many Western Polynesian languages. The opening lines of the famous Kumulipō[2] creation chant quoted above are the first of thousands outlining the generative relationships of the universe, from the night (pō) to the plants and animals of this world, to the chiefly ancestors of the ruling family of Hawai'i, and finally to the specific baby for whose birth this version of the chant was composed. Polynesian *pō* referred to the source of creation, the depths of the sea, the spirit world, and the time of darkness that followed each day of tropical sun. In this chapter, I consider the "anthropology of night" (Galinier et al. 2010) in ancient Polynesia, with particular attention to the Hawaiian case (figures 1.2–1.3). To this end, comparative data from three fields of anthropology (historical linguistics, cultural anthropology, and archaeology) are considered, first to understand the traditional meanings associated with night, then to build a model of nighttime practices, and finally, to examine possible avenues for the application of the model to archaeological analysis.

THE ORIGIN AND MANIFESTATIONS OF PŌ

In the absence of a written record, comparative historical linguistics has come to play a prominent role in understanding the cultures of ancient Polynesia, as well as its shared origins and many migrations (e.g., Kirch and Green 2001). Michel Brun and Edgar Tetahiotupa have assembled data on the origins and usage of the word *pō* throughout Polynesia (Brun and Tetahiotupa 2005). They begin with excerpts from the entry for *pō* from Edward Tregear's famous 1891 work, *The Maori-Polynesian Comparative Dictionary*, and proceed to examine the connotations and history of each meaning he documented. Each affords us insight into the symbolic and affective value of *pō* to pre-European-influence Polynesians. For example, the Kumulipō is a representation of the definition of *pō* as the "ancestor of all things"[3] (Brun and Tetahiotupa 2005, 63, after Tregear 1969). Brun and Tetahiotupa argue that when closely examined, even the second definition, "the night," has a more complex usage in some Polynesian languages.

In Hawaiian and other Eastern Polynesian languages, such as Tahitian, the word *pō* seems to have had a temporal function comparable to that of the word *day* in English (Brun and Tetahiotupa 2005, 63; see also Levy 1973, 149).[4] That is, just as English speakers may use the word *day* to refer to the "daytime," or the time when the sun is out, it can also be used to refer to a unit of twenty-four-hour time, as in the sentence, "I will harvest my sweet potatoes in three days." Thus Hawaiians used *pō* to indicate the night (in contrast to the day) as well as the marker of their twenty-four-hour unit of time, each of which was thought to begin as the sun set. So, it would make sense to say, "I will harvest my sweet potatoes in three nights." Clearly, this idea of the night, or darkness, as the start of a unit of time (aka *day* in English) both embodied and engendered a different relationship to evening for Polynesians than for Westerners. Our evening, a transition to an end, would have been felt as a transition to a beginning.

Pō is also used to refer to "the subterranean world from whence come beings and spirits and to which they return" (Brun and Tetahiotupa 2005, 63, after Tregear 1969). Thus in Polynesian philosophy, pō is both a time and place simultaneously; in pō (i.e., night), symbolically, if not literally, the world of humans becomes the world of spirits. Finally, *pō* is also defined as "the legendary land, origin of the Polynesian people" (Brun and Tetahiotupa 2005, 63, after Tregear 1969). This meaning once again affirms how time/place can be philosophically entwined. Brun and Tetahiotupa seek the linguistic origins of each of these meanings of *pō*, finding them in ancestral Polynesian phonemes such as *hu* and *ho*, tracing the transmutation of individual words for "day," "night," "beyond," "ocean," and "world" into the single homophone *pō* (Brun and Tetahiotupa 2005, 79–80) that came to invoke all of these meanings.

One of the other usages of *pō* in Polynesia is to refer to objects that are "below the horizon, below the sea," as referring to islands that appear on the horizon as you sail, visually emerging from pō (Brun and Tetahiotupa 2005, 76–79). Brun and Tetahiotupa believe that this is the most ancient Polynesian meaning of *pō*, before the additional meanings mentioned above condensed onto its phoneme. They argue, "numerous indications lead us to think that the pō of Polynesian legend had nothing to do with an imaginary and shadowy world of the night or submarine world, or even hell located underneath the world of the living, but refers, much more prosaically, to the faraway sea, that which can be found below the horizon" (ibid). Be this as it may, for a Hawaiian speaker in the centuries before European contact, the word *pō* would have invoked all of these meanings simultaneously, contributing to the inherent poetry of the language. Thus, if we reconsider the Kumulipō, quoted above, each use of the word *pō* should invoke all of the following, and more: in/of the night, under/beyond the sea, in/of the ancient past, and in/of the realm of spirits.

THE EXPERIENCE OF PŌ

Although it was not unusual for Hawaiians to experience seeing a manifestation of a god or goddess during the day, the night was the time when even an ordinary spirit might slip from the pō of their world and into the pō of this one. According to Mary Kawena Pukui, the souls of the deceased were thought to reside in pō, and there is some indication that the unborn, or souls of the future, were thought of as residing there as well (Handy and Pukui 1972). There is also the suggestion that during particular kinds of dreams, ordinary live humans may visit pō, meaning that the boundary of pō is permeable in both directions (Handy and Pukui 1972, 126). Similarly, Robert Levy (1973, 386) recounts an interview with a Tahitian man in which he explains that in some dreams it is "like your spirit goes and wanders . . . in the pō."[5]

This association of the night with crossover from/in pō, is common throughout Polynesia. For example, Margaret Mead makes multiple references to the care and concern Samoans took in moving about at night due to the presence of ancestors, spirits, and "ghosts and devils" (2001, 65). In considering these accounts of Polynesian beliefs of the night, one must be careful not to project a Western sense of spirits and ghosts as inherently frightening or bad. In the Polynesian universe, power and the divine (*mana*) existed in specific structural relationships with the profane (*noa*), structures that were governed by rules that had to be followed (*kapu*). Those who behaved with *aloha*, meeting appropriate rights and responsibilities with respect, were rarely at risk.[6] When encountering night spirits, if one did not see any familiar ancestors in the group, or could not remember the proper precautionary chants, the best course of action was to strip naked, lie down, and fake sleep until they passed (Beckwith 1970, 164).

In their review article, "Anthropology of the Night," Galinier and colleagues (2010, 825) assert that "in every society and culture, there are hypotheses concerning the relations between the nocturnal activity of the mind and knowledge, and the modes of its acquisition, conservation, or transformation during the night." This is certainly a prominent theme in the cultural ideas about pō in Polynesia. In her collection of Hawaiian proverbs and "poetical sayings," titled, *'Ōlelo No'eau*, Mary Kawena Pukui recorded multiple aphorisms along these lines. Most generally, *he hō'ike na ka pō*, literally, "a revelation of the night," is explained as "a revelation from the gods in dreams, visions, and omens" (Pukui 1997, 68, see also Handy and Pukui 1972, 143). Notice that pō here is understood as the realm of the gods and the time of dreaming (i.e., night). She notes another similar expression, *mai ka pō mai ka 'oiā'i'o*, which she translates as, "truth comes from the night (is revealed by the gods)" (1997, 225). Neither of these expressions uses the word for the gods or a god, *akua*.[7] In both, the role of pō as medium/ means of communication is emphasized.[8]

E. S. Craighill Handy and Mary Kawena Pukui include multiple examples of night knowledge in their famous study of Hawaiian life in Ka'u, Hawai'i (Handy and Pukui 1972). Dreams are taken seriously, they assert, "because they represent the most direct and continuous means of communication between those living in this world of light (*ao malama*) and the ancestral guardians (*'aumakua*) and gods (*akua*) whose existence is in the Unseen (Pō)" (Handy and Pukui 1972, 126–127). In return for appropriate respect and offerings, the beings of pō would most often offer knowledge and protection. These authors also report having met people who had learned a new hula or chant in pō, or came to know the proper name for a new baby (Handy and Pukui 1972, 99, 127).

Not surprisingly, given the association of generative pairing in the Hawaiian religion and cosmogony, night is also associated with sex in Polynesia. For one, it is considered possible to have a child sired by an *'aumakua* or ancestral spirit visiting from/during pō (Handy and Pukui 1972, 121; Pukui et al. 1972, 120–122). Night was also a time for flirtatious games and wooing.[9] Margaret Mead (2001) famously described clandestine meetings under the coconut trees for amorous Samoans, as did Robert Levy (1973) for Tahitians, and Handy and Pukui (1972) for Hawaiians. Raymond Firth (1983, 55) said of nighttime on the Polynesian island of Tikopia, "here is the opportunity for flirtation and intrigue, and from time to time an individual drifts off with some flimsy excuse to join a lover in a canoe shed or empty dwelling."

Hawaiian chiefs in particular were famous for staying up to indulge in all sorts of recreational excesses during the night. One common expression quoted by Pukui (1997, 98) is, *he pō moe ko na maka'āinana, he pō ala ko na li'i*, which she translates as, "commoners sleep at night, chiefs remain awake," meaning, she explains, that "commoners rest at night to be ready for the day's labor. Chiefs can well afford to spend the night in pleasure, for they can sleep during the day." It is worth noting Samuel Kamakau's point that at the height of the kapu system, there were some chiefs who were so sacred that if their shadows were to cross the path of a commoner, the commoner would have to be sacrificed. Says Kamakau (1991b, 10), "it was not right for them [chiefs of the most sacred status] to go out in the daytime; at night was the proper time for them to associate with other chiefs and people, when no shadow could be cast upon them." These chiefs received their tribute (pigs, etc.) at night as well, for they were like gods on earth (ibid.).

Mead (2001, 15) wrote a lovely and evocative description of evenings in a Samoan village: "After supper the old people and the little children are bundled off to bed. If the young people have guests the front of the house is yielded to them. For day is the time for the councils of old men and the labours of youth, and night is the time for lighter things." People sit and chat, and "if it is moonlight, groups of young men, women by twos and threes, wander through the village." There may be music, dancing, and "sometimes sleep will not descend upon the village until long past midnight; then at last there is only the mellow thunder of the reef and the whisper of lovers, as the village rests until dawn" (ibid). Similarly, Firth (1983, 52) describes late afternoon to evening in Tikopia as when "the social side of the village life becomes more evident." As in Samoa, "dancing, games and conversation on the beach may go on till any hour; there is no conventionally appointed time for retiring, but people trickle off as the desire for sleep comes upon them" (Firth 1983, 55). In their ethnography of life on a Polynesian atoll in Tuvalu, Keith and Anne Chambers describe similar evenings, as the work of the day winds down and is replaced by socializing and lighter tasks that can be done in a group (Chambers and Chambers 2001).

In his historical analysis of night (based primarily on preindustrial Europe), Ekirch (2006, 177) writes, "above all, nighttime commonly blurred the boundaries between labor and sociability. More than any time during the day, work and play intersected. Many tasks became collective undertakings, marked by a spirit of conviviality and companionship." Night fishing in Samoa is a perfect example of this phenomenon. Mead (2001, 15) describes the community reef fishing at night: "Half the village may go fishing by torchlight and the curving reef will gleam with wavering lights and echo with shouts of triumph or disappointment." In the late 1960s Barbara Smetzer (1969) witnessed an extraordinary Samoan phenomenon known as the night of the *palolo*.[10] The whole village stays up to participate in this once-a-year event. Younger men wade into the water with torches, searching for signs of the first sea worm. When it is sighted, the cry goes out, *ua sau le palolo!* ("the palolo comes") and young and old alike grab buckets, nets, baskets, flashlights, lanterns, and torches, and descend into the water laughing and shouting in order to catch this highly desirable culinary treat (Smetzer 1969, 65).

Not all Polynesian night-fishing practices involve the whole community. Firth (1983, 52) describes the sound of the night fishermen returning to the village with their catch as one of the first sounds of morning he would hear as others slept. Keith and Anne Chambers describe the near daily practice of night fishing for flying fish that they witnessed while living on the island of Nanumea in the 1970s. As dusk fell, fishermen would head out to sea as a "loosely organized flotilla" (Chambers and Chambers 2001, 115). The reflections from the canoes' lights (coconut-frond torches before propane lanterns) would startle the *hahave* fish to jump, and the fishermen would catch them midair in nets (ibid.). In their 1973–1974 dietary survey, the Chamberses (ibid.) found that this nighttime labor was a critical contribution to the food supply, hahave being eaten at one-quarter of all meals, and, once salted and preserved, serving as an important defense against food shortages.

Kamakau (1991b, 239), who describes similar canoe fishing by torchlight in Hawai'i, also stresses that "nighttime was the proper time for eel fishing" (Kamakau 1992, 83). In most cases this meant the trap was set before nightfall, left open overnight, and checked for results in the morning. However, there were some men who fished for eels by hand, wiggling their fingers to entice the eels to poke out of their rocky hiding places (Kamakau 1992, 86–87). Says Kamakau (1992, 86), "on a dark night when the sky was thickly studded with stars the eel fisherman . . . would say, 'There are fish tonight—the stars are twinkling.' This imagery is evocative, and once again draws a connection between the sky of pō and the sea of pō, between the plenty of the sea and the plenty of the night sky.

This deeply ingrained relationship between sea and sky is nowhere more apparent than in the ancient science of navigation. Observations of the heavens were critical to the Polynesians' lives as long-distance sailors (Finney 1979; Finney 2004; Lewis 1994). Although there were signs in wave patterns and bird movements during the day that could help indicate the direction of a landfall, it was really the night sky, bookended as it was with the rising and setting of the sun on the horizon, that brought a sense of location. At sea, at night, you knew where you were in the universe with a certainty that daytime in the middle of the ocean did not convey. Many authors have pointed out that to Polynesians, the Pacific Ocean was not conceived of as a treacherous expanse of dangerous ocean punctuated by tiny land safe spaces, but rather as a set of lands interconnected by the highway of the sea, or pō.[11] Similarly, I would argue that they saw the sky as being primarily about the stars, interconnected by the night, or pō. In other words, stars are the islands in the sea of the night.

Although historically there has not been much research into archaeoastronomy in Hawai'i, it is not surprising that once long-distance sailing was terminated, the great depth of knowledge of the night sky once harnessed to navigate the Pacific might be repurposed for organizing the built landscape (see, e.g., Kirch et al. 2013). This organization has begun to reveal itself in the orientation of temples, or heiau (Kirch 2004). On O'ahu, a walled enclosure site in the Honouli'uli District has been identified as a Makahiki festival gathering site based on its astronomical orientation, radiocarbon dates of construction and use, and supporting ethnographic details (Gill et al. 2015). Most likely, *kilolani,* or astronomical priests, responsible for reading the heavens for auspicious dates to build, wage war, and so on (Malo 1997, 75), were also responsible for reading the night skies to properly place these structures.

The basic calendar of the Hawaiians was twelve lunar months, each with thirty named days corresponding to the phases of the moon throughout the month (Malo 1997, 30–36). Handy and Handy (1991) have gathered extensive information on the planting and harvesting of native plants (and animals when relevant) in accordance with the traditional calendar. For example, a short summary of *mohalu* (the twelfth night), reveals that it is "good for planting flowers, which will be round and perfect like the moon on this night; and gourds, potatoes, and taro will grow well" (Handy and Handy 1991, 38). Handy and Pukui (1972) mention that residents of Ka'u, Hawai'i, timed their planting and harvesting cycles around not just the lunar months, but also the lunar days/nights. It was not unusual for farmers to rise at night and inspect nearby gardens, or to keep a small house, or *papa'i,* for sleeping among more distant fields (Handy and Pukui 1972, 13).

In addition to the sleeping and storage shelters of the uplands, Handy and Pukui (1972, 13–14) note that some families kept temporary sleeping shelters at the beach, canoe makers sometimes piled mats in their canoe houses to sleep near their work, and that rockshelters and lava tubes could serve as cool, dry places to sleep during warm nights. Ekirch (2006, 299) argues that a pattern of "segmented sleep" characterized preindustrial European practice, and that sleep was "less confined to nocturnal hours than it is in most Western societies today." Using historical sources, he concludes that the concept, and experience, of a first sleep, followed by a short period of wakefulness, or even rising to complete tasks, then followed by a second sleep period was commonplace (Ekirch 2006, 300–301). He (Ekirch 2006, 303) also cites anthropological accounts of the Tiv of Nigeria, who live a subsistence farming lifestyle, as having slept as it suited them, which quite often was a cycle of early sleep, wakefulness, and then a second later sleep. In short, Ekirch (ibid.) argues that "there is every reason to believe that segmented sleep, such as many wild animals exhibit, had long been the natural pattern of our slumber before the modern age, with a provenance as old as humankind." It is likely that the task oriented (e.g., farming, salt-collecting, canoe manufacture, etc.) temporary sleeping quarters mentioned by Handy and Pukui (1972) were part of accommodating segmented sleep patterns where moonlit nights were both an auspicious and convenient time for completing tasks.

For this reason, I think we have good grounds to imagine that precontact nights in Hawai'i were highly varied, with flexible schedules that may have involved subsistence activities such as night fishing, planting, or harvesting as the moon might dictate. Some nights would likely be spent asleep to be ready for an anticipated early rising, some in completing necessary rituals, and still others filled with dancing, singing, gambling, and games. It is likely that all of them included that most beloved of Hawaiian pastimes, "talking story," a Polynesian cultural constant also remarked upon by ethnographers Firth, Mead, Levy, and the Chambers.[12] The ancestors, or 'aumakua, would have felt particularly present at night, and an effort would have been made to avoid provoking ghosts or other malevolent spirits. Dreams, or other experiences in pō would make fertile conversation topics for the morning.

THE MATERIAL TRACES OF PŌ

As we think about developing a uniquely Hawaiian archaeology of the night, we must first consider the kinds of spaces where night activities might have taken place and then the kinds of material culture that would have supported those activities. Most activities related to fishing took place in canoes or along the shore in undesignated spaces with a toolkit that would not be particularly remarkable archaeologically. None of the games described as specifically nighttime activities involved unique spaces or much equipment that would be preserved archaeologically. Long-distance navigation, of course, took place on a canoe, and teaching navigation may have involved a calabash or set of interwoven sticks (Chauvin 2000), neither of which would preserve in anything but the most extremely dry rockshelters in Hawai'i's climate. However, any activities that took place after dark inside of structures, be they household or otherwise, might be expected to yield evidence of illumination. This evidence is likely to take several predictable forms archaeologically. These include the presence of (1) indoor hearths that would have provided illumination and warmth; (2) small stone lamps for burning oil; and (3) kukui (*Aleurites moluccana* endocarps) nut pieces. I consider each of these forms of evidence in turn.

It is immediately obvious that one can use a hearth during the day, as well as at night, for cooking, heat, and illumination; thus, a hearth's presence cannot automatically be taken as an indicator that a space was primarily used for after-dark activities. Similarly, regarding the small stone bowls that have been identified as lamps by many ethnographers and archaeologists, Peter Buck cautioned that "it is difficult at times to distinguish between mortars, stone lamps, dye cups, and other stone receptacles" (Buck 1993, 107). Buck suggests that stone lamps are distinguished by two features: first, they tend to have smaller and shallower central cavities (Buck 1993, 108) and, in some cases exhibit an "inner edge stained black with burnt carbon" from use (ibid., 107). He adds that plant oil was used in "stone mortars, with a wick made of *tapa*[13] and that the light was increased by adding more wicks" (ibid., 107).[14] Although basalt stone receptacles do not present preservation challenges, these lamps are not commonly found in archaeological contexts. One possible reason is that these are a distinctive and reusable piece of material culture that could be carried out by folks abandoning the countryside, and/or easily found by post-abandonment collectors in the early part of the twentieth century.[15]

The plant oil used in these lamps was most commonly derived from kukui, a tree whose endocarps are often found as macrobotanical remains in Hawaiian archaeological sites, both charred and uncharred. Stone lamps were called *poho kukui*,[16] and many ethnohistoric and ethnographic sources make reference to the burning of kukui, so much so that in many contexts kukui could be used as a synonym for light. In fact, electric lights were called *kukui uila* (Pukui and Elbert 1986, 474). Buck dedicated a section of his discussion of "Household Equipment" to "kukui-nut candles." He states that "the nuts were baked lightly, the hard shells cracked, and the oily kernels threaded on lengths of stiff midribs from dry coconut leaflets to form a primitive candle" (Buck 1993, 107). Long strings could be hung, wrapped together into torches, or laid into a poho kukui. A *makou* is a torch consisting of three kukui nut strings (Emerson 1909, 63).[17] Handy and Handy spend several pages on the uses of the various parts of the kukui tree, but cite Abraham Fornander 1916–1917, for the following description: "Torches were made by stringing kukui nuts on reeds about 4 feet long, binding several of these together with strips of *tapa* and then wrapping in *ti* leaves to prevent the oily kernels from burning too fast" (Handy and Handy 1991, 232). There is some suggestion that monitoring and maintaining the kukui nut strings was a job for the children of the household, as each nut had to be pushed off as it burned down (Krauss 1993, 59).[18]

Thus, it seems that the third type of material evidence for deliberate illumination after dark proposed above has the most potential; in short, tracing the distribution and concentration of kukui remains shows great promise as a building block in the Hawaiian archaeology of the night.[19] Theoretically, one might expect that places where nighttime activities requiring illumination repeatedly took place would be expected to yield larger concentrations of kukui remains. To explore the potential of this approach I consider here two archaeological data sets from leeward districts of Maui, one from intensive excavations of a handful of households, the other from test units spread extensively across the landscape.

Hawaiian households were clusters of functionally differentiated structures, most often with volcanic stone (basalt) foundations or windbreak walls that were capped with a wood-and-thatch superstructure.[20] Many types of *hale*, or house structures, are described in the ethnohistoric literature. Some of the most commonly mentioned types are *hale mua* (a men's eating and sleeping house, which also functioned as a household shrine), *hale noa* (a sleeping house for women and children, though men could also join their families here), and *hale 'aina* (a cooking and eating house for women). In addition to these core structures there might be others: for example, *imu* (earth oven) shelters, storage facilities, a canoe house, or even a menstrual house. It is also clear that outside areas were used extensively for all manner of tasks, including sleeping and socializing at night.[21]

In 1996, I undertook excavations at three household clusters (*kauhale*) of structures located within the Kahikinui District, Maui.[22] One was chosen in each of the three main habitation zones: *kai* (by the ocean), *waena* (in the heart of the agricultural/habitation area), and *uka* (at the top of the agricultural zone, bordering the upland forest). In each case, settlement pattern data derived from pedestrian survey were used to identify clusters of structures that seemed discrete and well defined. Extensive, household archaeology-style excavations were undertaken to facilitate identification of the function and patterns of use at each structure believed to be part of the cluster.[23] Radiocarbon dating yielded calibrated dates of occupation of the households no earlier than 1470 CE, with occupation terminated at or around European contact in the late 1700s and early 1800s.[24]

Several years before, a team from the State Historic Preservation Division Inter-Agency Office of Archaeology (undertaking archaeological work for the Department of Hawaiian Home Lands), had completed a pedestrian survey and testing project in the Kula District, Maui (Kolb et al. 1997). A total of 161 test units (ranging from .25 m × .25 m to 1 m × 1 m) were undertaken in 110 separate archaeological features, including 26 clusters identified as "major *kauhale*" (ibid., 98, 198). Calibrated radiocarbon dates from the Kula project suggest that more than 90% of the structures postdate 1400 CE, with the majority of the habitation sites showing intensive use between 1500 CE and European contact (ibid., 140).

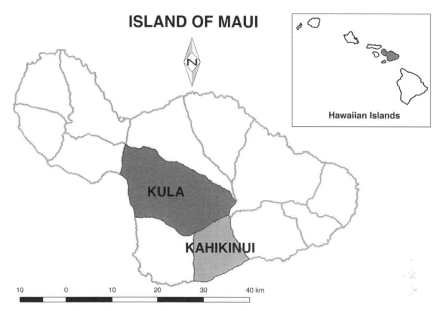

ISLAND OF MAUI

Hawaiian Islands

KULA

KAHIKINUI

10   0   10   20   30   40 km

FIGURE 8.1. *Kula and Kahikinui Districts, Maui Island.*

Kula and Kahikinui are both traditional land units (*moku*) that sit in the rain shadow of Haleakalā (figure 8.1). Their uplands were once covered in dryland forests, and neither had much (if any) perennial stream flow to support wet-taro crops; thus, they relied primarily on sweet potato and dry-taro farming. They were both somewhat marginal areas in the history and politics of the island of Maui, whose most powerful chiefly seats were both located in highly fertile windward areas: Wailuku of West Maui, and Hana of East Maui. In addition, both districts seem to have been intensively occupied during the same three centuries (1500–1800 CE). Most important, together these two data sets provide a sense of the information kukui distribution / counts might yield in an intensive household archaeology context, and in an extensive settlement pattern testing context, two types of projects commonly undertaken in Hawaiian archaeology.

Table 8.1 shows basic information on the kukui recovered from the Kahikinui household excavations. The deposits at the Waena household cluster stand out immediately, as they all contained significantly more kukui fragments than the structures in the other households, even taking into account that a great amount of square meters was excavated at the Waena household. From the depth of many of these deposits, it seemed clear that one factor at work was that Waena had been occupied much more intensively, and likely for a longer period of time than either of the other two households. Based on ethnohistoric descriptions of men's sleeping houses (hale mua), I anticipated that these structures would be

TABLE 8.1. Amount of kukui nut endocarp recovered by structure, from the Uka, Waena, and Kai household excavations, Kahikinui.

Household Cluster	Site Number	Description	Function	Kukui Count	Kukui Weight (g)	Excavated Area (m²)
Uka	44	Rectangular enclosure	Unspecified habitation	0	0	13
	45	Linear shelter with terrace	Unspecified habitation	21	1.8	13
	46	U-shaped enclosure	Men's house	0	0	7
	48	L-shaped shelter	Unidentified	0	0	5
Waena	742	Stone alignment	Men's house	1,109	868.6	18
	752-terrace	Terrace with wall	Unspecified habitation	117	30.4	20
	752-imu	Terrace	Earth oven	31	19.1	3
	1011	C-shaped shelter with yard	Earth oven	54	20.5	8
Kai	331	Linear shelter	Men's house	0	0	4
	334	Rectangular enclosure	Postcontact house	5	1.3	3
	335	Rectangular enclosure	Unspecified habitation	17	6.4	4

loci of nighttime activities, and thus characterized by significant kukui deposits. Men's houses were the locations of household shrines where offerings to the family's ancestral spirits ('aumakua) were made. It is the space in which relations between this world and the next were managed. It is where the men of the household slept and ate with their ancestors (Handy and Pukui 1972, 9). Thus, symbolically, these structures were an interface between this world and pō.

This kukui pattern was not borne out, however, and thus offers the opportunity to rethink when and how hale mua might have actually been used, or to rethink how we are currently identifying them in the archaeological record. In the Uka cluster, we interpreted site 46 as a possible hale mua and it contained zero kukui fragments. In the Kai cluster, we interpreted site 331 as a hale mua and it also did not yield any kukui. In the case of site 46, the interpretation was more of an unconfirmed negative. We had hypothesized via ethnohistoric and ethnographic sources, as well as previous excavations, that the hale mua would likely be placed at the highest elevation within the cluster, to honor Polynesian ideals of the relationship between status and height. There was nothing about the structure that contradicted that interpretation. In fact, the presence of slab paving in parts of the interior supported the idea that the structure had been

FIGURE 8.2. *Site 742, partially excavated, Waena household cluster, Kahikinui. (Photo by Cynthia Van Gilder)*

treated with special care. Site 331 was also at a higher elevation than others in the household cluster, but in addition, it contained many pig bones, and pig was a high-status food item reserved for men and the gods.[25] This bolstered our interpretation of this site as a space where men socialized, ate, and made offerings. It was site 742 (figure 8.2) at Waena (once again, the highest site in its cluster), with its lovely offering niche in the northeast corner (figure 8.3), that seemed to be structurally most convincing as a hale mua, although this site did not yield any pig remains.

As the data in table 8.1 illustrate, site 742 contained an extraordinary amount of kukui, even allowing for the amount of area excavated. Hale mua or not, this structure seems clearly to have been the site of extensive nighttime activities. The single living floor of site742 included 6 small-scale combustion features (on average, 50 cm × 50 cm), or concentrations of fire-altered stones set into shallow basin-shaped depressions (figure 8.3). In addition, two features consisting of dark ash and charcoal without associated rocks were found that may represent rake-out from one of the other small hearths. This location seems to have been a site where illumination was key.[26]

Table 8.2 shows only those structures in the Kula survey identified by Kolb and colleagues (1997) as permanent habitation sites in whose test units kukui was recovered. An additional fifty-six structures identified as permanent habitation

FIGURE 8.3. *Site 742, with niche and combustion feature, Waena household cluster, Kahikinui. (Photo by Cynthia Van Gilder)*

sites were tested and no kukui was found.[27] Of the seventeen structures containing kukui, only one (3237 E2) was designated as a possible hale mua, or men's house. Five other structures in the total project area were identified as possible hale mua, although the criteria for identification were different than those used

TABLE 8.2. Kukui nut endocarp recovered by structure (habitation), Kula.

Site number/ Feature number	Description	Function	Kukui Count	Kukui Weight (g)	Excavated Area (m²)
3200 P1	Platform (earthen)	Unspecified habitation	1	0.6	0.25
3217 WT1	Terrace with wall (multiple levels)	Multistructure	1	0.4	0.25
3218 P1	Platform (pebble paved)	Unspecified habitation	1	2.1	0.25
3220 WT1	Terrace with wall	Unspecified habitation	2	5.0	?
3223 WT3	Terrace with wall	Unspecified habitation	25	6.8	10.00
3225 WT1	Terrace with wall	Unspecified habitation	1	0.8	0.25
3237 E2	Rectangular enclosure	Men's house	12	1.1	2.50
WT1	Terrace with wall	Unspecified habitation	43	18.5	1.25
3247 WT1	Terrace with wall	Unspecified habitation	1	0.3	0.25
3259 WT1	Terrace with wall	Unspecified habitation	31	12.2	0.25
3261 WT1	Terrace with wall	Unspecified habitation	1	2.4	0.25
3262 E2	Rectangular enclosure	Unspecified habitation	6	3.9	0.50
3273 E3	Enclosure	Unspecified habitation	1[*]	0.2	?
3275 T1	L-shaped terrace	Unspecified habitation	45	20.6	0.25
3324 WT1	Terrace with wall	Unspecified habitation	1	0.5	0.25
3376 E1	Rectangular enclosure with C-shaped shelter	Multistructure	4	2.7	0.25
3200 WT2	Terrace with wall	Postcontact house	1	0.8	?
WT3	Terrace with wall	Postcontact house	1	1.7	?

in the analysis of the Kahikinui household data. In their discussion of permanent habitation sites, Kolb et al. use comparative size in square meters as the primary (if not only) criterion to identify men's houses (ibid., 104, see also 131). They identify habitation structures with an area within the range of 108 m² to 195

TABLE 8.3. Kukui nut endocarp recovered by ritual structure, Kula.

Site number	Description	Function	Kukui Count	Kukui Weight (g)	Excavated Area (m²)
1038	Notched, terrace with wall	Temple	2	0.2	4.00
1039	Notched enclosure	Temple	2	0.4	1.25
1040	Notched enclosure	Temple	18	2.9	6.25
3332	Notched enclosure	Temple	2	3.8	3.00

m² as possible men's houses (ibid., 104). Again, only one of the five sites identified as possible hale mua yielded kukui in its test unit.

The Kahikinui case study allows us to consider what the distribution of kukui remains might reveal about night activities within individual kauhale (household). In each of the three households considered, large concentrations of kukui are associated with the presence of extensive midden of all kinds. These structures (45, 752 terrace, 335) were each likely a kind of hale noa, or general living structure for the inhabitants where men, women, and children could mix freely. It may be that in Kahikinui, these kapu-free, general structures were the loci of night activities. Although one might have thought that hale mua would have yielded significant deposits of kukui, in only one case did a structure identified as a men's house based on other criteria yield kukui (742).

The Kula case allows us to consider what the distribution of kukui remains might reveal about night activities across a landscape. The pattern of finding kukui in the more intensively occupied, generalized habitation structures was borne out here, with most sites theoretically identified as men's houses containing no kukui (albeit in very small sample test units). In both Kahikinui and Kula, the site morphology most commonly associated with finds of kukui is a "terrace with wall." Structures of this configuration are very commonly associated with habitation sites throughout Maui before the influence of European contact. As a point of interest, none of the sixteen agricultural features tested in Kula contained kukui in its test units. Table 8.3 shows the kukui that was recovered from temple, or heiau, sites.[28] Of the eight sites sampled, four yielded kukui. There are ethnohistoric records of night rituals at temples lit by torches (Malo 1997, Kamakau 1991a), and it is conceivable that in the future, comparison of kukui concentrations might be a way to identify types of temples, or activity areas within heiau.

CONCLUSIONS

The rich ethnohistoric and ethnographic sources of Polynesia provide a record of nightly practices, meanings, and associations. For these islanders, experiences of the night were inextricably tied to their conceptions of the sea and the spirit world. These were places of power, danger, and potential, routinely navigated by both moon and starlight. Polynesians deliberately engaged in a variety of nocturnal activities, both mundane and sacred, from planting to harvesting, fishing, games, and religious rituals. Nights defined the "days," and like other nonindustrial societies, ancient Hawaiians presumably had a much higher tolerance for natural darkness than do modern Westerners. Nonetheless, one of the most surprising outcomes of this preliminary exploration of the archaeology of the night, is that there was not more kukui, or candlenut, debris found inside the excavated living spaces overall. Hawaiians may have relied heavily on hearths and fireplace-related illumination, or have spent the waking times of the dark outside of their household structures. Of course, there is also the nagging suspicion that plagues all archaeologists from time to time: that somehow living floors were being cleaned of daily debris much more thoroughly than we would like to suppose. Regardless, it is worth continuing to pursue an archaeological night vision, so that we can more clearly see what Hawaiians knew to be the source of all, pō.

ACKNOWLEDGMENTS

The St. Mary's College of California Office of Faculty Development helped support a writing retreat to complete a first draft of this chapter. Colleagues Catherine Marachi and Helga Lenart-Chang kindly double-checked my French translations, while Dana Herrera provided citation assistance. Editors Nancy Gonlin and April Nowell were supportive and encouraging. Finally, Anthony Talo helped with figures, formatting, and more, while Caitlyn and Diana patiently waited. Thanks to all!

NOTES

1. I have followed each source's use (or lack of use) of diacritics in the Hawaiian language. Where it is my own usage of a word, I have followed the spellings in Pukui and Elbert's (1986) *Hawaiian Dictionary.*

2. *Kumu* = source; *li-pō* = most profound *pō.*

3. All translations into English are by the author unless otherwise indicated.

4. In Samoa and Tonga (Western Polynesia) daytime and day are used in this manner (*ao,* Samoan; *aho,* Tongan) (Brun and Tetahiotupa 2005, 64).

5. Even today tales of the night marchers (*huaka'i pō*) are not uncommon in Hawai'i (Luomala 1983; Beckwith 1970, 22–24, 164).

6. Linnekin (1985, 40–41) writes that the Hawaiian rules of reciprocity governed relations with dead kinsfolk as well as living.

7. After the Christianizing of Hawai'i (1820), *akua* was used with the singular article *"ke"* to refer to the Christian god. With the plural article *"kau,"* it translates as "the gods." Neither form appears in these expressions.

8. This is quite possibly also invoking the sense of pō as a *kumu* (source or teacher).

9. See Malo 1977 (216–218) for descriptions of *ume and kilu* (nighttime games involving kissing and sometimes trading sex partners), as well as *puhenehene* (nighttime game involving teams and hiding a pebble).

10. Palolo are a kind of sea worm (*Palolo viridis,* also *Eunice viridis*) that spends most of its lifecycle attached to the limestone substrate of the islands' fringing reefs. Once or twice per year, at night, their posterior reproductive parts detach and float to the surface of the water to fertilize. These parts are considered a delicacy when baked into small cakes or eaten on toast.

11. Recent efforts at "cleaning up" the radiocarbon record (i.e., only using the most reliable dates from short-lived wood species, retesting old samples from the 1960s and 1970s, etc.) have resulted in a rethinking of the Hawaiian culture history chronology. Initial colonization of the archipelago is now believed to have occurred no earlier than 1000 CE, greatly shortening and intensifying the development of a unique Hawaiian culture (see Kirch 2011 for a summary).

12. Ekirch (2006, 4) claims that the artist Paul Gauguin found that Tahitian women do not sleep at night. I could find no evidence for this claim in the ethnographies and ethnohistories I consulted, but wonder if perhaps this was a case of segmented sleep patterns that were misunderstood by an outsider.

13. *Kapa* and *tapa* are cognate words referring to cloth made from the pounded bark of the paper mulberry tree (*Brousonnetia papyrifera*).

14. Buck references William T. Brigham's 1902 publication: "Stone Implements and Stone Work of the Ancient Hawaiians," *Memoirs of the Bernice Pauahi Bishop Museum,* vol. 1, no. 4. Honolulu, HI: Bishop Museum Press.

15. Similarly, whole basalt poi pounders are not rarely found very often in archaeological contexts, although all indications are that they were a common household implement.

16. *Poho* indicates a hollow or receptacle.

17. From his notes to Malo's *Mo'olelo Hawai'i: Hawaiian Antiquities.*

18. Viewers of the Disney animated film, *Moana* (2016), can see depictions of kukui torches and lamps in several scenes.

19. Although kukui was occasionally eaten, particularly in small amounts as a relish, it was much more commonly used to burn for the resulting light. In English it is referred to as candlenut.

20. See also Van Gilder 2001, 2005.

21. For more information on the Kahikinui Archaeological Project see Kirch and Van Gilder 1996; Van Gilder and Kirch 1997; Kirch 1997, Kirch 2014.

22. These excavations were completed in association with the Oceanic Archaeology Laboratory, University of California, Berkeley.

23. No excavations were undertaken in two structures in the Kai household for cultural sensitivity reasons. One of these appeared to be a sacred fishing shrine and the other appeared to include a post–AD 1800 intrusive burial.

24. For complete radiocarbon information, see Van Gilder 2005 and Kirch 2014.

25. Hawaiians were known to have practiced an eating taboo called the 'ai kapu. The terms of the 'ai kapu made certain foods taboo to women and others taboo to men. Additionally, men's and women's food were meant to be cooked separately (even if it was a non-taboo food, such as sweet potato) and eaten in gender-segregated eating houses. Young boys and girls ate with the women until the boys came of age and went to eat with the men. There were periods of the ritual calendar when the taboos were temporarily lifted. One of the most famous taboos was the consumption of pork by women. The 'ai kapu was officially abolished by Queen Ka'ahumanu in 1819.

26. In the Uka household, site 45 contained two slab-lined hearths, site 44 had one slab-lined hearth, while sites 46 and 48 had no evidence of combustion features. In the Waena household, site 742 is discussed above, 752-terrace also contained two slab-lined hearths, while sites 752-imu and 1011 both included extensive earth ovens. In the Kai household, only site 331 showed evidence of a combustion feature involving *in situ* burning, but no formal hearth or burnt rock. For more discussions of hearths and their significance to Hawaiian household organization, see Van Gilder 2001, 2005.

27. The total number of permanent habitation structures tested was seventy-three (Kolb et al. 1997, 87).

28. The project area was extended to include testing several historically known temple sites.

REFERENCES

Beckwith, Martha Warren. 1970. *Hawaiian Mythology*. Honolulu: University of Hawai'i Press.

Beckwith, Martha Warren. 1972 [1951]. *The Kumulipo: A Hawaiian Creation Chant*. Honolulu: University of Hawai'i Press.

Brun, Michel, and Edgar Tetahiotupa. 2005. "Réflexion sur Pō: jour et nuit." *Bulletin de la Société des Etudes Océaniennes (Polynesie Orientale)* 303/304:63–85.

Buck, Peter H. 1993 [1957]. *Arts and Crafts of Hawaii: Houses*. Honolulu, HI: Bishop Museum Press.

Chambers, Keith Stanley, and Anne Chambers. 2001. *Unity of Heart: Culture and Change in a Polynesian Atoll Society*. Long Grove, IL: Waveland Press.

Chauvin, Michael E. 2000. "Useful and Conceptual Astronomy in Ancient Hawai'i." In *Astronomy across Cultures: The History of Non-Western Astronomy*, ed. Helaine Selin and Xiaochun Sun, 91–125. Boston: Kluwer Academic. https://doi.org/10.1007/978-94-011-4179-6_4.

Ekirch, Roger A. 2006. *At Day's Close: Night in Times Past*. New York: W.W. Norton.

Emerson, Nathaniel. 1909. *Unwritten Literature of Hawaii*. Washington, DC: Government Printing Office.

Finney, Ben R. 1979. *Hokule'a: The Way to Tahiti*. New York: Dodd, Mead.

Finney, Ben R. 2004. *Sailing in the Wake of the Ancestors: Reviving Polynesian Voyaging.* Honolulu, HI: Bernice P. Bishop Museum Press.

Firth, Raymond. 1983 [1936]. *We, the Tikopia: A Sociological Study of Kinship in Primitive Polynesia.* Palo Alto, CA: Stanford University Press.

Galinier, Jacques, Aurore Monod Becquelin, Guy Bordin, Laurent Fontaine, Francine Fourmaux, Juliette Roullet Ponce, Piero Salzarulo, Philippe Simonnot, Michèle Therrien, and Iole Zilli. 2010. "Anthropology of the Night: Cross-Disciplinary Investigations." *Current Anthropology* 51(6):819–847. https://doi.org/10.1086/653691.

Gill, Timothy M., Patrick V. Kirch, Clive Ruggles, and Alexander Baer. 2015. "Ideology, Ceremony, and Calendar in Pre-Contact Hawai'i: Astronomical Alignment of a Stone Enclosure on O'ahu Suggests Ceremonial Use during the Makahiki Season." *Journal of the Polynesian Society (N. Z.)* 124(3):243–268. https://doi.org/10.15286/jps.124 .3.243-268.

Handy, E. S. Craighill, and Elizabeth Green Handy. 1991 [1972]. *Native Planters in Old Hawaii: Their Life, Lore, and Environment.* Honolulu: University of Hawai'i Press.

Handy, E. S. Craighill, and Mary Kawena Pukui. 1972 [1958]. *The Polynesian Family System in Ka-'U, Hawaii.* Rutland, VT: Tuttle Publishing.

Kamakau, Samuel M. 1991a. *Tales and Traditions of the People of Old: Nā Mo'olelo a Ka Po'e Kahiko.* Trans. Mary Kawena Pukui, ed. Dorothy Barrère. Honolulu: University of Hawai'i Press.

Kamakau, Samuel M. 1991b [1964]. *The People of Old: Ka Po'e Kahiko.* Trans. Mary Kawena Pukui, ed. Dorothy B. Barrère. Honolulu: University of Hawai'i Press.

Kamakau, Samuel M. 1992 [1976]. *The Works of the People of Old: Na Hana a Ka Po'e Kahiko.* trans. Mary Kawena Pukui, ed. Dorothy B. Barrère. Honolulu: University of Hawai'i Press.

Kirch, Patrick. 2004. "Temple Sites in Kahikinui, Maui, Hawaiian Islands: Their Orientations Decoded." *Antiquity* 78(299):102–114. https://doi.org/10.1017/S0003598 X00092966.

Kirch, Patrick V., ed. 1997. *Na Mea Kahiko o Kahikinui: Studies in the Archaeology of Kahikinui, Maui, Hawaiian Islands.* Oceanic Archaeological Laboratory, Special Publication No. 1. Berkeley: Archaeological Research Facility.

Kirch, Patrick V. 2011. "When Did the Polynesians Settle Hawai'i? A Review of 150 Years of Scholarly Inquiry and a Tentative Answer." *Hawaiian Archaeology* 12:1–26.

Kirch, Patrick V. 2014. *Kua'āina Kahiko: Life and Land in Ancient Kahikinui, Maui.* Honolulu: University of Hawai'i Press. https://doi.org/10.21313/haw aii/9780824839550.001.0001.

Kirch, Patrick V., and Roger C. Green. 2001. *Hawaiki, Ancestral Polynesia: An Essay in Historical Anthropology.* Cambridge: Cambridge University Press. https://doi.org /10.1017/CBO9780511613678.

Kirch, Patrick V., Clive Ruggles, and Warren D. Sharp. 2013. "The *Pānānā* or 'Sighting Wall' at Hanamauloa, Kahikinui, Maui: Archaeological Investigation of a Possible Navigational Monument." *Journal of the Polynesian Society (N. Z.)* 122(1):45–68. https://doi.org/10.15286/jps.122.1.45-68.

Kirch, Patrick V., and Cynthia L. Van Gilder. 1996. "Pre-Contact and Early Historic Cultural Landscapes in Kahikinui District, Maui: A Progress Report." *Hawaiian Archaeology* 5:38–52.

Kolb, Michael J., Patty J. Conte, and Ross Cordy, eds. 1997. *Kula: The Archaeology of Upcountry Maui in Waiohuli and Keokea*. Historic Preservation Division, Department of Land and Natural Resources. Report prepared for The Department of Hawaiian Home Lands.

Krauss, Beatrice H. 1993. *Plants in Hawaiian Culture*. Honolulu: University of Hawai'i Press.

Levy, Robert I. 1973. *Tahitians: Mind and Experience in the Society Islands*. Chicago: University of Chicago Press.

Lewis, David. 1994 [1972]. *We, the Navigators: The Ancient Art of Landfinding in the Pacific*. Honolulu: University of Hawai'i Press.

Linnekin, Jocelyn. 1985. *Children of the Land: Exchange and Status in a Hawaiian Community*. New Brunswick, NJ: Rutgers University Press.

Luomala, Katherine. 1983. "Phantom Night Marchers in the Hawaiian Islands." *Pacific Studies* 7(1):1–33.

Malo, David. 1997 [1903]. *Hawaiian Antiquities: Mo'olelo Hawai'i*. Trans. and annotated by Nathaniel B. Emerson. Honolulu: Bernice P. Bishop Museum Press.

Mead, Margaret. 2001 [1928]. *Coming of Age in Samoa: A Psychological Study of Primitive Youth for Western Civilisation*. New York: Harper Collins Publishers.

Pukui, Mary Kawena. 1997 [1983]. *Ōlelo No'Eau: Hawaiian Proverbs and Poetical Sayings*. Honolulu: University of Hawai'i Press.

Pukui, Mary Kawena, and Samuel H. Elbert, eds. 1986. *Hawaiian Dictionary: Hawaiian-English and English-Hawaiian*. Honolulu: University of Hawai'i Press.

Pukui, Mary Kawena. E. W. Haertig, and Catherine A. Lee. 1972. *Nana I Ke Kumu (Look to the Source)*, Volume I. Honolulu, HI: The Queen Lili'uokalani Children's Center.

Smetzer, Barbara. 1969. "Night of the Palolo." *Natural History* 78:64–71.

Tregear, E. 1969 [1891]. *The Maori-Polynesian Comparative Dictionary*. Netherlands: Anthropological Publications.

Van Gilder, Cynthia L. 2001. "Gender and Household Archaeology in Kahikinui, Maui." In *Proceedings of the Fifth International Conference on Easter Island and the Pacific*, ed. Christopher Stevenson, Georgia Lee, and F. J. Morin, 135–140. Los Osos, CA: Bearsville Press.

Van Gilder, Cynthia L. 2005. "Families on the Land: Archaeology and Identity in Kahikinui, Maui." PhD diss., University of California, Berkeley.

Van Gilder, Cynthia L., and Patrick Kirch. 1997. "Household Archaeology in the Ahupua'a of Kipapa and Nakaohu." In *Na Mea Kahiko o Kahikinui: Studies in the Archaeology of Kahikinui, Maui, Hawaiian Islands*, ed. Patrick V. Kirch, 45–60. Oceanic Archaeological Laboratory, Special Publication No. 1. Berkeley, CA: Archaeological Research Facility.

Nocturnal Ritual and Ideology

Night Moon Rituals

The Effects of Darkness and Prolonged Ritual on Chilean Mapuche Participants

TOM D. DILLEHAY

In recent years, the material signatures and the inferred meanings of public ritual in archaeological contexts have become major themes of study (e.g., Bell 2007; Kyriakidis 2007; Mithen 1997; Romain 2009). Archaeologists presume that some type of ritual behavior was associated with preindustrial "sacred places" and with large edifices displaying esoteric symbols used by elites to legitimize authority and power. It also is believed that a wide variety of ancient rituals were associated with human sacrifices, cremations, burials, and particularly with the elaborate tombs of important individuals. No doubt, rituals constituted a repetitive and widespread communal religious and political practice in ancient societies. Yet, the inferred material recognition of past ritual behavior is one thing, but interpreting its specific function and meaning is much more difficult: many aspects of ritual are not clearly expressed empirically, and they often produce patterning similar to that associated with nonritual practices, such as food preparation and consumption, the use of open spaces for various nonritual activities, and the work of small, specialized task groups. Studies of rituals vary widely in topic, method, and theory, with most focused on their relation to elite power

DOI: 10.5876/9781607326786.c009

and authority, others on amassing corporate labor for the construction of mon-umental projects, and so forth. Little archaeological attention has been given to the less-empirical aspects of ritual such as differences between daytime and nighttime activities and the emotion, sensory arousal, and psychological effects of ritual participation, and its symbolic and performative meanings among sha-mans and other figures (see Nowell, chapter 2, this volume). Obviously, these are difficult topics to study in material-oriented archaeology, and as Binford (1972, 127) has noted, "archaeologists are poorly trained to be paleo-psychologists." Despite this reservation, we still need to examine rituals in varied contexts and by different methods and concepts.

In articulating knowledge concerned with the material past, archaeology has to show things. It is not enough for us to just talk about the material world; it has to be visually demonstrated in artifacts, texts, maps, diagrams, illustrations, and photographs (e.g., Frieman and Gillings 2007; Llobera 1999; Mithen 1997; Renfrew and Scarre 1998; Skeates 2010). In archaeological analyses, these media are assumed most often to relate to the material record of daytime activities. While sight and vision are fundamental qualities of the material world, archae-ology has taken little interest in the other senses (e.g., smell, hearing, taste, touch), especially as they relate to the ritual behavior and meaning of nighttime activities. It is understandable why these less visible and detectable properties of past human behavior are neglected in archaeology. However, topics such as the differences between daytime and nighttime practices and the differential effects of ritual on shamans and non-shamanic participants provide an occasion to reconsider several issues concerning a range of senses, symbolism, altered states of consciousness, gender, authority, social power, and their relevance to the archaeological past.

There has been increased commentary in the anthropological and recently the archaeological literature about the neurological, symbolic, behavioral, emo-tional, perceptual, performative, and psychological effects (e.g., altered states of consciousness) of religious rituals on people, including shamans and other ritual leaders (e.g., Barrett and Lawson 2001; Boyer 1994; Boyer and Liénard 2006; Conan 2010; Johnson 2007; McCauley 2001; Romain 2009; Winkelman 2002, 2004). However, the effects of the physical and cognitive conditions of ritual on the senses, emotions, and behaviors of non-shamanic participants have received little scientific attention. A few studies, including McCauley and Lawson (2007, 237; cf. D'Aquili 1993; Laughlin 1996; Taheri 2007), have noted that the primary "means for producing arousal in ritual is to stimulate participants' senses in order to excite their emotions and to get them involved in the activity itself." However, the large majority of these studies center on daytime rituals. It is known that people participating in daytime rituals focus more on their senses of sight and sound and less on smell, touch, and taste. Nighttime rituals, often in less-familiar settings and with groups of people, however, require participants in the dark to *relearn* how to see and hear at the same time through the complementary modes of sensory engagement from smell and from the touch of nearby people (e.g., dance partners, marchers aligned in procession). In other words, other senses are required to excite emotion and involvement at night.

In this chapter, the primary concern is the effects of nighttime ritual on participants from an Andean region of South America (figures 1.2 and 9.1). The case study is the Mapuche people of south-central Chile who perform rituals under the full moon to communicate with important deities and ancestors and, in the case of female shamans, to implicitly reiterate equivalency and complementarity of political power with male secular leaders (Bacigalupo 1996, 2001, 2007; Dillehay 1985, 2007). Although this essay is not specifically about female shamans and power, these variables play into the agency and significance of the rituals discussed here. Also discussed briefly is an archaeological case: the 7500–4000 cal BP artificial mound site of Huaca Prieta (figure 1.3) on the north coast of Peru, where a dense accumulation of charcoal resulting from frequent fires and the use of torches formed a major part of the site and are believed to be associated with nighttime rituals (Dillehay et al. 2012). In both cases, I present more descriptive information than conceptual and cross-cultural insight, and briefly address their wider sociocultural implications for material and ritual studies in archaeology.

THE MAPUCHE

Today, the Mapuche number between seven and eight hundred thousand in south-central Chile and are the largest indigenous group in southern South America (INE 2010), with approximately half living on scattered *reducciones*, or indigenous lands (Faron 1962; Crow 2013; Dillehay 1985). About thirty thousand more Mapuche live in the Andean mountains to the east in Argentina. It was not until the end of the 1890s that the Mapuche were defeated by the Chilean and Argentine armies and confined to these lands (Bengoa 2003) where they have since suffered various atrocities and loss of social and resource rights. Although the rural Mapuche today are different from their late prehispanic and colonial ancestors, they still perform traditional public ceremonies where political and social issues are resolved and where they propitiate the deities and worship important ancestors. Despite profound historical changes in their society over the past few hundred years, in some areas there still are basic characteristics of the traditional Mapuche lifeway that have not been completely affected by these changes: for instance, kinship ideologies, land use and subsistence patterns, ethnic identity, and religion and cosmology (Dillehay 2007; Trentini et al. 2010). Traditional Mapuche were and still are a patrilineal, patrilocal, and bilateral society that resides in dispersed communities (Faron 1962). In the anthropological literature, the historical Mapuche are best known as mixed economists—*piñón* collectors

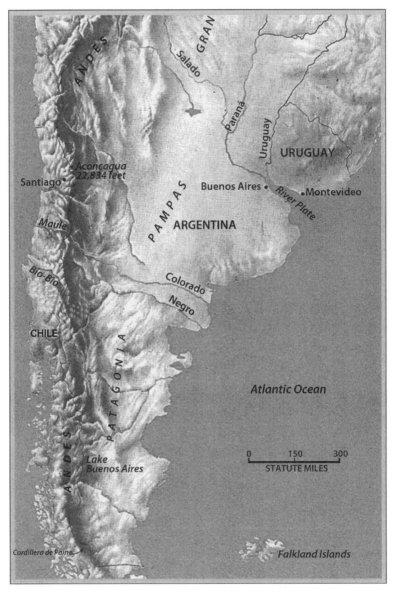

FIGURE 9.1. *The study area of the southern Andean region of South America.*

in the Andean highlands, and fisherfolk, hunters, gatherers, and horticulturalists in the central valley and foothills of the Andes in Chile and Argentina and along the Chilean Pacific coast. Past political organization was characterized by small to large autonomous "chiefdoms," except in times of war with the Spanish and Chileans, when more formally semicentralized polities formed to defend their lands. Today, the Mapuche continue to defend their lands and their ethnic rights, both through political demonstrations and public ceremonies and rituals.

During the sixteenth to nineteenth centuries, the transition from initial contact with the Spanish to widespread organized resistance by the Mapuche was marked by local centralization of political power at the *lof* (local patrilineal community) and *regua* (multipatrilineal communities) levels but regional noncentralization at the *ayllaregua* (multi-*regua* at the regional scale) and *butanmapu* (multi-*ayllaregua* at the interregional scale) levels. I say noncentralization because centralized political power among the Mapuche at the broader territorial level and at a specific center of government never existed, although they had an effective system of self-governance at all levels and designated regions of primary military operation. Political power, authority, and leadership within the historical warring Mapuche society were derived primarily from resistance and resilience and were linked to an assertion of absolute defense of their homeland, with the legitimacy of rule based on patriarchy, ancestor worship, religion, and large-scale public ceremonies. Public ceremonies performed during the day and night were highly significant events that solidified intergroup political alliances and developed the leadership skills of both secular and sacred leaders.

Changes in the countryside during wars with the Spanish and Chileans forced many Mapuche to eventually think and act beyond their own local kinship network and community affairs. The changing population and political conditions of war exacerbated social cleavages and altered the demographic dynamics in many communities. These conditions spurred the rapid appearance of new agencies of change such as a stratum of war leaders (*quen-toqui*), a stratum of warriors (*cona*), a stratum of new ritual leaders (machi, a term referring to both female and male shamans), and larger and more frequent public ceremonies (e.g., *coyantun, nguillatun, cahuin*) (figure 9.2), now organized to bring about greater political solidarity through the dual authoritative roles of secular chiefly leaders and sacred shamanic and priestly leaders, and widespread conscription in a new and growing ethnic consciousness (ethnogenesis and ethnomorphosis) and identity within the society at large (Boccara 1999; Leiva 1977; Bengoa 2003; Zavala Cepeda 2008; Dillehay 2016).

For reasons not well understood, the vast majority of shamanic leaders in modern times are female machi. Although all machi perform healing rites, the more respected and authoritative ones have detailed knowledge of the cosmological and religious world, which they employ during ceremonies to appease deities and ancestors and to engage the public in religious and political discourse. These practices provide machi with an external and unique source of power less available to secular leaders.

In summary, the Mapuche of the late prehispanic and colonial periods were not a unified, sovereign body, because they never attained a centralized political function and a formal territorial or state boundary. However, they had a clear and

FIGURE 9.2. *Large-scale, daytime nguillatun fertility ceremony at Rucalleco. (Photo by Tom Dillehay)*

coherent project to defend their independence, their ethnic integrity, and their governance system. This system was a "networking arrangement" of transterritorial, supraethnic, and interinstitutional leaders. It was a system that employed numerous large-scale public ceremonies to maintain religious, political, and social cohesion across fragmented territories and shifting alliances. It constantly reminded people of the strict adherence of *admapu* (ancestral customs) and the Mapuche way of doing things, discouraging the adoption of European ideas, goods, and technologies. (The exception here is the immediate adoption of the horse, some weaponry, and certain food crops such as wheat and barley from the sixteenth to the nineteenth centuries.) Thus, what best defines this population historically was not its unfettered independence or its legitimate use of violence to defend itself and its territory, as some traditional Western definitions might have it, but those everyday routines, rituals, activities, decisions, customs, religious beliefs, and policies that regulated the social making of meaning and of patriotic ethnic subjects. Many of these traditions still continue today, especially in regard to public ceremony, religious beliefs, and shamanic practices of machi.

NIGHTTIME RITUALS AND THEIR EFFECTS ON PARTICIPANTS

In this section, I briefly summarize the social and gender power of shamans, the observed effects of nighttime activity on the bodily senses of ritual participants, and how these effects influence people's support of shamanistic actions and people's belief in important deities, ancestors, and spirits whose existence regulates and depends upon human conduct and offerings. As noted above, the Mapuche continue to engage in both daytime and nighttime rituals for various purposes, including fertility, appeasement to deities for goodwill and well-being, social and political solidarity, and so forth. Traditionally, daytime rituals are administered by secular leaders (e.g., *lonkos*, *nguilltufes*) who are always men. Machi participate in daytime rituals but usually in a performative role through chanting and dancing. Shamans almost always lead nighttime rituals, which are usually performed under the light of a full or crescent moon, unless it is cloudy, but even then the moon is referenced and worshipped. Although the visual sighting of and reference to the moon are important, female machi draw not only on the power of the moon but also of the earth, water, air, and fire. To machi, the moon is more receptive to human petitions; it is life and it defends people (see Bacigalupo 2001). During traditional nighttime rituals, shamans light bamboo canes or branches of the sacred *canelo* or *foye* tree (*Drimys winteris*), often tipped with tree resin for burning, and make offerings of burning foye leaves. They sometimes smoke black tobacco to call on the combined power of the moon, fire, and smoke, and two fertility goddesses, *Kuyen-Kushe* and *Kuyen-Ulcha Domo* (see Bacigalupo 1996, 2007). During these rituals, female machi officiate as moon priestesses who obtain fertility and social power from the moon for the well-being of all.

Over the past forty years, I have participated in and conducted ethnographic and ethnoarcheological research on more than forty Mapuche daytime and nighttime rituals ranging from large-scale fertility rites (e.g., nguillatun) attended by several thousand people to small-scale shaman initiation rites (e.g., *rucatun*, *machitun*) practiced by ten to twenty persons. This is not the place to discuss the research problems, interdisciplinary methods, and concepts that my colleagues and I have employed to study these rituals; instead, the reader is referred to prior publications (Dillehay 1985, 2007). (I should note that most of these studies were in the late 1970s to early 2000s, when traditional rituals were more frequent. In recent years, due to the influence from evangelical movements, fewer shamans and participants are involved and many rituals have become less traditional or have disappeared.)

As a result of participating in these rituals, I have seen and personally experienced the effects of nighttime rituals on the human body, which can include overstimulation from song and dance, sleep deprivation and fatigue, drowsiness due to smoke inhalation from fires, and other external stimuli. Depending on a person's level of participation and on their mental and physical condition, these stimuli can lead to lethargy, daydreaming, and hallucination (Freeman 2000; Knight 2003; McCauley 1999; Taheri 2007; Tremlin 2006; Whitehouse and Martin 2004).

Specialists such as D'Aquili and colleagues (1979) assert that ritual accomplishes two important biological feats (see also Rappaport 1999; Turner 1987). First, it coordinates the neural systems and functions of ritual participants to allow for group action. That is, ritual behavior for most human and nonhuman species seems to be a way of overcoming social distance between individuals so that they can coordinate their activity in a way that would help the species survive environmentally, politically, or biologically. Mating rituals among certain animal species are the most obvious examples of this behavior, but ritual activity before coordinated group attacks or hunts are also common (D'Aquili 1993). Wolf packs, for example, go through ritual tail-wagging sessions and group howls, and ritual aggression among primates establishes social order and rank for possible battle (Avital and Jablonka 2000). The rhythmic and repetitious nature of ritual stimulation in both nonhumans and humans, through ear, eye, or bodily motion, increases a sense of unity of purpose between individuals. Further, it is thought to lead to coordinated arousal or discharge of the brain's limbic system, producing a sense of profound unity within the participants (Ashbrook and Albright 1997; Grimes 1995; Joseph 2002; Lakoff 1987; Mithen 1997; Pyysiäinen 2003). The second biological achievement of ritual is that it causes cognitive development or socialization within the individual organism. That is, ritual is "a mechanism for entraining and transforming the structure of the neuromotor subsystems in the developing organism" (D'Aquili et al. 1979, 37). Ritual teaches the younger members of the species what is important and how to behave in public.

To summarize, a cautionary point is in order here. As I venture into a topic unknown to me—the biology and neurophysiology of ritual activity—as an anthropological archaeologist, it is important for me to be aware of the temptation to move too easily from scientific accounts of the mind/brain to behavioral applications in Mapuche ethnography and back. In this case study, it is hard to resist the desire to take something I have observed in the field or have learned through readings about the science of the mind/brain and immediately hypothesize how certain kinds of ritual settings may stimulate certain mind/brain functions and how this may give rise to certain beliefs, myths, or religious patterns and ritual performances (D'Aquili 1993; Lawson and McCauley 1990; Laughlin 2009; McCauley 1999; McCauley and Lawson 2002, 2007). I refrain from this type of speculation. However, I make some observations and simply attempt to relate them to certain variables that I believe reveal some insight into the effects of nighttime rituals on shamans and participants and what this perception might mean to archaeology.

SHAMANS, PARTICIPANTS, AND THE EFFECTS OF RITUAL

Powerful machi often use light to mild altered states of consciousness (ASC) during public ritual to access non-ordinary reality to gain information and social power and to manipulate life forces and spirit entities (Dillehay 2007; Bacigalupo 2007). Although there are different scholarly opinions about the alleged ASC under which shamans perform rituals (Bahn 2001; Romain 2009; Tedlock 2005; Winkelman 2002), it seems that some machi can genuinely self-induce a light to moderate "diagnostic state" of ASC that can embody their spirits (filu). I have never observed these states induced by ingestion of any type of external mind-altering substances (e.g., *Latua publiflora, Datura* sp.). More specifically, most shamans, many of whom are forty-five to sixty years of age, have remarkable stamina that allows them to chant, sing, dance, pray, and lead ritual for several continuous hours under the physical and mental conditions described here. Machi inform us that it is the trance itself that helps them to concentrate their minds on the physical and mental requirements of prolonged ritual and the stamina to overcome fatigue. Once the multiday ritual ends, machi require solitude and rest for several days.

These conditions are somewhat different for non-shamanic participants. During nighttime rituals Mapuche informants tell us that to hear noise or even to sense silence in the dark is to hear or to imagine hearing things, some of which are not identifiable because they cannot be seen or directly engaged. This element adds a powerful esoteric, if not ethereal, sense to ritual that is rarely experienced during the daytime. When the body and mind are fatigued and in rhythm with dance, and music and chanting, some background noise such as the wind or the crackling of a distant fire, or the breathing of participants is resistant to the flow and meaning of real time and place. These sounds are seemingly limitless, continuous, unending, and unchanging and define their own perception and experience.

Mental fatigue and light or mild hallucinations from sleep deprivation, prolonged dancing and standing, chanting, excessive smoke exposure (smoke also affects the quality of nighttime photography, rendering images too fuzzy and unclear to reproduce here; camera flashes are strictly prohibited), and other factors are real during prolonged rituals. It is well documented that a common side effect of sleep deprivation is hallucination, as evidenced by, but not limited to, long-distance swimmers, ultramarathon runners, overly ambitious college students studying all night, ritual all-nighters, and others who excessively exert themselves (see D'Aquili 1993). According to one study (Alhola and Polo-Kantola 2007), at least 80% of people exhausted by excessive exercise or sleep deprivation will hallucinate if severely sleep deprived ("severe" meaning anything from getting only a few hours of sleep in a single night to going days without sleeping). Given such a high frequency, there seems to be a physiological basis for all-nighters that can induce in some people lethargic behavior, visions, or mild hallucinations of things not really there. In consulting with two neurologists familiar with the Mapuche, Enrique Edwards and Juan Liendo (personal communication, 1999–2002 and 2007–2011, respectively) and in interviewing Mapuche ritual participants, my colleagues and I have learned that prolonged ritual activity (generally 3–4 days), which involves interrupted or deprived sleep and light eating and excessive drinking (for some individuals), can invariably affect the human senses, often bringing about marked fatigue, restlessness, hallucinations, and blurred cognitive boundaries, especially during the night.

Based on observations provided by neurologists and informants, we believe that ritual in the dark transforms the sensibilities so that sensory perception is more centered upon hearing, smelling, and touching than upon seeing. The neurologists believe that nighttime ritual also brings about a more pronounced "mutualistic proprioception" of the world (e.g., Proske and Gandevia 2009; Robles De La Torre 2006). In other words, people's meaning and experience are derived not only from their own individual relative physical position in ritual, which is more defined during the daytime, but from the strength of effort they employ with other participants in their coordinated movement within the visually limited, dark world around them. That is, a person's mind/brain integrates information from the collective proprioception and from the vestibular system (the sensory system that provides a sense of balance and spatial orientation) for the purpose of coordinating movement with balance into an overall sense of body position and movement with others. Ultimately, this type of codependency among participants seems to produce greater social bonding and more arousal and probably "crowd control" by the shamans.

Although similar altered physical and mental states may take place during daytime rituals, their effects on Mapuche participants (including the author) are more accentuated in the total darkness of the night or under cloudy moonlight. There is no doubt that darkness connects people to deeper textures of the material world and qualities of corporeal experience. During nighttime ritual, people attempt to survey their surroundings with their ever-receptive ears and with their stumbling and bumping of others. Hearing and touching thus become the primary nighttime senses for detecting immediate and adjacent events and things. The multitude of sounds produced by companion elements, the wind, the trees, flowing water, animals, or other humans, the crackling of a distant bonfire, if present, all are factors in their activities.

In summary, the effects of intermittent ritual chanting, singing, marching, dancing, drum beating, and other activities for several days and nights are enhanced even more in the dark under a distant light source drawn from a full to partial moon or from large to small bonfires and from the effects of smoke and often fatigue. Most rituals at night take place in the dark or under limited moonlight. Fires are lighted during only certain times of rituals, which is usually in the early morning. Rhythmic singing, chanting, marching, and dancing can bring about low-level or semi-ASC not only among shamans but also among participants, depending upon their emotional, psychological, and physical conditions. By limiting and scheduling people's drink, food, and sleep, by the constant noise and movement of people, and by continuously exposing them to smoke and fatigue over several days, machi shamans help to facilitate varying degrees of physical and mental fatigue and, in some cases, mild hallucination, despair, and/or distorted cognition.

As was (and still is in a few areas) the case traditionally, the effects of prolonged rhythmic stimulation, regulated in ritual through these and other activities for three to four days, can change the focus of people's awareness. The incorporation of body movements in time to rhythmic beats in the dark can tend to negate a person's awareness of directional time and to abrogate historical time and oriented space. People singing, chanting, dancing, and marching together in the dark must rely on sound and the touch of the persons next to them for spatial orientation. This type of nighttime activity also can blur cognitive boundaries and the boundaries between the past and present and the real and unreal worlds. This mode of ritual engagement can take the form of what Pearson and Shanks (2013, 17) call "deep maps," which are rich collations and juxtapositions of the past and "the contemporary, the political and the poetic, the factual and the fictional, the discursive and the sensual; the conflation of oral testimony, anthology, memoir, biography, natural history and place."

Shamanic Influence

Machi can intentionally or unintentionally alter, to various degrees, the physical state and consciousness of the ritual participants in order to gain sociopolitical and religious sensibilities, if not support, and to strengthen the spiritual ties between the living, the dead, and the deities. In the shaman's universe, the ordinary world is intertwined with the invisible, ethereal world of important spirits, souls, gods, demons, ancestors, and other figures. The shamanistic manipulation of life forces and of the ritual public is usually for the purpose of bringing about changes in the world, such as improved food production, desired political outcomes, sustained relations with deities and ancestors, and restored cosmic and social order. This manipulation is often best achieved during the nighttime because this is when machi are perceived to be most powerful and without interference from or competition with secular leaders. The night belongs to the shamans.

Rituals provide the context for shamans to be more powerful, ethereal, and more influential as they speak to issues of the past and to Mapuche survival in the future. Post-ritual interviews with participants relate that they do not remember too much of the physical details of the ritual field, perhaps because they did not see them well or because they had mild to semi-ASC due to fatigue and symbolic overload, nor can they detail the specific messages of the shaman's discourses during nighttime rituals. They state that they do recall the overwhelming presence and cosmological position of shamans, their chanting and drum beats, how their own well-being and behavior were altered and regulated as a result of the complex entanglement of continuous dancing, chanting, and other activities and of the combined sights, sounds, smells, and tastes of nighttime rituals under the moonlight.

Yet, these shamanistic moonlight rituals are not just about religious discourse and the social bonding of the living and of the living and the dead. They also concern the display and complementarity of male secular and female sacred powers. Many female shamans officiating over nighttime rituals directly or indirectly seek to create gender equivalency through a complementarity in the balance of power. Female machi do not compete directly with male authorities, who perform during the daytime at multiday public ceremonies and who have considerable political jurisdiction in the secular political world. Female shamans complement their male counterparts through religious and ritual practices primarily at night and through support provided by the spiritual and ancestral world. Today, female machi also participate in Mapuche resistance movements because the recovery of ancestral lands, ancient forests, and traditions is central to their livelihoods and spiritual practices. The knowledge of all machi and their connections with spirit forces offer powerful symbolic tools for pursuing political goals alongside secular male leaders. But to gain and exercise this power, people must believe in spiritual forces and this is where the ritual practice of machi shamans during the nighttime moon is a significant influence on the thoughts and beliefs (*rakiduam*) and hearts (*piuke*) of participants.

While the beliefs, emotions, and other physical and mental aspects are not the agents of ritual, they define the necessary conditions for the success of machi as agents of ritual actions and sociopolitical influence. Public ritual and ceremony can be the primary context through which female shamans gain and demonstrate their power in the form of orations, and display of esoteric ancestral and cosmological knowledge. Public venues in more secular contexts where men traditionally perform are not infrequently available to female shamans, although more females are beginning to move into these contexts as a result of the "shamanization of Mapuche politics," rights, and identities (see Bacigalupo 2007, 249). As Bacigalupo (2007, 240–250) has described in her studies of female shamans, "in practice, both Mapuche men and women have gained prestige by holding positions of power external to their communities and by acting as intermediaries between Mapuche communities and government and politicians, in both the past and present . . . Female machi use their spiritual approach to politics to propitiate, honor, and manipulate politicians for good, evil, or pragmatic ends . . . As symbols of tradition and domesticity, female machi can sustain spiritual readings of power independently from male-dominant political ideologies and can legitimate a variety of gender-transgressive practices." Set in this context, female machi externalize their authority and power and locate it within the night under the spiritual power of the moon and in discourse with powerful deities and ancestors in the world above (*wenumapu*). In the absence of other sources of power, this external source is powerful. As Bell (2007, 286–87) contends, "ritual is the thing to do when one is negotiating for authority, and when the power that one needs to tap must have an extra-communal source. Yet everyone has to be empowered in some way or to some extent by such an appeal in order to bring power into the community from outside it. You do ritual when you are not exercising other forms of authority, control, or coercion." Empowerment for the female shamans comes from ritual performances connected to the authority of the deities and ancestors.

Material Signatures

Understanding the material and nonmaterial world of nighttime ritual calls for different modes of archaeological engagement and articulation. In the ethnographic case of the Mapuche, small campfires and large bonfires, ranging between 3 m and 7 m in diameter, serve as staging areas and ritual places associated with nighttime rituals. During daytime rituals, fires usually are no larger than 1.5–2.0 m, and these are associated with cooking by multiple families sharing hearth and food. Hearths and bonfires during the night tend to be around the edges of C- or U-shaped dance and procession plazas, while cooking hearths are aligned by families in rows around the edges of plazas. Furthermore, during night rituals only about 40–50% of the ritual spaces are used because participants aggregate closer by holding hands or sensing each other's presence in the dark, which facilitates more shared movement in the dark. During the daytime, the entire plaza is used and participants are more spatially structured in terms of dancers, machi, and so forth.

As mentioned below for the Huaca Prieta site, torches and excessive amounts of charcoal at archaeological sites also may signal nighttime ritual and activity. Although very difficult to determine in the material record, excessively clean spaces, especially where sharp objects such as ceramic, bone, and lithic fragments have been removed from dance and marching areas, is an indicator of places of congregation by barefooted people. Also, I have observed that during the nighttime, much smaller spaces are used for ritual because people move around less and stay confined to each other in order to adjust to darkness and not to stumble on each other or across logs and other objects. Trash also is tossed into limited areas, usually close to or into fires to burn it. Moreover, branches of the sacred tree, foye, are burned in torches, leaving its ashes and flecks of charcoal in a wider area at night. At night a resin or oil is applied to the tips of the branches to prolong burning. During the daytime only machi use foye branches, with their charcoal and ash intentionally deposited near the *llangi-llangi*, or *axis mundi*, in the center of ceremonial fields (Dillehay 2007), and no resin is used.

Set in a broader context, we can presume that the cognitive and physical worlds of the Mapuche (and other indigenous groups) are linked through the relations that ritual has with landscapes and skyscapes and the meanings people assigned to them. As Evangelos Kyriakidis (2007, 299) states, "rituals—especially communal ones—create cultural space, a *topos*, much like monuments. They

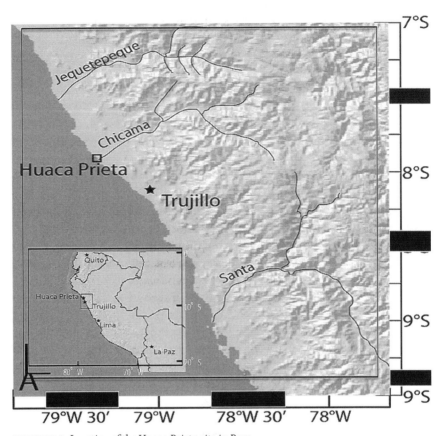

FIGURE 9.3. *Location of the Huaca Prieta site in Peru.*

may not affect the landscape physically, but they certainly affect it cognitively. Rituals, literally take place; they are performed in a specific location and are inscribed in the memories of the participants." This is especially true for the daytime Mapuche rituals when people see and experience the sacred landscape of ritual spaces and remember the acts and beliefs associated with them. During the night, however, people can only mentally envision the landscape, but it is not the same, because it cannot be seen and it has different sounds and smells. Ritual participation at night thus involves the memory of landscape, negotiated by expectation and anticipation in darkness, with only portions of it occasionally revealed by the light of fires.

Although I have mentioned a few material signatures of nighttime rituals, there is some indirect archaeological evidence for nighttime activity at the site of Huaca Prieta on the north coast of Peru (figure 9.3; Dillehay n.d.). Pioneering archaeological excavations conducted at Huaca Prieta by the late

FIGURE 9.4. *Large, dark mound at Huaca Prieta, Peru. (Photo by Tom Dillehay)*

Junius Bird in the mid-1940s revealed that the site has one of the densest, temporally longest and deepest middle-to-late Holocene cultural deposits in the world. The artificial portions of the mound at the site measure about 29 m high in some places, 65 m wide, and 162 m long. Bird's study of the site indicated different strategies of marine foraging and initial farming over time. The site was previously thought to date between about 5500 and 3500 cal BP and to have been only an occupational and burial mound (Bird et al. 1985), but our recent research at the site has dated the mound from about 7600 to 3800 cal BP (Dillehay et al. 2012).

The mound at Huaca Prieta is very dark, thus the name *prieta,* or "black," and it contains excessive amounts of ash and of specks of charcoal, revealing numerous burning episodes throughout time (figure 9.4). We believe that nighttime rituals were carried out at the site throughout its entire use during the middle-to-late Preceramic period in Peru, as more directly suggested by the presence of numerous burned torches made of long pine needles. The distal tips were burned and show stains of resin (figure 9.5). The torches were radiocarbon dated to about 5500 cal BP and were recovered from pathways leading to small (3 m × 4 m), demarcated ritual spaces at the top of the mound, which suggests that nighttime ritual processions took place across the sides and upper surface of the structure, but perhaps in limited places due to the inability to see the entire size and form of the mound at night. The archaeological evidence from the site suggests that rituals were related to the interment of important

FIGURE 9.5. *Burned torches excavated at the Huaca Prieta site. (Photo by Tom Dillehay)*

individuals in the mound and perhaps to pilgrimages by peoples from distant coastal and highland areas.

Even today, the meaning and perpetuity of the mound at Huaca Prieta continue as modern-day shamans, or *curanderos*, both males and females, from the north coast of Peru still visit and worship there, performing rituals under moonlight, and making offerings (usually coca leaves and *chicha* or corn beer) to deities and to pray for productive fertility from the sea and the land.

CONCLUSIONS

It has taken archaeology a long time to appreciate the social and symbolic dimensions of ritual activity in the past. Until poststructuralism developed in archaeology, archaeologists primarily classified ritual practices as either symbolic or functional in nature. Such a dichotomy often has led us to neglect the more integrative concepts of symbolism, psychology, and other effects of ritual participation. By examining these dimensions more, a wider spectrum of behaviors and more social and cognitive explanations of ritual can be offered. It is hoped that this brief essay on Mapuche nighttime rituals has contributed toward our understanding of these dimensions in both an ethnographic and an archaeological context, especially in regard to what archaeologists often refer to as ritual hearths or fires and large deposits of charcoal and evidence for burning. Some ritual hearths may be indicative of nighttime activities, which could have been associated with different effects on human behavior, including performance levels, the limited use of symbolic imagery to reinforce authority and power due to visual impairment, reduced physical activity and use of ceremonial space, and the reliance on sensory organs other than the eyes to participate in public congregation. These and other dimensions of nighttime activity also require archaeologists to reconsider the degree to which moderate- to large-sized ritual audiences can be regulated and addressed by leaders and the presumed effects that dance, song, and procession may have had on audiences from a political religious perspective.

ACKNOWLEDGMENTS

I wish to thank the shamans and members of the many Mapuche communities where my research team and I participated in public ceremonies. Most of this participation occurred while we were conducting archaeological fieldwork in communities and working with local people. Many individuals in these communities befriended us over the years, beginning in 1975. I also wish to thank Drs. Enrique Edwards (Hospital Regional de Concepcion) and Juan Liendo (Hospital Regional de Temuco and la Universidad de la Frontera, Temuco) for their professional experiences and insights into certain cognitive and neurological conditions that participants experienced during prolonged ritual. Over the decades, the National Science Foundation, the National Geographic Society, the University of Kentucky, Vanderbilt University, and the Guggenheim Foundation largely funded my research. I also wish to thank several colleagues who worked with me in the field during these rituals, particularly Gaston Sepulveda, Rene San Martin, Arturo Rojas, the late Americo Gordon, Jose Saavedra, Patricio Sanzana, and Arturo Rojas.

REFERENCES

Alhola, Paula, and Päivi Polo-Kantola. 2007. "Sleep Deprivation: Impact on Cognitive Performance." *Neuropsychiatric Disease and Treatment* 3(5):553–567.

Ashbrook, James B., and Carol Rausch Albright. 1997. *The Humanizing Brain: Where Religion and Neuroscience Meet.* Cleveland, OH: Pilgrim Press.

Avital, Eytan, and Eva Jablonka. 2000. *Animal Traditions: Behavioral Inheritance in Evolution.* Cambridge: Cambridge University Press. https://doi.org/10.1017/CBO 9780511542251.

Bacigalupo, Ana M. 1996. "Mapuche Women's Empowerment as Shamans/Healers." *Annual Review of Women in World Religions* 4:57–129.

Bacigalupo, Ana M. 2001. "The Mapuche Moon Priestess." *Annual Review of Women in World Religions* 6:208–259.

Bacigalupo, Ana M. 2007. *Shamans of the Foye Tree: Gender, Power, and Healing among Chilean Mapuche.* Austin: University of Texas Press.

Bahn, Paul G. 2001. "Save the Last Trance for Me: An Assessment of the Misuse of Shamanism in Rock Art Studies." In *The Concept of Shamanism: Uses and Abuses,* ed. Henri Paul Francfort, Roberte Hamayon, and Paul G. Bahn, 51–93. Budapest: Akadémiai Kiadó.

Barrett, Justin L., and E. Thomas Lawson. 2001. "Ritual Intuitions: Cognitive Contributions to Judgments of Ritual Efficacy." *Journal of Cognition and Culture* 1(2):183–201. https://doi.org/10.1163/156853701316931407.

Bell, Catherine. 2007. "Response: Defining the Need for Definition." In *The Archaeology of Ritual,* ed. E. Kyriakidis, 277–288. Los Angeles: Cotsen Institute of Archaeology.

Bengoa, José. 2003. *Historia de los Antiguos Mapuches del Sur.* Santiago: Catalonia.

Binford, Lewis R. 1972. *An Archaeological Perspective.* New York: Seminar Press.

Bird, Junius Bouton, John Hyslop, and Milica Dimitrijevic Skinner. 1985. *Preceramic Excavations at Huaca Prieta, Chicama Valley, Peru.* New York: Anthropological Papers of the American Museum of Natural History.

Boccara, Guillaume. 1999. "Etnogénesis mapuche: Resistencia y restructuración entre los indígenas del centro-sur de Chile (siglos XVI–XVIII)." *Hispanic American Historical Review* 79(3):425–461.

Boyer, Pascal. 1994. "Cognitive Constraints on Cultural Representations: Natural Ontologies and Religious Ideas." In *Mapping the Mind: Domain-Specificity in Culture and Cognition,* ed. Lawrence A. Hirschfeld and Susan A. Gelman, 391–411. New York: Cambridge University Press. https://doi.org/10.1017/CBO9780511752902.016.

Boyer, Pascal, and Pierre Liénard. 2006. "Why Ritualized Behavior? Precaution Systems and Action Parsing in Developmental, Pathological, and Cultural Rituals." *Behavioral and Brain Sciences* 29:595–613.

Conan, Neil. 2010. "*Neurotheology: This Is Your Brain on Religion.*" Andrew Newberg. Talk of the Nation, December 15. Philadelphia, PA: National Public Radio; http://www.npr.org, Accessed August 26, 2016.

Crow, Joanna. 2013. *The Mapuche in Modern Chile: A Cultural History*. Gainesville: University Press of Florida. https://doi.org/10.5744/florida/9780813044286.001.0001.

D'Aquili, Eugene G. 1993. "The Myth-Ritual Complex: A Biogenetic Structural Analysis." In *Brain, Culture, and the Human Spirit: Essays from an Emergent Evolutionary Perspective*, ed. James B. Ashbrook, 45–75. Lanham, MD: University Press of America.

D'Aquili, Eugene G., Charles D. Laughlin, and John McManus. 1979. *The Spectrum of Ritual: A Biogenetic Structural Analysis*. New York: Columbia University Press.

Dillehay, Tom D. 1985. "La influencia politica de los chamanes mapuches." *CUHSO* 2(2):141–157.

Dillehay, Tom D. 2007. *Monuments, Resistance and Empires in the Andes: Araucanian Ritual Narratives and Polity*. New York: Cambridge University Press. https://doi.org/10.1017/CBO9780511499715.

Dillehay, Tom D. 2016. "*Araucano Indomito*: Anti-Imperialism, Independence, and Ethnogenesis in Colonial (and Present-Day) Chile." *Chungara (Arica)* 46:698–736.

Dillehay, Tom D. n.d. *Where the Land Meets the Sea: Fourteen Millennia of Human History on the North Coast of Peru*. Austin: University of Texas Press.

Dillehay, Thomas D., Duccio Bonavia, Steven Goodbred, Mario Pino, Victor Vasquez, Teresa Rosales Tham, William Conklin, Jeff Splitstoser, Dolores Piperno, José Iriarte, et al. 2012. "Chronology, Mound-Building, and Environment at Huaca Prieta, Coastal Peru, from 13,700 to 4,000 years ago." *Antiquity* 86(331):48–70. https://doi.org/10.1017/S0003598X00062451.

Faron, Louis C. 1962. *Hawks of the Sun*. Urbana: University of Illinois Press.

Freeman, Walter. 2000. "A Neurological Role of Music in Social Bonding." In *The Origins of Music*, ed. Nils L. Wallin, Björn Merker, and Steven Brown, 411–424. Cambridge, MA: MIT Press.

Frieman, Catherine, and Mark Gillings. 2007. "Seeing is Perceiving?" *World Archaeology* 39(1):4–16. https://doi.org/10.1080/00438240601133816.

Grimes, Ronald L. 1995. *Beginnings in Ritual Studies*. Columbia: University of South Carolina.

INE. 2010. "Instituto Nacional de Estadísticas." Santiago, Chile.

Johnson, George. 2007. "God Is in the Dendrites." *Slate Magazine*. Accessed August 26, 2016. http://www.slate.com/articles/life/brains/2007/04/god_is_in_the_dendrites.html.

Joseph, Rhawn. 2002. "Dreams, Spirits, and the Soul." In *NeuroTheology: Brain, Science, Spirituality, Religious Experience*, ed. Rhawn Joseph, 411–425. San Jose, CA: University Press.

Knight, Christopher J. 2003. "Trauma, Tedium and Tautology in the Study of Ritual." *Cambridge Archaeological Journal* 13(2):293–295. https://doi.org/10.1017/S0959774303250162.

Kyriakidis, Evangelos. 2007. "Search of Ritual." In *The Archaeology of Ritual*, ed. Evangelos Kyriakidis, 1–8. Los Angeles: Cotsen Institute of Archaeology, UCLA.

Lakoff, George. 1987. *Women, Fire, and Dangerous Things: What Categories Reveal about the Mind*. Chicago: University of Chicago Press. https://doi.org/10.7208 /chicago/9780226471013.001.0001.

Laughlin, Charles D. 1996. "Archetypes, Neurognosis and the Quantum Sea." *Journal of Scientific Exploration* 10(3):375–400.

Laughlin, Charles D. 2009. "The Mystical Brain: Biogenetic Structural Studies in the Anthropology of Religion." Accessed August 26, 2016. http://www.biogeneticstruc turalism.com/docs/.

Lawson, E. Thomas, and Robert N. McCauley. 1990. *Rethinking Religion: Connecting Cognition and Culture*. Cambridge: Cambridge University Press.

Leiva, Orellana A. 1977. "Rechazo y Absorción de Elementos de la Cultura Española por los Araucanos en el Primer Siglo de la Conquista de Chile (1541–1655)." Tesis de Licenciatura. Santiago: Universidad de Chile.

Llobera, Marcos. 1999. "Landscapes of Experiences in Stone: Notes on a Humanistic Use of a Geographic Information System (GIS) to Study Ancient Landscapes." D.Phil. thesis, University of Oxford, Oxford.

McCauley, Robert N. 1999. "Bringing Ritual to Mind." In *Ecological Approaches to Cognition: Essays in Honor of Ulric Neisser*, ed. Eugene Winograd, Robyn Fivush, and William Hurst, 285–312. London: Lawrence Erlbaum Associates.

McCauley, Robert N. 2001. "Ritual, Memory, and Emotion: Comparing Two Cognitive Hypotheses." In *Religion in Mind: Cognitive Perspectives on Religious Experience*, ed. Jensine Andresen, 115–140. Cambridge: Cambridge University Press. https://doi.org /10.1017/CBO9780511586330.005.

McCauley, Robert N., and E. Thomas Lawson. 2002. *Bringing Ritual to Mind: Psychological Foundations of Cultural Forms*. Cambridge: Cambridge University Press. https://doi.org/10.1017/CBO9780511606410.

McCauley, Robert N., and E. Thomas Lawson. 2007. "Cognition, Religious Ritual, and Archaeology." In *The Archaeology of Ritual*, ed. Evangelos Kyriakidis, 209–254. Los Angeles: Cotsen Institute of Archaeology, UCLA.

Mithen, S. 1997. "Cognitive Archaeology, Evolutionary Psychology and Cultural Transmission, with Particular Reference to Religious Ideas." In *Rediscovering Darwin: Evolutionary Theory and Archaeological Explanation*, ed. C. Michael Barton and G. A. Clark, 67–74. Arlington, VA: American Anthropological Association. https://doi.org /10.1525/ap3a.1997.7.1.67.

Pearson, Mike, and Michael Shanks. 2013. *Theatre/Archaeology*. London: Routledge Press.

Proske, U., and Simon C. Gandevia. 2009. "The Kinaesthetic senses." *Journal of Physiology* 587(17):4139–4146. https://doi.org/10.1113/jphysiol.2009.175372.

Pyysiäinen, Ilkka. 2003. *How Religion Works: Towards a New Cognitive Science of Religion.* Leiden: Brill.

Rappaport, Roy A. 1999. *Ritual and Religion in the Making of Humanity.* Cambridge: Cambridge University Press. https://doi.org/10.1017/CBO9780511814686.

Renfrew, Colin, and Christopher Scarre, eds. 1998. *Cognition and Material Culture: The Archaeology of Symbolic Storage.* Cambridge: McDonald Institute for Archaeological Research.

Robles De La Torre, Gabriel. 2006. "The Importance of the Sense of Touch in Virtual and Real Environments." *IEEE MultiMedia* 13(3):24–30. https://doi.org/10.1109/MMUL.2006.69.

Romain, William F. 2009. *Shamans of the Lost World: A Cognitive Approach to the Prehistoric Religion of the Ohio Hopewell.* Lanham, MD: Altamira.

Skeates, Robin. 2010. *An Archaeology of the Senses: Prehistoric Malta.* Oxford: Oxford University Press.

Taheri, Shahrad. 2007. "Sleep and Metabolism: Bringing Pieces of the Jigsaw Together." *Sleep Medicine Reviews* 11(3):159–162. https://doi.org/10.1016/j.smrv.2007.03.005.

Tedlock, Barbara. 2005. *The Woman in the Shaman's Body: Reclaiming the Feminine in Religion and Medicine.* New York: Bantam Books.

Tremlin, Todd. 2006. *Minds and Gods: The Cognitive Foundations of Religion.* Oxford: Oxford University Press. https://doi.org/10.1093/0195305345.001.0001.

Trentini, Florencia, Sebastián Valverde, Juan Carlos Radovich, Mónica A. Berón, and Alejandro Balazoter. 2010. "Los nostálgicos deldesierto: La cuestión mapuche en Argentina y elestigma en los medios." *Cultura y representaciones sociales* 3:186–203.

Turner, Victor. 1987. "Body, Brain, and Culture." In *The Anthropology of Performance*, ed. Victor Turner, 156–178. New York: PAJ Publications.

Whitehouse, Harvey, and Luther H. Martin, eds. 2004. *Theorizing Religions Past: Archaeology, History, and Cognition.* Walnut Creek, CA: Altamira.

Winkelman, Michael. 2002. "Shamanism as Neurotheology and Evolutionary Psychology." *American Behavioral Scientist* 45(12):1875–1885. https://doi.org/10.1177/0002764202045012010.

Winkelman, Michael. 2004. "Shamanism as the Original Neurotheology." *Zygon* 39(1):193–217.

Zavala Cepeda, José Manuel. 2008. *Los Mapuches del Siglo XVIII: Dinámica Interétnica y Estrategias de Resistencia.* Santiago: Editorial Universidad Boliviarana S.A.

Where Night Reigns Eternal

Darkness and Deep Time among the Ancient Maya

JEREMY D. COLTMAN

The most notable quality of night is darkness, an experience recognized in all cultures despite temporal and spatial differences. In many cases, the darkness of night is significant because it has always been there. It is therefore little wonder that many cultures have developed origin myths in which darkness or night shares generative qualities with the original creation. In late antiquity and the Western European early Middle Ages, monastic life held both theological and cosmological significance that could be traced back to Judeo-Christian mythic traditions regarding a chaotic primordiality (Helms 2004). In Genesis for instance, God creates light and separates it from the darkness, which he called night. This implies that in Judeo-Christian thought, night was always there first and by itself while light was the "divine creation" (Schnepel and Ben-Ari 2005, 153). Helms (2004, 178) notes that "darkness stands even closer than light to ultimate cosmological beginnings in that darkness is often identified in lore and legend as one of the conditions that preceded the formation of the lighted world."

Unsurprisingly, these notions of night and darkness in Western thought are at home in the many rich mythic traditions regarding creation in Mesoamerica

DOI: 10.5876/9781607326786.c010

(figures 1.2–1.3). In colonial Nahuatl sermons for instance, the term used for darkness is not an abstract notion but a special or temporal locative that refers to a dark time or place:

> in indigenous usage this could refer to the disordered time (or time out of time) before cosmic order was established with the creation of the sun. To be in a dark place or a dark time is not quite the same thing as being in a metaphorical abstract "darkness" of the soul. However, the image of Christianity as a solar order contrasting with the chaotic darkness that preceded it fit Nahua conceptions quite well. (Burkhart 1988, 243)

Similar to the concept of "chaotic primordiality" in classical antiquity, the darkness of night for the ancient Maya symbolized the mythological past that predated the creation of the sun and the ordered world. Colonial texts that evolved from ancient lore certainly attest to this. For instance, the K'iche Maya *Popol Vuh* states that nothing yet existed in the primordial world but the night: "All lies placid and silent in the darkness, in the night" (Christenson 2003, 67–68). The Yukatek *Chilam Balam of Chumayel* also described a world of darkness prior to the creation of the sun and even of time itself (Roys 1967, 110). In ancient Maya thought, the night was linked to this primordial past and shared an iconography with the dark interior spaces of caves. While these dark abodes hosted frightful beings, they were also linked to emergence and creation and offered a preferred location for liminal rituals. This chapter explores why the darkness of night played a pivotal role in the religious iconography and ritual of the ancient Maya (see also Gonlin and Dixon, chapter 3, and Aveni, chapter 7, this volume, for the ancient Maya). While the general sign for darkness or night was ak'ab, another articulation corresponded closely to the *ch'een* glyph for "cave" and other dark spaces related to the dark and dangerous forest wilds. This motif, a combination of eyeballs and crossed bones, likely referred to the interior darkness of caves, the closely related forest wilds, and the "chaotic primordiality" that existed prior to the creation of the ordered world. Furthermore, it will be argued that the ch'een motif became reworked as it disseminated into Central Mexico by becoming a skull paired with crossbones. Despite this change in the motif, it still very much retained the meaning it carried for the Maya, a primordial darkness linked to caves, birth, and the original creation.

NIGHTLY LANDSCAPES

The night is well worth discussing since most of us spend almost half our lives in it (Galinier et al. 2010; Schnepel and Ben-Ari 2005). It is just as well that we spend this time sleeping. As most lore from around the world would attest, the night could be a dangerous and unnerving time. The blackness that accompanies night is cause enough for such distress. The ancient Maya perceived the color black as being largely related to "dark and foreboding places that humans fear to enter and where vision is deprived of external stimulus" (Houston et al. 2009, 35). One of the characteristics of night is the wild creatures that inhabit it, some of which would almost seem to defy logic; noisy furry creatures that fly for instance. The ancient Maya had a way of denoting these creatures as denizens of the night by marking them with a specific sign known as ak'ab, one of the twenty days in the calendar of the Maya of Yucatan representing "darkness/night" (Stone and Zender 2011, 58) (figure 10.1A).[1] Bats who have fiery speech and skeletal fireflies who smoke cigars are both frequently marked with the ak'ab sign (Brady and Coltman 2016; Stone and Zender 2011, 80) (figure 10.1B). Jars possibly containing *pulque* or other intoxicating beverages were also marked with ak'ab. The individuals holding them give some context to their meaning. Bees or wasps swarm around the opening of one such jar held by a being known as *Mok Chih,* whose name means "pulque sickness," a patron of alcoholic beverages and their inevitable aftereffects (Grube 2004) (figure 10.1C). The preeminent rain deity, *Chahk,* is known to appear with an ak'bal jar which in this case is the likely source of dark, black, rain-laden clouds (Taube 2004, 77:figure 6b). The Jaguar God of the Underworld (JGU) was a manifestation of the night sun. His spiral eyes are consistent with symbolism designating darkness and he frequently bears ak'bal signs on his cheeks (Houston and Taube 2000, 283–284). Early Classic stucco masks from the Temple of the Night Sun at El Zotz depict multiple images of this deity. The western orientation of the temple may be marking the descent of the sun into the dark western underworld (Taube and Houston 2015, 209–221). Much like the contrast between the diurnal and shining Maya Sun God, *K'inich Ajaw,* and the nocturnal aspect of the JGU, mirrors also denote such opposition. As Karl Taube (2016, 290) notes, the distinct surfaces of Classic Maya mirrors may allude to "the quality of reflective light, with one being the bright light of the day and the other, dark regions of the time of night."

Darkness and night were sometimes conveyed in unexpected ways, such as on the well-known Birth Vase, which depicts ancient Maya conceptions of supernatural birth that likely mimicked actual birthing practices (Taube 1994; K5113). These themes express some unique ways in which night and darkness were conveyed by the ancient Maya. One such expression is a serpent who has the markings and face of a jaguar (figure 10.1D). While this being appears in the context of birthing rites on this vase, the best representation appears well outside the Maya heartland on the north panel of Building A at Cacaxtla in modern-day Tlaxcala, Mexico. There, it is paired with a jaguar warrior and appears opposite a plumed serpent paired with an avian warrior on the south panel. The two opposed conjectural creatures and their associated warriors likely represent two diametrically distinct realms. While the plumed serpent and avian warrior refer to the east and the lustrous land of the Maya, the jaguar relates to the west and the darkness of night (Taube 1994, 666).[2]

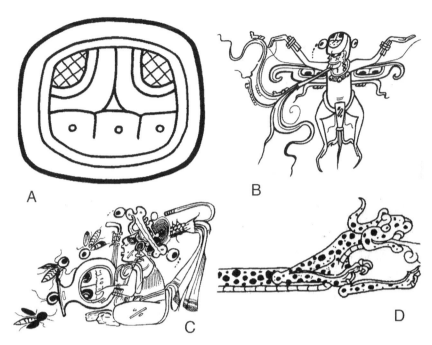

FIGURE 10.1. *Ak'ab and inhabitants of the night. (A) Ak'ab sign for "night/darkness" (from Stone and Zender 2011, 58); (B) skeletal firefly marked with ak'ab sign on its forehead (from Stone and Zender 2011, 80); (C) Mok Chih and his ak'bal-marked jar (from Stone and Zender 2011, 145); (D) Jaguar Serpent denoting darkness and the west (from Taube 1994, figure 6d).*

The aged creatrix and midwife known as Goddess O appears on the Birth Vase, assisting with the actual birth (figure 10.2A). She wears her customary skirt of eyes and crossed bones (figure 10.2A). As Miller (2005, 64) notes, Goddess O represents age in every respect: "her face, sometimes toothless, sags into a mass of wrinkles; her breasts hang down below the waist, shriveled and useless; her back is bent with advanced osteoporosis." In many cases Goddess O portrays jaguar features, further linking her to the night and darkness (Taube 1992, 99–105) (figures 10.2B, 10.2D). On the Birth Vase, a young woman in labor assisted by Goddess O stands on a *witz*, or mountain, which has a black hooked skeletal centipede pincer flanking it (Taube 1994, 661). The pincer of the skeletal centipede maw is regularly juxtaposed to the witz, thereby providing evidence of enclosures that relate to caves as liminal spaces where entities go to die and become reborn (Stone 2003). One example occurs in Drawing 19 from Naj Tunich cave with the skeletal centipede maw reading as a toponym referring to the cave as "black transformation place" (Stone 2003). In many respects, caves were considered part of the forest wilds that belonged to the night, as did the host of unruly

FIGURE 10.2. *Goddess O in Classic and Postclassic Maya Art. (A) The aged midwife and creatrix, Goddess O, assisting with a delivery on the Birth Vase (from Taube 1994, figure 2a). (B) Classic-period Goddess O as curer. Note jaguar features and eyes-and-crossbones motif (from Taube 1994, figure 2c). (C) Goddess O as caryatid (architectural support in female form), from Lower Temple of the Jaguars, Chichen Itza (from Schele and Matthews 1998, figure 6.11– A3). (D) Goddess O, Dresden Codex, p. 74 (from Taube 1992, figure 50e).*

supernatural beings who occupied this domain. Many of these occupants are marked by the ak'ab sign, including *way* spirits, grotesque animalistic spooks representing personified diseases and other misfortunes (Houston and Stuart 1989; Taube 2003; Stuart 2005b). These beings are still associated with the dark forest and are represented in modern Maya rituals. During contemporary *wayeb* and other period-ending rites, these forest spirits emerge from a periphery that lacks spatial order, which in turn also parallels its lack of social and moral authority. In other words, night was the chaotic antithesis to the bright diurnal day. Although the term *wayeb* remains obscure, it most likely refers to dreams and the night, both qualities of the forest (Taube 2003). Here the realm of the wild and the realm of the dead are linked with dream-consciousness (Pellizzi 2007, 240). Among contemporary Maya, dreaming can bring close encounters with a number of potentially dangerous beings, such as the *ik'al*, a winged, hypersexual entity that attacks souls that dare to fall asleep and brings them back to his cave

(Galinier et al. 2010; Blaffer 1972).. In rural Tlaxcala, there is a fear of blood-sucking witches who prey on children in the night, while in Tescopa, Distrito Federal, rain dwarves are thought to capture and enslave souls in their cave homes (Nutini and Roberts 1993; Madsen 1960). Closely linked to the realm of dreaming were beings mentioned in contemporary folktales of the Tzeltal Maya, such as "flesh dropper" and the Tzotzil creature known as "fallen flesh"—both of them akin to ancient Maya skeletal death gods whose domain was placed well within the darkness of night (Laughlin 1977; Stross 1978).

DARKNESS AND PRIMORDIAL TIME IN RITUAL

The wayeb and other period-ending rites among the modern Maya reflect ancient conceptions of the dark forest and primordial time. The animal beings that are portrayed during these rites recall the way beings known from the Classic period. The time period reflected in these modern rites was one of creation. During the Zotzil wayeb, the expression *ch'ay k'in* ("the period without sun") is used to refer to a ritual form of extended night, a return to primordial time when power-ful beings from the fringe of creation would enter the community, cause chaos, and then revert to the dark forest wilds (Taube 2003, 467). The idea that ritual is linked to creation and primordial origins was not unique and may have been more the rule than the exception. According to Eliade (1959, 81), the very act of creation was fundamental to all religion and ritual:

> The paramount time of origins is the time of the cosmogony, the instant that saw the appearance of the most immediate of realities, the world. This . . . is the rea-son that cosmogony serves as the paradigmatic model for every creation, for every kind of doing. It is for this same reason that cosmogonic time serves as the model for all sacred times. (Eliade 1959, 81)

While Eliade notes this in one broad sweeping stroke of customary compara-tive religion, I find it completely applicable for the ancient and contemporary Maya. In Mesoamerican curing rituals, creation myth is invoked as narration. Magicians and sorcerers invoke names of beings at the moment of their creation as they place themselves in the exact moment of creation by traveling across the barrier that is based on a profound belief in primogenital time (López Austin 1993, 89). An expression of this appears in Classic Maya texts and colonial incan-tations from the *Ritual of the Bakabs*.

Among the Classic Maya, the phrase *ch'ab'-ak'ab'* refers to creation and dark-ness, or "penance-darkness," and occurs on many monuments in the Peten that reference ritual events (Stuart 2005a, figure 11.7; Knowlton 2010, 22–30). This phrase, at least in Classic times, may have been related to the conjuring of ances-tors (Fitzsimmons 2009, 15). Stuart (2005a, 278) notes that this phrase "can be rightly regarded as one of the principal operating forces of kingship and its ritual duty." It may also relate to the invocation of primordial time rooted in the chaos of creation. This ancient invocation is mentioned a millennium later in the colonial Yukatek Maya *Ritual of the Bakabs*. Comprising forty-two incantations that are medical in nature, many of the personified diseases are named after animals (Roys 1965, xi, xviii; Braakhuis 2005, 185). In fact, many of the personified ailments in the *Ritual of the Bakabs* contain the root *uay* in their epithets, therefore suggesting a number of striking correspondences between supernatural entities designated as *uay* or *wayeb* in the eighteenth century *Ritual of the Bakabs* and the Classic-period way beings, which emphasizes the continuity between diseases and their personifications (Helmke and Nielsen 2009, 57). It is likely that way beings during the Classic period were invoked as personified diseases during this return to primogenital time.

In order for the curer to treat or combat the disease, they must cross over boundaries of the realm of human language into that of wild or mythological thought (Pellizzi 2007, 241). Linda Schele (1993, 2002) correctly noted that the incantations in the *Ritual of the Bakabs* are curing chants for the treatment of disease, and more specifically for attacking disease within the context of creation. The 4 Ajaw creation date is used repeatedly in the *Ritual of the Bakabs*, referring to the patient as the archetypal human being, *anom*, the "first human being" in Yukatek Maya mythology (Knowlton 2010, 257). While there is a strong sense of cosmological order with frequent mention of world directions and associated trees and world-directional colors associated with gods, illness interferes in the form of disease-causing spirits and winds. It is the curer's job to restore equilibrium, balance, and health to the body of the patient with an emphasis on the disease-causing spirit. As Schele (2002, 22) notes, most passages "begin with a description of the moment of creation that establishes time and place. Thereafter, the text recounts the genealogy, place, and context of the birth of the disease. By knowing the parentage and origin of the disease, the *h-men* gained control over it."[3]

CH'EEN AND THE EYES-AND-CROSSBONES MOTIF

The well-known skull-and-crossbones motif of the Late Postclassic International Style, like most symbols, evolved from an earlier form. The earliest example of this pairing occurs on a Late Preclassic façade on Structure B at Holmul, Guatemala. Infixed onto a witz ("mountain"), this is not only the earliest pairing of the skull and crossbones together but is also one of the earliest representations of the ch'een ("cave") mountain motif among the ancient Maya (Tokovinine 2013, 54). In most Mayan languages, the word *ch'een* carries the meaning of "cave," "well," and "grave." In ancient times, the ch'een glyph was frequently depicted as a profile enclosure with a blackened shadowing that could include either an impinged bone, a mandible, crossbones, or a disembodied eye infixed into the nocturnal field (Stone and Zender 2011, 133) (figure 10.3A). The nocturnal field is fitting, for on an empirical level caves can reveal the ancient Maya experience of intimate darkness and nullified senses.[4] Caves would have offered an "eternal night," making them prime destinations for liminal rites and the chosen abode of powerful supernatural forces that dwelled in perpetual darkness. That they were places of creation and emergence made them all the more significant and desired. Caves are naturally dark, so they share, at least on a general level, something with the night. Temples and houses can also be perceived as dark space. In the *Codex Borgia*, temples and caves are frequently shown as having an interior dark space with the typical iconographic conventions of eyeballs set against a darkened background, a convention and meaning not dissimilar from the Mayan ch'een sign figure 10.3B). A Late Classic Maya temple decorated with eyeballs also denotes it as a "house of darkness" (K5538). This convention of eyes set against a nocturnal field can also be seen on page 36 of the *Codex Madrid*, where an individual sits within a dark space surrounded by eyeballs (figure 10.3C). It is likely that the extruded eyeball is indicating strained vision or a lack of sight altogether within a dark space (Brady and Coltman 2016, 230). Furthermore, in Central Mexico, the day sign coinciding with the Mayan ak'bal is *calli* ("house"). Caves frequently display man-made architectural features that give them a temple quality. It is likely that caves served as the first temples and that is why the Classic Maya often depict their temples as anthropomorphic mountains with gaping maws as entrances, an architectural convention that mimics iconographic representations of caves. The Classic Maya were not alone in perceiving their temples with cave-like qualities. Neolithic Maltese and Egyptian temples were perceived as low, confined spaces that were both dark and convoluted, and they likely would have amplified sounds and smells, just like actual caves (Robb 2001).[5]

Such experiences mimicked the night, which for the ancient Maya could be fraught with danger, temporally distant, and inhabited by a cast of antisocial and unsavory beings. These denizens of the night belonged to the wilderness and dark forests that lacked internal order and spatial division (Stone 1995; Taube 2003). Indeed, natural environments tend to contain less clearly demarcated boundaries (Montello and Moyes 2012, 389). Caves are frequently dark, damp, and disorienting. The darkest part of caves known as "dark zones" in particular can be anathema to one's regular sensorium and in extreme cases might even entail what could be expected from isolation experiments (Montello and Moyes 2012, 389). Dark zones are often the chosen locale for most ritual activity. For instance, Lots designated as 5 and 8 at Midnight Terror Cave, Belize, are the darkest zones of the cave and also contain the most human remains. Deep within the dark zone of Naj Tunich cave a specific text reads *IL-li-BIH*, *'i-li-Way*, which according to Stephen Houston (2009, 169) signifies "away from surface light, and in textual references to acts of 'seeing' and, with one youth, the 'seeing

FIGURE 10.3. *Ch'een and the eyes-and-crossbones motif. (A) Two ch'een ("cave") signs, composed of an eye against a darkened or cross-hatched background. (From Stone and Zender 2011, 52.) (B) A dark temple. Note the eyeball denoting darkness in the interior. (Detail of* Codex Borgia, *p. 66; drawing by Jeremy Coltman) (C) An individual sitting within a darkened space. Note the extruded eyeball, which may relate to strained sight. (Detail of* Codex Madrid, *p. 36; drawing by Jeremy Coltman) (D) Eyes-and-crossbones motif against a black background, next to a caiman. (Detail of the Late Classic Vase of the Seven Gods, from Taube 2012, figure 4c) (E) Serving bowl depicting eyes and crossbones on the interior rim of vessel. Note way beings with detached eyeballs holding ak'bal jars. (Courtesy of Boston Museum of Fine Arts)*

of a road, seeing of a way, or companion spirit, as though by means of a vision quest into the recesses of the cave." Recent research has shown that kings could control or invoke these way beings, and some of these beings were personified diseases. This ability was a powerful political tool in ancient Maya ideology (Stuart 2005b). A number of other drawings in Naj Tunich suggests that caves for the Classic Maya may have served as locales where liminal rites and other acts such as intoxication and sexual exploration took place (Stone 1995; Houston et al. 2009). Dark zones were likely a prime locale for such liminal rites. Caves in general and dark zones in particular would have offered secrecy. While secrecy produces value through the exclusion of outsiders and the inclusion of insiders, it also must be performed in a public fashion so that it could be understood to exist (Jones 2014, 54; Herzfeld 2009, 135). This may be why caves served as locales for liminal-period rites, especially in the dark zones where the senses, especially sight became nullified.

As noted by David Stuart (Vogt and Stuart 2005, 157), the ch'een glyph corresponds to a recurring motif in Maya iconography: eyes and bones set against a nocturnal darkened background. The Late Classic Vase of the Seven Gods depicts the merchant deity God L presiding over six other deities during a creation event occurring on 13.0.0.0.0 4 ajaw 8 kumk'u (Houston and Stuart 1996, 293). The eyes-and-bones motif appears, suggesting that this creation event is taking place within a dark cave (Vogt and Stuart 2005, 157–159) (figure 10.3D).[6] The stacked zoomorphic witz, or mountain heads, behind God L's throne seem to confirm this. Closely related to this creation event was the setting up of the three-stone hearth as a symbol of cosmic order. Taube (2012, 18) notes that the three-stone hearth was probably erected as the world center on the date of 4 ajaw 8 kumk'u and could have possibly stood for the creation of light at the beginning of creation. An example from a Late Classic bowl on display at the Boston Museum of Fine Arts depicts the complete interior rim decorated with eyes and crossbones set against a solid black band (K1440) (figure 10.3E). It is likely that this bowl represents a symbolic cave. The two animal figures painted on the exterior of the bowl hold ak'bal jars and each has a detached eyeball extending far out of its socket. According to Grube and Nahm (1994, 692, figure 14), the *Ritual of the Bakabs* mentions the phrase *colop u uich* ("torn out eyes"), which is an epithet that refers to creator deities.

As previously stated, both darkness and primordial time were qualities that belonged to the forest wilds. Forests are dark, wild, and untamed. The crossbones motif appears in contexts that indicate that it marked such wild and untamed landscapes. Currently on display at the Metropolitan Museum of Art in New York, Stela 5 from Piedras Negras depicts a scene taking place within the dark confines of a cave or cave-like temple (Stuart and Graham 2003, 33–35). A ruler addresses his subordinate from his throne, a huge witz mountain that forms a looming arch over his head. Various creatures can be seen invading the scene from the periphery, including the JGU, a monkey, and a skeletal firefly smoking a cigar, an action that is providing light in an otherwise dark underground event. The bottom half of the stela, however, depicts a watery environment with a leafy band marked with crossbones. The leafy band is similar to another example in which the eyes-and-crossbones motif appears within a leafy arbor adorned with skulls and intertwined bones. Taube (2003, 477–478) notes that this arbor and those like it represent the ritual forest and are Classic Maya forms of the *tzompantli*, or skull rack, known from the Late Postclassic Aztec.

THE DARK SIGN OF BIRTH AND CREATION

The expression of the ch'een glyph with the corresponding eyes-and-crossbones motif represented the period of wild and untamed darkness and primordial time for the ancient Maya. While it has now become generally accepted that the motif set against a nocturnal background refers to the dark interior confines of caves, it frequently appears in yet another context: the skirt of the aged midwife and creatrix, Goddess O. Representations of Goddess O wearing this skirt are not only confined to the Classic period. Ix Chel, the Postclassic Yucatan version of Goddess O, frequently wears this skirt and retains her image as an aged grandmother and midwife, whose jaguar claws and skeletal features recall the destructive aspect as a devouring beast.[7] Diego de Landa (Tozzer 1941, 129) notes that Ix Chel was also the goddess of childbirth: "For their child-births they had recourse to the sorceresses, who made them believe their lies, and put under their beds an idol of a goddess called Ix Chel whom they said was the goddess of making children." It has been known for quite some time that Goddess O was the logical precursor to a number of Aztec goddesses who shared similar features and characteristics (Thompson 1950, 83; Taube 1992, 105; Miller 2005). These women were sometimes depicted as frightening and ferocious, which undoubtedly spoke to their destructive powers. As previously mentioned, these women were also creator deities who were the patronesses of healers and midwives. As Mary Miller (2005, 67), notes, "Aztec midwives called out to Tlaltecuhtli, as well as to Cihuacoatl and Quilaztli, and I would propose that they share common origins and practice in Goddess O—midwife, giver of life, and aged impending destroyer of the world."[8]

While her aged aspect made her the wise midwife par excellence, she was also a creator goddess of incredible antiquity. Reliefs from the Lower Temple of the Jaguars dating to Early Postclassic Chichen Itza depict four representations of the old man known as God N, which appear on the south column, while the north column depicts four images of Ix Chel, or Goddess O, several of which depict her in an eyes-and-crossbones skirt (Tozzer 1957, figures 195,

196, 615) (figure 10.2C). Schele and Matthews (1998, 215) note that the pairing of the Old Man and Ix Chel is likely due to these two old gods being a creator couple much like Xpiyacoc and Xmucane of the colonial *Popol Vuh*. Following Schele and Mathews, Simon Martin (2015, 218) enhances the argument that the representation of Goddess O at Chichen Itza invokes her as a powerful creatrix, particularly in her pairing with God N: "For Mesoamericans, the ultimate act of sorcery was the creation of the universe, and the founding gods are typically a male-female pair of elderly magicians." Martin goes on to show convincingly that this aged and powerful creator couple has parallels in Central Mexico with Ometecuhtli and Omecihuatl, Tonacatecuhtli and Tonacacihuatl, Citlallatonac and Citlalinicue, and Cipactonal and Oxomoco (Martin 2015, 221–223). For the sixteenth-century Pokomon Maya, Xchel and Xtamna, cognates of the Yucatec Ix Chel and Itzamna, are described as the old creator couple (Taube 1992, 99).

During the Terminal Classic period (AD 900) in the northern lowlands, skulls appear juxtaposed to crossbones and eyeballs. A key Terminal Classic example is the Uxmal Cementario Platform, where a skull is juxtaposed to crossed bones that are in a weave pattern, a probable allusion to textiles and the goddesses they represent (Stone and Zender 2011, 55) (figure 10.4A). This symbol system, which arises out of the ch'een glyph, would become the most likely origin of the skull-and-crossbones motif decorating platforms and skirts found among the Aztec-Mexica of Late Postclassic Mexico-Tenochtitlan.[9] Altar platforms uncovered during the excavations of Mexico City and Tenayuca (Batres 1902; Caso 1935) depict alternating skulls and crossed bones with fringe edging emanating from a rope, a convention known for textiles (figure 10.4B). In separate studies of the altars at Tenayuca and Tizatlan, Alfonso Caso (1935, 300, 1993, 43) noted that this convention denoting textile-fringe borders of these platforms represented the skirts of goddesses. His evidence for this was largely drawn from images of "strip goddesses" on pages 32, 39, 41, and 43–46 of the *Codex Borgia*. Following these initial insights, Cecelia Klein (2000) noted that these stone platforms symbolized the garments of the Tzitzimime and were petitioned to cure and heal the sick.[10] Folio 50r from the *Codex Tudela* depicts a *vieja hechizera*, or "old sorceress," holding a *manta* ("shawl") of skull and crossbones, a scene that is also associated with curing (Tudela de la Orden 1980, 279; Klein 2000, 5–6) (figure 10.4C). Klein (ibid.) further related this cloth manta to an image on *Codex Tudela* 76r, where a menacing skeletal figure stands on a practically identical skull-and-crossbones platform altar. These skull-and-crossbones altars recall those from Uxmal and Nohpat from the Terminal Classic northern lowlands. It is likely that they are serving as platforms of primordial darkness and creation, the same meaning ascribed to the ch'een glyph and corresponding eyes and crossbones of the Classic period.

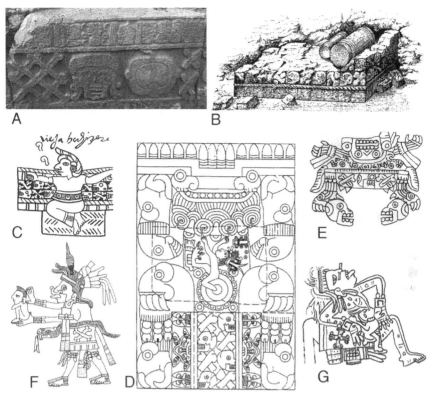

FIGURE 10.4. *The skull-and-crossbones motif in Maya and Late Postclassic Central Mexican art. (A) Terminal Classic altar with ch'een symbolism from the Cementario Platform, Uxmal. (Photo courtesy of David Stuart) (B) Stone platform of skulls and crossbones uncovered during excavations in Mexico City by Leopoldo Batres in 1900. Note the "rope" and crenellated edging suggestive of textiles. (C) The "Old Sorceress" (vieja hechizera) with textile of skulls and crossbones. (Codex Tudela 50r.; from Taube 2010, figure 6c) (D) Tlaltecuhtli giving birth to Tezcatlipoca though a chalchihuitl symbol on the date 2 Reed. (From Nicholson 1958, figure 4) (E) Tlaltecuhtli, underside of Stuttgart Statuette. Note skull-and-crossbones skirt as bowl. (Drawing by Jeremy Coltman) (F) Tlazoteotl with crossbone skirt and holding child. (Codex Laud, p. 29; drawing by Jeremy Coltman) (G) Goddess nursing a child. Note crossbones on skirt. (Codex Vaticanus B, p. 41; drawing by Jeremy Coltman)*

The most frequent use of the skull-and-crossbones motif is found on the skirt of the earth goddess, Tlaltecuhtli. To the Aztec-Mexica, Tlaltecuhtli was the primary primordial goddess, an aged creatrix whose origins lie at the beginning of time when the world was still in darkness (García Icazbalceta 1891, 231).[11] An Aztec myth from the *Histoyre du Mechique* (De Jonghe 1905) describes the creation of the universe from when Tezcatlipoca and Quetzalcoatl dismembered the body of Tlaltecuhtli. Whereas one half of Tlaltecuhtli became the sky, the other transformed into the earth, with her hair becoming the trees and grass, her eyes the pools, springs, and caves, her mouth the rivers and caverns, and her nose the valleys and mountains (Garibay 1965, 108). One relief of Tlaltecuhtli depicts her as a creator goddess giving birth to Tezcatlipoca through a *chalchihuitl* symbol, an act of creation that lies at the beginning of time (Nicholson 1958) (figure 10.4D). One of Tlaltecuhtli's most prominent characteristics and diagnostic attributes is a skirt emblazoned with skulls and crossbones. The goddess typically appears in a birthing stance, known generically as the "hocker," or *mamazouhticac*, parturition position (Nicholson 1967; Henderson 2007). This birthing position conceptualizes the earth goddess as "the great womb of life, the progenitress of mankind" (Nicholson 1958, 166). In a recent study of the Aztec *cuauhxicalli* (stone vessels to hold human hearts), Taube (2009) has demonstrated that Tlaltecuhtli's skull-and-crossbones skirt is sometimes depicted as a bowl firmly placed within her hips, a clear allusion to supernatural birth that can be seen on the base of the Stuttgart Statuette and Bilimek Pulque Vessel (Coltman 2007; Taube 1993; 2009, figures 6a–b) (figure 10.4E). Lacking a Tlaltecuhtli proper, the *Codex Borgia* depicts various figures in the parturition position with these "birth bowls" symbolizing this very mechanism (32, 40). What is clearly absent however is the skull-and-crossbones motif, which suggests that the motif is a primary characteristic of Aztec-Mexica art, particularly in relation to Tlaltecuhtli's skirt. However, several images in the Borgia Group depict Tlazoteotl wearing a skirt decorated with crossbones and engaged either in holding a child or nursing one (figures 10.4F–G). However, the precise pairing of the skull and cross-bones as articulated on the skirt of Tlaltecuhtli represents one of the clearest examples of Classic Maya influence on the artists of Tenochtitlan.

CONCLUSION

This chapter has briefly explored ancient Maya notions of the night with the primary argument centering on the idea that the importance of night was at least partly due to the fundamental role of darkness in creation. In a sense, night is a harkening back to primordial time before the creation of the ordered world. As in the incantations from Classic-period times to a millennium later in the colonial *Ritual of the Bakabs*, the phrase ch'ab'-ak'ab' may have explicitly linked creation to darkness, or something relatively close to it. In most Mesoamerican mythologies, the origins of the world have their beginnings in a time of primordial darkness prior to the creation of the sun. During the wayeb period and Carnival, there is a temporary return to chaos and the night. It was this return to primordial time and chaos that made the night so potent. Whether artificial night in the dark zones of caves, ritual forms of night during wayeb, or actual night when people dared lay their heads to rest, these periods were imbued with potentially dangerous power. It is this reason that the night continues to play such a central role in Maya thought.

This chapter has also addressed the eyes-and-crossbones motif as an expression of the ch'een sign for "cave." The ch'een motif invoked relations to a specific aspect of caves: primordial darkness and the impending creation. Marking dark cavernous spaces or the textiles of primordial deities, this motif began to appear with skulls on altars in the northern lowlands during the Terminal Classic at sites like Uxmal and Nohpat. This articulation of ch'ccn symbolism is the logical precursor to the skull-and-crossbones motif known for the Late Postclassic International Style, including the contact-period Aztec. While the motif underwent a slight change, it still retained its most basic meaning as a symbol of primordial darkness, caves, and birth. It is this continuity from the ch'een cave symbolism of the Classic Maya to the skirt of a Late Postclassic Aztec earth goddess that reinforces the importance of night as a temporary yet constant return to primordial origins when all lay in darkness.

ACKNOWLEDGMENTS

I would like to thank Nancy Gonlin and April Nowell for the kind invitation to contribute something to this fascinating topic. I owe a debt of gratitude to David Stuart for his incredible insight and encouragement regarding the writing of this chapter. Karl Taube and Marc Zender have made illustrations available to me with typical generosity. I would also like to thank John Pohl and James Brady for being excellent sounding boards, even when the sound may have become distorted at times. I owe a special debt to Cecelia Klein for her astute comments regarding an earlier version of the manuscript. Finally, many of these ideas were presented in a talk given at the 2017 Maya Meetings, January 13–14, University of Texas at Austin. I would like to thank both Astrid Runggaldier and David Stuart for their kindness and hospitality during my visit.

NOTES

1. The Contemporary Maya of Chichicastenango and Momostenango, Guatemala, frequently pair the day signs *ik'* (wind) with ak'bal (night) in various incantations. These tend to usually carry negative connotations and are indicative of disease, sorcery, misfortune, and antisocial emotions (Bunzel 1959, 280, 281, 346–351; Tedlock 1992, 126, 128–129). In Late Postclassic Central Mexico, the paramount sorcerer Tezcatlipoca was known as *yohualli, ehecatl*, which translates as "night, wind," essentially describing him as the personification of chaos.

2. Taube (1994, fig. 6e) has also called attention to the night sky's being depicted against a jaguar pelt at the Late Postclassic site of Tulum. Roys (1931, 331) notes that the Titzimin manuscript mentions that the spreading of jaguar skin in the market place was taken as a symbol of war, famine, and pestilence.

3. While Schele looked to the sky for the majority of these causes, most probably originated from deities linked to the earth, water, and wind, as these are the major sources of disease among contemporary Maya of Yucatan (Redfield and Redfield 1940).

4. The cave on the North Wall mural at Late Preclassic San Bartolo depicts an elaborate version of the *ak'bal* sign. Saturno et al. (2005, 15) note that instead of negative connotations generally associated with the night and darkness, this likely marks the cave as a sacred and ancestral place.

5. Early Medieval churches were also dark, cavernous, and enclosed spaces. However, the tombs of the enclosed abbey churches were conceptually linked to the sacred cave, "a powerful otherworldly place related to the land of the dead," where early Christian and Medieval images of salvation depicted the legend of the "Harrowing of Hell," in which Christ descended from his tomb into the vast darkness in order to break open the gates of hell and flood it with salvational light (Helms 2004, 185).

6. A caiman appears next to the eyes-and-crossbones motif, further emphasizing that this is a creation event. In Maya thought, the caiman symbolized the Earth and was sacrificed at the time of creation. A Classic Maya manifestation of this being, the "Starry Deer Crocodile," may have represented the night sky (Stuart 2005c; Velásquez García 2006).

7. Citing Landa, Taube (1992, 103) notes that Ix Chel was closely related to the spider. Landa (Tozzer 1941, 154) mentions that Yucatec curers carry not only small idols of Ix Chel but bundles containing stones known as *am*, the Yucatec word for "spider" used in divining. The spider is addressed in this passage from the *Ritual of the Bacabs*: "four days were you beneath the garden plot. The cochineal of your grandmother, the virgin Ix Chel, Chacal Ix Chel, Sacal Ix Chel is the symbol of the back of the green spider of wood, the green spider of stone" (Roys 1965, 53). Significantly, this passage mentions the spider in association with stone and wood, a pairing in Nahuatl known as *in tetl, in quiahuitl*, and that is indicative of castigation in Late Postclassic Central Mexico. *Codex Borgia* (pp. 49–52) depicts descending pairs of Cihuateteo and their male consorts as *tztzimime* (celestial demons) carrying objects of castigation such as stone and wood (Taube 1993). Furthermore, the first page of the narrative, or the "middle pages," depicts a creation scene of directional winds (*Codex Borgia*, p. 29). A yellow spider and a red spider appear along with the objects of stone and wood, indicating that creation is likely invoked in curing rituals.

8. In Late Postclassic Central Mexico, Toci, the aged aspect of Tlazoteotl, is associated with world creation and destruction, and is the goddess of diviners, midwives, and curers (Sahagún 1950–1982, bk. I:15). Taube (1992, 103) notes that Goddess O compares closely to Toci-Tlazoteotl as identified with creation and curing. One aged aspect of this goddess appears on one of the pillars from the Column 16 from Temple of the Warriors at Chichen Itza (Morris, Charlot, and Morris 1931, II:pl. 58). Her sagging stomach and breasts as well as chapfallen mouth clearly mark her as an aged creator goddess. Notably, she appears with a large weaving spool in her hair, one that recalls her image from the Birth Vase. This same instrument is found as one of the primary attributes of Tlazoteotl in Late Postclassic Central Mexico.

9. It is unlikely that the skull-and-crossbones motif had Central Mexican origins. While some skeletal imagery has been found at Teotihuacan, there are certainly no skull and crossbones paired together. The best evidence for a Central Mexican origin appears on an altar at El Corral, Tula (Acosta 1974). As previously mentioned, the skull and crossbones appear conflated together on a Late Preclassic Maya façade from Structure B at Holmul, Guatemala (Estrada Belli 2011). This is the earliest known example of the skull-and-crossbones theme by far. Furthermore, the skull and crossbones are infixed to a mountain with an old toothless man emerging from the open maw (Tokovininc 2013, 54–55). This important scene is the Old Man creator deity emerging from the cave maw of the mountain, with the skull and crossbones marking this as a primordial place of darkness and creation.

10. The tzitzimime embodied both positive and negative qualities in ancient Nahua cosmology. They were usually shown as ferocious skeletal women with menacing claws. Sahagún (1950–1982, VII:27) described them as frightful beings that would descend to earth to devour mankind during the appearance of a solar eclipse or if new fire could not be drilled at the end of the fifty-two-year cycle. I suspect that the prehispanic nature of the tzitzimime is far more complex than just idle "star demons" on standby waiting for an eclipse. For instance, they are well illustrated in the narrative cosmogony section of the *Codex Borgia* (29–46) and engaged in acts of creation and birth.

11. As a primordial creatrix associated with the night, Tlaltecuhtli frequently appears with a number of creepy crawly invertebrates such as spiders, centipedes, scorpions, and other creatures crawling in her tangled mop of hair (Caso 1967, figure 3). Spiders, centipedes, and scorpions are creatures associated with the earth and night and were related to sorcery and the magical arts in ancient Mexico.

REFERENCES

Acosta, Jorge. 1974. "La pirámide de El Corral de Tula, Hidalgo." In *Proyecto Tula*, 1ª parte, Colleción Científica 15, ed. Eduardo Matos Moctezuma, 27–49. México: INAH.

Batres, Leopoldo. 1902. *Excavations in Escalerillas Street, City of Mexico—1900*. México: J. Aguilar Vera & Co.

Estrada Belli, Francisco. 2011. *The First Maya Civilization: Ritual and Power before the Classic Period*. New York: Routledge.

Blaffer, Sarah C. 1972. *The Black-Man of Zinacantan: A Central American Legend*. Austin: University of Texas Press.

Braakhuis, H.E.M. 2005. "Xbalanque's Canoe: The Origin of Poison in Q'eqchi' Mayan Hummingbird Myth." *Anthropos* 100:173–191.

Brady, James E., and Jeremy D. Coltman. 2016. "Bats and the Camazotz: Correcting a Century of Mistaken Identity." *Latin American Antiquity* 27(02):227–237. https://doi.org/10.7183/1045-6635.27.2.227.

Bunzel, Ruth. 1959. *Chichicastenango: A Guatemalan Village*. Seattle: University of Washington Press.

Burkhart, Louise M. 1988. "The Solar Christ in Nahuatl Doctrinal Texts of Early Colonial Mexico." *Ethnohistory (Columbus, Ohio)* 35(3):234–256. https://doi.org/10.2307/481801.

Caso, Alfonso. 1935. "El Templo de Tenayuca estaba dedicado al culto solar (estudio de los jeroglíficos)." In *Tenayuca: Estudio arqueológico de la pirámide de este lugar, hecho por el departamento de monumentos de la Secretaría de educación pública*, ed. Juan Palacios, et al., 293–308. México: Talleres Gráficos del Museo Nacional de Arqueología, Historia y Etnografía.

Caso, Alfonso. 1967. *Los calendarios prehispánicos*. Series de Cultura Náhuatl, Monografías, 6. México: Instituto de Investigaciones Históricas.

Caso, Alfonso. 1993 [1927]. "Las ruinas de Tizatlán, Tlaxcala." In *La escritura pictográfica en Tlaxcala: Dos mil años de experiencia mesoamericana*, ed. Luis Reyes García, 37–53. Tlaxcala: Universidad Autónoma de Tlaxcala.

Christenson, Allen J. 2003. *Popol Vuh: The Sacred Book of the Maya*, trans. Allen J. Christenson. Norman: University of Oklahoma Press.

Coltman, Jeremy. 2007. "The Aztec Stuttgart Statuette: An Iconographic Analysis." *Mexicon* 29:70–77.

De Jonghe, Edouard. 1905. "Histoyre du Mechique, manuscrit français inédit du XVIe siècle." *Journal de la Société des Americanistes* 2(1):1–41. https://doi.org/10.3406/jsa.1905.3549.

Eliade, Mircea. 1959. *The Sacred and the Profane: The Nature of Religion*. New York: Harcourt, Brace, and World.

Fitzsimmons, James. 2009. *Death and the Classic Maya Kings*. Austin: University of Texas Press.

Galinier, Jacques, Aurore Monod Becquelin, Guy Bordin, Laurent Fontaine, Francine Fourmaux, Juliette Roullet Ponce, Piero Salzarulo, Philippe Simonnot, Michèle Therrien, and Iole Zilli. 2010. "Anthropology of the Night: Cross-Disciplinary Investigations." *Current Anthropology* 51(6):819–847. https://doi.org/10.1086/653691.

Velásquez García, Erik. 2006. "The Maya Flood Myth and the Decapitation of the Cosmic Caiman." *PARI Journal* 7:1–10.

García Icazbalceta, Joaquín. 1891. "Historia de los mexicanos por sus pinturas." In *Nueva colección de documentos para la historia de México 3*, ed. Joaquin García Icazbalceta, 228–263. México: Francisco Díaz de León.

Garibay, Angel Maria. 1965. *Teogonia e historia de los mexicanos: Tres opusculos del siglo XVI*. Mexico: Editorial Porrua.

Grube, Nikolai. 2004. "Akan: The God of Drinking, Disease and Death." In *Continuity and Change: Maya Religious Practices in Temporal Perspective*, ed. Daniel Graña Behrens, Nikolai Grube, Christian M. Prager, Frauke Sachse, Stefanie Teufel, and Elizabeth Wagner, 59–76. München: Verlag Anton Saurwein, Markt Schwaben.

Grube, Nikolai, and Werner Nahm. 1994. "A Census of Xibalba: A Complete Inventory of Way Characters on Maya Ceramics." In *The Maya Vase Book 4*, ed. Justin Kerr, 686–715. New York: Kerr Associates.

Helmke, Christophe, and Jesper Nielsen. 2009. "Hidden Identity and Power in Ancient Mesoamerica: Supernatural Alter Egos as Personified Diseases." *Acta Americana* 17:49–98.

Helms, Mary W. 2004. "Before the Dawn. Monks and the Night in Late Antiquity and Early Medieval Europe." *Anthropos* 99(1):177–191.

Henderson, Lucia. 2007. *Producer of the living, Eater of the Dead: Revealing Tlaltecuhtli, the Two-Faced Aztec Earth*. BAR International Series 1649. Oxford: BAR.

Herzfeld, Michael. 2009. "The Performance of Secrecy: Domesticity and Privacy in Public Spaces." *Semiotica* 175:135–162.

Houston, Stephen. 2009. "A Splendid Predicament: Young Men in Classic Maya Society." *Cambridge Archaeological Journal* 19(02):149–178. https://doi.org/10.1017/S0959774309000250.

Houston, Stephen, Claudia Brittenham, Cassandra Mesick, Alexandre Tokovinine, and Christina Warinner. 2009. *Veiled Brightness: A History of Ancient Maya Color*. Austin: University of Texas Press.

Houston, Stephen, and David Stuart. 1989. *The Way Glyph: Evidence for "Co-Essences" among the Classic Maya*. Research Reports on Ancient Maya Writing 30. Washington, DC: Center for Maya Research.

Houston, Stephen, and David Stuart. 1996. "Of Gods, Glyphs and Kings: Divinity and Rulership among the Classic Maya." *Antiquity* 70(268):289–312. https://doi.org/10.1017/S0003598X00083289.

Houston, Stephen, and Karl Taube. 2000. "An Archaeology of the Senses: Perception and Cultural Expression in Ancient Mesoamerica." *Cambridge Archaeological Journal* 10(2):261–294. https://doi.org/10.1017/S095977430000010X.

Jones, Graham M. 2014. "Secrecy." *Annual Review of Anthropology* 43(1):53–69. https://doi.org/10.1146/annurev-anthro-102313-030058.

Klein, Cecelia. 2000. "The Devil and the Skirt: An Iconographic Inquiry into the Pre-Hispanic Nature of the Tzitzimime." *Ancient Mesoamerica* 11(01):1–26. https://doi.org/10.1017/S0956536100111010.

Knowlton, Timothy. 2010. *Maya Creation Myths: Words and Worlds of the Chilam Balam*. Boulder: University Press of Colorado.

Laughlin, Robert M. 1977. *Of Cabbages and Kings: Tales from Zinacantán*. Smithsonian Contributions to Anthropology 23. Washington, DC: Smithsonian Institution Press. https://doi.org/10.5479/si.00810223.23.1.

López Austin, Alfredo. 1993. *The Myths of Opossum: Pathways of Mesoamerican Mythology*. Albuquerque: University of New Mexico Press.

Madsen, William. 1960. *The Virgin's Children: Life in an Aztec Village Today*. Austin: University of Texas Press.

Martin, Simon. 2015. "The Old Man of the Maya Universe: A Unitary Dimension to Ancient Maya Religion." In *Maya Archaeology 3*, ed. Charles Golden, Stephen Houston, and Joel Skidmore, 186–227. San Francisco: Precolumbia, Mesoweb Press.

Miller, Mary E. 2005. "Rethinking Jaina: Goddesses, Skirts, and the Jolly Roger." *Record of the Art Museum, Princeton University* 64:63–70.

Montello, Daniel R., and Holly Moyes. 2012. "Why Dark Zones Are Sacred: Turning to Cognitive and Behavioral Science for Answers." In *Sacred Darkness: A Global Perspective on the Ritual Use of Caves*, ed. Holly Moyes, 385–396. Boulder: University Press of Colorado.

Morris, Earl H., Jean Charlot, and Ann Axtell Morris. 1931. *The Temple of the Warriors at Chichen Itza, Yucatan*. Vol. II. Washington, DC: Carnegie Institution of Washington, Pub. 406.

Nicholson, Henry B. 1958. "The Birth of the Smoking Mirror." *Archaeology* 7:164–170.

Nicholson, Henry B. 1967. "A Fragment of an Aztec Relief Carving of the Earth Monster." *Journal de la Société des Americanistes* 56(1):81–94. https://doi.org/10.3406/jsa.1967.2272.

Nutini, Hugo, and John Roberts. 1993. *Bloodsucking Witchcraft: An Epistemological Study of Anthropomorphic Supernaturalism*. Tucson: University of Arizona.

Pellizzi, Francesco. 2007. "Some Notes on Sacrifice, Shamanism, and the Artifact." *Res: Anthropology and Aesthetics* 51:239–246. https://doi.org/10.1086/RESv51n1ms20167728.

Redfield, Robert, and Margaret Park Redfield. 1940. *Disease and Its Treatment in Dzitas, Yucatán*. Washington, DC: Carnegie Institution of Washington.

Robb, John. 2001. "Island Identities: Ritual, Travel and the Creation of Difference in Neolithic Malta." *European Journal of Archaeology* 42:175–202.

Roys, Ralph. 1931. *The Ethno-botany of the Maya*. Middle American Research Series 2. New Orleans: Tulane University.

Roys, Ralph. 1965. *The Ritual of the Bacabs: A Book of Maya Incantations*. Norman: University of Oklahoma Press.

Roys, Ralph. 1967. *The Chilam Balam of Chumayel*. Norman: University of Oklahoma Press.

Sahagún, Fray Bernardino. 1950–1982. *Florentine Codex: General History of the Things of New Spain*, trans. A.J.O. Anderson and C. E. Dibble. Monographs of the School of American Research 14. Santa Fe: School of American Research.

Saturno, William, Karl Taube, David Stuart, and Heather Hurst. 2005. *The Murals of San Bartolo, El Petén, Guatemala, Part 1, The North Wall*. Barnardsville, NC: Center for Ancient American Studies.

Schele, Linda. 1993. *Creation and the Ritual of the Bakabs*. Texas Notes on Precolumbian Art, Writing, and Culture No. 57. Austin: University of Texas Press.

Schele, Linda. 2002. "Creation and the Ritual of Bacabs." In *Heart of Creation: The Mesoamerican World and the Legacy of Linda Schele*, ed. Andrea Stone, 21–34. Tuscaloosa: University of Alabama Press.

Schele, Linda, and Peter Matthews. 1998. *The Code of Kings: The Language of Seven Sacred Maya Temples and Tombs*. New York: Simon and Schuster.

Schnepel, Burkhard, and Eyal Ben-Ari. 2005. "Introduction: 'When Darkness Comes . . . ': Steps Toward an Anthropology of the Night." *Paidemua: Mitteilungen zur Kulturkunde* 51:153–163.

Stone, Andrea. 1995. *Images from the Underworld: Naj Tunich and the Tradition of Maya Cave Painting*. Austin: University of Texas Press.

Stone, Andrea. 2003. "Principles and Practices of Classic Maya Cave Symbolism." Paper presented at the 68th Annual Meeting of the Society for American Archaeology, Milwaukee, WI, April 9–13.

Stone, Andrea, and Marc Zender. 2011. *Reading Maya Art: A Hieroglyphic Guide to Ancient Maya Painting and Sculpture*. London: Thames and Hudson.

Stross, Brian. 1978. *Tzeltal Tales of Demons and Monsters*. No. 24. Columbia: Museum of Anthropology, University of Missouri-Columbia.

Stuart, David. 2005a. "Ideology and Classic Maya Kingship." In *A Catalyst for Ideas: Anthropological Archaeology and the Legacy of Douglas W Schwartz*, ed. Vernon L. Scarborough, 257–285. Santa Fe: School of American Research.

Stuart, David. 2005b. "Way Beings." In *Sourcebook for the 29th Maya Hieroglyphic Forum (N.A.)*, 160–165. Austin: University of Texas.

Stuart, David. 2005c. *The Inscriptions from Temple XIX at Palenque: A Commentary*. San Francisco: Pre-Columbian Art Research Institute.

Stuart, David, and Ian Graham. 2003. *Corpus of Maya Hieroglyphic Inscriptions*, vol. 9, part 1, *Piedras Negras*. Cambridge, MA: Peabody Museum of Ethnology and Archaeology, Harvard University.

Taube, Karl. 2016. "Through a Glass, Brightly: Recent Investigations Concerning Mirrors and Scrying in Ancient and Contemporary Mesoamerica." In *Manufactured Light: Mirrors in the Mesoamerican Realm*, ed. Emiliano Gallaga and Marc G. Blainey, 285–314. Boulder: University Press of Colorado. https://doi.org/10.5876/9781607324089.c013.

Taube, Karl, and Stephen Houston. 2015. "Masks and Iconography." In *Temple of the Night Sun: A Royal Tomb at El Diablo, Guatemala*, by Stephen Houston, Sarah Newman, Edwin Román, and Thomas Garrison, 209–221. San Francisco: Precolumbia Mesoweb Press.

Taube, Karl A. 1992. *The Major Gods of Ancient Yucatan*. Studies in Pre-Columbian Art and Archaeology No. 32. Washington, DC: Dumbarton Oaks.

Taube, Karl A. 1993. "The Bilimek Pulque Vessel: Starlore, Calendrics, and Cosmology of Late Postclassic Central Mexico." *Ancient Mesoamerica* 4(01):1–15. https://doi.org/10.1017/S0956536100000742.

Taube, Karl A. 1994. "The Birth Vase: Natal Imagery in Ancient Maya Myth and Ritual." In *The Maya Vase Book*, vol. 4., ed. Justin Kerr, 650–685. New York: Kerr Associates.

Taube, Karl A. 2003. "Ancient and Contemporary Maya Conceptions about the Field and Forest." In *The Lowland Maya Area: Three Millennia at the Human-Wildland Interface*, ed. Arturo Gomez-Pompa, M. Allen, Scott L. Fedick, and J. Jimenez-Osornio, 461–492. New York: Haworth Press Inc.

Taube, Karl A. 2004. "Flower Mountain: Concepts of Life, Beauty and Paradise among the Classic Maya." *Res: Anthropology and Aesthetics* 45:69–98. https://doi.org/10.1086/RESv45n1ms20167622.

Taube, Karl A. 2009. "The Womb of the World: The Cuauhxicalli and Other Offering Bowls in Ancient and Contemporary Mesoamerica." In *Maya Archaeology*, ed. Charles Golden, Stephen Houston, and Joel Skidmore, 1:86–106. San Francisco: Mesoweb Press.

Taube, Karl A. 2012. "Ancient Maya Cosmology, Calendrics, and Creation: 2012 and Beyond." *Backdirt Annual Review of the Cotsen Institute of Archaeology at UCLA* 10–21.

Tedlock, Barbara. 1992. *Time and the Highland Maya*. Albuquerque: University of New Mexico Press.

Thompson, J. Eric. 1950. *Maya Hieroglyphic Writing: An Introduction*. Washington, DC: Carnegie Institution of Washington, Publication 589.

Tokovinine, Alexandre. 2013. *Place and Identity in Classic Maya Narratives*. Studies in Pre-Columbian Art and Archaeology, 37. Washington, DC: Dumbarton Oaks.

Tozzer, Alfred M. 1941. *Landa's Relación de Las Cosas de Yucatan*. Papers of the Peabody Museum of American Archaeology and Ethnology 18. Cambridge, MA: Harvard University.

Tozzer, Alfred M. 1957. *Chichen Itza and Its Cenote of Sacrifice: A Comparative Study of Contemporaneous Maya and Toltec*. Memoirs of the Peabody Museum of American Archaeology and Ethnology 11–12. Cambridge, MA: Harvard University.

Tudela de la Orden, José, ed. 1980. *Códice Tudela*, prologue by Donald Robertson; epilogue by Wigberto Jiménez Moreno. 2 vols. Text plus facsimile. Madrid: Ediciones Cultura Hispánica del Instituto de Cooperación Iberoamericana.

Vogt, Evon Z., and David Stuart. 2005. "Some Notes on Ritual Caves among the Ancient and Modern Maya." In *The Maw of the Earth Monster: Mesoamerican Ritual Cave Use*, ed. James E. Brady and Keith M. Prufer, 155–185. Austin: University of Texas Press.

The Emerald Site, Mississippian Women, and the Moon

SUSAN M. ALT

Night in the Mississippian world was not just for dreaming, although for many, dreams and visions could be as real or maybe more real, than daytime doings (Hallowell 1960; Irwin 1994; Ridington 1988). Night was also a time for personal interactions and storytelling. We might also say that the night in the Mississippian world belonged to women, because according to ethnohistoric accounts and Native American oral histories, the moon, the night sky, and reproduction were all aspects of feminine powers (Bailey 1995; Diaz-Granados et al. 2015; Emerson 1982, 2015; Hall 1997; Hudson 1976; La Flesche 1914, 1930; Prentice 1986; Reilly and Garber 2007). But because the night was more closely associated with women than men, archaeologists have not routinely considered the night or the power of women; we have not really been thinking about feminine powers in the Mississippian world (Emerson et al. 2016). Here, I consider Native American Siouan oral traditions,[1] archaeological evidence for ritual at a lunar shrine center, imagery on cave walls, and carved-stone figurines to help explicate ancient Cahokian Mississippian feminine powers of the night. Engaging more closely with Native American ontologies exposes the significance of night and

DOI: 10.5876/9781607326786.c011

women in Mississippian societies while avoiding representational interpretations. The impact of this perspective is profound. As I will demonstrate, the origins of North America's Mississippian culture and its first city, Cahokia, began in good part with feminine powers of the night.

Cahokia was located in west-central Illinois (figures 1.2 and 1.3) and is now understood to be composed of numerous mound centers, including East St. Louis, Lohmann, Mitchell, Pfeffer, and Emerald as well as the St. Louis Mound center located under the modern city of St. Louis, which contain many more than the 120 mounds located in what is called downtown Cahokia. Cahokia's import lies in that it was the place of origin for Mississippian civilization and that it was the only precolumbian city to develop north of Mexico. It was a multiethnic place that drew over one-third of its population from neighboring regions (Slater et al. 2014). Cahokia was notable not only for its monumental constructions but also for its complex social, political, and religious organization. The lifeways that began at Cahokia, now identified as Mississippian, came to cover an area that extended from southern Wisconsin to the Gulf of Mexico, and from eastern Oklahoma to northern Florida. Mississippian towns were most often mound-and-plaza centers that are typically—although not without controversy (see for example Pauketat 2007)—described as chiefdoms. Mississippian towns shared similar although regionally variable politics, economies, and religious practices.

To better understand ancient Mississippians, it is first necessary to recognize that Native American worldviews were and are very different from an academic worldview derived from Western intellectual and religious traditions (Cordova et al. 2007; Deloria 1995; Waters 2004; Watkins 2000). This disjuncture needs to be acknowledged and bridged if we are to better understand past peoples. Relational and symmetrical archaeologies are theoretical ways of thinking that scholars are using to attempt to build that bridge (e.g., Buchanan and Skousen 2015; Olsen et al. 2012; Watts 2013). Paying attention to Native voices is another means to better understand ancient Native American subjectivities (e.g., Silliman 2008). I attempt to build my own bridge by first recognizing that "reality" is subjective and culturally constructed. Native American realities in the past were full of other-than-human-persons, spirits, forces, and powers that at times were visible, and at times were not. Those persons and powers were real to people and therefore shaped their beliefs and actions; we can, at times, find traces of those actions (Bailey 1995; Bird-David 1999; Hallowell 1960, 1976; Harvey 2005; Viveiros de Castro 1998; Waters 2004).

Furthermore, we need to consider that images and icons were not mere representations to those who made them. That is, they were not just pictures or symbols but were instead aspects, incarnations, or dispersed elements of persons, powers, and forces (Alberti et al. 2013). They *were* things and they were agentive. For example, Francis La Flesche (1930) acquired a weaving loom used to make cloth for sacred bundles from an old woman because she feared that because her son and grandchildren were not trained in its handling, they would run afoul of the powers inherent to the loom and would be harmed by it. So, while it is commonplace for archaeologists to say that a Mississippian carved-stone figurine "represented" a god or goddess or mythic being, doing so misses the point. The carved figurine itself was actually an aspect, incarnation, or an other-than-human person—it had presence, power, and agency. This matters in important ways. It disperses power from persons to things and the relationships between them. It suggests that complex, if not dangerous, relationships could exist between persons and things—or rather, the nonhuman persons or powers that some things actually were (Brück 2006; Fowler 2004; Joyce 2008). It suggests that the actions of past people when engaged with some objects must be recognized as people responding to nonhuman persons, powers, and forces, not simply as people manipulating things.

A second matter of importance is to recognize that dreams and dream worlds were part of people's reality. In Western traditions we dismiss dreams as little more than an unconscious continuation of daily thoughts and worries. We tend to forget that for many people, Native Americans among them, dreams were instead another dimension of reality. Dreams did tell truths, predict the future, instruct people, reveal the sacred, and/or open portals to other dimensions (Bailey 1995; Deloria 2006; Fortune 2011; Irwin 1994; Murie 1981). Many ceremonies and rituals in Native American life, such as the Pawnee Morning Star sacrifice, could only be engaged when a dream came to the right person and dictated that it was the right time for that ceremony to occur (Murie 1981). When they came, dreams and the night were vital to an ability to communicate with the otherworld of spirits and forces who must be honored if life was to continue. According Vine Deloria (2006), the night was not just for dreams but was the time when important medicine rituals had to be undertaken. So then, it seems critical to understand the implications of what it might have meant for women to be more closely associated with the night than others.

The third key perspective to realign is that of gender ideologies. Native American gender roles, ideologies, and identities were and are very different than those that have become naturalized in Western society (and that inform academic discourse) because Native American gender roles were underpinned by very different world views. Western ideologies have often led to misunderstandings about Native beliefs and practices, for example, those surrounding third and fourth genders. As Anne Waters (2004, xxv) phrases it, "understanding specific gender and ethnic concepts, for example, from an American Indigenous philosophical perspective (Indigicentric) requires comprehending the conceptual logic of nondiscrete, nonbinary, dualist ontology (that stands as ontological backdrop) for these concepts." Gender in Native American society was not either/or, nor was male in opposition to female. Male and female genders were complementary parts of a whole that often included third, fourth, and fifth genders. Some have described Native American gender roles as focused on occupation rather than on biological sex characteristics or sexual preferences (Blackwood 1984; Holliman 1994, 2001; Jacobs 1994; Roscoe 1991).

GENDER AND RELIGION

Gender roles did, however, generally lead to different expectations for the activities and natures of men, women, third, fourth, and other genders in Native societies. However, Native societies were less likely to consider those roles as oppositional, bounded, fixed, or less valued. Rather than reinforcing male or female superiority and/or dominance, gender roles assisted in keeping societal needs balanced such that different genders were necessary to each other and for maintenance of a successful society. For many Native societies this kind of ideology not only permitted but also accepted and honored more than two genders. Overall, gender and identity were seen as more fluid and tied to a person's spiritual nature rather than immutably fixed to biological features (Blackwood 1984; Holliman 1994; Roscoe 1991). Yet ancient gender roles and gender's relation to sex are difficult to access as archaeological evidence for such is fragmentary at best, and information derived from ethnohistoric accounts has been unduly influenced by a Western patriarchal gaze (Blackwood 1984).

Given the preceding, perhaps it is not surprising that the power of the feminine is underestimated, if not unseen, by most Mississippian archaeologists who tend to focus on the day world, the sun, and the doings of men (but see Alt and Pauketat 2007; Emerson et al. 2016). But for Native American Siouan speakers there was a balance to the world and the cosmos that needed men and women and other genders. The sun and the moon, night and day, were aspects of a natural cycle that included people and other powers and forces (figure 11.1). The sun, according to many Siouan speakers of the eastern Plains, was related to men because of First Man who came from the sun and possessed the powers of the sun; men were of the sky. First Man was the most powerful male spirit and the sun was the most visible expression of *Wa-kan-da's* spirit, which is to say the sun was a holy power. Conversely, First Woman, related to the earth, but also to rain (water) and serpents/snakes, was mother of all things; she was the most powerful feminine spirit and she came from the moon (Bailey 1995; Diaz-Granados et al. 2015; Hall 1997). Female power was of night, related to the moon and stars, but night was also related to death—the night sky was the underworld revealed. But to be clear, to say that women were related to the moon is not to say that the moon referenced, represented, or cited female powers, but that the moon *was* feminine power, and given the permeability and unbounded nature of people, powers, forces, and things, flesh-and-blood women shared that power—they were of the moon (Prentice 1986).

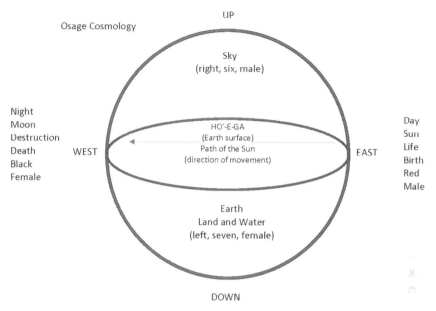

UP

Sky
(right, six, male)

Night
Moon
Destruction
Death
Black
Female

WEST

HO'-E-GA
(Earth surface)
Path of the Sun
(direction of movement)

EAST

Day
Sun
Life
Birth
Red
Male

Earth
Land and Water
(left, seven, female)

DOWN

FIGURE 11.1. *Osage cosmology. (Adapted from Bailey 1995, 33)*

MOUND 72 OR MISSISSIPPIAN MORTUARIES AND MYTHS

The archaeological focus on the sun, and on men, has been supported at Cahokia by interpretations of Mound 72, an elaborate mortuary mound. Mound 72 has long been considered evidence of a foundational male leader for Cahokia (Emerson et al. 2016). The focal point of the Mound 72 mortuary has been seen as one of the male burials on a beaded cape or blanket that was shaped like a falcon, and who was thought to be either a human inspiration for the Red Horn story cycle or a Red Horn impersonator (a description of the story follows) (Brown 2007, 2010; Pauketat 2008, 2010). The interred individual was described as surrounded by buried retainers, human (mostly female) sacrifices, and objects such as chunky stones, mica, copper, and stacks of perfectly crafted and hafted arrows—all items that were of great importance to Cahokians (Fowler et al. 1999). It was occasionally noted, but not well integrated into most interpretations, that more than one individual was buried on or under the beaded cape. When acknowledged, the second individual was also identified as male (Rose 1999).

The Red Horn story cycle, oft called upon in interpretations of the Mound 72 burials, tells of a hero or supernatural character who has many adventures, travels to the underworld, and who is killed by giants in the underworld. He is subsequently brought back to life by his two sons, in tales reminiscent of Mesoamerican hero twin sagas (Christenson 2007). The Red Horn stories are told in various versions as they have been recorded from different Native American tribes over time, although Radin's (1948, 1954) collected stories of the Winnebago are those most often cited. The central character, Red Horn, is given other names that reference his powers, such as "He Who Wears Human Heads as Earrings," and "He Who Is Hit by Deer Lungs" (Brown 2004, 2003, 2007; Brown and Kelly 2000; Hall 1989, 1991, 1997; Pauketat 2009; Radin 1948, 1954). The Red Horn saga is argued to have existed in some form prior to, or early in, the Mississippian period, because of art and artifactual evidence depicting themes or events described in the historically recorded stories (Brown 2003, 2007, 2010).

Some of the evidence for the antiquity of the Red Horn story include pictures depicted on cave walls at Picture Cave Missouri and at Gottschall Rock Shelter in Wisconsin (Diaz-Granados et al. 2015; Salzer 2005; Salzer and Rajnovich 2001). Red Horn is also thought to be portrayed on a Cahokian-made carved-stone fig-urative pipe (figure 11.2A) that was recovered from the great mortuary at Spiro (Brown 2004; Brown and Kelly 2000; Reilly 2004). Earrings, carved to look like human heads similar to those described in the Red Horn stories, are seen painted in the cave art and carved on the figurative pipe. Strikingly, such earrings have been found archaeologically, with some of them in burial contexts (Duncan and Diaz-Granados 2000; Hall 1991, 1997; Kelly 1991; Williams and Goggin 1956). This tale, seemingly supported by archaeological evidence in cave art and artifacts as well as the Mound 72 burials, have led to a focus on male power and domination at Cahokia and in Mississippian societies (Emerson et al. 2016). Evidence of femi-nine power has been ignored in the very same kinds of evidence that support the Red Horn associations. Now, new evidence refutes the old explanations. What follows will highlight some of that evidence.

Several new bioarchaeological analyses (Emerson et al. 2016; Slater et al. 2014; Thompson 2013; Thompson et al. 2015) require radically altered interpretations of the Mound 72 mortuary. The most important new data concern the central beaded-blanket burial, which is not of a male, or even two males, but of a male and a female laid out in extended positions, plus bundle burials of another male and female. The male "Red Horn" character is actually placed over a female indi-vidual, covering her right side with beads under the male and over the lower half of the female's body. The bundle burials were placed on or adjacent to the beaded area. Surrounding these burials are at least eight others, including males, females, and a young child (Emerson et al. 2016).

Rather than supporting a story about a key male individual, the configuration of the bodies better fits Native American traditions of complementarity in gen-der and social relations. According to Emerson and colleagues (2016, 22),

> if our assumption that the representations in 72Sub1 are connected to cosmic creation, world renewal, and fertility is correct, then the central burial pairs of males and females may be linked, as Romain (2016) proposes, to native creation

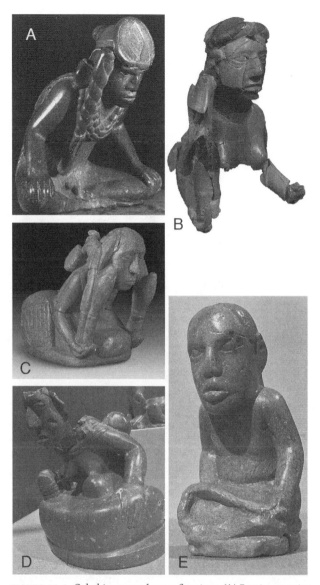

FIGURE 11.2. *Cahokian carved-stone figurines. (A) Resting warrior. (Courtesy of The University of Arkansas Museum Collections) (B) Sponemann figurine. (Courtesy of the Illinois State Archaeological Survey, University of Illinois) (C) Westbrook figurine. (Provided by and used courtesy of James Marlin) (D) Birger figurine. (Courtesy of the Illinois State Archaeological Survey, University of Illinois) (E) East St Louis figurine. (Courtesy of the Illinois State Archaeological Survey, University of Illinois)*

stories of the first man and woman (e.g., Dorsey 1906, 135; Hall 1997; Prentice 1986, 254–262; Weltfish 1965, 64).

If the Mound 72 mortuary complex is a reflection of past cosmological and ontological beliefs, then it reiterates what we know ethnohistorically; day/ male needs night/female and night/female needs day/male if the cosmos is to be in balance.

This interpretation makes sense because the sacred, for Siouan-speaking peoples, was not simply tied to a (male) deity, but was dispersed in many beings, things, places, essences, and persons. Religion was not a separable field of activity or belief but permeated all thought and all action. Wa-kan-da was not a person but part of nature, a force or a power that presented in numerous ways (Bailey 1995; Fletcher 1910; Hallowell 1976; Radin 1970). Wa-kan-da was an invisible creative power that animated the sun, the moon, and the stars. The cosmos "consisted of an indeterminate number of cycles of birth, growth, maturity and death . . . Everything moved from east to west, from birth to death" (Bailey 1995, 340). According to the Omaha and the Ponca, Wa-kan-da was a mysterious power or force that animated all things (Fletcher 1896). "The Osage believed that this great power [Wa-kan-da] resides in the air, the blue sky, the clouds, the stars, the sun, the moon and the earth," as well as all living and moving things (Bailey 1995, 31). The visible world was the purview of people; the invisible world was Wa-kan-da. Life depended upon Wa-kan-da, and human life was the product of intercourse between the father (the sky) and mother (the earth). This worldview in part explicates how North American indigenous religions are replete with spirits, forces, and powers that are embodied at various times by persons and things, but that otherwise remain unseen (Hall 1997; Hultkrantz 1967, 1981, 1987).

Native American oral histories document important other-than-human characters (besides Red Horn) who were often gendered male or female with powers and forces related to that of male and female corporeal persons. That is not to say that particular persons represented those beings, but that they shared powers. The sun, the moon, the stars, water, rain, wind, and lightning were commonly believed to be powers, forces, gods, or aspects of ancestors who shaped the world (Hall 1997; Pauketat 2008, 2012). For those historically known groups most closely associated with ancient Cahokia (Siouan speakers such as the Omaha, Osage, Ponca, Kansa, Quapaw), snakes and water monsters were also important other-than-human-beings who interacted with humans and who were part of the balance of the world. These same themes can also be found in Cahokian Mississippian imagery.

CAVE ART

Picture Cave, located fifty miles east of Cahokia, has been dated to the founding phase of Cahokia, which in turn was the first Mississippian center. Images inside of this cave seem to illustrate themes similar to those expressed in the Native American oral histories briefly reviewed above. The cave itself is interpreted by Diaz-Granados and colleagues (2015) as First Woman's vulva, or Womb of the Universe, a critical portal in the Mississippian world associated with the creation and continuation of the universe. Pictographs inside the cave include, among others, images of vulvas and Old Woman Who Never Dies / First Woman / Corn Mother. It is she who originally came from the moon (Diaz-Granados et al. 2015). It was the intercourse between First Woman and First Man that created human beings, important culture heroes, gods, and other critical forces and powers of the world.

In one of Picture Cave's images, First Woman is shown lying on her back with legs drawn up showing a "prominent pudendum in a coital position"; great serpent (a snake) approaches from below (Diaz-Granados et al. 2015, 224–225). While First Woman is the consort of First Man, she is also known through Osage stories to consort with serpents and snakes, who are lower-world spirits. Again, according to Diaz-Granados et al. (2015), vulvar motifs, including the First Woman image, were placed in the cave such that they caught sunlight. In this way First Woman can continue having intercourse with the sun and so could guarantee a continuing cycle of rebirth (Diaz-Granados et al. 2015). Caves are not the only Mississippian things that act as wombs. Hall (1997) noted that sweat lodges were considered wombs, because a supplicant enters the lodge and emerges as if reborn. Bucko (1998, 76) reported that Black Elk, of the Lakota, described emerging from the sweat lodge as if you are "like a baby coming out of your mother's womb, our real mother, the earth." Mooney (1896) reports a very similar sentiment among the Kiowa.

Hall (1997), drawing on Mesoamerican and North American ethnohistoric literature, as well as on Hopewell imagery, made the case that a hand is also something like a womb because a hand can "enclose and hold" and so was used by Mississippians as a womb metaphor. Mississippian images of hands were drawn such that the interior lines of the hand were shaped like a vulva, similar to the ancient images drawn on the wall of Picture Cave. This opening in the hand was a portal of sorts such that spirits (life) could emerge from the palm of the hand (Hall 1997, 127). The hand-and-eye motif, common in Southeastern Mississippian art, is similarly like the vulva, a portal for spirits. Likewise, carved-stone figurines share this imagery, and some interpret them as depicting women with plants to represent fertility (Emerson 1982, 1989, 2015; Emerson and Boles 2010).

CARVED-STONE FIGURINES

The Sponemann figurine[2] (figure 11.2B, found at the northern edge of Cahokia at the Sponemann site, has been argued to depict a woman, or more likely Corn Mother / First Woman, holding a plant stalk in each outstretched hand, thus representing fertility (Emerson 1982, 2015; Jackson et al. 1992). Instead, following Hall's (1997) identification of hands as vulvas, it is more likely that Corn Mother is giving birth to these plants through her hands. I suspect this figurine was not simply representing fertility, or women, or birth, but that it possessed forces or powers related to birth. It *was* a portal. This figurine and others like it were likely nonhuman persons to whom feminine power was distributed. Control of this power is why such figurines had to be killed and buried when decommissioned (see Jackson et al. 1992). The Sponemann carved person not only birthed plants from her hands but she also displayed elements of the underworld (the night) in the form of serpents entwined about her person, reminiscent of the suite of female and serpent images of Picture Cave.

A comparable stone figurine was found in Arkansas, but was sourced as having originated from Cahokia (Emerson et al. 2002, 2003). Called the Westbrook or McGhee pipe (figure 11.2C), this figurine, unlike the others, was found in a burial located in the center of a mound. The interment was believed to be that of a female individual who had a conch shell placed above her shoulders instead of her skull (Colvin 2012). The carved figure appears to be emerging from a funerary basket (the underworld) and like the Sponemann figure, is birthing plants from the outstretched palms of her hands.

Serpents are more prominent on the Birger figurine (figure 11.2D), found at the BBB motor site northeast of Cahokia, which has a female figurine holding a hoe "tilling" the back of a serpent. She also has gourds growing on her back (Emerson and Jackson 1984). The body of the serpent or snake nearly encircles the female's body, creating what Kent Reilly (2004, 134) has suggested is an *ogee*, a term used to denote a curved shape that is considered to be a portal to the underworld. In this case the ogee is likely better termed a vulva. Perhaps she is also emerging from the underworld but this time through the vulva (portal) created by the snake (both snakes and funerary baskets are of the underworld). It is the snake that becomes the vines that extend up the woman's back, linking her to the underworld (night), life and death. A more recently discovered carved-stone figurine draws in the feminine power of rain or water. This carving, called a fertility goddess, was found at Cahokia's East St. Louis site (figure 11.2E). It portrays a kneeling woman pouring water out of a marine shell cup (Emerson 2015; Emerson and Boles 2010). This shell iconography is reminiscent of the female whose head was replaced with a conch shell (described above), thus putting together themes of women and the night through associations of water, birth, and the underworld (serpents).

The described carved beings all relate women to serpents, the underworld, birthing, and life and death. But more significant, the figurines were not created to be representations or mnemonics. As has been well recorded for Siouan societies, objects can have and exercise great power (e.g., Bailey 1995; Fletcher and La

FIGURE 11.3. (A) Keller figurine (courtesy of the Illinois State Archaeological Survey, University of Illinois). (B) Image of initiate and portable shrine (from La Flesche 1930).

Flesche 1992). These objects were likely seen as actual portals or places from which spirits could emerge. They were things or actually nonhuman persons that could link feminine powers of life and death to flesh-and-blood people. They tell us that feminine powers of the night controlled life and death, and were associated with the underworld from where serpents and water emerge. They remind us that life for Cahokians did not always require flesh-and-blood bodies. Life or spirits could exist in many media, and spirits could and did move between forms and dimensions. The carved-stone objects were extraordinary because they could facilitate this movement and give us a hint of what that might have entailed.

However, it is the Keller figurine (figure 11.3A) that perhaps best connects the past, the present, and the powers of unseen forces and ties images on the carved-stone figurines to archaeological finds and to the Emerald shrine center. Alice Kehoe (2007) has written that the Keller figurine, which depicts a female character kneeling on a mat in front of what is often interpreted as a basket, actually might be a depiction of a woman weaving and engaged in the Osage *wa-xo'-be* ritual. The Keller figurine looks very similar to a drawn image in the La Flesche report (1930, plate 6, 563) of an initiate seated with both hands upon the portable shrine (figure 11.3B). Kehoe (2007, 2008) is likely correct that the Keller figurine is connected to a portable shrine resembling that described by La Flesche for the wa-xo'-be ritual. Both the historic ritual and the carved figurine place women in the midst of what is vital. The Osage wa-xo'-be ceremonies involved the creation of war medicine bundles, or portable shrines, for newly initiated priests and the ceremony required a woman, as part of the ritual, to weave the rush mat that enveloped a portion of the bundle.

According to La Flesche (1930) *wa-xo'-be* meant "sacred thing," a name also applied to sacred bundles, which were also called portable shrines. La Flesche reported in detail on the making of the Osage war bundle or shrine, which held a (symbolic) hawk. The shrine had three parts: a woven buffalo-hair bag, a deer-skin bag, and a woven-rush bag. The hawk was placed inside the woven-rush bag or envelope, rolled up inside of all three layers, and then tied. When the hawk was removed from the wrappings it was seen as a spirit "being born" (La Flesche 1930). A new wa-xo'-be shrine needed to be created when a man was to be initiated into the wa-xo'-be priesthood, a difficult calling to achieve. A woman was required to weave the rush envelope, which was the most sacred of the three layers of the bundle. The appointed woman was one who owned the proper *wi'-gi-e* (prayer song), as well as a sacred weaving frame, and who agreed to be paid for the task. She was given four days to weave the envelope and had to do so in isolation, either walled off in her home or in a separate building where no one else could enter, as the uninitiated could not be permitted to see the process or hear the wi'-gi-e. The envelope for the shrine was woven with rush, a water plant that had to be provided by people associated with water clans. The envelope was woven with designs equally representing the sky (undyed rush) and the earth (bands of light and dark). The wi'-gi-e sung by the weaver as she wove the rush shrine, as described by La Flesche (1930), indicates the Osage concern with the sky and earth which are home to Wa'-kan'-da, day and night, balance, and order. "To each of these four phases of the night, and to the sun and to the sky was a given a symbolic line in the shrine that typifies all the visible universe" (La Flesche 1930, 697). The lines of color for the wa-xo'-be described in the wi'-gi-e are surprisingly reminiscent of lines of color created by Cahokians when engaged in creating structured deposits on the floors of their shrine houses at the Emerald shrine center, as will be described in the next section.

The Emerald site, dated to the beginnings of Cahokia, was a place dedicated to spirits, powers, and the forces of wind, water, and most particularly the moon. It was located on a ridge in the uplands east of downtown Cahokia. To create Emerald, the Cahokians reshaped the natural ridge through earthmoving projects until it more perfectly aligned with a lunar standstill position (Pauketat et al. 2017), which is the most extreme position of the moon's long 18.6-year cycle and can be seen in the sky for a few months (Pauketat 2012). Just as important as the moon at Emerald were water and wind. The ridge sat upon a perched water table that caused water to ooze out of the sides of the ridge after rain (Alt 2018). The ridge also sat adjacent to a natural spring that provided water from deep underground. Wind is also prominent at Emerald, where a breeze can be felt when the air is still over the adjacent prairie and storms can be viewed as they approach from miles away (Alt 2016, 2018).

The Emerald ridge had twelve mounds built upon it organized into rows that are aligned to reference the lunar standstill. The ridge was covered in buildings, many of which were rebuilt numerous times, but few to none appear to have been for long-term living. While overbuilt with religious and public structures as well as with what we believe to be pilgrim housing, there is evidence of little other than religious activity, which occurred intermittently (Pauketat et al. 2017). Prominent among the structures were shrine houses and sweat lodges, many of which were also aligned with lunar standstills. Emerald was a place visited by people from all across the Midwest who traveled on roadways that led to Emerald from the south and away again toward Cahokia (Skousen 2016). It was a place where the new Mississippian religion was practiced, if not born, both before and after the rise of Cahokia as a major center (Alt 2018; Pauketat and Alt 2018; Pauketat et al. 2017).

I focus on shrine houses, which were buildings that were constructed at Emerald for religious purposes. They were notable for their applied yellow-clay-plastered floors. Their complex life histories of use and reuse reflect reengagement, even after being decommissioned (Alt 2016, 2018). In areas of the site with shrines there were also sweat lodges and large rotundas believed to be water temples (Pauketat et al. 2017). Sweat lodges, as mentioned, were often related to wombs in ethnohistoric accounts (Alt 2016, 2018), and the shrine houses just might be related to the portable shrines of the Osage. The twelve semisubterranean shrine-house basins (each up to a meter in depth) had several characteristics in common with each other. Some of those characteristics recall elements related to the Osage portable shrines. When each shrine house at Emerald was finally decommissioned it was refilled, but that infilling happened in a patterned way, and after being refilled, each basin had been reexcavated by the ancient Cahokians so that new offerings and rituals could be made. Every

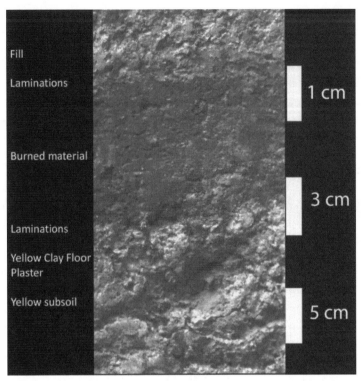

Fill

Laminations

1 cm

Burned material

3 cm

Laminations

Yellow Clay Floor
Plaster

Yellow subsoil

5 cm

FIGURE 11.4. *Soil profile of an Emerald shrine-house floor showing layers of color indicating fill, laminations, burned zones, and yellow-clay plaster on the floor, over subsoil. (Photo by Susan Alt)*

shrine was closed with water-washed silts, and on their floors most had burned materials, woven fabrics, and hides. The wi'-gi-e (prayer song) for the weaving of the wa-xo'-be describes a yellow line, a line of pallid hue, a crimson line, and a blue-black line (La Flesche 1930). The song describes the lines of yellow, which stand for the passing of night and the moon, a line of pallid hue for the coming of day, crimson for the approach of the sun, and a blue-black line for the return of night. These lines of color approximate the lines of color found in structured deposits of decommissioned shrines of Emerald (figure 11.4). Most of the shrines had yellow-clay-plastered floors that were covered over by water-washed silts (a pallid hue), red lenses from *in situ* burning (a crimson line), and layers of burned material (a blue-black line). While meaning in the Emerald deposits is certainly not identical to that in the Osage wi'-gi-e, it is likely that, given the repeated use of this depositional liturgy in nearly every shrine with an undamaged floor, it demonstrates a similar general concern and honoring of natural cycles and balance.

The floors of shrine houses further resonate with the creation of the Osage portable shrine in that many of the shrines thus far excavated have had burned hide and fabric on their floors, just as the portable hawk shrine had layers of woven-rush fabric and hide as part of its bundle. The orientation of shrines to the lunar standstill suggests that they were related not only to the moon and so to the night, but also to women, who shared feminine powers with the moon. The Emerald deposition and the Keller figurine, which features a woman with a portable shrine, seem to suggest that women and shrines might have been associated at the very beginnings of Cahokia.

The associations of women, water, the underworld (serpents), and the moon merge in other ways at Cahokia's Emerald shrine center. At Emerald, the body of a young human being, likely a female sacrifice, was buried in the post-hole from a large marker post (Alt 2015) that was placed along an alignment of constructions marking a lunar event—a cosmological happening visible at night (Pauketat 2012). But more important, her body was first covered by water-washed silts before being buried. That she was buried where a post was pulled might relate to the association of women with the underworld, or perhaps to the Siouan sacred pole rituals (Fletcher 1896). Her body might have been needed to mitigate the powers and forces released by the removal of the post. As seen in the shrine houses, water mattered greatly at Emerald.

Emerald sat above a natural spring and, as noted previously, nearly all of the Emerald shrine houses were decommissioned by the placement of burned offerings on their floors followed by water-washed silts (Alt 2016, 2018; Pauketat and Alt 2018). In Siouan cosmologies water was part of the earth, associated with feminine powers (Bailey 1995; Dorsey 1894, Fletcher and La Flesche 1992). Burned offerings found in shrines included items such as a tiny carved-clay figure clearly displaying breasts and a vulva, as well as sherds with vulva-form shapes applied to them. The sacrificed female was placed in what was a decommissioned post pit, but her body was encased by water-washed silts before she was finally covered over with soils and buried (Alt 2015, 2016). She was encased in both parts of the lower world, water and earth, and laid in a post pit that was aligned to a lunar standstill.

The Emerald site was created to reference the moon; the orientation of the ridge and nearly all important constructions that align to lunar standstills reinforce this fact (Alt 2016, 2018; Alt and Pauketat 2018; Pauketat and Alt 2017; Pauketat et al. 2017; Skousen 2016). Siouan oral histories tie the moon and earth to women, and the sun and sky to men. Carved-stone figurines and cave art reinforce the notion that these associations likely had a Mississippian if not an earlier derivation. Precise interpretations are not possible for the figurative art, since we must assume that specific meanings have shifted through time. However, it is not impossible that general relationships or associations of persons, things, and kinds of powers discussed in ethnohistorical reports might resonate with evidence from the deeper past. It is startling to find in deposition the same order of colors, kinds of materials, and groupings of things described ethnohistorically for portable shrines and the rituals for their making as well as a carved figurine that seems to tie together all of these items. The associations all point to an important role for women and the moon in the creation of Mississippian religion that occurred at Cahokia. The reanalysis of mound 72 reinforces that fact.

CONNECTING THE EMERALD SITE AND PICTURE CAVE

The Emerald site and Picture Cave both evoked the night, and thereby women, in more ways than those already mentioned. For example, at Emerald, shrine houses were dug deep into the ground, entailing dark interiors similar to sweat lodges. Both were places where I suspect prayer and renewals occurred, if not visions and sacred dreams, suggesting both were portals, or wombs, places where spirits traveled. Picture Cave, another dark interior place, had walls covered in images, or rather portals to or elements of sacred beings and events. But for the images to be placed on walls, someone must have envisioned them in a dream so that they could access the powers or forces that inhabited the images. For the Ponca and Omaha, the right to paint or wear a mystery image must originate in a dream (Dorsey 1890 cited in Diaz Granados et al. 2015, 205). If this more was violated, dream spirits would punish transgressors. Dreams are of the night. Emerald was also of the night, as the entire reconfigured ridge and its buildings were themselves a shrine to the moon.

CONCLUSIONS

The Mississippian night brought the moon and dreams. The night brought histories and stories of intercourse between mother earth and father sky that created the people, spirits, and the world. Dreams painted on walls and carved in stone tell us about some of the numinous beings in the Mississippian world. But more, they tell us that nonhuman persons were as much the founders of Cahokia as flesh-and-blood people were. The Emerald site and Picture Cave date to the foundations of Cahokia, so it follows that Cahokia could not have come to be if not for the dreams that were painted on cave walls, carved as other-than-human stone women, or the feminine powers of the moon. Dreams were reality, and stone carvings were persons who engaged with humans to order the Mississippian world. Every night Mississippian people would see the moon and remember First Woman, who had sex with the sun and who gave birth to so many persons and things. Night would remind everyone of the feminine powers that helped create the world.

Mississippian beginnings at Cahokia have most often been associated with male powers, the sun, and symbols of power such as birds of prey and falcon dancers. This association is often connected to the Mound 72 burial and the Red Horn story cycle. Evidence of feminine powers has been around for just as long but has not received nearly as much attention (Alt and Pauketat 2007; Emerson 1982, 2015; Emerson et al. 2016). The recently published reevaluations of Mound 72 burials, and the discovered gender balance in the main burials, should begin to change that story. Evidence for female power is equally present in Mound 72, and is further demonstrated on carved-stone figurines and in cave art. These images can still be related to ethnohistoric accounts of how Siouan speakers ordered their society and their ontological and cosmological understandings of how life worked, but need to be seen as a story of balance. Even the resting warrior pipe (figure 11.2A), which has been interpreted as an image of Red Horn, has an ogee carved on a circular disk that rests on his head. This form balances the overtly masculine sense of the carved male figurine by adding feminine powers (of the night) to it. We need to pay attention to the fact that male and female, day and night, were both honored by past people. As the Osage and the Cahokians knew, both were necessary to keep the cosmos balanced and ordered. They have told us so in their art and oral histories.

NOTES

1. I focus on Siouan traditions as it has become more common for Cahokia analysts to suggest that Siouan speakers are likely Cahokian descendants (Diaz-Granados et al. 2015; Kehoe 2007, 2008; Kelly and Brown 2012). Siouan groups today include Plains groups such as the Osage, Omaha, Quapaw, Ho-Chunk (Winnebago), Mandan, Dakota, Crow, Hidatsa, and others.

2. An unnamed and incomplete carved figurine was also found at the Sponemann site. There was just enough of it intact to determine that it had images of birthing powers similar to those of the Sponemann figurine (Emerson 1982; Jackson et al. 1992).

REFERENCES

Alberti, Benjamin, Andrew Meirion Jones, and Joshua Pollard. 2013. *Archaeology after Interpretation: Returning Materials to Archaeology.* Walnut Creek, CA: Left Coast Press.

Alt, Susan M. 2015. "Human Sacrifice at Cahokia." In *Medieval Mississippians: The Cahokian World,* ed. Timothy R. Pauketat and Susan M. Alt, 27. Santa Fe, NM: School for Advanced Research Press.

Alt, Susan M. 2016. "Building Cahokia: Transformation through Tradition." In *Vernacular Architecture in the Americas,* ed. Christina T. Halperin and Lauren E. Schwartz, 141–157. New York: Routledge Press.

Alt, Susan M. 2018. "Putting Religion Ahead of Politics: Cahokia Origins Viewed through Emerald Shrines." In *Archaeology and Ancient Religion in the American Midcontinent* (Archaeology of the American South: New Directions and Perspectives), ed. Brad Koldehoff and Timothy R. Pauketat, 208–233. Tuscaloosa: University of Alabama Press.

Alt, Susan M., and Timothy R. Pauketat. 2007. "Sex and the Southern Cult." In *The Southeastern Ceremonial Complex*, ed. Adam King, 232–250. Tuscaloosa: University of Alabama Press.

Alt, Susan M., and Timothy R. Pauketat. 2018. "The Elements of Cahokian Shrine Complexes and Basis of Mississippian Religion." In *Religion and Politics in The Ancient Americas*, ed. Sarah B. Barber and Arthur A. Joyce, 51–74. London and New York: Routledge Press.

Bailey, Garrick A. 1995. *The Osage and the Invisible World from the Works of Francis La Flesche*. Norman: University of Oklahoma Press.

Bird-David, Nurit. 1999. "'Animism' Revisited: Personhood, Environment, and Relational Epistemology." *Current Anthropology* 40(S1 supplement):67–91. https://doi .org/10.1086/200061.

Blackwood, Evelyn. 1984. "Sexuality and Gender in Certain Native American Tribes: The Case of Cross-Gender Females." *Signs (Chicago, IL)* 10(1):27–42. https://doi.org /10.1086/494112.

Brown, James A. 2003. "The Cahokia Mound 72-Sub1 Burials as Collective Representation." *Wisconsin Archeologist* 84:81–97.

Brown, James A. 2004. "The Cahokian Expression: Creating Court and Cult." In *Hero, Hawk, and Open Hand: American Indian Art of the Ancient Midwest and South*, ed. Richard F. Townsend and Robert V. Sharp, 105–121. New Haven, CT: Art Institute of Chicago and Yale University Press.

Brown, James A. 2007. "On the Identity of the Birdman within Mississippian Period Art and Iconography." In *Ancient Objects and Sacred Realms*, ed. F. Kent Reilly III and James F. Garber, 56–106. Austin: University of Texas Press.

Brown, James A. 2010. "Cosmological Layouts of Secondary Burials as Political Instruments." In *Mississippian Mortuary Practices: Beyond Hierarchy and the Representationist Perspective*, ed. Lynne P. Sullivan and Robert C. Mainfort, 30–53. Gainesville: University of Florida Press. https://doi.org/10.5744/florida/978 0813034263.003.0003.

Brown, James A., and John E. Kelly. 2000. "Cahokia and the Southeastern Ceremonial Complex." In *Mounds, Modoc, and Mesoamerica: Papers in Honor of Melvin L. Fowler*, vol. 27. ed. Steven R. Ahler, 469–510. Springfield: Illinois State Museum Scientific Papers.

Brück, Joanna. 2006. "Fragmentation, Personhood and the Social Construction of Technology in Middle and Late Bronze Age Britain." *Cambridge Archaeological Journal* 16(3):297–315. https://doi.org/10.1017/S0959774306000187.

Buchanan, Meghan, and B. Jacob Skousen, eds. 2015. *Tracing the Relational: The Archaeology of Worlds, Spirits, and Temporalities, Foundations of Archaeological Inquiry*. Salt Lake City: University Press of Utah.

Bucko, R. 1998. *The Lakota Ritual of the Sweat Lodge: History and Contemporary Practice*. Lincoln: University of Nebraska Press.

Christenson, Allen J. 2007. *Popol Vuh: The Sacred Book of the Maya: The Great Classic of Central American Spirituality*. Norman: University of Oklahoma Press.

Colvin, Matthew H. 2012. "Old-Woman-Who-Never-Dies: A Mississippian Survival in The Hidatsa World." MA Thesis, Texas State University, San Marcos.

Cordova, Viola F., Kathleen Dean Moore, Kurt Peters, Ted Jojola, and Amber Lacy. 2007. *How It Is: The Native American Philosophy of Viola F. Cordova*. Tucson: University Press of Arizona.

Deloria, Vine, Jr. 1995. *Red Earth, White Lies: Native Americas and The Myth of Scientific Fact*. New York: Scribner.

Deloria, Vine, Jr. 2006. *The World We Used to Live in: Remembering the Powers of the Medicine Men*. Golden, CO: Fulcrum Publishing.

Diaz-Granados, Carol, James R. Duncan, and F. Kent Reilly, III, eds. 2015. *Picture Cave: Unravelling the Mysteries of the Mississippian Cosmos*. Austin: University of Texas Press.

Dorsey, George A. 1906. "The Skidi Rite of Human Sacrifice." *International Congress of Americanists* 15:66–70.

Dorsey, James Owen. 1894. "A Study of Siouan Cults." In *Eleventh Annual Report of the Bureau of Ethnology*, dir. John Wesley Powell, 351–554. Washington, DC: Government Printing Office.

Duncan, James R., and Carol Diaz-Granados. 2000. "Of Masks and Myths." *Midcontinental Journal of Archaeology, MCJA* 25(1):1–26.

Emerson, Thomas E. 1982. *Mississippian Stone Images in Illinois,* Circular No. 6. Urbana: Illinois Archaeology Survey.

Emerson, Thomas E. 1989. "Water, Serpents, and the Underworld: An Exploration into Cahokia Symbolism." In *The Southeastern Ceremonial Complex: Artifacts and Analysis*, ed. Patricia Galloway, 45–92. Lincoln: University of Nebraska Press.

Emerson, Thomas E. 2015. "The Earth Goddess Cult at Cahokia." In *Medieval Mississippians: The Cahokian World*, ed. Timothy R. Pauketat and Susan M. Alt, 55–62. Santa Fe, NM: School for Advanced Research Press.

Emerson, Thomas E., and Steve Boles. 2010. "Contextualizing Flint Clay Cahokia Figures at the East St. Louis Mound Center." *Illinois Archaeology* 22(2):473–490.

Emerson, Thomas E., Kristin M. Hedman, Eve A. Hargrave, Dawn E. Cobb, and Andrew R. Thompson. 2016. "Paradigms Lost: Reconfiguring Cahokia's Mound 72 Beaded Burial." *American Antiquity* 81(3):405–425.

Emerson, Thomas E., Randall E. Hughes, Mary R. Hynes, and Sarah U. Wisseman. 2002. "Implications of Sourcing Cahokia-Style Flintclay Figures in the American Bottom and the Upper Mississippi River Valley." *Midcontinental Journal of Archaeology, MCJA* 27:309–338.

Emerson, Thomas E., Randall E. Hughes, Mary R. Hynes, and Sarah U. Wisseman. 2003. "The Sourcing and Interpretation of Cahokia-Style Figurines in the

Trans-Mississippi South and Southeast." *American Antiquity* 68(02):287–313. https://doi.org/10.2307/3557081.

Emerson, Thomas E., and Douglas K. Jackson. 1984. *The BBB Motor Site (11-Ms–595)*. American Bottom Archaeology, FAI-270 Site Reports No. 6. Urbana and Chicago: Published for the Illinois Department of Transportation by the University of Illinois Press.

Fletcher, Alice C. 1896. "The Emblematic Use of the Tree in the Dakotan Group." *Science* 4(92):475–487. https://doi.org/10.1126/science.4.92.475.

Fletcher, Alice C. 1910. "Wakonda." In *Handbook of American Indians North of Mexico*, ed. Hodge Frederick Webb. Bureau of American Ethnology. Washington, DC: Government Printing Office.

Fletcher, Alice C., and Francis La Flesche. 1992 [1911]. *The Omaha Tribe.* vol. 1 and 2. Lincoln: University of Nebraska Press.

Fortune, R. F. 2011. *Columbia University Contributions to Anthropology.* vol. 14. Omaha Secret Societies. Whitefish, MT: Literary Licensing.

Fowler, Chris. 2004. *The Archaeology of Personhood: An Anthropological Approach.* London: Routledge.

Fowler, Melvin L., Jerome C. Rose, Barbara Vander Leest, and Steven R. Ahler. 1999. *The Mound 72 Area: Dedicated and Sacred Space in Early Cahokia.* Reports of Investigations, no. 54. Springfield: Illinois State Museum.

Hall, Robert L. 1989. "The Cultural Background of Mississippian Symbolism." In *The Southeastern Ceremonial Complex*, ed. Patricia Galloway, 239–278. Lincoln: University of Nebraska Press.

Hall, Robert L. 1991. "Cahokia Identity and Interaction Models of Cahokia Mississippian." In *Cahokia and the Hinterlands: Middle Mississippian Cultures of the Midwest*, ed. Thomas E. Emerson and R. Barry Lewis, 3–34. Urbana: University of Illinois Press.

Hall, Robert L. 1997. *An Archaeology of the Soul: Native American Indian Belief and Ritual.* Urbana: University of Illinois Press.

Hallowell, Irving. 1960. "Ojibwa Ontology, Behavior, and World View." In *Culture in History: Essays in Honor of Paul Radin*, ed. Stanley Diamond, 19–52. New York: Columbia University Press.

Hallowell, Irving. 1976. "Ojibwe Ontology, Behavior and Worldview." In *Contributions to Anthropology: Selected Papers of A. Irving Hallowell*, ed. Irving Hallowell, 357–390. Chicago: University of Chicago Press.

Harvey, Graham. 2005. *Animism: Respecting the Living World.* New York: Columbia University Press.

Holliman, Sandra. 1994. "The Third Gender in Native California: Two-Spirit Undertakers Among the Chumash and Their Neighbours." In *Women in Prehistory:*

North America and Mesoamerica, ed. Cheryl Claassen and Rosemary A. Joyce, 173–188. Philadelphia: University of Pennsylvania Press.

Holliman, Sandra. 2001. "The Antiquity of Systems of Multiple Genders." In *The Archaeology of Shamanism*, ed. Neil Price, 123–134. London: Routledge.

Hudson, Charles. 1976. *The Southeastern Indians*. Knoxville: University of Tennessee Press.

Hultkrantz, Åke. 1967. *The Religions of the American Indians*. Berkeley: University of California Press.

Hultkrantz, Åke. 1981. *Belief and Worship in Native North America*. Syracuse, NY: Syracuse University Press.

Hultkrantz, Åke. 1987. *Native Religions of North America*. San Francisco, CA: Harper and Row.

Irwin, Lee. 1994. *The Dream Seekers: Native American Visionary Traditions of the Great Plains*. Norman: University of Oklahoma.

Jackson, Douglas K., Andrew C. Fortier, and Joyce Williams. 1992. *The Sponemann Site 2 (11-Ms-517): The Mississippian and Oneota Occupations*. American Bottom Archaeology, FAI-270 Site Reports No. 24. Urbana: University of Illinois Press.

Jacobs, S-E. 1994. "Native American Two-Spirits." *Anthropology Newsletter* November: 7. https://doi.org/10.1111/an.1994.35.8.7.

Joyce, Rosemary A. 2008. *Ancient Bodies, Ancient Lives: Sex, Gender, and Archaeology*. London: Thames and Hudson.

Kehoe, Alice B. 2007. "Osage Texts and Cahokia Data: Ancient Objects and Sacred Realms: Interpretations of Mississippian Iconography." In *Ancient Objects and Sacred Realms: Interpretations of Mississippian Iconography*, ed. F Kent. Reilly III, James F. Garber and Vincas P. Steponaitis, 246–261. Austin: University of Texas Press.

Kehoe, Alice B. 2008. *Controversies in Archaeology*. New York: Routledge.

Kelly, John E. 1991. "The Evidence for Prehistoric Exchange and Its Implications for the Development of Cahokia." In *New Perspectives on Cahokia: Views from the Periphery*, ed. James B. Stoltman, 65–92. Madison, WI: Prehistory Press.

Kelly, John E., and James A. Brown. 2012. "Search of Cosmic Power: Contextualizing Spiritual Journeys between Cahokia and the St. Francois Mountains." In *Archaeology of Spiritualities*, ed. Kathryn Rountree, Christine Morris, and Alan A.D. Peatfield, 107–129. New York: Springer.

La Flesche, Francis. 1914. "Ceremonies and Rituals of the Osage." In *Explorations and Field-Work of the Smithsonian Institution* SI-MC 63(8): 66–69. Washington, DC: Government Printing Office.

La Flesche, Francis. 1930. "The Osage Tribe: Rite of the Wa-Xo'-Be." Extract from the *Forty-Fifth Annual Report of the Bureau of American Ethnology*, ed. H. W. Dorsey. Smithsonian Institution, Bureau of American Ethnology. Washington, DC: Government Printing Office.

Mooney, James. 1896. "The Ghost Dance Religion and the Sioux Outbreak of 1890." *Fourteenth Annual Report of the Bureau of American Ethnology,* part 1, 653–1136. Washington, DC: Government Printing Office.

Murie, James R. 1981. *Ceremonies of the Pawnee,* ed. Douglas R. Parks. Lincoln: University of Nebraska Press.

Olsen, Bjornar, Michael Shanks, Timothy Webmoor, and Christopher L. Witmore, eds. 2012. *Archaeology: The Discipline of Things.* Oakland: University of California Press. https://doi.org/10.1525/california/9780520274167.001.0001.

Pauketat, Timothy R. 2007. *Chiefdoms and Other Archaeological Delusions.* Walnut Creek, CA: AltaMira.

Pauketat, Timothy R. 2008. "Founders' Cults and the Archaeology of Wa-kan-da." In *Memory Work: Archaeologies of Material Practices,* ed. Barbara Mills and William H. Walker, 61–79. Santa Fe, NM: School for Advanced Research Press.

Pauketat, Timothy R. 2009. *Cahokia: Ancient America's Great City on the Mississippi.* New York: Viking-Penguin Press.

Pauketat, Timothy R. 2010. "The Missing Persons in Mississippian Mortuaries." In *Mississippian Mortuary Practices: Beyond Hierarchy and the Representationist Perspective,* ed. Lynne P. Sullivan and Robert C. Mainfort, 14–29. Gainesville: University Press of Florida. https://doi.org/10.5744/florida/9780813034263.003.0002.

Pauketat, Timothy R. 2012. *An Archaeology of the Cosmos: Rethinking Agency and Religion in Ancient America.* London: Routledge.

Pauketat, Timothy R., and Susan M. Alt. 2018. "Water and Shells in Bodies and Pots: Mississippian Rhizome, Cahokian Poiesis." In *Relational Identities and Other-than-Human Agency in Archaeology,* ed. Eleanor Harrison-Buck and Julia A. Hendon. Boulder: University Press of Colorado.

Pauketat, Timothy R., Susan M. Alt, and Jeffery D. Kruchten. 2017. "The Emerald Acropolis: Elevating the Moon and Water in the Rise of Cahokia." *Antiquity* 91(355):207–222

Prentice, Guy. 1986. "An Analysis of the Symbolism Expressed by the Birger Figurine." *American Antiquity* 51(02):239–266. https://doi.org/10.2307/279939.

Radin, Paul. 1948. *Winnebago Hero Cycles: A Study in Aboriginal Literature.* Indiana University Publications in Anthropology and Linguistics, Memoir 1. Baltimore, MA: Waverly Press.

Radin, Paul. 1954. *The Evolution of an American Indian Prose Epic.* Bollingen Foundation Special Publications No. 3. Basel, Switzerland: Bollingen Foundation.

Radin, Paul. 1970 [1923]. *The Winnebago Tribe.* Lincoln: University of Nebraska Press.

Reilly, F. Kent, III., and James F. Garber, eds. 2007. *Ancient Objects and Sacred Realms: Interpretations of Mississippian Iconography.* Austin: University of Texas Press.

Reilly, F. Kent, III. 2004. "People of Earth, People of Sky: Visualizing the Sacred in Native American Art of the Mississippian Period." In *Hero, Hawk, and Open Hand:*

American Indian Art of the Ancient Midwest and South, ed. Richard Townsend, 125–138. New Haven, CT: Yale University Press.

Ridington, Robin. 1988. "Knowledge, Power, and the Individual in Subarctic Hunting Societies." *American Anthropologist* 90(1):98–110. https://doi.org/10.1525/aa.1988.90.1.02a00070.

Romain, William F. 2016. "Ancient Skywatchers of the Eastern Woodlands." Manuscript on file at Illinois State Archaeological Survey, Champaign.

Roscoe, Will. 1991. *The Zuni Man-Woman*. Albuquerque: University of New Mexico Press.

Rose, Jerome C. 1999. "Mortuary Data and Analysis." In *The Mound 72 Area: Dedicated and Sacred Space in Early Cahokia*, ed. Melvin L. Fowler, Jerome C. Rose, Barbara Vander Leest and, Steven R. Ahler, 63–82. Reports of Investigations, No. 54. Springfield: Illinois State Museum.

Salzer, Robert J. 2005. "The Gottschall Site: 3,500 years of Ideological Continuity and Change." *Ontario Archaeology* 79/80:109–114.

Salzer, Robert J., and Grace Rajnovich. 2001. *The Gottschall Rockshelter: An Archaeological Mystery*. St Paul, MN: Prairie Smoke Press.

Silliman, Stephen, ed. 2008. *Collaborating at the Trowel's Edge: Teaching and Learning in Indigenous Archaeology*. Tucson: University of Arizona Press and the Amerind Foundation.

Skousen, B. Jacob. 2016. "Pilgrimage and The Construction of Cahokia: A View from the Emerald Site." PhD diss., Department of Anthropology, University of Illinois, Urbana.

Slater, Philip A., Kristin M. Hedman, and Thomas E. Emerson. 2014. "Immigrants at the Mississippian Polity of Cahokia: Strontium Isotope Evidence for Population Movement." *Journal of Archaeological Science* 44:117–127. https://doi.org/10.1016/j.jas.2014.01.022.

Thompson, Andrew R. 2013. "Odontometric Determination of Sex at Mound 72, Cahokia." *American Journal of Physical Anthropology* 151(3):408–419. https://doi.org/10.1002/ajpa.22282.

Thompson, Andrew R., Kristin M. Hedman, and Philip A. Slater. 2015. "New Dental and Isotope Evidence of Biological Distance and Place of Origin for Mass Burial Groups at Cahokia's Mound 72." *American Journal of Physical Anthropology* 158(2):341–357. https://doi.org/10.1002/ajpa.22791.

Viveiros de Castro, Eduardo. 1998. "Cosmological Deixis and Amerindian Perspectivism." *Journal of the Royal Anthropological Institute* 4(3):469–488. https://doi.org/10.2307/3034157.

Waters, Anne. 2004. *American Indian Thought*. Oxford: Blackwell Publishing.

Watkins, Joe. 2000. *Indigenous Archaeology: American Indian Values and Scientific Practice*. Walnut Creek, CA: AltaMira.

Watts, Christopher, ed. 2013. *Relational Archaeologies: Humans, Animals, Things.* New York: Routledge.

Weltfish, Gene. 1965. *The Lost Universe: Pawnee Life and Culture.* Lincoln: University of Nebraska Press.

Williams, Stephen, and John M. Goggin. 1956. "The Long Nosed God Mask in Eastern United States." *Missouri Archaeologist* 18(3):3–72.

Illuminating the Night

CHAPTER 12

A Great Secret of the West

Transformative Aspects of Artificial Light in New Kingdom Egypt

MEGHAN E. STRONG

The ancient Egyptian worldview was very much shaped by the natural landscape. As Herodotus rightly pointed out, ancient Egyptian civilization (figures 1.2–1.3) was indeed the "gift of the Nile," as the yearly inundation provided the nutrient-rich silt and the river provided the water necessary to sustain agricultural production. Daily life was also very much governed by the continuous cycle of day and night. As with all things in ancient Egypt, the concepts of duality, balance, and right order (*ma'at*) were central to the interplay of light and dark. The bright, life-giving rays of the sun allowed plants to flourish in the fields, but at the same time could cause living creatures to suffer under its intense, scorching heat. Darkness offered a retreat from the constant, glaring sun but also provided cover for evil deeds. It is, therefore, not surprising that these two opposing forces of light and dark, day and night, were a core component of ancient Egyptian religious ideology, and consequently became the setting for numerous ritual performances. My examination of the "archaeology of the night" in ancient Egypt views artificial lighting as an intermediary between these two worlds of light and dark. This chapter focuses on the use

DOI: 10.5876/9781607326786.c012

of artificial lighting devices (see McGuire, chapter 13, this volume, for more on ancient lighting) during the funeral rites, as recorded in spell 137A of the *Book of the Dead*, a New Kingdom (1550–1069 BC) religious text. The inclusion of lighting implements among funerary goods placed in the burial chamber, and their appearance in the decorative program, are also considered.

The liminal stage of death was very much associated with the diurnal cycle of day and night in ancient Egypt. Just as the sun god, Ra, "died" in the west every day and plunged the Egyptian landscape into darkness, so the deceased also journeyed to the west, to brave the treacherous path to the Hall of Osiris, god of the underworld. Based on textual and iconographic evidence, Egyptologists know that artificial lighting played a part in the performance of the funeral ritual, and subsequent offerings to the dead throughout the year (Davies 1924; Gutbub 1961; Luft 2009). In contrast, the types of lighting used and the significance of employing lighting within this sacred space are minimally understood.

Before being able to discuss the ideology behind the funerary use of ritual illumination, it is necessary to understand the light sources themselves. Previous scholarship on illumination in ancient Egypt, however, has suffered from a lack of clearly defined terminology and typology of artificial lighting equipment. The Egyptians themselves were not particularly explicit in describing their ritual lighting devices and, as a result, the materials used to create these objects, their shape, color, and size, the context in which the lights would have been used, and the ritual significance of light sources is not always apparent. Unfortunately, academic investigation in this topic has further muddied the waters. What one Egyptologist refers to as a candle, another may describe as a lamp, torch, taper, or wick. An additional problem is the lack of textual material referencing lighting equipment. There may be, for example, only one text in the corpus of hieroglyphic writings that mentions a specific lighting device. Given these methodological limitations, it seems appropriate also to examine the material record of lighting paraphernalia in order to link, as best as possible, specific hieroglyphic words with associated physical objects. This, too, however, is not without its challenges. Egyptologists know very little about the physical objects that the ancient Egyptians used for illumination. As some have argued, this may be a problem of recognition on our part, but it may also be due to a lack of thorough analysis of the material (Robins 1939a, 185). There is in fact only a single three-page article that discusses lighting in ancient Egypt archaeologically (Robins 1939a). Since it was written, all subsequent mentions of artificial lighting equipment, albeit very few, have reiterated the same conclusions: (1) the ancient Egyptians used "floating-wick" oil lamps for illumination, an assertion based on Herodotus's (2.62) account of a festival celebration at Sais (Fischer 1980, 913; Forbes 1966, 143; Nelson 1949, 321–325; Robins 1939a, 185); and (2) the Egyptians must have also used some form of handheld torch/candle because of their depiction in temple and tomb reliefs from the New

Kingdom (Davies 1924, 9–14; Forbes 1966, 127–128; Nelson 1949, 321–325; Robins 1939a, 186). The entrenched acceptance of these conclusions into the scholarly literature has resulted in confusing terminology and a false idea that there is little information to gain from an archaeological examination of light. The first portion of this chapter therefore provides a typology of lighting devices. Significantly, all of the extant examples used to create this typology were found within mortuary contexts and are therefore directly relevant to a discussion on ritual lighting for the benefit of a deceased individual.

In contrast to the disparate opinions on artificial lighting paraphernalia, scholarly opinion on the symbolic meaning behind using ritual illumination in a mortuary context consistently centers on protection (Gutbub 1961; Haikal 1985; Régen 2010; Schott 1937). An element of protection is certainly implicit in the use of artificial lighting during the funeral rites. Several texts related to the afterlife specifically mention the use of lighting for the purposes of expelling enemies from the deceased:

> Father of Teti, father of Teti in darkness; Father of Teti, Atum, in darkness; bring Teti to your side that he may kindle a tkA [a light source] for you and protect you as Nun protected these four goddesses on the day they protected the throne, Isis, Nepthys, Neith, Serket.
>
> (UTTERANCE 362, TETI PYRAMID TEXTS[1])

> The eye of Horus [the light source] is your magical protection, Osiris, Foremost of the Westerners.
>   It exerts its protection over you, it overthrows all of your enemies."
>
> (SPELL 137A, BOOK OF THE DEAD, PAPYRUS OF NU, EA 10477)

What is problematic with previous interpretations of the ritual application of artificial lighting is the implication that this light is intended to protect against darkness (Davies and Gardiner 1915; Fischer 1977; Haikal 1985; Luft 2009). This gloss suggests a modern, classical interpretation of darkness, which has become entangled with connotations of evil, ignorance, and death (Galinier et al. 2010). As an alternative interpretation, the second half of this chapter suggests that artificial lighting was used as a ritual agent not to ward off darkness, but rather to embrace darkness as a necessary environment for the revitalization of the deceased. In this way, ritual illumination marked the transition between day (land of the living) and night (land of the dead), but also served as a marker of the deceased's rebirth and transformation into a divine spirit in the afterlife.

ARCHAEOLOGICAL EVIDENCE FOR ARTIFICIAL LIGHTING

Before entering into a discussion about why the ancient Egyptians used artificial lighting in rituals for the dead, it is necessary to understand what types of lighting paraphernalia they employed. The physical form(s) of artificial lighting devices during the Pharaonic period (2600–644 BCE) of ancient Egypt has seldom been discussed by scholars, with few conclusions put forward as to the form or composition of these sources of illumination. F. W. Robins (1939b, 44) in *The Story of the Lamp* perhaps summarized the issue best in that "the one thing that seems shrouded in mysterious darkness is that of Egyptian methods of artificial lighting." In fact, the majority of ideas published on artificial light were put forward in the early 1900s, with the most recent discussion in 1958 suggesting that "the story and chronology of lamps in ancient Egypt is yet to be studied properly" (Forbes 1966, 143). One of the great difficulties in identifying oil lamps, torches, and so on is a distinct lack of settlement evidence where artificial lighting certainly would have been used in domestic spaces. Therefore, the information that follows is primarily drawn from a mortuary context, which, though incredibly useful, is minimal. After a careful (re)examination of the existing literature, supplemented with personal museum visits, I have established a typology in order to identify and categorize lighting implements in the ancient Egyptian material record. I have purposefully avoided using abstract, twenty-first-century Western terminology, such as *torch* or *candle*, as earlier discussions of lighting devices have exclusively taken this type of etic approach in describing these implements. As much as possible, this study employs an emic perspective, describing the lighting devices in terms of the essential components emphasized by the ancient Egyptians, namely: the wick, a fuel source, and the form of vessel used to contain these two elements, if necessary. For a full discussion of the four types that I have identified—non-spouted open-vessel oil lamp, spouted open-vessel oil lamp, wick-on-stick, and wick-in-stick—see Strong (2021). In this chapter, I focus on the non-spouted open-vessel oil lamp and wick-on-stick types, as they are most relevant to a discussion of funerary lighting.

Non-spouted Open-Vessel Oil Lamp

The open-vessel oil lamp is the type used most commonly throughout the Pharaonic period. The vessels used to hold the cloth wick and fuel could be made of ceramic, stone, or metal, and ranged in form from simple, hand-made pieces to elaborately carved and painted items fit for a pharaoh.[2] This type of open-bowl lamp could also be used with or without wick holders in the form of ceramic disks (Brunton 1920; Petrie et al. 1923). Evidence from the New Kingdom (1550–1069 BC) cemetery at Deir el Medina suggests that simple oil lamps could also be enhanced by the addition of a lampstand (Bruyère 1939). One incredibly well-preserved piece was found in the tomb of Kha during Ernesto Schiaparelli's 1906 excavations (Schiaparelli 1937). This composite lamp, which bears more than a passing resemblance to a modern floor lamp, is made of two pieces: a bronze bowl formed in the shape of a lotus bud (although in the original publication it was described as a duck!) and a wooden column inserted into a hemispherical base that was painted to resemble a papyrus shoot. The bowl also contained remnants of a wick or a reed that rested up against the side of the vessel.

Wick-on-Stick Devices

As an alternative to placing a wick and fuel into a bowl to create an oil lamp, the ancient Egyptians attached the wick to a reed or stick, creating a rigid object that could be placed upright into a holder or carried in the hand. To my knowledge, the only extant example of this type of lighting device was found in the tomb of Tutankhamun (JE 62356; Egyptian Museum, Cairo) (figure 12.1). The wick is attached to a reed by a separate piece of cloth and then inserted into a small gilded tube, supported by a bronze personified *ankh* (the hieroglyphic symbol for "life"). Similarly shaped objects also appear in depictions of various rituals throughout the New Kingdom, including the illumination of thrones and the cult statue of the god in a temple (Nelson 1949; Wilson 1936). These are also the objects most frequently shown in tombs or funerary papyri as part of the offering of artificial light to the deceased (Davies and Gardiner 1915, plate XXVII).

USE OF ARTIFICIAL LIGHTING IN THE FUNERARY RITES

From the Eighteenth through Twentieth Dynasties, artificial light, particularly in the form of handheld implements of the wick-on-stick type, referred to as *tkA* (tek-ah) (singular) or *tkAw* (plural), became much more prominent in ancient Egyptian religious texts and tomb decoration. The presentation of tkAw to a deceased individual is described in spell 137A and B of the *Book of the Dead*, a collection of funerary spells and associated illustrations recorded on a papyrus scroll that would be buried with the mummy.[3] Some of the earliest examples of the *Book of the Dead* come from the beginning of the Eighteenth Dynasty (Munro 1988). One of these is the funerary papyrus of Nu (EA 10477), which serves as a reference point for this study as it contains the most complete version of spell 137A along with a vignette that illustrates aspects of the ritual performance (figure 12.2).[4] The instructions included within Nu's text also list the necessary equipment, people, and actions in order for the spell to be effective. First, four tkAw must be made of fine red linen and coated in Libyan oil. They are to be carried by four men whose arms are each inscribed with the name of one of the four sons of Horus. The tkAw are then lit and presented before the mummy while the spell is recited by a priest. At the culmination of the ritual the tkAw are extinguished in four basins of clay, which were mixed with incense and filled with the milk of a white cow. In the vignette from the papyrus of Nu, one can clearly see the tkAw (of the wick-on-stick type), their male carriers, and the four basins of milk, which are marked by hieroglyphs spelling out the ancient

FIGURE 12.1. *Lighting device of "wick-on-stick" type from the tomb of Tutankhamun (JE 62356) (c. 1336–1327 BC). The bronze ankh-holder is inserted into a roughly cut wooden base that is coated in a black resin. The lighting implement consists of a twisted linen wick attached to a reed, which extends approximately 10 inches above the top of the gilded tube in which it is placed. Two of these ankh-holders with gilded tubes were found in the tomb, but only this one retained its lighting device. (Copyright: Griffith Institute, University of Oxford)*

Egyptian word for "milk," *irtt*. The figure on the far right facing the procession represents the mummified body of Nu to whom the tkAw are being presented.

Many spells within the *Book of the Dead* descend from earlier corpora of funerary texts, namely the *Pyramid Texts* of the Old Kingdom (c. 2686–2125 BC), and the *Coffin Texts* of the First Intermediate Period (2160–2055 BC) and Middle Kingdom (2055–1650 BC). Spell 137A, however, appears to have no direct precursor in either of these texts.[5] In addition, it belongs to a unique category of spells referred to as sAxw, or "glorification texts." *Book of the Dead* spells belonging to the sAxw category differ from most *Book of the Dead* spells, which were intended to be recited by the deceased during their journey through the underworld. The

FIGURE 12.2. *Vignette of spell 137A from the papyrus of Nu (EA 10477), illustrating the performance of the ritual text. The four men, who represent the four sons of the god Horus, each carry a tkA. They are presenting the tkAw before the mummy of Nu, who is depicted on the extreme right of the image. Between the men and the mummy are four basins of milk in which the tkAw will be extinguished. (©The Trustees of the British Museum)*

sAxw, on the other hand, were recited by the living, at either the funeral or subsequent commemorative festivals, for the benefit of the deceased (Assmann 1990). The utterance of the sAxw and the performance of accompanying actions were intended to transfigure the deceased into a divine *akh*-spirit, a spiritual form associated with luminosity and light (Englund 1978).[6] Some of the sAxw texts were intended to revive the mummified corpse, such as the Opening of the Mouth ritual, which was employed to restore the senses to the deceased and to magically open the mummy's mouth so that he/she could breathe air again (Otto 1960). Other sAxw rituals included sacrificial rites, as well as spells for protection and provision of equipment for the deceased's journey in the afterlife. Previously, scholars have discussed spell 137A in the context of the latter category; a protective rite intended to provide illumination for the deceased on their long treacherous path through the underworld. This seems a logical and practical application of the light presented in spell 137A. However, in addition to the mundane function of illuminating the darkness of the underworld, I would suggest that this ritual also addressed aspects of revival and rebirth found in other sAxw texts, such as the Opening of the Mouth. This does not diminish the protective importance of artificial light. On the contrary, it illustrates that sAxw rituals could serve sympathetic functions during the transitional stage from death into afterlife.

The assertion that spell 137A played a role in the rebirth and transformation of the deceased centers upon the setting of the performance of the rite (Luft 2009; Strong 2009). As with other sAxw texts, spell 137A was most probably first performed as part of the funeral. Indeed, the postscript of the text explicitly states that in order for spell 137A to be read, the mummified body must be "reconstituted, perfected, and purified, and his mouth opened with metal" (lines 109–110).

The last of these conditions clearly refers to the Opening of the Mouth ritual, which would have been performed as part of the funerary rites. Descriptions of the Opening of the Mouth, as well as representations of it in tombs and funerary papyri, indicate that the mummy is to be placed upright in the forecourt of his/ her tomb, or perhaps just at the entrance, prior to his/her interment. The ritual is also meant to take place in broad daylight as captions from several Theban tombs provide instructions on standing the mummy up "before Ra":

> The day of burial, striding freely to his tomb.
> Performing the Opening of the Mouth at the . . . in the House of Gold,
> Set upright on the desert soil,
> Its face turned to the south,
> Bathed in light on earth on the day of being clothed.
>
> (THEBAN TOMBS 178 AND 259 [ASSMANN 2005, 317])

Referring back to the vignette in the papyrus of Nu, we may then infer that by drawing the mummy in an upright position, the scribe is indicating that the Opening of the Mouth ritual has been performed and the requirements of spell 137A for the deceased to be "reconstituted, perfected, and purified, and his mouth opened with metal" have been met. What is not explicitly stated in the directions of the spell is in what setting the presentation of the tkAw is meant to take place. Descriptions of the Opening of the Mouth ritual indicate that it was meant to be performed while the sun was still in the sky, so that the mummy could be "bathed in [natural] light." The use of artificial light, however, is something generally associated with nighttime. I propose that several lines from the text of spell 137A suggest the appropriate setting in which the tkAw are to be lit—namely at sunset, as Ra, the sun god, sets in the west (on the horizon) and begins his nightly journey through the underworld:

> It [the tkAw] comes for your ka . . . it comes announcing the night after the day.
> (Line 4)

> The sound eye of Horus [the tkAw] comes, shining like Ra in the horizon.
> (Line 33)

Performing the rite described in spell 137A at sunset imbues the artificial lighting implements, the tkAw, with several layers of meaning. First, as the text states, the light serves as a herald of the coming of night. In this capacity, the light source would mark not only the passage of time from day to night, but also the passage of the deceased from the land of the living, associated with the day, to the underworld, associated with night. It is possible that the tkAw rite was used as a culminating element of the funeral. The spell could be recited in the presence of the mourners outside of the tomb entrance, the light would be presented before the mummy, which at this point had been ceremonially awoken and prepared for his/her new existence in the underworld, and then the tkAw could be used to guide the mummy's way into the dark tomb chapel and down to the burial chamber where the deceased would finally be laid to rest. In this way, the artificial light source would mark both a physical transition (from outside the tomb to the burial chamber) and a spiritual transition (from inanimate corpse to ritually awakened to prepare for his/her journey to the Hall of Osiris).

ILLUMINATING THE BURIAL CHAMBER

Significantly, additional excerpts from spell 137A, along with depictions in tombs and papyri, imply that the presence of artificial light in the burial chamber symbolizes another transition of the deceased—becoming an *akh*. Of particular relevance is the fact that the text continually alternates back and forth between addressing the deceased and the god of the underworld, Osiris. In fact, by the New Kingdom, any deceased individual is commonly referred to as an Osiris— that is, Osiris Nu. So the presentation of artificial light in the form of tkAw is meant not only for the deceased as an Osiris, but for the actual god Osiris as well. Line 91 from the papyrus of Nu in fact explicitly states that the tkA should be lit for both the deceased individual and the god:

> Kindle this tkA for the *akh* and for Osiris Foremost of the Westerners.

The same line from spell 137A in the papyrus of Nebseni (EA 9900) is a bit more explicit in stating:

> Kindle this tkA for the *akh* in the necropolis in the presence of Osiris, the great god.

Paintings on the tympana of two Deir el Medina tombs, those of Pashed (TT3) and Amunnakht (TT 218), illustrate quite clearly the presentation of tkAw both for, and in the presence of, Osiris. Both scenes are painted within the burial chamber and in both instances the sarcophagus and coffin of the tomb owner would have been placed directly beneath these depictions. The vignette preserved on the tympanum of Pashed's tomb depicts an enthroned figure of the god Osiris wearing a gold-and-blue-striped *nemes*-headdress, which was reserved for ancient

Egyptian kings and gods, and holding the crook and flail, also symbols of royalty (Zivie 1979). In front of him, against the right side of the wall, is a seated deity who holds a bowl containing two ignited red-and-white-striped tkAw. Osiris sits in front of a depiction of the Theban hills, and behind his throne is a personified *udjat*-eye (a depiction of the eye of the falcon-headed god, Horus) with two arms extending the same type of bowl and tkAw as the deity. Directly beneath the outstretched arms of the eye, a miniature kneeling figure of the tomb owner, Pashed, raises his hands in adoration of Osiris. The line of hieroglyphic text in front of the tomb owner labels him as "Osiris, servant in the place of truth [Deir el Medina], Pashed." Behind the *udjat*-eye is a figure of Horus as a falcon, who is painted against the left side of the tympanum. The text, written along the right-hand side of the tympanum in six lines, is quite different from either form of spell 137 found in *Book of the Dead* papyri, aside from the title "Spell for kindling the tkA." The text reads, "Spell for kindling the tkA for Osiris, Foremost of the Westerners, in the necropolis. A way is opened for you in the darkness, a place that is in eternity. Your heart is powerful and broader than the sky. Osiris is the ruler of the Ennead, he remains with you for eternity" (Saleh 1984).

The tomb of Amunnakht (TT 218) is part of a tomb group for the father, Amunnakht, and his two sons, Nebenmaat and Khameteri (Porter and Moss 2004). The family had a joint offering chapel with three distinct niches for each man. All three tombs and their respective chapels are elaborately painted. While Amunnakht's sons only have one main burial chamber, Amunnakht's tomb is composed of two separate chambers, both of which are fully decorated. The depiction of the presentation of tkAw is found in the outer chamber, which would have served as Amunnkaht's burial chamber (figure 12.3). The scene is almost identical to the one in Pashed's tomb, but the text is radically shortened to only one line, "The tkA is lit for you" (Saleh 1984). Osiris remains the main figure in the scene, but he is depicted wearing the *atef*-crown. In addition to the *udjat*-eye and the Horus falcon behind Osiris, the arms of Nut receiving the sun disk within the western mountain (i.e., the horizon at Thebes) have been added. The addition of this figure and the narrowness of the chamber make the scene rather cramped, which may account for the shortening of the spell's text. In both Pashed and Amunnkaht's burial chambers, two registers of deities flank both sides of the tomb ceiling. They represent the tribunal in the Hall of Judgment and include Ptah, Thoth, Nut, Nephthys, Isis, Anubis, Wepwawet, and Khepri, among others. Both ceilings are also inscribed with hymns to Ra (Porter and Moss 2004).

Both of these scenes clearly illustrate the overlap of the presentation of tkAw to both the god Osiris and the tomb owner as an Osiris. Appropriately, the scenes are both painted on the walls of the burial chamber where the deceased would have been placed to live out his afterlife in communion with Osiris and the pantheon of other gods. Both scenes are also located on the western walls

FIGURE 12.3. *Tympanum from the burial chamber of Amunnkaht (TT 218) (1279–1213 BC). The god Osiris sits enthroned before the western hills of Thebes. Behind him the goddess Nut holds out her arms to receive the sun as it sets. Osiris is flanked by an udjat-eye and a seated god who together present four burning tkAw to Osiris. Luxor, West Bank, Deir el Medina. (Photo credit and permission for use granted by Dr. Mostafa Mohamed AlSaghir)*

of their burial chambers, further suggesting that the presentation of artificial light is linked to the west, the direction associated with the underworld, and the horizon where the sun would set below the Theban hills. There is, however, another deity who is present in these scenes: the sun god, Ra. He is visually referenced in the scene from Amunnakht's tomb as the sun disk being taken into the arms of Nut, the sky goddess. This further corroborates the hypothesis that the ritual described in spell 137A was meant to take place at sunset, because Nut would receive Ra every day as he set in the western horizon and bring him into her arms before swallowing him. He would then proceed through the starry body of Nut during his journey through the underworld at night and the goddess would give birth to him in the morning, propelling him into the sky from the eastern horizon. The hymns to Ra, which are recorded on the ceilings of Pashed and Amunnakht's burial chambers, also speak to the presence of the deity.

It is clear, therefore, that while the torches form a protective barrier flanking either side of the god Osiris and the tomb owner Osiris, they also signify the

FIGURE 12.4. *The ba of Ani, depicted as a human-headed bird, rejoining his mummy, as depicted in a vignette from his* Book of the Dead *(EA 10470) (c. 1250 BC). The mummy rests on a lion-bodied bed flanked on either end by lit open-bowl lamps on stands. (©The Trustees of the British Museum)*

light of Ra coming into the underworld (or in this case the burial chamber of the deceased) and rejuvenating both beings. This concept is expressed in one of the New Kingdom books of the underworld, called the *Amduat*, a text that records the nightly journey of the sun god, Ra in twelve hours or stages (Hornung 1999). In the sixth hour, as Ra descends to the deepest part of the underworld, the mythical burial chamber of Osiris, he encounters the mummified corpse of the god. It is at this point that Ra, as the *ba* or spirit of Osiris, joins with him and both gods are regenerated.

I would argue that bringing artificial light into the burial chamber (whether in actuality or just through their representation on the tomb walls) signifies this all-important moment of rejuvenation for the deceased individual within their tomb. The mummified corpse of the deceased, being equated with the god Osiris, is joined with his *ba* and regenerated as a divine *akh*-spirit that will live on in the underworld. The light from the tkAw provides a protective environment in which this rejuvenation can take place, and at the same time is a symbol of the resurrection of the mummified corpse. This idea is also represented in the *Book of the Dead*, such as in vignettes from the papyri of Ani (EA 10470) (figure 12.4) and Nebqed (Louvre N 3068). Since depictions of the hours of the *Amduat* were reserved for royal tombs, perhaps this option was a way for private individuals to depict the mythical reunion of Ra and Osiris through the joining of the deceased with their *bas*. Interestingly, the types of artificial light depicted in these vignettes are very similar in form to open-vessel oil lamps placed on lampstands found in the tombs of Kha and others. Just as the vignette of Ani depicts, the oil lamp and stand were placed just inside the entrance to the burial chamber at the foot of Kha's sarcophagus. It also seems from residue left within the vessel of the oil lamp that the lamp had been lit and left burning at the time the burial chamber was sealed—it seems in this instance that life did very closely imitate art.

CONCLUSIONS

The nighttime realm of the underworld in ancient Egypt was indeed a space that needed to be carefully navigated, and employing light for illumination and protection would certainly have been necessary. Contrary to previous studies, I believe night was not something to be avoided; rather, it was something that needed to be embraced. As this chapter has shown, the Egyptian funeral was a means of facilitating the transition from day/life to night/death and rebirth. Specifically, artificial light was used as a tool to mark this liminal stage during the performance of the tkAw ritual recorded in spell 137A of the *Book of the Dead*. By performing this ritual at sunset, the ancient Egyptians were connecting the movement of the deceased into the underworld with the "death" of the sun god, Ra, in the western horizon. In addition, the ritual light of the tkAw would be used to facilitate the physical movement of the mummy from the realm of the living outside of the tomb, down to the blackened burial chamber and the realm of the dead.

Offerings of light in the burial chamber, and/or depictions of these offerings on tomb walls and papyri, played a significant role in the next stage of the deceased's journey—transforming into a luminous, divine *akh*. Lit lamps or wick-on-stick implements created a protective environment within the burial chamber and symbolized the presence of the rejuvenating light of Ra reuniting with the mummified Osiris. Throughout this transition and transformation of the deceased, the light from the tkAw is not warding off night and darkness, but indicates that it is a necessary component in the process of regeneration and rejuvenation. For it is only through the union of the *ba*/soul and the mummy in the most sacred, blackened space of night that the deceased could achieve his goal of living on for eternity.

ACKNOWLEDGMENTS

I would like to sincerely thank the editors of this volume for their invitation to contribute to such a rich and engaging publication. I would also like to acknowledge Andrew Bednarski, Kate Spence, and Helen and Nigel Strudwick for their commentary on early drafts of this chapter.

NOTES

1. My own translation based on hieroglyphs published in Sethe (1908).

2. The beautifully crafted calcite lamp (JE 62111; Egyptian Museum, Cairo) from the tomb of Tutankhamun is an example of this type. For the original object record and photographs of this object, see the Howard Carter Archive, Griffith Institute, http://www.griffith.ox.ac.uk/gri/carter/173-c173-1.html.

3. Earlier examples have been found on mummy bandages and shrouds dating to the Seventeenth Dynasty.

4. For the publication of Nu's papyrus, including plates of the entire scroll, see Lapp (1997) For a synoptic publication of spells 137A, B, and later, see Luft (2009). All translations of this spell are my own based on the hieroglyphic text from the papyrus of Nu published in Luft (ibid., 234–305). Line numbers follow those listed in Luft's publication.

5. For a critical examination of the text of this spell and its origins, see Luft (2009).

6. The word *sAxw* translates as "to make into akhs."

REFERENCES

Assmann, Jan. 1990. "Egyptian Mortuary Liturgies." In *Studies in Egyptology: Presented to Miriam Lichtheim*, vol. 1. ed. Sarah Israelit-Groll, 1–45. Jerusalem: Magnes Press, Hebrew University.

Assmann, Jan. 2005. *Death and Salvation in Ancient Egypt*. Ithaca, NY: Cornell University Press.

Brunton, Guy. 1920. *Lahun I: The Treasure*. London: British School of Archaeology in Egypt.

Bruyère, Bernard. 1939. *Rapport Sur Les Fouilles de Deir El Médineh, 1934–1935; Le Village, Les Décharges Publiques, La Station de Repos Du Col de La Vallée Des Rois. (3e pt)*. Cairo: Institut français d'archéologie orientale.

Davies, Norman de Garis. 1924. "A Peculiar Form of New Kingdom Lamp." *Journal of Egyptian Archaeology* 10(1):9–14. https://doi.org/10.2307/3853990.

Davies, Nina M., and Alan Henderson Gardiner. 1915. *The Tomb of Amenemhēt (No. 82)*. The Theban Tomb Series. London: William Clowes and Sons, Limited.

Englund, Gertie. 1978. *Akh: Une Notion Religieuse Dans l'Égypte Pharaonique*. Uppsala Studies in Ancient Mediterranean and Near Eastern Civilizations, vol. 11. Uppsala: University of Uppsala.

Fischer, Henry G. 1977. "Fackeln und Kerzen." In *Lexikon Der Ägyptologie II*, ed. Eberhard Otto and Wolfgang Helck, 80–81. Wiesbaden: Harrassowitz.

Fischer, Henry G. 1980. "Lampe." In *Lexikon Der Ägyptologie III*, ed. Eberhard Otto and Wolfgang Helck, 913–917. Wiesbaden: Harrassowitz.

Forbes, R. J. 1966. *Studies in Ancient Technology*. vol. 6. Leiden: E. J. Brill.

Galinier, Jacques, Aurore Monod Becquelin, Guy Bordin, Laurent Fontaine, Francine Fourmaux, Juliette Roullet Ponce, Piero Salzarulo, Philippe Simonnot, Michèle

Therrien, and Iole Zilli. 2010. "Anthropology of the Night: Cross-Disciplinary Investigations." *Current Anthropology* 51(6):819–847. https://doi.org/10.1086/653691.

Gutbub, Adolphe. 1961. "Un Emprunt Aux Textes Des Pyramides Dans L'hymne À Hathor, Dame de L'ivresse." In *Mélanges Maspero I - Orient Ancien 4*, 31–72. MIFAO, 66. Cairo: Institut français d'archéologie orientale.

Haikal, Fayza. 1985. "Preliminary Studies on the Tomb of Thay in Thebes: The Hymn to the Light." In *Melanges Gamal Eddin Mokhtar*, ed. Paule Posener-Kriéger, 361–374. Bibliothèque d'étude 97. Cairo: Institut français d'archéologie orientale du Caire.

Hornung, Erik. 1999. *The Ancient Egyptian Books of the Afterlife*. Trans. David Lorton. Ithaca: Cornell University Press.

Lapp, Günther. 1997. *The Papyrus of Nu (BM EA 10477)*. vol. 1. *Catalogue of Books of the Dead in the British Museum*. London: Published for the Trustees of the British Museum by British Museum Press.

Luft, Daniela C. 2009. *Das Anzünden der Fackel: Untersuchungen zu Spruch 137 des Totenbuches*. Wiesbaden: Otto Harrassowitz.

Munro, Irmtraut. 1988. *Untersuchungen Zu Den Totenbuch-Papyri Der 18. Dynastie: Kriterien Ihrer Datierung*. Studies in Egyptology. London: Kegan Paul International.

Nelson, Harold H. 1949. "Certain Reliefs at Karnak and Medinet Habu and the Ritual of Amenophis I-(Concluded)." *Journal of Near Eastern Studies* 8(4):310–345. https://doi.org/10.1086/370936.

Otto, Eberhard. 1960. *Das Ägyptische Mundöffnungsritual*. vol. 1. Wiesbaden: Otto Harrassowitz.

Petrie, W. M. Flinders, Guy Brunton, and Margaret A. Murray. 1923. *Lahun II*. London: British School of Archaeology in Egypt.

Porter, Bertha, and Rosalind L. B. Moss. 2004. *Topographical Bibliography of Ancient Egyptian Hieroglyphic Texts, Reliefs, and Paintings*, Vol.1; Pt.1, *The Theban Necropolis; Private Tombs*. 2nd and augm. ed. Oxford: Griffith Institute, Ashmolean Museum.

Régen, Isabelle. 2010. "When a Book of the Dead Text Does Not Match Archaeology: The Case of the Protective Magical Bricks (BD 151)." *British Museum Studies in Ancient Egypt and Sudan*, no. 15:267–278.

Robins, F. W. 1939a. "The Lamps of Ancient Egypt." *Journal of Egyptian Archaeology* 25(2):184–187. https://doi.org/10.2307/3854653.

Robins, F. W. 1939b. *The Story of the Lamp (and the Candle)*. Oxford: Oxford University Press.

Saleh, Mohamed. 1984. *Das Totenbuch in Den Thebanischen Beamtengräbern Des Neuen Reiches: Texte Und Vignetten*. Vol. 46. Archäologische Veröffentlichungen / Deutsches Archäologisches Institut. Abteilung Kairo. Mainz am Rhein: von Zabern.

Schiaparelli, E. 1937. *La Tomba Del Dignitario 'Cha' Nella Necropoli de Tebe; Della Missione Archeologica Italiana, Egitto, 1903–1920*. Torino: Museo di Antichità.

Schott, Siegfried. 1937. "Das Löschen von Fackeln in Milch." *Zeitschrift für Ägyptische Sprache und Altertumskunde* 73(1):1–33. https://doi.org/10.1515/zaes-1937-0104.

Sethe, Kurt. 1908. *Die Altaegyptischen Pyramidentexte: Nach Den Papierabdrücken Und Photographien Des Berliner Museums.* Leipzig: J. C. Heinrichs'sche Buchhandlung.

Strong, Meghan. 2009. "Let There Be Light: A Study of Natural and Artificial Light in New Kingdom Egypt (1570–1070 B.C.)." Unpublished MA thesis, University of Memphis, Memphis.

Strong, Meghan E. 2021. *Sacred Flames: The Power of Artificial Light in Ancient Egypt.* Cairo: American University in Cairo Press.

Wilson, John A. 1936. "Illuminating the Thrones at the Egyptian Jubilee." *Journal of the American Oriental Society* 56(2):293–296. https://doi.org/10.2307/594676.

Zivie, Alain-Pierre. 1979. *La Tombe de Pached À Deir El-Médineh (No 3).* Vol. 99. Mémoires Publiés Par Les Membres de l'Institut Français D'archéologie Orientale Du Caire. Cairo: Institut français d'archéologie orientale.

Burning the Midnight Oil

Archaeological Experiments with Early Medieval Viking Lamps

ERIN HALSTAD McGUIRE

How did people in the past light up their houses at night? This fundamental question is one that archaeologists have not always explicitly addressed. One avenue of investigation is through the analysis of the material remains of light technologies within the archaeological record. For instance, many Viking Age houses contain evidence of both hearths and lamps, and yet little research has been conducted into the use of light in Viking homes. This case study aims to investigate Viking Age lamps through experimental archaeology, beginning with the reconstruction and testing of a closed-circuit steatite lamp. Such lamps are in the form of a bowl that is completely closed, as opposed to those that are U-shaped and have one end open.

The Viking Age falls at the end of what was once called the Dark Ages of Medieval Europe (figures 1.2–1.3). The image that we have of Viking houses is of smoke-filled, damp spaces, crowded with people and shrouded in gloom. However, among the house assemblages from across the Viking world, we find evidence of lamps, usually made from stone, ceramic, or metal. Trace evidence of fuels and wick materials, combined with ethnographic and historical sources,

DOI: 10.5876/9781607326786.c013

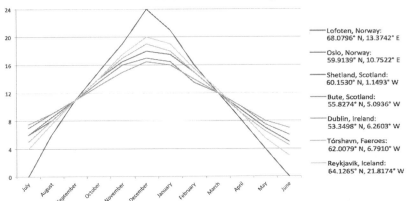

Hours of Darkness and Twilight

Lofoten, Norway:
68.0796° N, 13.3742° E

Oslo, Norway:
59.9139° N, 10.7522° E

Shetland, Scotland:
60.1530° N, 1.1493° W

Bute, Scotland:
55.8274° N, 5.0936° W

Dublin, Ireland:
53.3498° N, 6.2603° W

Tórshavn, Faeroes:
62.0079° N, 6.7910° W

Reykjavik, Iceland:
64.1265° N, 21.8174° W

FIGURE 13.1. *Approximate hours of darkness in the North Atlantic based on an annual cycle. Estimations are based on calculations from the fifteenth day of each month, using the SunriseSunset.com calculator.*

give hints as to how the lamps functioned, but as yet there has been limited research on Viking lamps in particular. Through the creation and analysis of an experimental Viking lamp, this chapter provides a fresh look at illumination in Viking Age houses and contributes to our knowledge about the anthropology of illuminosity, as put forth by Bille and Sørensen (2007). The research presented forms the beginning stages of a longer project; here the efficacy of various wick forms is analyzed, taking into consideration the quantity and quality of both light and heat produced by a single lamp. While initial tests were conducted in a modern setting, subsequent testing took place in a reconstructed Viking Age pithouse in southern Washington in 2016.

THE VIKINGS

The Viking Age marked a period of dramatic change in the North Sea and North Atlantic regions. In this period spanning the eighth through eleventh centuries CE, Norse raiders, traders, and settlers began expanding into new territories in the British Isles and as far west as the coast of North America, settling the islands of the Faeroes (c. 825 CE), Iceland (c. 875), and Greenland (c. 985) (Barrett et al. 2000). Coming from predominantly northern regions, they were familiar with extremes of light and dark—for some there would have been long periods with no sun at all in the winter (figure 13.1). Their new landscapes may have seemed familiar in many ways (Dugmore et al. 2006, 340–341), though the further south they went, the longer their days would have become, which would have led to subtle shifts in the growing seasons and in the rhythms of daily life.

As they expanded across the North Atlantic, the settlers carried with them familiar domesticated animals, such as sheep, goats, pigs, cattle, horses, and dogs. They also brought their traditional tools and other supplies from Scandinavia, importing objects of stone, metal, glass, pottery, and more. The material culture of the Viking Age is so distinct that it is sometimes described as a *landnám* (literally, "land-taking") package and can be used to identify the Norse presence in a given area (Amorosi et al. 1997, 501).

In their new settlements, the settlers used their imported goods and also produced new ones, following traditional models and creating novel forms according to their needs and desires. The houses that they lived in are classic examples of this trend. Typically, Vikings lived and worked on farms with multiple structures (Milek 2012, 85). The main house was often a large, rectilinear hall, heated by a centered hearth. Outbuildings included pithouse structures, built with a combination of timber and local materials, such as sod and stone. With minimal evidence for windows (although see Milek 2012, 94) and in regions with long, dark winters, light in these structures would have been limited. Eldjárn (1949–1950, 350) suggests that in Iceland, for instance, lamps may have been needed indoors from mid-September until mid-March. Experimental archaeology projects focused on air quality in Danish Viking Age houses suggest that the hearth was the main source of light and heat, but also produced sufficient smoke to have a negative health impact on residents (Christensen 2014; Christensen and Ryhl-Svendsen 2015). Given that lamps are present on a number of Viking Age archaeological sites, the experiments discussed here aim to explore the ways in which lamps may have further contributed to the living conditions in these structures.

A number of studies have looked at lamps in the archaeological record, though not with a Viking Age focus. These include Sophie De Beaune's (1987) early research on Paleolithic lamps (see also Nowell, chapter 2, this volume); recent work on Mesolithic lamps in Denmark (Heron et al. 2013); several projects looking at lamps from different periods in Egypt (e.g., Colombini et al. 2005; Copley et al. 2004) (see also Strong, chapter 12, this volume); Minoan lamps from Crete (Evershed et al. 1997); Late Roman ceramic lamps from Italy (Mangone et al. 2009; see Storey, chapter 15, this volume); and eighteenth-century Inuit sites in the Arctic (Solazzo and Erhardt 2007). While earlier studies aimed to identify objects as lamps, recent scholarship tends to focus more on identifying the materials used in lamp construction (as well as their origins and the implications for trade) and the fuel sources used in the lamps. Of particular interest to this project is the work by Dawson and colleagues (2007), who used experimental lamps and computer models to examine the quality of light in Arctic dwellings.

There is, as yet, no complete catalog of Viking Age lamps, thus, for this experiment a sample of lamps from several regions in the Viking world, including Norway, Sweden, Scotland, and Iceland, was compiled (figure 13.5) (for the selected catalog of Viking Age lamps, see table 13.2; see also Eldjárn [1949–1950], who presents a short catalog of steatite finds from Iceland, and Guðmundur Ólafsson [1987], who presents a short summary of light and light technologies from the Viking Age to the modern period in Iceland). The lamps are made primarily from stone, especially steatite, though there are pottery lamps as well. Some evidence also exists for metal lamps, such as the iron lamp from the Oseberg ship burial in Norway (table 13.2: Cat. 3), and a Late Norse/medieval bronze lamp found in Iceland (table 13.2: Cat. 25). Generally speaking, Viking Age lamps are closed-circuit bowl lamps, some of which have handles, while others are pierced at either end and are meant to hang. The lamps range from crudely built to highly worked, with varying degrees of finish. For instance, the stone lamps from Underhoull in Unst, Scotland, have very clear tool marks, especially inside the bowl area (figure 13.2, table 13.2: Cat. 12–13). Based on these tool marks, steatite lamps may have been primarily worked with knives and gouges, and then polished with sand (Bond et al. 2013; Turner et al. 2013, 167; see also Arwidsson and Berg 1983).

There is minimal evidence for what constituted wicks in Viking lamps. At Belmont, Unst, both flax and floss have been proposed (Bond et al. 2013; Turner et al. 2013, 196), while at Underhoull, Unst, flax and gut are mentioned as possible wick sources (Bond et al. 2013; Turner et al. 2013, 167). Ethnographic research from the Canadian Arctic highlights the use of moss and cotton-grass for wicking (Frink et al. 2012, 433). While mosses are widely available in the North Atlantic region, and have been used as wicking in the Arctic (Frink et al. 2012, 433) and possibly for Paleolithic lamps in France (De Beaune 1987, 575), I have yet to find reference to its use in a Viking context. Cotton-grass is a plant native to much of the northern hemisphere (Phillips 1954, 612) and may fit the description of grasses and floss, as noted in some of the reports on Viking lamps. Its use in lamps is discussed in the eighteenth-century text *Grasnytjar* by Björn Halldórsson (Kristjánsson and Sigfússon 1983, 254), which suggests that it certainly could have been used in the Viking Age.

To date, there has not been a significant amount of analysis of Viking Age lamps and fuel sources. In the case of the lamps from Shetland, archaeologists have posited the use of fish oil, and seal or whale blubber (Bond et al. 2013; Turner et al. 2013, 167, 196). These sources are compatible with the lipid analysis from Mesolithic lamps in Denmark, where Heron et al. (2013) identified the use of fish and seal oil as a fuel, even at inland sites. De Beaune's (1987, 575) experiments in reconstructing Paleolithic lamps indicated that sea-mammal oil was better than terrestrial-mammal oil, though she makes no mention of fish

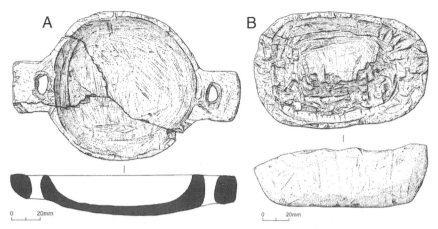

FIGURE 13.2. *Examples of two Viking Age lamps found at Underhoull, Unst, Scotland. (Images and permission from J. Bond)*

oils. Ethnographic and archaeological research from the Canadian Arctic suggests that sea-mammal oil and fish oil were the most widely used and efficient sources of fuel available to the various peoples of the Arctic (Frink et al. 2012, 433; Solazzo and Erhardt 2007, 17). As in Norway and Scotland, the most common lamp material in the Arctic appears to have been steatite, so it seems as though these materials work well together. Nilsen (2016) provides evidence for the likely extraction of oil from marine blubber at Nordic archaeological sites from the Mesolithic onwards through the application of experimental archaeology and an analysis of slab-lined pits. This suggests that marine oil could have been widely available through the Viking Age.

EXPERIMENTAL ARCHAEOLOGY

Experimental archaeology is the subdiscipline of archaeology centered on imitative or replicative experimentation (Saraydar 2008, 3). It is through the process of experimentation that we can test hypotheses about human behavior in the past (Ascher 1961, 793). A key advantage to experimental archaeology in the study of Viking lamps is the potential to answer questions about organic materials, which are so rarely preserved in the archaeological record (Hurcombe 2008). Finally, it is important to remember that a replicative experiment cannot tell us how something was done in the past, but may give us insight into what might have been (Saraydar 2008, 26). Thus, many experiments have focused on past technologies, including types of hunting tools, the use of agricultural tools, and so on. For surveys of some of this past work, see Saraydar (2008) and Ascher (1961). Moving beyond reconstructing technologies, Dawson et al. (2007) used replica Inuit *qulliq* lamps to measure light production. The results of these tests

FIGURE 13.3. *Reconstructed lamp, with wick of semi-processed linen tow and 30 ml of fish oil. (Photo by Erin McGuire)*

entered into computer simulations to measure the effects of light within a computer model of a Thule Inuit dwelling. Lacking a computer simulation of Viking housing, but having access to a reconstruction, the present study takes a more phenomenological approach to the question of light.

METHODS

In order to test the functionality of a steatite lamp, one closed-circuit bowl lamp was created (figure 13.3).[1] While not a precise replica, the lamp was modeled off an existing find from The Biggings, Papa Stour (table 13.2: Cat. 11, Crawford and Ballin-Smith 1999, SF521). The fuel source selected was a commercially available cod liver oil, chosen for both ease of access and consistency of product. The wick sources used include cotton-grass (*Eriophorum angustifolium*), flax (*Linum usitatissimum*), and moss (Svanberg 1997). The wick materials were tested both as raw/semi-processed fiber and as fully processed wicks (table 13.1). In each

TABLE 13.1. Wick materials, forms, and results from experimental archaeology project to re-create Viking lamps.

Material	Form	Results
Cotton-grass (dried)	Flower, seeds, stem 100 mm long flower 10 mm diameter	Flower end burned effectively for hours and could be relit to use again, stem did not burn at all
	Stem only 100 mm long	Would not light
	Spun flower fiber 150 mm long 3 mm diameter	Would not sustain bright flame for any length of time
Flax	Unprocessed stalk	Would not light
	Semi-processed tow	Tow burned effectively for hours and could be relit to use again
	Spun, unplied tow	Would not sustain fire
	Spun, plied tow	Would not sustain fire
	Spun, plied tow, with beeswax	Would not sustain fire
Moss	Loose	Would not sustain fire
	Spun	Would not sustain fire

instance, the wicks were soaked in 30 ml of oil in the lamp for fifteen to twenty minutes before being lit.

The effectiveness of each wick form was recorded on data sheets, though only two of the wicks proved to be viable for lamp use (table 13.1). Cotton-grass flowers are fine and fragile, and the individual seed heads fall easily off the stalk / stem. None of the sources consulted prior to the study discussed which part of the cotton-grass is used as the wick or how long or thick the wick should be. Three options were considered: the entire flower, seeds, and stem; the stem alone; or the flower fibers spun into a cord. While multiple seed heads / flowers could be spun together, the result was brittle and seemed unlikely to hold up under handling. Only the complete flower head worked effectively as a wick. Svanberg (1997, 151) notes that ethnographic research from Iceland indicates that the fluff of the flower is what was traditionally used for a wick, which confirms the testing conducted here.

In the case of flax, the wick options included the unprocessed stem / stalk of the plant, a length of tow (the coarse, broken fibers that result from the processing of flax into linen), a length of spun linen thread, and four-plied linen cord. In an attempt to improve the efficacy of the linen cord, it was also rubbed with beeswax, a process typical in making candle wicks. In the end, only the

FIGURE 13.4. *The pithouse, viewed from the front. (Photo by Erin McGuire)*

unspun linen tow worked effectively to sustain a flame. The two viable wick forms (cotton-grass flower and semi-processed tow) were then subjected to longer burn tests. Each was used for up to four hours' total burn time, across a two-day period. This step involved adding more fuel as needed, and relighting the wicks on the second day. The cotton-grass was tested in a darkened room in a modern home with the recording of fuel levels and brightness. The linen tow was tested in a reconstructed Viking pithouse, with fuel levels, brightness, temperature, and sensory observations being recorded.

Although the first tests were conducted in a modern setting, as noted above, the second set of tests were conducted at a hypothetical reconstruction of Viking Age pithouse on a private farm in southern Washington (figure 13.4). The house was built by a group of reenactors who form the *Vinnlig Stamme* community, and is based on both archaeological evidence and reconstructions at open-air museums in Europe. The pithouse's dimensions are approximately 3.5 m by 4.25 m internally, with the central peak reaching approximately 3.2 m high, making it comparable in size to the largest of the Icelandic pithouses (Milek 2012, 95). This reconstruction has a large window on the east face and a door on the west face, neither of which was completely closed during testing, as there is not yet a cover for it, although I did partially cover the window with a large animal hide. The resulting drafts undoubtedly had an impact on the test results. It should be noted that windows were not likely a common feature in pithouses, as they would have had a negative impact on insulation during winter months.

The group plans to better enclose the house in the future, by adding a door and a solid window cover.

Testing occurred from July 18 to July 20, 2016, a period during which the structure underwent further construction. Although the pithouse had a hearth at the start of testing, the hearth was dug out during the week of testing because it produced too much heat for the internal space of the house and was considered impractical. The lamp was placed centrally along the north wall of the house, and measurements were taken immediately in front of the lamp, at 30 cm, and at 60 cm toward the center of the room. Light was measured using a light meter app for iPhone.[2] Temperature readings were taken at the same distances, and a Seek thermal camera was used to record temperature variability on the north wall.

RESULTS AND DISCUSSION

In both instances, the lamp produced a low amount of light. On average, when the light levels were measured at close range, they produced between 7 and 9 lumens. For comparison, a typical paraffin wax candle produces 13 lumens, while a 15-watt compact fluorescent bulb will produce 800 lumens (Fouquet and Pearson 2006, 145). At the middle distance, the light meter read only 1–2 lumens. Unfortunately, the testing equipment proved insufficient to measure light levels beyond 1 foot away from the lamp. The lamp light in the small space of the pithouse felt sufficient for some kinds of work, such as food preparation or weaving, but was likely not bright enough for anything requiring close attention to detail, such as embroidery, unless seated directly beside the lamp itself. Indeed, it was apparently insufficient for any kind of work by modern standards (Dawson et al. 2007, 29). In spite of these low readings, the sense of those who experienced the light within the pithouse was that it was brighter than expected. A further point of consideration is whether brighter light was required by those accustomed to living and working in Viking Age buildings. Although modern mindsets tend to emphasize the importance of vision, other senses may have been equally, or even more, necessary (Dawson et al. 2007, 30–31; see also Bille and Sørensen 2007, 266). Finally, we do not know how many lamps would have been in use at a single time, but in the case of *Vinnlig Stamme*, two lamps were used simultaneously for a gathering one evening and the pithouse was perceived by users to be well lit.

In the immediate vicinity of the lamp, the temperature change was noticeable, but the lamp made little difference to the temperature of the room as a whole. This situation was likely at least partially because there was no door or window covering, and thus this aspect will need to be retested at a later date. There was a slow 1°C change approximately every half hour in the temperature of the air above the lamp, rising by about 3°C across three hours of testing. During this period, the flax wick appeared minimally affected by burning, and was seemingly unconsumed by the fire. It could be easily relit and used again. In comparison, the cotton-grass wicks tested earlier usually lasted three to four hours, and while they could be relit, they tended not to burn for more than an hour. The fuel consumption varied somewhat, but on average, 30 ml of fish oil lasted 2.5 hours.

The lamp was predicted to be smoky and to smell strongly of fish oil. Given that hearth fires contributed negatively to the quality of air in other reconstructed Viking Age houses (Christensen 2014, 18–19; Christensen and Ryhl-Svendsen 2015, 339), it was expected that the lamp would affect air quality as well, albeit not to the extent of a fire. Although no formal testing of carbon monoxide or carbon dioxide occurred, it was observed that smoke was only noticeable in a strong draft or when the flame was extinguished, much like snuffing out a candle flame. Moreover, the smell of the fish oil was minimally apparent in the modern setting, but not noticeable at all in the pithouse, where it competed with the smell of earth, timber, goat, and people.

It seems likely that lamps were lit by first lighting a stick or something similar in the hearth and using it to light the lamp's wick. Flint and strike-a-light tools only produce sparks, which would not be sufficient to light a lamp, unless they were used to light tinder, which could then be applied directly to the lamp's wick. A sustained flame is necessary to light most of the wick materials. Holding a steady flame to the oil-saturated cotton-grass or linen tow caused part of the wick to shrivel and blacken. Only once it had blackened did it seem to be able to burn for extended periods.

Wick form mattered more than expected and not in the way that was expected. It was anticipated that the hand-twisted wicks would be more effective, drawing more oil while burning longer and brighter. Instead, it appears that the "natural" wicks burned brighter, while consuming somewhat more of the fuel. This might be because the surface area of the flower and loose tow were larger, thus absorbing more oil while soaking. Moreover, they had a larger volume of material to burn. It was expected that these wicks would burn out faster, but both were useful for a minimum of three hours and were able to be relit hours later. Both wick forms would have been relatively easy to acquire in the Viking Age. Tow is a byproduct of linen production and would have been readily available as a material in areas of flax production, such as Norway and Scotland. While flax growth was perhaps more limited in Iceland and the Faeroes, cotton-grass is abundant, and was used as a wick even as recently as the last century (Svanberg 1997, 146–147). Collecting, drying, and storing the cotton-grass flowers would be very straightforward. Spinning the fibers of either the cotton-grass or the flax increased the effort and overall workload, but appeared to decrease the level of light, and in the case of the tow was unable to sustain a flame for any length of time. It is possible that the linen wick was too fine—a follow-up test with a thicker spun wick seems necessary.

Milek (2012, 122) argues convincingly that the Icelandic Viking Age pithouses were central elements of the domestic sphere, frequently functioning as buildings for textile production. She further proposes that this role would have been consistent with practices elsewhere in the Viking world. While many pithouses had small, enclosed hearths, and may have had windows (Milek 2012, 94), focused light in these spaces would have been limited, especially during darker seasons. Lamps would have provided portable light that could be moved and adjusted as needed. For instance, during the week of pithouse testing, the lamp was temporarily used to assist with outdoor cooking one evening. Because the steatite did not get overly warm at the handle end, the lamp was moved about to respond to various needs for light and its presence and absence was noticeable during this time. Interestingly, although the lamp had to be moved carefully, it proved to be highly portable even when full of oil and lit. Such a lamp could have been useful in the Viking Age to assist with fine-textile production (Ruffoni 2011, 37) and other work requiring extra illumination, if it was placed close to the work. From a distance, it only provides a soft, diffused light.

Milek (2012) sees pithouses as gendered spaces, associated with women's textile production. Lamps and lighting technologies may also have been associated with women's practices. The use of linen tow, a byproduct of weaving and the collection and use of cotton-grass could easily have fallen into the domestic sphere. Moreover, like the Inuit qulliq, Viking lamps need to be tended—fuel levels need to be monitored and wicks need to be adjusted to increase the length of time that they could be used. When burning the tow wick, for instance, fuel consumption was comparatively high and needed to be monitored. Extra oil was added to keep the lamp burning throughout the test period. If women were using the lamps within their work spaces and burning wicks produced by their own labor, it seems likely that they were also the ones who maintained the light.

The Oseberg ship burial, possibly the most significant female burial of Viking Age Norway, contained the bodies of two women and numerous grave goods, including a pair of iron lamps (table 13.2: Cat. 3). Even more intriguingly, one of the tapestries found in the grave has a repeated image of a woman carrying a lamp. The lamps in this grave and depicted on the tapestry have been interpreted as symbols of social status, fertility cults, and even life and death (Ingstad 1995, 144). Ruffoni (2011) challenges Ingstad's cultic interpretation of the Oseberg burial, preferring functional interpretations of objects such as lamps. She argues that lamps may have simply provided light, during the creation of the tapestries for example, but does not deny that they may have served a ritual purpose as well (Ruffoni 2011, 37). The majority of lamps included in the catalog below seem practical in nature, but intriguing details suggest the possibility of more—a lamp from Sweden has a cross inscribed in its bowl (table 13.2: Cat. 4), another from Iceland bears a possible inscription (table 13.2: Cat. 22). Moreover, many everyday objects may also serve ritual purposes, so categorizing them as one or the other may be meaningless. The symbolism of lamps, at least in the context of the burial at Oseberg, seems deeply connected with female identities and practices, both sacred and profane.

CONCLUSIONS

The results of this study demonstrate that experimental archaeology is a useful tool for examining how Viking Age lamps functioned, in a very practical sense. Through the creation of a steatite lamp and experimentation with wick materials and forms, it was possible to identify useable materials. Moreover, by measuring light levels in the interior of the reconstructed pithouse, it was possible to observe the character of the light produced. Given the low levels of light produced by the lamp, it seems likely that it would have been placed next to those who needed it most for their tasks.

This study emphasized the lamp itself, but in the future it would be useful to consider more fully the interactions of people using the light. Bille and Sørensen (2007, 266) examine the social dimensions of light, considering how the use of light shapes human experiences and connections. The *Vinnlig Stamme* group who built the pithouse are experienced reenactors with diverse skill sets. Over the course of the week at the site, I observed people practicing Viking Age weaving, stone carving, garment construction, cooking, and more. The majority of these activities took place outside, both in the daylight and after dark by firelight, but this was in part because the pithouse was given over to lamp testing at night. It would be valuable to work with the artisans in the future to assess how they interact with the light within the pithouse. In addition to observing the social uses of the space, it would be intriguing to see how the lower light levels affected the approach to specialized craft production (as with Dawson et al. 2007).

Hearths are regular features of Viking Age houses. In the traditional longhouse, they tend to be placed centrally, while in smaller pithouses they are more likely to occur in a corner or along a wall. Although it was outside the scope of the present study, analyzing the relationship between lamps and hearths within the house, through archaeological, textual, and ethnographic sources, would be a valuable endeavor in order to understand luminosity in Viking Age dwellings. Experimental approaches may also show us how lamp light and hearth light interplay in a reconstructed lightscape. In the case of the Washington pithouse reconstruction, the weather was too warm for a fire, but the sun set early enough to make lamp light essential. In a more northern environment, the sun sets later during the summer months, and so lamp light may not have been needed. Equally, as the seasons turn, the weather becomes colder, darkness falls sooner, and the hearth fires become necessary. This raises the question of what role the lamp might have played when the fires were lit. If hearths were

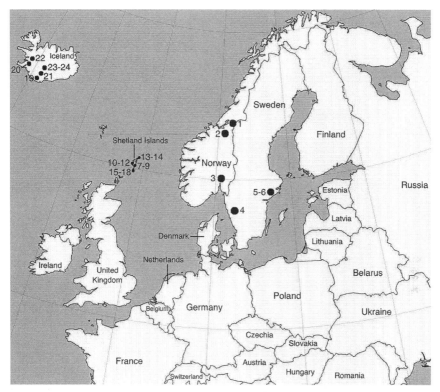

FIGURE 13.5. *Distribution map of lamps listed in the catalog. Numbers on map correspond to numbers in the catalog.*

enclosed in smaller spaces, as Milek (2012, 94) suggests, then they may have provided warmth without significant amounts of light. In the larger longhouses, with open central hearths, the light may not have reached all of the spaces in which it was needed, making portable light necessary.

Lamps, it seems, were an essential element of Viking daily (nightly?) life. They were capable of creating pools of light in dark spaces, illuminating the corners of the room, bringing to life the details of tapestries and weaving, and perhaps bridging the divide between day and night, sacred and profane, darkness and light. A dish of soapstone, a bundle of flax, a pool of oil—and a woman's hand to guide it?—were everything needed to bring light into the darkness.

TABLE 13.2. Selected catalog of Viking Age lamps

Country/ID	Site name	Lamp type	Material	Dimensions	Description	Date range	Source
NORWAY							
Cat. 1	Sulstugu, Vukus., Verdal, Nord-Trøndelag	bowl	steatite	10.2 cm wide, 3.7 cm high	Oblong, four-sided, flat-bottomed vessel	Viking?	Universitetsmuseenes Samlings-portaler, http://www.unimus.no/, item 15889
Cat. 2	Britannia Hotel's courtyard, Dronningens gt. 5, Trondheim	single-handled	steatite	14.8 cm dia., w/ 4.5 cm handle	Roughly made, slightly oblong, with single handle	Viking?	Universitetsmuseenes Samlings-portaler, http://www.unimus.no/, item 16568
Cat. 3	Oseberg ship burial, Vestfold	bowl (on spike)	Iron	15 cm dia., 6 cm deep, 44 cm spike	Round iron bowl mounted on a large spike(two lamps)	800–850	Kulturhistorisk museum, UiO, item Cf21674_12_C55000_138
Sweden							
Cat. 4	Kastellgården, Kungahälla, Ytterby, Bohuslän	bowl	other stone	17.5 cm × 16.4 cm, 5.5 cm high	Slightly oblong, dish-shaped, with central cross motif	1100–1200	Swedish Historical Museum, http://mis.historiska.se, item 118690
Cat. 5	Björkö, Adelsö, Uppland	bowl	ceramic	8 cm dia., 4.5 cm high	Round, straight-sided bowl, with central point	Viking Age	Swedish Historical Museum, http://mis.historiska.se, item 5208: 2370
Cat. 6	Björkö, Adelsö, Uppland	bowl	ceramic	unknown	Likely similar to SHM 5208: 2370, but severely fragmented	Viking Age	Swedish Historical Museum, http://mis.historiska.se, item 5208: 2371

continued on next page

TABLE 13.2—*continued*

Country/ID	Site name	Lamp type	Material	Dimensions	Description	Date range	Source
SCOTLAND							
Cat. 7	Kebister, Shetland	bowl	steatite	unknown	Sub-rectangular fragmented bowl, poor condition (re-used as weight?)	Iron-Age to 'Norse Period'	Owen and Lowe 1999: *Kebister: The Four-Thousand-Year-Old Story of One Shetland Township*, Section 5.5.8, SF1820
Cat. 8	Kebister, Shetland	bowl	steatite	~8.5 cm dia., ~3 cm high	Fragmented sub-rectangular bowl, sanded?	Iron-Age to 'Norse Period'	Owen and Lowe 1999: *Kebister: The Four-Thousand-Year-Old Story of One Shetland Township*, Section 5.5.8, SF2293
Cat. 9	Kebister, Shetland	bowl	steatite	10 cm × 5 cm, 3.4 cm high	Unfinished, sub-rectangular flat bottomed vessel	Iron-Age to 'Norse Period'	Owen and Lowe 1999: *Kebister: The Four-Thousand-Year-Old Story of One Shetland Township*, Section 5.5.8, SF3010
Cat. 10	The Biggings, Papa Stour, Shetland	single-handled	steatite	8.4 cm dia, overall length inc. handle 10 cm, 3.6 cm high	Round bowl, with handle	Iron Age?	Crawford and Ballin Smith 1999: *The Biggings, Papa Stour, Shetland: The History and Archaeology of a Royal Norwegian Farm*, Section 7.2.4, SF521
Cat. 11	The Biggings, Papa Stour, Shetland	hanging	steatite	~10.5 cm × 7.2 cm, ~3 cm high	Oval lamp with two suspension lugs, one broken	Viking Age	Crawford and Ballin Smith 1999: *The Biggings, Papa Stour, Shetland: The History and Archaeology of a Royal Norwegian Farm*, Section 7.2.4, SF522
Cat. 12	The Biggings, Papa Stour, Shetland	single-handled	steatite	10.1 cm × 2.8 cm, 2 cm high	Small oval lamp, possibly portable, with perforated handle.	Viking Age?	Crawford and Ballin Smith 1999: *The Biggings, Papa Stour, Shetland: The History and Archaeology of a Royal Norwegian Farm*, Section 7.2.4, SF434

continued on next page

TABLE 13.2—*continued*

Country/ID	Site name	Lamp type	Material	Dimensions	Description	Date range	Source
Cat. 13	Underhoull, Shetland	hanging	steatite	~11.5 cm dia., 17.5 cm overall length including suspension lugs, ~2.5 cm high	Fragmented, unfinished, shallow, circular hanging lamp with lugs	Viking Age	Bond et al. 2013: "Excavations at Hamar and Underhoull," pp. 166-67, SF's 1639, 1858, 1997
Cat. 14	Underhoull, Shetland	bowl	steatite	~14.5 cm × 9.5 cm, ~5 cm high	Incomplete, broken during construction, smooth outer face, partially hollowed bowl	Viking Age	Bond et al. 2013: "Excavations at Hamar and Underhoull," pp. 166-67, SF 1931
Cat. 15	Jarlshof, Shetland, floor of House 2	bowl	steatite	~10 cm dia., ~1.2 cm deep	Small, circular dish, with evidence of burning	Viking Age?	Hamilton 1956: *Excavations at Jarlshof, Shetland*, figure 54, 13, p. 185
Cat. 16	Jarlshof, Shetland, floor of House 2	bowl	steatite	~12 cm long	Oval lamp	Viking Age?	Hamilton 1956: *Excavations at Jarlshof, Shetland*, figure 54, 19, p. 185
Cat. 17	Jarlshof, Shetland, phase VI house	hanging	steatite	~12.5 cm × 11.5 cm, ~1.2 cm deep	Oval hanging lamp with suspension lugs	ca. 1150	Hamilton 1956: *Excavations at Jarlshof, Shetland*, pp. 184-85
Cat. 18	Jarlshof, Shetland, phase VI house	hanging	steatite	19 cm × 11.5 cm, ~2 cm deep	Flat, sub-rectangular plate, with suspension lugs on short sides.		Hamilton 1956: *Excavations at Jarlshof, Shetland*, pp. 184-85, F300.
ICELAND							
Cat. 19	Herjólfsdalur, Vestmannaeyjar	bowl	basalt	16 cm × 15 cm, 12 cm high	Bowl carved into basalt. Evidence of burning.	850-1100	*Sarpur: Menningarsögulegt gagnasafn* (Archives: Cultural database, Iceland), item HJD/VE/81-584/2001-21-584

continued on next page

TABLE 13.2—continued

Country/ID	Site name	Lamp type	Material	Dimensions	Description	Date range	Source
Cat. 20	Suðurgata 3–5, Reykjavík	bowl	other stone	24 cm × 21 cm, 3 c m deep	Irregular, hollowed out stone. Soot in bowl.	900	*Sarpur: Menningarsögulegt gagnasafn* (Archives: Cultural database, Iceland), item S3-5-571
Cat. 21	Sámsstaðir 1, Fljótslíð, Rangárvallasýsla	hanging	steatite	16.8 cm dia., 3.9 cm high	Large, flat, circular dish with two suspension lugs. Norwegian?	870–930	*Sarpur: Menningarsögulegt gagnasafn* (Archives: Cultural database, Iceland), item 5375 /=906-42; *Eldjárn*, 1949–50: "Kléberg á Íslandi," *Árbók Hins íslenzka fornleifafélags*, bls. 5-40
Cat. 22	Ingunnarstaðir, Kjós, Kjósarsýsla	single-handled	tuff	20.8 cm × 12 cm, 9.5 cm high	Square, flat-bottomed bowl with large handle. Possible inscription on handle.	900–1100	*Sarpur: Menningarsögulegt gagnasafn* (Archives: Cultural database, Iceland), item 1959-1962
Cat. 23	Stöng, Þjórsárdalur, Árnessýsla	bowl	granite	11 cm dia. 6.5 cm high, 1.9 cm deep	Round, shallow bowl, evidence of burning	900–1100	*Sarpur: Menningarsögulegt gagnasafn* (Archives: Cultural database, Iceland), item 13879/1939–1943; A. Roussell 1943: "Stöng, Þjórsárdalur," in *Forntida gårdar i Island* (Copenhagen: Einar Munksgaard), 72–97
Cat. 24	Stöng, Þjórsárdalur, Árnessýsla	bowl	tuff	10 cm dia., 5 cm high, 2 cm deep	Round bowl, flat bottomed, broken but glued together	900–1100	*Sarpur: Menningarsögulegt gagnasafn* (Archives: Cultural database, Iceland), item 13877/1939-43; A. Roussell 1943: "Stöng, Þjórsárdalur," *Forntida gårdar i Island* (Copenhagen: Einar Munksgaard), 72–97.
Cat. 25	Unknown	bowl	bronze	10 cm dia., 2.5 cm high	Round bronze bowl, possibly had a handle	1000–15000	*Sarpur: Menningarsögulegt gagnasafn* (Archives: Cultural database, Iceland), item 6663 /1914-101

NOTES

1. See Viking Lamp Project for details: https://onlineacademiccommunity.uvic.ca /vikinglamps/making-the-first-lamp/.

2. The light meter tool used was the "Light Meter—lux measurement tool" by Elena Polyanskaya, available in the Apple App Store. It was recommended by a photographer, though it turned out not to be as sensitive as I might have preferred.

REFERENCES

Amorosi, Thomas, Paul Buckland, Andrew J. Dugmore, Jon H. Ingimundarson, and Thomas H. McGovern. 1997. "Raiding the Landscape: Human Impact in the Scandinavian North Atlantic." *Human Ecology* 25(3):491–518. https://doi.org/10 .1023/A:1021879727837 http://www.jstor.org/stable/4603254.

Arwidsson, Greta, and Gosta Berg. 1983. *The Mästermyr Find: A Viking Age Tool Chest from Gotland.* Stockholm: Vitterhets-, historie- och antikvitetsakad.

Ascher, Robert. 1961. "Experimental Archeology." *American Anthropologist* 63(4):793–816. https://doi.org/10.1525/aa.1961.63.4.02a00070 http://www.jstor.org/stable/666670.

Barrett, James, Roelf Beukens, Ian Simpson, Patrick Ashmore, Sandra Poaps, and Jacqui Huntley. 2000. "What Was the Viking Age and When Did It Happen? A View from Orkney." *Norwegian Archaeological Review* 33(1):1–39. https://doi.org/10.1080/00293 650050202600.

Bille, Mikkel, and Tim F. Sørensen. 2007. "An Anthropology of Luminosity: The Agency of Light." *Journal of Material Culture* 12(3):263–284. https://doi.org/10.1177/1359 183507081894.

Bond, Julie M., with contributions by S. J. Dockrill, Z. Outram, C. E. Batey, J. Summers, R. Friel, L. D. Brown, E. Campbell, J. Cussans, G. Cook, R. Legg, W. Marshall, J. G. McDonnell, A. Mustchin, M. Church, L. E. Hamlet, and I. A. Simpson. 2013. "Excavations at Hamar and Underhoull." In *Viking Unst: Excavation and Survey in Northern Shetland, 2006–2010,* ed. Val Turner, Julie Bond, Anne-Christine Larsen, and Olwyn Owen, 123–79. Lerwick: Shetland Amenity Trust.

Christensen, Jannie M. 2014. "Living Conditions and Indoor Air Quality in a Reconstructed Viking House." *EXARC Journal* 1:16–19. https://doi.org/10.1111/ina.12147.

Christensen, Jannie M., and Morten Ryhl-Svendsen. 2015. "Household Air Pollution from Wood Burning in Two Reconstructed Houses from the Danish Viking Age." *Indoor Air* 25(3):329–340. https://doi.org/10.1111/ina.12147.

Colombini, M. P., G. Giachi, F. Modugno, and E. Ribechini. 2005. "Characterisation of Organic Residues in Pottery Vessels of the Roman Age from Antinoe (Egypt)." *Microchemical Journal* 79(1–2):83–90. https://doi.org/10.1016/j.microc.2004.05.004.

Copley, Mark S., Fabricio A. Hansel, Karim Sadr, and Richard P. Evershed. 2004. "Organic Residue Evidence for the Processing of Marine Animal Products in Pottery

Vessels from the Pre-Colonial Archaeological Site of Kasteelberg D East, South Africa." *South African Journal of Science* 100(5–6):279–283.

Crawford, Barbara E., and Beverly Ballin-Smith. 1999. *The Biggings, Papa Stour, Shetland: The History and Excavation of a Royal Norwegian Farm.* Edinburgh: Society of Antiquaries of Scotland and Det Norske Videnskaps-Akademi.

Dawson, Peter, Richard Levy, Don Gardner, and Matthew Walls. 2007. "Simulating the Behaviour of Light inside Arctic Dwellings: Implications for Assessing the Role of Vision in Task Performance." *World Archaeology* 39(1):17–35. https://doi.org/10.1080/00438240601136397.

De Beaune, Sophie. 1987. "Palaeolithic Lamps and their Specialization: A Hypothesis." *Current Anthropology* 28(4):569–577. https://doi.org/10.1086/203565 http://www.jstor.org/stable/2743501.

Dugmore, Andrew J., Mike J. Church, Kerry-Anne Mairs, Thomas H. McGovern, Anthony J. Newton, and Guðrun Sveinbjarnardóttir. 2006. "An Over-Optimistic Pioneer Fringe? Environmental Perspectives on Medieval Settlement Abandonment in Þórsmörk, South Iceland." In *Dynamics of Northern Societies: Proceedings of the SILA/NABO Conference on Arctic and North Atlantic Archaeology, Copenhagen, May 10th–14th, 2004*, ed. Jetter Arneborg and B. Grønnow, 335–345. Copenhagen: Aarhus University Press.

Eldjárn, Kristján. 1949–50. "Kléberg á Íslandi." *Árbók Hins íslenzka fornleifafélags* 50:41–62.

Evershed, Richard, Sarah J. Vaughan, Stephanie N. Dudd, and Jeffrey S. Soles. 1997. "Fuel for Thought? Beeswax in Lamps and Conical Cups from Late Minoan Crete." *Antiquity* 71(274):979–985. https://doi.org/10.1017/S0003598X00085860.

Fouquet, Roger, and Peter J. G. Pearson. 2006. "Seven Centuries of Energy Services: The Price and Use of Light in the United Kingdom (1300–2000)." *Energy Journal* 27(1):139–177. https://doi.org/10.5547/ISSN0195-6574-EJ-Vol27-No1-8 http://www.jstor.org/stable/23296980.

Frink, Liam, Dashiell Glazer, and Karen G. Harry. 2012. "Canadian Arctic Soapstone Cooking Technology." *North American Archaeologist* 33(4):429–449. https://doi.org/10.2190/NA.33.4.c.

Hamilton, John R. C. 1956. *Excavations at Jarlshof, Shetland.* Edinburgh: H. M. Stationery Office.

Heron, Carl P., Søren H. Andersen, Anders Fischer, Aikaterini Glykou, Sönke Hartz, Hayley Saul, Valerie Steele, and Oliver E. Craig. 2013. "Illuminating the Late Mesolithic: Residue Analysis of 'Blubber' Lamps from Northern Europe." *Antiquity* 87(335):178–188. https://doi.org/10.1017/S0003598X00048705.

Hurcombe, Linda. 2008. "Organics from Inorganics: Using Experimental Archaeology as a Research Tool for Studying Perishable Material Culture." *World Archaeology* 40(1):83–115. https://doi.org/10.1080/00438240801889423.

Ingstad, Anne Stine. 1995. "The Interpretation of the Oseberg Find." In *The Ship as Symbol in Prehistoric and Medieval Scandinavia*, ed. Ole Crumlin-Pedersen and Birgitte Munch Thye, 139–149. Copenhagen: Nationalmuseet.

Kristjánsson, Gísli, and Björn Sigfússon, comp. 1983. *Rit Björns Halldórssonar í Sauðlauksdal*. Reykjavík: Búnaðarfélag Íslands.

Mangone, Annarosa, Lorena C. Giannossa, Rocco Laviano, Custode S. Fioriello, and Angela Traini. 2009. "Investigations by Various Analytical Techniques to the Correct Classification of Archaeological Finds and Delineation of Technological Features: Late Roman Lamps from Egnatia: From Imports to Local Production." *Microchemical Journal* 91(2):214–221. https://doi.org/10.1016/j.microc.2008.11.006.

Milek, Karen. 2012. "The Roles of Pit Houses and Gendered Spaces on Viking-Age Farmsteads in Iceland." *Medieval Archaeology* 56(1):85–130. https://doi.org/10.1179/0076609712Z.0000000004.

Nilsen, Gørill. 2016. "Marine Mammal Train Oil Production Methods: Experimental Reconstructions of Norwegian Iron Age Slab-Lined Pits." *Journal of Marine Archaeology* 11(2):197–217. https://doi.org/10.1007/s11457-016-9153-8.

Ólafsson, Guðmundur. 1987. "Ljósfæri og lýsing." *Íslensk Þjóðmenning I*: 347–369. Reykjavík: Bókaútgáfan Þjóðsaga.

Owen, Olwyn, and Christopher Lowe. 1999. *Kebister: The Four-Thousand-Year-Old Story of One Shetland Township*. Edinburgh: Society of Antiquaries of Scotland.

Phillips, Marie E. 1954. "Eriophorum Angustifolium Roth." *Journal of Ecology* 42(2):612–622. https://doi.org/10.2307/2256893.

Roussell, A. 1943. "Stöng, Þjórsárdalur." In *Forntida gårdar i Island*, ed. M. Stenberger, 72–97. Copenhagen: Einar Munksgaard.

Ruffoni, Kirsten. 2011. "Viking Age Queens: The Example of Oseberg." MPhil thesis, University of Oslo.

Saraydar, Stephen C. 2008. *Replicating the Past: The Art and Science of the Archaeological Experiment*. Long Grove, IL: Waveland Press, Inc.

Solazzo, Caroline, and David Erhardt. 2007. "Analysis of Lipid Residues in Archaeological Artifacts: Marine Mammal Oil and Cooking Practices in the Arctic." In *Theory and Practice of Archaeological Residue Analysis*, British Archaeological Reports International Series 1650, ed. Hans Barnard and Jelmer W. Eerkens, 161–178. Oxford: Archaeopress.

Svanberg, Ingvar. 1997. "The Use of Rush (*Juncus*) and Cotton-Grass (*Eriophorum*) as Wicks: An Ethnobotanical Background to a Faroese Riddle." *Svenska landsmål och svenskt folkliv* 1997–1998:145–157.

Turner, Val, Julie Bond, Anne-Christine Larsen, and Olwyn Owen. 2013. *Viking Unst: Excavation and Survey in Northern Shetland, 2006–2010*. Lerwick: Shetland Amenity Trust.

Nighttime Practices

CHAPTER 14

Engineering Feats and Consequences

Workers in the Night and the Indus Civilization

RITA P. WRIGHT AND ZENOBIE S. GARRETT

WHAT IS AN ARCHAEOLOGY OF THE NIGHT?

Nighttime and darkness are intangible concepts that leave few physical traces (except perhaps archaeological depictions of night skies). Indeed to suggest that certain activities would be inherently nighttime activities is anthropologically problematic, in that it assumes an environmental determinism governing human behavior. The very concepts of night and day themselves are social constructs, and as archaeologists we cannot assume that past cultures would have made a similar distinctive dichotomy.

However, despite the challenges presented in doing an archaeology of the night, it is eminently a worthwhile process. Certainly the acute development of human vision encourages a focus on those groups and activities easily seen, and invites an avoidance of those events that go "bump in the night." Modern constructed fears and fictions surrounding the night are even subsumed into popular presentations of archaeology—illustrations and reenactments of the past that include a nighttime component occur in dark places, often a conscious rhetorical device meant to "Other" the activity and its associated human agents. This

DOI: 10.5876/9781607326786.c014

culturally constructed ignorance of activities that happen after dark is problematic for modern researchers in that it overlooks the power of human beings to adapt and encourages a form of sensory snobbery—where the power of other senses to inform human action is ignored. An archaeology of the night invites us as researchers to consider how past groups may have conceived, navigated, and responded to nighttime settings, and invites us to consider alternative interactions and perceptions of the world around us.

More important, however, an archaeology of the night forces us to think about those activities and the peoples doing them that occur in the dark today. Whether these same activities may have occurred in the dark in the past is irrelevant; the major point is that activities that occur at night in the present are hidden and unseen, and by extension, those groups are left in the academic and historical dark. Reflecting on activities that occur at night in our own society in service of the archaeology of the night provides a platform for "seeing" the unseen activities around us and the unseen groups enacting them.

The theme of this volume has forced us to consider and grapple with what activities occur at night and how that can be applicable to the archaeological record of the Indus civilization. In doing so we have focused on water and sewage system maintenance, a traditional nighttime activity of the modern world, to demonstrate how the common spaces and activities of maintenance would have constructed a shared sense of belonging for participants and/or imposed shared identities upon them by outside viewers.

While social inequality is ultimately the focus of this chapter, the case studies provided here in the context of the nighttime are intended to suggest that, at times, the regulation of activities to the night can be part of a socially exclusionary act. At the same time, sewage and water workers, as well as other modern nocturnal agents, have been socially excluded from anthropological study; thus the greatest benefit of an archaeology of the night in many cases is simply to shed light on these groups and invite us to better understand them.

Indus cities (figure 1.2) in present-day Pakistan and India were among the first to emerge in world history during the third millennium BCE (ca. 2600–1900 BCE) and much like other urban centers, they faced the hazards encountered when people established densely populated settlements. Among Indus contemporaries in Mesopotamia and Egypt as well as in other early urban environments, water and sewage systems provided facilities that were attempts to cope with the pollution problems caused from "foul effluent" (Jansen 1993, 15) and the need for potable water.

This chapter focuses on the Indus's sophisticated water systems and sanitation technology, which is known from at least three of its cities. There are no written records that inform us about how the system was maintained but their built features are testimony to what shaped the tasks required. We know virtually nothing about the workers who kept the system functioning and whether they operated independently or were part of a centralized bureaucracy. That they worked at night is inferred from the types of work required, the odiferous nature of the trash pits they cleaned, and the presence of many of the amenities along the main thoroughfares. We begin by providing a general description of the Indus civilization, paying particular attention to the major Indus cities of Harappa, Mohenjo-daro, and Dholavira, and then delve into the significance of water and sanitation technologies in early state societies. These sections are followed by a description of these technologies at the Indus city of Mohenjo-daro, and using analogies from historical sources in New York City and elsewhere, we reenact the tasks performed by the workers who maintained them.

THE INDUS CIVILIZATION

The Indus civilization was located in what is now Pakistan and India and at a small settlement in northern Afghanistan (Kenoyer 1998; Possehl 2002; Wright 2010). Its chronology is based on a division into three periods, the Early (3300–2600 BCE), Mature (2600–1900 BCE), and Late Harappan (1900–1400 BCE) (figure 1.3). Each of these periods can be broken down into phase categories with variations in the several regions in which they developed. Often referred to as the Indus Valley civilization, the settlements were actually nurtured by two water systems, the Indus River in Pakistan and the Ghaggar–Hakra system in northwest India (Wright 2010).

The regions into which these rivers flowed, where the largest Indus cities—Harappa, Mohenjo-daro, and Dholavira—are located and which are described in this chapter, have diverse ecologies that can be broken down, using their urban centers as benchmarks. In the Pakistan province of Punjab (figure 14.1), the city of Harappa was located in a semiarid zone. It was provisioned by the Indus and its tributaries, the Ravi, Chenab, and Jhelum Rivers. Archaeological sites contemporary with Harappa on a dry river bed of the Beas River that ran parallel to the Ravi River, where Harappa was located, formed an ecological niche in which rural settlements interacted with the urban center (Wright et al. 2008; Wright 2010). In addition to the riverine water system, precipitation was derived from seasonal monsoon and winter westerly rains (Wright 2010). The lowest excavated occupation levels at Harappa and along the Beas River go back to the Early Harappan period. In contrast to the region around Harappa, the city of Mohenjo-daro, in the Sindh province of southeastern Pakistan, is a region with precipitation from seasonal monsoons and intermittent rains. During large parts of the year, modern Sindh lies in a desert-like environment. Thus far, attempts to plumb to levels at Mohenjo-daro that date to before the Mature Harappan have not been successful (Jansen 1993). Unlike Harappa, which shows evidence of pre-urban activity and settlement, Mohenjo-daro, as the evidence currently

FIGURE 14.1. *The Indus civilization with sites referred to in the chapter. (© Rita Wright)*

stands, appears full-blown in its urban form and may have continued into the Late Harappan. Finally, the ancient city of Dholavira is located in Kutch in the province of Gujarat, India, near the coast, where a number of settlements in its surrounding regions were rich in maritime and other natural resources. Levels that extend back to the Early Harappan have been discovered in the city proper. However, it appears that a major river system is not what attracted settlers to the site. Water was provisioned by reservoirs and dams that drew from a runnel (seasonal stream) from which water was channeled into the city (Bisht 2005). Initially, the water was restricted to a sector of the city, but over time engineers developed a magnificent system of reservoirs and dams. As water was released from the reservoirs, it cascaded down into the town and was used for drinking water in the upper city, and in the lower city for domestic needs and irrigation. In addition, two other major Indus cities have been discovered: Ganweriwala, in the Cholistan desert in Pakistan, is known only from surface survey (Mughal 1997) and Rakhigarhi, in northwest India's Haryana province, is a topic of ongoing archaeological research, so therefore neither will be addressed here.

The varied surroundings of the major Indus cities described above are indicative of the widescale environmental diversity characteristic of the region and the variety of resources available to Indus peoples. These resources likely played a role in attracting early agricultural and pastoral communities from the mountains and low-lying areas, and eventually encouraged the building of Indus cities. In Sindh people were initially drawn to the area by chert quarries that were exploited well back into the Paleolithic (Biagi and Cremaschi 1991). In Gujarat, shell and carnelian were much-desired resources for ornaments. The sole Indus settlement, thus far, in northern Afghanistan, is in the area of Badakshan, the location of the world's largest source of lapis lazuli. Other precious minerals exploited in the area were gold, silver, copper, and tin. Throughout the Mature Harappan period, especially, but also earlier and later, the Indus civilization drew on natural resources from these outlying regions (Law 2008).

Finally, in its time, the Indus was known in a world that extended beyond its borders. Texts from Mesopotamia (present-day Iraq), tell of a place named Meluhha that was known for its trade and other forms of contact (Steinkeller 2006) and that is believed to be the Indus civilization. These records demonstrate the civilization's extensive contacts that were maintained by maritime transport up the Persian Gulf with stops in each of the modern-day Arabian states and overland in Iran and beyond.

WATER WORKS AND SANITATION IN EARLY STATES

The varied nature of hydrology across the Indus civilization required a lavish system of water amenities for storage and distribution as well as a large labor force to maintain them. The primacy of these systems to the maintenance of urban centers is reflected in the title of the most recent research conducted at Mohenjo-daro, which describes the site as a *City of Wells and Drains* with a subtitle of *Water Splendour 4500 Years Ago* (Jansen 1993). The two types of water works addressed in this chapter are those that provided potable water and sanitation systems.

In order to situate the Indus in its historical context and to appreciate the challenges of urban upkeep met by other early civilizations, we provide a brief review of how the earliest urban centers coped with the challenges of maintaining water systems. The two technologies, potable water and sanitation, complemented each other, but they often were managed separately. The following is not a comprehensive timeline for each of them but is designed to draw attention to the challenges of city life in the earliest states. Its purpose is to provide a framework from which to understand the significance of these same amenities in the Indus civilization, which we describe subsequently.[1]

Potable Water

Even before the development of cities, people sought potable water wherever they went. This need is reflected by the migrations of nomads whose treks followed the paths of oases. In the earliest settled communities, for example at Jericho in the Levant, people were attracted by its springs (Kenyon 1957). Water was carried from the springs to households, either in ceramic jars or containers made of other impermeable materials. Later when people moved to the alluvial plain in Mesopotamia, rainwater was collected for household use. In Early Dynastic Egypt, the Nile River supplied the major source of drinking water. In the New World at the Classic Maya city of Tikal (250–900 CE) people drew water from existing springs and channeled it through a natural ravine into artificially constructed reservoirs and dams (Scarborough et al. 2012). A sand filtration system cleansed the water, making it potable.

Sanitation Systems

The earliest evidence in the Old World for a sanitation system dates to the fourth and third millennia BCE. At the Chalcolithic site of Habuba Kabira, Syria (ca. 3400–3000 BCE), people channeled water and debris away from residences by producing earthenware pipe sections through which the effluent flowed (Jansen 1993, 15).[2] In the late fourth and early third millennia in Mesopotamia, drainage systems were created for storm-water control. They included vaulted sewers, gutters and drains for household waste and surface runoff, and cesspools under some houses over which people squatted through a floor opening (De Feo et al. 2014, 3938). During the same period, there were toilets at Skara Brae in Scotland connected to a drainage system that ran below residential floors (De Feo et al. 2014, 3939). In Early Dynastic Egypt at Hierakonpolis, waste was removed from the settlement and taken outside of inhabited areas, probably to the rivers. There also were bathrooms fitted with stone slabs. A drainage channel ran from the baths into a vessel and into the desert, while in less well-off households, excrement was deposited into ceramic bowls and collected in jars with sand. This waste was emptied into rivers and streets. A similar system was employed by those even less well-off who used a simple stool over a bed of sand. In the pyramids, a more sophisticated system employed clay pipes to guide water and effluent through the sewage system (De Feo et al. 2014, 3942).

A more spectacular system of storm-water management was developed in the Minoan and Mycenaean civilizations between 3200 and 1100 BCE. It included conduits and pipes that moved water and human waste from toilets that were flushed out with jars of water. Later, toilets in the palace at Knossos had wooden seats and the pipes were connected to a central drainage system. In addition, stone conduits were used to move rainwater to reduce the risk of flooding (De Feo et al. 2014, 3939). In China, four thousand years ago in early settlements on the Yellow River, earthenware and earthen pipelines were placed under the street for drainage. In the later Shang dynasty, urban drainage systems included sewers and an elaborate system that extended (in some cities) over 15 km^2 (De Feo et al. 2014, 3943). Very sophisticated hydraulics at the Classic Maya site of Palenque (600–700 CE) in the New World prevented flooding that occurred due to landscape alterations and temperature changes (French et al. 2013). These changes included the construction of a paved plaza and subsequent deforestation. The effects of the changes were ameliorated by the construction of an aqueduct, one of the largest urban features at the site. Using hydroarchaeological modeling Kirk French and colleagues (2013) determined that during a ten-year peak event due to a reduction in temperature and a drought urban flooding was reduced.

LIVING AT MOHENJO-DARO: POTABLE WATER AND SANITATION

Mohenjo-daro is one of the best vantage points from which to observe an Indus city (ca. 2600–1900 BCE) and its water amenities. The city's baked-brick architecture has been reconstructed and, wherever possible, renovated (figure 14.2). It is a UNESCO World Heritage site and even today, visitors are able to walk through many of its city streets and examine bathing areas in residences and the well-known Great Bath. Built on a north-south, east-west axis, with slight divergences, its builders relied on astronomical data based on the positions of the sun and fixed stars that were integrated with elements from the physical landscape and provided orientation points (Wanzke 1984, 35). After its initial construction there were modifications in some street plans and alterations to its amenities such as changes in the water consumption points in specific blocks (Jansen 1993, 126).

The evidence for water works at Mohenjo-daro and other centers discussed in the preceding paragraph add a new "craft" to the archaeologist's repertoire of technologies. Interestingly, while archaeologists have not considered their significance to modern urbanism, other scholars have investigated water works as models for sustainability in contemporary societies (Bond et al. 2013; Singh et al. 2015). Others look more closely at what lies beneath our cities (Ascher 2005) by conducting ethnographic studies of the consumption and managing waste (Royte 2006). Some prepare Maintenance Art (Kennedy 2016; Ukeles 2016), a practice that regards trash as cultural artifacts. They, along with historical analogies discussed later, have come a long way toward understanding the complexity

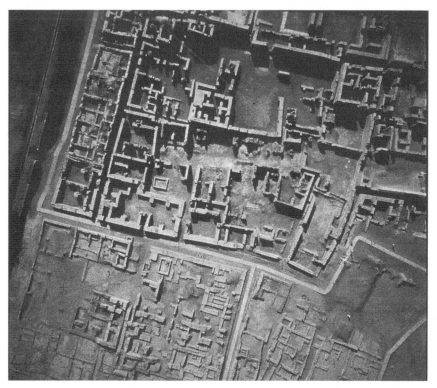

FIGURE 14.2. *Aerial view of the streets and houses at Mohenjo-daro. (Photo courtesy of M. Jansen, Aachen Research Project, Mohenjo-daro)*

of the technologies employed in the past and provide possible insights into workers in the past.

The water system at Mohenjo-daro combined the distribution of drinking water and sanitation throughout a city that was densely clustered in tightly packed neighborhoods (figure 14.2). Designed in a gridlike pattern, infrastructural features such as water sources and sewage disposal were built into its city streets. The system of wells was a vital resource and the principal source of potable water. The wells were constructed of specially designed wedge-shaped bricks that provided a tight fit to prevent seepage. Wells were produced using a method still known today in Pakistan as "shaft-sinking." A cylindrical wooden ring is set in the ground and weighted with bricks. As the ring is lowered, it compresses the dirt, which is then "removed from the center and beneath the ring: the procedure continues as the ring sinks under its own weight until water is reached" (Livingston 2002, 20; see also Jansen 1993, 118). Notable is that this identical well technology has been discovered at small Indus villages and towns that one of us surveyed in rural areas along the Beas drainage, where they remain visible in spite of agricultural development and the establishment of modern villages and towns (Wright 2010).

At Mohenjo-daro wells were either shared by several residences or were for use in an individual household. They were located at convenient points in neighborhoods, while some were built in rooms in the interiors of houses. In one room, for example, a well was surrounded by a brick floor where specially designed small depressions were constructed, "as stands for vessels with pointed base[s]" (Jansen 1993, 108, figure 126). However, whether wells were maintained by neighborhood groups in the districts where they were located or by a municipal bureaucracy is unknown.

Many ceramics were used to store water and these artifacts were carefully documented by the early excavators at Mohenjo-daro (e.g., Mackay 1938). Though produced in different styles, their persistent presence in certain interior locations across the city, suggests that they were produced for specific purposes. They came in various sizes and shapes, some of which were so large that the impressions from string drawn around the exteriors while they were drying before being kiln fired are still visible. While some were small, others were up to three feet or more in height or with maximum body diameters of three feet. Many were sunk deeply into floors. Several types were coated with thick slips on their interiors and exteriors; other exteriors were covered with sandy mixtures. Additional jars in the interior of houses captured water that was fed into drains carefully leveled with gravel (Jansen 1993). These jars were often set into specially produced stands while others were found in hollows in burnt-brick pavements supported by bricks to stabilize the container or to prevent water from leakage. Damaged jars were recycled and some were placed outside of houses to serve as drains. Overall, many of the vessels found in the interiors of houses were in bathing areas and well rooms that were positioned at the end of streets. Nonetheless, their presence in residential interiors that were not part of the original city plan may have been the responsibility of household members.

The exterior drainage system was complex and required regular cleaning and a large workforce to flush and clear deposits (Jansen 1993, 121). Its upkeep and variety suggest that workers were part of a municipally organized system. Three major features contributed to the sewerage system in the city's streets that have been fully documented by Jansen's research team. First, drains were located along major residential streets. These were produced from baked bricks and in several shapes that were either left open or covered (figure 14.3; see also figures in Jansen 1993, figures 142 and 143, for dimensions). Second, where the drains had to overcome curves or met several drains, cesspits were installed. As effluent flowed into their specially designed shafts, it spilled out to the other side. Suspended matter that sunk to lower levels was removed by workers

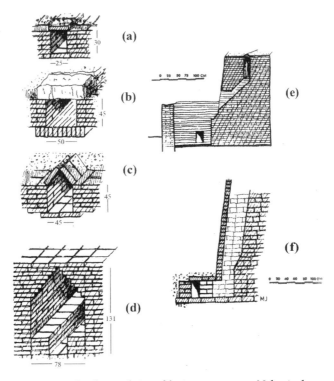

FIGURE 14.3. *Graphic rendition of drainage systems at Mohenjo-daro. (Courtesy of M. Jansen, Aachen Research Project Mohenjo-daro)*

who descended a set of steps into the pit, brought the sewage to the top, and removed it. Finally, soak pits—absorbent pits used to soak up waste—were usually installed on the largest streets. These pits needed to be scooped out and cleaned as well (Jansen 1993). If a street drain was at too great a distance from a building, a catchment vessel was installed under vertical chutes and cleaned by tipping them out onto the street. There were various other features, depending upon need. For example, in places where the toilets or bathing platforms were positioned on the wall adjacent to the street, chutes channeled water and waste directly into the drains below.

In some parts of the city, there were bathrooms in every household (Jansen 1993, 122). The effluent in each residence flowed from the interiors of houses to the outdoor street drains and spilled into pits at street level. Some houses had terracotta pipes that carried water from their interiors alongside streets and dumped their contents onto the main street, where they flowed into the pits (Wright 2010). The effluent spilling from the terracotta pipes carried the waste several blocks so that their owners were relatively free of the smelly odors while

FIGURE 14.4. *Plan of houses at HRA-B Mohenjo-daro. At top left, House VIII has a terracotta pipe (dashed lines) extending from its interior out to the main street. (Courtesy of M. Jansen, Aachen Research Project Mohenjo-daro)*

people who lived in houses adjacent to the soak pits (figure 14.4), often directly at the front, on the street side of the residence, were not so lucky. Odors would have been most offensive where restrictions in gravity flow caused clogging (Jansen 1993). Suspended matter would have to be removed in order to keep waste flowing into the pits, thus emitting more odors.

These days, in a walk through Mohenjo-daro, you would not have to bear witness to the smell of trash radiating from the sump pits on "off" days. But there were other potential downsides of the system. The area around Mohenjo-daro is susceptible to torrents of rainwater during seasonal storms and we know that the streets were largely unpaved, since only a few *in situ* pavements (brick and pottery fragments) have been discovered. Most streets, likely, were covered with packed earth. During rainy seasons, water and debris from households that were left on streets would have flowed through the town. Reflecting on the potential result, Jansen believes that it would "have turned the city into a sea of muck" (Jansen 1993, 78).

Until now, the presence of cleanup crews at Mohenjo-daro or in any of the other Indus cities has been an invisible and rarely considered side of life. Our basic assumption that the work took place at night is based on several factors. The trash pits and other sanitation structures that flanked housing would have been an even more odiferous presence during the day, when people moved about the streets, than at night. While maintaining the system was a year-round task, in summer, when the desert warms up, choosing to work at night makes sense. Drawing on the writings of the British military and local officials, they describe summer months as hot with fierce unrelenting winds, while others describe the land as "parched" (Dalrymple 2013; Seaton 1875; Mirza 'Ata 1952). Still, the careful planning that went into removal and prevention of clogging of streets drains, cesspits, and soak pits required sustained and specialized care in order to prevent noxious substances from littering the landscape and had to be carried out throughout the year. The scale and intricacies of Mohenjo-daro's sanitation system would have undoubtedly required significant care, a task too large to be confined to the daylight hours.

Historical records from New York City between 1895 and 1906 provide some details of night work that match the types of technologies available at Mohenjo-daro. There were four tasks mandated for municipal cleaning in late-nineteenth-century New York City that provide insights into the nature of work and the people who performed it at Mohenjo-daro. They include cleaning the streets and removing dust and trash, keeping water jars filled to capacity, and the more unpleasant tasks of keeping drains free of debris and scouring pits or sewers.

The equipment needed to perform the work included water, brooms, wooden carts and draft animals, and when working at night or in deep pits, portable light. Brooms are easily fashioned from lower tree branches or bushes. For light, different phases of the moon would have been convenient but intermittent. A better choice would have been torches, a form of light used by people well before the advent of cities. Animal fats are an obvious choice as fuel, but the tree sap or pitch from local plants would be even better. Certain trees—the jujube (*Ziziphus jujube*), for example—were well known to Indus people. It emits pitch that might have provided an enduring light. Whether this substance could be used deep inside of the pits is problematic.

1. *Carting away Debris.* Wooden carts, for which we have evidence at Mohenjo-daro from clay models, would have been a convenient way in which to move necessities around the city. In New York City wooden carts were used to carry away horse manure that was scooped up by workers. In the Indus, carts were pulled by zebu cattle, as attested to by the scarring on the bones of zebu in the archaeological record (Miller 2004).

2. *Sweeping Streets and Removing Dust.* In addition to sewage and garbage, streets would have to be swept. Airborne dust, especially on the dirt streets at Mohenjo-daro, would have been a health hazard. It has long been known (e.g., Hippocrates in the fourth century BC, and Pliny the Elder in Rome) that dust is a health hazard. The United States Occupational Safety and Health Administration (OSHA) standards identify silica dust found in road dirt to have serious health effects (http://www.safetyworksmaine.gov/pdf/swt0402.pdf). In the State of Maine, Department of Labor (SWT0401) directives, workers are mandated to wet down areas before sweeping in order to keep dust from becoming airborne. In New York City in the nineteenth century, streets were paved with brick or dirt; they were wetted down to control the dust and swept clean with brooms. To sweep the dirt or paved streets at Mohenjo-daro and to avoid creating additional dust, sprinkling with water would be a relatively easy matter by broadcasting water on the surface. The city had wells on almost every street and large water jars that would have served as a ready supply of liquid.

3. *Keeping Water Jars Filled.* Keeping a source of water nearby would have been crucial in any urban environment, but particularly for urban areas in an arid environment. In New York City, water from an upstate reservoir was piped to the city by the mid-nineteenth century. At Mohenjo-daro, upkeep on wells was necessary to maintain a ready supply for drinking water and keeping the water jars full for maintenance workers.

4. *Scouring the Pits.* Clogged drains and removing solid matter from the pits is obviously dirty work, no matter how it is described. Descending the steps in the pits with light from torches, scooping out the wet consolidated debris, and hauling it to the surface were not mechanized but were performed manually, in nineteenth-century New York City. At Mohenjo-daro, most liquids would drain out into the soil, but collecting more solid matter and hauling it to the surface were necessary. Yannis Hamilakis (2014) in his book, *The Archaeology of the Senses*, would refer to the experience as less visual and more sensorial in nature. Approaching the consolidated but wet trash, workers would have encountered a sensorial assemblage that would have lived in memory long after the tasks were completed. Other contributors to this volume (see, for example, Kamp and Whittaker, chapter 4) might think of it as entering a liminal landscape between civil society and its underside, while other authors could refer to it as a senses-cape. By any definition, having come to terms with its material substances, it was a unique and not easily forgotten sensory experience.

CULTURAL PERCEPTIONS AND IDENTITIES

Elsewhere, one of us (Wright 2010, 242), interpreted the proximity of some of the features and locations of drains, sump pits, and cesspits at Mohenjo-daro as signaling social differences between households. When thinking about the upkeep of the system, it followed that the workers, who were exposed to its odors and disease and who were responsible for its management, would be near the bottom of the social hierarchy. This interpretation was based on assumptions about "dirty," uninteresting, low-paid work. In the context of this volume, one could argue (as we have above) that if such activities did happen at night, their restriction to the cover of darkness may have underscored and contributed to the construction of social differentiation and inequality. While nighttime would have been an attractive time for maintenance for a number of reasons, it may have also served to conceal the workers and their contributions from the society that benefited from them.[3] With rare exceptions, the modern day (or, more accurately, modern night) occurrence of sewage and water maintenance restricts engagement with sanitation workers. While urban dwellers may appreciate the benefits of this work completed at night, they are often oblivious to the labor force involved in the upkeep of urban infrastructure. This modern-day blindness to nocturnal activities has important ramifications for archaeological study. To date, Indus water and sanitation workers have not been studied, even though the work they performed was essential to the well-being of the city.

Ignorance of these groups archaeologically no doubt stems from modern society's aversion to the unpleasant realities of sanitation work, a disinterest in the perceived "menial" tasks of sanitation crews, and their invisibility in society. Nevertheless, as we have argued throughout this chapter, these workers would have provided crucial services to burgeoning urban populations, and indeed the progress and promise of urban life would not have been possible without them (Nagle 2013). Understanding how these workers fit into society and civic life is a critical component of overcoming the current archaeological darkness on the subject and can provide insight into whether nighttime worked to conceal and/or suppress certain groups. Because no archaeological studies on Indus sanitation workers exist, we consulted modern and historical records in two parts of the world that do not share the same history or culture. The comparisons are between the sanitation workers in Kolkata (Calcutta), India and the other, the Department of Sanitation in New York City from the late nineteenth- and early twentieth-century historical records referred to earlier. Both conduct part of their work at night (Basu, Dey, and Ghosh 2013; Dhar 2014; Oatman-Stanford 2013). By looking at these two examples, we as archaeologists can start to understand the varied perceptions of nighttime workers in society and use this evidence to think more deeply about the societal roles that those who worked at night may have inhabited in the past.

The sanitation system of Kolkata was built by the British nearly a century and a half ago. Although modern at the time, poor management has made it unable to handle the modern sanitation needs of the city (Singh et al. 2015). The sanitation workers in Kolkata and in many other cities in India are Dalits. They are at the bottom of the social hierarchy of Indian society, an untouchable caste considered unclean. They have tolerated the humiliating conditions of the work for the measly compensation provided (up to $3 a day) and conditions that make them most susceptible to disease, death, and injuries. The private firm that regulates sanitation does not provide adequate protective equipment, forcing the workers into intimate contact with the effluent as they emerge from sewers walking in bare feet, sometimes with their limbs and torsos uncovered. When accidents occur while working, sanitation workers who die on the job may be left in the contaminated sewage water, and the sludge is dumped in the Hugli River (Stockton 2014).

In contrast, conditions for sanitation workers in New York City underwent major reforms in the late nineteenth century, but prior to 1894 the system may have looked something like Kolkata. It was considered one of the filthiest and "stinkiest" cities. Sailors said that they smelled the city "six miles out to sea" (Schmidt 2010, 1). There were epidemics, dirt, dead animals in the street layered with manure, and all sorts of domestic debris, from food to furniture. The situation changed in 1894 when Colonel George Waring was appointed to clean up the city. The new commissioner used his military background and experience as a sanitary engineer in Memphis, Tennessee to establish a first-rate team of sanitation workers and alerted the city's citizens to the value of the work being conducted by his department. Under Waring's direction, the potable water supply of the city was greatly expanded and sanitation across the city became a top priority.

In response to Waring's directives, there was a sea change in the level of respect bestowed on the sanitation workers. Whereas in the past, they had been greeted by residents in some neighborhoods with broken crockery, now they were a welcome sight. Unlike the Dalits of Kolkata, who are socially ostracized and viewed as unclean, the workers were in some sense thought of as "heroes" (Nagle 2013, 2), likely because of the marked reduction in deaths and diarrheal diseases as a result of the clean streets.

An insight into how the sanitation workers in New York viewed themselves appeared in the 1906 *New York City Sanitation Journal* (see vol. xxi, no. 5, page 110, for the full text). This micro-melody (containing seven different interval scales) was titled "A Song in Praise of Helminthes" and was sung by the workers themselves. Prescient are the final lines in which the workers describe some "old friends" (lice, for example) and "enemies." The exact words are: "Fussy little microbes, billions at birth, Make our flesh and blood and bones, Keep us on the earth" (*New York Sanitation Journal* 1906, 110).

This jolly song not only celebrates their collective identity as New York City sanitation workers but also anticipates the latest theories of evolutionary medicine. The "old friends" hypothesis was developed in 1989 (Rook et al. 2014) and distinguishes it from "crowd" infections. Researchers in evolutionary medicine have suggested that helminths and other "old friend" parasites are rarely harbored by humans these days, but could provide health benefits to their hosts, regulating the immune system and discouraging or inhibiting certain diseases. Whereas old friends had health benefits, crowd infections are a phenomenon of urban living and they lack the health benefits of old friends. Old friends are missing from some urban populations because many do not have contact with the natural environment or green spaces.[4]

If the evolutionary medicine specialists are right, then the sanitation workers in New York reaped a benefit from their street work, which contributed to a more positive perception of their nighttime activities. The song indicates an awareness of harboring helminths and the medicinal advantages they provided in an urban setting. More important, it promotes a shared collective identity among these nighttime workers. These same workers not only united together to celebrate their positions through song, but took pride in their nocturnal activities.

Research into modern sanitation workers in Kolkata and nineteenth- and twentieth-century historical records from New York City revealed different management strategies and managers that held different social/cultural views regarding the sanitation workers. For the Indian workers, already suppressed by their inferior status as Dalits, their sanitation work, and the disregard of authorities for the importance of that work, reproduced their identity as an inferior category of citizens. It is providing them with a political platform from which to challenge their low status and to garner support for better working conditions and improvements in the sanitation system. (see *countercurrents.org*—August 15, 2016). On the other hand, the New York City sanitation workers labored through the night under an efficient and lasting regime instituted by Colonel Waring. As respected members of the department and community, they achieved a positive sense of identity, proudly displaying their pride in a poetic rendering that commemorates the tight bonds among these sanitation workers and their self-professed value.

In both of these cases strong group identities were reinforced by the restricted nature of work in the night. However, the social perception and value of these groups varied greatly. These two examples suggest that nighttime can play a critical role in the formation and support of group identity. However, the role of nighttime in the social value of these groups is much more complex. While at times, nighttime may help underscore social differences, they may not always be perceived in the same way. Such information is a crucial step in building models for archaeological investigation and interpretation of night activities and can be used as a springboard for asking questions about night workers in the archaeological record.

CONCLUSIONS

In this chapter, we have reconstructed the kinds of sanitation infrastructure needed to maintain Mohenjo-daro and the Indus civilization. Keeping in mind that many of these activities likely happened at night, we have examined some of the day-to-day activities they conducted and how nighttime affects group identity and social value, through examples drawn from modern-day Kolkata and historic New York City. While these examples indicated that nighttime work could result in strong group identity, the social value of these groups varied greatly. Of particular significance to the social worth of these groups was the management success of the urban infrastructures.

The "water splendour" at Mohenjo-daro was a masterly achievement that lasted for at least six hundred years (Jansen 1993), much of which likely happened in the dark. Throughout these 219,000 nights, sanitation standards likely fluctuated, but although some of the amenities were dysfunctional and were abandoned in the final period, for the most part, the city thrived, suggesting that the waterworks were maintained. How this management affected the social value of sanitation workers cannot be said, but this chapter has provided evidence that such questions can and should be asked by archaeologists. Urban maintenance is a twenty-four-hour job, and much of the work happens at night. This observation is true today, and was likely true in the Indus as well. Much of this chapter relies on the well-developed archaeological documentation of the technical features of Mohenjo-daro's amenities. We employed modern analogies when discussing the specifics of day-to-day maintenance. Finally, we questioned the cultural value and especially of how those "invisible" nighttime workers may have been regarded culturally. We hope we have shown that groups involved in nightly urban upkeep would have been crucial to the sustainability of urban life and should therefore play a critical role in archaeological theories surrounding the formation of urban societies. That these groups could have inhabited a range of social roles makes them an essential key to understanding the value of urbanization in society.

NOTES

1. Karl Wittfogel's hydraulic theory proposed that irrigation technology caused the development of early states, but Wittfogel's theory itself was limited (Wittfogel 1957). Although it recognized the importance of irrigation in supplying water to groups, it failed to take into account the numerous ways water was socially used and the economic investment and accompanying social consequences of these supply systems. In reality, people drew pleasure in drinking potable water, bathing in it, keeping their homes and streets clean, and maintaining a healthy population.

2. Our discussion is based on the most comprehensive analysis of prehistoric water installations in prehistory by an industrial engineer, Geovanni De Feo. In it, he brought together the research of colleagues in the fields of architecture, archaeology, and water history (De Feo et al. 2014).

3. Rare exceptions are the long-term ethnographic study of sanitation workers (Nagle 2013) and Merle Ukeles, who produces maintenance art. An exhibition at the Queens Museum presents the current status of her work (Kennedy 2016; Ukeles 2016).

4. Researchers in evolutionary medicine believe that twenty-first-century humans rarely harbor the kind of parasites that derive nourishment from their hosts. The parasites are protozoa and are called helminths. They believe that diseases like allergies, Parkinson's disease, and Crohn's disease could benefit from these parasites. The thesis made the popular press in the *New York Times,* August 3, 2016, front page: "Barnyard Dust Offers a Clue to Stopping Asthma in Children" (Kolata 2016).

REFERENCES

Ascher, Kate. 2005. *The Works: Anatomy of a City.* New York: Penguin Press.

Basu, Nilangshu Bhusan, Ayanangshu Dey, and Duke Ghosh. 2013. "Kolkata's Brick Sewer Renewal: History, Challenges and Benefits." *Proceedings of the Institution of Civil Engineers–Civil Engineering* 166(2):74–81.

Biagi, Paolo, and Mauro Cremaschi. 1991. "The Harappan Flint Quarries of the Rohri Hills (Sindh, Pakistan)." *Antiquity* 65(246):97–102. https://doi.org/10.1017/S0003598X0 0079321.

Bisht, Ravindra Singh. 2005. "The Water Structures and Engineering of the Harappans at Dholavira." In *South Asian Archaeology 2001,* Vol. 1, ed. Catherine Jarrige and Vincent Lefèvre, 11–25. Paris: Editions Recherche sur les Civilisations.

Bond, T., E. Roma, K. M. Foxon, M. R. Templeton, and C. A. Buckley. 2013. "Ancient Water and Sanitation Systems: Applicability for the Contemporary Urban Developing World." *Weather Science and Technology*: 935–938.

Dalrymple, William. 2013. *Return of a King: The Battle for Afghanistan, 1839–42.* New York. Alfred Knopf.

De Feo, Giovanni, George Antoniou, Hilal Fardin, Fatma El-Gohary, Xiao Zheng, Ieva Reklaityte, David Butler, Stavros Yannopoulos, and Andreas Angelakis. 2014. "The Historical Development of Sewers Worldwide." *Sustainability* 6(6):3936–3974. https://doi.org/10.3390/su6063936.

Dhar, Sujoy. "A Journey into the 140-Year-Old Tunnels Below Calcutta." April 11, 2014. Accessed October 6, 2016. https://nextcity.org/daily/entry/a-journey-into-the -140-year-old-tunnels-below-calcutta.

French, Kirk D., Christopher F. Duffy, and Gopal Bhatt. 2013. "The Urban Hydrology and Hydraulic Engineering at the Classic Maya Site of Palenque." *Water History Journal* 5(1):43–69. https://doi.org/10.1007/s12685-012-0069-4.

Hamilakis, Yannis. 2014. *Archaeology of the Senses: Human Experience, Memory, and Affect.* Cambridge: Cambridge University Press.

Jansen, Michael. 1993. *Mohenjo-daro: City of Wells and Drains, Water Splendour 4500 Years ago.* Bonn: Bergisch Gladbach Frontinus-Gesellschaft.

Kennedy, Randy. 2016. "An Artist who calls the Sanitation Department Home." *New York Times*, September 21.

Kenoyer, Jonathan Mark. 1998. *Ancient Cities of the Indus Valley Civilization.* Karachi: Oxford University Press.

Kenyon, Kathleen M. 1957. *Digging up Jericho.* London: Praeger/Ernest Benn Limited.

Kolata, Gina. "Barnyard Dust Offers a Clue to Stopping Asthma in Children." *New York Times*, August 3, 2016. Accessed October 6, 2016. http://www.nytimes.com/2016/08/04/health/dust-asthma-children.html.

Law, Randall H. 2008. "Interregional Interaction and Urbanism in the Ancient Indus Valley: A Geologic Provenance Study of Harappa's Rock and Mineral Assemblage." PhD Diss. University of Wisconsin, Madison.

Livingston, Mona. 2002. *Steps to Water: The Ancient Stepwells of India.* Princeton, NJ: Princeton Architectural Press.

Mackay, Ernest J. H. 1938. *Further Excavations at Mohenjo-daro, Being an Official Account of Archaeological Excavations carried out by the Government of India between the years of 1927 and 1931.* Vols. 1 and 2. New Delhi: Government of India Press.

Miller, Laura J. 2004. "Urban Economies in Early States: The Secondary Products Revolution in the Indus Civilization." PhD diss., New York University, New York.

Mirza 'Ata, Mohammad. 1131, AH/1952. *Naway M'arek.* Nashrat i Anjuman-I tarikh, no. 22.

Mughal, Mohammad R. 1997. *Ancient Cholistan: Archaeology and Architecture.* Rawalpindi: Ferozsons.

Nagle, Robin. 2013. *Picking Up: On the Streets and Behind the Trucks of the Sanitation Workers of New York City.* New York: Farrar, Straus and Giroux.

New York City Sanitation Journal. 1906. 21(5):110.

Oatman-Stanford, Hunter. 2013. "A Filthy History: When New Yorkers Lived Knee-Deep in Trash." *Collector's Weekly*, June 24, 2013. Accessed August 28, 2016.http://www.collectorsweekly.com/articles/when-new-yorkers-lived-knee-deep-in-trash/.

Possehl, Gregory L. 2002. *The Indus Civilization: A Contemporary Perspective.* Walnut Creek, CA: AltaMira Press.

Rook, Graham, A.W. Christopher, A. Raison, C.L. Lowry, and Charles L. Raison. 2014. "Microbial 'Old Friends' Immunoregulation and Socioeconomic Status." *Journal of Translational Clinical and Experimental Immunology* 177(1). https://doi.org/10.1111/cei.12269.

Royte, Elizabeth. 2006. *On the Secret Trail of Trash.* New York: Little, Brown and Company.

Scarborough, Vernon L., Nicholas P. Dunning, Kenneth B. Tankersley, Christopher Carr, Eric Weaver, Liwy Grazioso, Brian Lane, John G. Jones, Palma Buttles, Fred Valdez, and David L. Lentz. 2012. "Water and Sustainable Land Use at the Ancient Tropical City of Tikal, Guatemala." *Proceedings of the National Academy of Sciences of the United States of America* 109(31):12408–12413. https://doi.org/10.1073/pnas.1202881109.

Schmidt, Sarah. 2010. "Digging into New York City's Trashy History." *OnEarth Magazine*, October 15, 2010. Accessed August 28, 2016. http://archive.onearth.org/article/digging-into-new-york-citys-trashy-history.

Seaton, Major-General Sir Thomas. 1875. *From Cadet to Colonel: The Record of a Life of Active Service*. London: Hurst and Blackett.

Singh, Ram Babu, Senaul Haque, and Aakriti Grover. 2015. "Drinking Water, Sanitation and Health in Kolkata Metropolitan City: Contribution Towards Urban Sustainability." *Geography, Environment Sustainability* 8(4):64–81. https://doi.org/10.15356/2071-9388_04v08_2015_07.

Steinkeller, Piotr. 2006. "New Light on Marhaši and Its Contacts with Makkan and Babylonia." *Journal of Magan Studies* 1:1–17.

Stockton, Richard. 2014. "The Three Worst Jobs in the World." June 30, 2014. Accessed August 28, 2016. http://all-that-is-interesting.com/worst-jobs.

Ukeles, Merle Laderman. 2016. *Maintenance Art at the Queens Museum*. New York: Prestel.

Wanzke, H. 1984. "Axis Systems and Orientation at Mohenjo-Daro." In *Interim Reports on Fieldwork Carried out at Mohenjo-Daro 1982–83*, vol. 2. ed. M. Jansen and G. Urban, 33–44. Aachen, Roma: Forschungprojekt "Mohenjo-Daro."

Wittfogel, Karl A. 1957. *Oriental Despotism: A Comparative Study of Total Power*. New Haven, CT: Yale University Press.

Wright, Rita P. 2010. *The Ancient Indus: Urbanism, Economy, and Society*. Cambridge: Cambridge University Press.

Wright, Rita P., Reid Bryson, and Joseph Schuldenrein. 2008. "Water Supply and History: Harappa and the Beas Settlement Survey." *Antiquity* 82(315): 37–48.

All Rome Is at My Bedside

Nightlife in the Roman Empire

GLENN REED STOREY

The dawn and gloaming most invite one to Musement; but I have found no watch of the nychthemeron that has not its own advantages for the pursuit.

—CHARLES PIERCE

There is no place for either thinking or resting in the city, Sparsus, for a poor man. In the morning, the school teachers negate life, by night, it is the bakers . . . Whoever can count the losses of sluggish sleep could say how many hands in the city strike the pots and pans whenever the moon in eclipse is set upon with a Colchian noisemaker . . . The laughter of the crowd passing by awakens me and all Rome is at my bedside. Whenever I am overcome by fatigue and sleep would be pleasant, I go to my villa.

—MARTIAL *Epigrams* 12.57.3–17, 26–28

Et ad cubile est Roma ("all Rome is at my bedside").[1] So complained the Roman poet Martial in the second century CE. That is because the city of Rome was a wonderful example of the *nychthemeron*, (literally, "night today," in Greek; Galinier et al. 2010, 820), the twenty-four-hour extent of a "day" in the most

DOI: 10.5876/9781607326786.c015

fundamental sense (figures 1.2, 1.3). There was no respecting the common notion that the nighttime needed to be quiet so people could sleep. The origin of Martial's specific complaint is still true; one is kept up by the sounds of people in the street in various states of sobriety or just in good spirits (or ill). Another challenge specific to Rome is also still true. While tossing and turning with jet lag once, while in Rome for an epigraphy conference, I was treated to the sound of the trash pick.up outside my hotel at 2 a.m. (see Wright and Garrett, chapter 14, this volume, for a discourse on trash pickup in the Harappan civilization). I grumpily admitted to myself "aha! That goes back a long way" because that is what would have transpired in Rome after the ordinance of Julius Caesar that prohibited wheeled traffic in the city during a good portion of the day:

> As many streets as are or will be in the city of Rome, within those areas of con-tiguous habitation, let no one . . . introduce or drive in those streets a wheeled vehicle during the day: after sunrise until the 10th hour. Exceptions: necessary conveyance or transport for building sacred temples for the immortal gods and for public works. Introduction and driving of conveyances will be permitted, under the terms of this law, to particular individuals for particular reasons. (*Lex Iulia Municipalis*, the "Julian Law of Municipalities")

Depending on the season (Roman practice was to have twelve hours of day-light and twelve hours of darkness every day, the length of the hour changing daily), wheeled traffic in Rome was prohibited from sunrise to between 2 p.m. and 7 p.m., roughly. Of course, one can appreciate that exceptions were probably common and allowing of private traffic was helped by bribes. Nevertheless, the result is a lot of noisy wheeled delivery of commodities to the shops of Rome by night, and a lot of human communication commonly carried on in the dark. Daveluy (2010) emphasized the acoustic dimension of the night, and here we have it richly illustrated.

Thus, immediately we know that Rome was alive at night and (in contrast to many past societies) we have substantial evidence for what people did when darkness fell. For the remainder of this chapter, I discuss several examples of this wealth of evidence. I do so using as a framework the order of discussion set out in Roger Ekirch's (2005) history of the night. I begin with terrors of the night: darkness—disease, ghosts, accidents and alcohol, plunder and violence, and fire—and then consider aspects of night life: artificial lighting, night labor, sex, writing at night, (k)nightwalking (to be explained later), and last, patterns of sleep. In the course of this recital of nightly activities, I highlight archaeologi-cal evidence of nightlife that complements and enhances the rich documentary record we have for night in the Roman Empire.

Darkness

It is hard to say specifically how the effect of darkness might be best illustrated. It seems that the dark night was frightening to the Romans. That is perhaps best demonstrated by a famous line of the poet Catullus, who, in Poem 5.5–6, says to Lesbia that they should live and love because *nobis cum semel occidit brevis lux, nox est perpetua una dormienda* ("when once this brief light sets for us, night is one long perpetual thing to be slept," meaning death). As Ekirch (2005, 3–15) clearly sets out, night holds its terrors largely because its darkness is reminiscent of death.

Disease

Regarding disease, Rome has long been considered an important exemplar of the "urban graveyard effect," the idea from historical demography that urban centers in the preindustrial world were notoriously unhealthy places—even to the point of being "demographic sinks" because mortality, due to disease and malnutrition, were notoriously high (Storey 2006). Although none of the evidence equates the epidemics and pandemics that struck Rome as purely nocturnal scourges, Juvenal (*Satires* 3, 232) does comment that "in Rome, most illnesses end in death from insomnia," because the noise of the city at night does not allow sleep and therefore results in insufficient rest for convalescence. It is also clear that death's carrying off of infected individuals in great numbers during the hours of darkness was quite usual. Rome did have an institution to record daily deaths in the city and provide a venue for funerals—the temple of Libitina. On several occasions, the capacities of this institution were overwhelmed, as noted in the sources. In 174 BCE, Livy reports (*From the Founding of the City* 41.21.76) that "the slave population suffered the highest mortality. Piles of unburied slaves could be found beside all the roads. The temple of Libitina could not provide funerals for just the free born, let alone the others." Suetonius (*Nero* 39.1, events of 65 CE) stated that "there was a pestilence in the autumn during which 30,000 funerals were recorded in the lists of Libitina." St. Jerome, in his *Khronikon* ("Chronicle" 188, events of 79 or 81 CE), wrote that "a huge pestilence arose at Rome of such magnitude that almost 10,000 dead were entered into the daily lists" of Libitina. These sources suggest the wrenching experience of relatives having to deal with the dead bodies of loved ones who had succumbed during the night, as they tried to make arrangements with officialdom to have the deaths recorded and attended to as morning dawned.

As bad as these totals of death were, they became worse in episodes of major pandemics. The first was the Antonine Plague (possibly smallpox) that ravaged the Roman Empire from 165 to 189 CE (Lo Cascio 2012). Here Dio Cassius in his *Rhomaikon* (*Roman History* 73.14.3, events of CE 189) noted that "the greatest plague of which I have knowledge appeared. On numerous occasions, 2,000 people died in one day in Rome." The Antonine Plague was so detrimental to the demography of the city of Rome (Paine and Storey 2006, 2012) that Rome was only just finally recovering when the next major pandemic struck the city during the short-lived reign of the Emperor Decius (*Augustan History*, "The Two Gallieni" 5.5, events of 251 CE): "So terrible a plague rose up, both in Rome as well as the cities of Greece, that in one day, 5,000 people died of the same sickness." Perhaps the worst of all was the Plague of Justinian that struck the Empire in 542 CE. Procopius, in his *Hyper ton polemon* (*History of the Wars* 2.23.1–2, events of 542 CE) echoed all the sources we have just reviewed: "the disease passed through Constantinople in four months, reaching its height in three. In the beginning, the dead numbered only a few more than normal, then, a little later, when the sickness increased, the count of the corpses reached upwards of 5,000 per day, and then it went up to 10,000 and even more." All of these accounts share the common image of greatly elevated daily mortality that played out in the most terrifying dimension for the countless infected individuals who lived out their last suffering moments in the darkness of the preindustrial urban night. Although it is difficult to tell whether the statistics given were approximately accurate, the scale of death striking down hundreds and thousands, day and night, is not in dispute.

Ghosts

The Romans believed in ghosts. Perhaps the most obvious example of this is from Petronius's *Satyricon*, an early form of the novel. Because it is focused on the Roman low life, with not-at-all respectable characters, much of its action takes place at night, and thus should be required reading for anyone interested in the Roman nychthemeron. Ghosts appear in the story in the following way: during the famous *Cena Trimalchionis*, the dinner party thrown by a wealthy but unsophisticated freedman named Trimalchio, two ghost stories are told. The first, about a werewolf who devours a flock of sheep (63.4–14), is told by a freedman named Niceros, egged on by Trimalchio to tell the story. Both clearly believe it, but some of the Roman freeborn guests react with the same skepticism that Pliny the Elder, in his *Natural History* (34.2–3), demonstrated in his dismissal of the truth of such stories—only Greeks believe in werewolves! (Sokolowski 2013).

Trimalchio tells the second story about witches who appear for only an instant and steal away the dead body of a boy at his wake and turn it into straw (64.4–8). These witches were supposed to be shapeshifters and behave like screech owls. Most tellingly, Trimalchio (63.9) echoes a common Roman view of women: *sunt mulieres plussciae, sunt nocturnae, et quod sursum est, deorsum faciunt* ("women know too much, are nocturnal, and they make everything topsy-turvy"; literally, "what is pointed up, they make pointed down"). Women are thus characterized as nocturnal owls. As we shall see later, in the discussion of sex and night, the Romans were not very explicit about equating night and sex, but possibly they did not need to do so, if this was a common male conceit (Sokolowski 2013).

Witches appear to have been more credible to the Romans than werewolves. Apuleius, in his novel *The Golden Ass*, written in the mid-second century CE, also has witches. These witches act primarily in the context of sex and love (Ogden 2002, 135–136). They interact with humans but usually do so to punish males. Obviously this is part and parcel of Roman fear of women wielding power. Despite his skepticism over werewolves, Pliny the Elder is clear that some aspects of the supernatural were quite real: "there is no one who is not afraid to be bewitched by dire incantations" (*Natural History* 28.4.19). Of course, night-time is an excellent time for casting spells and fearing them.

Accidents/Alcohol

The issue of safety was much on the minds of people, especially during the night-time darkness, which is probably why accidents were common. The Roman poet Juvenal was not at all sure how safe a city was where lots of people were active at night, as was the case in Rome:

> Consider now the many and diverse dangers of the night. What a distance there is to the lofty roofs from which a tile brains you! How often mutilated and cracked crockery falls! With what dead weight they mark and mar the pavement! You can be considered unbusinesslike and improvident of sudden disaster if you go to dinner intestate. There are so many ill-fated events in the night which the watchful windows hold in store for you as you pass by. Therefore, you must hope and pray silently to yourself that the windows be content only to shower you with open piss pots. (*Satires* 3, 268–277, after 100 CE)

If you think that perhaps Juvenal was exaggerating a bit (he *was* an entertainer, after all), consider this next passage, quoted *in extenso* to show both how the Romans invented "legalese" and to what extent their legal system did try to find out who was responsible for illegal action. Because throwing or pouring things out of the windows of the ubiquitous upper stories of Roman buildings was illegal, it was clearly done more often at night, to take advantage of the cover of darkness. No one on the third or fourth floor of an apartment building is neces-sarily going to take the trouble of walking down the flights of stairs at night to use the latrine (not necessarily connected to the sewer system but often was just a cesspit). They would just do their business out the window. The Roman jurists Ulpian, Paul, and Gaius (*Digest of Justinian* 9.3.1–5) write about the legal action for attempting to control this behavior by punishing the guilty parties:

The praetor [Rome's chief judicial official] said concerning those who throw down or pour things out of buildings: I will grant judgment for double damages against whoever lives in a place from which something has been thrown down or poured out onto a public thoroughfare or place of congregation . . . This legal action for an act will be commenced against whomever inhabits the place from which the throwing or pouring took place and not against the owner of the building, for the fault is with the former . . . If a son, still in the power of his father, lives in a rented apartment and something is thrown down or poured out from it, the action is not directed against his father, because the relation does not arise from contract of hire, but this action proceeds against the son himself . . . If many people inhabit the same apartment, from which there was a throwing down, this action can be commenced against any one of them for the whole sum of the damages . . . since, clearly, it is impossible to know which one of them did the throwing or pouring . . . but if one of them is brought up for legal action, the rest will go free . . . If many people inhabit an apartment divided into sections, action will be brought against whomever inhabits the part from which the pouring took place . . . If someone is managing an apartment, occupying the greater part of the apartment themselves, this person alone will be held accountable. But if someone is managing an apartment occupying only a modest portion of the unit and has rented the rest to many others, they all will be held accountable, as the occupants of this apartment from which something was thrown down or poured out . . . it will be proper for the Praetor, moved by a sense of fairness, to begin action rather against whomever possesses the bedroom or sleeping area from which there was a throwing down. In the case where many people inhabit the apartment, it is more just if the action stand against all when something is thrown down from the heart of the apartment.

Turning to alcohol, it is clear that Roman cities were not bastions of temperance. After all, one of the Roman words for a "bar" was *taberna*, from which we derive the word *tavern*. The archaeology of both Pompeii and Ostia is full of these establishments. I will return to this point below. I first consider Rome and its night life in the bars. We do not know precisely what alcoholic beverages were consumed in them; clearly, wine was a must, and it was likely to have been cheap kinds of wine. The poet Martial lets us know that wine from the territory of Veii, just north of Rome, produced wine for Rome, implying that Veientan wine was for drinking at home and dining out required more expensive brands (*Epigrams* 2.53, 85 or 86 CE). We also know that Pompeii actually produced wine in great quantities for the Roman market. However, Pliny the Elder (*Natural History* 14.70) said that Pompeiian wine (though improving for up to ten years in the amphora) gave one a headache. Pliny was a wealthy man so he probably only drank superior varieties of wine. Veientan and Pompeiian wines were probably a staple for the common people of Rome, and they found them aplenty in the tabernae that served drinks.

Headaches probably resulted more from excess than the quality of wines per se. The word *taberna* (possibly an Etruscan word) originally meant a simple shelter such as a "tent," "shack," or "hut." In later usage, the term meant habitation in general, and further developed the specialized meaning of "shop"—a "hut for business" (Isidorus of Seville, died CE 636, *Etymologies* 15.2.43). Thus the word *taberna* implied both a place of business and a residence—humble in comparison to the private mansions of the wealthy. Ulpian (*Digest of Justinian* 50.16.183, between 212 and 217 CE) states simply: "the term *taberna* ["house"] designates every building usable for living, not just a building that is closed by doors." So, for the common people of Rome, many had a taberna for a home. Equally, many repaired to them for refreshment, especially in the area of Rome called the *Subura*. Juvenal (*Satires* 3, 5–9) characterized that part of town thusly: "I prefer a desert isle to the Subura. What have we seen so miserable, so lonely there that you would not rather shun the fires, the incessant caving-in of roofs, and the thousand other dangers of the cruel city?" We revisit fires and cave-ins below. For our purposes, the Subura was a notorious slum that was especially dangerous at night. So dangerous that Augustus, when he built his Forum, with his Temple of Mars the Avenger backing up onto the Subura, built a huge retaining wall to cut off the public forum area from the Subura. A remnant of the wall still stands today (figure 15.1).

To illustrate what the tabernae looked like in Rome, we turn to one piece of valuable evidence: fragments of the Marble Plan of the city constructed and displayed at the orders of the emperor Septimius Severus between 205 and 208 CE (Reynolds 1996). Figure 15.2 presents a famous fragment that shows a residential district along the Vicus Patricius not far from the modern Santa Maria Maggiore church and the Baths of Diocletian. All of these establishments sold commodities to the citizens of Rome, and many of them sold food and drink. Many closed at night, but many remained open.

Figure 15.3 shows a well-preserved but presumably typical taberna/bar in Ostia, the port of Rome. Such facilities were even more common in Pompeii. The facility in Ostia even seems to have a pleasant outdoor terrace in the back of the structure to allow people to eat and drink in the open. These kinds of establishments catered to the night life in Roman cities. But for those who were visiting a city and needed a place to stay, the Romans did have the equivalent of hotels and motels. Figure 15.4, from Pompeii, shows one on "the strip" just outside Pompeii's main gate on the road to Herculaneum. This one undoubtedly had bar facilities to feed and refresh travelers. Yet again, another venue for night life.

FIGURE 15.1. *The Subura retaining wall built by Augustus. (Photo by Glenn Storey)*

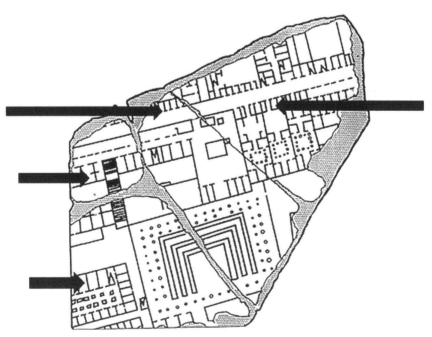

FIGURE 15.2. *A fragment of the* Forma Urbis Marmorea *("the Marble Plan") of Rome, dating from the early third century CE. The arrows indicate tabernae—shops and food establishments. (Map by Glenn Storey)*

FIGURE 15.3. *A thermopolium ("hot drinks bar"—purely a modern designation) at Ostia. (Photo by Glenn Storey)*

Plunder and Violence

It seems likely that human conspecific violence is more likely at night so that it might hide under cover of darkness. That it happened at Rome at night was much commented upon in the sources. Consider the previously mentioned *Satyricon* of Petronius and how much of it takes place at night due to the unsavory character of the action. Here is an excerpt:

> the caterer interrupted with part of the modest fare . . . "are you drunk, run-away slaves, or both? . . . By heaven, you weren't going to pay for your room, and you were going to skip out into the street in the dark, weren't you? You won't get away with it. I'll learn you that this *insula* [apartment building] isn't just the property of some feeble widow, but belongs to Marcus Mannicius." "Are you threatening us?" exclaimed Eumolpus . . . Meanwhile, the cooks and the *insularii* [agents of the landlord] were thrashing him [Eumolpus] outside. Someone was threatening to poke him in the eyes with hissing meat on a spit while someone else had taken up the stance of a gladiator brandishing a fork snatched from the pantry. (Petronius *Satyricon* 95. 1, 8; description of the mid-first century CE)

We know that fighting in the streets of Rome, especially at night, was very common, mostly resulting in simple assault and theft (Carcopino 1940, 47–48; Paoli 1963, 38–40). We also know that there were bands of marauding youths who, either due to high spirits or the need to make some easy cash, specialized in beating up defenseless individuals who happened to be in the streets in the darkness. (A famous case is discussed below under the heading "(K)nightwalkers.") In any event, most people avoided going out at night, and if they did, they were wise to take

FIGURE 15.4. *(Left) A motel just outside the Herculaneum Gate at Pompeii, facing Vesuvius, located by the arrow in relation to the rest of the city (right). (Photo and map by Glenn Storey)*

an escort. The wealthy did this commonly with slave bodyguards. Shopkeepers, unless they owned bars, shut up for the night with a solid wooden barricade that fit into a groove in the stepping stones at the entrance of the shop. They are commonly seen in Pompeii and Ostia. Figure 15.5 is an example from Ostia.

Fires

It seems that one of the greatest night fears for denizens of preindustrial urban contexts was that of fire. Fire was a particular challenge in Rome because of the closely crowded, built-up structures. Although many Roman cities were clearly planned (e.g., many European cities started life as Roman military camps, which were set out on a grid), Rome itself showed little central planning in its growth. Roman administration had to play catch-up to the way the city grew up organically (Robinson 1992). The frequency of fire had the result of producing building rubbish that accumulated in the city over the centuries, as noted by Frontinus (*On the Water Supply of the City of Rome* 1.18, Trajanic age, 98–117 CE): "The hills of Rome have been gradually built up by the rubbish from ruined buildings because of the frequency of fires."

The very real terror of fire, especially at night, was captured vividly by Juvenal (*Satires* 3, 197–202): "In other places, it is possible to live where there is no fire and nights are free from the fear of somebody next door yelling 'fire!' while carrying out his trifling possessions, and the third floor is already smoking around you. You don't know it because, if the alarm is raised at the foot of the stairs, you will burn last of all in your spot at the top, with only the roof tiles to protect you."

FIGURE 15.5. *Groove for a barricade to a shop entrance for closing up at night. (Photo by Glenn Storey)*

To address these last two night fears—crime at night and the problem of fire—the Emperor Augustus instituted the *vigiles*, a joint police and fire-brigade (our words *vigil* and *vigilantes* are clearly related to this term). There were seven cohorts (a cohort was about 800 men) of these patrolmen, largely made up of ex-slaves, commanded by a member of the equestrian order. His duties are described in detail in the *Digest of Justinian* (Paul, Severan age, first quarter of the third century CE, 1.15.1–4; events of 6 CE):

> Therefore he [Augustus] stationed seven cohorts at useful locations, so that each and every cohort should watch over two of the official regions of the city. Tribune officers were set to command them and in overall command was a man of equestrian rank called the Prefect of the Vigiles. Because, for the most part, fires are the fault of the inhabitants, he is responsible for corporal punishment of those who have kept their household fires negligently, or he can remit the punishment, with a strongly worded warning. Robberies occur mostly in the apartment blocks and warehouses, where people store the most precious portion of their possessions, whether in a storage room, cupboard or chest . . . It must be understood that the Prefect of the Vigiles must keep watch all through the night, patrolling accompanied, and in proper military footwear, with hooks and axes, to admonish tenants to take care, lest any fire incidents should occur through their negligence. In addition, let him warn each and every tenant that they should have water in their apartments.

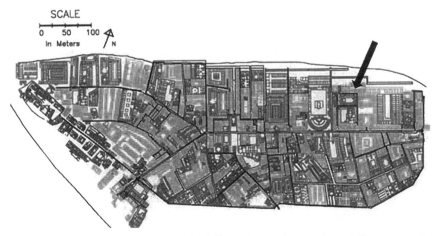

FIGURE 15.6. *Computer map of Ostia. The different shades of gray indicate different types of facilities: warehouses, rental properties, public structures, private mansion townhouses, and craftsmen association properties. The arrow points to the Barrack of the Vigiles, with the Baths of Neptune below it to the south. (Map by Glenn Storey)*

The prefect's duties are further outlined with the amazing revelation that, after being up all night, he holds morning court at the tribunal and tries the malefactors caught during the night. It speaks volumes about Roman efficiency that the judge was to be a man who was sleep deprived and thus not in any mood to put up with any legalistic nonsense. The vigiles were barracked in an *excubatorium*, one for each cohort, distributed throughout the city. In a notable irony, when the Great Fire of 64 CE broke out in the shops of the Circus Maximus, the cohort for that region was barracked across the river in Region 14, Transtiberim (Trastevere). When inhabitants were fleeing the fire, they blocked the bridge and prevented the vigiles from arriving in a timely manner.[2]

The vigiles were also rotated in and out of the city of Ostia, the port of Rome and the warehouse for much of the city's comestible commodities. The Barrack of the Vigiles is well known to even the tourists of Ostia. It was a converted apartment block and probably two to three stories tall—the very kind of venue producing the horrors from above outlined by Juvenal (the building had to house perhaps 250 patrolmen detached and rotated from the cohorts in Rome). Figure 15.6 is a computer map of Ostia showing the location of the Barrack of the Vigiles, with the Baths of Neptune just next to it.

Figures 15.7 and 15.8 feature the courtyard of the barrack with figure 15.7 showing the tribunal (the raised platform on which the judges sat; it could have statues of the emperor and other magistrates) with the bases for statues of emperors, and figure 15.8 highlighting the east entrance. The barrack would be very active

FIGURE 15.7. *Courtyard of the Barrack of the Vigiles, Ostia. The tribunal is along the back wall. (Photo by Glenn Storey)*

FIGURE 15.8. *East entrance to the Barrack of the Vigiles, Ostia. Very likely, the foreground was the nightly mustering point for the guards on watch. (Photo by Glenn Storey)*

at night because units would be on duty every night, and they almost certainly mustered and prepared in the courtyard, as well as returned to it. The courtyard was focused on the official iconography of the current emperors and their administrators. Perhaps as in Rome, we can easily picture a weary official settling into the courtyard in front of all the statues with patrolmen tiredly trudging in with their prisoners for judgment as the dawn is coming up, and summary justice was about to be meted out to the thieves caught in the night sweeps. Galinier and colleagues (2010) deal with the issue of "thieves of the night" and how law applies more strictly and summarily for nighttime law-breaking than that during the day, which the judgments of the Prefect of the Vigiles were likely to exemplify. After all, as Ekirch put it (2001, 84), night gave birth to the rule of the law.

ASPECTS OF THE NIGHT

Night Labor

As we have seen, the vigiles and their prefect, as well as the troublemakers they were watching out for, were very busy at night with their various labors. The first issue we addressed at the beginning was the noise of delivery wagons bringing in the commodities for the support of the city because they were not allowed in at daytime. Clearly, many transporters were hard at work at night, as described by Juvenal (*Satires* 3, 232–238): "Sleep in the city is the prerogative of great wealth only. Here is the crux of the disease: the passage of heavy transport vehicles in the narrow curve of the streets and the curses wafting up from blocked traffic." Also at the outset, Martial told us that while teachers were noisy in the daytime—plus a host of others, as described by Seneca in a description of the public baths (Seneca the Younger *Epistulae* 56, 1–2, between 63 and 65 CE)—it was the bakers who were noisiest at night. Bakers were crucial to the stability of the city of Rome because they are literally producing Rome's "daily bread." There were special incentives given to bakers to produce as many loaves as they could, many for free distribution to the citizens on the dole. So, although undoubtedly a demanding life (one with plenty of sleepless nights at work), it was also a profitable profession. Figure 15.9 shows the tomb of Marcus Vergilius Eurysaches (whose non-Roman *cognomen*—the last of the standard Roman citizen's three names—strongly suggests that he was of servile origin), a prominent baker who fashioned a mausoleum in the shape of his baking oven. A number of other professions that probably had a fair amount of night work are touched on in Joshel (1992).

Sex and the (Roman) City

The striking thing about Roman sex is that it does not seem to have been exclusively a nighttime activity. That may sound naïve, given that humans can engage in sex at any time, night or day. Perhaps it is the Christian element of life since Roman pagan times that has emphasized the "sinfulness" of sex and driven it into the darkness of the night, as the only appropriate time to engage in it, or it simply may be a Western notion. The pagan Romans seemed to have found anytime the right time for sex. Many people know about the brothels of Pompeii (figure 15.10) and how they are full of "dirty" pictures. That is something of a

FIGURE 15.9. *Funerary monument of the baker Marcus Vergilius Eurysaches, near the Porta Maggiore. (Photo by Glenn Storey)*

misapprehension; explicit depictions of the sex act are more frequently found proudly displayed in the most public portion of the wealthiest houses of Pompeii (Clarke and Larvey 2003). It did not detract from the reputation of the owner to display pictures of explicit sexual activity prominently. Was it a way to show good taste, like displaying a copy of the Mona Lisa or a replica of the statue of David?

In the literature exploring Roman prostitution and the archaeological example of brothels or sex shops at Pompeii, there is virtually no discussion of aspects of prostitution that distinguish between its daytime and nighttime dimension (McGinn 2013). Nighttime or not, the Romans were not shy about depicting sex. Perhaps there *was*, after all, a strong association of that activity with nightly hours. Figure 15.11 shows a typical sex scene on a Roman olive oil lamp, found in the 2015 University of Iowa summer field school at Gangivecchio, Sicily. The scene, showing a man lifting high the leg of his partner to facilitate intercourse, is quite common (Clarke and Larvey 2003). Was lighting the lamp at nightfall supposed to turn one's thoughts in that direction?

Writing at Night

Because of the efficiency of olive-oil lamps, the Romans were able to make use of the hours of darkness to do work. Emperors, especially, used the night for

FIGURE 15.10. *The main brothel of Pompeii, an unprepossessing two-story structure. (Photo by Glenn Storey)*

answering correspondence and making decisions on all kinds of policies (Millar 1977). Of course, it was the so-called "good" emperors who were remembered for using the nighttime hours to work for the benefit of the empire. A prime example of this attitude is provided by Pliny the Elder, a first-century CE author and politician. His workday was described by his nephew and eventual adopted son, Pliny the Younger. Pliny the Elder died a hero's death. As commander of the Roman fleet at Misenum, when Vesuvius erupted in August of 79 CE, he immediately boarded his flagship in order to assist victims of the disaster but also to satisfy his own curiosity about this spectacular natural phenomenon. He died, overcome by the gases from the eruption in Stabiae, the next town over from Pompeii.

We know the round of Pliny's day. He was up writing before dawn; he then held his *salutatio* (salutation or *levée*) when an elite Roman greeted his clients and gave them gifts of cash. He then went off to the emperor's *salutatio*. The

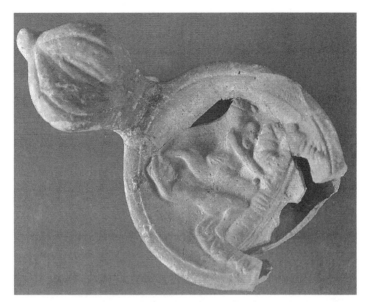

FIGURE 15.11. *Scene from a Roman lamp, Gangivecchio, Sicily. (Photo by Santo Ferraro; courtesy of Santo Ferraro and the Museum of Gangi, Sicily, and the Archaeological Superintendency of Palermo)*

Emperor was Vespasian, who also was working during the hours of darkness. He would often send for Pliny in darkness, long before the hour of the *salutatio*, because Pliny was Vespasian's "filing cabinet." As the author of a *Natural History*, of which we possess only a portion, Pliny was an expert on the different regions of the empire, so when Vespasian had a question about correspondence he received from some far-flung region of the empire, he would call Pliny to come and tell him about the place. After all that, Pliny then sat down to write. He then had a midmorning snack followed by a rest, when he had slaves read to him while he lay in the sun. He took a short cold bath, played ball, and took a short siesta. He wasted little time and took only a light and rapidly eaten *prandium* (lunch). So, when other Romans knocked off work, Pliny set to work again. Unless he was going to dinner out, he took only a late evening supper (probably around dark). He then worked by lamplight until around 1 a.m.

The Romans insisted on twelve hours of darkness and twelve hours of light, every day of the year. So, the length of the hour shifted every day. At the winter solstice, one daytime hour was equal to 44⁴⁄₉ modern minutes; one nighttime hour was 75⁵⁄₉ minutes; the day was 8 hours 54 minutes; the night was 15 hours, 6 minutes. These intervals were exactly reversed at the summer solstice. In table 15.1 we approximate what the hours were like between winter and summer. So, at both ends of the day, it is easy to see that in wintertime, especially, busy

TABLE 15.1. Intervals of the changing Roman hours of the day

	Winter Solstice	Summer Solstice
Hora Prima	7:33 a.m.–8:17 a.m.	4:27 a.m.–5:42 a.m.
Hora Secunda	8:17 a.m.–9:02 a.m.	5:42 a.m.–5:58 a.m.
Hora Sexta	11:15 a.m.–12:00 p.m.	10:44 a.m.–12:00 p.m.

people almost by definition had to use artificial light to do their work. For writers, emperors, and bureaucrats, that meant working by lamplight.

(K)nightwalkers

The term *knightwalker* was coined by Ekirch (2005, 210–226) to refer to the habit of elite individuals going out to participate in roles of nightly conflicts as either policemen or malefactors (which we touched on previously under the heading of "Plunder and Violence"). Quite obviously, the best example of the Knightwalker is the aforementioned Prefect of the Vigiles, who was, by definition, of knightly status, what the Romans called an *eques*, the station just below that of senator. He is the brave member of the forces of order, who lost sleep in order to suppress crime and destruction by fire. A good example of an elite on the other end of the continuum would be the Emperor Nero.

> Immediately after dark, taking up a freedman's cap or a wig, he would go into dives and wander about the neighborhoods, having fun, but not without making mischief. He habitually beat up people returning from dinner, seriously wounded anyone fighting back, and gave them a good dunking in the sewers. He also broke into shops and looted them. Every fifth day, as if a market day, was designated at the Palace, where part of the takings were sold at auction. He then squandered the proceeds. Often, in the brawls of that type, he risked danger of life and limb, once nearly being beaten to death at the hands of one member of the senatorial order, whose wife Nero had assaulted. Hence, never thereafter did he put himself out in public at that time of the night without tribunes of the imperial bodyguard following at a distance, but hidden. (Suetonius *Nero* 26)

Tacitus, in his *Annals* (13.25), expanded the account and provided the names of Nero's senatorial adversary, one Julius Montanus, who fought Nero off:

> When Quintus Volusius and Publius Scipio were consuls [56 CE] there was peace abroad but outrages at Rome because Nero wandered about the whore houses and bars, made up in disguise wearing slave outfits. His companions would steal items exhibited for sale in shops and inflict wounds on anyone who got in their way. The victims were so clueless that Nero himself took his licks, which showed on his face. Then, when it had become well known that the one who was on the prowl was

Caesar, the injuries visited upon notable men and women actually increased, and certain individuals, under the name of Nero, carried out the same activities (without penalty) with their own gangs. Night took on the character of a city under occupation. Julius Montanus, of the senatorial order, but not yet embarked on his career of office-holding, by chance tussled in the dark with the emperor. Because he had resisted vigorously as Nero was attempting violence, then asked pardon once Nero had been recognized, Montanus was forced to commit suicide, as if his actions had been an accusation. Consequently, Nero, more fearful for the future, surrounded himself with soldiers and a good many gladiators, who allowed the start of brawls of a modest character, as if of a private nature. But if the situation was resisted more energetically by the injured parties, they brought their weapons into play.

This is quite a tale of a sitting Roman emperor going out and committing crimes at night, with impunity. This recital dramatically illustrates the dangers of night in Rome and why people needed to be afraid, because who knows, your assailant might have been the emperor himself. Of course, in the countryside of the Roman world, such fears were probably significantly lessened. The *Pax Romana* did fill the Mediterranean world with a large army that did suppress brigandage for a very long time, and the disappearance of that integrated system did entail an overall dramatic loss of security.

Nightwalker is a term that did not exist in Latin. The closest equivalent is *noctivagus* ("night-wanderer"). One wondered if this *might* refer to either the expression of nighttime proclivities such as Nero's or to, perhaps, prostitution. In its feminine form, *noctivaga*, has been translated as a "night hag." There is also the term *noctipuga*, which literally means "night buttocks, rump" but refers to the female genitalia (Glare 2015). These rarely used terms indicate some association of night with females, again showing the Roman male penchant for blaming the ills of the night on women. The term *night-wanderer* is used, however, mostly with regard to deities associated with the moon and stars or possibly with nighttime worshippers of those nighttime deities. Clearly, some religiously motivated nighttime observances were made; these appear to be rural in nature. There are hints of some notion that such activities were not very respectable and something to be feared. The Romans were suspicious of nighttime rituals from the Roman Republic through to late antiquity. In 186 BCE, the Roman Senate famously decreed against Bacchic (Dionysiac) cult practices imported from Greece. To the Romans, nighttime ritual implied prostitution, magical rites, and even human sacrifice, and thus very much looked down upon them. Christianity (although much of its early liturgy had had to be carried on at night) adopted a similarly intolerant approach to night ritual (Kahlos 2016, 172).

One thing that aided this focus on nighttime activity, especially in Roman cities, was the layout of houses. What is interesting about Roman apartment houses is

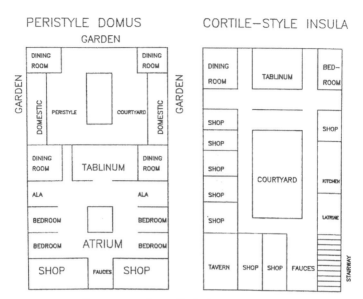

PERISTYLE DOMUS

GARDEN

DINING ROOM · DINING ROOM

GARDEN · DOMESTIC · PERISTYLE · COURTYARD · DOMESTIC · GARDEN

DINING ROOM · TABLINUM · DINING ROOM

ALA · ALA

BEDROOM · BEDROOM

BEDROOM · ATRIUM · BEDROOM

SHOP · FAUCES · SHOP

CORTILE–STYLE INSULA

DINING ROOM · TABLINUM · BED–ROOM

SHOP · SHOP

SHOP · COURTYARD · KITCHEN

SHOP · LATRINE

SHOP · SHOP

TAVERN · SHOP · SHOP · FAUCES · STAIRWAY

FIGURE 15.12. *Comparative plans of (*left*) the Roman elite townhouse (domus) and (*right*) the Roman apartment building. (Drawing by Glenn Storey)*

that they are a combination of a Roman townhouse (or *domus*) and a multiple-residence apartment block. As seen in figure 15.12, the Roman townhouse of the elites is a locus that is fundamentally inward looking. This is reflected in modern Mediterranean-inspired housing, which is centered on a courtyard and shows blank walls to the street, punctuated by a large entrance gate. It is assuredly a daytime venue. The Ostian apartment house also has a courtyard where considerable inward-looking activity was concentrated, but, as the converted Barrack of the Vigiles reflects, were primarily outward-looking, often having balconies that allowed inhabitants to interact with individuals in the street—interactions that might include throwing objects down onto passersby, whether deliberately or accidentally, most commonly at night. It just might be that Nero's fun was enhanced by his realization of the fact that people in the apartment houses could probably look down on the scuffles and hear the rowdiness of Nero and his companions, either to their mild amusement or disgust. Roman apartment houses (as illustrated by the archaeology of Ostia) were thus almost like an "architectural theater" for night life, both in courtyard and rooms overlooking the street and the shops below.

In terms of private housing, the Roman suburban villa was also a theater for the Roman elite to parade their wealth. We have one extensive description of a Roman suburban villa of the High Roman Empire, provided in one of the letters of Pliny the Younger (*Epistles* 2.17). Pliny describes his Laurentine Villa, eleven

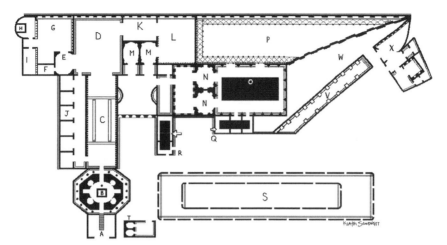

FIGURE 15.13. *Plan of Pliny's Laurentine Villa, based on his textual description proceeding as if in a straight line. The key is based on the text of Pliny's Letters 2.17, translated by Betty Radice (1963). (Original drawing by Keaton Scandrett)*

Roman miles from Rome, on the Tyrrhenian coast. Numerous attempts have been made to "reconstruct" the villa; literally hundreds of artists and architects have tried their hand at making a replica (Du Prey 1994), including the one presented here, the work of student archaeological illustrator, Keaton Scandrett.

For our purposes, one of the features that Pliny emphasized, is the pains he took to build a private "retreat" into the plan. The plan is represented by figure 15.13, which is based on Pliny's description, illustrating this retreat, which includes a terrace (W) and enclosed passageway (V) to a suite of private rooms (X). Pliny liked this wing of the villa (his "favorite," described as *amores*, "loves") because during the Festival of the Saturnalia (December 17–24, a solstice festival when houses were decorated with evergreens, people exchanged gifts, and slaves acted like masters—clearly the forerunner of Christmas), he could escape the December partying of his household, which would have had to go into the hours of darkness due to the short span of daylight at that season. It was very much his nighttime retreat (he could keep writing, away from the merrymaking, and in the dark) and we likely have the archaeological correlate of his description in the ruins of the Villa of Palombara, although it is not the only possible candidate and the featured wing shows only the barest traces just beside the large square enclosure on the right of the diagram, figure 15.14.

Patterns of Sleep

The Romans appeared to have recognized Ekirch's (2001, 2005) division of sleep into two main periods, which demonstrated how common it was in European

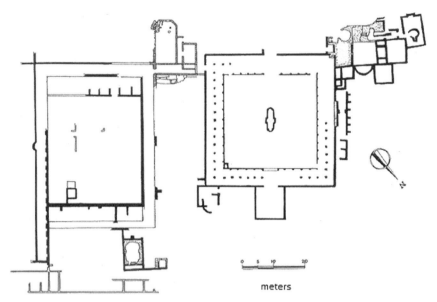

FIGURE 15.14. *Villa of Palombara, possible archaeological correlate for Pliny's Laurentine Villa. (Based on Ramieri 1995, figure 3)*

history for people to go to sleep at nightfall and then, around midnight, to get up for a while (perhaps an hour or two) to talk, write, do chores, have sex, and so on, and then go to sleep again to arise at dawn. The first sleep, as Ekirch defines it, was indeed referred to by the Romans. It is even mentioned by Thucydides (*History of the Peloponnesian War* 7.43), who says *apo protou hypnou* ("after first sleep"). The Romans called it *primus somnus* ("first sleep"), *prima nox* ("first night"—this is used heavily by military writers such as Julius Caesar and the historian Livy to describe attacks soon after nightfall)—*concubia nox* ("lying down in bed at night"), *prima sopor* "first sleep"), or *prima quies* ("first quiet, or sleep"). References to the first sleep are found all the way from Ennius, the earliest Roman poet (*Annals* 2.27 in the second century BCE) who used the phrase *noctu concubia* ("bedding down time of night"), through Plautus, Livy, Cicero, Pliny the Elder, and others, all the way to Macrobius (*Saturnalia* 1.3.12 and following) and Sidonius Apollinaris in the fifth century CE. What is less clear is what the Romans called the interval between the two sleeps, and what they called the second sleep. The fully expectable *secundus somnus* ("second sleep") is not attested to in a comprehensive digital database such as the Packard Humanities Index. In any event, it does seem that the first sleep characterization is reasonably clear.

The phrase that seemed to produce the most relevant information is *prima quies*, literally "first quiet" or "first sleep." In Book 2.268 of Virgil's *Aeneid* (in which Aeneas describes the Fall of Troy to Queen Dido), Aeneas tells of when the Greeks, hidden in the Trojan Horse, are about to make their move: *tempus erat quo prima quies mortalibus aegris incipit et dono divuum gratissima serpit* ("that time when first quiet begins for sad mortals and, most thankfully, as a gift of the gods, creeps up on people"). That is probably a military context and thus perhaps is not so informative of routine patterns of sleep. In the same vein, Ovid in his *Metamorphoses* 8.83, in the story of Minos, Scylla, and her father, Nisus, paints a picture: *nox intevenit, tenebris audacia crevit, prima quies aderat, qua curis fessa diurnis pectora somnus habet, thalamus taciturna paternos* ("night cropped up, and her daring was increased by reason of the darkness; first quiet started, when sleep takes hold of breasts tired out by daily cares, and silent was the parental bedroom"). Once again, the time is highlighted because action starts, but the description does suggest a period of initial sleep, where a following wakefulness is implied. Vergil gives us another line in Book 8.407: *ubi prima quies medio iam noctis abactae curriculo expulerat somnum* ("when first quiet has expelled sleep, in the middle of the course of the night which has been driven away"). This is more promising, telling us that the first quiet (sleep) is broken up at some point (expels sleep), and that in the middle of the night, nighttime has been driven away—that is, everyone has been awakened and they treat the time as daytime. The phrase *medio curriculo noctis* ("the mid-course of the night") could be the designation for that break in sleep identified by Ekirch (2001, 2005). So, these passages strongly suggest the pattern of a first sleep, followed by a "mid-course" interval and then a second period of sleep. Although the second period of sleep has been harder to identify, it may be referred to in a couple of phrases: *tertia vigilia* ("third watch of the night")—the Romans seemed to divide the night into three or four periods, in this case just three, with first sleep, a period of activity in the "middle of the night," and then the third period again for sleep—or *gallicinium* ("cock crowing time")—that is, the second sleep ends when the cock crows to greet dawn.

CONCLUSIONS

The city of ancient Rome, and Roman society in general, is very ripe as a subject for study in the context of an Anthropology/Archaeology of the Night. It is an excellent example of the nychthemeron. From the ethnohistoric record, it is clear that the acoustic dimensions of nightly activities were really a concern of ancient commentators, as were the dangers of the night in the preindustrial urban context. The Roman legal system was also put very much into play to deal with illicit activities of the night, and we know that night malefactors were dealt with harshly by the vigiles as they also patrolled to prevent fires that terrified the ancient cities of the world. We briefly explored issues of artificial lighting and the less-terrifying aspects of the night in terms of nightly activities, as well as patterns of sleep. Finally, it was demonstrated that the urban residences were built and maintained with some attention to the nightly activities that went on in the cities of the empire. For the Romans, at least in their urban guise, were truly a twenty-four-hour a day people.

NOTES

1. All translations from the Latin are my own unless otherwise indicated. The citation of ancient sources in this chapter follows the standard classical scholarship practice: all ancient sources have a standard reference that allows scholars to cite a passage without referring to a modern version or translation, and thus the citations have no date, and do not appear in the References.

2. One can, with some difficulty, see a portion of the *excubatorium* for the cohort guarding Regions 11 (Circus Maximus) and 14 (Transtiberim) in some holes in the piazza in front of the McDonalds in Trastevere.

REFERENCES

Carcopino, Jerome. 1940. *Daily Life in Ancient Rome: The People and City at the Height of the Empire*, ed. with bibliography and notes by H. T. Rowell. Trans. from French by E. O. Lorimer. New Haven, CT: Yale University Press.

Clarke, John R., and Michael Larvey. 2003. *Roman Sex: 100 BC to AD 250*. New York: H. N. Abrams.

Daveluy, Michelle. 2010. "Comment on 'Anthropology of the Night: Cross-Disciplinary Investigations.'." *Current Anthropology* 51:837–838.

Du Prey, Pierre de la Ruffinière. 1994. *The Villas of Pliny from Antiquity to Posterity*. Chicago: University of Chicago Press.

Ekirch, A. Roger. 2001. "Sleep We Have Lost: Pre-Industrial Slumber in the British Isles." *American Historical Review* 106(2):343–386. https://doi.org/10.2307/2651611.

Ekirch, A. Roger. 2005. *At Day's Close: Night in Times Past*. New York: W. W. Norton.

Galinier, Jacques, Aurore Monod Becquelin, Guy Bordin, Laurent Fontaine, Francine Fourmaux, Juliette Roullet Ponce, Piero Salzarulo, Philippe Simonnot, Michèle Therrien, and Iole Zilli. 2010. "Anthropology of the Night: Cross-Disciplinary Investigations." *Current Anthropology* 51(6):819–847. https://doi.org/10.1086/653691.

Glare, P.G.W. 2015. *Oxford Latin Dictionary*. 2nd ed. Oxford: Oxford University Press.

Joshel, Sandra R. 1992. *Work, Identity and Legal Status at Rome: A Study of the Occupational Inscriptions*. Norman: University of Oklahoma Press.

Kahlos, Maijastina. 2016. "Artis heu magicis: The Label of Magic in Fourth Century Conflicts and Disputes." In *Pagans and Christians in Late Antique Rome: Conflict, Competition and Coexistence in the Fourth Century*, ed. Michele Renee Salzman, Marianne Sáhgy, and Rita Lizzi Testa, 162–177. New York: Cambridge University Press. https://doi.org/10.1017/CBO9781316274989.007.

Lo Cascio, Elio, ed. 2012. *L'Impatto della "Peste Antonina." Pragmateiai. Collana di studi e testi per la storia economica, sociale e amministrativa del mondo antico.* vol. 22. Bari: Edipuglia.

McGinn, Thomas A. J. 2013. "Sorting Out Prostitution in Pompeii: The Material Remains, Terminology and the Legal Sources." *Journal of Roman Archaeology* 26:610–633. https://doi.org/10.1017/S1047759413000482.

Millar, Fergus. 1977. *The Emperor in the Roman World, 31 BC–AD 337.* Ithaca, NY: Cornell University Press.

Ogden, Daniel. 2002. *Magic, Witchcraft and Ghosts in the Greek and Roman Worlds: A Sourcebook.* New York: Oxford University Press.

Paine, Richard R., and Glenn R. Storey. 2006. "Epidemics, Age-at-Death, and Mortality in Ancient Rome." In *Urbanism in the Preindustrial World: Cross-Cultural Approaches*, ed. Glenn R. Storey, 69–85. Tuscaloosa: University of Alabama Press.

Paine, Richard R., and Glenn R. Storey. 2012. "The Alps as a Barrier to Epidemic Disease During the Republican Period: Implications for the Dynamic of Disease in Rome." In *L'Impatto della Peste Antonina*, ed. Elio Lo Cascio, 179–191. Bari: Edipuglia.

Paoli, Ugo Enrico. 1963. *Rome: Its People, Life and Customs.* Trans. R. D. MacNaghten. New York: Longman.

Radice, Betty. 1963. *The Letters of the Younger Pliny.* Trans. Betty Radice. New York: Penguin Classics.

Ramieri, A. M. 1995. "La villa di Plinio a Castel Fusano." *Archeologia Laziale* 12:407–416.

Reynolds, D. W. 1996. "Forma Urbis Romae: The Severan Marble Plan and the Urban Form of Ancient Rome." PhD diss., University of Michigan, Ann Arbor.

Robinson, Olive F. 1992. *Ancient Rome: City Planning and Administration.* New York: Routledge.

Sokolowski, Deborah. 2013. "Folklore and Superstition in Petronius' *Satyricon*." *Parnassus* 1:70–86.

Storey, Glenn R., ed. 2006. *Urbanism in the Preindustrial World: Cross-Cultural Approaches.* Tuscaloosa: University of Alabama Press.

Midnight at the Oasis

Past and Present Agricultural Activities in Oman

SMITI NATHAN

Oases hold significant social and economic value to communities living in arid environments. In addition to the availability of important natural resources, such as fertile land and water, oases provide crucial junctures along desert trading routes, defense against invaders and harsh environmental conditions, and potential areas to settle permanently. For permanent oasis dwellers, a sound subsistence strategy is vital. One strategy employed by oasis communities around the world is *oasis agriculture*—a term describing agrarian subsistence practices that occur in an oasis setting (Stevens 1972). While there is an awareness of the numerous oasis agriculture practices that occur during the day, less is known about those activities that occur at night. This chapter examines the role of the night in past and present agricultural activities in Oman, a country with a long history of oasis agriculture.

Oman, officially known as the Sultanate of Oman, is located on the southeastern coast of the Arabian Peninsula, where it borders the countries of Yemen, Saudi Arabia, and the United Arab Emirates and major bodies of water including the Indian Ocean, the Gulf of Oman, and the Arabian Sea (figure 16.1;

DOI: 10.5876/9781607326786.c016

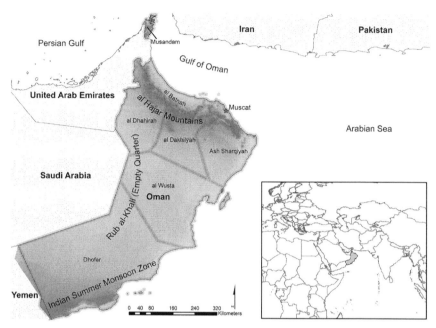

FIGURE 16.1. *Major geographical and geological areas in Oman. (Map by Smiti Nathan)*

see also figures 1.2–1.3). Oman possesses a diversity of environments. Over 2,000 km of coastline span the eastern and southern edges of the country. In the south, specifically, in the region of Dhofar, the Indian Ocean monsoon provides ample rainfall, which results in lush vegetation that covers the landscape from mid-June to mid-September. This environment rapidly shifts if one ventures northeast from Dhofar and into the sandy dune deserts of the Rub al-Khali, also known as the Empty Quarter. Throughout the country *sabkhat* (salt flats; sing. *sabkha*) and *wadis* (intermittent rivers; sing. *wadi*) are present. In the northeastern portion of the country, the al Hajar Mountains are rich with ophiolites, which are parts of the Earth's oceanic crust that have risen and are now exposed above sea level. The geological history of these mountains has resulted in a variety of resources (copper ore, chlorite, clays, etc.) that have been exploited by humans since antiquity (Blackman et al. 1989; David 2002; Glennie 2005; Hauptmann et al. 1988).

The country is ruled by Sultan Qaboos bin Said al-Said, who overthrew his father in a bloodless coup in 1970. Since then, Sultan Qaboos initiated extensive national infrastructure programs (e.g., road works, education access, and health-care) to modernize the country. Much of Oman's current economic prosperity derives from oil. The country's oil reserves are not as large as those of its Gulf neighbors and an integral part of the Oman's national narrative is the acceptance that these resources are limited (Limbert 2010). Prior to the ascension of Sultan

Qaboos, agriculture formed the vast majority of Oman's economy. While this is no longer true, agriculture still retains social and economic importance in Oman.

This chapter begins by providing an overview of the archaeological foundations of oasis agriculture in Oman. This is then followed by an investigation of the role of the night in agrarian activities through case studies that explore the following three questions: (1) Which activities exclusively occurred at night? (2) If an agricultural activity could occur at any time, why was the night selected? (3) Who was participating in nighttime agricultural activities?

In order to answer these questions, three types of sources are examined in this chapter: previous research on historical agrarian practices, environmental data, and the results of a recent ethnoarchaeological study. Previous work on historical oasis agriculture practices in Oman is reviewed and situated in the context of the archaeology of the night. Oman is a region that has undergone major socioeconomic and infrastructural changes during the last half century, which have impacted oasis agriculture in significant ways. Past research provides valuable information on practices prior to and after major twentieth-century changes. The integration of environmental data, notably temperature records and crop tolerance estimations, are used here to consider nightly practices.

Finally, this chapter is also informed by ethnoarchaeological data derived from the author's own study (Nathan, in prep). During the winter of 2016, I conducted an ethnoarchaeological study investigating local agrarian practices in the al-Dhahirah governorate[1] of northern Oman (figure 16.1), specifically in communities located in the alluvial plains of the al Hajar Mountains. The study examined crop selection, water and irrigation, agriculture location and organization, ownership and labor division, and purpose and memory. Consequently, this chapter focuses on agricultural practices in northern Oman. This location was chosen for two reasons. First, it contains many archaeological sites evidencing human occupation, sedentism, and oasis agriculture dating back to the Bronze Age. Second, agrarian activities continue in this region today. The next section provides a brief overview of the archaeological foundations of oasis agriculture in Oman.

THE ARCHAEOLOGICAL FOUNDATIONS OF OASIS AGRICULTURE IN OMAN

Archaeological investigations in Oman have occurred since the 1970s (de Cardi et al. 1976; During Caspers 1970; Frifelt 1975; Hastings et al. 1975; Whitcomb 1975). Oman has received less attention by the scholarly community in comparison to other areas of the Near East. Recently, there has been a growing interest in various aspects of Oman's archaeological record, which dates to the Paleolithic period (Petraglia and Rose 2010; Whalen 2003). This overview of the archaeology of Oman aims to contextualize the prehistoric foundations of oasis agriculture in northern Oman, but it is important to note that many prehistoric findings in northern Oman are similar to those found immediately across the Oman and United Arab Emirates (UAE) border. These areas shared similar cultural complexes in antiquity, though they are now distinct geopolitical areas. Nonetheless, those sites in the UAE that display similar cultural complexes are also referenced.

The foundations of oasis agriculture date to the Bronze Age (ca. 3100–1300 BCE) (Al-Jahwari 2009; Cleuziou 1982, 1996; Frifelt 1989). Unlike other areas of the Near East, which saw agriculture during the preceding Neolithic period, agriculture in Oman arrived millennia later. Agriculture did not completely replace other forms of subsistence or form the dominant subsistence strategy at certain sites. Recent archaeological evidence from Oman indicates that oasis agriculture occurred in conjunction with pastoralism (McCorriston et al. 2012; Uerpmann and Uerpmann 2008; Vogt and Franke-Vogt 1987), hunting (Bökönyi 1992; Bökönyi and Bartosiewicz 1998; Uerpmann and Uerpmann 2008), foraging (McCorriston 2006), and fishing (Beech 2004; Hoch 1995). While oasis agriculture was not the only significant food procurement strategy, agrarian communities made a lasting impact on the landscape.

The onset of the Bronze Age has been heralded as a period of major transformations due to increased socioeconomic complexity, which materialized in several ways (Cleuziou and Tosi 2007). Increased sedentism by many communities led to the construction of large settlements surrounding tower-like structures (Cable and Thornton 2013; Cleuziou and Tosi 2007; de Cardi et al. 1976; Frifelt 1975; Hastings et al. 1975; Weisgerber 1981). Other structures, like multichambered, collective burial monuments, also emerged on the landscape (Blau 2001; Cleuziou and Vogt 1983; Salvatori 1996; Vogt 1985).

During the Bronze Age, the toponym *Magan* began to appear in Mesopotamian texts (Crawford 1973; Leemans 1960). The location of Magan, a powerful socioeconomic polity, eluded scholars for centuries. Through the discovery of copper deposits, of which Magan was a key supplier (Kmoskó 1917; Wellsted 1838), in southeastern Arabia, specifically northern Oman and bordering areas of the UAE, the location of Magan was firmly identified. The lack of a known written script in Oman during the Bronze Age probably contributed to the delay in identifying Magan's location.

The inhabitants of Magan exploited local natural resources from the al Hajar mountains, which included not only copper but clays and chlorite. Local clays were used to create ceramics (Blackman et al. 1989; Méry 1991, 2000) and chlorite was manipulated to create softstone vessels (David et al. 1990; David 2002; Mouton 1999; Ziolkowski 2001). In addition to domestic usage, these objects were exported to neighboring areas like Mesopotamia (Begemann et al. 2010; Crawford 1973; Gensheimer 1984; Piesinger 1983) and the Indus (Blackman et al. 1989; Edens 1993; Méry 1988; Potts 2000; Vogt 1996). This interaction was not one-sided and evidence of Mesopotamian and Indus imports are present

FIGURE 16.2. *The oasis village of Majzi near Ibri, Oman. Date palm groves are a prominent feature of oasis agricultural systems in northern Oman. (Photo by Smiti Nathan)*

at Bronze Age sites in southeastern Arabia (Edens 1993; Piesinger 1983; Potts 2010; Vogt 1996).

In conjunction with increased sedentism and intensified interregional trade, the Bronze Age witnessed the onset of oasis agriculture (Al-Jahwari 2009). The catalyst driving the adoption of this subsistence strategy is still debated. Ecologically driven hypotheses are based on environmental evidence, including lacustrine sediments in southeastern Arabia that reveal moister conditions that coincide with the emergence of oasis agriculture communities (Parker et al. 2006). Others have pointed to socioeconomic factors, such as increased settlement intensification driven by the exploitation and trade of copper ore with Mesopotamia and the Indus (Cleuziou and Tosi 2007). Nonetheless, the evidence of oasis agriculture during this period is largely based on archaeobotanical finds, specifically the date palm (*Phoenix dactylifera* L.) The date palm is a critical component in the functioning of modern and historical oasis agriculture systems in Oman (figure 16.2). These trees provide food with their fruit, raw construction materials, and fuel from their wood-like meristem, and the ability to propagate other plants (e.g., cereals, legumes, citrus fruits) under their shading (Tengberg 2012). The discovery of hundreds of date stones (seeds of the date palm) and mud-brick impressions of stem/leaf fragments in Bronze Age contexts suggest that date palms were also integral to prehistoric oasis agriculture practices (Cleuziou 1989; Tengberg 2012; Willcox 1995). In addition to date palms, domesticated imported cereals like wheat (*Triticum* sp.) and barley (*Hordeum vulgare* L.)

FIGURE 16.3. *The falaj system. (Top left) The falaj coming in from the mountains; (top right) the falaj in the oasis; (bottom left) water being distributed from the falaj and onto agricultural land; (bottom right) agricultural squares irrigated with water from the falaj. (Photos by Smiti Nathan)*

are evidenced directly through charred seeds (Costantini 1979; Tengberg 1998) and indirectly through artifacts like grinding stones (Potts 2000).

While the first evidence of major components of oasis agriculture, like sedentism in oases and the cultivation of date palms and cereals, emerge in the Bronze Age, the subsequent Iron Age period (ca. 1300–300 BCE) is the accepted time frame for the emergence of another key component in modern and historical oasis agriculture practices: the falaj system (Al-Tikriti 2010; Avanzini and Phillips 2010; Wilkinson 1977). The falaj system is a series of subsurface channels that use gravity to move groundwater across long distances from the mountains and into settlement areas to irrigate crops (Al-Tikriti 2002).[2] This system is similar to *qanats*, found in neighboring Iran and other areas of the Near East, which also used tunneled structures and gravity to move water into settlement areas (Al-Ghafri et al. 2003; Boucharlat 2003).

Historically, the falaj was a key source of water for irrigating crops within oasis communities (figure 16.3). Other water management methods, such as groundwater wells and channels, were also present in antiquity (Charbonnier 2015; Desruelles et al. 2016; Frifelt 1989). Nonetheless, the introduction of falaj irrigation is thought to be a primary factor behind the continued growth of oasis agriculture subsistence (Bellini et al. 2011; Potts 2008). While oasis agriculture has certainly changed over the course of millennia, centuries, and in the past few years, this subsistence strategy retains its socioeconomic importance to modern-day inhabitants.

Which Activities Exclusively Occurred at Night? Stargazing as a Water Management Method

Modern and historical observations of the falaj system, including water management and redistribution practices, show that communities needed to actively share water sources (Al-Marshudi 2007; Al Sulaimani et al. 2007; Nash 2015; Sutton 1984; Zekri et. al 2014). The night was, and still is, a component of many time-based water redistribution systems in oasis communities. In many places, water from the falaj flowed continuously, twenty-four hours a day, and redistribution was based on time. Water from the falaj typically flows into one agricultural area at a time (Al-Marshudi 2007); thus, an important aspect of water management in this system is knowing the time when one is allocated water. Water allotments were not restricted to just the day, but could occur during the night. Harriet Nash conducted extensive research on the use of stars as a method of time-keeping during the night (Al-Ghafri et al. 2013; Al Sulaimani et al. 2007; Nash 2007, 2010, 2011, 2015; Nash and Agius 2009, 2011, 2013; Nash et al. 2014). While there is a fair degree of regional variation with this method, there are two basic variables for this system: stars and observation points.

The stars, also known as falaj stars, can be a single star or a group of stars. They are usually watched rising or setting over different observation points, which could be natural or human-made horizons (Nash 2015). In my interviews, many of my informants remembered this method of time-keeping for water allocation, yet, no one was part of a community that continued this practice. Star-based timekeeping was important for many villages, but it fell out of use with the introduction of wristwatches in the 1960s (Nash 2015).

While star-based timekeeping is not as widely used as it was in the past, the night still plays a role in water allocation. The terms *badda* and *athar* are often used to describe different units of water times in northern Oman.[3] Badda usually refers to a twelve-hour period—there is a day badda and night badda—and an athar usually refers to a thirty-minute period, which includes the night (Al-Marshudi 2001, 2007). In some villages in northern Oman, these units were sold as water shares and differential pricing has been reported based on day and night divisions and seasonality. Usually water shares that were bought, sold, or mortgaged with a nighttime allotment were cheaper than day-time allotments (Al Sulaimani et al. 2007).

In addition to the falaj, groundwater wells were also a source of water for many families practicing oasis agriculture. In terms of night use, some interviewees from my study reported that daytime and nighttime watering using wells was shared among family members. In this scenario, my informants reported that waking up to water plants at night was inconvenient, thus, nighttime watering was usually rotated among family members so no one person was consistently burdened.

If an Agricultural Activity Could Occur at Any Time, Why Was the Night Selected? Temperature Considerations for Plant Propagation

In northern Oman, there can be a stark contrast between day and night temperatures, especially according to the season. During the winter months (roughly October to March) average day temperatures around the city of Ibri (near where my fieldwork was conducted) in the al-Dhahirah governorate range from 25°C to 38°C, whereas average night temperatures range from 13°C to 24°C. During the summer months (roughly April to September), average day temperatures range from 37°C to 45°C, whereas average night temperatures range from 21°C to 30°C.[4]

These stark temperature ranges impact agricultural potential and decision-making. In northern Oman and neighboring areas with similar temperatures in the United Arab Emirates, there are further linguistic and conceptual divisions in seasonality based on climatic features such as rainfall, wind, and temperature (Yateem 2009). In many areas of northern Oman, there are specific local terms for the hottest summer months,[5] roughly May to August, where average daytime temperatures range from 42°C to 44°C. Some farmers in my study discussed different growing strategies in the context of local seasonal terms. These local terms indicate a keen awareness of extreme temperatures and subsequent strategies to maintain agricultural output during these months. Consequently, the winter months are usually when the majority of harvesting occurs in northern Oman and temperature relief is a contributing factor to this strategy. Nonetheless, there are plants that are grown and maintained year-round, despite harsh temperature highs. For example, date palms, which are vital for oasis agriculture systems, are maintained year-round and can tolerate temperatures ranging from 10°C to 52°C, which makes them suitable to withstand scorching hot summer days and cooler winter nights (Food and Agriculture Organization of the United Nations, n.d.).

From the Bronze Age to the present, Oman has incorporated foreign cultivars in its agricultural strategy (Bellini et al. 2011; Costantini 1979; Potts 1994; Tengberg 2003; Willcox 1995). Barley, a cereal introduced in the Bronze Age, can tolerate temperatures ranging from 2°C to 40°C, while wheat, specifically *Triticum aestivum*, is a bit more sensitive, with an absolute temperature tolerance ranging from 5°C to 27°C (Food and Agriculture Organization of the United Nations, n.d.). Barley and wheat are still grown today and continue to be important crops for many oasis communities. Furthermore, climatic conditions in northern Oman, with the exception of select aridification events, have been relatively similar from the Bronze Age to the present (Parker et al. 2006). Thus, an awareness of temperature and, perhaps, temperature tolerance might have also contributed to decisions surrounding crop selection and plant propagation in antiquity.

The night can provide relief from harsh temperatures, for both humans and plants. Over the course of my interviews, some of my informants mentioned they would water their crops at night as it was too hot during the day. Here, the night mitigated the potential adverse effects of conducting agricultural activities, such as irrigating crops, which would otherwise occur during the day. For plants, nighttime watering, specifically during the early evening or before sunrise, can reduce evaporation. Thus, plants are able to retain more moisture than if watered during the day. Moisture retention during the night can also impact the harvesting of certain crops during the winter months. Numerous informants from my ethnoarchaeological study reported that they cut alfalfa (*Medicago sativa* L.) before sunrise because they felt the crop was fresher, thus, making it more marketable. While irrigating during the summer months or harvesting crops during the winter months can occur during daytime hours, the nighttime was specifically selected for its advantages in temperature relief and water retention.

Who Was Participating in Nighttime Agricultural Activities? Ethnoarchaeological Insights from Northern Oman

During the winter of 2016, I conducted an ethnoarchaeological study investigating agrarian practices in the al-Dhahirah governate of northern Oman through interviews with local farmers. Interviews had two main parts. The first part was a thirty-two-question survey, with English and Arabic translations. This survey formed the basis of inquiry for this study. The second was a tour of cultivation areas owned or maintained by each interviewee. Translators were key for understanding the answers of interviewees, especially when communicated in local dialects. In total, twenty-six interviews were conducted that encompassed responses from fifty-nine people. The main aim of the study was to collect much needed-background information regarding oasis agriculture in northern Oman, specifically in regions with evidence of Bronze Age habitation in the al Dhahirah governate.

I directly asked interviewees, "What agricultural activities occur at night?" The most popular answer was irrigation. As demonstrated in the previous sections, irrigating plants is an agricultural activity with numerous nighttime components and facets. Indeed, the night serves an important role for this agricultural activity. However, the question remains—who are the people who undertake such tasks?

If communal falaj irrigation was a community's primary water source, farmers were responsible for knowing their allocated time for watering their fields. If there was an issue, they would turn to the person who was in charge of managing the falaj, often known as the *wakil*, to resolve disputes (Al-Marshudi 2001). I was able to speak with two people who held the position of wakil. They explained that one of their major responsibilities was knowing the times when each farmer received water and both informants knew how to tell time using stars. Additional responsibilities of the wakil include overseeing the sale, rental, and maintenance of physical parts of the falaj system (Al-Marshudi 2001).

Historically, the wakil position followed stringent gender boundaries, in that, the post has been exclusively occupied by men. This gender norm is also reflected in agricultural activities related to falaj irrigation. Throughout the course of my interviews, both men and women participated in numerous agricultural activities and stages of farming, including planting, weeding, and harvesting. Activities surrounding irrigation, however, were reported to be primarily conducted by men. Nonetheless, in a few of the households that I interviewed, women would take on this role. This situation was usually explained in one of two ways. First, some women asserted that they were deeply interested in agriculture and wanted to perform this activity. Second, if a male figure of adult age was not present due to stints in the military or death, then women would assume watering duties. Such watering responsibilities would extend into the night and a few women reported that they would oversee the watering of crops at night.

Over the course of the last three decades, there has been an increase in hiring foreign workers, typically from South Asian countries like Bangladesh, Pakistan, and India, to undertake agricultural tasks for a given farm. If one ventures around northern Oman, the vast majority of quotidian agricultural activities are performed by foreign workers. Usually, a worker is assigned to a family for a one- or two-year period. Persons needed for a shorter duration of time, ranging from a few hours to a few days, can be hired for just that period of time. A few families reported that they hired foreign workers who completed short-term tasks at night. This schedule was due to two main reasons: either the family preferred a certain task to be conducted at night or the hired worker had another job during daytime hours and was available only at night.

DISCUSSION

In order to examine the role of the night in past and present agricultural activities in Oman, three questions were posed: (1) Which activities exclusively occurred at night? (2) If an agricultural activity could occur at any time, why was the night selected? (3) Who was participating in nighttime agricultural activities? Focused case studies provided a starting point in which to assess these questions.

Water, specifically practices surrounding irrigation, arose as a common theme in nightly practices. The falaj system and groundwater wells are the main sources of water for agriculture. Though other water sources exist, they are nowhere near ideal. For example, while rainfall can bring about lush vegetation in southwestern Oman, precipitation is notably quite limited in northeastern Oman. The members of modern communities with whom I spoke during my interviews reported that they did not rely on rainwater to directly water their plants, but instead on rains that produced wadis, which would recharge water tables. The lack of water from direct rainfall is consistent with the results of a twenty-seven-year study that examined rainfall throughout Oman (Kwarteng et al. 2009). On average, precipitation of more than 1 mm occurred only thirteen days per year, but most of those days received less than 10 mm of rain. Reliance on rainwater for agricultural purposes is simply not viable.

Water is a resource that is often in high demand for oasis agricultural communities. To ensure that all community members could access the resource in a way that continually met their agricultural needs, harnessing the night was necessary. Prior to the introduction and widespread usage of wristwatches, sundials were commonly used to keep track of time during the day, while falaj stars were used at night (Nash 2007). Irrigation that continuously occurs throughout the day and night allows water to rotate more quickly among the fields of community members.

Though the night is often considered as a time for rest in Oman, there are some advantages to nighttime irrigation. First, in some water markets, the monetary cost of night irrigation is less than the day. Second, nighttime watering during the summer months mitigates heat stressors on both humans and plants. Still, nighttime irrigation comes with its disadvantages. First, if watering or changes in water allocation start at night, this means that a person must be awake to oversee this activity, which is often viewed as an inconvenience because modern farmers have other jobs and tasks that must be completed during the day. Communities and families often compensate for this by rotating night allotments or reducing the monetary cost of night irrigation.

Agriculture in Oman has changed rapidly, especially in recent decades. In addition to new and improved technologies (e.g., electric pumps for wells, tractors, sprinklers for irrigation), there is also an increase in hiring foreign workers to complete daily agricultural tasks that were once done by both male and female family members. These workers might complete nighttime agricultural activities as part of a short-term job or as part of their long-term job placement. Unfortunately, the scope of my study did not include interviews with these foreign workers. Hopefully, future studies will include their perspective in modern oasis agricultural practices and subsequent nighttime agrarian activities.

Water sharing and the practices associated with it clearly demonstrate the historical role of the night. While informants consistently report these practices to be quite old, it is difficult to assign an accurate time-depth to such practices beyond a couple centuries. While the emergence of agriculture dates back to the Bronze Age and the falaj system dates back to the Iron Age, examining the role of the night is challenging for these foundational periods in Oman's agrarian history. Still, there are a number of possibilities for theorizing about the role of the night for ancient oasis agricultural communities in Oman.

First, the lack of a known written script in the region during the Bronze Age and limited evidence during the Iron Age (Magee 1999) eliminates the possibility of deferring to domestic textual sources for clues about nighttime activities in antiquity. However, foreign textual sources from neighboring regions, such as Mesopotamia, could be a possibility for nighttime activities, in general. Second, a reevaluation of the material finds at Bronze and Iron Age archaeological sites that evidence agrarian activity in the context of nighttime practices could prove quite useful, especially using examples from the work of other authors in this book as inspiration. Finally, the creation of models based on environmental data, such as day and nighttime temperatures, could be an interesting entry point for considering the role of the night in ancient oasis agriculture activities with regards to irrigation and plant propagation, especially since the overall climate in Oman has been relatively similar from the Bronze Age to the present (Parker et al. 2006).

While this chapter has examined the role of the night in Oman in the context of agricultural activities, there are other social contexts in which nightly practices emerge. The night can be a time for recreation and gathering. In my experience, early morning archaeological work was often filled with stories from my young male workers about late-night socializing and barbecuing in the wadi that occurred just hours before. The night also can be a time of vulnerability. As one drives around northern Oman, numerous remains of Islamic-period watchtowers and forts are present. Was nighttime watch against potential invaders practiced? The remnant architectural evidence certainly suggests this possibility. The night can also be a significant time in religious observations. Currently, most of Oman's population practices Islam. During Ramadan, a holy month that entails fasting during the day, Muslims only eat and drink after dusk. Ramadan in Oman must be full of modern nightly activities. Oman is rich with potential for examining nightly practices, not only for oasis agriculture, but other modern, historical, and archaeological contexts.

CONCLUSIONS

This chapter has examined the archaeology of the night in Oman, specifically oasis agricultural activities. Previous research on historical agrarian practices and environmental studies (e.g., paleoenvironmental models, temperature records, precipitation research) provided valuable information informing our understanding of what agricultural activities occurred at night, why the night was selected, and who was undertaking these tasks.

Ethnoarchaeological research has demonstrated that there are nighttime activities associated with oasis agriculture in northern Oman. Water management, particularly irrigation, stood out as an agrarian activity with several nighttime components. While assigning a definitive time-depth to such water-related night activities is currently not possible, the historical and modern role of these oasis agricultural practices are clear. Such an interrogation of the night could be applied to other societies around the world where irrigation was, and still is, used.

Furthermore, this chapter has offered numerous rationales as to why certain agricultural activities occurred at night, such as maximizing water access, differential water pricing, and labor considerations. Temperature was highlighted as a potential driver of nighttime irrigation activities and crop selection strategies. The night offered relief from scorching hot summer days for both humans and plants.

Oman is a country experiencing rapid development and changes and it was essential to capture current perspectives on both modern and near-past agricultural activities; thus, a recent ethnoarchaeology study was necessary. This study provided relevant data regarding nighttime oasis agricultural activities around the al-Dhahirah governate, while offering an update on the current nature of certain nighttime activities, such as star-based timekeeping and water allocation, and of the people assigned nighttime tasks. The combination of historical research, environmental studies, and ethnoarchaeology provided an entry into examining the archaeology of the night in Oman's oasis agriculture communities. Such multidisciplinary approaches might be useful in future investigations and theorizing of the night.

ACKNOWLEDGMENTS

I would like to thank Oman's Ministry of Heritage and Culture (MHC) for permitting me to conduct the ethnoarchaeological research portions of this chapter. I am particularly grateful to the MHC's office in Bat, Oman, specifically to Sumaia al-Marmari, Samia al-Shaqsi, Asma al-Jassasi, and Wadha al-Marmari, who located interviewees and translated many interviews. My other translators include Fatma al-Matralfi, Aadil Salim al Moqbali, Ahed al Moqbali, Ibrahim al-Moqbali, Mohammed Zayid al Moqbali, and Sultan Saif. Additional logistical support was provided by MHC staff members, Sulaiman al-Jabri, Ismael al-Matralfi, and Badr al-Moqbali. Special thanks is due to the Archaeological Water Histories of Oman (ARWHO) Project led by Michael Harrower, who arranged for my permit and visa, and provided invaluable research support. Also, I appreciate that the Bat Archaeological Project (BAP) and Social, Spatial, and Bioarchaeological Histories of Ancient Oman Project (SoBO) permitted me to conduct interviews in their research area. Abdulrahman al-Hinai of the Oman Botanic Garden provided invaluable advice and discussions surrounding the fieldwork component of this project as well as botanical insights. The initial conference manuscript of this chapter benefited from feedback from Sneh Pravinkumar Patel, Eli N. Dollarhide, John O'Hara, Katherine French, and Pam Crabtree. The final manuscript benefited from feedback from Christian Staudt, Brooke Norton, Eli N. Dollarhide, Zenobie S. Garrett, Taylor Zaneri, and Joelle Nivens. Institutional support for writing this manuscript was provided by New York University, specifically my adviser, Rita Wright, and the Goethe University, where I am hosted by Katharina Neumann. Finally, financial support for the initial presentation of this chapter at the 2016 Annual Meeting of the Society for American Archaeology was provided by New York University's Graduate School of Arts and Sciences Dean's Student Travel Grant Program and the New York University's Student Senator's Council Conference Fund; the ethnoarchaeological research of this chapter was funded by a dissertation fieldwork grant from the Wenner-Gren Foundation.

NOTES

1. As of 2011 Oman is made up for eleven governorates: Ad Dakhiliyah, Al Dhahirah, Al Batinah North, Al Batinah South, Al Wusta, Ash Sharqiyah North, Ash Sharqiyah South, Muscat, Musandam, Dhofar, and Al Buraymi. Each governorate is made up of provinces known as *wilayat* (sing. *wilayah*). Al Dhahirah is made up of three wilayat: Ibri, Yanqul, and Dhank. This chapter incorporates data spanning all three wilayat.

2. The term *falaj* can be used to describe a number of conceptually similar, though distinct, irrigation methods. A 2007 report on falaj use in Northern Oman by Zaher bin Khalid Al Sulaimani (Al Sulaimani et al. 2007) recorded three types of falaj systems: the *da'ūdī falaj* uses an underground tunnel to connect a groundwater well to settlement areas; the *ghailī falaj* uses an open channel to connect wadi base flows to settlement areas; and the *ʿainī falaj* describes a system of subsurface channels that use gravity to move groundwater across long distances from the mountains and into settlement areas in order to irrigate crops, which is closer to the conceptualization that most scholars associate with the falaj system.

3. Some villages have additional terms, along with *badda* and *athar*, to describe water allotment.

4. Temperature averages based on data from 2000–2012 from https://www.worldwea theronline.com/v2/weather-averages.aspx?locid=1778735&root_id=1777320&wc=local_ weather&map=~/ibri-weather-averages/az-zahirah/om.aspx.

5. Seasonal terms in Oman were confirmed through personal communications with Abdulrahman al-Hinai of the Oman Botanic Gardens.

REFERENCES

Al-Ghafri, Abdullah, Takashi Inoue, and Tetuaki Nagasawa. 2003. "Daudi Aflaj: The Qanats of Oman." In *Proceedings of the Third Symposium on Xinjang Uyghor, China*, 29–36. Chiba: Chiba University.

Al-Ghafri, Abdullah, Harriet Nash, and Mohammed Al-Sarmi. 2013. "Timing Water Shares in Wādī Banī KharūB, Sultanate of Oman." *Proceedings of the Seminar for Arabian Studies*: 1–10.

Al-Jahwari, Nasser Said. 2009. "The Agricultural Basis of Umm an-Nar Society in the Northern Oman Peninsula (2500–2000 BC)." *Arabian Archaeology and Epigraphy* 20(2):122–133. https://doi.org/10.1111/j.1600-0471.2009.00315.x.

Al-Marshudi, Ahmed Salim. 2001. "Traditional Irrigated Agriculture in Oman." *Water International* 26(2):259–264. https://doi.org/10.1080/02508060108686912.

Al-Marshudi, Ahmed Salim. 2007. "The Falaj Irrigation System and Water Allocation Markets in Northern Oman." *Agricultural Water Management* 91(1–3):71–77. https://doi.org/10.1016/j.agwat.2007.04.008.

Al Sulaimani, Zaher Bin Khalid, Tariq Helmi, and Harriet Nash. 2007. "The Social Importance and Continuity of Falaj Use in Northern Oman." In *The 4th Regional Conference and 10th International Seminar on Participatory Irrigation Management (PIM)*, 2–5. May 2007, Tehran, Iran.

Al-Tikriti, Walid Yasin. 2002. "The South-East Arabian Origin of the Falaj System." *Proceedings of the Seminar for Arabian Studies* 32:117–138.

Al-Tikriti, Walid Yasin. 2010. "Heading North: An Ancient Caravan Route and the Impact of the Falaj System on the Iron Age Culture." In *Eastern Arabia in the First Millennium*, ed. Alessandra Avanzini, 227–247. Rome: L'Erma di Bretschneider.

Avanzini, Alessandra, and Carl Phillips. 2010. "An Outline of Recent Discoveries at Salut in the Sultanate of Oman." In *Eastern Arabia in the First Millennium*, ed. Alessandra Avanzini, 93–108. Rome: L'Erma di Bretschneider.

Beech, Mark J. 2004. *In the Land of the Ichthyophagi: Modelling Fish Exploitation in the Arabian Gulf and Gulf of Oman from the 5th Millennium BC to the Late Islamic Period.* Oxford: Basingstoke Press.

Begemann, Freidrich, Andreas Hauptmann, Sigrid Schmitt-Strecker, and Gerd Weisgerber. 2010. "Lead Isotope and Chemical Signature of Copper from Oman and Its Occurrence in Mesopotamia and Sites on the Arabian Gulf Coast." *Arabian Archaeology and Epigraphy* 21(2):135–169. https://doi.org/10.1111/j.1600-0471.2010.00327.x.

Bellini, Cristina, Chiara Condoluci, Gianna Giachi, Tiziana Gonnelli, and Marta Mariotti Lippi. 2011. "Interpretative Scenarios Emerging from Plant Micro- and Macroremains in the Iron Age Site of Salut, Sultanate of Oman." *Journal of Archaeological Science* 38(10):2775–2789. https://doi.org/10.1016/j.jas.2011.06.021.

Blackman, M. James, Sophie Méry, and Rita P. Wright. 1989. "Production and Exchange of Ceramics on the Oman Peninsula from the Perspective of Hili." *Journal of Field Archaeology* 16(1):61–78. https://doi.org/10.2307/529881.

Blau, Soren. 2001. "Fragmentary Endings: A Discussion of 3rd-Millennium BC Burial Practices in the Oman Peninsula." *Antiquity* 75(289):557–570. https://doi.org/10.1017/S0003598X00088797.

Bökönyi, Sándor. 1992. "Preliminary Information on the Faunal Remains from Excavations at Ras Al-Junayz, Oman." In *South Asian Archaeology, Paris 1989, Monographs in World Archaeology 14*, ed. Catherine Jarrige, 45–48. Madison, WI: Prehistory Press.

Bökönyi, Sándor, and László Bartosiewicz. 1998. "Animal Husbandry, Hunting and Fishing in the Ras Al-Junayz Area: A Basis of the Human Subsistence." In *Archaeozoology of the Near East III*, ed. Hijlke Buitenhuis, László Bartosiewicz, and Alice Mathea Choyke, 95–102. Publications 18. Groningen: ARC.

Boucharlat, Rémy. 2003. "Iron Age Water-Draining Galleries and the Iranian Qanat." In *The Emirates in Antiquity*. Proceedings of the First International Conference on the Archaeology of the U.A.E., ed. Daniel T. Potts, Hassan Al Nabooda, and Peter Hellyer, 161–172. Abu Dhabi: Trident Press Ltd.

Cable, Charlotte M., and Christopher P. Thornton. 2013. "Monumentality and the Third-Millennium 'Towers' of the Oman Peninsula." In *Connections and Complexity: New Approaches to the Archaeology of South Asia*, ed. Shinu Anna Abraham, Praveena Gullapalli, Teresa P. Raczek, and Uzma Z. Rizvi, 375–399. Walnut Creek, CA: Left Coast Press.

Charbonnier, Julien. 2015. "Groundwater Management in Southeast Arabia from the Bronze Age to the Iron Age: A Critical Reassessment." *Water History* 7(1):39–71. https://doi.org/10.1007/s12685-014-0110-x.

Cleuziou, Serge. 1982. "Hili and the Beginning of Oasis Life in Eastern Arabia." *Proceedings of the Seminar for Arabian Studies* 12:15–22.

Cleuziou, Serge. 1989. "Excavations at Hili 8: A Preliminary Report on the 4th to 7th Campaigns." *Archaeology of the United Arab Emirates* 5:61–87.

Cleuziou, Serge. 1996. "The Emergence of Oases Towns in Eastern and Southern Arabia." In *The Prehistory of Asia and Oceania*, ed. Gennady Afansas'ev, Serge Cleuziou, John R. Lukacs, and Maurizio Tosi, 159–165. Berne: UISPP.

Cleuziou, Serge, and Maurizio Tosi. 2007. *In the Shadow of the Ancestors: The Prehistoric Foundations of the Early Arabian Civilization in Oman*. Muscat: Ministry of Heritage & Culture, Sultanate of Oman.

Cleuziou, Serge, and Buckhard Vogt. 1983. "Umm an-Nar Burial Customs: Evidence from Tomb A at Hili North." *Proceedings of the Seminar for Arabian Studies* 13:37–52.

Costantini, Lorenzo. 1979. "Palaeoethnobotany: Identification of Two-Rowed Barley and Early Domesticated Sorghum." *Archaeology in the United Arab Emirates* 2/3:70–71.

Crawford, Harriet E. W. 1973. "Mesopotamia's Invisible Exports in the Third Millennium B.C." *World Archaeology* 5(2):232–241. https://doi.org/10.1080/00438243.1973.9979570.

David, Hélène. 2002. "Soft Stone Mining Evidence in the Oman Peninsula and Its Relation to Mesopotamia." In *Essays on the Late Prehistory of the Arabian Peninsula (Serie Orientale, 93)*, ed. Serge Cleuziou, Maurizio Tosi, and J. Zarins, 317–335. Roma: Istituto Italiano per L'Africa e L'Oriente.

David, Hélène, Monique Tegyey, Joël Le Métour, and Robert Wyns. 1990. "Les Vases En Chloritite Dans La Péninsule d'Oman: Une Étude Pétrographique Appliquée À L'archéologie." *Comptes-Rendus de l'Académie Des Sciences, Paris* t. 311(Série II):951–958.

de Cardi, Beatrice, Stephen Collier, and Donald Brian Doe. 1976. "Excavations and Survey in Oman, 1974–1975." *Journal of Oman Studies* 5:61–94.

Desruelles, Stéphane, Eric Fouache, Wassel Eddargach, Cecilia Cammas, Julia Wattez, Tara Beuzen-Waller, Chloé Martin, Margareta Tengberg, Charlotte M. Cable, Christopher P. Thornton, et al. 2016. "Evidence for Early Irrigation at Bat (Wadi Sharsah, Northwestern Oman) before the Advent of Farming Villages." *Quaternary Science Reviews* 150(October):42–54. https://doi.org/10.1016/j.quascirev.2016.08.007.

During Caspers, Elisabeth. 1970. "Trucial Oman in the Third Millennium B.C.: New Evidence for Contacts with Sumer, Baluchistan and the Indus Valley." *Origini* 4:205–276.

Edens, Christopher M. 1993. "Indus-Arabian Interaction during the Bronze Age: A Review of Evidence." In *Harappan Civilization: A Recent Perspective*, 2nd ed., ed. Gregory Possehl, 335–363. New Delhi: Oxford & IBH Publishing Co.

Food and Agriculture Organization of the United Nations. n.d. "Ecocrop." *Ecocrop*. http://ecocrop.fao.org/ecocrop/srv/en/home. Accessed July 31 2016.

Frifelt, Karen. 1975. "On Prehistoric Settlement and Chronology of the Oman Peninsula." *East and West* 25(3/4):359–424.

Frifelt, Karen. 1989. "Third Millennium Irrigation and Oasis Culture in Oman." *Old Problems and New Perspectives in the Archaeology of South Asia* 2:105–113.

Gensheimer, Thomas R. 1984. "The Role of Shell in Mesopotamia: Evidence for Trade Exchange with Oman and the Indus Valley." *Paléorient* 10(1):65–73. https://doi.org/10.3406/paleo.1984.4350.

Glennie, Ken W. 2005. *The Geology of the Oman Mountains: An Outline of Their Origin.* 2nd ed. Bucks, UK: Scientific Press Ltd.

Hastings, Ann, James H. Humphries, and Richard H. Meadow. 1975. "Oman in the Third Millennium BCE." *Journal of Oman Studies* 1:9–55.

Hauptmann, Andreas, Gerd Weisgerber, and Hans-Gert Bachmann. 1988. "Early Copper Metallurgy in Oman." In *The Beginning of the Use of Metals and Alloys*, ed. Robert Maddin, 34–51. Cambridge, MA: MIT Press.

Hoch, Ella. 1995. "Animal Bones from the Umm an-Nar Settlement." In *The Island of Umm an-Nar*, Vol. 2, *The Third Millennium Settlement*, ed. Karen Frifelt, 249–256. Jutland Archaeological Society Publications vol. 26(2). Aarhus: Aarhus University Press.

Kmoskó, Mihály. 1917. "Beiträge Zur Erklärung Der Inschriften Gudeas." *Zeitschrift für Assyriologie und Vorderasiatische Archäologie* 31(1-2):58–90. https://doi.org/10.1515/zava.1917.31.1-2.58.

Kwarteng, Andy Y., Atsu S. Dorvlo, and Ganiga T. Vijaya Kumar. 2009. "Analysis of a 27-Year Rainfall Data (1977–2003) in the Sultanate of Oman." *International Journal of Climatology* 29(4):605–617. https://doi.org/10.1002/joc.1727.

Leemans, Wilhelmus F. 1960. *Foreign Trade in the Old Babylonian Period.* Leiden: Brill.

Limbert, Mandana. 2010. *In the Time of Oil: Piety, Memory, and Social Life in an Omani Town.* Stanford: Stanford University Press.

Magee, Peter. 1999. "Writing in the Iron Age: The Earliest South Arabian Inscription from Southeastern Arabia." *Arabian Archaeology and Epigraphy* 10(1):43–50. https://doi.org/10.1111/j.1600-0471.1999.tb00126.x.

McCorriston, Joy. 2006. "Breaking the Rain Barrier and the Tropical Spread of Near Eastern Agriculture into Southern Arabia." In *Behavioral Ecology and the Transition to Agriculture,* ed. Bruce Winterhalder and Douglas Kennett, 217–236. Berkeley: University of California Press.

McCorriston, Joy, Michael Harrower, Louise Martin, and Eric Oches. 2012. "Cattle Cults of the Arabian Neolithic and Early Territorial Societies." *American Anthropologist* 114(1):45–63. https://doi.org/10.1111/j.1548-1433.2011.01396.x.

Méry, Sophie. 1988. "Ceramics from RJ-2." In *The Joint Hadd Project: Summary Report on the Second Season, November 1986–January 1987,* ed. Serge Cleuziou and Maurizio Tosi, 41–47. Naples: Instituto Universitario Orientale.

Méry, Sophie. 1991. "Origine et Production Des Récipients de Terre Cuite Dans La Péninsule d'Oman à l'Âge Du Bronze." *Paléorient* 17(2):51–78. https://doi.org/10.3406/paleo.1991.4552.

Méry, Sophie. 2000. *Les Céramiques d'Oman et l'Asie Moyenne: Une Archéologie Des Échanges À l'Âge Du Bronze.* Paris: Éditions du CNRS.

Mouton, Michel. 1999. "Le Travail de La Chlorite À Mleiha." In *Mleiha I. Environnement, Stratégies de Subsistance et Artisanats (Mission Archéologique Française À Sharjah),* ed. Travaux de Pouilloux, 227–243. Lyon: Maison de l'Orient et de la Méditerranée.

Nash, Harriet. 2007. "Stargazing in Traditional Water Management: A Case Study in Northern Oman." *Proceedings of the Seminar for Arabian Studies* 37:157–170.

Nash, Harriet. 2010. "Lesser Man-Made Rivers: The Aflaj of Oman and Traditional Timing of Water Shares." In *History of Water: Rivers and Society,* Volume II, ed. Terje Tvedt and Richard Coopey, 221–235. London: I.B.Tauris.

Nash, Harriet. 2011. *Water Management: The Use of Stars in Oman.* Oxford: Archaeopress.

Nash, Harriet. 2015. "Star Clocks and Water Management in Oman." In *Handbook of Archaeoastronomy and Ethnoastronomy,* ed. Clive L. N. Ruggles, 1941–1948. New York: Springer; https://doi.org/10.1007/978-1-4614-6141-8_201.

Nash, Harriet, and Dionisius A. Agius. 2009. "Folk Astronomy in Omani Agriculture." *Proceedings of the International Astronomical Union* 5(S260):166–171. https://doi.org/10.1017/S1743921311002249.

Nash, Harriet, and Dionisius A. Agius. 2011. "The Use of Stars in Agriculture in Oman." *Journal of Semitic Studies* 56(1):167–182. https://doi.org/10.1093/jss/fgq063.

Nash, Harriet, and Dionisius A. Agius. 2013. "Star Charts from Oman." *Proceedings of the 24th Congress of the Union Européenne des Arabisants et Islamisants*, ed. V. Kleem and N. Al-Sha'ar. Leuven: Peeters.

Nash, Harriet, Muhammad bin Hamad al Musharifi, and Ahmad bid Saif al Harthi. 2014. "Timing Falaj Water Shares in the Hajar Ash Sharqī." *Journal of Oman Studies* 18:63–75.

Parker, Adrian G., Andrew S. Goudie, Stephen Stokes, Kevin White, Martin J. Hodson, Michelle Manning, and Derek Kennet. 2006. "A Record of Holocene Climate Change from Lake Geochemical Analyses in Southeastern Arabia." *Quaternary Research* 66(3):465–476. https://doi.org/10.1016/j.yqres.2006.07.001.

Petraglia, Michael D., and Jeffrey I. Rose, eds. 2010. *The Evolution of Human Populations in Arabia: Vertebrate Paleobiology and Paleoanthropology.* Dordrecht: Springer Netherlands; https://doi.org/10.1007/978-90-481-2719-1.

Piesinger, Constance Maria. 1983. "Legacy of Dilmun: The Roots of Ancient Maritime Trade in Eastern Coastal Arabia in the 4th/3rd Millennium B.C." PhD diss. University of Wisconsin, Madison.

Potts, Dan T. 1994. "Contributions to the Agrarian History of Eastern Arabia II: The Cultivars." *Arabian Archaeology and Epigraphy* 5(4):236–275. https://doi.org/10.1111/j.1600-0471.1994.tb00071.x.

Potts, Dan T. 2000. *Ancient Magan: The Secrets of Tell Abraq.* London: Trident Press Ltd.

Potts, Daniel T. 2008. "Arabian Peninsula." In *Encyclopedia of Archaeology*, ed. Deborah Pearsall, 827–834. Cambridge: Academic Press. https://doi.org/10.1016/B978-0123 73962-9.00395-2.

Potts, Dan T. 2010. "Cylinder Seals and Their Use in the Arabian Peninsula." *Arabian Archaeology and Epigraphy* 21(1):20–40. https://doi.org/10.1111/j.1600-0471.2009.00319.x.

Salvatori, Sandro. 1996. "Death and Ritual in a Population of Coastal Food Foragers in Oman." In *Trade as a Subsistence Strategy: Post Pleistocene Adaptations in Arabia and Early Maritime Trade in the Indian Ocean* (UISPP Colloquium XXXII), ed. Gennady Afanasiev, Serge Cleuziou, John R. Lukacs, and Maurizio Tosi, 205–223. Forli.

Stevens, John H. 1972. "Oasis Agriculture in the Central and Eastern Arabian Peninsula." *Geography (Sheffield, England)* 57(4):321–326.

Sutton, Sally. 1984. "The Falaj—a Traditional Co-Operative System of Water Management." *Waterlines* 2(3):8–12. https://doi.org/10.3362/0262-8104.1984.005.

Tengberg, Margareta. 1998. "Paleoenvironnements et Economie Vegetale." In "Milieu Aride—Recherches Archeobotaniques Dans La Region Du Golfe Arabo-Persique et Dans Le Makran Pakistanais." University of Montpellier II.

Tengberg, Margareta. 2003. "Archaeobotany in the Oman Peninsula and the Role of Eastern Arabia in the Spread of African Crops." In *Food, Fuel and Fields: Progress in African Archaeobotany*, ed. Katharina Neumann, Ann Butler, and Stefanie Kahlheber,

229–237. Africa Praehistorica, Monographien zur Archaeologie und Umwelt Afrikas. Koeln: Heinrich-Barth-Institut.

Tengberg, Margareta. 2012. "Beginnings and Early History of Date Palm Garden Cultivation in the Middle East." *Journal of Arid Environments* 86:139–147. https://doi .org/10.1016/j.jaridenv.2011.11.022.

Uerpmann, Margarethe, and Hans-Peter Uerpmann. 2008. "Animal Economy during the Early Bronze Age in South-East Arabia." *Archaeozoology of the Near East VIII*, ed. Emmanuelle Vila, Lionel Gourichon, Alice M. Choyke, and Hijkle Buitenhuis, Emmanuelle, 49(1):465–485.

Vogt, Buckhard. 1985. "Zur Chronologie Und Entwicklung Der Gräber Des Späten 4.–2. Jtsd.v. Chr. Auf Der Halbinsel Oman." PhD diss. Georg-August Universität zu Göttingen.

Vogt, Buckhard. 1996. "Bronze Age Maritime Trade in the Indian Ocean: Harappan Traits on the Oman Peninsula." In *The Indian Ocean in Antiquity*, ed. Julian Reade, 107–132. London: Kegan Paul International.

Vogt, Buckhard, and Ute Franke-Vogt, eds. 1987. *Shimal 1985/1986. Excavations of the German Archaeological Mission in Ras Al-Khaimah, UAE. A Preliminary Report.* Berlin: Dietrich Reimer Verlag.

Weisgerber, Gerd. 1981. "Mehr Als Kupfer Im Oman—Ergebnisse Der Expedition 1981." *Der Anschnitt* 33:174–263.

Wellsted, James Raymond. 1838. *Travels in Arabia.* London: Murray.

Whalen, Norman. 2003. "Lower Palaeolithic Sites in the Huqf Area of Central Oman." *Journal of Oman Studies* 13:175–182.

Whitcomb, Daniel. 1975. "The Archaeology of Oman: A Preliminary Discussion of the Islamic Periods." *Journal of Oman Studies* 1:123–157.

Wilkinson, John Craven. 1977. *Water and Tribal Settlement in South-East Arabia: A Study of Aflaj in Oman.* Oxford: Clarendon Press.

Willcox, George. 1995. "Some Plant Impressions from Umm an-Nar Island." In *The Island of Umm An-Nar: The Third Millenium Settlement*, ed. Karen Frifelt, 257–259. Aarhus: Jutland Archaeological Society Publications, Aarhus University Press.

Yateem, Abdullah A. 2009. "Agriculture and Pastoralism in the Hajar Mountains of the Emirates : A Historical Ethnography." *Journal of the Gulf and Arabian Peninsula Studies* 35(135):17–85.

Zekri, Slim, Dennis Powers, and Abdullah Al-Ghafri. 2014. "Century Old Water Markets in Oman." In *Water Markets for the 21st Century*, ed. K. William Easter and Qiuqiong Huang, 149–162. Dordrecht: Springer Netherlands; 10.1007/978-94-017-9081-9_8.

Ziolkowski, Michele C. 2001. "The Soft Stone Vessels from Sharm, Fujairah, United Arab Emirates." *Arabian Archaeology and Epigraphy* 12(1):10–86. https://doi.org/10 .1111/j.1600-0471.2001.aae120102.x.

Fluid Spaces and Fluid Objects

Nocturnal Material Culture in Sub-Saharan Africa with
Special Reference to the Iron Age in Southern Africa

SHADRECK CHIRIKURE AND ABIGAIL JOY MOFFETT

As a block of time, the night is an integral part of human existence that is experienced in several culturally specific ways. The beginning of the night might have seen the continuation of activities performed during the day; however, in some instances darkness opened the windows to distinctive public practices while in others it inaugurated more private, intimate performances. Archaeologically however, the evidence does not preserve in discrete categories such as "used only during the day," "used only during the night," and "used during both day and night." For this reason, the study of nightly practices in the last two thousand years of the sub-Saharan African past (figures 1.2, 1.3) poses many difficulties to archaeologists due to the ambiguity of the material and nonmaterial evidence. This period, the Iron Age (200–1900 CE), is associated with the archaeology of farming communities in the region. Yet, the anthropology and sociology of various communities resident in sub-Saharan Africa (e.g., Bourdillon 1976, 1987; Gelfand 1973; Hammond-Tooke 1993) reveal the presence of daily and nightly practices, suggesting that despite the ambivalence of the archaeological record, some effort must be invested into considering the archaeology of

DOI: 10.5876/9781607326786.c017

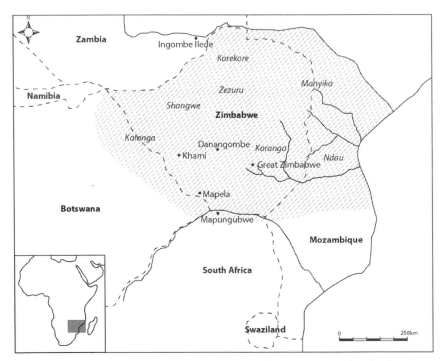

FIGURE 17.1. *The southern African region, with some of the sites mentioned in the chapter and the approximate distribution of speakers of different Shona dialects.*

nightly practices. This effort requires a nuanced conversation that involves the material and nonmaterial records belonging to the past and the present. Under such circumstances, it would be extremely dangerous to commit to a purely uniformitarian argument (see Wylie 1985) that the past and the present are the same. Rather, in this chapter, we engage in a conversation between the past and the present, as sources of information that might help us to comprehend a very significant but archaeologically slippery aspect of past human behavior that may be dissimilar to the present.

Across sub-Saharan Africa the transition from day to night is associated with gendered cultural behaviors such as learning, song and dance, smelting, hunting, and in some cases farming. Depending on the context and specific cultural group, the performance of different nightly activities required a great deal of scheduling and was culturally determined and culturally embedded. For example, although folktales performed a didactic role in traditional Shona societies of southern Africa (figure 17.1), the nightly practice of storytelling was taboo at certain times of the year, restricted to the period between the end of the harvest and the beginning of the new agricultural cycle to help ensure that people remained focused on their work (Hodza 1983). Often carried out with the benefit of moonlight, hunting, farming, and smelting are some of the sociotechnical activities that were performed during the night (see Gonlin and Dixon, chapter 3, and Nathan, chapter16, this volume, for more on nightly subsistence activities). For example, the Njanja iron smelters of southeastern Zimbabwe (Mackenzie 1975) operated iron furnaces at night just as the Dogon smelters of Mali did (Huysecom and Agustoni 1997). Furthermore, performances associated with leisure and pleasure, such as sexual intercourse, were also conducted under the shroud of the night. Juxtaposed with these deeds were some illicit nightly practices such as raiding, adultery, stealing, and witchcraft. This Shona proverb best summarizes the "dark side" of nightly practices: *zvakaipa zvose zvinoitwa murima* ("all the bad deeds are done under the cover of darkness"). However, what is good in one nightly context may be bad in another.

While technical performances such as iron smelting were generally executed along gender- and status-based lines, others such as tilling the land were implemented in gender-inclusive ways. The anthropological record is replete with examples of quotidian and technical practices that took place under the cover of the night. While we benefit from observation of and participation in nightly practices in the recent past in southern Africa, it is archaeologically challenging to separate daily from nocturnal behaviors, particularly given that some of the nightly practices were an extension of those taking place during the day. Like daily activities, nightly practices also included material culture production, use, and discard, thereby contributing, over time, to the archaeological material and nonmaterial records. To add to this complexity, the cultural behaviors that are archaeologically recoverable are conditioned by surviving material evidence and the absence thereof. Even so, archaeological evidence is an aggregate of events and activities that happened during the day and the night. Despite this aggregation, rarely do Africanist archaeologists pause to consider what the material and nonmaterial remains from nightly performances might look like.

Against a background of the significance of nightly practices in human existence, this chapter strings together anthropological and archaeological insights to initiate a conversation about the archaeology of nocturnal activities. Our main conclusion is that in general the material manifestation of daily performances is difficult to differentiate from that of nocturnal practices due to overlaps in human behaviors. However, the use of "daily" material culture during the night, in contexts associated with ritual, sex, and other nocturnal adventures, should alert archaeologists to issues of day-night (cross-time) overlaps in material culture use. Particular objects had context and time-defined meanings that changed from day to night, in spaces based on status, age, and gender relations, and from the public to the private, and back to the public. Such observations expose the multiple layers of complexity associated with studying the archaeology of the night using material culture. Rather than perceiving this complexity as a limitation, it is an opportunity to introduce the much-needed nuance to the study of nightly cultural behaviors in the African past.

THE ANTHROPOLOGY OF NIGHTLY PRACTICES IN SOUTHERN AFRICA

As with many cultures in the world, the onset of darkness in southern Africa marked the beginning of essential performances, several of which continued from daytime (Hammond-Tooke 1993). Some of these activities were associated with different spaces and material culture, and were sometimes performed in private and public areas, often along age-, gender-, and status-based categories (Gelfand 1962, 1973). Learning and instruction are vital components of societies, and these aspects are no less applicable to communities in southern Africa. Among the Shona people, whose distribution covers much of Zimbabwe and adjacent regions in Mozambique, South Africa, and Botswana, it was the duty of the elders to educate the youngsters as they passed through different life stages (Hodza 1981, 1983). While the practical instruction occurred during the day, much of the theoretical instruction took place around a fire (for warmth and light), under the cover of the night, during the performance and delivery of folktales (*ngano*) by elderly men and women.

The process of storytelling was often gendered such that old women were responsible for telling stories to young girls in the cooking hut (*imba yokubikira*) while old men were responsible for the delivery of folktales to young boys at the *dare* (Ellert 1984). According to Gombe (1986), the dare as a space had dual meanings: (1) the male space in each homestead and (2) a court where judicial matters were resolved in a community. This discussion is based on the first meaning because the second meaning mostly applied in daily and often ad hoc contexts. As a male space, the dare was an open area on the edge of the homestead while the cooking hut was conceptually a female space (Bourdillon 1976). The fireplace in the cooking hut belonged to the wife and it was associated with reproductive metaphors and symbolism. Gendered though these different spaces were, spatial boundaries were often relaxed, with men using the kitchen and women also going to the dare, depending on context. Also, there were times when ngano were narrated to both girls and boys. Performed for entertainment and relaxation purposes, ngano were didactic and imparted to growing children skills about role-playing in life (Atkinson 1986; Kileff 1987). They also instilled virtues such as tolerance that encouraged learners to be selfless members of society. Typically, villains got punished while heroes were generously rewarded. For example, in a folktale titled *Mutongi Gava* (Judge Jackal), a leopard caught in a hunter's trap implored a passerby to set him free, but once loose, the leopard attempted to eat the man. The two struggled until a wise jackal passed by. Upon hearing the story, the jackal pretended that he did not understand the argument and encouraged the warring parties to restore the initial set up. Once the leopard was inside the trap, the jackal advised the man to continue with his journey, leaving the captive leopard to die. The moral of the story is that one cannot be cruel to somebody who has helped him/her (Hodza 1983).

Most interestingly, the main characters in most ngano included a combination of human beings, animals, and trees that taught youngsters about human life and ecology (Mutasa et al. 2008). Despite the didactic function of ngano, taboos mandated that they were performed only between the harvest and rainy seasons. This scheduling was aimed at ensuring that all the effort was invested into the agricultural cycle. As a type of cultural performance, storytelling was mainly verbal but in the process, humans used material culture and spaces similar to those used during the day.

Under moonlight, a number of activities such as community dances were also performed and most boys and girls of marriageable age met their future partners during these gatherings (Gombe 1986). The night also presented an opportunity for the continuation of more mundane activities that were often carried out during the day. Reputed Shona farmers, known as *hurudza*, sometimes ploughed their fields using moonlight. Hunters, too, exploited the cover of the night to hunt for nocturnal and non-nocturnal animals. Typically, the material culture such as drums (song and dances), spears (hunting), and hoes (horticulture) used during these nightly events was similar to that used during the day. However, the scheduling of nightly activities was governed by rituals and taboos known as *miko nezvierwa* that made it possible to perform some, but not all, behaviors during the night.

The cover of darkness opened the door to different types of ritual performances. For example, as far as divinity was concerned, the Shona believed in a God to whom they could speak only via intercessory ancestors (Beach 1980). In times of need and during the beginning of the rainy season, the head of the house prayed to God via ancestors for good health, good harvests, and good luck (Gelfand 1962). The prayers were performed at the back of the cooking hut on a platform known as *chikuva* and under the leadership of the homestead head. During the prayer, beer was often poured on the floor, symbolizing the ground where the dead were buried. Material culture that includes calabashes, clay pots, and wooden plates was used during the ceremonies. Outside of rituals, this back platform was used for storing pots that were closely associated with the feminine in use and material properties (Aschwanden 1987), thereby emphasizing the fluid and shared nature of spaces.

The night was a theater through which various ritual performances—good and bad—were enacted. In times of ill health, the Shona consulted traditional healers (*n'angas*). Diagnosis was performed through the use of material culture such as divining dices (*hakata*) (figure 17.2) (Ellert 1984; Gelfand 1956). Typically,

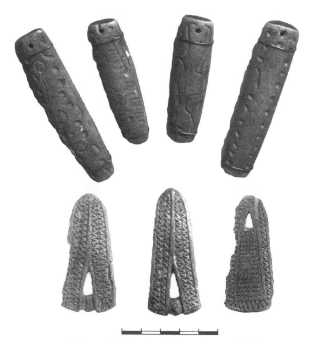

FIGURE 17.2. *(Top row) Wooden divining dice on display at the Natural History Museum, Bulawayo, Zimbabwe. (Photo by Abigail J. Moffett) (Bottom row) Ivory divining dice recovered from Khami. (Adapted from Robinson 1959, Plate 5)*

divining dices were composed of four pieces: one representing male, the other one female, and the other two representing good and bad luck. When thrown to the ground, the n'anga would interpret the upward-facing sides before conveying the message to the fortune seekers. Solutions were subsequently prescribed and often these included the use of medicines and ritual cleansing, which was mostly performed at night. It was common for every homestead to be conceptually fortified by medicines planted into the ground to protect the families from malevolent spirits and witches (Gelfand 1962).

Although controversial and difficult to verify, witchcraft is yet another nightly practice that was part of the Shona worldview. The opposite of traditional healers, witches (*varoyi*) could cast bad luck, disease, and death to other members of the community. Traditional healers neutralized the power of witches. Allegedly, Shona witches practiced their nightly trade in the nude. Before embarking on their expeditions, they left mortars beside their husbands as decoys so that, under a spell, they would not recognize that their wives were away. Interestingly, witches were believed to fly in winnowing baskets that flew at supersonic speed, covering a return journey of thousands of kilometers in a single nightly expedition. Upon landing, witches then traveled on the backs of hyenas. The paraphernalia of witchcraft, such as winnowing baskets and mortars and pestles, are similar to material culture used in a number of daytime and nighttime contexts.

Some of the charms typically associated with witches were decorated with black, white, and red glass beads, similar to ones used to represent traditional healers. White, red, and black are deeply embedded in the symbolic schema of many southern African communities (Hammond-Tooke 1981). These beads, when worn by traditional healers, were active in the materialization of healing and divining (Gelfand 1956). The colors of the beads could also be associated with the presence of evil spirits, with their meaning transformed in different ritual settings associated with witchcraft, thereby exposing the complexity of symbols. Similarly, other artifacts, such as the seemingly mundane mortar and pestle used for processing food during the day, took on new meanings at night in which they became embodied objects.

Aside from ritual, there are some nightly performances that were aimed at intimate and more private leisure and pleasure. Sexual intercourse is a pleasurable performance that often took place in private in a dedicated space, the sleeping hut (imba yekurara). Sex crystallized each and every marriage and was taken very seriously because it was the key to reproduction. It also oiled the relationship between a husband and a wife. Boys and girls approaching marriageable age were taught about sexual performances for them to be successful in their marriages (Shoko 2009). As a performance, sex was associated with complementary bodily moves made by both men and women. Often, women wore a waist belt made of glass beads known as *mutimwi* or *chuma chechikapa* (*chikapa* refers to the gyrations made by women during sex). Believed to enhance women's fertility, the husband played with the beads before, during, and after sex. The sound from the friction of strands of beads making up the mutimwi created melodious acoustics that provided a musical background to the entire sexual experience. Each woman had a calabash known as *chinu* that symbolized her sexuality (Shoko 2009). The calabash contained oil that was used for massaging during and after sex. Apart from mutimwi and chinu, other material culture associated with sexual performance includes the sleeping mat known as *bonde*. All these items were owned by a woman and were inalienable possessions so closely associated with her personhood that they were buried with her (after Weiner 1985).

Some individuals who were known to possess some medicine known as *mubobobo* that enabled them to sneak illicitly into other people's sleeping huts. They cast a spell on the couple and then had sex with the wife without either the husband or wife realizing it. This illicit sexual activity could be stopped only by traditional healers, who neutralized the power of the mubobobo. Yet some men 'locked' their wives, through spells, so that they could not commit adultery.

FIGURE 17.3. *Anthropomorphic iron-smelting furnace from Nyanga, Eastern Zimbabwe. (Photo by Shadreck Chirikure)*

If the wife performed adultery, whether during the day or night, the illicit pair would not uncouple until caught, and the spell could be reversed only after the payment of reparations. Together with beliefs about witchcraft, the mubobobo is difficult to verify tangibly but remains a belief among certain people in Shona communities today.

Most communities performed sociotechnical activities such as iron smelting, during the night. In Bantu societies, iron smelting was metaphorically associated with human copulation and reproduction (Childs 1991; Schmidt 1997, 2009). Typical Bantu iron-smelting furnaces symbolized a female body and were often decorated (figure 17.3) with breasts, female genitalia, and navels. The actual process of smelting symbolized sexual intercourse that generated heat, resulting in transformations that produced a baby. Not surprisingly, the iron bloom symbolized a child. The blowpipes (*tuyeres*) that transported air into the furnace during smelting symbolized the penis. Interestingly, tuyeres are known as *nyengo* in Shona and often sexual intercourse is known as *kunyengana*. According to Childs

(1999), tuyeres also symbolized the penis among the Toro of Uganda. In a smelting reconstruction conducted in Tanzania, the Bachwezi smelters performed gestures similar to those performed during sexual intercourse when pumping bellows (Reid and MacLean 1995). Not surprisingly, in Bantu Africa, iron smelters were often mandated by taboos to practice sexual abstinence with their human wives when smelting. Failure to observe this precaution would result in unsuccessful smelts, or a "stillborn" baby. In some cases, men performed smelting away from the public gaze, just as intercourse, but in others, it was done in the homestead precinct under the cover of darkness.

DISCUSSION: FLUID SPACES AND FLUID OBJECTS

Archaeological formation processes (Schiffer 1987) aggregate daytime and nighttime behaviors, with the result that Africanist archaeologists, as with their counterparts elsewhere, rarely engage with nocturnal activities, thereby creating a somewhat limited picture of the past. However, life today does not stop with the setting of the sun, nor did it stop during the night for the ancients. Time is a sociocultural construct that is perceived differently by various communities (Lucas 2004). For example, among the many Bantu communities resident in Africa south of the equator, as elsewhere, time is compartmentalized into daytime and nighttime. Groups such as the Shona divide their time into *mangwanani* (morning), *masikati* (afternoon), and *manheru/usiku* (night). However, there are overlaps between late night/early morning, late morning/early afternoon, and late afternoon/early night, which often precipitated a great deal of continuity and scheduling of various performances. Although human behavior sometimes overlapped between day and night, some performances were mostly enacted under the cover of the dark.

Perhaps the most pertinent question is, What are the archaeological signatures of these essential but intangible nightly practices? Storytelling, a gendered performance of the night, was associated with gendered spaces used during the day. During storytelling, the male space (dare) and the female space (imba yekubikira) were reserved respectively for men and women. However, boundaries shifted and were often relaxed, depending on the context, resulting in gender crossovers. As an open space, in the homestead, the dare was not a built environment. While archaeology is biased in favor of the readily preserved built environment, identifying intangible nightly practices carried out in open spaces remains challenging. Furthermore, identifying culturally meaningful open spaces such as the dare is complicated by the fact that archaeologists do not often open up areas large enough to expose the full spatial layout of a site during excavation. Certainly, the 1 m² or 2 m² test trenches that are fashionable during most excavations do not help in this regard. Middens are known to have accumulated next to the dare but often a midden's location within the homestead meant that rubbish from various areas of the homestead ended up in one place.

In contrast to the dare, the cooking hut was a built environment with features such as a fireplace, a bench, a back platform (chikuva), and pot sockets. All these features were observed on house floors dating from the Early (200–1000 CE) and Late Iron Ages (1000–1900 CE) (Huffman 2007). However even in the case of the kitchen hut with its archaeologically identifiable features, it might be dangerous to infer storytelling from the presence of fireplaces, back platforms, and benches from huts dating to the deep past, since spaces and their contextual use likely may have changed over time, as it did from day to night. Similarities in features may not necessarily correlate with a similarity in use (Lane 1994). Indeed, the shifting meaning of space based on the materials and persons using it observed ethnographically among Shona communities provides further caution about associating specific spaces with fixed cultural behaviors.

Ritual is another very significant cultural behavior that was practiced during the night. In terms of Shona religion, the head of a house prayed at the chikuva to God via male and female ancestors. While the prayer was a verbal performance, it was associated with different categories of material culture such as wooden plates, pots, ritual axes, and spears. While this ritual is a known cultural behavior, in most cases, the material culture used also applied to daily practices. However, that the chikuva was also a female space where pottery was kept in the house and was also a key shrine demonstrates that spaces were associated with various functions and that they were shared between genders. This usage underscores the importance of space sharing and exposes the fluid nature of boundaries between performances and within the homestead. If the view is considered that the house is a container that symbolizes the female body (Chirikure et al. 2015), then the fact that important family rituals were conducted in a conceptually female body has greater implications for the conceptualization of gender than the more conventional archaeological and anthropological reconstructions permit.

The analysis of spatial patterning in first- and second-millennium CE sites in the southern African region has been dominated by a Central Cattle Pattern model (Huffman 2007). Framed in terms of cognitive structuralism, the model allocates specific spaces into gender binary activity areas. Thus, the cattle kraal that in some cases was located at the center of the settlement is associated only with men. The open space near the kraal is often interpreted as a court (dare), similarly associated with men. In contrast, houses, usually located in a ring around the cattle kraal, are designated female spaces. Proponents of the model argue that the centrality of male activity areas in the settlement pattern of Iron Age communities reflects a social system of male hereditary leadership in patrilineal societies for over two millennia in the archaeology of southern Africa.

While the model can make a vital contribution to the study of the past when applied flexibly, the dichotomization of space into rigid male and female spaces contradicts the observation that taboos were often relaxed and that women owned cattle, women could herd cattle, and that men slept in the houses that were gendered as female. Therefore, by returning to the house at night, men were conceptually going back to the womb, as the house was often symbolically conceived to be. This relaxing of taboos exposes the complicated nature of symbolic behavior, which renders inappropriate the apportionment of different spaces to men and women without considering the night. During the night, men did not sleep at the dare but they retreated into the houses where they performed some of the activities outlined above. Thus at night, a settlement layout with a centrally located cattle kraal would assume a different meaning from that applicable to some contexts during the day. In any case, both the cattle kraal and the houses were circular and thus were symbolic containers and bodies essential to societal renewal.

Witchcraft is yet another example of a ritual that affected the lives of Shona people. It is believed that witches operated in the dark when they cast bad luck, ill health, and disease to others. Identifying objects, receptacles or containers of medicine, or items involved in healing and spirituality in the archaeological record is difficult (Insoll 2011). Often, the material culture associated with witchcraft included winnowing baskets and mortars and pestles similar to those used during the day. Some of these items are, however, perishable and do not preserve well. Although operating in the nude, witches are known to have used charms decorated with glass beads (black, white, and red) and cloth. The malevolent power of witches was neutralized by that of traditional healers, or n'angas. Guided by good spirits and even ancestors, n'angas used material culture such as divining tablets that were often gendered.

Ivory divining dices/tablets (figure 17.2, bottom) were recovered from the site of Khami (1300?–1650 CE), a World Heritage site situated approximately 22 km west of the modern town of Bulawayo and one of the former capitals of the Torwa-Changamire state (Pikirayi 2002). These dice, five in total, were retrieved from underneath the burnt rubble at the entrance to a hut built on an elaborately constructed dry-stone-walled platform at the site. The dice were found buried in association with two small ivory carvings of felines, three ivory pallets, the head of an ivory staff, and a cowry shell (Robinson 1959, 53). In contrast, little to no material remains were recovered from other surveyed and excavated hut floors at Khami, indicating that this cache was unique. The materials recovered and the depositional context associated with the front entrance of the hut indicate that these items may have had a symbolic/ritual association possibly linked to healing and divination. Furthermore, these ancient dice indicate some form of continuity in healing practices into the deeper past.

Sexual intercourse is yet another nightly practice that was central to reproduction and enjoyment. Because of the importance of sex, many groups mentored girls and boys of marriageable age to ready them for the institution of marriage. The process of instruction involved the use of training aids such as figurines that anatomically resembled males and females. During instruction, eligible young-sters were taught about the human body, sexually sensitive body parts, and what to do during sex. To aid the performance, the waist belt, mutimwi, worn by Shona women, was made of numerous strands of glass beads. Furthermore, the sacred calabash, chinu, played an important role in the institution of sexual intercourse. The gestures accompanying the performance are intangible and are therefore archaeologically unrecoverable, but the chinu and mutimwi were often buried with their owner.

The glass beads used in southern Africa during the Iron Age (700–1900 CE) were imports from trade networks connected to the Indian Ocean rim. The dominant archaeological narratives in the region associate glass beads with pres-tige and status (Killick 2009; Wood 2012). For example, the so-called royal burials, particularly those of women recovered from Mapungubwe Hill (1200–1290 CE), contained within them thousands of glass beads. Part of the interpretation of the graves as elite burials stems from the quantity of beads in the deposit (Huffman 2007). However, as we have seen, waist belts made of glass beads played a central role during sexual intercourse. Without a waist belt, a wife might be asked to return to her parents' home to retrieve one. Explorations of the use of materials such as glass beads in nightly contexts indicate the different functions of objects in different usages, some of which are linked to personhood, sexuality, and much more. More important, some glass beads were used in rit-ual contexts because colors such as red, white, and black appealed to ancestors. Therefore, archaeological interpretation must be alert to multiple possibilities beyond prestige alone.

Technological acts such as iron smelting were also performed during the night. Indeed, some ethnographic reconstructions of traditional iron smelting carried out among the Dogon of Mali exposed that smelting took place for three days nonstop, including day and night (Huysecom and Agustoni 1997). Other simi-lar examples include the Bassar of Togo. Although sub-Saharan archaeologists have excavated hundreds of smelting furnaces, rarely have they attempted to identify what smelts might have been carried out during the night. Scientifically, there is no way of differentiating smelts that were conducted during the day from nightly ones because physically and chemically, the process, product, and byproducts remain the same. Across sub-Saharan Africa, indigenous iron smelt-ing was wrapped up in ideas about transformation and reproductive metaphors (Herbert 1993). The smelting furnace was gendered as female and was thus a sym-bolic wife of the smelter. In some contexts, it has been attested that rituals and taboos relating to privacy and sexual abstinence determined the location of fur-naces away from homesteads. However, some archaeologically known furnaces are from homestead precincts (Chirikure et al. 2015; Ndoro 1991; Schmidt 1997). Rather than interpreting that such furnaces were not contemporary with associated homesteads, as believed by some (e.g., Greenfield and Miller 2004), it is possible that such smelts were carried out under the cover of darkness. We fully recognize that such a view flirts with the limits of archaeological inference, but suggest that archaeologists have overlooked the magnitude of the night as a parameter affecting smelting.

So far, the examples discussed have demonstrated that there are a host of cultural behaviors that were performed during the night and in some cases, they are similar to daily practices. This observation brings the prominence of lighting into the center of the discussion because it is lighting that makes darkness visible. In this regard, moonlight played a luminary role in the scheduling of activities. Public dances involving many community members were often done when there was moonlight (see Dillehay, chapter 9, this volume). During the spring season, moonlight is usually at its brightest in southern Africa, therefore, many people could gather at night. It also meant that those with a habit of carrying out illicit and illegitimate deeds could be "clearly seen." In more private settings, fire was a main provider of light, warmth, and heat. The fireplace, whether at the dare or in the house, constituted a vital space. The house fireplace, *choto*, was a significant locus of transformations such as cooking. In fact, most "containers" for transformation were gendered as female (e.g., pots, houses, and smelting furnaces). In all these transformations, just as in sex, heat was an essential transformative agent.

Archaeological reconstructions of the worldviews of Iron Age communities in southern Africa, derived from structural interpretations of statically gendered spaces, have ascribed little agency to the users of those spaces and objects. However, gender is constructed, contested, and negotiated in space, time, and materiality (Conkey and Gero 1997; Conkey and Spector 1984). A review of the intersection of space, objects, performance, and day-night time in Shona communities further articulates this point. Furthermore, the prominence of fertility symbolism, which dominated the Shona worldview, indicates the centrality of the feminine in both conventionally male- and female-gendered spaces. Therefore, women physically, symbolically, and metaphorically played an active role in daily and nightly practices. The serious challenge is to identify such intangible beliefs in the deep past without conflating them with the present.

CONCLUSIONS

Under the cover of the night, quotidian and technical performances unfolded, some of which were specific to the night but others of which carried over from the day. The timing of performances was critical to ensuring that life functioned properly. The fire, whether in the kitchen hut or at the dare, was a locus of sociocultural performances such as storytelling and rituals. Fire's link with heat, the ultimate source of transformation, made the fireplace in the hut, a space gendered as female, vital. Private and public, gender- and age-based performances took place during the night, with illumination from the fire or the moon. Spaces, places, and genders were fluid between performances and times of the day (day and night), such that, often, many boundaries were severally enforced, severally relaxed, and severally reinforced in a single day or night, depending on context.

Material culture is an indicator of cultural behaviors such as nightly practices. However, some of the material culture used during the night often was similar to that used during the day, while the context of use differed. A winnowing basket for grain processing during the day provided "transport" for witches during nocturnal ritual activities, while mortars were used as decoys in the same context. Pots and wooden plates used for nocturnal rituals during ancestor supplication were similar to those used for daytime activities. Furthermore, glass beads used during the day for ornamentation and bodily decoration were used as performance aids during sexual intercourse, an act that may have taken place at night. These changing meanings present significant challenges for archaeologists because the same objects, usually identified with the same name when used during the day, have different meanings when used during the night. As a locus of cultural performances, the night is a critical time segment that produced material culture. Therefore, it is incumbent upon archaeologists to attempt to explore in detail the archaeology of nightly practices.

REFERENCES

Aschwanden, Herbert. 1987. *Symbols of Death*. Gweru: Mambo Press.

Atkinson, Norman D. 1986. "Traditional African Stories as Learning Materials." *Zambezia: The Education* 5(Supplement):51–62.

Beach, David N. 1980. *The Shona and Zimbabwe 900–1850: An Outline of Shona History*. London: Heinemann.

Bourdillon, Michael F. 1976. *The Shona People: An Ethnography of the Contemporary Shona with Special Reference to their Religion*. Gweru: Mambo Press.

Bourdillon, Michael F. 1987. *The Shona People*. Gweru: Mambo Press.

Childs, S. Terry. 1991. "Style, Technology, and Iron Smelting Furnaces in Bantu-Speaking Africa." *Journal of Anthropological Archaeology* 10(4):332–359. https://doi.org/10.1016/0278-4165(91)90006-J.

Childs, S. Terry. 1999. "After all, a Hoe Bought a Wife: The Social Dimensions of Ironworking Among the Toro of East Africa." In *The Social Dynamics of Technology*, ed. Marcia-Anne Dobres and Christopher R. Hoffman, 23–45. Washington, DC: Smithsonian Institution Press.

Chirikure, Shadreck, Simon Hall, and Thilo Rehren. 2015. "When Ceramic Sociology Meets Material Science: Sociological and Technological Aspects of Crucibles and Pottery from Mapungubwe, Southern Africa." *Journal of Anthropological Archaeology* 40:23–32. https://doi.org/10.1016/j.jaa.2015.05.004.

Conkey, Margaret W., and Joan M. Gero. 1997. "Programme to Practice: Gender and Feminism in Archaeology." *Annual Review of Anthropology* 26(1):411–437. https://doi.org/10.1146/annurev.anthro.26.1.411.

Conkey, Margaret W., and Janet D. Spector. 1984. "Archaeology and the Study of Gender." *Advances in Archaeological Method and Theory* 7:1–38. https://doi.org/10.1016/B978-0-12-003107-8.50006-2.

Ellert, Henrick. 1984. *The Material Culture of Zimbabwe*. Harare: Longman.

Gelfand, Michael. 1956. *Medicine and Magic of the Mashona*. Cape Town: Juta.

Gelfand, Michael. 1962. *Shona Religion*. Cape Town: Juta.

Gelfand, Michael. 1973. *The Genuine Shona: Survival Values of an African Culture*. Gweru: Mambo Press.

Gombe, Jairos M. 1986. *Tsika Dzavashona*. Harare: College Press.

Greenfield, Haskel J., and Duncan Miller. 2004. "Spatial Patterning of Early Iron Age Metal Production at Ndondondwane, South Africa: The Question of Cultural Continuity between the Early and Late Iron Ages." *Journal of Archaeological Science* 31(11):1511–1532. https://doi.org/10.1016/j.jas.2004.03.014.

Hammond-Tooke, W. David. 1981. *Boundaries and Belief: The Structure of a Sotho Worldview*. Johannesburg: Witwatersrand University Press.

Hammond-Tooke, W. David. 1993. *The Roots of Black South Africa*. Johannesburg: Jonathan Ball Publishers.

Herbert, Eugenia W. 1993. *Iron, Gender, and Power: Rituals of Transformation in African Societies*. Bloomington: Indiana University Press.

Hodza, Aaron C. 1981. *Shona Registers*. Harare: Mercury Press.

Hodza, Aaron C. 1983. *Ngano Dzamatambidzanwa*. Gweru: Mambo Press.

Huffman, Thomas N. 2007. *Handbook to the Iron Age*. Pietermaritzburg: University of KwaZulu-Natal Press.

Huysecom, Eric, and Bernard Agustoni. 1997. "Inagina: l'ultime maison du fer/The Last House of Iron." Geneva: Telev. Suisse Romande. Videocassette, 54 min.

Insoll, Timothy. 2011. "Introduction: Shrines, Substances and Medicine in Sub-Saharan Africa: Archaeological, Anthropological, and Historical Perspectives." *Anthropology & Medicine* 18(2):145–166. https://doi.org/10.1080/13648470.2011.591193.

Kileff, Clive, ed. 1987. *Shona Folk Tales*. Gweru: Mambo Press.

Killick, David. 2009. "Agency, Dependency, and Long-distance Trade: East Africa and the Islamic World, ca. 700–1500 CE." In *Polities and Power: Archaeological Perspectives on the Landscapes of Early States*, ed. Steven E. Falconer and Charles L. Redman, 179–207. Tucson: University of Arizona Press.

Lane, Paul. 1994. "The Use and Abuse of Ethnography in the Study of the Southern African Iron Age." *Azania* 29–30(1):51–64. https://doi.org/10.1080/00672709409511661.

Lucas, Gavin. 2004. *The Archaeology of Time*. London: Routledge.

Mackenzie, John M. 1975. "A Pre-Colonial Industry: The Njanja and The Iron Trade." *NADA (Salisbury)* 11(2):200–220.

Mutasa, Davie E., Shumirai Nyota, and Jacob Mapara. 2008. "Ngano: Teaching Environmental Education using the Shona Folktale." *Journal of Pan African Studies* 2(3):33–54.

Ndoro, Weber. 1991. "Why Decorate Her." *Zimbabwea* 3(1):60–65.

Pikirayi, Innocent. 2002. *The Zimbabwe Culture: Origins and Decline of Southern Zambezian States*. Walnut Creek, CA: Altamira Press.

Reid, Andrew, and Rachel MacLean. 1995. "Symbolism and the Social Contexts of Iron Production in Karagwe." *World Archaeology* 27(1):144–161. https://doi.org/10.1080/00438243.1995.9980298.

Robinson, Keith Radcliff. 1959. *Khami Ruins*. Cambridge: Cambridge University Press.

Schiffer, Michael B. 1987. *Formation Processes of the Archaeological Record*. Albuquerque: University of New Mexico Press.

Schmidt, Peter R. 1997. *Iron Technology in East Africa: Symbolism, Science, and Archaeology*. Bloomington: Indiana University Press.

Schmidt, Peter R. 2009. "Tropes, Materiality, and Ritual Embodiment of African Iron Smelting Furnaces as Human Figures." *Journal of Archaeological Method and Theory* 16(3):262–282. https://doi.org/10.1007/s10816-009-9065-0.

Shoko, Tabona. 2009. "Komba: Girls' Initiation Rite and Enculturation among the VaRemba of Zimbabwe." *Studia Historiae Ecclesiasticae* 35(1):31–45.

Weiner, Annette B. 1985. "Inalienable Wealth." *American Ethnologist* 12(2):210–227. https://doi.org/10.1525/ae.1985.12.2.02a00020.

Wood, Marilee. 2012. *Interconnections: Glass Beads and Trade in Southern and Eastern Africa and the Indian Ocean—7th to 16th Centuries AD*. Department of Archaeology and Ancient History, Studies in Global Archaeology 17. Uppsala: Department of Archaeology and Ancient History, Uppsala University.

Wylie, Alison. 1985. "The Reaction Against Analogy." *Advances in Archaeological Method and Theory* 8:63–111. https://doi.org/10.1016/B978-0-12-003108-5.50008-7.

The Freedom that Nighttime Brings

Privacy and Cultural Creativity among Enslaved Peoples at Eighteenth- and Nineteenth-Century Bahamian Plantations

JANE EVA BAXTER

BAHAMIAN NIGHTTIME AND JUNKANOO

The Junkanoo Festival is among the most celebrated and iconic features of contemporary Bahamian Culture (Bethel 1991, 2000, 2003; Dean 1995; Ferguson 2000, 2003) (figure 1.2). Over the course of each year and in great secrecy, organized groups create costumes and props made from paper and wire in special locations known as "shacks," they practice call-and-response-style music of African origins using goatskin drums, cowbells, and brass instruments, and they prepare coordinated, choreographed dance routines (Ferguson 2000). In the middle of the night, at precisely 12:01 a.m. on Boxing Day (December 26) and again New Year's Day, the festival of Junkanoo begins, and a parade of costumed dancers and musicians roll down Bay Street performing their routines until the sun rises (figure 18.1). After the event, costumes are left out in the open air to decompose in the warm sun and tropical rains. Now a highly organized event with judges, sponsorship, and prizes, today's Junkanoo is a modern manifestation of a celebration with very deep historical roots.

DOI: 10.5876/9781607326786.c018

FIGURE 18.1. *Bahamian Junkanoo celebration on December 26, 2003, in Nassau. (Photo by ebrodie; licensed under Creative Commons, https://commons.wikimedia.org/wiki/File:Junkanoo.jpg)*

When the Bahamian scholar and educator Arlene Nash Ferguson wrote her book on the annual Junkanoo festival (Ferguson 2000), she wove historical insights into a plausible narrative for the origins of this important event. Enslaved peoples, who had been brought to the Bahamas carrying only intangible culture, had limited outlets in their day-to-day lives to express memory, culture, and identity. The three days off given to enslaved people at Christmastime offered time and distance to remember, to enact, and to create, and in that time, to celebrate freedom, personhood, and self. Darkness and nighttime figured quite prominently into her narrative. In an abbreviated account, Ferguson (2003, 96–99) wrote:

> And so you steal away into the Bahamian bush under cover of night to reclaim yourself. You have come from too many places in Africa and are too diverse to reestablish all of the conditions of your homelands, but you now have the opportunity to reconcile reality with the past. Here, now, is the opportunity to reclaim abandoned aspects of your culture, albeit modified. It is an exercise in freedom, and you assemble your weapons.
>
> You are aided and encouraged by the protective folds of the darkness. The familiar drumming patterns echo the once familiar natural rhythms of nature. The fire

brings light to the darkness, and the promise of new life. The masking and costuming disguise the present reality, and provide the opportunity to transform, conceal. The dance unleashes the power within, and the camaraderie of forbidden associations shore up the soul for the all too swift return to the harsh reality.

This narrative of Junkanoo is a powerful starting place for thinking about nighttime on Bahamian plantations in the late eighteenth and early nineteenth centuries (figure 1.3). Junkanoo or "Johnny/John Canoe" was once more widespread with reported occurrences in nineteenth-century North Carolina, Belize, and Jamaica (Ferguson 2000). Junkanoo in the Bahamas, with the exception of an imposed hiatus by British authorities in the mid-twentieth century, is unique, as it has been an unbroken tradition dating back to at least 1801 (Dean 1995; Ferguson 2000). Junkanoo also has strong, well-established West African roots, and is clearly an amalgamation of many different African cultural traditions that became uniquely combined in the context of Bahamian slavery (Bethel 2003; Dean 1995; Ferguson 2000).

Despite this longstanding tradition, there is a kind of historical darkness around the festival. There are vague, brief, and irregular mentions of Johnny/John Canoe in the newspapers in the capital city of Nassau dating back to 1801 (Bethel 1991; Dean 1995). More specific references are quite rare, such as a mention in the *Nassau Guardian* in December 1864 that there was "no Christmas pantomime" that year (Sands 2003, 14). This historical silence and misnaming of the event in a newspaper founded in 1844 primarily for the island's white community speaks to the secrecy and privacy of these proceedings.

Early in the twentieth century, these same newspapers report on Junkanoo with a bit more frequency, but with a clear outsider's perspective. An editorial that ran in the *Tribune* on January 3, 1911, quipped, "the New Year holiday was heralded early on Monday morning by the customary noise of horns, bells, and drums, and the grotesque masqueraders disported themselves along Bay Street with an energy and vigour which if put into their pursuit of their avocations during the year will be to some purpose" (Bethel 1991). Outside the Afro-Bahamian community it is clear that Junkanoo was little known, not well understood, and not highly regarded in the nineteenth and early twentieth centuries. Despite this metaphorical historical darkness, the materials and traditions of Junkanoo have been passed down through generations of Afro-Bahamians and are a powerful form of indigenous history and symbols of freedom—not enslavement. As Stan Burnside said (in Bethel 2003, 121), "Bahamians were never slaves, because of Junkanoo."

In addition to its deep history and African origins, Junkanoo is traditionally a festival of nighttime. Current debates about the modern Junkanoo festival pit the traditionalists against more progressive forces seeking to expand Junkanoo events, and one of the key areas of debate is the essential element of nighttime.

For many, and traditionally, Junkanoo is not Junkanoo unless it takes place after dark (Bethel 2003, 125).

THEORIZING NIGHTTIME IN THE CONTEXT OF SLAVERY

Even with Junkanoo as a point of departure, the nature of nighttime on nine-teenth-century Bahamian plantations exists primarily in the realm of theory. While we know nighttime happened, the absence of any particular, identifiable technologies devoted to nighttime, such as devices or features made exclusively to provide light in the darkness (see Church, chapter 5; Strong, chapter 12; and McGuire, chapter 13, this volume), makes the dividing of spaces, places, and activities into nocturnal and diurnal a task that extends well beyond material certainty. It is this very ambiguity about nighttime that makes this Junkanoo narrative particularly significant.

It is not unusual to think of nighttime as a naturally occurring cover for things deemed transgressive, clandestine, or forbidden by cultural norms, legal con-structs, or social obligations (see Gonlin and Dixon, chapter 3; Coltman, chapter 10; and Chirikure and Moffett, chapter 17, this volume). Polly Wiessner (2014) has provided convincing evidence that social relations, narrative styles, and interactive forms become altered in darkness and by firelight. In the context of slavery, it is easy to see how nighttime offered a cover for all types of activities, including extreme events such as escape or rebellion, to more mundane activi-ties prohibited by slave owners as a means of control. Historical accounts of the famous 1831 Southampton Insurrection in Virginia emphasize how Nat Turner's organization of the rebellion occurred through conversations, meetings, and movements after dark (Kaye 2007). Other sources from the United States report that the religious practices that helped inform and empower slave resistance and rebellion were also common nighttime activities (Rucker 2001). This idea of nighttime as a time and space of resistance is relevant and poignant, but also somewhat limiting.

The Junkanoo narrative is not just one of resistance and transgression but also one of cultural creativity, ethnogenesis, and memory practice where identi-ties and meanings were shaped and formed through intentional and deliberate actions. Theorizing nighttime as when activities defined as forbidden by planters could be undertaken, limits the interpretive possibility that enslaved communi-ties had their own cultural knowledge, rituals, and agendas that they did not want to share with those outside the community. Darkness in such a context is not just a way of taking part in things deemed forbidden, but also for keeping the intangible heritage of a community away from others. Hiding activities at night to avoid punishment or repercussion is very different from keeping things hidden to protect their integrity and sanctity. The first emphasizes reaction, the second creation and agency.

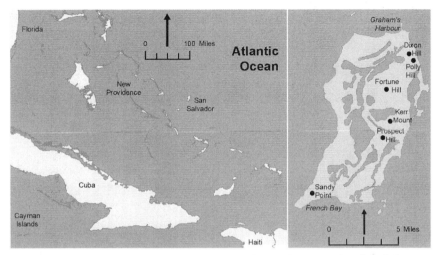

FIGURE 18.2. *The Bahamian island of San Salvador, showing locations of excavated planta-*
tion sites and those mentioned in the documentary record for the island. This map gives a
sense of distances that could have been traveled in a single day on the island. For example, we
know people from Prospect Hill regularly made round trip journeys to Dixon Hill and occa-
sionally to French Bay or Graham's Harbor in a single day. Others traveled from Sandy Point
to Polly Hill in the same time. (Map by Christopher Milan)

This understanding of nighttime inspired by the particularly Bahamian tradition of Junkanoo offers a way to reconsider the lives of enslaved peoples on
plantations in the Bahamas. Using the case study of the island of San Salvador,
three lines of evidence are combined here to consider the possibilities of nighttime activities taking place in the early nineteenth century, and to illustrate the
broader implications for those activities when considering the archaeological
and historical records. First, plantation landscapes are considered in terms of
affordances particular to nighttime that might have enabled independent activities on the part of enslaved peoples. Second, the documentary record is analyzed
for information that offers insights into nighttime activities. Finally, ethnographic
information about lighting the darkness is presented to illustrate potential plantation-period technologies that would have facilitated nighttime activities.

SELECT BACKGROUND ON THE NINETEENTH-CENTURY BAHAMAS

It is essential to begin with some background on the Bahamas in the nineteenth
century, because these islands have a unique history when compared to other
island colonies in the region. The Bahama Archipelago (figure 18.2) was very
sparsely populated until the arrival of the British Loyalists in the 1780s shortly
after the American Revolution. The influx of Loyalists and their slaves from the

new American nation almost doubled the population of the colony and tripled the population of enslaved peoples. The Loyalists also brought with them a different sensibility toward race relations, and what had been a largely integrated community was transformed into one of residential and social segregation (Craton and Saunders 1992).

The Loyalists created new settlements on previously uninhabited islands in the archipelago, including San Salvador. Initially, the Loyalists tried to replicate the economy of the mainland United States by establishing cotton plantations, but within a decade or two the plantation system collapsed due to soil erosion and infestations by agricultural pests. Although salt-raking continued in the southern Bahamas, by the early nineteenth century most enslaved peoples were no longer working in cash-crop agriculture, but rather were expending much of their labor on subsistence farming, either on their own or alongside their masters (Craton and Saunders 1992).

The collapse of the plantation system led most planters to return to Nassau from the outer islands, leaving management of their plantations and slaves to slave overseers. These planters took up mercantile and professional positions in the capital city, and took little if any direct interest in their Out Island plantations. The few planters who remained on the outer islands actively engaged in economic activities tied to their own subsistence, with very little commerce transpiring with Nassau (Burton 2006).

Although no demographic record was kept of the slaves brought by the Loyalists, it is known that the mainland population from which they were drawn had undergone a period of creolization, and by the end of the Revolution, only about 20% of the mainland slaves were African born. The abolition of the slave trade in 1807 did bring new people from Africa into the colony with some regularity as slave ships were captured and passengers relocated to safety, but most of these free populations were concentrated on the island of New Providence. The sex ratio of enslaved people seems to have been evenly balanced, allowing for family formation where families did not already exist, and the population of enslaved people grew rapidly through natural increase, at a higher rate than for whites in the early nineteenth century. Overall, most Bahamian slaves were healthy; disease was not widespread in the nineteenth century. With a generally healthy climate and easy access to seafood, especially conch, even slaves on relatively poor plantations had a better diet than those on the US mainland or on the sugar-producing islands of the West Indies. Moreover, slaves continued to live in relatively small units of fewer than forty, more like the tobacco plantations in the southern United States than the sugar islands elsewhere in the Caribbean.

Bahamian slavery, therefore, contrasted sharply with the Caribbean in general; although still unjust and morally corrupt, it was less harsh than its counterparts in other parts of the Americas. In addition, the Amelioration Acts, passed by the

British Parliament in the 1820s, gave slaves more legal protection than in the United States during the same period. As Emancipation neared in 1834, many slaves on the outer islands had far greater autonomy than slaves on mainland American plantations, as white planters moved to Nassau, or left the Bahamas completely (Craton and Saunders 1992; Johnson 1996). On San Salvador, only two plantations had white owners in residence at the time of emancipation, with the rest of the plantations being overseen by slaves, or having renters or agents overseeing the property.

PLANTATION LANDSCAPES AND NIGHTTIME AFFORDANCES

At least eight plantations, and most likely a greater number, were established on the island of San Salvador between 1780 and 1834. Five of these plantations have been the subject of archaeological study (Baxter 2015; Baxter and Burton 2006, 2011; Baxter, Burton and Wekenmann 2009; Gerace 1982, 1987) and the landscapes and material culture of these sites are among the best documented for the period on the islands. Unlike prehistoric sites, which were predominantly coastal, Loyalist planters built their plantations on high ridges that afforded the best access to breezes for cooling and insect control, mimicked design choices elsewhere in the Caribbean and mainland United States, and offered access to the inland lakes that made the transportation of goods to port easier than overland routes (figure 18.2). The outer islands of the Bahamas are generally small and were not regularly connected to one another through shipping traffic. As such, there was little concern that enslaved peoples would be able to escape, and features for surveillance were more symbolic than practical qualities of landscape design.

Most, but not all of these plantations had slave quarters or a yard with individual houses and provisioning fields for use by the enslaved (figure 18.3). All had some residential structures for enslaved peoples, and slave registers for the period indicate that they were living in nuclear families in single- or multigenerational households (Burton 2004; Craton and Saunders 1992). These domestic areas were separated from the planters' and overseers' residences by a significant distance (figure 18.3) and the built environment created visual barriers that afforded mutual privacy to the residents of the slave quarter and planter household alike.

Plantation soundscapes, particularly for the consideration of privacy, were tested during archaeological investigations at Polly Hill and Prospect Hill Plantations and during site visits to Sandy Point Plantation (figure 18.2). For these tests, small groups were dispatched to both the planter residence and slave quarters of the plantation. Noisemaking episodes were coordinated using two-way radios, and each group took turns producing sounds of different volumes and types (e.g., singing, talking, work-related noises occurring both inside and outside of buildings) while the other group noted whether those sounds carried to the other location. These experiments were conducted using different prevailing winds, and it was found that one could engage in normal conversation and in many

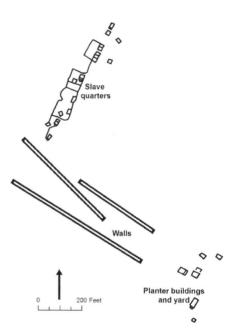

FIGURE 18.3. *The plantation landscape at Prospect Hill Plantation, representative of plantation layouts on the island, where the structures designed for use by the planter/overseer and family and the enslaved population were separated by distance and often physical barriers such as walls. (Map by Christopher Milan)*

cases loud conversation without being overhead. These experiments suggest that if one were to be intentionally quiet, conversation and activity taking place in one residential area of the plantation would not be overhead in the other.

It is useful to think of these plantation landscapes and soundscapes in the context of affordances (Gibson 1977, 1979; Aveni, chapter 7, this volume). Kamp and Whittaker (chapter 4, this volume) illustrate how sensory perceptions and landscape affordances are altered at nighttime, and how darkness offers both limitations and possibilities for actions and interactions. In the case of Bahamian plantations, the possibility of independent, undetected movement and activity was enabled by the nature of the landscape. While planters' houses were located on high points on the landscape to a panoptical effect, the darkness of nighttime would have negated this limited advantage in elevation for oversight. The separation of spaces both in both visual and auditory realms offered a reasonable degree of privacy at nighttime and opportunities for activity by enslaved peoples that would have been undetected and unrecorded by the planters or overseers.

NIGHTTIME IN HISTORICAL SOURCES

Historical sources for the island of San Salvador are quite sparse. Because of the archipelagic nature of the then-colony and the circumstances that concentrated the white planter class in Nassau, very little was written about the Bahamas outside of New Providence (Craton and Saunders 1992; Saunders 2002). Annual reports made by Island Commissioners were based on visits lasting less than one week a year, and were focused primarily on institutions managed on behalf of the colonial government.

San Salvador does have two exceptional sources that shed some light on the island during the nineteenth century. The first is the UNESCO World Heritage Document, "A Relic of Slavery," commonly known as "Farquharson's Journal." This journal details the daily events of nearly two full years at Prospect Hill Plantation (figures 18.2 and 18.3) as reported by its owner, Charles Farquharson, in the years leading up to emancipation (Farquharson 1957). The second source is the testimony of several island residents after the murder of an enslaved person by his slave overseer at Sandy Point Plantation in 1833 (figure 18.2). This record is a very rare instance in which depositions were taken from enslaved people as well as planters and overseers, allowing for a particularly complex and nuanced view of the events at the time (Burton 2004). Farquharson's Journal establishes patterns for the day-to-day operations of a plantation, and the sworn testimony gives very specific details of a few exceptional days of plantation life. The two sources complement one another well, and while they do emphasize daytime activities and are written from the perspective of an island planter and the courts in Nassau, they also provide meaningful insights for a study of nighttime.

These two sources report that enslaved people worked six days a week on tasks defined and assigned by others, with Sundays being left unscheduled. Under manumissions laws, this day off allowed slaves to work their own provisioning fields, care for their own homes and yards, and make and repair clothing and other household items. This consistent scheduling and demanding workload suggests that many activities, including numerous social, ritual, and communal activities, quite often would have been deferred to nighttime hours.

These sources also indicate that enslaved people and planters traveled among plantations during daylight hours, and that round trips between plantations were made in a single day (figure 18.2). For enslaved peoples, these trips were made primarily for cooperative day labor during times of harvest, but also for sanctioned social events such as the funeral for a member of their community (Farquharson 1957). For planters, day trips allowed for socializing among members of a very small group of individuals comprising the "planter class" on the island. It was a rare and notable occurrence for people to stay somewhere on the island other than their own home. Charles Farquharson specifically notes the very unusual event of his son James and two of his "hands" staying at French Bay when a ship was in port.

Perhaps most significant, on December 26, 1832, Charles Farquharson penned the following in his journal: "Some of our people gon abroad to see some of their friends and some at home amusing themselves in their own way threw the day, but all of them at home in the evening and had a grad dance and keep it up until near daylight." This passage, referring to the "gra[n]d dance" taking place until near daylight on Boxing Day is considered by many to be a reference to Junkanoo at Prospect Hill Plantation (Bethel 1991; Dean 1995; Ferguson 2000). It certainly is a unique depiction of nighttime revelry among the enslaved peoples for the two years reported in the journal, and is an exceptional description of plantation life for the Bahamas as a whole.

A RELIC OF NIGHTTIME TECHNOLOGY: LIGHTING THE DARKNESS

There is a remnant technology of nighttime still in use on San Salvador that may have its roots in the plantation period. The contemporary population of San Salvador has shifted to four primary locations along the Queen's Highway that rings the island (figure 18.2). Residents venture into the island's interior (known colloquially as "the bush") for two main reasons. The first is to access plantains, bananas, and other crops that grow in depressions in the limestone bedrock called "banana holes." These holes and the plants that grow in them are understood to be the possession of individual island residents, and such ownership is commonly respected without official enforcement. The second is to seasonally hunt land crabs, an activity that takes place only at night during the summer. While the locations of people's banana holes are well known, spots for crabbing are among the most carefully guarded secrets of island residents.

While flashlights are widely available, they are not considered by many to be the appropriate technology for crabbing. Emptied beer bottles are filled with slow burning oil and a cloth wick that is lit and carried into the bush. These lights look like very slow burning Molotov cocktails and provide a dim but efficient and steady light. Elderly island residents (80+ years old) remembered using these same lights as children and considered them to be a technology that comes from even earlier generations. This technology also uses materials that would have been readily available to island residents in the nineteenth and early twentieth centuries. This traditional form of lighting is considered both "lucky" for hunting crabs and a superior light for attracting and mesmerizing the crabs for capture. They also do not give off as much ambient light as flashlights, and help keep an individual's crabbing activities a secret from others who might be out in the bush. Discarded bottle lights are a common discovery on archaeological surveys of the island's interior.

CONCLUSIONS: RETHINKING SAN SALVADOR'S
PLANTATIONS AS NIGHTTIME SPACES

This chapter has covered a great deal of ground combining the Bahamian festival of Junkanoo with plantation landscapes, the documentary record, and finally the use of traditional objects in contemporary Out Island practices. In essence, this combination of sources creates a structure to understand the potential means, motives, and opportunities for nocturnal activities on Bahamian plantations during the nineteenth century.

Plantation landscapes were not designed to duplicate the island's own effect of keeping populations in place, and instead afforded a degree of autonomy and privacy to both the few planters and overseers on the island and the much larger enslaved population. While current analyses of daytime activities on these plantations emphasize the differential use of plantation landscapes by planters and enslaved peoples (Chapman 2010; Delle 2000; Epperson 1999), further analysis illustrates that nighttime significantly changed these landscape dynamics. These landscapes offered the opportunity for enslaved peoples to interact without being overseen or overheard in the darkness, and therefore presented the possibility of unscheduled time at night to be used for interactions and actions that could be kept secret within the confines of the slave community.

Evidence for daytime round-trip travel across long distances indicates it also would have been possible for enslaved peoples to have moved among plantations for their own purposes at night, unbeknownst to their overseers. Pathways and landscape features used during the daytime would have provided a somewhat familiar setting for nighttime movements, particularly if technologies for portable illumination were in use.

This awareness of how nighttime altered the affordances of the island landscape and the likely presence of technologies to illuminate the darkness forces a reconsideration of the social lives of enslaved peoples on San Salvador during the nineteenth century. In both history and archaeology, the analytical unit of the plantation has dominated scholarship. Slave registers record plantation demographics for individual plantations and have become the analytical basis for historical thinking. The site boundaries of individual plantations define and guide archaeological research. These analytical patterns have been based on the presumption that enslaved people's lives were largely restricted to their own plantation, and their social interactions and physical mobility were constrained by owners and overseers. Recognizing that the same round trips made during the daytime could also be made in silence and darkness at night, offers the possibility of entire new social worlds and interactions that took place away from individual plantations and instead at intermediate places on the landscape. These places may have been physically ephemeral and therefore archaeologically invisible, but would have had ramifications for the social structures and relationships on individual plantations during the daytime as well.

The Bahamian festival of Junkanoo is illustrative of the types of social and ritual connections that can be made during nighttime that transcend into daytime worlds and into the days, weeks, and months between nighttime gatherings. Many of these connections have no direct material manifestations, but have profound social and psychological consequences for those participating in Junkanoo.

However, while Junkanoo is in many ways a celebration of intangible culture and heritage, it is also deeply connected to the material world and offers guidance for rethinking archaeological evidence from plantations.

There is archaeological evidence for rituals at many plantation sites during the plantation and post-plantation periods. Tableaus of ship graffiti in a singular motif are found across the Bahama Archipelago and are a material manifestation of traditional knowledge being shared among the communities of these islands (Baxter 2010). Excavations at slave residences have revealed carved shell, animal jawbones, ochre, and other items stashed under the foundations and floors. These types of ritual activities are both widespread and localized, and may represent a type of shared cultural knowledge created and affirmed by connections made at nighttime. Similarities in ritual expression among individual plantations have often been attributed to a shared African heritage, but it has not been understood as having connections to contemporaneous ritual practices involving community members from multiple plantations.

Ceramic distributions at San Salvador plantation sites are typified by a pattern on which a single ceramic ware is well represented at a single site and is found in very small quantities (one or two sherds) at one or more of the other plantations (Baxter 2015). This distribution pattern has typically been interpreted as a result of the means of acquisition and distribution of goods from Nassau by the planters. These mechanisms include the practice of shipping mixed-crate ceramics to outer islands (Wilkie and Farnsworth 1999) or, in the case of a single family on San Salvador, having the funds and connections to purchase and distribute ceramics and other goods and across the island. However, this pattern may also be material evidence for social connections among enslaved peoples at various plantations, where pieces of broken ceramics common in one household or plantation community were shared with those at others to symbolize clandestine relationships, affirm connections among the broader community, and provide material reminders of events and activities that transpired intermittently in the lives of enslaved people.

Junkanoo may have been an annual celebration, but it is also a historical practice that calls us to be mindful of how nighttime afforded opportunities for enslaved populations across the Bahama Archipelago. The ability to move in the night undetected in silence and darkness, to meet with people from across the island, and to transform spaces undefined by plantation economies, owners, and overseers create a powerful reimagining of the Bahamian past. Such a perspective offers a potent way to theorize processes of ethnogenesis, identity formation, and memory practice for a population at a time when the daytime was not their own, and to rethink the material worlds of plantations as simultaneously bound and shaped by economic forces and transcended by social and ritual connections made under cover of darkness.

ACKNOWLEDGMENTS

First, I want to thank Nan Gonlin and April Nowell for the invitation to participate in this project. Thinking about plantations on San Salvador at nighttime has been an exercise in creative and analytical thinking that has enriched my perspective on sites I thought I knew quite thoroughly. I am indebted to Meg Conkey, Polly Wiessner, and fellow volume participants whose work and commentary has helped improve my own contribution greatly. Archaeological fieldwork for this project was codirected by Dr. John D. Burton, relied on laboratory analysis led by Susan Wiard, and involved dozens of students from DePaul University over a series of field seasons. Funding for portions of this research was provided by the DePaul University Research Council and the College of Liberal Arts and Social Sciences. I am grateful to my many Bahamian colleagues who support this research, including those from the Antiquities Museums and Monuments Corporation, the College of the Bahamas, the Department of Archives, and the Gerace Research Centre. Finally, a very special thanks to my friend Arlene Nash Ferguson whose telling of the Junkanoo story has inspired my thinking and stirred my soul for years—I am grateful for this opportunity to bring our worlds of Junkanoo and archaeology together in this narrative.

REFERENCES

Baxter, Jane Eva. 2010. "A Different Way of Seeing: Casting Children as Cultural Actors in Archaeological Interpretations." In ¡Eso no se toca! Infancia y cultura material en arqueología, ed. Marga Sanchez-Romero. Complutum 21(2):181–196.

Baxter, Jane Eva. 2015. "A Comparative View of San Salvador's Plantations." In Proceedings of the Fifteenth Symposium on the Natural History of the Bahamas, ed. Ron Morrison and Robert Erdman, 99–108 San Salvador: Gerace Research Centre.

Baxter, Jane Eva, and John D. Burton. 2006. "Building Meaning into the Landscape: Building Design and Use at Polly Hill Plantation, San Salvador, Bahamas." Journal of the Bahamas Historical Society 28:35–44.

Baxter, Jane Eva, and John D. Burton. 2011. "Farquharson's Plantation Revisited: New Historical and Archaeological Insights from Two Seasons at Prospect Hill." Journal of the Bahamas Historical Society 33:17–26.

Baxter, Jane Eva, John D. Burton, and Marcus Wekenmann. 2009. "Kerr Mount: The Archaeological Record of a Plantation-Period Plantation." Journal of the Bahamas Historical Society 31:31–42.

Bethel, E. Clement. 1991. Junkanoo: Festival of the Bahamas. London: MacMillan Education LTD.

Bethel, Nicolette. 2000. "Navigations: The Fluidity of National Identity in the Post-Colonial Bahamas." PhD diss., Cambridge University.

Bethel, Nicolette. 2003. "Junkanoo in the Bahamas: A Tale of Identity." In *Junkanoo and Religion: Christianity and Cultural Identity in the Bahamas*, ed. Jessica Minnis, 118–130. Nassau: College of the Bahamas.

Burton, John D. 2004. "The American Loyalists, Slaves, and the Creation of an Afro-Bahamian World: Sandy Point Plantation and the Prince Storr Murder Case." *Journal of The Bahamas Historical Society* 26:13–22.

Burton, John D. 2006. "'A Tierra Incognita': Life on Post-Emancipation San Salvador." *Journal of the Bahamas Historical Society Volume* 28: 1–11.

Chapman, William. 2010. "White and Black Landscapes in Eighteenth-Century Virginia." In *Cabin, Quarter, Plantation*, ed. Clifton Ellis and Rebecca Ginsburg, 121–140. New Haven, CT: Yale University Press.

Craton, Michael, and Gail D. Saunders. 1992. *Islanders in the Stream: A History of the Bahamian People*. vol. 1. Athens: University of Georgia Press.

Dean, Lisa Carol. 1995. "Preserving Junkanoo: A Traditional Festival of Music and Culture." *Journal of the Bahamas Historical Society* 17:11–22.

Delle, James. 2000. "Gender, Power, and Space: Negotiating Social Relations under Slavery on Coffee Plantations in Jamaica, 1790–1834." In *Lines That Divide: Historical Archaeologies of Race, Class, and Gender*, ed. James Delle, Steven. Mrozowski, and Robert Paynter, 168–201. Knoxville: University of Tennessee Press.

Epperson, Terrence. 1999. "Constructing Difference: The Social and Spatial Order of the Chesapeake Plantation." In *"I, Too, Am America": Archaeological Studies of African American Life*, ed. Theresa Singleton, 159–172. Charlotte: University Press of Virginia.

Farquharson, Charles. 1957. *A Relic of Slavery: Farquharson's Journal 1831–32*. Nassau: The Deans Peggs Research Fund.

Ferguson, Arlene Nash. 2000. *I Come to Get Me: An Inside Look at the Junkanoo Festival*. Nassau: Doongalik Studios.

Ferguson, Arlene Nash. 2003. "The Symbolism of Junkanoo." In *Junkanoo and Religion: Christianity, and Cultural Identity in the Bahamas*, ed. Jessica Minnis, 95–99. Nassau: College of the Bahamas.

Gerace, Kathy. 1982. "Three Loyalist Plantations on San Salvador, Bahamas." *Florida Anthropologist* 35(4):216–222.

Gerace, Kathy. 1987. "Early Nineteenth Century Plantations on San Salvador, Bahamas: The Archaeological Record." *Journal of The Bahamas Historical Society* 9(1):22–26.

Gibson, James J. 1977. "The Theory of Affordances." In *Perceiving, Acting, and Knowing*, ed. R. Shaw and J. Bransford, 67–82. New York: Lawrence Erlbaum.

Gibson, James J. 1979. *The Ecological Approach to Visual Perception*. New York: Houghton Mifflin.

Johnson, Howard. 1996. *The Bahamas: From Slavery to Servitude, 1783–1933*. Gainesville: University of Florida Press.

Kaye, Anthony E., and the Kaye Anthony E. 2007. "Neighborhoods and Nat Turner: The Making of a Slave Rebel and the Unmaking of a Slave Rebellion." *Journal of the Early Republic* 27(4):705–720. https://doi.org/10.1353/jer.2007.0076.

Rucker, Walter. 2001. "Conjure, Magic, and Power: The Influence of Afro-Atlantic Religious Practices on Slave Resistance and Rebellion." *Journal of Black Studies* 32(1):84–103. https://doi.org/10.1177/002193470103200105.

Sands, Kirkley C. 2003. "Junkanoo in Historical Perspective." In *Junkanoo and Religion: Christianity, and Cultural Identity in the Bahamas*, ed. Jessica Minnis, 10–19. Nassau: College of the Bahamas.

Saunders, Gail. 2002. "Slavery and Cotton Culture in the Bahamas." In *Slavery without Sugar: Diversity in Caribbean Economy and Society Since the 17th Century*, ed. Verne Shepherd, 129–151. Gainesville: University Press of Florida.

Wiessner, Polly W. 2014. "Embers of Society: Firelight Talk among the Ju/'hoansi Bushmen." *Proceedings of the National Academy of Sciences of the United States of America* 111(39):14027–14035. https://doi.org/10.1073/pnas.1404212111.

Wilkie, Laurie, and Paul Farnsworth. 1999. "Trade and the Construction of Bahamian Identity: A Multiscalar Exploration." *International Journal of Historical Archaeology* 3(4):283–320. https://doi.org/10.1023/A:1022850626022.

Concluding the Night

Afterword

A Portal to a More Imaginative Archaeology

MARGARET CONKEY

These chapters and the symposium sessions that generated them give us a most welcome trajectory for an archaeology that can push beyond its own borders and often times self-imposed limitations. Our editors have provided us with both an introduction to and a thematic overview of the stimulating and original chapters that have come up with an array of topics, contexts, data, and interpretations that would challenge those who might have said "How can you know *that?*" about an archaeology of the night. Fortunately, that question has been asked often and responded to often in archaeology, and this is no exception to a veritable panoply of surprises and "Ah ha" moments that have resulted. As with several other "How can you know *that?*" projects with which I have been associated over the decades (e.g., Gero and Conkey 1991; Schmidt and Voss 2000), the resultant chapters here bear the imprint of thoughtful revision, recalibration, and reworkings in a domain that has no immediate precedents. This is hard revision work, but the results are rewarding, not just to the authors or other participants but to a much-enriched archaeological enterprise. There are numerous concepts and nodal connections that this inquiry into the night implicates and

DOI: 10.5876/9781607326786.c019

there is a kind of "work" that night-thinking does for archaeology. If ambitious enough, one could generate a "mind map" for where this work takes us, but, for now, just a few possible observations will have to do.

Most people, and even archaeologists, have never thought there might be an archaeology of the night, much less that there could be archaeological "signatures" of the night. Does the darkness we associate with the night translate into a darkness of knowledge? Are we so strongly enmeshed in an epistemology of the primacy of "seeing" (Ong 1977; Jay 1993)? Do most of us live in such an electrified world until we decide to sleep that we have not thought about activities in the dark—or the variously lit-up night? That there are no traces in or of the dark? It suddenly seems so obvious that many activities are carried out in both daylight and the night and that there are, as so many chapters demonstrate, specific activities *for* the night, activities that leave as much archaeological evidence as daylight activities do and that, furthermore, can enrich and expand what we infer about daytime itself. The project of this volume is a powerful suggestion: to ask us to think again about our archaeological areas and materials through the framework of an archaeology of the night or an archaeology of the dark! One stands in admiration for the editors who managed to find so many smart scholars who were willing to "think through again" and/or who were already engaging with dimensions of an archaeology of the night.

In fact, this is one of the important nodes in a "thought map" for archaeology that this volume highlights, namely, by questioning the centrality of vision as a dominant sense, some authors are making an important intervention into an archaeology that has not (until quite recently, e.g., Hamilakis 2013) been attuned to or engaged with senses other than the visual and usually it is *OUR* visual: what can we, as archaeologists, "see"? Where is the tangible, visible even touchable evidence that an overly empiricist archaeology continues to demand, though in much muted form? This archaeology of the night project then provides a key and important focus on a multisensorial archaeology; in fact, this is a strong intervention into whatever a multisensorial archaeology can be. It pushes it toward not just a different subfield of archaeology, but all of the chapters are asking what kind of archaeology emerges if we approach it from the multisensorial perspective, doing archaeology as a multisensorial practice (Tringham, pers. comm., December 2016). We read of several compelling examples here of how navigating one's self in the night and in a dark (or less well-lit, or differentially lit) context makes for powerful embodied experiences, different embodied experiences. We are reminded that learning to navigate in the dark or the semi-lit is indeed something to learn and experience; it reminds us of the power of liminal experiences and makes these essays an anthropology of liminality in a way that is different from the classic anthropological treatises (e.g., Turner 1967; Van Gennep 1960), if only because what we learn about here is a much more expansive notion of liminality, more than primarily "rites of passage" but actions and practices often woven into the very fabric of everyday life. In fact, these studies open up the inquiry into the centrality of liminality in human life: we learn about activities that are structured "as if it were night," even if it is not night outside. And we are reminded as well of the association between night activities and such cultural phenomena as smoky intoxication, night witches, "other worlds," other bodily and cognitive states, and an other embodied person. Further, the question is even raised: is night gendered? And not just because there may well have been certain night activities for certain engendered persona?

The readers of these chapters should have their very understandings of the way in which "light" works in human life expanded. We learn about the night technologies, how some practices actually require "the night" (e.g., star-based timekeeping), about the technologies of light, ranging from fire and ways to capture it (e.g., torches, lamps, ceramic braziers), how natural phenomena such as lightning at night may be culturally understood and used, to sophisticated props to reveal and conceal. In many instances, we learn that technologies of and for the night are much more than techniques and objects, but are themselves part of integral metaphors and practices: night is to be embraced and not avoided. And if ever an important dimension to archaeological inquiry, archaeoastronomy, needed yet another way in which to demonstrate its potential to enhance our archaeological understandings, an archaeology of the night is it.

While a recent New Yorker cartoon elicits our usual amusement when it depicts several purportedly "prehistoric" people running across the landscape, chasing, it appears, the sun so low in the sky, calling out "come back, come back," we are also moved to note that this underestimates both the longstanding human understandings of the day-and-night cycles, and does not allow for the rich world of life after dark, a dark that can, yes, hide and conceal, but can also enlighten, reveal, establish connections with other worlds, spirits, and reaffirm cultural knowledge and practice. I am moved to bring in a particular ethnographic example that has several "lessons" for us. It is a description (Ray 1963) of a Klamath-Modoc (California/Oregon group) of a curing ceremony (making it clear that it was something that took place only at night):

> The first spirit to be called gained no precedence, but was thus honored as a strong spirit. Frog was perhaps the most frequent choice for the initial call. The logic of the selection was this: most illnesses are caused by an intrusive object; food is the commonest means of entry; and Frog is a keen analyst of foods. Or if Lightning were chosen: the task is to find the source and nature of this illness, the possibilities are many, but Lightning makes the night as bright as day and spreads everywhere. Surely Lightning can help. (Ray 1963)

That is, Lightning illuminates the night sky and thus helps to see the spirits, to see their medicine. And Lightning, as it happens, is made material in the form of what we would call a "zigzag" design in Klamath-Modoc rock art, rock art that on many grounds is associated with, and the recognized work of, the curers or shamans (David 2010). In the chapters in this volume, there is much lightning that allows us to not only "see in the dark" (ouch, again there is that visuality epistemology!) but to see that the dark can have its illuminations and revelations that often have their own materialities.

So, in the end, there is only a beginning, and we can make our list of the archaeological themes that have emerged—perhaps unexpectedly?—from the query into an archaeology of the night. The portal opens to new ways to engage with such core and crucial archaeological topics and subjects: into liminality, gendered times and spaces, the transformative experiences of human life, embodiment, the multisensorial, the experiential, the strategic, the reorienting of lives, the changed affordances, the cosmologically potent, the hidden that is simultaneously revelatory, and into memory and practice. What more could we ask for in pushing archaeology into a more imaginative inquiry and practice. Bravo to the editors and contributors! What's up next?

REFERENCES

David, Robert J. 2010. "The Archaeology of Myth: Rock Art, Ritual Objects and Mythical Landscapes of the Klamath Basin." *Archaeologies* 6(2):372–400. https://doi.org/10.1007/s11759-009-9108-x.

Gero, Joan, and Margaret Conkey, eds. 1991. *Engendering Archaeology: Women and Prehistory*. Oxford: Basil Blackwell Publishers.

Hamilakis, Yannis, ed. 2013. *Archaeology and the Senses: Human Experience, Memory and Affect*. Cambridge: Cambridge University Press. https://doi.org/10.1017/CBO9781139024655.

Jay, Martin. 1993. *Downcast Eyes: The Denigration of Vision in Twentieth-Century French Thought*. Berkeley, Los Angeles: University of California Press.

Ong, W. J. 1977. ""I See What You Say": Sense Analogues for Intellect." In *Interfaces of the Word: Studies in the Evolution of Consciousness and Culture*, ed. Walter J. Ong, 121–144. Ithaca, NY: Cornell University Press.

Ray, Verne. 1963. *Primitive Pragmatists: The Modoc Indians of Northern California*. Seattle: University of Washington Press.

Schmidt, Robert, and Barbara Voss, eds. 2000. *Archaeologies of Sexuality*. London: Routledge.

Turner, Victor. 1967. *The Forest of Symbols: Aspects of Ndembu Ritual*. Ithaca, NY: Cornell University Press.

Van Gennep, Arnold. 1960 [English trans.; orig. 1909]. *The Rites of Passage*. Chicago: University of Chicago Press.

Contributors

Susan M. Alt is professor of anthropology at Indiana University and an archaeologist working on issues of religion, violence, gender and migration as related to social and political complexity at Cahokia and the greater American Midwest. She is the author of the book *Cahokia's Complexities: Ceremonies and Politics among the First Mississippian Farmers*, editor of the volume *Ancient Complexities: New Perspectives in Pre-Columbian North America*, and coeditor of *Medieval Mississippians: The Cahokian World*.

Anthony F. Aveni is the Russell Colgate Distinguished University Professor of Astronomy, Anthropology, and Native American Studies at Colgate University, where he has taught since 1963. Originally trained in the astrophysical sciences (PhD, University of Arizona, 1965), his work now focuses on cultural astronomy, the role of cosmology in city planning, and the perception and expression of time in the indigenous cultures of Mesoamerica and Peru. He has published on these topics in journals including *American Scientist*, *History Today*, *American Antiquity*, and *Latin American Antiquity*. Aveni is the author of *Skywatchers: A Revised Updated Version of Skywatchers of Ancient Mexico* (2001), a standard textbook in the ethnosciences. His most recent books include the edited Dumbarton Oaks volume on *The Measure and Meaning of Time in Mesoamerica and Peru* (2015) and *In the Shadow of the Moon: The Science, Magic and Mystery of Solar Eclipses* (2017). He was the recipient of the H. B. Nicholson Medal for Excellence in Mesoamerican Studies, given in 2004 by the Peabody Museum, Harvard and, in 2013, the Fryxell Medal for Interdisciplinary Research from the Society for American Archaeology. In 1982, Aveni received the Professor of the Year Award from the Council for the Advancement and Support of Education, Washington, DC, America's highest national award for teaching.

Jane Eva Baxter is associate professor and chair of anthropology at DePaul University (PhD, University of Michigan, 2000). She is a historical archaeologist working in the United States and the Bahamas on issues of labor and identity, as well as childhood and gender. Her current project is a longitudinal study of the sisal and lumber industries on the Bahamian island of Abaco, focusing on migratory labor, issues of sustainability, and gender and identity formation in the late nineteenth and early twentieth centuries. Baxter's publication record includes many works on the archaeology of childhood and archaeological pedagogies as well as those reporting on her field projects in Chicago and the Bahamas.

Shadreck Chirikure is professor and head of the Department of Archaeology, University of Cape Town, South Africa. He has an MA in artifact studies and a PhD in archaeology from the Institute of Archaeology, University College London. Since his training crossed many disciplinary spaces, interdisciplinarity comes naturally to his research, which follows three separate but interrelated strands: the first combines techniques from earth and engineering sciences with those from archaeology, anthropology, and history to study precolonial technologies such as mining, metallurgy, pottery making, and other high-temperature processes; the second focuses on heritage management and conservation, emphasizing the role of local communities in heritage interpretation and conservation; and the third collapses the first two, exploring the development of African-centered knowledge that responds to the needs of the post-colony.

Minette C. Church is professor at the University of Colorado, Colorado Springs, and faculty director of the UCCS Heller Center for the Arts and Humanities. She was a visiting research fellow in the Department of Archaeology and Palaeoecology in the School of Natural and Built Environment, Queen's University, Belfast, Ireland. Church currently serves on the Colorado Governor's Historic Preservation Review Board. Her areas of geographic interest are Belize, Central America, and the United States-Mexico borderlands; in both regions she focuses on the archaeology of parenting and childhood, landscape archaeology, border regions, and colonial/postcolonial transnational identities.

Jeremy D. Coltman has taught in the Department of Anthropology at California State University, Los Angeles; Santa Monica College; and University of California, Riverside. He is fascinated with the ideological and artistic influence of the ancient Maya on the Late Postclassic Nahua and Aztec civilizations, a subject on which he has published in a number of journals including *Mexicon*, *Latin American Antiquity*, and *Ancient Mesoamerica*. His current research involves an investigation of the Maya solar cult at the site of Chichen Itza, Yucatan, Mexico.

Margaret (Meg) Conkey is the Class of 1960 Professor Emerita of Anthropology at the University of California, Berkeley, with previous faculty positions at Binghamton University and San Jose State. She has served as president of the Society for American

Archaeology and of both the Archaeology Division and the Association for Feminist Anthropologists of the American Anthropological Association. Her field research has been based in the French Midi-Pyrénées for the last twenty-five years directing "Between the Caves," a Paleolithic regional survey, and codirecting excavations at an open-air Middle Magdalenian site. Conkey's scholarship has focused on issues in the study of Paleolithic art and visual culture and on the feminist practice of archaeology.

Tom D. Dillehay is the Rebecca Webb Wilson University Distinguished Professor of Anthropology, Religion, and Culture and Professor of Anthropology and Latin American Studies in the Department of Anthropology at Vanderbilt University, and professor extraordinaire and honorary doctorate at several universities in Chile and Peru. Dillehay has carried out numerous archaeological and anthropological projects in Peru, Chile, Argentina, and other South American countries and in the United States. He has been a visiting professor at several universities around the world. Dillehay has published twenty-two books and more than three hundred refereed journal articles and book chapters. He has received numerous international and national awards for his research, books, and teaching. He is a member of the American Academy of Arts and Sciences and the Latin American Academy of Sciences.

Christine C. Dixon-Hundredmark is a tenured faculty member in Anthropology at Green River College, Washington. She has conducted fieldwork in Mexico, Honduras, Belize, El Salvador and Costa Rica, as well as Hawaii. Her research focuses on sociopolitical economy, especially as it relates to farmer autonomy..

Zenobie S. Garrett is a visiting scholar in the Department of Anthropology at New York University. She specializes in landscape approaches to cultural complexity, with a regional focus in Europe. She has worked in Peru, the United States, England, France, Ireland, and Oman. Garrett is a member of the Register of Professional Archaeologists and serves on the Committee for Public Education for the Society for American Archaeology.

Nancy Gonlin is Registered Professional Archaeologist 16354 who investigates Classic Maya commoners, household archaeology, and archaeology of the night. She is co-editor of the journal *Ancient Mesoamerica*. Her co-edited volumes and contributions are *Commoner Ritual and Ideology in Ancient Mesoamerica*, *Ancient Households of the Americas*, *Human Adaptation in Ancient Mesoamerica*, and *Night and Darkness in Ancient Mesoamerica* (forthcoming). She has co-authored a case study, *Copán: The Rise and Fall of an Ancient Maya Kingdom*, and a textbook, *The Archaeology of Native North America*.

Kathryn Kamp teaches at Grinnell College where she is the Earl D. Strong Professor of Social Studies. Her work is primarily in the American Southwest, although she has also done research in Belize, Cyprus, Syria, and Turkey. Her primary interests are in the interpretation of the past, the archaeology of childhood, ethnoarchaeology, and experimental archaeology. She coedits the journal *Ethnoarchaeology: Journal of Archaeological, Ethnographic, and Experimental Studies*.

Erin Halstad McGuire is an archaeologist and associate teaching professor at the University of Victoria, British Columbia. She is interested in the Viking expansion, funerary rituals, and the life-course. Most recently, she has been exploring experimental archaeology, as both a research and a teaching tool. In 2016, she was honored to be the inaugural recipient of the award for Excellence in Teaching for Experiential Learning at the University of Victoria.

Abigail Joy Moffett earned her PhD in the Department of Archaeology at the University of Cape Town, South Africa. Her research interests cover several aspects of the political economy of Iron Age farming communities in southern Africa, from crafting and cross-craft gender relations, local and regional political dynamics, to the construction and negotiation of value through the exchange and consumption of local and imported objects.

Jerry D. Moore is professor of anthropology at California State University, Dominguez Hills. His research focuses on the archaeology of cultural landscapes in Peru and Baja California. His archaeological fieldwork has been supported by the National Science Foundation, National Geographic Society, Wenner-Gren Foundation for Anthropological Research, Center for Pre-Columbian Studies at Dumbarton Oaks, and other agencies and foundations. Moore has been a fellow at Dumbarton Oaks, the Sainsbury Centre for the Arts, University of East Anglia, the Getty Research Institute, and the Institute of Advanced Study, Durham University. His books include *Architecture and Power in the Prehispanic Andes: The Archaeology of Public Buildings*; *Visions of Culture: An Introduction to Anthropological Theories and Theorists*; *Cultural Landscapes in the Prehispanic Andes: Archaeologies of Place*; *The Prehistory of Home* (2014 Society for American Archaeology Book Award); *A Prehistory of South America: Ancient Cultural Diversity of the Least Known Continent*; *Incidence of Travel: Recent Journeys in Ancient South America*; and numerous articles, book chapters, and reviews. He is currently editor of *Ñawpa Pacha: Journal of Andean Archaeology*.

Smiti Nathan is an archaeologist specializing in interdisciplinary approaches to food and resource decision-making strategies of ancient societies around the Indian Ocean region, specifically in Oman and Ethiopia. She received her PhD in the Department of Anthropology at New York University and is currently an Assistant Director of Life Design at the Johns Hopkins University.

April Nowell is a Paleolithic archaeologist and professor of anthropology at the University of Victoria. She specializes in the origins of art, language, and other symbolic behavior, in the emergence of the modern mind and in the growth and development of Middle to Late Pleistocene children. Currently, Nowell directs an international team in the excavation of Lower and Middle Paleolithic sites in Jordan and codirects a study of European Upper Paleolithic finger flutings with Leslie Van Gelder. She is the editor of *In the Mind's Eye: Multidisciplinary Perspectives on the Evolution of Human Intelligence* and coeditor of *Stone Tools and the Evolution of Human Cognition* with Iain Davidson. Her recent research has been published in numerous venues, including *American Anthropologist*, *Journal of Human Evolution*, *Cambridge Archaeological Journal*, *Journal of Archaeological Science*, and *Evolutionary Anthropology*.

Scott C. Smith (PhD 2009, University of California, Riverside) is an associate professor in the Department of Anthropology at Franklin & Marshall College. He studies landscape, architecture, and the development of social complexity in the Andes. Since 2009 he has codirected the Proyecto Arqueológico Machaca Desaguadero (PAMD) in the Upper Desaguadero Valley of Bolivia.

GLENN REED STOREY is jointly appointed in the Departments of Classics and Anthropology at the University of Iowa. He has coauthored a book with his sister, Rebecca Storey, Mesoamerican bioarchaeologist at the University of Houston: *Rome and the Classic Maya: Comparing the Slow Collapse of Civilizations.* He is completing a monograph in Italian on the Greco-Roman site of Gangivecchio in Sicily, where he is excavating a Roman villa. Storey continues working on issues of the archaeology of ancient cities, demography and economy of the Roman Empire, and the application of ground-penetrating radar techniques to Roman archaeology, as well as historical cemeteries in Iowa.

MEGHAN E. STRONG is an adjunct assistant professor in the Classics Department at Case Western Reserve University and an archaeology research associate at the Cleveland Museum of Natural History. She also serves as co-director of the Nuri Archaeological Expedition, which studies the royal pyramids and necropolis of Nuri, Sudan.

CYNTHIA L. VAN GILDER earned her MA and PhD from the University of California, Berkeley, where the National Science Foundation funded her research on gender, households, and social change in precontact Hawai'i. Since joining the anthropology faculty at St. Mary's College of California, Van Gilder has continued to publish on the use of practice theory in Hawaiian archaeology, microhistory approaches to archaeological data, sociopolitics of archaeology, and narratives of cultural/ethnic identity. Currently serving as the director of academic advising at St. Mary's, she has also researched mentorship and learning in academia, including national and international presentations on building creative collaborations to support undergraduate student success. A dedicated proponent of four-field anthropology, Van Gilder's current research is on the anthropology of tourism, specifically how narratives of cultural identity shape the Hawaiian tourist experience in Las Vegas, Nevada.

ALEXEI VRANICH earned his PhD from the University of Pennsylvania and has been working in South America since 1995. He has extensive research experience with early complex societies around the world in Spain, Italy, India, Peru, Bulgaria, and Costa Rica. Vranich has been recognized by the National Science Foundation for the innovative application of technology to the study of the past. His present research and publication projects center on the city of Cusco, Peru, capital of the Inca empire and largest precolumbian empire in the New World.

JOHN C. WHITTAKER is professor of anthropology at Grinnell College. He has worked in the American Southwest for more than thirty years, running an archaeological field school near Flagstaff, Arizona. He coedits the journal *Ethnoarchaeology: Journal of Archaeological, Ethnographic, and Experimental Studies*, and has done archaeology and ethnography in the Middle East, Turkey, and United States. Whittaker plays and experiments with prehistoric technologies, especially stone tools (*Flintknapping: Making and Understanding Stone Tools*; *American Flintknappers: Stone Age Art in the Age of Computers*) and projectiles, and coaches the world's first collegiate atlatl team.

RITA P. WRIGHT is professor emerita of anthropology at New York University. Her research interests include comparative studies of urbanism, state formation, gender, and cycles of change in early societies. She has conducted field research in Afghanistan, Pakistan, and Iran, and used secondary sources from Mesopotamia to study the organization of production. She specializes in ancient technologies with a focus on the production and distribution systems of ceramics and textiles and exchange networks. Wright's major field work has been at the city of Harappa and a study that she directed of rural sites in a landscape and settlement survey along a now-dry bed of the Beas River that ran parallel to the nearby Ravi River, where Harappa is located. She is especially interested in planned cities, their sociopolitical organization, and their management of water technologies. Wright is founder and chief editor of *Case Studies in Early Societies*, editor of *Gender and Archaeology*, coeditor with Cathy L. Costin of *Craft and Social Identity*, and author of *Ancient Indus: Urbanism, Economy, and Society*.

Index

Page numbers in italics indicate illustrations.

burial chambers, Egyptian, 250, 257–61
burials: at Cahokia, xxvi, 227–28, 232, 237, 239; Huaca Prieta, 193; Iron-Age Africa, 364; Polynesia, 172(n23); Shona, 364; Viking, 275; at Xultun, 148

Cacaxtla, 203
Cahokia, xxv–xxvi; carved figurines from, 229, 231–34; iconography at, 224–25; male and female power in, 223–24, 238–39; Mound 72 burials at, 227–28
calabashes, Shona use of, 359, 364
calendar, 110, 140; Hawaiian, 161, 173(n25); Maya, 203
Calendar Round, and New Fire Ceremony, 61–62, 63
camelids, 123–25, 134
campfires: Mapuche use of, 191; Upper Paleolithic, 31–32
camping, Colorado–New Mexico borderlands, 102, 103, 104, 107
candlelight, xxi, 115
candlenut. See kukui nut
candles, xix, xxi, 16, 31, 99, 100, 107, 109–11, 114–15, 163; Egyptian, 250–52; wicks, 271, 273–74
cannibalism, 145
Cañones, resistance to electrification, 115–16
caravan routes, Lake Titicaca Basin, 126–27
carnivores, Classic Maya concepts of, 59–60
carts, wooden, 298
castes, sanitation workers, 301
Catholic Church, 114, 124; community rituals, 110–11
cattle drives, 104
cave paintings: Mississippian, 223, 228, 237, 239; Upper Paleolithic, 29, 31, 33–35
caves: acoustics of, xxi–xxii; dark zones in, 208, 210; iconography of, 202, 207, 213, 215; lighting in, xx, 30–31; as liminal spaces, 204–5; Mississippian use of, 230–31
ceilies, 95, 99
celebrations, xxiii, 46, 60–62, 121–22, 144, 148; Junkanoo, 369, 370, 380
celestial phenomena, xxv, 16, 66; navigation using, 160–61
Celestial River (Mayu; Milky Way), xxiv, 125
Cena Trimalchionis, 310
censers, Classic Maya use of, 58, 60
Central Cattle Pattern, 362–63
ceramics, 29, 252, 265, 267, 389; Classic Maya, 53, 55, 56, 57, 58, 66; Indus Valley, 292, 295; Magan, 336; San Salvador, 380

ceremonies, xxi, xxii; curing, 389–90; dream-sanctioned, 225; Mapuche, 183, 184
Cerén, 15, 46, 48–49, 61; darkness, 59–60; environmental setting, 50–51; household architecture, 51–52, 58; night soil, 56; sacbe at, 65; sleeping benches, 54–55
Cerro Chijcha, 127, 131
Chahk, 203
Chalcolithic, sanitation system, 292
Chamula Maya, cannibalism metaphors, 144–45
chaotic primordiality, 201, 202
charcoal and ash, 58, 60, 167, 181, 191, 193, 195
Chauvet cave, 31, 32, 33, 34
ch'een glyph, 202, 207–8, 213, 215; and darkness, 209, 210–11; and Goddess O, 211–12
Chichen Itza, 212, 216(n8)
chiefdoms, Mapuche, 182–83
chiefs, Hawaiian, 159
chikuva, 357, 362
Chilam Balam of Chumayel, 202
childbirth, 211, 214. See also birth
children, as field guides, 86
Chile, Mapuche in, 181
China, sanitation systems, 293
Chorti, 13, 56
Christianity, 216(n5), 315. See also Catholic Church
chronobiology, 7. See also circadian rhythms, circadian cycle
Cipactonal, 212
circadian rhythms, circadian cycle, 7, 8–9, 37–38, 79
Citlalinicue, 212
Citlallatonac, 212
Classic Maya, 6, 11, 15–16, 45, 65, 67, 208; darkness and creation, xxiii, xxv, 66, 206–7; eclipse prediction, 145–49; hearths and braziers, 57–58; nighttime practices, 51–57; rituals and feasting, 60–63; torch use, 58–59; urban vs. rural areas, 59–60; water and sanitation systems, 292, 293. See also astronomy; Calendar Round; Cerén; Copan
climate, 79, 98, 103, 162, 374; neotropical, 50–51; Oman, 340–41; Upper Paleolithic, 28, 29
Codex Borbonicus, 62, 63
Codex Borgia, 209, 212, 214, 216(n7), 217(n10)
Codex Laud, 213
Codex Madrid, 208, 209
Codex Tudela, 212, 213
Codex Vaticus, 213
Coffin Texts, 254
cognition, 28, 152

cognitive changes, in Mapuche shamanic rituals, 180, 186, 187–89, 191, 192, 195; development, 100
cognitive states, 389
cognitive structuralism, 362
color, Mississippian symbology, 236
Colorado–New Mexico borderlands: Catholic Church rituals in, 110–13; homesteads in, 100–102, 109; irrigation in, 105–7; nighttime travel on, 102–3, 107–8; Penitente rituals in, 113–14; work and travel in, 96–97, 103–5
combustion features, in Hawaiian households, 167, 168
commoners: Classic Maya 16, 47, 49, 51, 53, 54, 58, 67; Hawaiian, 159
communal drives, Upper Paleolithic, 31
communication, with other world, 225
community-building, 95; Colorado–New Mexico borderlands, 110–11
conch shells, 232, 374
conflict: between moon and sun, 143; water management, 106–7. See also violence
Constantinople, Plague of Justinian in, 310
constellations, 66; in Andean ethnoastronomy, xxiv, 125–26, 131. See also stars
cooking and cooked food, 8, 12, 31, 57, 58, 80, 87, 89, 100, 143, 149–50, 163–64, 173(n25), 191, 275, 276, 315, 365
cooking huts, Shona, 356, 357, 362. See also kitchen
Copan, 15, 46, 47–48, 59, 65, 66; benches at, 53, 55; dancing platform, 60, 61; environmental setting, 50–51; household architecture, 51–52, 58; New Fire Ceremony at, 62
cordholders, Classic Maya sites, 52, 55
Corn Mother/First Woman, figures of, 231–34
cosmology: Andean, 125–26; Cahokian, 228, 230; Siouan, 226, 227
cotton-grass (Eriophorum angustifolium), wicks of, 268, 270–71, 272, 274
cotton plantations, in Bahamas, 374
Coyote, 81
crabbing, in San Salvador, 378
creation, xix, 216(n6), 231; darkness and, xxii–xxiii, xxv, 201–2, 206–7; Tlatecuhtli and, 213–14
creator couple, Maya, 212. See also First Man; First Woman
crime, in Rome, 311–12, 315–16, 317
cross-bones motifs, 208, 209, 210–11
cultural ecology, 15–16
culture, perception and, 78–79. See also parallax effect

curanderos, at Huaca Prieta, 194
curing, skull-and-crossbones symbol, 212
Cushing, Frank, Zuni Folk Tales, 82

Dalits, as sanitation workers, 301
dance, xviii, 60, 89, 98, 109, 159, 162, 181, 185, 187, 188, 189, 195, 239; in Bahamas, xxiv, 369, 371, 377–78; hunter-gatherer, 27–28; sub-Saharan Africa, 354, 357, 365; Upper Paleolithic, 32–33, 36
dance and procession plazas, Mapuche, 191
dancing platforms, Copan, 60, 61
dare, 356; archaeology of, 361–62
Dark Ages, xx, 265
dark beings, Maya, 17
dark cloud constellations, 125–26
darkness, xx, xxiv, xxvii, xxviii, 5–7, 9, 12, 13–15, 201, 202; in Classic Maya sites, 59–60, 208; and creation, xix, xxii–xxiii, xxv, 206–7, 214; Egyptian concepts of, 249; Maya concepts of, 46, 66, 203; in Rome, 309; slavery and, 372; solar eclipse, xxv, 141, 152–53; theatricality of, 89; wild and, 210, 211
dark spaces, Maya, 17
dark zones, in caves, xxii, 208, 210
date palms (Phoenix dactylifera L.), 337
day and night cycles, 389; Roman lengths of, 323–24. See also circadian rhythms
death, xix, xxii, 13, 66, 141, 144, 148, 226, 230, 232–33, 250, 251, 256, 261, 275, 301, 309, 324, 358
death gods, Maya, 206
debt payment, during solar eclipses, 150–51, 152
Decius, Emperor, 310
Deir el Medina tombs, 252; images in, 257–60
deities/gods, xxiii, 123, 143, 144, 152, 190, 230–32; ancient Egyptian, 250–51, 253, 255, 256–58, 259, 260–61; Classic Maya, 46, 56, 57, 60–62, 66, 203–4, 205, 206–7, 210–12, 213, 214–15, 216(n3, n8), 217(n9); 148, 149; Hindu, 149, 150; Mapuche, 181, 183–85, 189–91, 194; Mississippian, 225, 231–32; in Polynesia, 157–59, 167, 171(n7); Puebloan, 81; Roman, 308, 325, 329; Shona, 357, 362; Sioux, 230. See also names of individual deities
Desaguadero valley, 122, 127
Dholavira, 289, 290–91
dice, divining, 357–58
Digest of Justinian, 317
Dio Cassius, Rhomaikon, 310
disease, in Roman Empire, 309–10
ditch judges, 106
divination, xxiii; Shona, 357–58, 359

Dogon, iron smelting in, 355, 364
Dowd, Marion, 14
drainage systems, Mohenjo-daro, 295–96
dream consciousness, 205
dreams, dreaming, xxvi, 13, 46, 52, 157, 158, 162, 203, 225, 238; dangers of, 205–6
dream worlds, Native American, 86, 225
Dresden Codex, eclipse prediction in, 145, 146, 147–48
Drimys winteris, 185, 191
dust, removing, 299
dynastic power, sun and moon and, 143–44
dynasty, 7, 48, 62, 149, 253, 262(n3), 293

eagles, in Pueblo stories, 82
Early Bronze Age, Oman, 18
Early Dynastic Egypt, 292
Early Middle Ages, xviii, xix, 201, 216(n5)
earrings, in Red Horn stories, 228
earth, 7, 28, 37, 60, 65, 97, 143, 144, 149, 185, 214, 216(n6), 217(n11), 230, 231, 234, 237, 256, 301, 334; and First Woman, 226
East St. Louis site, 224; figurine from, 229, 232
eclipses, 217(n10); solar, xxv, 17, 140–41
ecology, of night, 6–7
eel, Hawaiian fishing of, 160
Egypt: xx, xxii, 292; artificial lighting, 17, 249–52; burial chambers, 257–61; funerary rites, 253–57; oil lamps, 252–53
Ekirch, A. Roger, xvii, xxi, xxvii, 18, 96, 159, 161, 162, 172, 308, 309, 320, 324, 327, 328, 329
El Bosque (Copan), 59
El Cerén. *See* Cerén
electricity, 6, 9, 96, 115, 139, 163, 343
electrification, 16, 100, 388; resistance to, 115–16
electronic media, traditional beliefs and, 150
elites, 12, 179–80; Classic Maya rituals and, 61, 62–63
El Salvador, 15; Classic Maya in, 46, 48. *See also* Cerén
El Zotz, Temple of the Night at, 203
emancipation, British Empire, 375
Emerald site, xxvi, 224, 234; shrine houses at, 235–38
emotion: in music, 15, 28, 36, 38–40; night, darkness and, 14, 36, 38; ritual and, 16, 180–81, 190, 215(n1); senses and, 89, sleep and, 36–38
emperors: marauding by, 324–25; Roman, 321–23
Ennius, 328
environment, 79; neotropical, 50–51. *See also* climate

epigraphy, Classic Maya, 46
Eriophorum angustifolium, wicks of, 268, 270–71, 272, 274
ethnoarchaeology: Mapuche, 185, 186, 191, 195; of oasis agriculture, 335, 341–42, 345
ethnogenesis, 372
ethnographic accounts, ethnography, xxi, xxiv, 8, 13, 17–18, 40, 46, 54, 56, 81, 89, 114–15, 142, 159, 161–63, 166, 170, 172, 185, 265, 271, 276, 293, 304, 362, 364, 373, 389; analogy, 30, 38, 58, 82, 86, 268–69
ethnohistory, 46, 56
Europe, xx; Upper Paleolithic, 28–29
experimental archaeology, 17, 30, 265, 267, 269, 271, 276
eye-and-crossbones motif, 207–8, 216(n6); and *ch'een* glyph, 209, 210–11; and Goddess O, 211–12
eyeballs, as darkness symbol, 208
eyesight, biology of, 79

falaj system, xxvii, 338–39, 341–43, 346(n2)
farming: in Bahamas, 374; Shona, 357. *See also* irrigation systems; oasis agriculture
farmsteads, Purgatoire River, 96, 98–99
farolitos, 114
Farquharson, Charles, 377–78
"Farquharson's Journal," 377–78
feasts and feasting, 13, 60; Classic Maya, 48, 60, 61
female / feminine power; Mississippian iconography of, 232, 237; night and, 226
Ferguson, Arlene Nash, on Junkanoo, 370–71
fertility, hands as symbols of, 232
fertility rites: Huaca Prieta, 194; Mapuche, 184, 185
festivals, Junkanoo, xxiii–xxiv, 18, 370–72. *See also* celebrations
fields, xxvi, 9, 48, 104, 106, 109, 124, 161, 249, 341, 357, 375, 377; Sinagua, 85–86
fighting, in Rome, 315
figurines, figures: agency of, 225; Cahokian Mississippian, 223, 228, 229, 231–34; Shona, 364
finger fluting, 32
fire(s), 8, 9, 17, 87, 188; in Rome, 316–17; and sociocultural practices, 365–66; Upper Paleolithic use of, 31–32
fire features, Sinagua, 87–88
fireflies, 66, 211; and *ak'ab* glyphs, 203, 204
firelight, cognitive development and, 100. *See also* cognition

Ovid, *Metamorphoses*, 329
owls, 7, 50, 81, 114, 310, 311
Oxomoco, 212

Pajcha Pata, 127
Pakistan, 288, 289, 291; well construction, 294–95
Palenque, hydraulics, 293
Paleolithic. *See* Upper Paleolithic
palm prints, Upper Paleolithic, 32, *33*
palolo (Palolo viridis), 160, 172(n10)
Palombara, Villa of, 327, *328*
pandemics, Roman Empire, 309–10
Panel of Lions (Chauvet), 34
Papua New Guinea, solar eclipses, 151–52
parallax effect, 6
parasites, 302, 304(n4)
Pashed, 257, 258, 259
pastoralism and agropastoralism, 123–24, 134. *See also* camelids
Paul, 311–12
Pawnee Morning Star sacrifice, 225
Penitente Brotherhood, 113–14
percussive instruments, Upper Paleolithic, 34–35
performance, performative acts, Upper Paleolithic, 32, 39–40
Petronius, *Satyricon*, 310, 315
Pfeffer site, 224
Phoenix dactylifera L., 337
pictographs: Mississippian, 230–31; Red Horn story, 228, 239
Picture Cave (Missouri), 228, 230–31, 232, 238
Piedras Negras, 60, 210–11
pigs, in Hawaiian sites, 159, 167
pipes: musical, xxi, 34; sanitation, 293, 296–97; smoking, 228, 232
pitch, as fuel, 100, 298
pithouses, 78, 91; Sinagua, 78, 87; Viking, 267, 272–73, 275, 276
placemaking, xxiv, 95, 96
Plague of Justinian, 310
plantations, 371, 372, 379–80; daily operations of 377–78; land- and soundscapes on, 375–76; slavery and, 373–74
planters, 374, 375, 379; socializing of, 377–78
platform, 134; at Tiwanaku, 132–33
Pliny the Elder, xxvi, 299, 328; on supernatural, 310, 311; on wine, 312–13; work habits, 322–23
Pliny the Younger, 322; Laurentine Villa, 326–27, *328*

pō, xxiii; archaeological evidence of, 162–70; in Hawai'i, 155–56; origin and meanings of, 156–59, 160, 161, 172(n8)
Pokomon Maya, 212
police and fire brigades, Roman, 317–20
political power: feasting and, 60; Mapuche shamans, 181, 182–83, 190–91; Maya, 60, 210; sanitation workers, 300–303; Titicaca Basin, 126, 132
Polly Hill Plantation, *373, 375*
Polynesia/Polynesians, xx–xxi, xxiii, xxiv, 17, 166, 170–71, 171(n4); navigation, 160–61; *pō* in, 155–59; sleeping shelters, 161–62
Pompeii, *316*; brothels in, 320, 321, *322*; wine in, 312–13
Ponca, and Wa-kan-da, 230
Popol Vuh, 202, 212
portals, 225, 232, 233, 238, 390
practice theory, 10, 11–12, 18, 49, 50
predators, 31, 81, 100
prefects, duties of, 317–18, 320, 324
priestesses, 56, 63, 111, 114, 122, 161, 183, 185, 234, 253
priests, 161
privacy, 59, 90, 364, 371, 375, 376, 379
processions, Catholic, 111, 112–14; Egyptian funereal, 254, *255*; Hawaiian, 171(n5); at Huaca Prieta, 193, 196. *See also* rituals
Procopius, *Hyper ton polemon*, 310
procreation: Classic Maya elites, 62; and *pō*, 158–59
Prospect Hill Plantation, *373, 375, 376*; "Farquharson's Journal" and, 377–78
prostitution, Roman, 320, 321, 325
public ceremonies, Mapuche, 181, 183, 184, 190
Puebloans, stories, 81–82
Pukui, Mary Kawena, 157, 159; *'Ōlelo No'eau*, 158
pulque, 203
Purgatoire River, 96; irrigation systems on, 104–5, 107
Pyramid Texts, 254

Qaboos bin Said al-Said, 334, 335
Quetzalcoatl, 213–14
Quimsachata Mountain, and Southern Celestial Pole, 122, 126, 130, 132

Ra, 250, 256; images of, 258, 259–60
rabbit, and Maya moon goddess, 66
radio, 9, 96, 99, 115, 375
radiocarbon dates: Hawaiian, 164, 172(n11); Huaca Prieta, 193

ship graffiti, 380
Shona, 10, 18, 365; agriculture and storytelling in, 354–55; gendered space, 356, 361–62;
homestead ownership, 362–63; illicit activities, 359–60; iron smelting, 360–61; sexual
intercourse, 363–64; witches, 358–59
shrines: 63, 233; Classic Maya ancestor, 60,
61; Hawaiian ancestral, 164, 166; houses,
at Emerald site, xxvi, 234, 235–38, 236;
Mississippian, 223, 235–38; sacred bundles as,
234, 237; Shona, 362
Sidonius Apollinaris, 328
siestas, 98, 323
Sinagua, 16, 77–78; fire features, 87–90; movement within pueblos, 83–85; sensescapes,
xxii, 91; viewsheds, 86–87; village structure,
82–83
singing, 32, 86, 109, 108, 112, 162, 188, 189, 375
Siouan speakers, 223, 226, 230, 239, 239(n1). See
also Mississippian culture; Osage
Sipán tombs, 9
skeletal imagery, 217
skull-and-crossbones motif, Mesoamerican,
202, 212–14, 217(n9); skirts with, 211–12
sky, skyscapes: Colorado–New Mexico borderlands, 97–98; Lake Titicaca Basin, 124–25;
and landscape, 63, 65. See also night sky
Skyband bench, at Copan, 66
slaves, slavery, 309, 380; in Bahamas, xxiii–xxiv, 18,
370–76, 379; in Rome, 315–16, 317, 323, 324, 327;
socializing of, 377–78; in United States, 96
sleep, xxi, 7, 46; and emotion, 36–38; gendered
patterns of, 107, 164; in Rome, 309, 320,
327–29; segmented, 161–62, 172(n12). See also
first sleep; second sleep
sleep deprivation, 36–37, 185, 187
sleeping huts, Shona, 359
sleeping shelters/houses, Polynesia, 161–62, 64,
166–67
Smetzer, Barbara, 160
smoke exposure, 187, 274
snakes, 81, 90, 125, 226, 230, 231, 232
soak pits, Mohenjo-daro, 296–97, 298
social inequality, 288; sanitation workers and,
300–303
socialization, sociability, 13, 36, 109; fire/hearth
and, 32, 58, 89–90, 109, 365–66; Polynesia, 159,
160; ritual and, 186; labor and, 160
social memory, 97, 103, 104, 115
social reproduction, on Colorado borderlands,
96, 104, 115

solar alignments, at Tiwanaku, 132–33
solar eclipses, xxv, 17, 46, 122, 153, 217(n10);
animals during, 141–42; biting and eating
metaphors in, 144–45; Hindu mythology,
149–51; human reactions to, 142–44; Maya
prediction of, 145–49; Papua New Guinea,
151–52; total, 140–41
"Song in Praise of Helminthes, A," 301–2
souls: during solar eclipses, 151–52; pō, 157
sound, soundscapes, xxiv, 7, 79–80, 81, 85, 91;
Bahamian plantations, 375–76; Mapuche
ritual, 187, 188, 189; Polynesia, 160; in Rome,
308; rural and urban, 59; Shona, 359; Upper
Paleolithic, xxi–xxii, 19, 27–28, 34, 39–40. See
also music
South Africa, 356
Southampton Insurrection, 372
Southern Celestial Pole, 132; Tiwanaku sunken
court, 125, 130, 133
South Sudan, solar eclipse in, 142–43
Southwest, American, xxi, 16. See also Sinagua
space: on Bahamian plantations, 375–76, 380;
dark, 202, 204–5, 208, 209, 215, 216(n5);
Egyptian ritual, 250, 261; gendered, 82, 356,
361–63, 365–66; Hawaiian use of, 162–70; at
Huaca Prieta, 193–94; Mapuche ritual, 189,
191–92; in Viking houses, 273, 275, 276–77
Spain, Upper Paleolithic music, 34, 35
spells: in Deir el Medina tombs, 258; in
Egyptian Book of the Dead, 250, 251, 253–57,
261; Roman, 311; Shona, 358, 359–60
spiders, 216(n7), 217(n11)
spirits: Egyptian, 255, 260; Mapuche, 186, 189,
190; Maya, 46, 61, 205, 207, 210; Polynesian,
157–59, 170–71; portals for, 232, 233; Shona,
358, 359, 363; Siouan, 226, 226, 231, 234, 238.
See also ancestors; ghosts
Sponemann figurines, 229, 231–32, 239(n2)
stars, xviii, 389; navigation via, 160–61; timing
irrigation by, 105–6, 339
stealing, Shona, 355
stellar observations, 121–22; navigation and,
160–61; sunken courts, 129, 130–31
stories, storytelling, 36, 89, 96, 99, 114; hunter-
gatherer, xviii–xix, 27–28; Polynesian, 162;
Pueblo, 81–82; Red Horn cycle, 227–28,
230; sub-Saharan Africa, 354–55; Upper
Paleolithic, 33–34
storm-water management, 292, 293
street sweeping, 299
Stuttgart Statuette, 214